EXPERIENCING TOTALITARIANISM

THE INVASION AND OCCUPATION OF LATVIA
BY THE USSR AND NAZI GERMANY
1939-1991

A Documentary History

Edited by
Andrejs Plakans

authorHOUSE®

AuthorHouse™
1663 Liberty Drive, Suite 200
Bloomington, IN 47403
www.authorhouse.com
Phone: 1-800-839-8640

First published by AuthorHouse 8/15/2007

ISBN: 978-1-4343-1573-1 (sc)

Library of Congress Control Number: 2007904217

Printed in the United States of America
Bloomington, Indiana

This book is printed on acid-free paper.

Dedicated to the memory of Dr. Alfreds Rimša
(1919-2005)

CONTENTS

Editor's Preface

The idea of this documentary collection came into being during the years immediately following the collapse of the USSR, when in 1991 the republic of Latvia renewed its statehood. One consequence of this turning point in the history of Latvia was the arrival into Latvian archives of an immense amount of heretofore inaccessible documentation of the decades during which Latvia had not been able to shape its own destiny, namely, the approximately sixty years between the signing of the Hitler-Stalin Pact in August, 1939, and the momentous events of 1991. Dr. Alfrēds Rimša of San Marcos, California, one of the thousands of Latvians who had fled their homeland in 1944 and eventually settled in the US, had maintained a lively interest in the subsequent history and fate of his homeland, and in the mid-1990s proposed to the Institute of History of the Latvian Academy of Science (now of the University of Latvia) the creation of a documentary collection of the 1939-1991 period. An agreement was signed between the Institute and Dr. Rimša in 1997. The ultimate goal of the project was a documentary history in English that would lay out to the reader the mechanisms of totalitarian rule – those of Nazi Germany, which had occupied Latvia during the course of WWII between 1941 and 1944, and of the Soviet Union, which first occupied the country in 1940, held power for a year, and then returned to power in Latvia after the defeat of Nazi Germany in 1945. The documents were to be selected from the many hundreds of thousands available since 1991 for public scrutiny for the first time, and presented with other documents, sometimes available earlier, that would round out the story.

The Institute of History, headed in 1997 by Dr. Andris Caune, created a working group of scholars to scrutinize the Latvian archives, and other collections and repositories, for the documents best exemplifying the story. The working group was headed by Dr. Irene Šneidere and consisted of Dr. D. Bleiere, Dr. R. Vīksne, E. Pelkaus, Dz. Ērglis, and A. Žvinklis – all of them historians and specialists in various aspects of the history of the Latvia in the 20th century and all also subsequently active contributors to the reformulation of Latvian history in the post-Soviet period. Dr. Andrejs Plakans of the Department of History of Iowa State University was invited to become the general editor of the English-language version of the manuscript. As the collection neared completion, Dr. Aldis Pūrs, who holds a doctorate in history from the University of Toronto and writes about various topics in twentieth-century Latvian history, was contracted by Dr. Rimša to do the first English-language translation. Dr. Rimša remained an active participant in the project throughout, even as his health began to deteriorate. It was his vision that guided the project, and he continued to believe that the collection would be of interest not only to those of his compatriots whose lives were affected by the events the documents describe, but also to younger people, especially university and college students, for whom these decades of the twentieth century are fast becoming ancient history.

Unfortunately, Dr. Alfreds Rimša did not live to see the project to completion. Therefore, the collection is dedicated to his memory.

To finish the project, the general editor of the present volume was able to secure in 2006 a Publication Subvention Grant from the Office of the Provost of Iowa State University. The general editor is very grateful to Iowa State University for its help.

As noted, this collection is the product of the collaborative efforts of many persons. Roughly speaking, the division of labor was the following: Irene Šneidere and her team gathered the documents from the Latvian archives and other collections, made translations where necessary, wrote the introductions to the collection and its four parts as well as comments on particular documents, and annotated the documents; Aldis Pūrs did the first translation of the entire document into English; and the general editor of the English version reviewed and adjusted the translation, reorganized and renumbered the documents where necessary; provided additional annotations where they seemed to be needed for the English-language reader; and standardized as much as feasible the many institutional references in the documents. His work was facilitated by the publication of many of these documents in Russian and Latvian in a collection entitled *Latvija padomju režīma varā [Latvia under the Control of the Soviet Regime]*, edited by Irēne Šneidere (Riga: Latvian Institute of History, 2001).

The general editor of the present volume expresses his gratitude to the Latvian Institute of History, especially Dr. Šneidere and her team; to Aldis Pūrs in tackling the daunting task of translation; and, finally, to Vidvuds Beldavs of AuthorHouse for his suggestions and advice.

A note about translation

The translation of documents from German, Latvian, and Russian, which are highly inflected languages, into English, which is not, is a formidable challenge. In addition, most of the documents published here were written by government and Party bureaucrats, *apartchiki*, and functionaries for each other and contain all the hallmarks of this genre of writing: convolution, obliqueness, institutional references, acronyms and other abbreviations, the passive voice, procedural directions, repetition of titles of persons and of earlier promulgations of superiors and the Party, and various kinds of formalizations typical of internal documents. This is especially so of those documents – frequently marked "secret" or "top secret" – that were meant only for the eyes of the small elites whose word was final in these totalitarian systems. The tension between absolutely precise translation, on the one hand, and readability, on the other, is always present, and the general editor hopes that neither has been severely compromised in the final English version of these documents. There are also a lexical problem, namely, what linguists call the problem of "false friends," which could be expanded to "nearly false friends": words in different languages that look alike but have different or differently shaded meanings. Thus, for example, the word *milicija* (which came into Latvian from the Russian during the Soviet period), means "police" and not "militia." The word *bandīts* (singular, and again from the Russian) does not translate straightforwardly into the English "bandit," because in Soviet-era nomenclature a bandit was a person who performed an armed attack on institutions of Soviet power or on official Soviet personnel. The Soviet-era terms from the Russian – in Latvian *aģitācija, aģitet* – were used in Communist parlance to refer to different kinds of activism (for example, electoral) and did not have the somewhat negative connotation of the English terms *agitation, to agitate*. Also, in Communist parlance the word *propaganda* does not carry with it the suggestion of fabrication as it does in English. And so on. The choices made in the present translation could at times be debatable.

Since the source of each document is provided, it is possible, at least in principle, for the reader to check the final translation against the original. In any event, the general editor takes full responsibility for the final product.

Andrejs Plakans
Professor Emeritus, Department of History
Iowa State University, Ames, Iowa 50011, USA
April, 2007

INTRODUCTION

The principal events in the history of the twentieth century in Latvia are connected to the acquisition of statehood after World War One and its renewal at the end of the century. Both of these events involved the collapse of empires. At the beginning of the century there was the Russian Tsarist Empire, on whose ruins the independent Baltic States – Latvia, Lithuania, and Estonia – were formed. In 1991, when the empire of the USSR began to crumble, the former Baltic Soviet Socialist Republics that had been occupied and annexed by force were the first of all of the Republics of the USSR to re-acquire their independence. They received international recognition without much delay.

If the creation of the Republic of Latvia was connected to the First World War, it was the Second World War that destroyed the Latvian state. Latvia was pulled into the events of World War Two against its wishes even before the war had begun, because the country's destiny was decided in secret treaties between Nazi Germany and the Soviet Union. Latvia had become an object to be divided by two dictatorial great powers. Throughout World War II, Latvia was powerless against these great-powers machinations. Other, more powerful states with much older democratic traditions were also occupied. Two occupational regimes replaced each other in Latvia. They changed the life of Latvia and affected not only the whole of the state and society, but all persons individually. On June 17, 1940, the army of the Soviet Union invaded Latvia and occupied it. The USSR acted subtly and deceitfully in Latvia as well as in the other Baltic States. Citizens of the country appeared to be conducting the process of annexation, but the real decision-makers were the Embassy of the USSR, Moscow's Special Emissary Andrei Vishinski, and also the Red Army. A whole contingent of well-known and democratically-minded politicians and socially prominent figures from the period of Latvia's parliamentary period (before 1934) expressed their desire to participate politically and formed lists for the parliamentary elections. Their efforts, however, were in vain and were soon declared to be "a serious, counter-revolutionary crime." In Stalin's Soviet Union, this meant a death sentence or at least ten years in a prison camp.

Europe's democratic states and the diplomatic representatives of the USA in Latvia observed these "changes in state order."

In order to partially mask the truth of military aggression, immediately after the armed forces of the USSR entered, mass demonstrations were organized, the participants of which "unanimously" supported the actions of the collaborationist government of Augusts Kirchenšteins. Very quickly, however, participations in demonstrations became mandatory and non-participation met with the threat of punishment. In the twentieth century, even in the year of 1940, good propaganda required that conquerors arrive as "true bringers of freedom." In the inter-war period, no other state in the world (with the possible exception of Nazi Germany) so loudly proclaimed its "love for peace" and its "general attempts for universal disarmament" as the Soviet Union. It also proclaimed itself as the "only state of free workers and peasants to which the entire civilized world's working peoples dreamt of belonging." The entrance of the Red Army into Latvia was explained in terms of defense needs of the country in case of war. The people were promised the renewal of democracy and the right of free elections. Actually, the Soviet government prepared the inhabitants of Latvia for a large-scale theater performance that was to be called a "socialist revolution." Through all of the years of Soviet occupation, even to the end of the 1980s, historians, philosophers, and lawyers of the Latvian SSR had to demonstrate this "revolution's" objective preconditions, to uncover its development, to falsify events, and to glorify its result.

The Stalinist regime in the Soviet Union can be characterized with the words "police terror." This regime was forced upon Latvia. At the beginning, however, no one could even imagine what miseries it would bring the country's inhabitants. The Peoples' Commissariat of the Interior of the Latvian SSR spearheaded this work. Soon after the annexation of Latvia, the "Criminal Code of the Russian Soviet Federal Socialist Republic" was introduced, together with its comprehensive 58th paragraph. According to this paragraph, any inhabitant could become the "enemy of the people," subject to repression, because he or she had lived in a bourgeois state and had participated in its elections. They might have had sung "songs hostile to class" in the country's song festivals, for instance. The Commissariat of the Interior carefully collected and indexed denunciations and created its web of agents and informants. The task of the latter was to report on the prevailing public mood and to uncover "enemies of the people." A wave of arrests swept over Latvia. On June 14, 1941, about 15,000 residents of Latvia, including infants, were deported to Siberia.

Initially, Soviet power in Latvia held sway only for one year (1940-1941) but it was able to so alter the attitudes of the inhabitants that a large part of the people awaited the next occupiers – the Germans of the Hitler regime -- as "liberators from Bolshevism." On July 1, 1941, many of the inhabitants of Rīga went out on the streets to joyfully greet German soldiers. One year of terror under the Soviet regime erased the centuries-long hostility that Latvians had nursed toward earlier German-speaking conquerors of the country.

The Germans of the Third Reich, now Latvia's second occupiers, very deceitfully exploited Latvian hostility towards the former communist regime by unmasking and underscoring the latter's repressive rule.

Both regimes were similar in their efforts to destroy even the memory of the years of independence (1918-1940) of the Latvia state. For both regimes, Latvia was raw material for their own designs and a source of labor, as well as cannon fodder for their military forces. Nevertheless, there were differences in the attitudes of the two occupier's attitudes toward the administrative organization of the territory under their control. The Soviet Union, following its old dream of a soviet socialist regime, created a formal unit – the Latvian Soviet Socialist Republic. The leaders of Nazi Germany, however, gave priority to their own plans for a "Thousand-Year Reich" and included the former USSR northeastern territory now under their control into a unified, separate creation called *Ostland* or Eastern Land.

From the first days of Nazi German occupation, Latvia's inhabitants were told that Jews, who according to Nazi racial theory were not even humans but in the best case a "generation of vipers" – as they were called in the Latvian-language newspaper *Tēvija*, were guilty of all of the previous misery and the crimes of the Soviet regime. This was why the land had to be "cleansed" of all Jews (the wealthy and the poor, women and children). "Nationalistically inclined Latvians" were invited to do this dirty work. There were not many such people, but those that did get involved in the "purification actions," and particularly their leaders, contributed to the Nazis' "final solution" doctrine in a most shameful and condemnable manner.

In 1943, Nazi Germany suffered repeated defeats on the Eastern front and was suddenly in need of more soldiers. In Latvia, mobilization was undertaken of a "Latvian SS Volunteer Legion." This designation was chosen to hide the violation of international law that forbids the mobilization of the inhabitants of occupied territories into the army of the occupier. Thus the inhabitants of Latvia came to be fighting in the armies of both Nazi Germany and the Soviet Union. In 1944 on Latvian territory, Latvian soldiers were positioned against each other at different places of the front: father against son, brother against brother.

During this whirlwind of tragic events, the opinion of the Ambassador of the Republic of Latvia to the USA went unheard. He clearly and straightforwardly defined the Nazi regime as an occupation, and asked the inhabitants of Latvia not to collaborate in its criminal acts.

In spite of the fact that neither the USA nor Great Britain recognized the 1940 annexation of the Baltic States, including that of Latvia, the fact of the matter remains that in the post-World War II period the Soviet Union was able to resume its occupation. The Moscow government was convinced that this time the "power of the working masses" would last forever. Expressing this belief, the newspaper of the Latvian Communist Party, *Cīņa*, wrote in January of 1949: "Of course there are still some backward-crawlers with us, leftovers from an old era that have not forgotten the bourgeois past and do not even know what they are now hoping for."[1]

In the Latvian SSR, a governing structure was created that was similar to those existing in other Union Republics (see Appendix 4). Until the reacquisition of independence in 1991, this basic structure did not change. The 1977 Constitution (and its 6th paragraph), however, constitutionally reinforced the Communist Party's dictatorial role in the state (in the words of the Constitution – "the leading role"). Every tool was used in Latvia to guarantee the realization of "socialist transformation" and to suppress any resistance , with the end being the creation of a people conceived of as an obedient mass (in Soviet propaganda, the inhabitants of the state were designated as "the peoples' masses," "the working peoples' masses," or the "peasant masses"). During Stalin's rule (until 1953), terror was practiced against the residents of the state (see Appendix 5) as well as complete surveillance of them. Later, methods of control were changed, but political censorship existed until the end of the 1980s.

Of course, the Stalinist regime cannot be compared to what existed in the USSR or in the Latvian SSR in the 1970s and 1980s. In the latter decades, after gradually overcoming the destructiveness that accompanied agricultural collectivization in Latvia, collective farms were able to guarantee the inhabitants with food. A large part of the agricultural product was taken to other regions of the USSR. In all of the post-World War II years in Latvia, there continued a rapid industrial development, in line with planning originating in Moscow. The growth of industrial production required additional labor. Since existing labor reserves in Latvia were already exhausted by 1950, in subsequent decades needed labor was recruited in unlimited numbers from other regions of the USSR. This process had many negative consequences. For one, it gradually diminished the proportion of Latvians among the inhabitants of Latvia. By the end of the 1980s Latvians did not account for more than 50% (see Appendix 1-3) of the total population of the country, which fact threatened the very existence of the Latvian nation in the state entity that bore their name. Second, the rapid growth in the number of urban dwellers reduced the standards of living in the cities because of inadequate development of infrastructure and lagging construction of apartments. The labor recruited from elsewhere in the Soviet Union, however, was still ready to live in Latvia, even if in barracks, because in other regions of the USSR living conditions were even worse. Third, because industrial enterprises were located primarily in Rīga, this ultimately led to basic differences in the level of development of different regions of Latvia. Fourth, the development of industry did not necessarily raise living standards because most of production was aimed at meeting the demands of the military- industrial complex, particularly in the years from the 1960s to the 1980s.

All of these problems greatly influenced Latvia's economic and social development even after the country had regained its independence in 1991.

· ·

The collection consists of archival documents, the majority of which are published here in English for the first time. Many documents from the post-war era were kept in secret collections or in special files inaccessible to researchers. In order to more widely reflect the events in Latvia, documents from different levels of governing institutions and organizations have been used, including the Latvian SSR Council of Ministers, the Latvian SSR Supreme Soviet, and the Latvian SSR Ministry of Finance.

Important documents were kept in the archive of the former Party Institute of History of the Latvian Communist Party Central Committee. These documents now reside in the Latvian State Archive as a separate collection -- the section of social-political documents. Particularly informative is the voluminous material from the collection of the Latvian Communist Party Central Committee. Since the Party's Central Committee concentrated power in its hands, this material reflects practically all of the spheres of social life.

A very specific group of the sources is the archival material of the former Latvian SSR State Security Committee. These documents (primarily investigative files) have also been turned over to

Latvian State Archive and constitute Fond (collection) No. 1986. The publication of these documents is important, first of all because they describe the mechanisms of the terror apparatus in the USSR; second, because they testify to the powerlessness of human logic and understanding in confrontation with the regime; and thirdly, because they demonstrate that there were still brave souls that struggled against the brutalities of the system.

Chronologically, the collection ends with the reacquisition of independence in 1991.

The editors have tried to present the complete text of the documents, deleting only trivial sections or sections not relevant to the question being illustrated. The documents are divided by thematic groups in order to facilitate understanding. Within these groups, the documents are generally in chronological order. Each chapter has an introduction that is meant to enhance orientation in each of the complicated periods of the contemporary Latvian history.

The peculiarities of the language and its style are preserved in the documents as much as possible, but grammatical mistakes have been corrected when they were apparently typographical. Also, translation of the documents into English has made their peculiarities less obvious. Words or parts of words missing from the text have been included in brackets; at times, brackets are used to add words to make the meaning clear. The title reflects the type of document and its contents as well as the place and date of its origin. If the document was created in Rīga (and there are many of these), then this is not shown in the title. Following the document is its key to its source: archive or source abbreviation, *fond* (collection) number, *apraksts* (directory) number, *lieta* (file) number, page number(s). Since the majority of the documents are published here in English for the first time, the key also draws attention to those that are reprinted. Since most of the documents are typed (this is also not shown in the key), this fact is stressed only if the document was hand-written. All documents were written in Russian, German, or Latvian languages, which is also noted in the key.

Commentary is attached to those documents that need additional information on the document's contents. The document collection as a whole is supplemented with information in the form of appendixes.

REPOSITORIES, COLLECTIONS, AND SOURCES USED

Each document in the collection is followed by a sometimes abbreviated reference to the source in which it can be found.

Andersons = E. Andersons and L. Siliņš, *Latvijas Centrālā padome. Latviešu nacionālā kustība 1943.-1945* (Uppsala, 1994).

Atmoda. (Principal newspaper of the post-Soviet "Awakening" movement and of the Latvian Popular Front)

BA = Bundesarchiv Koblenz, Germany

Brīvā Zeme. (Newspaper of the Latvian Farmers Union, published between 1919 and 1940)

Cīņa. (Main newspaper of the Latvian Communist Party; started publication in 1904 as a newspaper of the Latvian social-democratic movement)

Daugavpils Vēstnesis. (A newspaper in the Latvian city of Daugavpils)

Diena. (A leading daily newspaper of post-Soviet Latvia)

Dokumenty = *Документы внешней политики: 1939 год.* Том XXII. Книга вторая (Moscow, 1992)

Fronte = *Latvijas Tautas fronte. Gads pirmais.* Rīga, 1989.

Helsinki-86 = *Latvijas cilvēktiesību aizstāvēšanas grupa "Helsinki – 86." Dokumentu krājums. 07.86.-04.88.* Rīga: Neatkarīgās informācijas centra izdevums, 1989.

Komunistiskā = *Komunistiskā totalitārisma un genocīda prakse Latvijā.* Rīga, 1992.

Krievijas = *Krievijas Latviešu biedrība; Ceļš uz tās izveidošanu, dibināšanas konferences materiāli un darbības pamatmeti pirmajā gadā.* Rīga, 1990.

Kurzemes Vārds. (Newspaper published in Liepāja from 1918 to 1944)

Latvian Legion = A. Ezergailis, ed. *The Latvian Legion: Heroes, Nazis, or Victims? A Collection of documents from OSS WAR-Crimes investigation files 1945-1950.* (Rīga, 1997).

Latvijas okupācija = *Latvijas okupācija un aneksija: 1939-1940. Dokumenti un materiāli.* (Riga, 1995). Document collection prepared by I. Grava-Kreituse, I. Feldmanis, J. Goldmanis, and A. Stranga.

Latvijas Republikas = I. Šneidere and A. Žvinklis, ed. *Latvijas Republikas Ministru kabineta sēžu protokoli: 1940. gada 16. jūnijs- 19. jūlijs* (Rīga, 1991).

Latvijas Tautas Saeimas = *Latvijas Tautas saeimas 1. sesija. 1940. gada 21.-23. jūlijā. Stenogramu atreferējums* (Rīga, 1940).

LKP = *LKP, LKJS un Sarkanās palīdzības revolucionārās lapiņas*. 1920-1940 (Rīga, 1963).

LVA = Latvijas Valsts Arhīvs (Latvian State Archive)

LVVA = Latvijas Valsts Vēstures Arhīvs (Latvian State Historical Archive)

Meyer = Meyer, Alfred, ed. *Das Recht der besetzten Ostgebiete. Estland, Lettland, Litauen, Weissruthenien und Ukraine* (München and Berlin, 1943).

Niurnbergskii protsess = *Нюрнбергский процесс над главными военными преступниками*. Том I (Moscow, 1965).

Polpredy = *Полпреды сообщают .. Сборник документов об отношениях СССР с Латвией, Литвой и Эстонией: Август 1939 г. – август 1940 г* (Moscow, 1990).

Prozess = *Der Prozess gegen die Hauptkriegsverbrecher vor dem internationalen Militargerichtshof: Nürnberg 14, November 1945 – 1 Oktober 1946. –* Band XXIX, *Amtlicher Text Deutsche Ausgabe, Urkunden und anderel Beweismaterial, Nummer 1850 – PS bis Nummer 2233 – PS* (Nürnberg, 1948).

Rīgas IKA = Rīga Municipal Executive Committee Archive

Rīkojumu Vēstnesis. (A government newspaper of the German occupation period of Latvia, 1941-1944, which published in Latvian the official decrees and orders of the occupation authorities)

Tauta = *Tauta. Zeme. Valsts. Dokumentu krājums* (Rīga, 1995).

Tēvija. (The main daily Latvian newspaper during the German occupation of Latvia 1941-1944).

Valdības Vēstnesis. (The official newspaper of the government of Latvia, published 1918-1940)

Valters = Valters, M. *15. maija apvērsums un ārkārtējās pilnvaras ar pilnvaru tekstu* (Stockholm, 1951).

Verkundungsblatt = *Verkundungsblatt des Reichskommissars für das Ostland* (Official publication of the directives of the *Reichskommissar* for *Ostland*).

Verordnungsblatt = *Verordnungsblatt des Reichsministers für die besetzten Ostgebiete* (Official publication of the directives of the *Reichsminister* for the Eastern Occupied Territories).

Ziņotājs = *Latvijas PSR Augstākās Padomes Prezidija Ziņotājs* (News organ of the Presidium of the Supreme Soviet of the Latvian SSR)

PART I: The Eve of Invasion, August 1939 to June 17, 1940

At the beginning of World War II, the government of Latvia declared absolute neutrality (September 1, 1939), but unfortunately was unable to realize this policy. The fate of the country had already been decided before the beginning of the war. This was done by Nazi Germany and the Soviet Union in the August 23, 1939, Non-Aggression Treaty, the so-called Molotov-Ribbentrop Pact (see Document No. 1). An essential component of this treaty was the secret supplementary agreement (protocol) concerning the division of Eastern Europe into spheres of influence. This meant that the Soviet Union acquired complete freedom of action regarding Latvia, whose independence it had recognized earlier by signing the peace treaty with Latvia on August 11, 1920, and with whom the USSR had signed a Non-Aggression Treaty on February 5, 1932.

The government of Latvia was informed of the contents of the secret agreement of the Molotov-Ribbentrop Pact, but could do nothing to change the situation. The Baltic States, including Latvia, were in effect isolated. This happened because of several factors. First of all, there was no unity between the Baltic States, which fact the USSR exploited very successfully; secondly, Great Britain and France showed no desire to stand up for the preservation of the sovereignty of Latvia, Lithuania, and Estonia, leaving these states to their fate; thirdly, Germany's strategic, military interests were directed against Western Europe.

Pursuing its expansionist objectives, the USSR forced Latvia to sign a Mutual Assistance Pact -- or the so-called Bases Treaty (see Documents No. 4 and 5) - on October 5, 1939 (Estonia on September 28, and Lithuania on October 10). The discussion of this treaty took place in Moscow at the Kremlin, and it was very short. At the beginning, Stalin underlined that a division of spheres of influence between Germany and the USSR had already happened and with this, Latvia could be occupied. Thus one more step was taken towards the destruction of Latvian statehood.

As the former President of Latvia, Kārlis Ulmanis, later wrote in his notes from prison in the USSR: "Latvia did not sign the treaty voluntarily... I was worried about the increase and spread of Communist agitation in Latvia; I was also bothered about demonstrating an impact to the inhabitants of Latvia as well as by the international evaluation of the situation; with the signing of this treaty Latvia lost its ability of autonomous political action."[2]

The government of Latvia fulfilled all of its treaty requirements, hoping to demonstrate its good faith and hoping also that the USSR would be satisfied and Latvia could preserve its independence, even with restricted sovereignty.

On September 28, 1939, along with the Treaty of Friendship and Borders, Germany and the USSR signed a secret agreement about the departure of German citizens and people of German descent from the territories that were a part of the USSR's interest sphere. Following this secret agreement between the two Great Powers, Germany, and Latvia signed a treaty on October 30, 1939, concerning the departure of Latvian citizens of German nationality to Germany. Preparations for the implementation of this treaty had already taken place. Latvia signed the treaty due to political pressure from Germany; in this international situation there was no other option. The departees, according to the treaty, had the right to take their movable property with them. Their immovable property would transfer to a fiduciary departees' joint stock company, called *UTAG* (acronym for *Umsiedlungs-Treuhand-Aktien-Gesellschaft*), created just for this task (see Document No. 7). Even at this critical moment, the government of Latvia was able to forbid the removal of property that had cultural-historical value, such as antiquities, archives, and works of art.

The departure of Germans with Latvian citizenship continued until the spring of 1940, but at the moment of Latvia's occupation by the USSR on the 17th of June, 1940, there were still around 10,000 Germans in Latvia.[3]

World War II affected the economic conditions of Latvia very negatively (see Documents No. 8 and 9). As a result of the blockade of the Baltic Sea, external trade was reduced substantially, and it was not possible to guarantee a steady supply of raw materials for factories. Keeping in mind that Latvia's industrial plants used predominantly imported raw materials (in some industries they amounted to more than 50% of all raw materials), the work day and work week were reduced for those with work, and unemployment increased. By contrast, in agriculture, with the summer season approaching, a labor shortage became apparent. Until World War II, more than 40,000 foreign agricultural workers (primarily from Lithuania and Poland) were used for seasonal labor in Latvia. With the beginning of war, rural workers from Poland could no longer arrive and the number of workers fell considerably.

Despite the economic difficulties caused by the war, the domestic politics of Latvia remained mostly stable, even though leftist agitators (primarily the underground Latvian Communist Party) tried to destabilize the political situation by calling on the people to overthrow the Ulmanis government (see Document No. 13). They were unable to accomplish this, even though some in the population were dissatisfied with economic conditions and with the rise in prices.

In the first half of 1940, the pressure exerted by the USSR on Latvia increased. There were repeated requests to increase the number of troops at the Soviet bases in Latvia, and there was considerable though surreptitious construction work going on at these bases.

Simultaneously, the USSR continuously and without foundation accused the government of Latvia of not fulfilling the provisions of the October 5, 1939, Treaty (see Document No. 12). At the same time, military activity by Nazi Germany increased on the Western front: in April and May of 1940, Germany invaded Denmark, Norway, Belgium, the Netherlands, and France. Both of these factors influenced the Latvian Cabinet of Ministers to issue the decree of May 17, 1940, that granted authority to the Latvian Ambassador in London to represent Latvia's interests abroad in case of an emergency (see Document No. 14). As a result of this decree, as well as the later policy of the Western countries of not recognizing the occupation of the Baltic States, the Republic of Latvia continued to exist *de jure* even after Soviet occupation.

Already in the spring of 1940 in the Leningrad and Moscow military districts, special cadres were being formed and trained (see Document No. 19). These consisted primarily of Latvian members of the All-Union Communist (Bolshevik) Party who knew the Latvian language, some well and some poorly. They were being prepared to be sent into Latvia where they were to assume positions of authority after the occupation. This underlines the planning that preceded Latvia's occupation and annexation.

In the middle of June of 1940, events unfolded very rapidly in the Baltic States. On June 14th, the government of the USSR presented Lithuania with an ultimatum, demanding that it change its government and allow the entrance of additional Soviet forces into the state (the 9th-12th divisions). On June 15th, Lithuania accepted the ultimatum without protest. On the night of June 15th, Soviet armed forces attacked Latvia's border posts (see Document No. 15). On June 16, the government of the USSR submitted similar ultimata to Estonia and Latvia (see Document No. 16). Both states accepted the demands. On the evening of June 16, 1940, the Latvian Cabinet resigned (see Document No. 17). Facing the facts that Lithuania was already occupied and the armed forces of the USSR (numerically superior to Latvia's army, which had roughly 20,000 soldiers) were already on the territory of Latvia, the Latvian government decided to not resist in order to prevent loss of life and destruction of property. In this situation, resistance would not have preserved Latvia's independence. On the morning of June 17th, the armed forces of the USSR entered Latvia's territory in an open fashion, by contrast with the fall of 1939, when the Red Army soldiers were moved to the agreed-upon bases in closed echelons. The occupation of Latvia was completed quickly (see Document No. 18).

DOCUMENTS NO. 1-2: GERMAN-SOVIET RELATIONS

Document No. 1

Secret protocol of the German-Soviet Non-Aggression Treaty of August 23, 1939

In Moscow, August 23, 1939

Secret Supplementary Protocol

Relevant to the signing of the non-aggression pact between Germany and the Union of Soviet Socialist Republics, the authorized representatives of both parties signing this pact in specific, confidential discussions considered the question of delineating the spheres of interest of both sides in Eastern Europe. The results of these discussions were the following:

1. In the event of territorial, political restructuring in the Baltic States (Finland, Estonia, Latvia and Lithuania), the regions belonging to the north of the northern border of Lithuania are the border between German and USSR spheres of influence. Lithuania's interests with respect to the Vilnius province are recognized by both sides.

2. In the event of territorial, political restructuring in the territories belonging to Poland the approximate border of Germany's and the USSR's spheres of influence will be the line of rivers Narev, Visla and Sana. The question of whether the preservation of an independent Polish state serves the interests of both sides and what its borders should be will be completely clarified by future political developments. In any event, both governments will resolve this question in the spirit of friendly cooperation.

In the southeast of Europe the Soviet side emphasizes Soviet interests in Bessarabia. The German side confirms its complete political disinterest in this region.

Both sides will keep this pact in complete secrecy.

Moscow, August 23, 1939

In the name of the German government   Authorized by the government of the USSR
       J. von Ribbentrop   V. Molotov

Source: *Polpredy, pp. 17-18; Latvijas okupācija, pp. 71-72. Original in Russian..*

Comment*: The German-Soviet Non-Aggression Treaty was signed in Moscow at the same time as the secret protocols. Further expanding the said agreement, on September 28, 1939 in Moscow, the USSR, and Germany signed a treaty of friendship and borders. In the third paragraph of this treaty, it was said that the governments of both states could undertake the "necessary state changes" in their zones of interest.*

The USSR denied the existence of this published document for fifty years. During the International War Crimes Tribunal in Nuremburg (from November 20, 1945-October 1, 1946), the representatives of the victorious states agreed that the question of the existence of this pact, its contents, and its influence on the development of the following events would not be discussed. Only at the beginning of 1948 did the US State Department in cooperation with the Ministries of Foreign Affairs of Great Britain and France publish the document collection Nazi-Soviet Relations, 1939-1941, *which included the text of the secret protocols.*

Excerpts from the notes of G. Hilger, advisor to the German Embassy, about conversations between Stalin and Joachim von Ribbentrop concerning the USSR's plans regarding the Baltic States.

In Moscow, September 27-29, 1939

[…] About the third point – "the Baltic" – the Minister[4] announced the following:

It follows from the report of Ambassador Graf von der Schulenburg, that the Soviet government from this moment has begun to work on this matter, which unquestionably is related to the discussions that are currently under way with the Estonian government. The German Ambassador in Estonia reported that the Soviet Union offered Estonia a military convention for five years (Stalin corrected this to ten years) and requested the creation of bases in Estonia's territory for Soviet naval forces and airplanes and for close cooperation. This apparently must be seen as the first step in resolving the Baltic question. Germany currently finds itself in a state of war and would welcome the step-by step solution to the Baltic question. It is clear that we are not interested in the affairs of Estonia and Lithuania. But we would be grateful if the Soviet government would inform us when and how they are preparing to solve this set of questions so that the German government, in relation to the accepted agreement, could formulate its position. What follows from the report of Graf von der Schulenburg is that the Soviet side expects from our side clear agreement (Stalin added: we expect a favorable attitude). […]

[…] On the question of the Baltic, Stalin reported that the Soviet government requested that the Estonian government provide bases for their naval forces in Estonian ports and the Dago and Ösel islands[5], as well as bases for their air forces. To guard these bases, the Soviet government will place in Estonia one infantry division, one cavalry brigade, one tank brigade, and one air force brigade. All of these events will happen under cover of the Soviet Union and Estonian Mutual Aid Agreement; Estonia has already agreed.

To the minister's question if the Soviet government foresaw in this way to slowly push in to Estonia and potentially also Latvia, Mr. Stalin responded affirmatively, adding that irrespective of this, in Estonia the current government system, ministries, etc. would stay in place for the time being.

Regarding Latvia, Stalin reported that the Soviet government intends to offer similar recommendations to it. But if Latvia resists the offer of a mutual aid pact on the same terms as Estonia then the Soviet army will "settle accounts" with Latvia in the shortest period of time.

Regarding Lithuania, Stalin reported that the Soviet Union will include Lithuania in its requests in the event of a concluded, relevant agreement with Germany about the "exchange" of territory. In the first part of the discussion[6], Stalin did not state his intentions regarding the seizing of Lithuania very clearly. […]

When this part of the discussion ended[7], the Minister asked Stalin to report in what way the Soviet government foresaw the realization of its plans regarding the Baltic.

Mr. Stalin answered that the Estonian government agreed to the Soviet Union's suggestions and that is why the relevant conclusion of an agreement with Estonia can be expected already this evening, and at the latest tonight. Then Stalin told us the contents of the agreement with Estonia (currently arrived at). Not only that, but Stalin told us that in the text of the agreement about the stationing of Soviet naval forces the decided-upon place is Baltisport[8], but at the same time in a special, confidential discussion it had already been agreed upon that ships will also be stationed in Tallinn because Baltisport is not yet fully ready. As far as the maximum number of troops to be brought into Estonia, Stalin said 25 thousand. In the earlier discussions he mentioned the number of aviation brigades as three regiments. At the conclusion, Stalin repeated that at the present time there were no changes foreseen in the current political and economic systems in Estonia or the establishing of the Soviet system. For the time being, the Estonian constitution and ministries will continue their work. For the time being also, Estonia will even resolve its own foreign policy matters. [...]

Source: *Dokumenti, pp. 610-611. Original in German.*

DOCUMENTS NO. 3-6: THE USSR FORCES ITS MILITARY BASES ON LATVIA

Document No. 3

Minutes of an emergency session of the Cabinet of Ministers of Latvia about discussions with the USSR

October 1, 1939

Present:

Minister President	Dr. K. Ulmanis
Deputy Minister President and Minister of War	Gen.J. Balodis
Minister of the Interior	K. Veitmanis
Minister of Education	Prof. J. Auškaps
Minister of Social Affairs	A. Bērziņš
Minister of Transportation	B. Einbergs
Minister of Welfare	J. Volonts
Minister of Agriculture	J. Birznieks
Minister	J. Čamanis
State Comptroller	H. Apsītis

Minutes: Minister of Justice

Meeting began at 18:10.

The President gave a report on why the emergency session of the Cabinet of Ministers had to be called. In quick order the question of sending a delegation to Moscow was raised. The Minister of Foreign Affairs reported about his discussions with our Ambassador in Moscow about the sending of representatives of the Latvian government to Moscow to undertake discussions with the government of the USSR. The necessity of the trip was called for by the treaties that were ratified with Germany on September 28th of this year and the other – with Estonia. Decided to send on October 2 to Moscow the Minister of Foreign Affairs, V. Munters.

The President placed before the Cabinet the projected report about the upcoming discussions with the government of the USSR and the delegating of the Minister of Foreign Affairs to Moscow.

The report brought forward was accepted.

In the discussions about the delegation's assignment there was made the unanimous decision to preserve peace in the state and to defend with all possible tools the interests of the Latvian nation and state.

Meeting closed at 20:10

State and Minister President	K. Ulmanis
Minister of Justice	H. Apsītis

Source: *LVVA, 1307. f., 1. apr., 315. l., p. 213; Latvijas okupācija, pp. 115-116.Original in Latvian.*

Comment: On September 28, 1939, the USSR and Germany signed a treaty of friendship and borders in Moscow; on the same day the Estonia-USSR Mutual Assistance Treaty was signed.

The discussions of the delegations of Latvia and the USSR began on October 2nd late in the evening. Stalin also participated in them.

On October 3rd in an extraordinary session the Cabinet of Ministers decided:

"2. to assign to the Minister of Foreign Affairs the task of using all efforts to improve the text of the Estonia-Russia treaty, trying, if possible, to get the most favorable conditions for the USSR treaty with Latvia;

3. to authorize the Minister of Foreign Affairs, V. Munters, to sign the Mutual Assistance Treaty between Latvia and the USSR." [LVVA, 130. f., 2. apr. 1.l., p. 98]

Document No. 4

Mutual Assistance Pact between Latvia and the Union of Soviet Socialist Republics

Moscow, October 5, 1939

The President of the Republic of Latvia on one side and the Presidium of the Supreme Soviet of the USSR on the other side, with the purpose of developing the friendly relations founded upon the Peace Treaty of August 11, 1920; and recognizing of independent statehood on each side and non-interference in each other's domestic affairs; recognizing that the Peace Treaty of August 11, 1920, and the Non-Aggression Treaty of February 5, 1932, and the peaceful path of resolving conflicts remains the strong foundation of their mutual relations; are convinced that the interests of both equal parties are served by the precise definition of the guaranteeing mutual security, and recognize the necessity of concluding between them the following mutual assistance pact, and for this purpose appoint as their authorized agents:

For the President of the Republic of Latvia: Vilhelms Munters, Minister of Foreign Affairs,

For the Presidium of the Supreme Soviet of the USSR: V. M. Molotov, Chair of the Soviet of People's Commissars and Commissar of Foreign Affairs,

Who mutually have demonstrated their authorizations that were found to be in the necessary and appropriate form, agreed to the following:

Paragraph I
Both Equal Parties undertake to provide assistance to each other, including also militarily, in the event of a direct attack or if the threat of attack would arise from any European Great Power on the Equal Parties' sea borders with the Baltic Sea or on their land borders with Estonia or the territory of the Republic of Lithuania as well as on the bases mentioned in the pact's third paragraph.

Paragraph II
The Soviet Union undertakes to extend assistance to Latvia's army on beneficial terms in the form of armaments and other war materiel.

Paragraph III
The Republic of Latvia, in order to guarantee the security of the Soviet Union and also to strengthen its own independence, grants to the Soviet Union the right to maintain, in the cities of Liepāja and Ventspils, naval bases and some aviation airfields on the basis of a lease for a determined price. The specific place for the bases and for the airfields shall be determined, and their borders defined, on the basis of mutual agreement.

In order to defend the narrows of Irbe, the Soviet Union is granted the right, on the same terms, to place a coastal artillery base on the seashore between Ventspils and Pitrags. The naval bases, airfields, and coastal artillery bases, in order to defend the Soviet Union, have the right to keep on these bases and airfields at the mentioned places and at their own cost a strictly limited number of Soviet armed land and sea forces, whose maximum number will be determined with a separate agreement.

Paragraph IV
Both Equal Parties undertake to not form any unions and to not participate in any coalitions that are aimed against one of the Equal parties.

Paragraph V
The implementation of this pact can in no way impinge on the sovereign rights of either Equal Party, including their structures of government, economic and social system, and military behavior.

The bases and airfields (paragraph III) shall remain Latvia's territory,

Paragraph VI
This pact takes effect upon the exchange of ratified documents. The exchange of ratified documents will happen in Rīga in six days time counting from the day of signing.

This pact is in force for ten years after which, in the event that one of the Equal Parties does not recognize the necessity of abrogating this pact one year before its expiration, it will automatically remain in force for the next ten years.

In confirming this, the above mentioned authorized agents signed the treaty and affixed their seals.

Drawn up in Moscow in two originals in the Latvian and Russian languages on October 5, 1939.

V. Munters   V. Molotov

Source: *Valdības Vēstnesis, October 10, 1939. Original in Latvian.*

Comment: *The Presidium of the Supreme Soviet of the USSR ratified the pact on October 8, 1939, and Latvia's Cabinet of Ministers on October 10th. The exchange of ratified documents took place in Rīga on October 11th.*

The Peace Treaty between Latvia and the Soviet Union (August 11, 1920) mentioned in the document ended the state of war between both countries. Russia recognized the independence of the state of Latvia "without protest and for eternity" and renounced any claims on Latvia's land or people (2nd paragraph).

The Non-Aggression Treaty between both states was signed for three years, but on April 4, 1934, was extended to ten years. The first paragraph of this treaty said that "both above mentioned parties mutually attempt to refrain from any kind of attack against each other, as well as from any violent actions that are intended against the other parties 'territorial integrity and inviolability or political independence, regardless of whether such an attack or violent act would happen independently or together with some other states, declaring or not declaring war." [Valdības Vēstnesis, July 5, 1932]

Document No. 5

Confidential Protocol of the Mutual Assistance Pact between Latvia and the USSR

October 5, 1939

Attachment
Confidential Protocol

I
It is decided that in order to avert and bring an end to attempts to draw the Equal Parties into the war currently in Europe, the USSR has the right during this war to keep on the places that are meant for airfields and bases (Pact, 3rd p.), and in specific land and air armed force garrisons, altogether up to twenty five thousand persons.

II
The assistance defined in the first paragraph of the pact is extended after the request of the other side; moreover, after mutual agreement, the side whose obligation it is to offer aid to the other side, in the event of war with a third state, can remain neutral.

III
In order to implement this pact and to solve any questions that may arise, a joint commission will be created on the principle of parity that will work out its own internal rules.

In the event of disagreements about the place for bases and airfields and the definition of their borders, as well generally concerning the work of the Joint Parity Commissions, disputed questions will be decided through diplomatic channels or through direct discussions between governments.

IV
This confidential protocol is an attachment to the Mutual Assistance Pact between the USSR and Latvia concluded on October 5, 1939.

In Moscow, October 5, 1939

V. Molotov
V. Munters

Source: *Polpredy, pp. 86-87. Original in Russian.*

Comment: *A Joint Commission was created to address practical questions relating to the stationing of the armed forces of the USSR on bases in the territory of Latvia. It began its work on October 14, 1939. On Latvia's side the Commission was led by General M. Hartmanis, on the USSR side – Corps Commander I. Boldin. In concert with the protocol of the signed agreement, Soviet bases were created in two of Latvia's port cities on the Baltic Sea (Liepāja and Ventspils), as well as in other towns in the western part of the country. On October 29th, the Soviet armed forces began entering Latvia's territory.*

Report of the USSR *chargé d'affaires* **in Latvia, I. Čičajev, to the People's Commissar of Foreign Affairs of the USSR, V. Molotov, about the mood of the Latvian population regarding the signing of the Latvia-USSR Mutual Assistance Pact**

October 10, 1939

The mutual assistance pact signed this year on October 5 in Moscow[9] has reduced to a certain degree the tension and confusion evident among government personnel in the last while.

Still, the pact has not created complete calm. The ruling class, together with its government, does not believe that the pact has created a stable and long-lasting condition. Fear of a potential Bolshevization of Latvia is tied to the expected arrival of our military units to guard the naval bases and the airfields. The ruling class also is afraid of the appearance of revolutionary activities within the country. They base this on the mood of the mass of the working people that openly shows sympathy for the Soviet Union. Among these inhabitants there is the conviction that the days of fascist dictatorship in Latvia are numbered and that in the near future there will be a Soviet Latvia. Rumors have spread that in Latgale a temporary underground revolutionary action committee has already begun to create a movement.

In the ranks of government there is a characteristic mood that was exemplified by the Minister of Agriculture, Birznieks, in his speech of October 6, in which he said: "if conditions are created that demand of us certain responsibilities and sacrifices, then we do not have to hang our heads and do not have to be concerned with empty gossiping. We have to do our job the same as before." This can be said to be official recognition of the need to bear "sacrifices," which the government has done. Unofficially, however, there are many more open conversations that depict the signing of the pact as yielding to the threat of force. The Commander of Latvia's Army, General Berķis, displayed such a sentiment in discussion with our military attaché, by asking acidly: for what purpose were 280 tanks concentrated on the Latvian border?

A desire to show the USSR in the role of the "aggressor" is also evident in the so-called "democratic" camp, including in some social democratic leaders (Bastjānis) who spread shameless libel "about the attack of Russian reactionaries," "the intentions of USSR imperialism" etc.

Nevertheless, an important segment of the influential ranks (Finance Minister Valdmanis, Credit Bank Director A. Bērziņš and others) understand the pact as the "lesser evil" and say that it is better to be under Russian influence than German because with the Russians the Latvians save their identity, but that Germans will not only destroy their national culture, but also the Latvians themselves.

The most striking example of the attitude of the government ranks toward the pact is reflected in the behavior of the press that is under the strict control of the Ministry of Social Affairs. Commentary on the meaning of the pact for Latvia appeared in the Latvian newspapers only four days after its signing. Before that time, no newspaper expressed its attitude to the pact. Still, it must be noted that the published comments are notable for extreme terseness and the repetition of dry facts. Apparently the newspapers were given a directive to not describe the pact in particulars and in that way to minimize its value and usefulness for Latvia. In the last few days the voice of the press has become a little freer and it is beginning to give the pact more attention, but I still do not detect truthfulness and a desire to appropriately value the pact's usefulness to Latvia.

In characterizing the government's position, the following facts are interesting to note: they are almost openly saying that before the pact was concluded the Ulmanis government heightened its attempts to find some support for its position in Berlin. It decided to conclude the pact only when it received the answer that Germany had no interests, other than economic, in the Baltic. Apparently, the habit of harmonizing its actions with Western European countries continues to influence the government even in these times.

As distinct from the attitude of the ruling elite, the majority of the classes of the Latvian nation – workers, poor farmers, - particularly Russians and the progressive intelligentsia accepted the mutual assistance pact with unhidden joy. They call us by telephone, send letters, come in person, to express their satisfaction with the growth of the Soviet Union's influence in the Baltic. They only regret that the Soviet Union has accomplished too little, yielding to the Latvian government side. Our friends would like, if not quite a Soviet Latvia, than at least the freeing of the country from the dictatorship of the Ulmanis government.

The turn forced upon the Latvian government's foreign policy has called forth different conversations and guesses here about the goals of Ulmanis. For an example, they say that he is getting ready to create a coalition government with social democratic participation. These speculations include the names of the future social democratic ministers – P. Kalniņš, Lorencs, and others. In the thinking of the masses, this is related to Moscow's requests that were supposedly presented to Munters during the conversations in Moscow. In the same manner, they evaluate the resignation of the Chief of the Army General Staff, General Hartmanis, who had a germanophilic reputation.

Some guesses refer to delays in talks about a trade treaty. The opinion is widespread that Moscow is dragging out the trade talks on purpose in order to worsen the economic conditions and to thereby engender more dissatisfaction among the people's with the Ulmanis government.

In the last few days, the situation has been complicated by the beginning of the German government's activities to repatriate the local German ethnic inhabitants to Germany – about which I informed you by telegram. You will find far more detailed news about this question in material that we are transmitting on the TASS line.

Chargé d'affaires of the USSR in Latvia   I. Čičajev

Source: *Polpredy, pp. 99-100. Original in Russian.*

DOCUMENTS NO. 7- 15
ADJUSTING TO DANGER

Document No. 7

Confidential review of the General Secretary of Latvia's Ministry of Foreign Affairs, M. Nukša, about the discussions with Germany's Ambassador, U. von Kotze, in relation to the departure of the Baltic Germans and its process

November 7, 1939

Overview of the Repatriation of Baltic Germans[10]

The Baltic German repatriation is already occurring very rapidly and intensively...

On October 6th at about 10:00 in the morning, Germany's Ambassador, von Kotze, called me, and asked if I could accept him in the forenoon because he had some urgent news. We agreed on the time: 11:15, but the Ambassador arrived at 11:30.

The Ambassador apologized and then immediately referred to the just-signed treaty with the USSR[11]; he feels very much with Latvia in this difficult time, but hopes that Latvia will be able to soften the final solution to the question as was the case with the Estonians.

Then the Ambassador verbally (as the Ambassador affirmed) presented the news that his government had told him to give to the Latvian government.

In recent days, the Ambassador began, in relation to ongoing events, there has been a noticeable increase in hostility towards Germans in Latvia. The uninformed masses supposedly wish to blame Germany and Germans for what has happened, even though it is known that Germany is without guilt. There were hostile posters in Jelgava; in the streets, the staff of the German embassy heard it said that Germans should be killed, that Germans don't have any business here etc. Even an officer used such words in a store. Furthermore, relative to the introduction of the ration system, Germans have had to surrender their passports and because of that they are left without personal documents.

Therefore following the assignment of his government he had come to give us verbal notification of the following:

The Latvian government should know about the growth of hostility and is asked that all necessary steps be taken to make more secure the German nationality group;

Taking into account the troubled conditions, the German government offers the particular protection of the German nationality group (*besonderen Schutz*);

The Latvian government is asked to allow those ethnic German Latvian citizens (the local Germans) that would like to leave Latvia to do so through simplified procedures, particularly with respect to various formalities (visa, currency, luggage, etc.);

From all of this it was apparent that the Ambassador was delivering his information in a great hurry. His statements were not precise; the formulation was not prepared; they were created bit by bit after many questions from my side.

I answered that I had personally not noticed any hostility toward the German element, and that the Ministry of Foreign Affairs also knew nothing of it; but that in respect to safety, the government had always taken all steps to maintain order and legality and would continue to do so in the future.

After inquiries at the Ministry of the Interior, it turns out that some of the phenomena noted by the Ambassador really had happened, for example: the posters in Jelgava, angry comments. The nation was feeling importance and consequences of events.

I asked von Kotze what is meant by *besonderen Schutz*? About that he had been told nothing precise, but here it could have the meaning of "taken away," *Abtransport*, perhaps in those cases when legal departure could not be guaranteed. (So things would not happen as in Bromberg – the Ambassador remarked).

Closing the discussion, I remarked that I would familiarize the Minister of Foreign Affairs with the Ambassador's notification.

An hour later Hitler gave his speech to the Reichstag in which he described as untenable that ethnic German splinter groups are located in Eastern Europe. These groups were the precise cause of constant international troubles. Therefore, one of the most far-sighted tasks aimed at bringing order to European life was the rearrangement of the inhabitants of Eastern Europe.

After several days, the German Ambassador came with an official suggestion regarding this question, and also received the Latvian Government's consent to proceed. At the same time, German ships arrived in a great hurry to take away the repatriating Germans and in the same hurry experts arrived to continue the discussions. Some of them had not even been able to get Latvian visas.

From our side, we told the German Ambassador that departure could take place only in an organized manner and on the basis of a treaty. The Cabinet of Ministers created a specific commission on October 10th to deal with the question relating to the departure to Germany of the relatives of the ethnic Germans. The Minister of Justice, Apsītis, was appointed the chair of the commission and its members were the Deputy Minister of the Interior Legzdiņš, General Secretary of the Ministry of

Foreign Affairs Nukša, Director of the Agriculture Department Grāvis and the LTR Chamber General Secretary Zalts.[12]

In the Germany delegation, the participants were Ambassador von Kotze as Chair with about 10 delegates – experts. Specialists were invited into Latvia's delegation – lawyers and representatives from economic organizations.

Latvia's viewpoint was briefly summarized in the State President's message (12.10): "If someone wants to leave, let them leave" … These words defined the fundamental principles of departure rules: the deciding factor is the departee's free will, rather than objective statistics [about ethnic membership]. Besides, in what way could one obtain really convincing, objective proof about belonging to a known ethnicity a short time before departure? In Estonia the same question was easier to answer because there every German is noted in the German Cultural Self-Administration Rolls.

On October 13 there took place the first joint collective meeting of both delegations. They achieved agreement through discussion on fundamental theses. Further work was done in sub-commissions. This work was wide-reaching and very complicated. Liquidation, after all, affects things, connections, relations, and values that have been created over many centuries and that have merged with our life in certain areas of life. How to separate out from this accumulation of a lifetime which is separatable, and how to take from the Germans that which is impossible to remove without violating our own Latvian economic and social conditions - that is a task to which solutions must be found with the greatest amount of attention.

The "Treaty about the repatriation of ethnic German citizens of Latvia to Germany" was signed this year on October 30th as a result of these discussions.

The Treaty's fundamental theses are:

Repatriation will happen as a one-time action at the conclusion of which the German minority ceases to exist in Latvia for all time.

In principle, each citizen, starting with those of 16 years of age, can freely choose to repatriate, or, stay in Latvia without any minority rights.

The departee can take or dispose of movable property, excluding that property that is described in the supplemental minutes and which will have a special manner of disposition.

The transfer of immovable property, beginning from the day of the owner's departure, will be made to a special fiduciary Repatriation Joint Stock Company for supervision and action only, with rights to dispose of it in 2 years time (until December 31, 1941). Regarding immovable property that is not sold by the mentioned date there will be a further agreement or it will be transferred on the basis of an assessment to assenting Latvian institutions, using the Bank of Latvia's promissory notes without interest.

Rural immovable property will go to assenting Latvian institutions with free action in the same manner – against promissory notes – already by January 31, 1940.

All active liquidations will be paid into a special account in the Bank of Latvia. This sum then transfers to Germany in principle as payment for the additional export goods to Latvia periodically for many years.

In addition, it is also noted that with the conclusion of the repatriation actions, all questions that are related to the German minority in Latvia will end for all time: schools, churches, congregations, societies, certain charity offices etc.

Even though in principle each citizen freely chooses departure from or remaining in Latvia, after constant requests from the Latvian delegation there was included in the treaty an option to review the ethnicity in those cases in which unconscientious citizens – Latvians – want to depart in order to take their capital to Germany, due to fears of Bolsheviks and confiscations. Concerning the signing of the Latvian-USSR Mutual Assistance Pact and the pending departure of Baltic Germans, all sorts of rumors are spreading among the people; there is a noticeable feeling of insecurity and even fear. There are substantiated suspicions that a large part in the creation of the rumors was played by local

German leadership in order to hasten the departure. The President of the country has also pointed to the creators of this turbulence in his note.

With the German departure, great changes in the economic life will take place, particularly in Rīga. Many enterprises will have to be sold, as well as real estate, and many apartments will open up. Energetic reordering is expected from the government. If this were left to private persons, or general society had complete freedom of action, considerable disturbances could easily be created: some enterprises would end and unemployment would be created; a swift movement of inhabitants from suburbs to the center would happen where the great majority of German apartments would become free; these apartments would soon come into the hands of wealthy foreign nationals, and the same would happen with real estate. A decree had to be issued hurriedly that the apartments that became free due to the departure of their tenants must be registered with the police without delay. Furthermore, renting can only happen with the agreement of the prefecture. The purchase of real estate still needs the permission of the Minister of Justice. Hopefully in this way it will be possible to limit the immovable property of the Rīga center from passing into the hands of Jews and also to avoid the possibility that suburban owners of buildings, who are mostly Latvians, are left without renters and would come to the edge of bankruptcy.

The Repatriation Registration Office has just begun its work. It is functioning successfully; to this day about 7,500 people have been released from Latvian citizenship. Insufficient time has passed to estimate how large a percentage of the 60,000 Germans will depart. During the treaty discussions, the German delegates claimed that almost all would repatriate; that from Rīga, for example, of the 39,000 Germans at least 38,000 would depart. Still, from many sources comes the news that on the question of departure the Germans are not as unanimous as their leadership claims. Clearly, one can not deny that departure is happening with a heavy heart. The phenomenon has developed differently than some of the local German leaders had imagined it. When the German military prepared its march on the East some of the Baltic Germans had placed high hopes on it, as some say and affirm. But the mountain did not come to Mohammed, - now Mohammed is going to the mountain.

The Latvian public looks at these preparations without hostility, without envy, or taunts, and even with a certain empathy for the departing persons.

In Estonia, repatriation began a few days earlier than in Latvia. Also, there the basis of the repatriation is a written treaty between the two states. There are many fewer Germans in Estonia – 15,000, therefore also a smaller percentage.

Germany has not turned to Lithuania with a suggestion for an official repatriation.

M. Nukša
General Secretary

Source: *LVVA, 2570. f., 1. apr., 466. l., pp. 2-9. Original in Latvian.*

Comment: *According to the statistics of the 1935 census, 62,144 Germans lived in Latvia (3.19% of the total population), of whom 56,441 were citizens of Latvia. By April 15, 1940, 53,172 people had renounced their citizenship and departed, of whom 45,559 were Germans. The second period of departure was in the spring of 1941. This occurred according to the pact concluded between the USSR and Germany on January 10, 1941. At that time, about 17,100 people left Latvia, and of those about 11 or 12 thousand were Germans. Those that left Latvia were relocated to the western provinces of occupied Poland (the Poznan-Bidgošč region).*

The institution created for the purpose -- UTAG (Umsiedlung Treuhand Aktiengesellschaft) -- took care of the possessions and accounts of the departees by means of a fiduciary departees share society. UTAG was created in November of 1939 and continued its work after the Soviet occupation and the annexation of Latvia to the USSR.

From a speech entitled "Peace is not for the tired!" by President Kārlis Ulmanis to an evening audience at Skibe "Ezerkleiši" and to the radio audience

February 10, 1940

[…] Citizens of Latvia!

A blizzard is blowing outside and the frost is crackling, but in the larger world a hostile storm is brewing. People are burdened with daily worries about family, about farms, but further out – about the nation, about the state. […]

We are pressed upon if not exactly by the horrors of war, then a war blockade and we feel its weight. […]

But speaking about the war blockade I want to say that the pressure will become greater and continue to grow. At the same time, being a brave people, let us tell ourselves that we do not even know what all the future hides. And we can not allow ourselves to think and can not lull ourselves with thoughts that everything will become better. The opposite can also be true. And that is why we must be ready to stand against hardships, to overcome them, to be victorious over them, so that always in all of the future we can live in our own land and in our state. […]

[…] But we must keep another thought in our heads – that there could come a moment when not only will there be fewer foreigners among us, but our own youth might be invited and called upon for a different job, to fulfill a different assignment. […]

If that serious, decisive moment comes, then from each rural home one man will have to put on a uniform. You can realize that in Rīga there is no one warehouse where there is enough room to store all the needed supplies, speaking first of clothes and boots. And then know that you must prepare to have at least two shirts and other relevant clothing accessories – two towels, and also a few pairs of good boots, socks, and stockings. Begin to prepare these and keep them ready. And if some farm does not have enough material or another is incapacitated, then talk among yourselves, become sincere and friendly boys again, and get the materials together. And if the materials will never be needed and if they will remain as a surplus, then you will use them yourselves. But be ready with supplies and prepare for that day. If it were not an important thing then I would not talk about it now. And this does not apply only to farms, but to all of the households in the cities as well. […]

Source: *Brīvā Zeme, February 12, 1940. Original in Latvian.*

From Commander of the Army of Latvia, General K. Berķis: Circular Number 45111 to commanders of all units of the armed forces and war office personnel about economic condition and the question of army supplies

February 15, 1940

Rush

The last speech of the President[13] awakened in society and also among soldiers wide-ranging discussions, but in some places its meaning was misunderstood as if we were finding ourselves on the eve of war.

The President's speech was addressed primarily to rural people so that in these present times they would not only help themselves, but that they would also volunteer to help the state with its difficulties with imports and in overcoming the consequences. With the existing war blockade, our purchases in foreign lands will shrink, particularly the acquisitions of cotton and cotton goods. That is why the President invited rural women to take up the spinning-wheel and knitting tools without delay and to supply not just people in their homes, but also other people with shirts, towels, and sheets. That is particularly important for the needs of the army, because every year clothing has had to be ordered from factories that produced them from imported materials. Therefore it would be good if the countryside helped, because a situation could arise when factories could not meet the needs of the army because of a lack of material, and then clothing will have to be purchased from small producers.

There are no "horrors of war" hiding behind the request to again return to our grandfathers' far-sightedness in keeping in each homestead seed and bread for the needs of one year. That is an ancient belief of Latvian farmers – to protect oneself against failed harvests. In present times, when we have to make do with our own strength, this belief is worth remembering respectfully because a failed harvest now would have evil consequences.

It is the same with the instruction about shoes. Every man in each home eligible for military service or in the reserve or of age for serving in the home guard must keep boots at home. That is foreseen in the military obligation law that says each person called up must arrive with two changes of clothing and a good pair of his own boots. Those that might have forgotten these instructions are now reminded of them.

The leaders of the state are doing and will do everything to safeguard us from being pulled into war, but we must always be ready for everything because others will then factor in our preparedness.

Inform you soldiers about what is mentioned above.

General Berķis
Army Headquarters Chief
General Rozenšteins

Source: *LVVA, 1526.f. 1. apr., 543. l., p. 13. Original in Latvian.*

Excerpts from the minutes of a staff meeting in the Ministry of the Interior about relations of the inhabitants of Latvia with the soldiers stationed in the USSR's garrisons in Latvia.

February 21, 1940

This year on the 21st of February at 12:00 noon the Minister of the Interior, K. Veidnieks, convened for a conference in the Ministry's meeting hall the senior staff of the Ministry. The following participated: Deputy Minister J. Legzdiņš; Border Guard Brigade Commander General L. Bolšteins; Directors J. Zankevics, P. Miezis, E. Dimiņš, J. Fridrihsons, A. Austrums and J. Legzdiņš; Police Inspector J. Ķīselis; Police Inspector for Special Assignments P. Pommers; Prefect K. Jansons; Criminal Police Board Chief J. Silarājs; Passive Air Defense Board Chief Colonel J. Ozols; Deputy Directors J. Pūpols, G. Caucis; Assistant Senior Prefect F. Šauberts; Railroad Police Chief K. Briedis; and Section Leaders V. Zariņš, O. Krauze, V. Šalka, and J. Ziemanis.

The conference was opened at 12:03 and was directed by Minister of the Interior K. Veidnieks. Secretary A. Kāps took minutes.

[…] Speaking about the relations between our citizens and the soldiers stationed in USSR garrisons in Latvia, it should be noted that there are still some regrettable misunderstandings and incidents. For example, not long ago an unnecessary incident was occasioned by a Russian military attaché who was traveling by train from Liepāja to Rīga. He did not like the "reserved" sign that had been placed in the carriage and he began an argument with the conductor, asking him to take down the sign. When the conductor did not do this because the sign was placed there following an agreement with the Russians, the attaché ripped own the sign and threatened the conductor by saying that the conductor could no longer travel by train. In part, perhaps, this Russian's tactless behavior can be explained by the fact that a German citizen was traveling in the same carriage. The Russian apparently wanted to show off in front of him. Another Russian officer in recent days, in Liepāja at the Kalpaks Bridge, pulled out a revolver and threatened our police officer in charge who would not let him cross the bridge without a permit. But it turned out that the same Russian had not been allowed to go into Tosmare without a permit. With respect to the people of Ventspils, they have begun to complain about the Russian airplanes that train in the sky and about the use of live ammunition. Falling to the ground, some of the bullets have knocked out windows. Complaints have also come in that Russian tractors have knocked down trees on the side of the road. A particularly large number of these cases have occurred recently. It is noticeable that on the Russian side the needed steps are not being taken to keep these incidents from recurring. There is, of course, a Joint Commission established for dealing with such questions of cohabitation, but this Commission reviews questions dealing primarily with the general environment. Incidents of a military character will have to be addressed differently. They should be addressed to the Chief of the Army Staff in writing, who will then take them up them with the USSR Corps Commander. Incidents that are not of a military character, as well all of the most important military incidents, should be reported to the Minister of Foreign Affairs who will then contact the Russian Ambassador. The Join Commission Chair, Kampe, is currently ill and his place is temporarily being filled by General Hartmanis. From now on, submit all of the files about conflict with the Russians for registration and afterwards notify me. Together we will clear up all things and make decisions who should be notified further in each case. […]

In discussions concerning these matters, Vice Director Caucis related the following – A few days ago when I was in Liepāja I observed that the Russians were buying things as actively as if on the eve of a big holiday. Almost all of the officers had their hands filled with large and small suitcases. The local inhabitants said that the Russians buy everything they can get, and especially manufactured goods. The most active business in Liepāja is nevertheless done on Fridays, count as free days for the Russian soldiers. They pay any price that a store owner asks. Locally, it is also said that the Russians send what they buy to the USSR. Along with this, the question is raised from an economic perspective: can we allow such [mass] purchasing of our goods? For the Russian rubles that have no value in the USSR they can buy a lot here. Not just that, but many inhabitants complain that recently the Russians fly and dive over the city in airplanes, thereby getting on many people's nerves.

Returning to Rīga from Liepāja in the train I again noticed that our people impose themselves unnecessarily on the Russians. As an example, when the train stopped in Saldus station, some drunken peasant fell over a Russian's boots inside the car. A conflict was avoided only with the help of police who were called by the same Russian. Comparing our citizens with the Russians, the latter were more reserved towards strangers in the carriage.

Mister Minister – Russian purchases currently do not present the government with major concerns. The primary purchasers are sailors and officers. News has come in that just recently the Russians' money has dried up. The Russians get Latvian money through the established mechanism. If they buy goods, the Ministry of Finance pays *lats* into their account which the Russians then pay out to their soldiers. Currently we are not afraid that they will buy all of our goods because as long as it is still possible to replenish our stores the Russians, with their purchases, do not create worries. The only evil is that the Russians might purchase all of the best clothing. We can, however, still satisfy our needs with common cloth. If at some point the moment arrives when there is a shortage of cloth then we will introduce rations for clothes and shoes. With that the Russians will be denied their chance of buying. If currently the Russians are buying a lot, then that is only good for the people of Liepāja who have the opportunity to earn a lot. Directions have come in that the Russians are particularly active in buying watches.

With respect to violations of the directions for getting along, it should be noted that no directions have yet been ratified and all things are addressed case-by-case basis. With respect to all undesirable incidents in everyday life the leadership of the Russian army units is notified in a timely manner. Director Austrums will have to write to the Chief of the Army headquarters about these questions and ask him to address them to the leadership of the Russian armed forces. If our Army headquarters will not be able to do anything to help address these conflicts of everyday life, then we will notify the Ministry of Foreign Affairs which will be able to complain about Russian behavior to the leadership in Moscow.

To avoid [further] incidents caused by our own citizens, we have assigned the Chief of the Railroad Police the task of eliminating them. It would be desirable if the main supervisor of a train would more frequently walk through those wagons in which Russian soldiers are traveling.

Chief of the Railroad Police, Mister Briedis – It has been noticed that the Russians do not like traveling in the compartments reserved for them. In the event that they do use them, they behave peacefully. This is explained by the Russians thinking that there are listening devices in the walls of the carriages.

General Bolšteins – I have noticed that private persons often push into the wagons where the Russians are, with no real need to be there.

Minister – Assign to the Security and Order Police Departments the job of controlling this phenomenon more strictly. They should determine the guilty citizen's identity in an unobtrusive manner, away from the Russians. Also assign to the Security Police in the trains where there are many Russians traveling the job of listening to what our inhabitants are saying about the Russians and to see how they act towards them. If there is the need, in an unobtrusive manner, determine the guilty parties' identities and give them a severe fine, not excluding expelling them from the city.

Director Dimiņš – I doubt that we will be able to end these incidents by using only the police. Would it not be correct to invite the press and radio to help in a discreet manner by describing the need for citizens of avoiding any contact with the Russians? If the Russians have already been ordered not to have contact with Latvians, we could do just the same with Latvians.

General Bolšteins – Crawling on their stomachs before the Russian is still in the nature of many Latvians, and therefore no delicate instructions through the press can help us. In these cases, the only useful means are truncheons. It would also help to give administrative punishments which would very quickly convince the masses. The nature of some of the Latvian crawlers is explainable as an attempt to insure against an unknown future.

Minister – We will nevertheless not be allowed to give directions to our citizens about behavior toward Russians in travel situations through the press or through the radio, because that would have had to be done in the beginning when the Russians entered, as it was in Estonia for example. In all of these undesirable events the police have to act energetically and tactfully, in every case avoiding detaining the guilty party in front of the Russians.

Speaking about questions of internal affairs, continued the Minister, I want to spend some time on the ramifications of the President's radio speech. The objective of this speech was to warn citizens not to fall asleep, but to always be ready for any possibility or horror. That which was hoped for has been achieved. The people are awake and active and are beginning to approach all things more seriously. As in conditions of war, we must always be ready so that in the moment of need we would be able to face, and be prepared for, any danger. This speech, however, scared many, and some have said that war will begin in the spring. Rumors are also spreading that a Russian garrison will be stationed in Rīga, that other new quarters for Russians are being sought, and that the Russians have presented us with new demands. This, however, is all made- up rumor and there have been no new demands presented to us. [...]

Conference closed at 14:35

Riga, February 28, 1940

K. Veidmanis, Minister of the Interior
A. Kāps, Minister's secretary

Source: *LVVA, 1368.f., 3.apr., 51.l., pp. 52-55 .Original in Latvian.*

Excerpts from the minutes of a meeting of the Committee to Supply the Soviet Garrisons, of the Agricultural Ministry of Latvia, concerning purchases by Red Army soldiers of goods for personal use

March 1, 1940
Secret

[...] The Soviet Garrison Supply Committee received news that in those regions where Soviet garrisons are stationed, the garrisoned soldiers are purchasing goods in stores in an unusually large volume for their personal use. As a result some categories of goods are starting to run out and there is a noticeable rise in prices; this is particularly true of the cities of Liepāja and Ventspils. The local inhabitants are not happy with this kind of behavior from the soldiers. Through surveys of stores, the Committee gathered information about these purchases through the months of November 1939 to January 31, 1940. The meeting participants were introduced to the collected data. In the reviewed period, according to information provided by stores, the following purchases were made, measured in terms of *lats*: of manufactured goods 189,713 *lats*; of leather goods 43,277 *lats*; of groceries 16,768 *lats*; of sweets 7,715 *lats*; of excise goods 1,365 *lats*; of watches, knives, precious metal goods 22,727 *lats*; of bicycles, radios and gramophones 12,643 *lats*; of glass, ceramics, glazed pottery, porcelain goods 4,233 *lats*; of other small purchases, including writing supplies and perfumes 11,523 *lats*. Altogether 310,054 *lats*.

The statistics are only approximate; in reality the purchases are for a higher total. According to the view of the authorized regional agent of the Committee, [the total amount of] purchases of manufactured, leather goods, and watches could be doubled. The soldiers buy most the goods that are unavailable in the Soviet Union: suits (particularly in light colors), Boston suits, black cloth, women's clothing, leather jackets, leather suitcases, shoes, watches, and razors. The purchases by the Soviet soldiers would not create disturbances in our economy if they would use their purchases here and not send them away. There are suspicions that the soldiers'purchases are being sent as packages in the mail carriage of trains that move often in both directions and are not controlled by our institutions. Voices are being raised to create a supplemental to the treaty concerning mail wagons in trains, in the hope that we can curtail the sending of private packages in this manner. Such a supplemental, however, would still not give the hoped-for results because the packages could still be sent on ships.

It is expected that in the summer such purchases will increase, and therefore this would be a question of some urgency so as to make sure that certain goods needed locally will not start to run out.

In the meeting it was determined that the outflow of woolen goods and thick sole leather would not be desirable, because precisely these goods are necessary for our own use. The sale of other excise goods, however, could occur without any obstacles because there is little of the material here relevant to the sale prices.

A suggestion was made to bring in a rationing system for those goods (woolen goods and sole leather) that could harm our economy if they became scarce. In this manner the unnecessary purchase of these goods would be ended. Bicycles and their tires could be sold only to those that have drivers'licenses. The rationing system would be a burden and it should be used only in the most necessary cases.

The question can still be raised if the sale of goods needing protection should be limited by a law, but such sales would be difficult to control and this kind of restriction could relatively easily be circumvented. [...]

The Committee will continue to gather information on the purchases of Soviet soldiers and report it to interested institutions.

Committee Chair [J. Krīsbergs]
Staff [J. Valainis]

Source: *LVVA, 2570.f., 13. apr., 1715. l., pp. 35-36 (Copy of original). .Original in Latvian.*

Document No. 12

Report of the Ambassador to the USSR of the Latvian Republic, F. Kociņš, to the Minister of Foreign Affairs, Vilhelms Munters, about the unobstructed expansion of the number of service personnel at the USSR's military bases

March 16, 1940, Moscow

Embassy of Latvia
Number 45/ secret

Most honorable Minister,

Pursuant to your directions I asked for a meeting with Molotov. On March 15th, this year, he received me at the Kremlin.

As the first thing, I raised the question about the understanding of the treaty on the part of the commander of the naval forces in Liepāja, according to whom apparently naval forces are not counted as part of the contingent of armed forces. I presented our opinion and asked for the settlement of each potential misunderstanding that needed to be averted because of such interpretations of the pact.

Molotov listened to my explanations and superficially read through the memorandum handed to him and answered that also from his point of view the naval forces found in the bases are not counted as part of the contingent. The contingent mentioned in the treaty is meant only as the base's defense. After that he dryly added that he would give a written reply to the submitted memorandum.

When I informed him thoroughly about the Voentorg servants, I remonstrated that despite our not coming to an agreement, we had understood their needs and had already handed out more than 100 visas, but that in order to keep good order we asked how many of these servants were expected to be sent to Latvia, and to count them in the contingent with the right to only be stationed in the determined institutions.

Molotov listened to my explanations and in a highly raised voice said: "What kind of pact will this be when servants, carpenters, ditch diggers, and salt and bread carriers will be given the assignment to guard bases." He did not agree that our request – to count this servant personnel and workers in the contingent – seriously desired to clarify the meaning of the pact.

I remonstrated that in this event the meaning of contingent had lost its sense because, for example, according to the Soviet Ambassador's explanations to the Lithuanian government, the number of servants in Lithuania could reach 1,500 and we have to know how large this number might be with us.

Molotov answered that he would notify us over the number and that it would not be large. They would send only a limited number, but that we should also understand that cobblers and carpenters cannot be counted as defenders of the bases.

No motivations or explanations helped: Molotov remained with his idea that the Voentorga servants cannot be counted in the contingent. All that remained was to inform his opinions to our government.

No less difficult was the question of construction battalions and workers.

I inform you that on March 4th of this year, Zotov gave you a request by the Soviet Union to grant expedited permission to allow into Latvia:

> construction battalions: 1,200 persons
> 1,500 free contract workers and
> 150 engineers and workers

to which the Ambassador replied that the mentioned workers would not be counted in the contingent and that he did not know how many more would need to be admitted. [...]

F. Kociņš [signature]
Ambassador to the USSR

Source: *LVVA, 2570.f., 13. apr., 1715.l., pp. 20-21 (copy of original).Original in Latvian.*

Document No. 13

Proclamation entitled "Oppressors!" by the Latvian Communist Party, including a call to overthrow the existing government by means of revolution

May 1940

May 15 is approaching and Ulmanis with his clique is going into the last year of governing. Are we not premature in saying that it is the last? No! Our call is founded on facts and the necessity of natural development.

In six years our own fascists have little by little sold out the state of Latvia. They sold it and betrayed it. Those hundred million *Lats* paid to realize the plans of Greater Germany – just a trifle to the repatriated German Junkers. Our government, sick with megalomania in which historical precedent plays no role, allowed provocative and provoking behavior against the real and true friend of the nation of Latvia – the Soviet Union, against the state that protects the Latvian nation from the horrors of war and with that guarantees our state's independence and permanence. The government, thinking only of its class interests, destroys our factories, closes enterprises, and turns workers into slaves! Intoxicated by its power, the government has allowed the crippling of social legislation, giving it a hollow ring. What has become of our health insurance? Who is running it and how are people healed? Knowledge and experience do not matter, what are important are relatives and membership in certain student fraternities. Even the doctors complain about the directives from the existing leadership of the health insurance board: to prescribe fewer and cheaper medicines, to refuse even necessary operations, to not allow vacations for those unable to work. X-rays and offices of physical therapy serve only to decorate the health insurance board. The Rīga municipal government has given an instruction to its affiliated institutions not to allow workers to leave who have reached their pension years. That means that the pension fund is empty. All of this happens in the name of "thrift." Thrift! But is the Palace of Justice thrifty? Is the Museum of War thrifty? Is the addition to Ulmanis'palace thrift? Is the multiplying of Ministers and Directors thrift? Is the newly created State Defense Council thrift? This council -- for what and against what was it created? Is this again the rattling of sabers? Are there not already enough shortages and unemployment, are we to be pulled into the slaughter of the nation? Is the President not getting peace from the "laurels" of the Finnish fascist militarists or maybe he is scared of his former friends, as attested to by the driving away of Balodis, Einbergs and company from the government. Maybe! But those are also fears of the people, those are also fears of the awakening resistance of the working class; the government sits on a powder keg. Out of blind hatred and a desire to survive it does not want to see that the working nation's patience is at an end. Work in the factories is reduced, but the working day is lengthened. With every day the cost of living rises in relation to a day's pay. Arbitrarily and coercively the factory workers are sent to the fields, swamps, and forests to work in inhumane conditions. The farms of the smallest farmers auctioned off for non-payment of high taxes. Arbitrarily, the working peasants of Latgale are sent to the farms of the Grey Barons of Vidzeme and Kurzeme. Political terror, overcrowded prisons. Workers killed in the streets and in the torture chambers of the political overseers. Look how active the six years of Ulmanis government have been. It is enough for the working nation to open its eyes.

The working class and the working peasants as the leading force of revolution will undertake to sweep the grave diggers of the Latvian Republic from the face of the Earth through the path of Revolution. The working nation will create on the ruins of this government a new, free, democratic republic with a government elected by all of the people.

Great tasks confront the Latvian working masses – to concentrate all power and organization for the last assault on Ulmanis'band of thieves.

Long live free, democratic Latvia!

Latvia's Communist Party

Source: *LKP, pp. 545-546.Original in Latvian.*

Comment: *From 1920 onward Latvia's Communist Party worked underground. This party did not recognize an independent Republic of Latvia; its goal, in accord with contemporary Communist ideological doctrine, was a "socialist revolution" (in other words, a coup) and Latvia's attachment to the USSR. By comparison with other political parties that had legally existed until Ulmanis'coup d'etat of May 15, 1934, the Communist Party had relatively few members (generally about 600-900) and was uninfluential. Nevertheless, unlike the legal parties, the Communist Party maintained its structure and ability to function after May 15, 1934. The Party in Latvia was in the same category as other illegal organizations and groups the goal of which was to change the country through violence. The Party in Latvia was also weakened by repression and terror in the USSR. From 1919, Latvia's Communist Party found itself under the complete control of the Communist International (in real terms, the Communist Party of the USSR). It received financial and material aid as well as orders for action directly from Moscow or through the embassy of the USSR. Stalin's purges killed almost all of the Latvian state, party, and military figures who were living in the USSR. Stalin also held a negative view of Latvia's communists: in 1936 in Moscow a decision was accepted to liquidate the leading organ of Latvia's Communist Party – the Central Committee. Latvia's Communist Party did not play a significant role in the country's life until the end of June 1940, after Latvia's occupation. In the first half of April in 1939, 67 underground members were arrested in Latvia, which was practically all of the leadership of the Party.*

The small numbers of the Party in Latvia and its weak influence among the citizenry did not help in the creation of provocations or internal unrest that could be used to justify the coming occupation. There were, however, a few such attempts, as, for example, in Liepāja, where there was a large Soviet garrison and large workers' protests were organized on May 1, 1940. These, however, did not have the desired results.

Report of the State Chancellery to Latvia's Minister of Foreign Affairs, V. Munters, concerning the decision of the Cabinet of Ministers to grant emergency powers to Latvia's ambassador in London, K. Zariņš

May 18, 1940

State Chancellery
Number 48
Valdemārs Street 3, apartment 4, Rīga

To the Minister of Foreign Affairs

The State Chancellery announces that the meeting of May 17 the Cabinet of Ministers resolved:

If because of war it is becomes impossible to maintain contact with Latvia's diplomatic and consular missions in Western Europe, to grant to Latvia's Ambassador in London, Kārlis Zariņš, emergency authority.

The Minister of Foreign Affairs will determine when the authority takes effect by giving the relevant order to the Ambassador in London and stating what missions are assigned to the emergency authority.

If for technical reasons the Minister of Foreign Affairs can not give the order to the Ambassador in London, the latter will be granted the emergency authority automatically.

The Ambassador in London tests this by sending a telegraph message to the Minister of Foreign Affairs and in the event of not receiving a reply in twenty-four hours, acts on the foundation of the emergency authority until communications are renewed with the Minister of Foreign Affairs.

To the Ambassador in London, Kārlis Zariņš, is attached the emergency authority relating to all of Latvia's diplomatic and consular missions, except for missions in the following states: Estonia, Lithuania, Finland, Sweden, Germany, and the Soviet Union.

If Ambassador Kārlis Zariņš during the time that he has the emergency authority dies or loses the freedom to act, with this decree the granted emergency authority transfers to Latvia's Ambassador in the USA, Alfrēds Bīlmanis.

The emergency authority provides the following rights:

To defend the interests of Latvia to the best ability in all lands except Estonia, Lithuania, Finland, Sweden, Germany and the Soviet Union;

For this purpose to give relevant orders to all of Latvia's missions excepting those missions in the aforementioned states;

To use the state's resources and moveable and immovable property that is in the relevant missions' control;

To temporarily suspend Ambassadors as well as to remove or transfer all mission employees;

To liquidate missions, except the legation in the USA;

To appoint delegates to meetings and conferences;

In extraordinary circumstances that limit the use of these rights, to transfer this authority to Ambassador Alfrēds Bīlmanis.

Signed   R. Bulsons
Acting Deputy Director of the State Chancellery
B. Roze
Acting Deputy Department Director

I confirm the accuracy of the transcript: T. Anševics
Director of the Administrative Department

Source: *Valters, pp. 278-280. Original in Latvian.* .

Comment: *After the occupation of Latvia on June 17, 1940, the government did not give the order to K. Zariņš to use his emergency authority. However, Latvia's diplomatic representatives in foreign lands were not adequately informed about the real conditions in Latvia. Only in the second half of July did some of the diplomats understand and correctly evaluate the situation, namely, that an occupation had occurred. The Ambassadors in London, K. Zariņš, in Berlin, E. Krieviņš, and in Washington, DC, A. Bīlmanis, submitted protests to the governments of Great Britain, Germany, and the USA about the Soviet occupation and invited them to not recognize it. The Western states accepted K. Zariņš' emergency authority. Nevertheless, in future years different states held different opinions regarding his authority to appoint diplomatic representatives of the Republic of Latvia in their states.*

The authority granted to Zariņš did not give him the right to create a government of Latvia in exile. Nevertheless, in the fall of 1940, Zariņš turned to the government of Great Britain with the request that he be permitted to open the question of the establishment of a Latvian exile government, but he received a negative response. After Latvia's occupation such a government-in-exile was never created.

Document No. 15

Telephonogram, number A 11 – 851, sent by Captain Holanders, Latvia's Border Guard Brigade, to the Border Guard Brigade Commander, General Bolšteins, about armed provocation by the USSR on Latvia's borders

June 15, 1950, 12:45

To the Commander of the Border Guard Brigade

The following has happened at the headquarters of the 1st unit of the III Abrene Battalion:

At 3:00 a.m. this morning, June 15, as the sun was rising, border guards of the USSR crossed the border and attacked the building of the 2nd guards at Masļenki, which surprised the mentioned guards.

As a result: the guard building was burned down. In the smoldering wreck were found the corpses of the guard commander's wife and one of the guards. Another guard's corpse, shot from behind, was found in his underwear 100 meters behind the building. Besides this, the following were found heavily injured – the wife of a guard and the 14- year-old son of the guard commander. The Red Army units captured and took with them as they departed three guards from the mentioned guard post. At the place of the incident, the Red Army units left behind the following physical evidence: 20 spent shell casings, 1 hand grenade, 1 wire-cutter with which telephone lines were cut about 150 meters from the guard post, and one individual packet which was handled by an injured person because a trail of blood can be seen going to the border. At the same time an attack was happening on the 3rd Guards post in Šmaiļi. Here. according to the eyewitness, the wife of the Guard Ozolnieks, the attack came from about 15 Red Army troops, divided into two groups: one of them went to the rear and looked for the guards and their families in the private apartments, but the other captured the guards in the post without a fight. In the post the receiver was ripped from the telephone. From here the Red Army troops took four guards across the border, the wife of one guard, and the miller Smukkalns with his family and workers. Seeing the fire at the 2nd guard post, a sheepherder from the Kareļi windmill, Vītoliņš, went to report it to the 1st post. From there the commander of the guard and two guards hurried to help, but, arriving at the 2nd guard post, they were captured and taken across the border with the others. Not counting the above mentioned persons, the commander of the 4th guard post who had gone to inspect the 3rd post at about 03:20 was also captured and taken across the border.

In summary: shot and killed - 2 guards and 1 woman; wounded - 1 woman and 1 boy; taken across the border -- 2 guard commanders, 9 guards, 1 wife of a guard, and as was later determined, 27 private individuals.

There was not the slightest reason for the Red Army's attack and acts of violence. Our border guards had not experienced, and there have not been, any border conflicts with border guards of the USSR.

Capt. Holanders
3rd Battalion War District Acting Chief

Source: *LVVA, 2574.f., 2. apr., 7082.l., p. 4; Latvijas okupācija, pp. 334-335. Original in Latvian.*

Comment: *At the same time as the attacks on Latvia's border guards took place, there were also attacks on Lithuania's border posts. Latvia's Minister of the Interior created a special commission to investigate this incident. On June 16, 1940, the Ambassador of the Republic of Latvia in Moscow, F. Kociņš, informed the People's Commissar of Foreign Affairs of the USSR, V. Molotov, about the attack and asked him to investigate the event. But neither in the summer of 1940, nor later, did the government of the USSR give any official explanation.*

DOCUMENTS NO. 16-19
THE ARMED FORCES OF THE USSR ENTER LATVIA

Document No. 16

Communication by the government of the USSR to the Government of Latvia, with the demand that the government be changed and that the entrance of Soviet armed forces into the territory of Latvia be guaranteed

June 16, 1940, Moscow

On the basis of material facts that are in the possession of the Soviet government, and on the basis of the exchange of ideas that occurred recently in Moscow between the Chair of the Soviet of People's Commissars of the USSR, Molotov, and the Minister President of Lithuania, Merkys, the Soviet government has concluded that the government of Latvia has not only failed to dismantle the anti-Soviet military union which was established with Estonia prior to the signing of the Soviet-Latvian mutual assistance agreement, but has expanded it by bringing Lithuania into the union and is trying to also involve Finland.

Before the conclusion of the Soviet-Latvian Mutual Assistance Pact in the fall of 1939, the Soviet government could still put tolerate the existence of such military unions, even if in essence they went against the earlier concluded Non-Aggression Pact between the USSR and Latvia. But after the conclusion of the Soviet-Latvia Mutual Assistance Pact, the Soviet government sees the existence of anti-Soviet military unions between Latvia, Estonia, and Lithuania not only as impermissible and intolerable, but also as deeply dangerous and threatening to the security of the borders of the USSR.

The Soviet government had calculated that after the conclusion of the Soviet-Latvia Mutual Assistance Pact, Latvia would withdraw from military unions with other Baltic States and in this manner the military union would be liquidated. But Latvia together with other Baltic states worked at the revival of the abovementioned military union and its expansion. This is shown by such facts as the calling of two secret three-Baltic-State conferences in December of 1939 and February of 1940 – and [the publication] Revue Baltique, which is published in English, French and German languages in Tallinn, and other such things.

All of these facts prove that the government of Latvia crudely violated the Soviet-Latvia Mutual Assistance Pact that forbids both sides from "concluding any unions or participation in coalitions, that are aimed against one of the signatory parties" (4th paragraph of the treaty)[14].

This crude violation of the Soviet-Latvia Mutual Assistance Pact by the government of Latvia has happened at the time when the Soviet Union has implemented and is continuing to even more firmly implement pro-Latvian policies and is fulfilling conscientiously all of the demands of the Soviet-Latvia Mutual Assistance Pact.

The Soviet government finds that such a state of affairs can no longer be tolerated.

The government of the USSR sees the following as completely essential:

Without delay, the establishment in Latvia of a government that would be able and ready to guarantee the honest implementation of the Soviet-Latvia Mutual Assistance Pact;

Without delay the guaranteeing of the free entry of Soviet armed forces into the territory of Latvia the stationing of them in the most important centers of Latvia in numbers sufficient to guarantee the implementation of the Soviet-Latvia Mutual Assistance Pact, and the averting of any potential provocative acts against the Soviet garrison in Latvia.

The Soviet government sees the fulfillment of this request as an elementary step without which it is impossible to honestly and faithfully fulfill the Soviet-Latvia Mutual Assistance Pact.

The Soviet government will wait for a reply from the government of Latvia until 11:00 at night, June 16. The failure of the government of Latvia to respond by this time will be seen as a refusal to fulfill the abovementioned requests of the Soviet Union.

Source: *Polpredi, pp. 386-387. Original in Russian.*

Comment: *The charges against the government of Latvia in the demand were completely unfounded. In Tallinn on December 10, 1939, there was created an office of cooperation between Estonia, Lithuania, and Latvia. Its publication,* Revue Baltique, *was to follow events in the Baltic States and to disseminate information about these states to all countries in the world.*

Latvia's government was given nine hours to submit a reply to the ultimatum. The Republic of Latvia's Ambassador in Moscow, F. Kociņš, arrived in the Kremlin on June 16th at 14:00 at the request of the People's Commissar of Foreign Affairs of the USSR, V. Molotov. V. Molotov read him the ultimatum, noting that if no response was received by the mentioned time, force would be used. During the discussion, Kociņš asked for an extension of the time in the ultimatum, but that was not taken into account. The next discussion took place at 19:45 when F. Kociņš gave V. Molotov the response of the Latvian government that included the request to put off the entry of armed forces for at least one day and to not immediately publish the ultimatum. V. Molotov refused to fulfill these requests. F. Kociņš again arrived at the Kremlin at 22:30 and officially reported that the government of Latvia accepted the demands of the USSR.

The next day the text of the ultimatum of the government of the USSR was published in Valdības Vēstnesis *and* Izvestija, *but without the last lines.*

Document No. 17

Minutes of the meeting of the Cabinet of Ministers of Latvia, Number 40, about accepting the demands of the USSR ultimatum

June 16, 1940

Present:

Minister President	Dr. K. Ulmanis
Minister of Foreign Affairs	V. Munters
Minister of the Interior	K. Veidnieks
Minister of War	General K. Berķis
Minister of Transport	A. Kāposts
Minister of Justice	H. Apsīts
Minister of Trade and Industry	J. Blumbergs

Minutes taken: Acting Deputy Director of the State Chancellery   R. Bulsons

The meeting begins at 19:00.

The Minister of Foreign Affairs, V. Munters, reports on the ultimatum that the Chair of the Soviet of Commissars of the USSR had submitted to Latvia's Ambassador in Moscow on June 16, 1940 at 14:00 (at 13:00 Latvian time).

Decide to accept the request of the government of the Soviet Union about additional armed forces entering into Latvia.

Decide to inform the President of the resignation of the Cabinet of Ministers and to immediately report this decision to President Kārlis Ulmanis.

The meeting concluded at 22:00.

> Minister President K. Ulmanis
> Acting Deputy Director of the State Chancellery R. Bulsons

Source: *LVA, 270.f., 1. apr., 2.l., p. 84; Latvijas Republikas, p. 9.Original in Latvian.*

Document No. 18

Protocol of agreement between representatives of Soviet armed forces and Latvia's Army about the order of entry of armed forces of the USSR, their movement, and supply

June 17, 1940 Joniškos (Lithuania)

On behalf of the Soviet side, Tank Division Colonel General Pavlov; on behalf of Latvia's side, Colonel Ūdentiņš.
On June 17, 1940 both sides accepted the following points:

1.

The Soviet Armed Forces will be allowed to be stationed in the following regions of Latvia:

Cēsis (Venden) – Valmiera;
Rīga – Jelgava - Bauska;
Tukums – Talsi;
Ventspils (Vendava) - Kuldīga (Goldingen) - the state's border from Piķeļi to the sea;
Jaunjelgava (Friedrichstadt) - Madliena (on Russian maps "to Litve");
Birži (Buschhof) - Jēkabpils (Jakobstadt) - station Jaunkalsnava (st. Novo-Kalsenav);
Višķi (Dubni) – Ilūkste - the state's border with Lithuania from Novoaleksandrovsk (Zarasai) region – Jozefova;
Dricēni Baranaja – Ludza (Ljutsin) – Rēzekne;
Ape (Hoppenhof) – station Gulbene (Alt-Gulbene) – Balvi (Bolovsk) only – Alūksne (Marienburg), including the lake.

2.

The stationing of armed forces, except for the regions mentioned in the concluded basic agreement and supplementary agreements of the governments of the USSR and Latvia, is temporary and it will be reviewed by a special commission.

3.

Shipments by rail to the Soviet armed forces either from the USSR as well as from Lithuania will be accepted without examination or delay by the government of Latvia without bothering the normal rail traffic.

4.

Grant to units of the Soviet [armed forces] the right to use telephone and telegraph networks in the territory of Latvia according to the regular order. Communications between the most important Soviet armed forces garrisons in Latvia, if possible, will be given direct lines.

5.

To grant the Soviet military command through the appropriate administrative institutions of Latvia the right to hire workers from the inhabitants of Latvia for the purpose of building and maintaining aerodromes and airfields.

6.

The supply commanders of the Soviet armed forces (no lower than the division supply commander) are given the opportunity to purchase all the necessary groceries and fodder from Latvia's available resources through the appropriate administrative institutions that should facilitate this.

7.

The question of the naval forces of the USSR was not considered; it will be considered in a special agreement. The protocol was hand-written in two copies on two pages in the Russian language and signed.

> For the Soviet Side
> Tank Armed Forces Colonel General Pavlov
> For Latvia's side
> Colonel Ūdentiņš

Source: *Polpredy, p. 386-387. Original in Russian.*

Comment: *The protocol was signed after the armed forces of the USSR had already crossed Latvia's border early in the morning. On June 18, 1940 the government of Latvia ratified this protocol.*

Document No. 19

From a hand-written autobiography of a former staff member on special assignment from the USSR's Peoples Commissariat of the Interior. He was assigned to the Latvian Army Staff in 1940 and wrote about his arrival in Latvia in the summer of 1940

August 1951

[…] On May 9, 1940, I was again called to active military duty in the Leningrad War Province's Political Supervision Group that was being created by the All-Union Communist Bolshevik Party and the USSR People's Commissariat of the Interior to be sent into Latvia.

On June 11, 1940, I was sent from Leningrad to Rīga as a part of this group under the command of the 3rd Soviet Army. After arriving in Rīga [June 12] we were placed under the command of the Latvian Communist (Bolshevik) Party Central Committee which sent us as advisors in July of 1940 to different state institutions. […]

E. Kerre

Source: *Polpredy, pp. 395-397. Original in Russian.*

Comment: *E. Kerre, the author of the autobiography was a functionary in the USSR People's Commissariat of the Interior and a cadre in the Red Army, but in 1938 he was removed from his post and worked as a military training instructor in the education section of the Kubishev region. After being sent into Latvia, he worked as the representative of the USSR People's Commissariat of the Interior at the headquarters of Latvia's army. From September 15, 1940, he worked as the Chief of the Special Section of the Latvian SSR People's Commissariat of the Interior, as the Chief of the 3rd Section of the 181st territorial Infantry division.*

Normally, similar autobiographies (even those written in 1940) it is stated only that the author arrived in Latvia "in the summer of 1940." This document is different from the others in that it mentions concrete dates. This is exactly why it is unique, because it demonstrates that already in May of 1940 the USSR began to create special groups of Latvians for sending into Latvia. This group of Latvian functionaries entered Latvia even before it was occupied. The following persons entered Latvia in the same way: the soon-to-be Deputy People's Commissar of Education of the Latvian SSR, P. Valeskalns; the soon-to-be leader of the Department of Marxism-Leninism at the University of Latvia and editor of the newspaper Cīņa from 1940-1941, O. Miške; the Deputy Minister of Finance from 1940-1941 and later the Deputy People's Commissar of Light Industry of the Latvian SSR, E. Leitmanis; the Chief of the Latvian SSR Statistical Board from 1940-1941, J. Ādamsons; the Chief of the Supreme Court of the Latvian SSR from 1940-1941, F. Dombrovskis, and many others.

PART II: THE OCCUPATION AND ANNEXATION OF LATVIA BY THE USSR: JUNE 17, 1940 TO THE END OF JUNE 1941

In the early morning of June 17, 1940, Soviet armed forces crossed Latvia's border and occupied the state. At the same time the USSR occupied Estonia, and it had already entered Lithuania on June 15th. On June 17th, at about noon, the USSR entered Latvia's capital – Rīga - and occupied important, strategic points (see Document No. 2). According to some reports, the Soviet Union moved between 300,000 to 500,000 soldiers into the Baltic States. Moreover, due to the treaties concluded in the fall of 1939, there were already Soviet military bases in Latvia, Lithuania, and Estonia.

Latvia's army, not receiving any orders, put up no resistance to the occupying forces because after the acceptance of the USSR's ultimatum of June 16, 1940[15], armed resistance was impossible.

From June 17, 1940, the Soviet side began to actively interfere in the life of the state, and gained quick control over its domestic and foreign policy. On June 18, 1940, A. Vishinski, Deputy Chair of the Soviet of Peoples Commissars and the USSR's authorized representative in Latvia, officially entered Rīga. A. Vishinski and the functionaries of the USSR embassy became the actual decision-makers about everyday life in Latvia. The primary task of the representative of the government of the USSR was to facilitate the incorporation of the Republic of Latvia into the Soviet Union. A. Vishinski acted surreptitiously and carefully. This is why, at the beginning, he was able to confuse both international observers and Latvian society about the real goals of his mission.

On July 4, 1940, the new Latvian government, headed by A. Kirhenšteins, ratified the law concerning elections to the *Saeima* (parliament) and a new *Saeima* electoral law (see Documents No. 9 and 10). The elections were organized in a great hurry, with only nine days allowed for all preparations. The Central Electoral Commission accepted candidate lists for only three days (July 8-10). This is why Latvia's Communist Party, which was informed of the elections on July 2nd (before the government decision about elections to the *Saeima*), had the opportunity of participating in the elections (see Document No. 8).

After the announcement that elections would take place, a group of well-known political figures in Latvia (former ministers and former deputies to the *Saeima*) showed that they believed the announcement. Vishinski met with the well-known political leader and Minister of Education from 1931 to 1933, Atis Ķeniņš, and said that the elections would happen according to the newly ratified electoral law. In other words if at least 100 electors'signatures were collected, a list of candidates could be submitted. The group therefore created the "Democratic Latvian Electorate" electoral list (see Document No. 11). This bloc's electoral platform was based on general, democratic principles:

> [...] 1. A free, independent, democratic Latvia.
> 2. Close, permanent cooperation with the USSR to reach the goals of the October 5, 1939 Mutual Assistance Treaty and to further develop it.
> 3. The internal reconstruction of the state the on foundations of progress, democracy, and faithful cooperation with Latvia's workers and their organizations. [...]
> 9. The development of the future life of the state on strict, legal principles, guaranteeing inviolability of each person and property, as well as democratic freedoms such as speech, assembly, press, religion and others. [...]

They were able to secretly make multiple copies of this platform and distribute it partially. But already on July 9th the bloc's activity was curtailed. The "Democratic Latvian Electorate" bloc also had difficulty collecting the needed number of electors'signatures (see Document No. 12). In order to prevent the bloc's candidate list from being registered at the Central Electoral Commission, the

Ministry of Social Affairs forbade presses to take any print orders relating to the elections without permission from the Ministry. At the same time, potential organizers of electoral lists for the *Saeima* were asked to publish typographically their electoral platforms and to distribute them among the inhabitants. In these conditions, only the Latvian Communist Party's "Working People's List" could meet the official requirements.

The "elections" to the People's *Saeima* took place from "July 14-15." The armed forces of the USSR supervised them (see Document No. 15). A prolific propaganda campaign and mass demonstrations throughout Latvia accompanied the elections. The inhabitants' participation in the elections was encouraged by raising their hopes that a newly elected parliament would create a just and democratic state. Veiled threats were used against the rest in suggestions that not participating in the elections would be viewed as a sign of disloyalty to the new order. Since only one list – the Communist sponsored "Working People's Bloc" – was allowed to be put forward, regardless of the actual electoral results the official result was a foregone conclusion. Nevertheless, many changes were made voting procedures, making the manipulation of votes easier; there were also many other procedural violations (See Document No. 14). On July 23, 1940, the Central Electoral Commission reported that 94.8% of the eligible citizens had participated in the election and that 97.8% voted for the "Working Peoples bloc" list. Though there is no direct documentary proof that the electoral results were invented, they nevertheless are difficult to believe. In the 1920s and 1930s, the inhabitants of Latvia participated in elections actively, in comparison with other democratic states, but the proportion that voted was never more than 75-80%.

The Moscow government exploited this election farce to legitimize the fact of Latvia's occupation. The elections had to shown to be organically linked to old electoral system when Latvians were in charge, when in reality the organizers of the 1940 election remained hidden. The most accurate description of this was given by the Secretary of the Central Committee of the Latvian Communist Party, Žanis Spure, who said: "Many of our members have the wrong outlook, [when they say] that the LCP does not have a particularly important assignment, and that it is the Red Army in Latvia that will attach us to the Soviet Union. This is the incorrect view: the Red Army has not come to attach us we have to make it happen that we [are seen to join] the USSR."[16] This was said on July 6th. Thus the Communists already knew about the plans to incorporate Latvia into the USSR even though in the platform of the "Working Peoples Bloc," and also in demonstrations that were organized before the elections, the demand that Latvia enter the USSR was not made. Instead, the slogans voiced in demonstrations calling for such a step were punished as provocative behavior. But in the demonstrations after the election, slogans about joining the USSR became the principal theme.

On July 21, 1940, the People's *Saeima* declared the establishment of "Soviet power" in Latvia and ratified a law about joining the USSR (see Documents No. 21 and 22). The Republic of Latvia was declared the Latvian Soviet Socialist Republic (Latvian SSR). These laws were clearly unconstitutional according to Latvia's 1922 Constitution, which said that laws concerning changes in the nature of the state or concerning major steps such as joining the USSR must be approved by a national referendum in order to have the force of law.

The direction of events surprised foreign diplomats in Rīga, who walked out of the session of the *Saeima* that was accepting these changes. On July 28th, A. Vishinski returned to Moscow, having successfully completed his task. Latvia's incorporation into the USSR was formally recognized on August 5, 1940, with a law from the Supreme Soviet of the USSR (see Document No. 23). All citizens of the Republic of Latvia were declared citizens of the USSR (see Document No. 24).

Having eliminated Latvia's independence, it was very important for the USSR that all the institutions of the old state, such as the diplomatic corps and embassies in foreign lands, disappear as well. Until the parliamentary elections, the diplomatic representatives of Latvia in foreign countries were left without information about what was happening, which reduced their ability to fully do their work (see Document No. 27). It was difficult for the new government in Latvia to recall diplomats and take over the representation because the majority of foreign governments refused to recognize the incorporation of Latvia, and the ambassadors did not return. In these cases Latvia's diplomats were declared "traitors to the state" (see Document No. 29), and the behavior of the foreign states was described as unfriendly to the USSR.

The other attribute of state sovereignty that the USSR liquidated after the annexation of Latvia was the armed forces (see Document No. 20). The sovietization of Latvia's Army began in the first days in July (see Documents No. 16 and 17), and led to its inclusion into the Red Army (see Documents No. 18 and 19). The officers' corps was liquidated almost entirely, with some officers forced to retired and others were arrested, imprisoned, or deported (see Document No. 43).

No less important to the USSR was the exploitation of the economic potential of the annexed territory, which in practice meant the transfer of the wealth of Latvia and its inhabitants to the Soviet state. Along with the declaration of Soviet power came the nationalization of banks, industrial and trade enterprises, as well as apartment buildings (see Document No. 25). In less than a year practically all industrial enterprises were nationalized. By June of 1941 small private enterprises, basically workshops, accounted for less than 5% of total industrial production. From October, 1940, onward Latvia's industries were included in the planned economy of the USSR.

Furthermore, all land was declared the property of the people, i.e. nationalized (see Document No. 26). An agrarian reform was enacted the goal of which was to create in the countryside a class of grateful but economically unviable smallholders who later could become the basis of collectivization. The agrarian reform in all of Latvia was done with shocking speed and was finished by September 25, 1940. At the beginning of 1941, 50 machine and tractor stations, and 504 machine and horse rental points, were created as visible signs of the state's aid to farmers but, in reality, as the first step towards collectivization. The reforms concentrated not only land, but also the equipment needed to work the land, in its own hands.

The resources of private and juridical persons were confiscated through the nationalizing of banks. Immediately after the occupation of Latvia, in June of 1940, out-payments from the accounts and investments of private persons were restricted. From August 1 on, persons could not withdraw more than 100 *lats* a month (after November 25, 100 rubles). Later, all savings of private persons exceeding 1,000 *lats* were confiscated. The second path toward the confiscation of money was through the transition to Soviet currency. In the government's announcement it was said that "all transactions must be done according to the exchange: 1 *lats* equals 1 ruble."[17] According to economists' calculations, the real exchange rate of rubles to *lats* was approximately 4 to 1. Living conditions declined despite the increase in wages for some categories of work precisely for this reason (see Document No. 37). It must be taken into account, also, that at the same time prices for groceries and manufactured goods were raised because they were lower in Latvia than in the Soviet Union (see Document No. 36). On March 21, 1941, the Soviet of Peoples Commissars of the USSR ratified a law concerning the annulment of the *lats* as the basic currency as of March 25th.

After Latvia's incorporation, the comprehensive censorship system (see Documents No. 30-32) and the organs of control that existed in the Soviet Union – Peoples Commissariat of the Interior of the Latvian SSR, Prosecutor of the Latvian SSR, Peoples Commissariat of Justice of the Latvian SSR - received jurisdiction over those institutions that were directly under the control of the Soviet Union. The next step, beginning on November 26, 1940, was to apply the "legal" basis of the terror apparatus of the USSR – the RSFSR Criminal Code – to Latvia (see Document No. 40). From this point on, paragraph 58 of the RSFSR Criminal Code was used officially in Latvia, although it had already been used in repression against inhabitants before its official introduction, for crimes of a political nature against the Soviet state (anti-Soviet agitation, aiding the international bourgeoisie, serving in the Russian Tsarist army or police to 1919, etc.) which at the time in the USSR were classified as criminal offenses. In this way the systematic political repression that already existed in the USSR was brought into Latvia, and political, social or other work performed in pre-1940 Latvia (see Document No. 41), including serving in the army or police, was criminally punishable.

The regime that emerged from the Soviet occupation did not encounter organized or effective opposition from the inhabitants of Latvia. The development of events in the first weeks of occupation was very swift, and the occupiers'real political goals were well-disguised. Not only that, but the repressive apparatus of the new state worked very effectively from the first days -- our current information is that at least 143 people were arrested by the end of June and early July, but by August more than 300. As the goals and methods of Soviet politics became more apparent, however, opposition grew. The most widespread form of protest came from small groups of schoolchildren and youths engaged in underground activity, which included the writing and dissemination of handouts and recognition of Latvia's traditional state holidays (see Documents No. 38 and 39). Even these small signs of dissatisfaction were brutally suppressed. Arrests happened secretly; people simply disappeared from the local view. In this way an atmosphere of fear was created that prepared the way for much-larger-scale repressive actions.

The most serious violence against Latvia's inhabitants in the first year of Soviet occupation was the June 14, 1941 mass deportation. It was an action that was carefully planned. Even before the occupation and annexation of the Baltic States, the repressive organs of the Soviet Union began to devise a plan for the implementation of mass deportations. Preparation required a lot of time because it was necessary to plan camps for receiving deportees, create special trains and coordinate their movements with existing schedules, and organize needed local personnel to manage the movement of tens of thousands of people. Furthermore, all of these plans had to be made secretly in order to limit any opposition to or avoidance of the deportations. In one of the completely confidential instructions regarding this action, it was underlined that "care must be taken so that the operation occurs without noise or disturbance not only among the deported, but also among those inhabitants who are known to be hostile to Soviet power."

On May 14, 1941, the All-Union Communist (Bolshevik) Party Central Committee and the Council of Peoples Commissars of the USSR ratified the completely confidential law called "About the deportation of socially foreign elements from the Baltic Republics, western Ukraine, western Belarus, and Moldavia." Involved was all of the territory that had been occupied by the USSR as a result of the August 23, 1939, Secret Agreement of the Molotov-Ribbentrop Pact (see Part I, Document No. 1).

In Latvia and the other Baltic States the deportations happened during the night of June 13-14. Entire families with children were deported. Altogether 4,202 people were arrested (primarily heads of families), and they were sent to camps separately from their families. Family members that were deported by administrative order (that is, without any foundation even in the Soviet legal system) were sent to places of settlement where they lived under the strict surveillance of the local security organs. In 1941, the deported were sent primarily to Western Siberia in the USSR (in the Krasnoyarsk region). Altogether, 14,194 people were deported from Latvia. 80.4% were Latvian; 12.5% Jewish; 3.8% Russian; and 3.3% members of other nationalities (Poles, Germans, Belorussians, etc.). Those that were considered „socially foreign elements" were deported also – persons who had been prominent in the Republic of Latvia in government structures, economic life, or politics; those who owned certain kind of property, officers in Latvia's army, police, etc. The real goal of this action was the consolidation of the totalitarian regime through the use of terror.

After World War II, the ideologues of Latvia's Communist Party tried to justify this inhumane action as a security requirement necessary on the eve of war. The invasion by Nazi Germany of the Soviet Union actually saved inhabitants of Latvia from further deportations.

Documents No. 1-4
The first day of Soviet occupation

Document No. 1

The last speech of K. Ulmanis, President of the State and President of the Cabinet of Ministers, to the people of Latvia regarding the occupation of Latvia.

June 17, 1940

Citizens!

The events of the last 24 hours have stirred all of us, and thus I see it as my duty, as I have always done during such important moments, to tell all of you what the government is thinking and doing at this moment.

As of this morning Soviet armed forces are coming into our land. This is happening with the government's knowledge and assent which derives from the existing friendly relations between Latvia and the USSR. Therefore, I would ask that the inhabitants of our land look upon the entering armed forces with friendship. At the same time, you must understand that the movement of these armed forces must happen without disturbances and that you can facilitate this by restraining unnecessary curiosity and by refraining from bothering their movement.

This morning you also heard the news that the entire government offered its resignations to me and that I have told the ministers to remain at their posts until a new government is created. The first assignment for all of us is to maintain the unity and desire to work that we have had up to this point; to stay in our places and to continue to serve the ideal we hold as the highest and holiest – the interests of Latvia and our nation.

It is inevitable that the currently experienced events will bring a certain restlessness and distress in the heretofore peaceful rhythm of our lives. This is a temporary phenomenon that we will get over after a few days. At this moment, I invite you to show in your thoughts, work, and behavior the strength of the people's spirit that was created by the golden years of renewed Latvia. Then I will be sure that all that will now happen will turn out to be good for the future of our state and nation and for our good and friendly relations with our great Eastern neighbor, the Soviet Union.

This is our most important collective assignment. It transcends all the details of our daily lives, and we will devote in these days our best will and our best efforts to further it.

But this moment also demands the rapid performance of many new practical tasks. At this moment I am speaking during a break in a cabinet session in which we are discussing the most urgent issues. I am convinced that you will understand the orders that the government has given, and will give, even if on some occasions they are strict and even harsh. Fulfill them conscientiously because they have no other goal than your peace and well-being. May a sense of obligation and unrelenting work guide all of you.

My heart is with you and I feel that your hearts are beating in a friendly response. Let us go forward and do our work. I will stay in my place, you stay in yours.

Source: *Valdības Vēstnesis, June 18, 1940. Original in Latvian.*

Comment: *All informational radio programs were forbidden after the entry of some of the units of the Red Army into Rīga; only music was played. On the evening of June 22 at 22:15, K. Ulmanis was allowed to speak on the radio during an intermission in the Cabinet of Ministers session. The speech was approved in advance by the representative of the government of the USSR in Latvia, A. Vishinski.*

K. Ulmanis had occupied the post of Minister President from 1934. In 1936 he also became the President of the State. He occupied both of these highest posts until Latvia's occupation. After that, until July 21, 1940, K. Ulmanis continued to formally fulfill the functions of the State President by signing all of the decrees of the newly created government. After the announcement of Soviet power in Latvia, K. Ulmanis was deported to the USSR to Voroshilovsk (currently Stavropol) where he was under house arrest. After the invasion of the USSR by Nazi Germany in June, 1941, he was imprisoned in the Voroshilovsk Prison on July 5, 1941. K. Ulmanis died on September 21, 1941 in the Krasnovodska Prison hospital (in Turkmenistan). Until the re-aquisition of Latvia's independence in 1991, the KGB denied that they had any information on the fate of the last State President of Latvia after his deportation. Even to this day, materials about the later days of K. Ulmanis remain in Moscow.

Document No. 2

From a telegram of the authorized representative of the USSR, V. Derevjanski, to the Peoples Commissar of Foreign Affairs of the USSR, about the entrance of Red Army units into Rīga

June 18, 1940

[…] At about 1:00 in the afternoon the advance tank units began to come into Rīga and they quickly occupied the most important points in the city. The authorities had not expected such a quick arrival and fast work from our side, because at 12:30 Ulmanis was still calmly driving around the city streets [..] The tanks were stopped by crowds of people. They embraced, kissed, and gave flowers to the Red Army soldiers. In some places there were attempts to organize demonstrations. Red flags were raised among the crowds. There was conflict with the police. As a result of the conflict, 30 police were injured and just as many inhabitants were injured. […] Our commanders took steps to reestablish order in the city. It was enough for our commanders to turn to the inhabitants with the request that peace and complete order be restored within 30 minutes, and by 11:00 in the evening the city was already calm. […] Together with the command authorities I asked for the prohibition of demonstrations and other types of disturbances, but also that, if they did happen, that military force not be used to quell them. […]

Today, June 18th, the creation of a new government is being awaited - the founding of a new regime in the state and, among other things, the freeing of political prisoners. […] Yesterday[18] evening we allowed radio programs with the condition that from now on all broadcasts must be approved by us and that no reports disloyal to he USSR or the Red Army are allowed. Today in the morning we allowed work to resume in the harbor. We asked that a special decree be promulgated forbidding the acceptance of Soviet money in exchange for local currency or as payment for goods in stores, and this was done without delay. We requested that a special institution be created to supply our [military] units with all that is needed, which was created under the leadership of General Hartmanis. The President and the government are currently fulfilling their duties.

Derevjanskii

Source: *Polpredi, pp. 400-401.Original in Russian.*

From the minutes of the interrogation of A. Austrums, the Director of the Department of Police of the Ministry of Interior, about the disorder in Rīga on June 17, 1940, after the arrival of the Red Army

July 5, 1940

[...[On the day of June 16, I was called from my apartment to see General Rozenšteins at army headquarters, who told me that the Red Army was coming during the night and that the police had to make sure that there was order. I also went to Minister Veidnieks in his office where Fridrihsons, General Bolšteins, and I think other leading members of the Ministry, were present. The Minister directed that we destroy all of our secret files that describe the political condition of the state. In relation to this I gave an order to my subordinates to destroy all of the secret files that related to political conditions. In my office I took last months'reports from my cabinet and gave them to be destroyed. I did not know until now that my subordinates also destroyed the files of those who had been administratively punished as well as the reports. On the day of June 17, the Rīga prefect told me by telephone that there was unrest around the prefecture. At around 17:00 o'clock I escorted Minister Veidnieks when he drove to the prefecture. At the time there were many people on the street, but the general mood was peaceful. The Prefect told the Minister that there had been unrest earlier. The Minister expressed his dissatisfaction and said that the guards had probably not acted correctly enough. Several times the Minister refused to allow the summoning of the Red Army and ordered that order and the free movement of the armed forces be ensured without use of weapons. While we were at the prefecture, shooting began at the station and the Minister gave the order to restore order without using weapons, which was achieved by pushing the crowd back to Dzirnavu Street. After that, however, the crowd again came to the prefecture and now the Minister asked by telephone for the armed forces to take the preservation of order into their hands because the police were unable to do it by themselves. After the arrival of the armed forces, I heard shots near the post office – they said that a Red Army tank fired and afterward there was no conflict and everything calmed. I stayed in the prefecture all night. I did not see any of the public detained there. The next day the prefect told me that in one or two cases the guards had beaten some private persons. I told him to make an investigation and to give the file to the prosecutor. In relation to administrative punishments, I gave directions to carefully punish only the truly guilty and to use the typical level of punishment in order to not cause any nervousness. [...]

Source: *LVA, 1986.f., 2. apr., 6203.f., pp. 9-11 (handwritten report).Original in Latvian.*

From the service report of J. Fridrihsons, the Director of Security Police of the Ministry of the Interior, to the Minister of the Interior about the mood and activity of Communists.

June 19, 1940

The Communists are excited and happy because of what has happened. In meetings that have been held it is made clear that the founding of Soviet order in Latvia is only a question of time. Immediately a citizens'government will be installed that is acceptable to the Communists and that will prepare the path for further events; the government that is now being formed will soon be exchanged for a Communist government. The Communists anticipate that the new government will be asked to give Communists wide freedoms – even legalizing them. They are not clear on what and how the Red Army leadership wants to present requests, and how concretely they, the Communists, should behave. One thing is clear: they have to prepare the path for a major event. Currently they are carefully looking for contacts and want to clarify the plans of the Red Army leadership. They, the Communists, have difficulties with the current shortage of adaptable printing presses. They have a very primitive one that works very slowly. One proclamation was distributed, which is already dated. The Communists consider their upcoming work to be: to prepare to submit demands, to go out in demonstrations, to show enthusiasm for the Red Army, etc. About the events at the Station[19] and at Marija Street – they react against them as hooliganism and maintain that these events are bad for them, the real communists. The Communists are even beginning to say that these were organized by certain institutions for provocative means to hinder the Communists because home guards in private clothing were seen in the masses. One thing is clear from these events, the nation agrees with the Communists in celebrating and waiting for the founding of Soviet order.

On June 18th, news came that workers from the "Rīga Silk" factory, numbering about 100, wanted to gather at 13:00 o'clock to elect a delegation to go to the Russian government. This was immediately reported to the Labor Chamber that sent its representative to Director Baumanis (a former Legionnaire[20]). Baumanis said they anticipated discussion about restructuring work hours due to the prohibitions on movement between 22:00 and 4:00 in the morning. Later it was clarified that the meeting was held and that the worker Žurgin spoke, but because he is not an adept speaker, he asked the worker Baus to continue. The latter said that there was a need to go and agitate at the factories in order to create soviets from which a government would be created. The workers received this rather coolly. An order has been issued to arrest Žurgin and Baus. The question about one day of celebration was discussed with Director Baumanis who did not agree to it, but said that they would get it.

Feliks Rževuskis and Francis Velmunskis agitated at the port to stop working; an order has been issued to arrest both. [...]

The region of Valmiera reports: within the borders of the Valmiera region everything is calm except for Gaujiena parish where a certain Vītols hung out a red piece of clothing with the words: Long Live the Red Army, Long Live Stalin. In Sermukša parish, the former member of the council said that he was not going to return.

J. Fridrihsons
Security Police Department Director

Source: LVA, 1986.f., 1.apr., 43894.l. (surveillance report), p. 133. Original in Latvian.

DOCUMENTS NO. 5-7
THE CREATION OF THE PUPPET GOVERNMENT

Document No. 5

The minutes of the session of the Cabinet of Ministers about the creation of the new government

June 21, 1940

Present:

State President	Dr. K. Ulmanis
Minister President, acting Minister of Foreign Affairs	Prof. A. Kirhenšteins
Minister of the Interior	V. Lācis
Minister of War	Gen. R. Dambītis
Minister of Social Affairs	P. Blaus
Minister of Transport	J. Jagars
Minister of People's Welfare	J. Lācis
Minister of Justice	J. Pabērzs
Deputy Minister of the Interior	V. Latkovskis

Minutes taken by the Acting Director of the State Chancellery   R. Bulsons

The meeting begins at 10:15.

State President Kārlis Ulmanis, opening the first meeting of the Cabinet of Ministers, speaks to the members of the Cabinet of Ministers:

"Taking into account that on June 16th of this year the entire Cabinet of Ministers submitted their resignations[21] to me, I invite Prof. Dr. A. Kirhenšteins to the post of Minister President and the following as the Cabinet of Ministers: as Minister of war, Gen. Dambītis, as Minister of the Interior, V. Lācis, as Minister of Social Affairs, P. Blaus, as Minister of People's Welfare and acting Minister of Education, J. Lācis, as Minister of Justice and acting Minister of Finance, J. Pabērzs, as Minister of Transport, J. Jagars, as Deputy Minister of the Interior and Chief of the Political Police, V. Latkovskis, and as Commander of the Army, General Kļaviņš.

Having received the assent of the Minister President and the members of Cabinet, I proclaim the government as founded and prepared to fulfill its duties. I wish you success in resolving the complicated assignments. These assignments include the maintenance of order and security, the guaranteeing of the ability to continue normal work, and careful maintenance of good and friendly relations with our neighbors and particularly with our friendly, great Eastern neighbor – the Soviet Union. Take into your hearts to loyally work to station the units of the armed forces of the Soviet Union that are in our land and in helping them with their living conditions."

The Minister President, Prof. A. Kirhenšteins, responds to the State President:

"Highly esteemed Mister President! In the name of the Cabinet and myself I thank you for your good wishes. We will try to fulfill these demanding duties that we have accepted in this difficult moment. We thank you for your work. We have long known of your concern for the people's welfare, education, and health. The "Friendly Invitation" has a particularly important meaning in the improvement of the people's education. You have suggested and invited young people to work, taught them to work, particularly in the countryside. The "Mazpulki" network covers the whole land with hard-working young people. In this difficult moment you have facilitated good relations with foreign countries, particularly with our great neighbor – the Soviet Union. We promise to work for Latvia, to continue, maybe with different methods, the work which you, Mister State President, and the previous government had begun."

The session concluded at 10:25.

State President K. Ulmanis
Minister President A. Kirhenšteins
Acting Director of the State Chancellery R. Bulsons

Source: *LVA, 270.f., 1. apr., 2.l., p. 91.Original in Latvian.*

Document No. 6

Declaration of the Government of the Republic of Latvia

June 21, 1940

Having undertaken to fulfill high state obligations, the government announces to the people of the Republic of Latvia: [...]

The new government sees as its responsibility to facilitate and improve the people's material and spiritual welfare, to guarantee freedom and the rights of people, to guarantee the interests of the state and all of its citizens regardless of their material condition, confession, education, or nationality.

Taking these assignments into account, the government of the Republic of Latvia proclaims an amnesty for all who have struggled for freedom and the people's fortune, for all whose freedom was taken by the previous government due to their political, democratic beliefs.

The new government sees as its first task the guaranteeing of the honest fulfillment of the Latvia and Soviet Union Mutual Assistance Treaty of October 5, 1939, and based on this treaty the creation of a close union between Latvia and the Soviet Union with every resource being used to avert any hindrance to this important state task.

The fact that on the territory of Latvia are stationed the friendly armed forces of the Soviet Union, whom the nation of Latvia received with happiness and sincerity, is the best proof of the true friendship of our peoples with this force. This is also proof of our great neighbor – the Union of Soviet Socialist Republics -- friendly relations with our fatherland.

The government is strictly and indubitably convinced that the friendship of the people of Latvia and the Union of Soviet Socialist Republics will continue to develop and strengthen and that only in this manner can our fatherland's continued development and flowering be guaranteed.

The government's firm conviction is that the indissoluble friendship of the great Soviet Union and the people of the Republic of Latvia will be a great and real force in the future that will guarantee the independence of the state of Latvia, mutual security, and peaceful, successful cooperation between both states.

The government's principle in its foreign policy is to guarantee peace-loving and friendly relationships with all states, and first of all with the Soviet Union.

The government will concern itself with completely implementing the Constitution of the Republic of Latvia according to the real desires of the people.

The government invites the people of the Republic of Latvia to join hand in hand on collective work on behalf of our dear fatherland – Latvia.

A. Kirhenšteins, Minister President
General R. Dambītis, Minister of War
V. Lācis, Minister of the Interior
P. Blaus, Minister of Social Affairs
J. Lācis, Minister of People's Welfare
J. Pabērzs, Minister of Justice
J. Jagars, Minister of Transportation
V. Latkovskis, Deputy Minister of the Interior

Source: *Valdības Vēstnesis, June 22, 1940. Original in Latvian.*

Document No. 7

The Radio Speech of V. Lācis, the Minister of the Interior of the People's Government of Latvia, about the assignments of the Ministry of the Interior in the cleansing of the state and administrative apparatus.

June 23, 1940

Free Citizens of Latvia!

[…] The Red Army being in the territory of Latvia, and the happy reception that our inhabitants gave the Red Army, is solid proof and a guarantee of our stable relations and our brotherly friendship with the USSR. […]

The most important assignment that the Ministry of the Interior must do is completely and thoroughly clean out the state apparatus of reactionary elements and the enemies of the people.

The enemies of Latvia and of the Latvian nation spread the most provocative rumors in attempting to shake our trust in the mutual assistance pact, to sow in the nation mistrust of the new government and of our great friend – the Soviet Union.

The Ministry of the Interior in the most exact and careful way must fight against them and in the future fight similar provocative works of scoundrels, to attach the most severe punishment for each transgression of state order. In this work a major role falls on the people. We call on our society, our societal organizations, and all conscientious people, all of our land's true patriots, to support us. […]

Already a part of the work has been done in choosing the state and administrative apparatus. The decisions of the previous government are being reviewed in order to rescind those that do not match the principles of Latvia's Constitution and the declaration of the new government of June 21, 1940[22]. Legislative acts in the field of general state and administrative construction are being prepared, grounded in the June 21, 1940, declaration, whose assignment is to guarantee particularly:

1. the inviolability of people and citizens' property;
2. the protection of state and society's property and its inviolability;
3. all of the functionaries' responsibility to their state obligations and transgressions of state discipline. […]

Source: *Valdības Vēstnesis, June 25, 1940. Original in Latvian.*

DOCUMENTS NO. 8-15

ELECTIONS WITHOUT THE RIGHT TO CHOOSE

Document No. 8

Excerpts from the minutes of the conference of Regional Secretaries of the Rīga Municipal Committee of the Latvian Communist Party about preparations for the *Saeima* elections

July 4, 1940

9 region Secretaries participating.

Day's Order:
1. *Saeima* elections. [...]

1. Comrade Spure reports that regarding the order from the International and the decision of the Secretariat, the elections to the *Saeima* must take place soon. The elections will be held on the basis of the first Constitution. The latter's limitations are repealed. The elections must be prepared quickly. The elections must happen on the 14th and 15th of July. The election campaign begins tomorrow, July 5th. We must explain our two suggestions that the *Saeima* is not popular because 1) There are no constitutional limitations; 2) The Workers Bloc – workers, peasants, the working intelligentsia and representatives of the army will go into the bloc. Parties, excluding the Communist Party, are not legalized and that is why they can not be legalized in practical terms in two weeks time. The results will be dependent on our work and abilities. The regions must take into account that the apparatus that participated in the election of factory committees must be broadened and supplemented. Their work must be concentrated in the regions if possible.
All Latvia is divided into 5 electoral provinces. In Rīga 21 candidates, in Latgale – 27, in Vidzeme – 22, in Kurzeme – 15, in Zemgale – 15.
How will the elections happen: lists will be drawn up, organization meetings will be called that will choose authorized agents for an authorized, collective meeting that will draw up candidates. The region assignment: to push forward candidates from the meetings of the region's authorized agents. The regions must have concrete suggestions tomorrow in regards to representatives and candidates – from different classes and nationalities.
All lists of candidates will be submitted to the Central Electoral Commission workers'bloc. The following will be elected at the meeting of the Central Election Commission: 2 – from the LCP, 2 – from trade unions, 1 each – from the Ministry of Justice, Interior, and the Statistical Board. From the party – Buševics and Deglavs. From the trade unions – Šics and Vecvagars. [...]

Source: *LVA PA, 102.f., 1.apr., 5.l., p. 8.Original in Latvian.*

Comment: *The document shows that the elections were organized according to the Communist International (which existed from 1918-1943), or according to orders from Moscow, and that only the Communist Party could participate in them and as well that it would be a new type of parliament in which only one party is represented. It should be noted that the Central Electoral Commission was first ratified at this meeting and only afterward at a session of the Cabinet of Ministers (see Document No. 9).*

Excerpts from the Minutes of the Session of the Cabinet of Ministers about adding Latvian Communist Party representatives to the government, about the *Saeima* elections and preparations for them

July 4, 1940

[...] The meeting begins at 19:20.

[...] 2. Ratified:

      1/ Law about political leaders in the Army[23],

      2/ Law about the Liquidation of Latvia's Labor Central. [...]

12) Ratify the following decree: [...]

The government of the Democratic Republic of Latvia recognizes as its task the guaranteeing of the people of Latvia of the ability to freely express their desires in matters that have currently arisen before our fatherland in the areas of building and governing the state, and in recognizing that no delays can be allowed in these most important affairs of state, decrees:

      To carry out elections to the *Saeima* without delay under the rules of the 6th paragraph of the Constitution of the Republic of Latvia that elections should be general, equal, direct, secret, and proportional.

      To set the time of the elections of the *Saeima* as July 14 and 15, 1940.

      To adopt the election law and to immediately implement it.

13) Ratify the law about the elections to the *Saeima*[24]. [...]

15) Appoint to the Central Electoral Commission:

from the Ministry of Justice – A. Meņģelsons, from the Ministry of the Interior – Ansis Leja, from the Ministry of Social Affairs – Oskars Gulbis, from the State Statistical Board – A. Maldups, from the Latvian Communist Party – Ansis Buševics and Arnolds Deglavs and from the trade union organizations – K. Šics and Vecvagars. [...]

17) Agree with the suggestion of the Minister of Transportation that soldiers of the USSR traveling on Latvia's railroads enjoy the same fares that exist for soldiers of Latvia's army.

18) Decide to assign all state and local government institutions to acquire the state flag of the USSR.

19) Decide to unite the Finance and Trade and Industry Ministries into one Finance Ministry that will be led by Minister of Finance K. Karlsons and with N. Priede as Deputy Minister of Finance with voting rights in Cabinet.

20) Regarding the acceptance of the *Saeima* electoral law, decide to send the following thank you and congratulatory telegram:

      1. To Josef Vissarionovich Stalin, the Leader of the people of the Union of Soviet Socialist Republics and of all of the working masses of the world:

      "The government of the Democratic Republic of Latvia today ratified a law about elections to the *Saeima*. After 6 years of no rights and repression this will again give the people of Latvia their freedom, the right to decide for themselves their fate and the ability to work together with the great Union of Soviet Socialist Republics and its peoples in true friendship. At this great historical moment the government of the Republic of Latvia on behalf of the people of Latvia send you, the genial Leader of all of the world's working masses, thanks for our freedom and justice.

      Long live the friendship of Latvia and the USSR, long live the close and indivisible union of the Republic of Latvia and the USSR, long live the leader and best friend of the working peoples, Josef Vissarionovich Stalin!" [...]

Session ends at 21:40

Minister President Prof. Dr. A. Kirhenšteins
Acting Director of the State Chancellery R. Bulsons

Source: *LVA, 270.f., 1. apr., 2. l., pp. 103-104. Original in Latvian.*

Comment: *This meeting took place after the authorized agent of the USSR, A. Vishinski, returned to Rīga from consultations in Moscow. Due to his suggestions the government was expanded (deputy ministers were included) and supplemented with members of the Latvian Communist Party (A. Tabaks, K. Karlsons, N. Priede).*

Document No. 10

From the new government's Law about elections to the *Saeima*

The Cabinet of Ministers has ratified on July 4, 1940 and the State President has published as the law:

Law about elections to the *Saeima*

Part I
Voting Rights

1. All of Latvia's citizens have voting rights who on the day of the elections have reached 21 years of age. [...]

Part II
Election Commissions

4. The elections to the *Saeima* are organized by the Central Electoral Commission that consists of eight members appointed by the Cabinet of Ministers.
5. The Central Electoral Commission is called to its first meeting by the Minister President; the Commission elects its chair and secretary. [...]
9. In each electoral province the elections to the *Saeima* are organized by the provincial electoral commission: In Rīga province – in Rīga, Vidzeme – in Valmiera, Latgale – in Rēzekne, Kurzeme – in Liepāja, Zemgale – in Jelgava.
Five members appointed by the Cabinet of Ministers work in the provincial electoral commissions. [...]

Part III
Submitting Lists of Candidates

14. Voters have the right to submit a list of candidates until July 10, 1940 at 20:00 o'clock. [...]
19. Each submitted list of candidates for deputy to the *Saeima* must be signed by at least 100 voters. The first three signatures are seen as the submitters of the candidate list and take on responsibility for the correctness of all of the submitted documents. Each voter can sign only one list of candidates. [...]

Part IV
Order of Elections

23. The election hall must be open from 8:00 to 22:00 on July 14 and 15 for the submission of ballots.

24. The electorate will be informed in a timely manner of the election's time and place. In the countryside this information will be distributed by parish boards notifying each homestead individually, but in the cities the municipal boards will do it through advertisements. [...]

26. [...] The electoral commission writes down on a special list the names of the electors and their passport numbers that receive lists of candidates.

27. In the election hall a closed room or compartment will be provided where the voters by themselves can choose, according to their view, one electoral list, fold it four times, and personally deposit it in the sealed box. Before putting it into the box, the chair of the electoral commission or his deputy marks the exterior of the electoral list. [...]

33. Beginning with the opening of the election hall on the first day, the electoral commission keeps minutes of the election process. The electorate has the right to ask that their complaints and protests be recorded in the minutes. [...]

38. Lists are viewed as spoiled if: a) the form or sample is ambiguous and b) there are crossed out portions or new candidates written in. [...]

This law goes into effect from the day of its publication.

July 5, 1940, Rīga

K. Ulmanis
State President

Source: *Valdības Vēstnesis*, July 5, 1940. *Original in Latvian.*

Comment*: In order to guarantee the desired election results the A. Kirhenšteins government ratified a new electoral law in the place of the existing 1922 electoral law, which was like the previous one only in its structure but not in its essence. This law (see paragraph 14 and 23) was meant for only one election. Therefore it was already clear to the compilers of the law that these were the last elections of a* Saeima*. Also, this law, unlike the previous one, introduced a double control over the electorate because the electoral commission not only pressed the appropriate seal in voters' passports, but also compiled lists of the electorate. This was the first step to the introduction of the Soviet electoral system that was based on lists of electors. Furthermore, these lists helped identify those persons that had made corrections in their electoral ballots. Any correction to the electoral ballots was recognized as "counter-revolutionary behavior" and those persons that had behaved this way were later imprisoned and harshly punished (LVA, 1986. f., 2. apr., 2, 7514., pp. 52-54). Relating to the new law (see paragraph 38), the electorate's responsibility was simply to throw the only electoral ballot into the voting urn, thereby proving their loyalty to the existing order.*

The minutes of the interrogation of H. Celmiņš, imprisoned by the NKVD, about the attempted creation of the "Democratic Latvian Electorate" bloc before the beginning of the elections to the *Saeima* in July of 1940

November 11, 1940
Completely Secret

Accused Celmiņš, Hugo son of Pēteris
Interrogation minutes

November 11, 1940
Interrogation begun at 10:25

Question: In the period of preparation of the elections of the people's *Saeima*, did you hold some kind of illegal conference of former active functionaries of the "Farmers Union"?

Answer: Yes, together with "Democratic Center" functionaries I actively participated in the preparation of the so-called illegal „Democratic Latvian" bloc's list.

Question: Tell us who was in the illegal "Democratic Latvian electorate."

Answer: The leading members of the "Democratic Latvian Electorate" bloc were: the lawyer Atis Ķēniņš, the lawyer Pēteris Berģis, Voldemārs Zāmuels, the author Kārlis Skalbe and me, that is Celmiņš, Hugo.

Question: What assignments did your "Democratic Latvian Electorate" bloc give to you?

Answer: The "Democratic Latvian Electorate" bloc saw as its goal the grouping together of other former right-wing parties and Mensheviks to form a united "Democratic Latvian Electorate" bloc list, and in this way get the landowners, factory owners and merchants to participate in the new people's *Saeima*, that is, to participate in the legislation of the new order in Latvia.

Question: But in practice what did your "Democratic Latvian electorate" bloc do?

Answer: Our bloc suggested candidates for the new *Saeima* from all of the right-wing parties. We collected signatures for the submission of the "Democratic Latvian Electorate" bloc list of candidates, campaigned among the local electorate inviting them to vote for the "Democratic Latvian Electorate" bloc list.

Question: Thus you worked against the "Working People's" bloc?

Answer: Yes, we campaigned among the electorate for the "Democratic Latvian Electorate" bloc list by gathering signatures for our candidate lists.

Question: Then the landowners, manor owners, merchants and others did not recognize the working people's chosen list?

Answer: I do not know if landowners recognized the "working people's" list.

Question: Who did your bloc suggest as candidates for the new *Saeima*?

Answer: The "Democratic Latvian Electorate" bloc picked the following as candidates for the new *Saeima*: from the „Farmers Union -- me, Hugo Celmiņš, General Balodis; from the "Democratic Center – Atis Ķēniņš, the lawyer Peteris Berģis, the lawyer Voldemars Zāmuels, the author Kārlis Skalbe; from the new farmers - Mīlbergs, Skuju Frīdis; from the right – the lawyer Ansis Petrēvics and a whole row of other people whose surnames I do not remember right now. I remember from the Mensheviks (radical democrats) - Holcmanis (I do not remember his name).

Question: Therefore your "Democratic Latvian Electorate" bloc wanted, though struggle, to create the conditions in the new *Saeima* for landowners, merchants, factory owners and other right, opposition parties to come to power.

Answer: Yes, the "Democratic Latvian Electorate" bloc wanted by the electoral path to create the conditions for landowners, merchants, factory owners and other right, opposition parties to participate in the legislation of the new order in Latvia.

The minutes, read to me, are recorded correctly as to my words, to which I also sign:

(Celmiņš)

Interrogated by Sergeant Andrejenko , Investigator of the Investigative section of the LSSR Peoples Commissariat of the Interior's State Security Board

Source: *LVA, 1986.f., 2. apr., 9047. l., pp. 35-37.Original in Russian.*

Comment: *H. Celmiņš was a noted political and social figure in the Republic of Latvia in the 1920s and 1930s. He was the Minister of Agriculture and Education. From 1924 to 1925 and 1928 to 1931 he was the Minister President and later the Mayor of Rīga.*

Not taking into account that the "Democratic Latvian electorate" bloc was not allowed to contest the elections to the Saeima, many of its members were imprisoned and harshly punished for the attempt to create an alternative electoral list, which act was seen as illegal and counter-revolutionary behavior. H. Celmiņš was arrested on October 10), 1940, and later deported to the USSR where in 1941 he was sentenced with and received the death penalty.

Document No. 12

From the minutes of the interrogation of A. Ansulis about collecting signatures for the candidate list "Democratic Latvian Electorate" bloc

July 11, 1940 in Liepāja

[…] On July 7 this year at roughly 10:00 o'clock in the morning three strange men escorted by Voldemārs Peņķis from the Ķeira homestead in Pērkone parish arrived at our house. […] The strangers said that they needed 150 signatures so that they could turn in a list so that the list's candidates could defend farmers'interests. […] Tuesday evening coming home from work I saw that our shepherd's father, Baškovs, who lives in Liepāja at Number 20 Roze Street together with some unfamiliar man had come to our house. The unfamiliar man said that in the "Communist" editorial there was news that some signature collectors had been walking around our parish. They, that is Baškovs and the unfamiliar man, reacting to this news, had come to see if that was true. He also explained to me that the Working People's bloc list was composed of workers, farmers and the working intelligentsia. He also said that this list unites all of the working people of Latvia and that other lists aren't even needed. The unfamiliar man then had me sign a list where I withdrew my earlier signature because I now understood that I had been deceived. […]

A. Ansulis
Chief of the Board of the Liepāja Regional Political Police, J. Šalms

Source: *LVA, 1986.f., 2. apr., 1547. l., vol. 1, p. 141. Original in Russian.*

Comment: *In order not to allow the submission of any list but the "Working Peoples bloc" to the Central Electoral Commission, the Chief of the Political Police, V. Latkovskis, gave orders for greater surveillance of the inhabitants to prevent the creation of alternative lists or the collection of electors'signatures. To accomplish this assignment, all possible resources were used, including forcing inhabitants that had signed candidate lists to withdraw their signatures.*

Document No. 13

The Latvian Communist Party's Instructions to the electorate "Electorate, take notice!" published in the newspaper *Cīņa*

July 14, 1940

1. The election will take place on July 14 and 15 – today and tomorrow.
2. Votes must be cast at election posts or sub-posts between 8:00 in the morning until 10:00 in the evening. The election posts are advertised in the press.
3. Do not wait for the last minute to cast your vote – go during the voting post's times.
4. Make sure that all of your family members, associates, and neighbors also participate in the election. If they are undecided or wavering, convince and encourage them. Ask them if they have fulfilled their duty as citizens.
5. Take care that all of the sick and those that can not walk are taken to the voting posts or call the traveling election post to them.
6. You can only vote in person and once – in any election post or sub-post.
7. Do not forget to take your passport.
8. In the urn you can only submit the list of Latvia's working people's bloc that you will receive at the election hall on the election day.
9. You can not strike candidates'names from the list, and you can not add new ones. The list must be submitted unchanged.
10. Do not listen to provocateurs that invite you to not take part in the elections or to strike names or ruin candidate lists.

Source: *Cīņa, July 14, 1940. Original in Latvian.*

The Central Electoral Commission's instructions to the Provincial Electoral Commissions

July 14, 1940

Central Electoral Commission
July 14, 1940
Number 125

To the Provincial Electoral Commissions

News has come into the Central Electoral Commission that in some election posts due to the fault of the post's commission the submission of lists in the urns without the official post (sub-post) commission seal has been allowed.

In these events the Central Electoral Commission has determined to count these lists as valid when the number of submitted lists is determined and corresponds to the number marked in the electoral process minutes.

Central Electoral Commission Chair   A. Buševics
Deputy Secretary   O. Gulbis

Source: *LVVA, 1308.f., 9. apr., 3824. l., p. 144. Original in Latvian.*

Comment*: The Central Electoral Commission violated paragraph 27 of the Law on the election to the Saeima (see Document No. 10) with these instructions. First, the Central Electoral Commission overstepped its authority; second, invalid ballots were recognized as valid, and; third, this gave the opportunity for one elector to place into the electoral urn many ballots.*

From the minutes of the Aizviķa election post electoral commission of Liepāja district in the Kurzeme electoral province, about the participation of Red Army representatives in supervising the election process

July 14, 1940

The commission in the presence of the electorate examined 1 box (urn) that was found to be undamaged and empty, it was sealed and at 8:00 o'clock the voters were permitted entry. In the voting hall there were the following representatives of submitted candidate lists authorized by the 22nd paragraph of the Law about the elections to the *Saeima*:

At the beginning of the election, the representatives of the candidate list had not arrived.

These minutes as well as all of the election material in an unsigned way must be sent to the province electoral commission.

Election process

(Noted are the most important obstacles to the process of the elections and the voters'requested complaints and protests. If in these minutes there is not enough space for all of the notes, create separate minutes to attach to these minutes.)

At 10:00 in the election hall there arrived our friendly USSR soldiers as representatives of the Latvian Communist Party's Lejaskurzeme organization 1) M. Ratņikov and 2) T. Kuprikov and from the periodicals *Kommunist* and *Krasnoje znamja* editorial staff 3) T. Ivanov.

At about 16:00 o'clock in order to gather information representatives from the provincial electoral commission arrived in the election hall and confirmed that the election hall was set up according to the directions of the election instructions and that the election process proceeded without incident.

Source: *LVVA, 1308, f., 9. apr., 3096. l., p. 5. Original in Latvian. .*

Comment: *Drawing from the minutes of other electoral commissions, representatives from the Red Army with mandates from the Latvian Communist Party actively involved themselves in the process of supervising the elections in all of the territory of Latvia. For example, in the electoral commission minutes of the Bārta Parish electoral district one can find the following: "Participating as the representatives of the LCP were the Red Army officers Nikolaj Sizin and Ivan Djadin..." (LVVA, 1308.f., 9. apr., 3096.l., p. 21). This means that representatives of the occupying army actually controlled the electoral process in Latvia. The results of such an election can not be and were not internationally recognized.*

The Latvian Communist Party, following directions from the Embassy of the USSR, organized the elections and Communists decided who was on every level of the electoral commissions. The Communists' and their supporters' supervision of the electoral process and the work of the commissions was not disguised. In the report of the Central Electoral Commission it was stated that: "the supply of electoral material began at 13:00 on July 12 and ended the evening of July 13. [...] At the same time as the arrival of the electoral supplies, the institution's commission's work at organizing the elections was examined on the spot. In this regard, strong support was provided by the Latvian

Communist Party in providing to the Central Electoral Commission trustworthy employees who used automobiles as transport to those places where the local commission's effectiveness was in doubt."
(LVVA, 1308.f. 9.apr., 800/1.l.,, p. 6).

DOCUMENTS NO. 16-20
THE DESTRUCTION OF LATVIA'S ARMY

Document No. 16

From the Law about political leaders in the army

On July 4, 1940 the Cabinet of Ministers ratified and the State President declares the following law:

Law about Political Leaders in the Army

[…] In order to completely implement the steps necessary for the realization of true democracy in the army, as well as to strengthen military discipline and organization of all soldiers, the Cabinet of Ministers decides:

1. To establish the post of political leader in Latvia's Army.
2. The Political Leader post is established:
    a) at the Army headquarters;
    b) at divisions and brigades;
    c) at regiments;
    d) at individual units such as military institutions and garrisons.

The Cabinet of Ministers appoints the Army's political leaders from candidates proposed by social, political organizations. […]

4. The Political Leader and the personnel under his authority are assigned the following tasks:
    a) to introduce the soldiers to the government's laws and decrees and explanation of them;
    b) to educate all of the army's soldiers in the spirit of the state's democratic changes, as well as to organize and lead social, political work in the army;
    c) to facilitate the strengthening of organization and military discipline;
    d) to organize and lead the military press.

This law takes affect the day of its publication.

July 8, 1940, Rīga
State President K. Ulmanis

Source: *Valdības Vēstnesis, July 8, 1940. Original in Latvian.*

Comment: *The beginning of the sovietization of Latvia's army began with the ratification of this law. The Political Leader Institute in the USSR's Red Army was created in 1919. The political leaders in the army had the same authority as commander. In other words, in the armed forces of the USSR (until the fall of 1942) there existed the principle of dual power according to which all of the work of commanders was controlled by political leaders. Since all of the political leaders were appointed by the Communist Party, the USSR was guaranteed strict control over the armed forces, which showed not only in the training of soldiers in the spirit of communist ideology, but also in purely military issues.*

With this law the existing principles of the Red Army were brought into Latvia's Army. After occupation, the Communist Party was the only social, political organization in Latvia; therefore, in view of the 2nd paragraph of the law, only it had the right to nominate candidates for the political leader posts. The Chief of Army Headquarters order of July 18, 1940, even before the announcement of Soviet power, required all units to subscribe only to Latvian Communist Party periodicals (LVVA, 1527.f.,1. apr., 227.l., p. 165). One other task of political leaders was to inform on the mood in the army and to draw up a "list of untrustworthy officers that should be retired from the army" (see Document No. 19).

Document No. 17

Vidzeme's Division Commander's Circular Number 3652 about the political training of soldiers according to the lesson plan ratified by the Commander of Latvia's Army, General R. Kļaviņš, on July 24, 1940

August 17, 1940

To: The aide of the Vidzeme Division Commander
Commander of the 4th Valmiera Infantry Regiment
5th Cēsis [Infantry Regiment Commander]
6th Rīga [Infantry Regiment Commander]
Vidzeme Artillery [Regiment Commander]
5th Cēsis Infantry Regiment Commander's Aid
Vidzeme Artillery Regiment Commander's Aid

In order to ease the work of the regiment political leader in the general political training of soldiers and to animate the political instruction lesson plan for soldiers of Latvia's army ratified by the Army commander, [you are instructed to] find in each regiment and in individually stationed garrisons 2-3 officers or non-commissioned instructors with carefully prepared lesson plans with defined themes. Send the list of mentioned officers and non-commissioned instructors, to be chosen in consultation with the political leaders, to me by August 20 of this year.

The assignment of these officers and non-commissioned instructors will be to help the regiment political leaders in the event that they are unable to lead political activity:
    1) Because of too large an audience,
    2) Because the regiment units are sent to too many different garrisons,
    3) When they are on business, holiday and other similar reasons.

For leaders of political activities, officers and non-commissioned instructors who speak Russian well and are gifted oratorically should be chosen.

The material for preparing the anticipated questions in the lesson plan should be acquired with the Regiment's budget.

The regiment commanders should pay particular attention to the political activities of those units that are stationed outside of the regiment's political leader's permanent place of residence (units outside of Rīga, guard and work companies).

The changed times place a responsibility on those soldiers that have not mastered the Russian language to learn it. It will ease the work if all units can be organized for training in the Russian language. The responsibility for achieving this goal is placed on the chiefs of the units.

<u>Attachment</u>: political training lesson plan copy

Confirmed
Commander of Latvia's Army
General Kļaviņš
July 24, 1940

Lesson Plan for Political Activities of the Soldiers of Latvia's Army

	Title of Theme	Anticipated number of hours for given theme	Learning supplies
1.	The *Saeima* declaration about State power and Latvia's entry into the USSR	2 hours	*Saeima*'s declaration published in the newspapers *Cīņa* and *Proletarian Truth* from 07/22/40
2.	The *Saeima*'s Declaration about Land	2 hours	Above 07/23/40
3.	*Saeima*'s Declaration about the nationalization of banks, enterprises and factories	2 hours	Above 07/23/40
4.	USSR's Constitution (Fundamental Law)	10 hours	Red Army's Political training manual, section 7, pages 27-37 from the article in *Proletarian Truth* of 07/22/40. "Constitution of the USSR" in the Latvian language in the newspaper *Cīņa* 07/23/40
5.	Red Army and Navy, USSR's Armed Support	6 hours	Red Army political training book, section 2
6.	The Ceremonial Oath to the Workers-Peasant Red Army	2 hours	Red Army political training book, section 2, pages 29-37
7.	The Second Imperialist War and the USSR's Foreign Policy	4 hours	Collection of articles: "USSR's Foreign Policy"
8.	The Non-Aggression Pact and Friendship and Border Treaty between the Soviet Union and Germany	2 hours	Comrade Molotov's speech to the meeting of the Supreme Soviet of the USSR

9.	USSR – Great industrial superpower	4 hours	Red Army political training book, 3rd section
10.	The victory of collective farm structures in the USSR	4 hours	Red Army political training book, 4th section
11.	The peoples' material and spiritual condition in the USSR	4 hours	Red Army political training book, 5th section
12.	USSR – Soviet Union as a great co-operator and friend of peoples	4 hours	Red Army political training book, 6th section
13.	All-Union Communist (Bolshevik) Party as the organizer of socialist victory and the leader of the USSR	4 hours	Red Army political training book, 8th section
14.	Lenin-Stalin: heroes of the Soviet peoples and international working masses	8 hours	Red Army political training book, 9th section. "Comrade Stalin's short biography." "Comrade Stalin about Lenin."
15.	Comrade Voroshilov - Red Army Leader	2 hours	Red Army political training book, section 2, pages 70-75

Teaching to be done four times a week for two hours a day.

July 23, 1940

Br. Kalniņš
Political Leader of the Army

A. Zirnītis
Chief of the Cultural Propaganda Supervisory Unit

Correctly transcribed:
Chief of the Cultural Propaganda Supervisory Unit
(A. Zirnītis)

Source: *LVVA, 1526.f., 1. apr., 543. l., pp. 34-36.Original in Latvian.*

Comment: *In preparing Latvia's army for its inclusion into the Red Army even before the annexation of Latvia, stress was placed on improving the teaching of Russian language to the soldiers and officers. After the example of the Red Army, soldiers of Latvia's Army were expected to engage in so-called political activities. Because there were not enough specially-trained political leaders for this work, there was a decision to create political leader assistants. Even though formally still in an independent state (the plan for political activities was ratified on July 24, 1940), these personnel were ordered to teach soldiers the constitution of a different state, the biographies of its leaders, and to have them read celebratory accounts of this order from articles in newspapers, brochures and "the instructional books of the Red Army" – i.e. collection of communist dogma. This is how the political training and ideological indoctrination of Latvia's soldiers began, following the example of the Red Army.*

Document No. 18

Excerpt from the People's Commissar of Defense of the USSR, S. Timoshenko, Order number 0141 "About the Establishment of the Baltic Military Province, the Disbanding of the Kalinin Military Province and the Renaming of the Belorussia Special Military Province as the Western Special Military Province"

July 11, 1940

1. I order that by August 1, 1940 a Baltic Military Province be established and that it is headquartered in Rīga. [...]

3. The Commander of the Baltic Military province will be Colonel General A. D. Loktionov, the commander of the military province's headquarters will be Lieutenant General P. S. Klenov.
4. The Baltic Military Province will include the territory of the Republics of Latvia and Lithuania as well as the military units and installations stationed in the western section of the Kalinin province, [...]
7. The Chief of the Red Army General Headquarters has been given a list of armed forces units and organizations that:
    a) Are to be included in the Baltic Military province. [...]
8. The establishment of the Baltic Military Province will be reported to the commander of the armed forces on July 31, 1940.
9. This order takes effect when it is distributed
    telegraphically.

USSR People's Commissar of Defense
Marshall of the USSR, S. Timoshenko

Source: *Polpredi, pp. 462-463. Original in Russian.*

Comment: *This order, given before the "free, democratic" elections in the Baltic States and the subsequent decisions to "voluntarily" join the USSR, again demonstrates that the belief of the leaders of the Soviet state was that the elections were just technical matters designed to disguise the fact that the occupation had already happened in the Baltic States and that their complete annexation was just a question of time.*

From the order of the USSR's People's Commissar of Defense, S. Timošenko

August 17, 1940

All-Union Communist (Bolshevik) Party Central Committee and the Soviet of Peoples' Commissars ratify the following decree transforming the armies of the Estonian, Latvian and Lithuanian SSRs:

1. To preserve for one year the existing armies of the Estonian, Latvian and Lithuanian SSRs, to purge the disloyal elements and to transform each army into a territorial rifles' corps. It is taken into account that the commanding personnel in this time period will finish acquiring Russian language and military re-training, after which the territorial corps will be changed for ex-territorials, based on general formations [...]

3. To include all of the existing armed units of the Estonian, Latvian and Lithuanian armies, with their arms, transport and war material into the formed corps. To give the leftover war material in working order, after the reorganization of the army, to army warehouses.

4. To strengthen the political contents of cadres, give the Peoples' Commissar of Defense the assignment of choosing [cadres] from the ranks of the Red Army's appropriate ethnic and Russian commanders for a section for commanders and political activity.

5. To introduce the Red Army's program and rules to the transformed corps, to give to the Peoples Commissar of Defense the assignment to have these translated into the relevant ethnic languages.

6. To assign the transformed corps to the Red Army and to designate them: the Estonian SSR 22nd Rifles Corps, the Latvian SSR 24th Rifles Corps and the Lithuanian 29th Rifles Corps under the command of the Baltic Military Province.

7. The 22nd, 24th, and 29th Rifles Corps should keep their existing uniforms, but it is suggested that they remove the shoulder insignia introduce the Red Army's command symbols.

8. In two months time, the transformed corps's entire personnel will take the military oath in accordance with the USSR Supreme Soviet Presidium's decree of January 3, 1939 concerning the taking of the military oath. [...]

In order to fulfill the order: [...]

5. Together with the government of the USSR, to examine the Estonian, Latvian, and Lithuanian army cadres and to purge the disloyal elements. To send the personnel files of the Estonian, Latvian, and Lithuanian armies' officers – those that leave the army and those that are disloyal – to the Red Army Cadres Board. [...]

> USSR Peoples Commissar of Defense
> Soviet Union Marshal S. Timošenko
> Chief of Staff of the Red Army
> Soviet Union Marshal B. Šapašņikov[25]

Source: *Polpredi, pp. 505-508 Original in Russian.* .

Order Number 28 of the Minister of War of the Latvian SSR, R. Dambītis, about the liquidation of the Ministry of War and the inclusion of Latvia's army into the Red Army

August 31, 1940

With the decision of the Council of Peoples'Commissars of the Latvian SSR the Latvian People's Army is admitted into the Red Army.

Local Military Boards (Military District Chiefs) are renamed as Military Commissariats.

Military Educational institutions are reorganized as the Red Army's normal infantry school.

The War Ministry of the Latvian SSR, in accord to the Constitution, is liquidated. All goods, weapons, war reserves, apartments, land, money and accounts belonging to the Latvian Peoples'Army and the Ministry of War are transferred to the Baltic Military Province.

Relevant to the mentioned decree:

1. To transfer personal contents, material and currency valuables, dwellings, apartment and accounts, live and dead stock that belongs to the Latvian Peoples Army and the Ministry of War – to the control of the Military Council of the Baltic c Military Province, for its use according to its decisions.

2. To liquidate the Ministry of War and all of the boards, institutions and enterprises under its control, to turn over the personal materials that are associated with military service, all property, files and archives to the Military Council of the Baltic Specific Military Province. […]

4. Goods, weapons, war reserves and other valuable material assigned to the Latvian Peoples Army for all of its armed forces units and institutions; to close all supply of goods and account books by September 1st of this year.

To prepare a list of all transferred goods, dwellings and their contents.

To accomplish the mentioned work by September 10th of this year.

To turn over the goods according to the instructions of the commission appointed by the War Council of the Baltic Specific Military Province.

To draw up files of the transfer of materials in six copies: to leave one copy with the unit, to send two to the chief of the Supply Board of the Latvian People's Army and three copies to the Goods Receiving Commission. […]

Minister of War
General Dambītis

Commander Peoples'Army
General Kļaviņš

Source: *LVA PA, 101.f., 2. apr., 280. l., p. 9. Original in Latvian.*

Comment: With this order many categories of soldiers in Latvia's army were retired from active military service, continuing the retirement of officers and soldiers from the army that had began after the occupation of Latvia in June. From June to July, 55 officers were effectively driven out of the Army (including all of the army's clergymen). For example, on July 30, 1940, 18 officers, 6 of whom were decorated with the highest military medal of recognition in Latvia – the Lačplēsis Military Order, for accomplishments in battle during Latvia's War of Independence from 1918 to 1920, were retired with one written command (LVVA, 1303.f.,1. apr.,4. l., pp. 11, 14). The soldiers that had participated in the war for Latvia's independence from 1918 to 1920 (particularly in battles against the Bolsheviks), as well as those that were awarded military decorations, were the first to be recognized by the occupying army as unwanted, hostile and useless.

Documents No. 21-24
Latvia's incorporation into the Soviet Union

Document No. 21

Declaration of the Peoples *Saeima* about Soviet power in Latvia

July 21, 1940

Declaration Concerning State Power

[...] Expressing the will of all of the free working people of Latvia, the *Saeima* hereby announces the establishment of Soviet power on all of Latvia's territory.

Latvia, with the acceptance of this declaration in the *Saeima*, is renamed a Soviet Socialist Republic. This law of the *Saeima* takes effect without delay.

From this day on, all power in the Latvian Soviet Socialist Republic belongs to the working masses of the city and countryside, represented by the working masses'Councils of Deputies.

The *Saeima* is strongly convinced that all of the inhabitants of Latvia will rally around Soviet power for the complete victory of the people's will, for Latvia's economic and cultural flowering, and for our nation's freedom and fortune.

Long live the Latvian Soviet Socialist Republic!
Long live the working masses'Councils of Deputies!
Long live the Soviet Union – the fatherland of all the world's working masses!

Source: *Latvijas Tautas Saeimas, pp. 30-32.Original in Latvian.*

Declaration about Latvia's admission in the Union of Soviet Socialist Republics

July 21, 1940

[…] With its politics hostile to the nation, the old, plutocratic government took Latvia to the brink of ruin.

As a result of the criminal, treasonous politics of the former reactionary clique in power, Latvia was threatened with the horror of becoming the spoils of imperialists.

The former criminal clique of Latvia's rulers tried with artificial measures to wall off the Latvian nation from the nations of the Union of Soviet Socialist Republics, and tried in every way to delay the brotherly coming together of our and the Soviet nations, our friendship and close, unbreakable union with our great neighbor – the invincible Union of Soviet Socialist Republics.

The old government tried to dodge the fulfillment of the October 5, 1939, mutual assistance pact between Latvia and Union of Soviet Socialist Republics. The old government, breaking its word, violated this agreement, traitorously driving our land into war and destruction.

In place of the friendship of nations, the reactionary clique that earlier ruled our land, in many ways fueled and kept alive national cleavages and intolerant chauvinism.

Now, when the Latvian nation has overthrown the old regime – the unjust and repressive regime – and has begun a full and bright new life on the path to social reconstruction and a new state, when the great historical moment has struck, when completely and for all time all barriers between Latvia and the Union of Soviet Socialist Republics must be taken down, [we must initiate] the legal process to strengthen the close, stable union of the Latvian Republic with the Union of Soviet Socialist Republics.

The Latvian Peoples *Saeima* now gathered is convinced that only by entering the Union of Soviet Socialist Republics is our state's real sovereignty guaranteed; our industrial, agricultural, and national culture's true flowering [ensured]; the Latvian people's material and cultural welfare situation improved. Our loved homeland's development and prosperity will be great.

Our nation is tied to the brotherly nations of the Union of Soviet Socialist Republics with close bonds that were created in the many years of revolutionary struggle against tsarism, against capitalism, and against manorial owners that oppressed Russian and Latvia's workers and peasants.

The time has come to seal these bonds for all time.

The nation of Latvia, entering the community of brotherly and great socialist lands and fortunate nations, will unleash all of its wealth-creating forces and hand in hand with the working masses of the Union of Soviet Socialist Republics will go forward along the new life's path of construction.

Only in the Union of Soviet Socialist Republics will Latvia's nation heal the wounds that it received from the many years of slavery. Only with its great friend's – the Soviet Union – help, and as an equal brotherly member of the Soviet Union's community, will the Latvian nation be able to raise its economy, develop its national culture, guarantee equality of nations, guarantee peace, bread and real freedom for Latvia's working masses.

Based on the unanimously voiced will of Latvia's nation, the *Saeima* decides:

To ask the Supreme Soviet of the Union of Soviet Socialist Republics to accept the Latvian Soviet Socialist Republic into the Soviet Union as a Union Republic on the same terms that the Union of Soviet Socialist Republics accepted the Ukrainian Soviet Socialist Republic, Belorussia and other Union Soviet Socialist Republics.

Long live Soviet Latvia!

Long live the great Union of Soviet Socialist Republics!

Source: *Latvijas Tautas Saeimas, pp. 33-35. Original in Russian.*

The Law of the Supreme Soviet of the USSR concerning the acceptance of the Latvian Soviet Socialist Republic into the USSR

Kremlin, Moscow, August 5, 1940

Having heard the declaration of the authorized commission of the *Saeima* of Latvia, the Supreme Soviet of the Union of Soviet Socialist Republics declares:

i. To fulfill the request of the *Saeima* of Latvia and accept the Latvian Soviet Socialist Republic into the Union of Soviet Socialist Republics as a Union Soviet Socialist Republic with equal standing.

ii. To organize elections in accordance with paragraphs 34 and 35 of the Constitution (Basic Law) of the USSR in the Latvian Soviet Socialist Republic for deputies to the Supreme Soviet of the USSR.

iii. To assign to the Presidium of the Supreme Soviet of the USSR the task of declaring the day of the election.

Chair of the Presidium of the Supreme Soviet of the USSR, M. Kalinin
Secretary of the Presidium of the Supreme Soviet of the USSR, A. Gorkin

Source*: Valdības Vēstnesis, August 12, 1940. Original in Russian.*

Decree of the Presidium of the Supreme Soviet of the USSR about the order in which citizens of the Lithuanian, Latvian, and Estonian Soviet Socialist Republics acquire USSR citizenship

September 7, 1940

1. In connection with paragraph 1 of the August 19, 1938 Union of Soviet Socialist Republics' Citizenship law, the citizens of the Lithuanian, Latvian and Estonian Soviet Socialist Republics, beginning from the day that these republics were accepted into the USSR, are citizens of the USSR.

2. The citizens of the Lithuanian, Latvian, and Estonian Soviet Socialist Republics who at the moment of this decree's publication are located outside of the borders of the USSR and for whom these Republics' Soviet governments have not rescinded citizenship, must register as Soviet citizens with authorized USSR representatives or consulates no later than November 1, 1940, either by arriving in person or by sending a specific request through the mail and attaching the national passport.

   Persons who will not have registered as Soviet citizens with authorized USSR representatives or consulates by November 1, 1940, can acquire USSR citizenship on the basis of the general instructions in the 3rd paragraph of the citizenship law of the Union of Soviet Socialist Republics.

3. Those ethnic minorities who were stateless and could not acquire Lithuanian, Latvian or Estonian citizenship in view of the political regimes that existed in Lithuania, Latvia and Estonia until the founding of Soviet power, acquire USSR citizenship according to the

procedure outlined in this decree's first and second paragraphs.

The remainder of the stateless persons that permanently live in the territory of the Lithuanian, Latvian, and Estonian Soviet Socialist Republics can acquire USSR citizenship according to the procedures in the 3rd paragraph of the Citizenship Law of the Union of Soviet Socialist Republics.

4. Persons whose Soviet citizenship was rescinded by the All-Russian Central Executive Committee and the Soviet of Peoples' Commissars of the RSFSR decree of December 15, 1921, and who are currently located on the territory of the Lithuanian, Latvian, and Estonian Soviet Socialist Republics will be equated the stateless persons, as described in this decree's 3rd paragraph, second section.

Kremlin, Moscow, September 7, 1940

Chair of the Presidium of the Supreme Soviet of the USSR, M. Kaļiņin
Secretary of the Presidium of the Supreme Soviet of the USSR, A. Gorkin

Source: *Ziņotājs, September 11, 1940. Original in Russian.*

DOCUMENTS NO. 25-26
CONFISCATION OF THE PROPERTIES OF THE LATVIAN STATE AND OF ITS INHABITANTS

Document No. 25

Declaration of the nationalization of banks and large enterprises

July 22, 1940

In Latvia's bourgeois republic, the same as in all capitalist lands, big industrial enterprises and the banking system were tools to impoverish the working nation and to allow a small group of bankers and factory owners to live from the labors of workers, peasants, tradesmen, and the working intelligentsia. The people's possessions went into the pockets of the wealthy, factory owners and other speculators, making them wealthy on the basis of other peoples' work; this created unemployment and mass poverty, and traumatized the people's economy by robbing the working masses' of faith in their future, by creating uncertainty about tomorrow.

During the *Saeima*'s elections from July 14 to 15, all of the working nation of Latvia unanimously asked for an end of this state of affairs.

The *Saeima* of the Republic of Latvia, in answering these just demands of the nation, has decided to nationalize all large trade and industrial enterprises and banks in all of the territory of Latvia. From this moment, the *Saeima* declares that all large trade, industrial and transport enterprises, as well as banks, and all of their possessions are the property of the people, that is, the state's property. (Prolonged applause, Deputies give a standing ovation.) With this great historic legislative act a new page in the people's history of Latvia opens, the conditions for the rapid blossoming of the nation's welfare and fortune are created.

The People's *Saeima* is convinced that this law reflects entirely the peoples'and state's interests.

The people's *Saeima* assigns to the government the task of drawing up and ratifying without delay a list of enterprises and institutions to nationalize.

Source: *Latvijas Tautas Saeimas, p. 50-51.Original in Latvian.*

Comment: *The beginning of the nationalization of Latvia's large and medium sized industrial enterprises began at the end of July 1940 and ended at the beginning of September. During this time, about 800 enterprises were nationalized. The nationalization process did not end with the nationalization of large and medium enterprise, however. On February 21, 1941, the Soviet of People's Commissars of the Latvian SSR ratified the law "About the nationalization of small, private enterprises that have a local, state or industrial importance." The nationalization of these enterprises was to be done in one week's time. Altogether in Latvia, 1,648 small enterprises were nationalized.*

In August of 1940, all banks were nationalized. Preliminary work for this was already done in July when several banks were consolidated.

Document No. 26

The Latvian SSR government's law about the creation of the State Land Fund and the rules for its distribution

July 29, 1940 the Cabinet of Ministers ratified and the State President published the following law:

Law about Land

3. The State Land Fund, established with the July 22, 1940 *Saeima* declaration about land as the peoples' property, is the recipient of the following types of land:
   (1) All the current state land used for agriculture that is not directly needed by the state;
   (2) All church, congregation, and cloister land regardless of its size;
   (3) That part of the land that exceeds 30 hectares of existing land owners' land, not including the land of the enemies of the people and of land speculators which is transferred in its entirety to the Fund.
4. The State Land Fund is used for supplying the landless and small landholders with land, as well as to satisfy the needs of socially used land.
5. First, from the State Land Fund, additions will be made to the land of the small landholders whose farm does not reach the size mentioned in paragraph 4.
6. New farms are distributed at the size of 10 hectares.
7. Farms from the State Land Fund are distributed to citizens of the Latvian Soviet Socialist Republic who were working primarily in agriculture as of July 22, 1940. Farms are also distributed to those citizens in active military service who were primarily working in agriculture until they were called into active service.
8. All the land of the Latvian Soviet Socialist Republic distributed by the Fund, as well as the land left to the current owners, is distributed and ratified through reference to the land book deeds, and is given over for use for life to working peasants until the time when one of their legal, direct heirs takes over the working of the land.
9. Each working peasant's responsibility is to work the land for his own use and improve it, to maintain the farm buildings and to build and direct the entire farm according to the newest achievements of agriculture, putting all energy and knowledge into this work.

10. The parish boards, in which there are 2 authorized agents of the Ministry of Agriculture, apply the law about land to everyday life [in their localities]. Complaints about the decisions of the local government in land affairs will be resolved by the Land Use Committees at the Ministry of Agriculture, whose make-up is decided by the Cabinet of Ministers. The decisions of the Land Use Committees are final and can only be appealed to the Senate.

11. This law does not apply to land in the administrative borders of municipalities about which a separate law will be issued.

12. All ratified land use contracts are rescinded from April 23, 1941.

13. Directions, instructions and decrees on how to implement this law will be given by the Minister of Agriculture.

14. This law takes effect on the day of its publication.

Prof. Dr. A. Kirhenšteins
State President

Source: *Valdības Vēstnesis, July 31, 1940. Original in Latvian.*

Comment: *After the nationalization of land, the agrarian reform created about 50,000 new farms. Because these farms were no larger than 10 hectares, they were not economically viable, but viability was not the goal of the agrarian reform. The agrarian reform was mean to ensure support for Soviet power from the poorest section of farmers and at the same time prepare for the collectivization of agriculture. Officially, it was maintained that there would be no forced collectivization.*

DOCUMENTS No. 27-29

SANCTIONS AGAINST THE AMBASSADORS OF THE REPUBLIC OF LATVIA IN FOREIGN COUNTRIES

Document No. 27

From the report of K. Zariņš, Ambassador of the Republic of Latvia to England, to the Minister President, A. Kirhenšteins

July 11, 1940

[…] Not much is spoken about us in the press or in public, but some facts are given, sometimes by the reporters from Stockholm and Helsinki, as it has always been, trying to fill out the colors, but there is no commentary. Private interest is large. Often I am presented with questions about what is really happening in the Baltic, are we still the decision-makers in our own homes or are we completely under the Russian truncheon. Also many ask for explanations about the elections. I keep my replies distant and refrain from more precise information because of disrupted communications. This is how it is; for a long time I have not seen Latvian periodicals and the special news broadcasts do not give enough material to satisfy all of the questions. [You yourselves will understand that news once a week or once per ten days reading of reports for three quarters of an hour does not create enough of a landscape.] Not counting our own citizens, English public representatives come to the embassy and even official institutions for all sorts of information. This is also completely natural because the state's official representative is in the right place to receive authentic news. But we can not completely satisfy requests and we have to make do with citations from various speeches of our ministers. I am placed in an uncomfortable situation, which goes counter to all of our accepted traditions. I would be very thankful if more complete information could be found. [...]

Source: *LVVA, 3574.f., 4. apr., 7662.l., pp. 102-103.Original in Latvian.*

Document No. 28

The Ministers of Justice of the Latvian SSR's explanation of the addenda and changes in the law about citizenship

July 29, 1940

In such historical times as the current ones, when we are developing and stabilizing a new order in the state, it is not in the interests of the state that a part of the citizens are located outside of the state's borders unnecessarily. Such citizens not only do not help in the great new work of construction, but, not knowing the conditions, they cannot relate to others in foreign lands truthful information about the new order; such citizens, even without knowing it, can harm the new order by staying in foreign lands. Because of this it is believed that the government has the right to request that the citizens who are unnecessarily located in foreign lands need to return to Latvia, and has the right also to use certain sanctions against those that do not listen to this request.

Source: *LVVA, 1307. f., 1. apr., 232. l., p. 121.Original in Latvian.*

Document No. 29

Excerpts from the minutes of the session of the Cabinet of Ministers about the rescinding of citizenship from K. Zariņš and A. Bīlmanis

July 30, 1940

[...] The session begins at 13:00.

Based on rules in the 8th paragraph of the law about citizenship, it is decided to rescind citizenship of the former Ambassador in London, Kārlis Zariņš, and the former Ambassador in Washington, Alfreds Bīlmanis, and based on the rules in the third section of the ninth paragraph of the same law, it is decided to confiscate the possessions of Kārlis Zariņš and Alfreds Bīlmanis. Kārlis Zariņš and Alfreds Bīlmanis are traitors against the state and are hereby proclaimed to be in violation of the law.
The session closes at 14:00.

Minister President, Prof. Dr. A. Kirchenšteins
Acting Director of the State Chancellery V. Stalažs

Source: *LVA, 270. f., 1. apr., 2. l., p. 137. Original in Latvian.*

Documents No. 30-32
The introduction of the censorship system

Document No. 30

The law of the Latvian SSR about the Chief Literary Board

3. The Chief Literary Board resides within the Ministry of Interior and it controls the content and the technical production of:
    (1) Printed work prepared by a mechanical or chemical processes;
    (2) Reproductions of articles, artistic representations and music scores meant for distribution;
    (3) Published products from foreign lands.
4. The Chief Literary Board is headed by the Board's Chief, who is appointed by the Cabinet of Ministers.
5. The editorial staff and the political editors in publishing houses are responsible for the contents of published periodicals and non-periodicals, but for technical publications – the [responsible persons are the] technical editors.
    (1) Note: Political editors can also work with several publishing houses.
6. The Chief of the Chief Literary Board appoints the political editors.
7. The press or the shop's responsible leader send 2 examples of the first 20 copies of published periodicals and the first 15 examples of non-periodical published work, such as photographs and other similarly prepared items, without delay to Rīga, to the Chief Literary Board. Along with this, the editor of the publishing house must supply the number of published copies of the periodical on request from the Chief Literary Board or local chief of the peoples'militia.
8. The Post-Control Bureau, whose leader is appointed by the Minister of Interior on the suggestion of the Board Chief, is located at the Chief Literary Board to review the prepared and distributed published material.
9. Additional decrees on applying this law will be given by the Minister of the Interior.
10. This law goes into affect on the day of its publication.

August 10, 1940

Saeima Chair P. Briedis
Deputy State President

Source: *Valdības Vēstnesis, August 10, 1940. Original in Latvian.*

The decision of the Latvian SSR government about the closing of all periodicals and about the permitted publications list

August 10, 1940

The Cabinet of Ministers, acting on the liquidation of the Department of the Press and Societies and the founding of the Chief Literary Board, declares that all permits issued to date for the distribution of periodicals are annulled. From August 10, the Cabinet of Ministers allows only the following periodicals to be distributed:

Struggle	Locomotive
Proletarian Truth	Working Woman
Free Peasant	Justice
Soviet Latvia	Latgale's Truth
Workers Magazine	Flame
Labor	Free Daugava
Red Soldier	Zemgale's Communist
Government Herald	Communist
Red Sport	Free Venta
Pioneer	Talsi District Reporter
Rīga Crocodile	Flag
Free Youth	Relaxation
Red Aid	Latvia's School
Agitator and Propagandist	State Statistical Board Reports
Radio Wave	Labor Peasant

Deputy Minister President, Minister of the Interior V. Lācis
Deputy Social Affairs Minister, Minister of Foreign Affairs, Comrade A. Jablonskis

Source: *Valdības Vēstnesis, August 10, 1940. Original in Latvian.*

Order 158 of the Board of Artistic Affairs of the Soviet of Peoples Commissars of the Latvian SSR about the censoring of all manner of programs of cultural events and entertainment

March 22, 1941

The Artistic Affairs Board of the Soviet of Peoples Commissars of the Latvian SSR with this order defines the method for submitting artistic programs for permission:

1. All theaters, circuses, stages, artistic creations, cinema entertainments, and restaurant programs before and after censoring, as well as the permission granted to [perform and show] them, belong to the Artistic Affairs Board of the Soviet of Peoples Commissars of the Latvian SSR independent of who organizes these events or who the organizers are responsible to.
2. Events with an artistic program can not happen if they do not have the necessary performance permits.
3. The preparation of work that has not yet been allowed can not begin if it does not have the needed permits.
4. Work for review directly from the author is not accepted.
5. For the acceptance of programs the following material must be submitted, identifying the authors and also the translators:
   a. Plays, sketches, etc. (published) must be submitted in 1 copy,
   b. Plays, sketches, etc. (unpublished) must be submitted in 2 copies,
   c. Song notes in 1 copy, but text in 2 copies,
   d. Poems in 2 copies,
   e. The copy of the full program showing the event's place and time in three copies.
   Note. This paragraph's a, b, and c points do not apply to the repertoire list accepted by the Artistic Affairs Board.
6. The programs of one-time events must be submitted for acceptance to the Artistic Affairs Board no later than 10 days before the event.
Note. If the event is repeated at a different place or at a different time, the permit must be requested anew.
7. After the program is accepted, it is forbidden to alter it without the permission of the Artistic Affairs Board. For violating this paragraph, both the organizer and performer are held responsible.
8. In all events with a program of an artistic character there must be 2 places reserved, not further back than the 4th row, for employees of the Artistic Affairs Board's Performance and Repertoire Control Section.
For not obeying this order, the guilty will be held criminally accountable.

H. Līkums

Source: *Ziņotājs, March 27, 1941. Original in Latvian.*

DOCUMENTS NO. 33-34
THE LATVIAN COMMUNIST PARTY – THE IMPLEMENTERS OF MOSCOW'S POLICIES

Document No. 33

From the stenogram of the speech of the Chair of the Soviet of Peoples Commissars of the Latvian SSR, V. Lācis, at the IX Congress of the Latvia's Communist Party

December 17, 1940

Comrade Lācis: (speaking in the Latvian language)

Comrades, not quite a full half year has gone by since Latvia's Communist (Bolshevik) Party was legalized. The Party was legalized not by some capitalist government, not some bourgeois, democratic parliament, it was done by itself. The situation when this legalization happened is still fresh in everyone's memories. It would be a waste for me to repeat precisely the analysis of this situation, to look at how our political condition became confused and then how they cleared, and how in the Baltic Sea provinces this led to the growth of the political weight of the Union of Soviet Socialist Republics, on one hand, and on the other, the demise of the local, pseudo-national government.

We know that for the government of the Soviet Union and for the Communist Party these events were not accidental. The events on the shores of the Baltic Sea came as a surprise to others – first of all to the local plutocratic clique, made stupid by their power, who called its leadership "the nation's rebirth" and "unified government," but used its power for politics hostile to the nation. It also came as a surprise to the imperialist beasts[26] that had speculated on the division of the USSR and are now pulled into a new slaughter that they must fight alone. [...]

Where there is a lack of political education, class instinct takes its place. But that does not mean that the political training of the working masses is not seen as one of the most important assignments for the party. [...]

Source: *LVA PA, 101. f., 1.apr., pp. 1, 15, 20. Original in Russian.*

Comment: *The Latvian Communist Party went from an illegal and uninfluential party with few members in the Republic of Latvia to being the only and decisive political force in the Latvian SSR. But it still must be kept in mind that the LCP lost even the limited autonomy that it had in the 1920s and 1930s when it worked under the control of the Comintern. At the end of 1940, it had 2,800 members. Nevertheless, the local communists comprised only few of this membership. The dominance of Red Army soldiers and party functionaries and administrators who arrived from the Soviet Union was now very noticeable. In December of 1940, the IX Congress of the Latvian Communist Party took place in Rīga; of the 218 delegates, 55% were Latvian, 34% of the representatives were from the Red Army of the USSR and the State Security organs. This reflected the real organization of power in the territory of Latvia. The Politburo of the LCP created at the Congress included the Chief of the Political Board of the Baltic Special Military Province, Division Commandeer F. Shamanin – the chief commissar (political leader) in the Red Army in the occupied Baltic.*

From the Minutes of a meeting of the Politburo of Latvia's Communist (Bolshevik) Party Central Committee

January 2, 1941

Participated: Politburo members: Comrades Kalnbērziņš, Augusts, Neilands, Plēsums, Šamaņin, V. Lācis, F. Deglavs. Noviks;
Politburo candidate (members): comrades Pugo, Ļestjev;
Central Committee members: Comrades Paldiņa-Rūsis, Avotiņš, Pavlov and Gailis.

1. HEARD: About the re-issue of "Short Course of the History of the All-Union Communist (Bolshevik) Party."
    /Reporter Comrade Deglavs /.
    DECIDED: 1) To recognize that it was particularly urgent to re-issue without delay the "Short Course of the History of the All-Union Communist (Bolshevik) Party" in the Latvian language in a print run of 1,000 copies. To appoint comrade Deglavs, Fricis, as the editor responsible for the translation, and to release him from all other party assignments until January 15th, and to assign him the responsibility of working at the State Plan (Commission)[27] for four hours every day (from 8:30 until 12:30).
    To free comrade Ozoliņš, Kārlis, from work at the editorial staff of *Cīņa* and to assign the proofreader Mazuks to special work on the "Short Course of the History of the All-Union Communist (Bolshevik) Party" until January 12th.
    The book must be published by January 15th of this year.
2. To determine that the price of the book "Short Course of the History of the All-Union Communist (Bolshevik) Party" will not be more than 3-5 rubles.
3. To assign to comrade GUSTSONS to guarantee the needed paper for the publication of "Short Course of the History of the All-Union Communist (Bolshevik) Party."

2. HEARD: About the assigning of leading workers to party, Komsomolsk, trade union, and soviet and economic organizations.

DECIDED: After listening to Comrade PAVLOVS' report about the conditions of assigning leading workers to the apparatus of the party, Komsomolsk, trade union, soviet and economic organizations, Latvia's Communist (Bolshevik) Party Central Committee Politburo determined that despite the considerable work accomplished in the screening and assignment of leading workers, there is still a noticeable shortage of responsible workers in the mentioned organizations; furthermore some organizations are polluted with people that are not appropriate for our political needs (the Peoples Commissariat of State Control, The Peoples Commissariat of Agriculture, the Peoples Commissariat of Education, the Peoples Commissariat of Trade, etc).

In line with our acceptance of the old bureaucratic apparatus with the goal of strengthening this apparatus with employees that have work experience, Latvia's Communist (Bolshevik) Party Central Committee Politburo decrees:

1. To ask the All-Union Communist (Bolshevik) Party Central Committee for help in forming responsible cadres and for it to send to the Latvian SSR leading workers for the following jobs:
    a. In the apparatus of Latvia's Communist (Bolshevik) Party Central Committee:
        i. Deputy Leader of the School Section.
        ii. Leader of the Central Committee's Party Activist House.

      iii.   Leader of the Party School.

      iv.   Assistants to the Secretary of the Central Committee – 4 people.

      v. Central Committee Instructors – 12 people.

      vi.   Lecturers for the foundations of Marxism-Leninism – 10 people.

      vii.   Political editors – 10 people.

      viii.   Leader of the Party Archive.

      ix.   A responsible coder for the specific section – 1 person.

      x. Stenographers in the Russian language – 1 person.

    b.   In the apparatus of the Party Municipal and District Committees:

      i. Section leaders – 15 people.

      ii. Instructors – 29 people.

      iii.   Periodical Editors – 15 people. [...]

  f. In the Peoples Commissariat of Agriculture:

      i. Deputy Peoples Commissar (agronomist).

      ii. [Deputy] Chief of a Scientific Research Institute.

      iii.   Beekeepers Section Deputy Chief.

      iv.   Deputy Chief of the State Seed Control Inspectorate.

      v. Agricultural Construction Section [Deputy Chief].

      vi.   Livestock Board [Deputy Chief].

      vii.   Equestrian Section [Deputy Chief].

      viii.   Small stock husbandry [Section Deputy Chief].

      ix.   Land-Reclamation Section [Deputy Chief].

      x. Veterinarian Board [Deputy Chief].

      xi.   Finance Board [Deputy Chief] [...]

o. In the Commissariat of People's Education

      i.   Deputy People's Commissar.

      ii.   Director of the Museum of the Revolution.

      iii.   Deputy Chief of the Political Education Board.

      iv.   Deputy Chief of the Cadres Section.

      v.   Lecturers of Marxism-Leninism School Faculty for the State University and the Agricultural Academy – 12 people. [...]

3. HEARD: About the order of visits from district and municipal Party Committee Secretaries to the Latvian Communist (Bolshevik) Party Central Committee.

DECREED: Latvia's Communist (Bolshevik) Party Central Committee has determined that individual district and municipal party committee secretaries are taking independent trips to RĪGA and to other places beyond the borders of their district or municipality without a permit from Latvia's Communist (Bolshevik) Party Central Committee.

The Politburo of Latvia's Communist (Bolshevik) Party Central Committee views such trips as intolerable and in order to bring in the needed discipline determines:

1. To ban all district and municipal party committee secretaries' trips to RĪGA and other places outside of their district and municipal borders taken without a permit from Latvia's Communist (Bolshevik) Party Central Committee leadership.

2. To assign as a responsibility to municipal and district party committee secretaries to harmonize every occurrence of a trip outside of their district or municipality borders with the secretariat of Latvia's Communist (Bolshevik) Party Central Committee and to travel only with their permission.

3. To determine that district and municipal party committee secretaries' calls to sections of Latvia's Communist (Bolshevik) Party Central Committee must happen only with the permission of the Secretary of the Central Committee of

Latvia's Communist (Bolshevik) Party. [...]

5. HEARD: About the decision of the Jelgava Municipal Committee of Latvia's Communist (Bolshevik) Party (comrade Gailis)

DECREED: The December 21, 1940 decision of the Bureau of the Jelgava Municipal Committee of Latvia's Communist (Bolshevik) Party about the admission of ROZENBERGS, A. as a candidate comrade of the All-Union Communist (Bolshevik) Party is rescinded for violating party statutes.

Explain to the First Secretary of the Jelgava Municipal Committee of Latvia's Communist (Bolshevik) Party, comrade Šubs, that those that were in other parties are admitted only in exceptional cases, and only after the recommendation of five party members: three of whom must have 10-year party status and two must have standing from before the Revolution[28], together with an obligatory ratification from the All-Union Communist (Bolshevik) Party Central Committee. [...]

8. HEARD: About the accomplished work of re-pricing a wide variety of consumer goods.

DECREED: Latvia's Communist (Bolshevik) Party Central Committee and the Soviet of Peoples Commissars of the Latvian SSR have discovered that in the work to re-price a wide variety of consumer goods, mistakes were allowed and a distortion of price politics led to increases on sewed products, wool and half-silk cloth, partially on haberdashery (neck ties), knitted fabric (gloves), and work shoes, and as a result has decreed:

1. To assign to the People's Commissar of Trade (comrade PUPURS), People's Commissar of Light Industry (comrade ŠICS), People's Commissar of Local Industry (comrade KARLSONS), People's Commissar of Wood Processing (comrade GUSTONS) to review the prices of all consumer goods in ten days time and to re-price them completely according to the existing price guides of the USSR, and to submit this for ratification to the Central Committee of Latvia's Communist (Bolshevik) Party and the Soviet of People's Commissars of the Latvian SSR. [...]

3. To assign to the Republic's prosecutor, comrade SOLDNIEKS, to investigate the distortions in determining the prices for individual goods and to call the guilty parties to justice.

9. HEARD: About the growth of the party [ranks]. (Reporter comrade Gailis).

DECREED: The Central Committee of Latvia's Communist (Bolshevik) Party has determined that Latvia's Communist (Bolshevik) Party district, municipal and regional committees are not fulfilling the decision of the IX Congress of Latvia's Communist (Bolshevik) Party about the growth of the party's ranks. The Congress assigned to party organizations the responsibility of examining the question of accepting new members into the ranks, and to be careful about and strictly examine the individual [candidate's] approach. Nevertheless, individual party organizations in chasing growth in their numbers, have overstepped the statutes of the All-Union Communist (Bolshevik) Party by forgetting the principles of Leninist-Stalinist screening in accepting new members, lowering the requirements for those that are joining the party, and by retreating from the party's statutes that ask that only workers, peasants and intellectuals that are conscientious, active believers in communist affairs be accepted into the ranks of the All-Union Communist (Bolshevik) Party [...]

11. HEARD: About the creation of a Livestock Sector at Latvia's Communist (Bolshevik) Party Central Committee's Agricultural Section.

DECREED: To create a Livestock Sector at the Agricultural Section of the Central Committee of Latvia's Communist Party and to ask the All-Union Communist (Bolshevik) Party Central Committee to ratify this law.

12. HEARD: About strengthening the apparatus of the Party, Komsomolsk, and Soviet-economics with leading employees.

DECREED: 1) In order to strengthen the Party, Komsomolsk, trade unions and Soviet-economic apparatuses with leading employees, the Politburo of the Central Committee of Latvia's Communist (Bolshevik) Party deems it necessary to ask the Central Committee of the All-Union Communist (Bolshevik) Party Central Committee and the Authorized Agent of the Soviet of Peoples Commissars of the USSR, comrade Derevjanski, for the following members for the apparatus:

1. Ļitvinov
2. Štrodah
3. Šapovalov
4. Rīdziņš
5. Kalugin
6. Smirnov
7. Vikuļin [...]

3. To ask the Central Committee of the All-Union Communist (Bolshevik) Party to ratify this decision.

Secretary of the Central Committee of Latvia's Communist Party J. Kalnbērziņš

Source: *LVA PA, 101.f., 1. apr., 12. l., pp. 22-30.Original in Russian.*

Comment: *The published document demonstrates that no question in the social or economic life of Latvia could be decided without the consent of the leadership of the Latvian Communist Party. The communists also placed private life under their control.*

One of the chief tasks of the LCP was the ideological indoctrination of the inhabitants. Concurrent with the closing of periodicals that were not wanted by the new order, strict censorship was introduced (see Document No. 30-32). Books with contents that did not match Soviet ideology, were removed from libraries, and the leadership of the Communist Party tried with all of its might to force communist dogma on the inhabitants. Already in July of 1940, the LCP newspaper Cīņa began to publish the All-Union Communist (Bolshevik) Party Short Course of History, *which for many years (including after the death of Stalin) was the only officially recognized handbook of Soviet ideology and propaganda. Meetings were organized in enterprises and institutions for the study of this book.*

Even before the occupation of Latvia, people were sent into the country by the USSR who later occupied leading posts in institutions and in the army (See Part I, Document No. 19). Drawing only on the totals in published minutes, more than 200 persons were requested from the USSR for leading positions in Latvia's organizations and institutions. The majority of those that arrived were not highly qualified specialists, did not speak Latvian, and did not know the local conditions. Their assignment was to control the local employees and to consolidate the Soviet regime in Latvia.

Documents No. 35-37
Introducing Soviet standards of living

Document No. 35

Decree of the Presidium of the Supreme Soviet of the Latvian SSR about the confiscation of apartments and their use in municipalities

September 12, 1940

1. In order to achieve the rational use of living space, and to guarantee citizens with a supply of apartments, as well as to acquire the needed rooms for institutions, organizations, and enterprises, the People's Commissar of Communal Economy has the right to tell cities to create Apartment Commissions, as well as to tell them that the confiscation of the unoccupied apartments or parts of them needs the permission of the Apartment Commissions in cities.

2. The Apartment Commission consists of a Chair, who is assigned by the deputies of the local city Soviet of working people, but until this Soviet is founded, by the local municipal government; and three members – representatives of the People's Militia, Latvia's Communist Party, and Trade Unions.
    The Apartment Commission can invite representatives of other interested institutions or organizations as needed.

3. The Apartment Commission in a particular city determines the use and supply of buildings in harmony with the orders and instructions of the People's Commissariat of Communal Economy. In particularly, they agree:
    (1) To decide about the distribution of unoccupied apartments to those that have requested them and to issue the needed permits for taking them;
    (2) To supervise and insure that the defined minimum density of inhabited apartments is observed;
    (3) To assign lodgers to apartments that have not received the relevant number of lodgers in a timely manner;
    (4) In particularly pressing cases, in contact with the People's Commissariat of Communal Economy, to decide about the relocation of inhabitants from one apartment to another.

4. In a municipality defined by the People's Commissar of Communal Economy, permits for inhabitation cannot allow more than the following living space:
    (1) one person without a family – one living room;
    (2) one family with up to four people – three living rooms, but for each additional two people – one more living room.
    (3) If a living room is not included, a room whose size is less than 12 square meters. If in one apartment there are 2 or more such rooms, then each 2 such rooms are counted as one. Rooms whose size is larger than 35 square meters must be counted as two living rooms.
    (4) If a family or an individual person keeps a house servant and in the apartment there is a specific house servant's room, then the latter is counted as a living room independent of its size. [...]

7. A family or persons that occupy a greater number of rooms than allowed by the existing rules, in the time defined by the People's Commissar of Communal Economy, must take

on the relevant number of lodgers. In case of this request not being met, the Apartment Commission has the right to assign lodgers.

1. The People's Commissariat of Communal Economy has the job of supervising the work of the Apartment Commission.
2. In order the fulfill this decree the People's Commissar of Communal Economy can give orders and instructions.

> Prof. Dr. A. Kirhenšteins
> Latvian SSR Supreme Soviet Presidium Chair
> P. Blaus
> Latvian SSR Supreme Soviet Presidium Secretary

Source: *Ziņotājs, September 13, 1940. Original in Latvian.*

Comment: *The next step in the centralization of the apartment board was the nationalization of buildings. On October 28, 1940, the law "About the nationalization of large buildings" was ratified. The owners were left with a small area defined by the norms in this published document's 4th paragraph. In Rīga and in other cities, not only were many apartment houses nationalized, but so were private houses the total sizes of which were larger than defined norms.*

Document No. 36

Decision Number 1756 – 716 CS of the Soviet of People's Commissars of the USSR and the Central Committee of the All-Union Communist (Bolshevik) Party about the transition to Soviet currency in the Latvian SSR

September 21, 1940

Completely Secret

Sample Number
Kremlin, Moscow

The Soviet of People's Commissars of the USSR and the All-Union Communist (Bolshevik) Party Central Committee decides:

To realize the transition to Soviet currency in the Latvian SSR and to avert the difference in currency value, to guarantee that the wages of workers and servants in the Latvian SSR relate to the existing work wages of the USSR, as well as to realize economic aid to those peasants who have little land, and those peasants who had land distributed to them anew, and to guarantee the improvement of material conditions in the fields of health care and education in the Latvian SSR, to allow in September and October of this year to increase the emission of Latvia's *Lats* in the necessary amounts, and to carry out the following practical steps:

I

1. Beginning with September 16, 1940, to raise the wages of the working masses of the Latvian SSR to the following medians:
   a. Industrial, transport, communications, construction and communal economy workers – by 40%. The Soviet of People's Commissars of the Latvian SSR together with the

All-Union Trade Union Society Central Council defines the wage increase amounts in industrial branches and to individual worker categories;

b. Grade school and high school teachers – by 40%;

c. University professors and lecturers – by 40%;

d. Agronomists – by 40%;

e. Doctors in cities – by 25%;

f. Doctors in the countryside – by 30%;

g. Middle and junior medical personnel – by 40%;

h. Engineer-technical personnel and enterprise and institution servants – by 30%.

2. To liquidate the existing inequality in pay for women, establishing for them the principle of equal work equal work pay with men.

3. To assign to the Soviet of People's Commissars of the Latvian SSR until October 15th of this year the task of submitting to the Soviet of People's Commissars of the USSR their suggestions about the existing wage system of the USSR and the introduction of its rules to the Latvian SSR.

4. With the beginning of this academic year to rescind tuition in universities.

5. As of November 1 of this year, to rescind payments for workers, servants, and peasants for medical care in hospitals, clinics, out-patient centers, and doctors' offices.

6. As of November 1 of this year, to create social insurance for all workers and servants of the Latvian SSR. As of November 1 of this year, to ascribe to all of the state co-operative enterprises, organizations, and enterprises of the Latvian SSR the existing social insurance tariffs of the USSR. [...]

9. To increase the purchase of agricultural products from state and co-operative organizations. To allow in the period beginning on October 1 of this year until November 1 an increase in the purchase prices for all agricultural products excepting grain-crops by 10-25%. To purchase agricultural products, excepting grain-crops, after November 1 of this year according to market prices, but not exceeding the purchase prices that exist in the USSR. To keep the purchase prices of grain-crop cultures at the existing level.

10. Beginning October 1, 1940, to raise the prices of industrially manufactured grocery items by 25%, but industrial items – by 50%.

11. From November 1 of this year, to undertake a second increase in prices in industrial as well as industrially manufactured grocery goods.
The Soviet of People's Commissars of the Latvian SSR will decide the scale of price increases by harmonizing them with the Soviet of People's Commissars of the USSR no later than October 20 of this year.

12. To keep the existing prices for household soap, matches, petroleum and salt.

13. To assign to the Soviet of People's Commissars of the Latvian SSR, together with the People's Commissariat of Trade of the USSR, the task of working out and submitting by November 1, 1940, to the Soviet of People's Commissars of the USSR for ratification a price index for industrial and industrially manufactured grocery goods (not groceries) related to the prices that exist in the USSR. To implement this price index beginning with November 16 of this year. [...]

15. To assign the Soviet of People's Commissars of the Latvian SSR the task of submitting a bill with the needed increase in the emission of Lats related to the prices in this law to the Soviet of People's Commissars of the USSR no later than September 25 of this year.

II

16. To bring into circulation in the territory of the Latvian SSR, beginning with November 16, 1940, Soviet currency along with the *lats*. The date with which the circulation of *lats* will

75

end must be determined by a law of the Soviet of People's Commissars of the USSR.

17. In the period of the circulation of two currencies, in order to standardize the exchange rate, [the following will be the case] one *lats* = one ruble.

18. In the period of the circulation of two currencies, all wages of workers in enterprises and institutions and the bills for agricultural products purchased by the state and by co-operatives will be paid with Soviet currency only, but *lats* arriving in banks will be kept there and not allowed back into circulation, and they will be accepted, without comment, for payment according to the exchange rate defined in the 17th paragraph.

19. Current accounts and investments belonging to private enterprises and persons that were opened in *lats* in banks and credit offices, and do not exceed 1000 *lats* at the moment when the *lats* is withdrawn from circulation, will be paid out in Soviet rubles, according to the stated exchange rate, up to the sum of 1000 rubles.

20. Current accounts of private enterprises and private persons, and investments that were opened in *lats* and exceed 1000 rubles will be paid out in Soviet rubles up to the sum of 1,000 rubles. Active amounts above 1000 rubles in these accounts will be transformed into Soviet currency, to be distributed from these current accounts for production and trade needs.

21. The existing money in accounts of state and co-operative enterprises, and accounts of institutions, that are kept in banks and credit offices, and that were opened in *lats*, from the moment of the withdrawal of *lats* will be paid out in Soviet currency.

III

22. To suggest to the Soviet of People's Commissars of the Latvian SSR to use a decree of the acting Presidium of the Supreme Soviet to do everything to speed nationalization of trade enterprises whose yearly trade circulation is 100,000 *lats* and more. Nationalization must be completed from September 27 to 29, 1940. [...]

Chair of the Soviet of People's Commissars of the USSR
V. Molotov
Secretary of the Central Committee of the All-Union Communist (Bolshevik) Party
J. Stalin

Source: *LVA, 270.f., 1.s.apr., 2.l., pp. 16-22. Original in Russian.*

Comment: *As per the instructions in the document above the law about the nationalization of trade enterprises with a yearly circulation of more than 100,000 lats (at the time there were 1,114 such enterprises) was ratified, on September 28, 1940. The nationalization of trade enterprises continued, and this process also included medium and small enterprises. By June of 1941, private trade enterprises accounted for only 10% of the circulation of all of Latvia's trade.*

From the report of the People's Commissar of Social Insurance of the Latvian SSR, I. Paldiņa, to the secretariat of Deputy Chair of the Soviet of People's Commissars of the USSR, A. Kosygin, about reduction of the level of the guaranteed pension in 1941

February 22, 1946

[...] There were 504 teachers and family members of deceased pedagogical workers enrolled in the pension fund of the Rīga municipality in 1938 for whom in a year pensions were paid out to an overall sum of 880,663 *lats*. In other words, the average pension amount was 1,747 *lats* in a year for each person receiving a pension. Because the family members of deceased teachers received on average about 1/3 of a teacher's pension, the actual teacher's pensions average was more than the teacher's pension in the Soviet Union (1800 rubles).

In 1941, in accommodating Soviet legislation and in reference to the All-Union Trade Union Central Council Secretariat decision number 507, 6th paragraph (ratified on March 29, 1941 by the Soviet of People's Commissars of the USSR, Decision collection , number 11, 182) pensions were reduced in all similar cases.

The real level of guaranteed pension was also strongly affected by the transition to Soviet currency. Although officially the amount was leveled to the ruble, at the time Soviet currency was introduced there was the increase in prices and wages for workers and servants. In that way the buying power of the *lats* in 1940 was tangibly higher than the ruble's buying power in 1941. [...]

As a result of this, the general dissatisfaction among old pensioners with the reduction of the guarantee level was noted in 1941. [...]

People's Commissar of Social Insurance of the Latvian SSR
I. Paldiņa

Source: *LVA, 1169.f., 3. apr., 8. l., p. 1.Original in Russian.*

Documents No. 38-45
The justification of terror

Document No. 38

The Rīga student and youth underground organization "Latvia's Liberators'"appeal entitled "Never Forget!"

September-December 1940

Never forget!

Never forget that only because of our disunity did we come to live for many years under foreign powers and suffer many wrongs. That has also happened now, when because of differences in the nation and due to lack of seriousness, we must suffer. Never believe in the possibility of eternal peace as the "red robber bands" say, because as you know yourself, that has never happened. Those who surrender in a cowardly fashion are robbed and killed. Such things now go in our land. Your responsibility, new soldier, is to stand guard and be alert about our autonomy and freedom. That which you have inherited from your Fathers, you must also keep!

The land is ours.
We won't give it to strangers
Not Zemgale, not Latgale
Not Selians, not Kurs.

Source: *LVA, 1986.f., 2. apr., 10462. l (surveillance report, handwritten).Original in Latvian.*

Comment: *In December of 1940, the 8 members of the underground Rīga youth organization "Latvia's Liberators," the youngest of whom was only 16 years old and the oldest 20, were arrested. In February of 1941, their file was sent for review to the Special Conference of the USSR People's Commissariat of the Interior. The organization's participants were accused of "counter-revolutionary activity" and all of them were sentenced to ten years in a punishment camp.*

Report of police official E. Spilners, of the Cēsis section of the police board of the People's Commissariat of the Interior of the Latvian SSR, about the inhabitants' behavior at cemeteries and their attempts to put flowers [on graves]

November 17, 1940

I, police official Elmārs Spilners of the worker-peasant militia board, Cēsis section, on November 17, 1940, was on guard at the Cēsis cemetery, where the Cemetery of the Brethren is also located, in order to observe who places flowers at the monument to the fighters for Ulmanis'Latvia. At about 11:00 I saw two citizens (females) coming from the cemetery toward the monument. Having approached the monument, as far as I could see, they wanted to place flowers. I called out: Stop! At that moment I saw two more citizens (females) also coming from the cemetery toward the monument, and I also called for them to stop! The first two began to flee through the gate that leads to the highway that goes from Cēsis to Raiskums. As the latter two were closer to me, that exit was not available to them. I took them to the side of the cemetery and asked them to show me their personal documents, and one of them showed me a Cēsis union card with the name of Velta Evelīte. I asked her to show me what was under her coat, and then I observed that citizen Evelīte had flowers hidden under her coat, and then she asked if laying flowers was not allowed. They said that they lived in some house not far from the cemetery outside of Cēsis. The second citizen (female) did not have any documents and I also did not see any flowers on her. During this time the first two that fled were on the road opposite the place where I found myself with the latter two citizens (female). I called for them to return, which they did. I do not know if they had flowers and I invited all four to go with me to the militia station. Having brought them to the station I turned them over to the militia staff on duty for further interrogation. Returning to the cemetery, I found by the cemetery gate some flowers and by a nearby bush more flowers that could have belonged only to the fleeing citizens, who could have placed them there in order to return later. Along the road were shredded flowers, which they could have shredded while being picked up, because it was somewhat dark and it was not easy for one person to observe four people.

I have told all: E. Spilners, Workers-Peasant Police Board Cēsis section police

Source: *LVA, 1986.f., 2. apr., 8402. l. Original in Latvian.*

Announcement about the standardization of RSFSR Codes of Criminal Law and Criminal Trials , Civil Law and Civil Trials, Labor Law, and Marriage, Family, and Guardian Law in the territory of the Latvian SSR

November 25, 1940

With respect to the November 6, 1940, decree of the Presidium of the Supreme Soviet of the USSR about the temporary standardization of the RSFSR criminal, civil and labor legislation in the territory of the Latvian, Lithuanian and Estonian Soviet Socialist Republics (*Reporter of the Supreme Soviet of the USSR*, November 18, 1940 number 46), the Soviet of People's Commissars of the Latvian SSR reports information and execution of the following:

1. Temporarily, until the publication of the All-Union Code, beginning with November 26, 1940, in the territory of the Latvian SSR the following codes are standardized with RSFSR Codes: Criminal Law, Criminal Trial, Civil Law, Civil Trial, Labor Law, and Marriage, Family and Guardian Law. .

2. The verdicts that the courts have made in criminal and civil affairs before the founding of Soviet order in Latvia, and have not been carried out, are not implementable. The files on these must be reexamined by the judicial organs of the Latvian SSR for their consistency with the RSFSR codes temporarily in force.

3. Crimes committed on the territory of Latvia prior to the founding of Soviet order, as well as those proposed for investigation or the application of justice from the relevant Latvian organs before the founding of Soviet power, will be held to responsibility according to the relevant codes of the RSFSR.

4. Property disputes involving civil and other juridical matters, independent of when they began, must be examined by the judicial organs of the Latvian SSR according to the relevant RSFSR codes temporarily in force and other USSR government and Latvian SSR government laws and decisions.

Chair of the Soviet of Peoples Commissars of the Latvian SSR
V. Lācis
Peoples Commissar of Justice of the Latvian SSR
A. Jablonskis

Source: *Ziņotājs, November 26, 1940. Original in Latvian.*

Appeal of the Former Minister of Justice of the Republic of Latvia, H. Apsītis, to the Justice Collegium of the Supreme Court of the RSFSR, about his illegal trial

Astrahkhan prison, October 17, 1941

On October 13-14, 1941, the Astrahkhan Regional Court Justice Collegium sentenced me to the supreme punishment – execution by shooting according to the RSFSR Criminal Code's 58-4 and 16-58-13 paragraphs.

I see this verdict as incorrect for the following reasons:

[1)] I never admitted, and cannot admit, myself guilty of the criminal acts as they are stated in the written accusation.

My work in various professions in the Republic of Latvia can not be categorized as criminal, because I carried out those tasks in an independent state whose sovereignty was recognized, and not just ratified, by the Soviet Union. The principle of a Nation's self-determination was declared by Soviet power and the Communist Party even before the creation of the USSR. Therefore from November 18, 1918, Latvia as an independent state had its laws and none of the [actions] of that state's employees could have any relevance to the laws of foreign states, including the RSFSR, and the employees did not need to [such laws] r act according to them.

I brought this to the attention of the Court, among other things referring to two important international treaties: the August 11, 1920 Peace Treaty with the Soviet Union and the October 5, 1939 Treaty about Military Bases in Latvia. I also drew attention to many others, for example treaties on trade and general economic matters, on cultural and diplomatic contacts, etc. I also mentioned the fact that both Latvia and the USSR were equal members of the League of Nations. All of this demonstrates that not only according to the general principles of international justice, but also according to the relations and concrete acts in relation to the USSR, Latvia[ns] could create their state and social life according to their reason and their perspectives, not taking into account any foreign state. The court did not account for my motivations and therefore exceeded the relevant decisions of the Criminal Process Code.

2) If at any time, I as an employee of the court, as a soldier, and later as a member of government was not bound to the laws of foreign states, then it is completely incorrect to refer my completely legal activities to the 58th paragraph, 4th and 13th points of the Criminal Code of the RSFSR, attaching to these paragraph the power of retroactive law. Each criminal act requires that it be threatened with punishment of prohibited [behavior] at the moment it is committed. The idea of the criminal act requires that I had intent to commit the crime, but I had no such intent and could not have it, because I fulfilled my legal responsibilities in Latvia, not in the USSR. I could violate the laws of the USSR theoretically and practically only beginning with August 5, 1940, that is, from the moment Latvia entered the Soviet Union, which understandably did not happen before that date.

3) The applicability of the 4th and 13th points of the 58th paragraph is incorrect on the basis of the idea that all of the asked for descriptives of this paragraph are not apparent [in the actions being punished]. As an example, the government of Latvia could never be counter-revolutionary because there was no revolution in Latvia. In all of the time the independent Latvian state existed there was never in Latvia a civil war (see the 13th point of the 58th paragraph), which is attributed to me in the contents of the written offences according to the criminal law. Also, Latvia's army was never a criminal organization, but the organ that exercised state sovereignty (that was recognized in the treaty of August 11, 1920). If the participants in Latvia's army can be seen as criminals, then there would not have followed, not only the August 11, 1920 Treaty, but several thousand former soldiers would need to be called to responsibility which Soviet power in Latvia did not do and also could not do.

4) All of the time I was acting, and am still acting, as a citizen of Latvia, but not as a Soviet citizen (see also in the written accusation!). Therefore even if I admitted (but honestly that is not

the case!) that I had committed some *political* crime in Latvia *before* the entry of Soviet armed forces, then I could be tried for this affair by a competent Latvian court in the territory of Latvia, but not <u>beyond</u> its borders and in the court of another republic according to the laws of a foreign state. This is clear according to generally accepted criminal and criminal court principles, according to the decisions of the Criminal Process Code of the RSFSR and, particularly importantly, according to the Stalin Constitution. Beyond the borders of Latvia I could use the <u>rights of sanctuary</u>, but a <u>local</u> court in Astrahkhan is not allowed to try me. If, nevertheless, it is done this way, then the court has overstepped its powers, according to the Criminal Trial Code. According to the Constitution of the USSR, I could only be deported.

5) The court in reviewing my file and recognizing me as guilty violated still other decisions of the Criminal Trial Code. For example, it charges me as guilty of being close to the reactionary party "Farmers Union," but in the written accusation I am not even mentioned as guilty of this. Later, the permitted witnesses in the file, Fridrihsons and Karčevskis, in the previous investigation were not even interrogated on my case, but their testimony was added to my investigative file from other files <u>after</u> the conclusion of the investigation.

Furthermore, the court did not call during the investigation my chosen witnesses – Andrejs Kampis (located in the Astrakhan Prison), who is Former Director in Latvia's Ministry of Foreign Affairs and who participated in the 10.05.1939 military base treaty negotiation in Moscow; he could testify that not long before the arrival of Soviet forces in Latvia, the leaders of the USSR, Stalin and Molotov, talked about Latvia's sovereignty and independence. I have to add that in the October 5, 1939 treaty there is a paragraph that clearly states that the USSR <u>completely recognizes Latvia's social, that is state and society's, order.</u>

6) Astrahkhan's regional court, sentencing me to execution, itself admitted that there is no <u>direct</u> proof against me, that there is no behavior shown by me that is <u>directly</u> mentioned in the Criminal Code of the RSFSR; but it found me guilty according to the 16th paragraph, that is, according to analogy. If that is so, then it is incomprehensible that I was sentenced to the ultimate punishment because usually criminal trials do not recognize analogy.

7) Also it must be taken into account that the court threw out a considerable number of accusations against me: as an example, I am vindicated from the charge that I had fought against the working class and against the USSR, which is very important.

Based on everything mentioned here, I submissively ask the Supreme Court to <u>end</u> the process against me for lack of evidence, or if the court does not agree with this, to rescind the Astrahkhan Regional Court verdict and to ask that a different sentence with a different sanction of my behavior in the affair be meted out.

H. Apsītis

Source: *LVA, 1986. f., 1. apr., 37194. l., pp. 242-244 (handwritten). Original in Russian.*

Comment: *The contents of the most voluminous 58th paragraph of the RSFSR Criminal Code (14 sections) served the Soviet regime in its struggle against real and imaginary enemies, using as its basis the principle of class and an interpretation of past events in the interests of the regime. In the Latvian SSR this code was given retroactive force. This gave the regime the ability to repress everyone who had worked in the government institutions, and in social or political organizations of the independent Republic of Latvia. H. Apsītis, the last Minister of Justice of an independent government of Latvia, was one such person. He was arrested on October 19, 1940. Afterwards he was deported to the USSR, where he was tried. Being a professional lawyer, H. Apsītis wrote an appeal founded on legal and juridical, principles; the argument demonstrates the unfounded nature of the charges against him. Of course, at the time no one took such arguments into account. H. Apsītis was executed January 19, 1942.*

Document No. 42

Top secret letter of the Chair of the Soviet of People's Commissars of the Latvian SSR, V. Lācis, and the Secretary of the Central Committee of the Latvian Communist Party, J. Kalnbērziņš, to the Secretary of the Central Committee of the All-Union Communist (Bolshevik) Party, A. Andrejevs, with the request to allow the introduction of compulsory labor in Latvia

June 5, 1941

Construction and industrial enterprises are experiencing a shortage of labor. At the same time, a noticeable number of unemployed who are supported by the state avoid work, continuing to openly purchase goods for resale (for speculation).

The Central Committee of Latvia's Communist (Bolshevik) Party and the Soviet of People's Commissars of the Latvian SSR sees it as obligatory to introduce obligatory labor for this category of inhabitants on the basis of the following directives:

All people able to work will be subject to compulsory labor, including those living on unearned income saved in former times and currently not working in enterprise and institutions of the state, of co-operatives and of social organizations. These people include: former owners of industrial enterprises and their co-owners who employed paid labor; former owners of trade enterprises and co-owners, former building owners, former owners of intermediary offices, non-working people who live on capital or income acquired from nationalization of enterprises; people who had their farms nationalized in 1941.

The head of the family and the members of the family able to work are subject to compulsory labor in the following age groups: men aged from 18 to 60, and women from 18 to 55.

Work compensation will be take place according to the wage norms that exist in the enterprises and work to which the mentioned persons are sent.

These categories of inhabitants will first be used for loading and unloading work, and as workers'assistants in new construction and major renovations.

Submitting this as a proposed law, the Central Committee of Latvia's Communist (Bolshevik) Party and Soviet of People's Commissars of the Latvian SSR ask for permission to ratify the idea.

Source: *LVA PA, 101. f., 1. apr., 52.l., p. 129.Original in Russian.*

The Plan for the use of the property of the inhabitants deported from Latvia on June 14, 1941

[Not later than June 17, 1941]

Secret

1. In order to organize and control the use of the property of those deported from the municipalities of the Latvian SSR, a special commission is created and attached to the Central Committee of Latvia's Communist (Bolshevik) Party. [The commission is composed of] the following:

1. KRUMIŅŠ – Deputy Chair of the Soviet Trade section of the Central Committee of Latvia's Communist (Bolshevik) Party
2. ĶĪSIS – Deputy Chair of the Soviet of People's Commissars of the Latvian SSR
3. CINIS – Deputy People's Commissar of State Security
4. KOROĻEV – Representative of the People's Commissariat of the Interior
5. DEGLAVS – Chair of the Executive Committee of the municipality of Rīga
6. TABAKS - People's Commissar of Finance
7. PAEGLE – People's Commissar of Trade.

To suggest to the secretaries of party municipal, district and region committees and to the chairs of municipal, district and region executive committees to choose authorized agents from the ranks of the party and Soviet activists, to guarantee they have documents authorizing them to act on behalf of the executive committees, and to assign them, together with house superintendents, groundsmen, and persons whom the deported person trusted with the use of their property, the task of making, no later than June 17, 1941, an inventory of the apartment and the possessions [of the deported person], and to add to the list all of the deportee's property that is meant for expropriation for the good of the state, and to guarantee the guarding of the latter and its safekeeping until use.

The following property of the deportee is requisitioned for the working masses for the good of the state:

1. Transport equipment: automobiles, motorcycles, bicycles, carriages, coaches, etc, and horses if they are on the property, as well as livestock.
2. Radio receivers.
3. Valuable musical instruments: pianos, grand pianos, accordions, wind instruments, etc.
4. All copying equipment, typewriters, presses etc.
5. Historical and artistic valuables: furniture, paintings, all sorts of prized trophies and other goods.
6. Precious metals: silver, gold, platinum jewelry and melted currency, precious stones, crystal etc.
7. Different kinds of weapons and their ammunition as well as all explosives.
8. Medical and laboratory instruments and supplies.
9. All libraries.
10. All safes.
11. Photo cameras and their supplies.

3. To create a special commission near the municipality to appraise the property expropriated for the good of the state, but in Rīga [the appraisal will be] by the region and district executive committees, consisting of:

1. Representatives of the Executive Committee (Commission Chair)
2. Representative of the Party Organization
3. Representative of the People's Commissariat of the Interior

4. Representative from the Financial Sections

5. Representatives from the State Co-Operative Organizations.

Depending on the amount of the Commission's work, several district commissions attached to the executive committee can be created in the same manner. In necessary cases the committee can co-opt specialists in the appraising of property.

The commission compiles a list of the expropriated property for the good of the state, with appraisals in 4 copies. The first copy remains with the commission, the second goes to the trade organizations to whom the goods are given for use, the third copy goes to the finance section for control (review) and the fourth copy goes to the central Control Commission (review).

All property that is not expected to be used by trade organizations is given to state institutions and organizations only with the permission of the Central Commission.

4. To assign to comrade ĶĪSIS, the Deputy Chair of the Soviet of People's Commissars of the Latvian SSR, to give warnings to the chairs of the municipal and district committees to quickly take into their control all of the deportees' apartments and to not allow the arbitrary occupation of apartments, but to distribute them to workers, responsible employees, and the working intelligentsia only with the decision of the municipal and district executive committee.

Source: *LVA PA, 101. f., 1. apr., 52. l., pp. 126-128.Original in Russian.*

Document No. 44

The informative report of the Secretary of the Daugavpils Communist Party Municipal Committee, Treimanis, to the Central Committee of Latvia's Communist Party about occurrences of armed resistance in Daugavpils district during the deporting of inhabitants on June 14, 1941

June 18, 1941

During the time of the removal operation of counter-revolutionary elements from Kalupe parish, Daugavpils district, there occurred armed resistance. BABRIS, Ivans, born in 1904, a former policeman and home guard, used the fact that his brother claimed to be he, and ran into the house and through a half-opened door fired a revolver and killed the group's leader – comrade SLICIS, the district authorized agent of the militia, and wounded the arm of comrade JOZĀNS, the authorized agent of the municipal party committee and All-Union Communist (Bolshevik) Party candidate member. Comrade Jozāns' wound is not serious, neither bones nor joints are damaged. The criminal, using the fact that one of the militia was killed and the other wounded, fled on a bicycle and hid, taking with him a weapon from the killed comrade SLICIS. He has still not been caught.

Along with this there has been a noticeable spread of provocative rumors such as: "The war will start soon, that is why the deportation of enemies has begun."

(Secretary of the Daugavpils Municipal Communist Party Committee, comrade Treimanis, informative report)

Leader of the Section of Organizational Instructor Units of the Central Committee of Latvia's Communist (Bolshevik) Party: /Solovjov/

Source: *LVA PA., 101. f., 2. apr., 279. l., p. 57. Original in Russian.*

From the request of the former officer of Latvia's Army, L. Atvars, to the General Prosecutor of the USSR about rehabilitation

March 27, 1957

To the General Prosecutor of the USSR

From: Atvars, Leonīds son of Anufrijs
Living in the Taimira National Province
Dudinka municipality, Liņejnaja Street, apartment number 4
Number 2

Submission

Would you please review my trial file and rehabilitate me. I describe my file in this submission.
[…]

I was accepted into the Rīga War School[29] in September of 1937, which I completed with distinction in 1939. In the same autumn I was sent to a regiment as a platoon commander at the rank of lieutenant.

The Red Army came into the territory of Latvia in the summer of 1940. The regiments of Latvia's Army were gradually incorporated into the Red Army. In this way our regiment, as well as myself, was counted into the 24th Territorial Baltic Corps[30] as components of the 227th Rifles Regiment. At the beginning of 1941, soldiers and officers changed their old Latvian uniforms for the uniforms of the Red Army, swore the oath, and became full Red Army men.

In 1941, being stationed at the summer camp by Litene near Rīga, on the 14th of June, by the order of the regiment commander and commissar, all of the regiment officers went out on tactical exercises. [Our] guide was the regiment commissar who led us through the brush orienting himself by previously broken bush branches. When we came to a gathering place, we, the former officers of Latvia's army, found ourselves alone, surrounded by old cadre Red Army soldiers and officers. They opened fire, some of us fell and immediately we heard the commissar's command: "Hands up!" They took our weapons, removed our insignia and took everything that was in our pockets. They placed us in automobiles and took us to the nearest train station, placed us in wagons with bars which were always a sign of a convoy of hostiles. The train took [us] to the East. In August of 1941, we were brought to Krasnojarsk. There, after a month of work in the Žlobino base, (those like me) about 1000 people, were seated on barges that took us along the Yenisei River to Dudink - a municipality, but after that by train to Noriļsk municipality.

Until December of 1941, I worked in the Latvian brigade in the construction combine in Noriļsk city. Until December of 1941, I was called out tens of times to interrogations. Accusations that the investigator placed before me were lies, I had not participated in the [described activities]. During interrogations the investigator constantly tried to get me to admit to anti-Soviet activity. Still, for four months I did not admit to anything, because there were no criminal charges [against] me. Not paying attention to my repeated denials of anti-soviet agitation, the investigator used moral and physical pressure against me. I held out against the obscene lies for a long time. But I was threatened with a weapon, fists were used against me, and I was beaten, forced to stand on my feet for a long time[31], and in many ways belittled, threatened, weakened with famine. I am ashamed to even write that you have known about these things for a while; in the ice cellar I was forced to sign the investigator's deceitful accounts about me, not taking into account that I was never even given [the document] to be read.

Tortured, famished and plagues by fear, I agreed to sign everywhere the investigator pointed to with his finger. I still felt ambiguous about signing the deceitful documents because all that I had suffered had become unbearable and intolerable.

Immediately after signing I was sent to prison. That happened on the 25th of December. On the same day they called me from the prison barracks to the prison office where in a few seconds the harsh sentence was read to me: freedom taken from me for 10 years and rights for 5 years, removal of officer's rank and confiscation of property according to the 58th paragraph, 10th point section II. Immediately, maybe an hour or two after the sentence was read, together with others I was sent to the punishment camp for work in the rock quarry. The inhabitants of Noriļsk municipality always saw us as German prisoners, which gnawed at our morale even more because at the time, as well as now, I saw myself as an honorable soldier, not as an anti-Soviet agitator.

Until March of 1943, I worked in Norilsk municipality in its industrial construction brigade. I was highly valued, but unexpectedly in 1943, I was taken in a convoy to the regional court in Dudinka municipality where they showed me the file I had signed that the above-mentioned lying investigator had written.

Again they threatened me with a weapon, intimidating me, and a second time I was forced to sign the same never-read page. After a few minutes I was taken to the judges who read me their sentence: that I was to receive the supreme punishment – execution by shooting, according to the earlier mentioned paragraph. They took me again to Noriļsk prison and put me in the barracks for those condemned to death and forced me to write a complaint to Moscow. I sat in the wing for those condemned to death for 5 months. Just as unexpectedly I was sent to the punishment camp at Kalargon, without a time limit (until a special decree).

In the fall of 1944, I arrived at mine number 13 where I worked until the end of the time [punishment] and on June 14, 1951 I was freed. [...]

Atvars

Source: *LVA PA, 101. f., 2. apr., 279.l., p. 57.Original in Russian.*

Comment: *This document represents the tragic fate of officers after Latvia's army was transformed into the 24th Territorial Corps of the Red Army. Altogether more than 500 of the corps' Latvian officers were repressed. At the shooting of officers in the forest near Litene described in the document, 28 officers were killed. The rest were deported to the USSR. L. Atvars, together with three other corps officers, L. Gutbergs, L. Kociņš and A. Induss, were tried after deportation in December of 1941 by the sitting session of the Taimir Regional Court. They, as well as all the other officers, were charged with anti-Soviet activities, and lying about the work of the Communist Party and Soviet government. L. Kociņš and A. Induss were immediately given the death penalty. They were shot in June of 1942. L. Gutbergs died in prison in January of 1943. L. Atvars' file, by request of the prosecutor, was re-examined and in March of 1943 he was sentenced to the death penalty. In June of 1943 the USSR's Supreme Court's Court Collegium changed the supreme punishment to loss of freedom for 10 years, loss of rights for five years (in reality, police surveillance) and confiscation of property. Of all of the repressed Latvian officers of the 24th territorial corps, only every fifth returned from the camps.*

PART III: THE OCCUPATION REGIME OF NAZI GERMANY: 1941-1945

Military activity began on the territory of Latvia on the first day of war between Germany and the Soviet Union, June 22, 1941, and by July 7th, German armed forces had occupied all of Latvia's territory.

A special ministry, the Eastern Lands or *Ostland* State Ministry, was created to rule the occupied Eastern provinces, and Alfred Rosenberg was appointed as the *Ostland* leader.

On July 16, 1941, with an order from Hitler, the *Ostland* State Commissariat (*Reich Kommissariat*) was created as a special administrative unit, consisting of Lithuania, Latvia, Estonia and Belarus. Heinrich Lohse was appointed the *Ostland* Reich Commissar, and stationed in Rīga. Otto-Heinrich Drechsler became the General Commissar of Latvia.

At first, it was the German army that fulfilled governing functions. With the creation of the Reich Commissariat, however, the territory of Latvia west of the Daugava River (Kurzeme and Zemgale) was turned over to civilian administration. In the rest of Latvia (in Vidzeme and Latgale), and in Estonia, civilian rule began on September 1.

Latvia's territory was divided into six administrative units - regions[32] (*Gebiete*) - that were ruled by Regional Commissars (*Gebietskommissar*). The regions were further divided into municipalities and parishes (in German called *Gemeinde*).

Before the beginning of the war against the Soviet Union a plan had already been drawn up outlining the basic principles of rule for these occupied eastern provinces as well as the basic political policies pertaining to the nationality groups in them. Latvia was to become a German outpost in the East. This was to be done by Germanizing "the useful racial elements" (see Document No. 1). The idea of a Latvia (as well as of an Estonia and a Lithuania) had to be eradicated (see Document No. 8). The occupational regime sought to underscore the fact that Latvia did not exist as a state or as a unique administrative unit. Differences of opinion existed only about how large a portion of the local population, and over what period of time, could be assimilated, as well as what to do with the racially unfit elements among the Latvians and other nationalities in their midst. These plans were kept secret from the local population. The only time they were made public was in the lead article of the SS and SD newspaper *Das Schwarze Korps* entitled "Germanization?" (August 20, 1942) in which it was clearly stated: "Our task is not to Germanize the East in the old sense, that is, to teach German language and German laws to the people of the region, but to make sure that there reside there only people with real German, Teutonic blood..."[33]

The first days of the occupation start of the start of the genocide of Jews. It began with a mass propaganda campaign that equated Jews with Communists, and blamed Jews for the repressions against the inhabitants of Latvia in 1940-1941.

By October of 1941, almost all Jews living in small towns and in the countryside had been killed. In Rīga and in two other large cities, Daugavpils and Liepāja, ghettos had been created (see Document No. 20). Almost all of the Jews interned in these ghettos were killed as a result of mass shootings organized specifically to exterminate them. During the implementation of this genocidal policy, more than 63,000 Jews with Latvian citizenship were murdered. SD units, the so-called *Einsatzkommando*, carried out the killings. After the mass murders nearly emptied the Rīga ghetto, about 20, 000 Jews were brought to the ghetto from all of Europe for liquidation.

As in other territories occupied by Germany, the Nazis tried to involve local residents in genocidal activities. The SD auxiliary unit led by Viktors Arājs (the Arājs Commando), which shot to death more than 26,000 people, is one such particularly odious example.

The same fate as awaited the Jews was also meted out to (Roma) Gypsies. During the time of the Nazi occupation, more than 2,000 Roma, about half of all of Roma in Latvia, were murdered. The genocide was not just a tragedy for these two peoples, but also created a heavy and irreplaceable loss to the whole nation of Latvia. It must be added also that more than 2,000 mentally ill people were liquidated as well. These crimes against humanity also included the shooting of hostages in order to intimidate the inhabitants in several places in Latvia (see Document No. 24).

The occupation of Latvia by the USSR and the subsequent terror in 1940-41 created a situation in which a considerable part of the Latvian nation saw the German army as saviors from mass deportations and from physical destruction. They greeted the German army as liberators in the hope that Latvia's state framework and governing structures would be renewed. In the first days of July 1941, a Latvian government began to form from a group of Latvian organizations. In the days immediately after the German armed forces entered Rīga, the Bank of Latvia also renewed its work, and sought to renew the national currency by emitting the *lats*.[34] A temporary municipal government and other institutions in Riga also attempted to organize themselves. But these activities were curtailed by the German occupiers in the first half of July. Latvian military formations were banned, and all weapons and munitions had to be surrendered (see Document No. 5).

The institutions created by the German occupation forces had to resolve a difficult dilemma. On the one hand, they did not want to create any kind of Latvian administration or anything that would resemble a government. On the other hand, they needed to include Latvians in administration because there was no other way too govern the land efficiently and ensure that Latvia's economic and human resources could be used by Greater Germany and in the war effort. Furthermore the people that worked with the occupiers had to enjoy authority in Latvia.

Several different plans were drawn up and there was a struggle between two governance models: representatives of a hard line spoke against any Latvian autonomy, against any Latvians involvement in governance, and were for the complete germanization of Latvia and its complete inclusion into the German state. The representatives of a more "liberal" line believed it was necessary to guarantee the cooperation of Latvians in order to more effectively realize Greater Germany's goals, as well as to make Latvians equally responsible for implemented policies. It must be stressed that these differences of opinion were purely tactical, because the basic opinion – that Latvia and the other Baltic States had to become an integral component of Greater Germany – was the same on both sides. The balance tilted toward one opinion or the other depending on the progress of the war, the opinions of the Nazi high command in Germany, and views among the local representatives of occupational power. At the beginning of the war, without a doubt, the hard-line exponents dominated. As the situation at the front worsened, the more liberal approach became dominant, but generally the final answer to the question was put off until the end of the war. Suggestions about projects that anticipated limited renewal of Latvia's sovereignty were made in order to obtain the support of influential people in Latvian society for the mobilization of Latvia's inhabitants into the German army, and in order to maintain the illusion that by working with the occupational authorities the renewal of Latvia's independence (even if limited) could be facilitated.

During the first weeks of occupation the Self-Administration of the Land (*Landselbstverwaltung*) began to be formed, but officially it began to work on March 18, 1942. Rosenberg's official approval was received two months later -- on May 12. This new administrative apparatus consisted of General Directorates. Each General Directorate had departments, the leaders of which called Directors.

It must be stressed that this institution was not a government and not even true self-administration. The Self-Administration of the Land (henceforth SAL) did not have a hierarchical structure and it was not a collegiate organ. The General Directors were responsible to parallel German administrative structures that controlled their work, and to the Reich Commissar who could rescind any decision made by the SAL or Director General (see Document No. 10). Although the SAL did make decisions and submitted protests as a collegiate organ, these measures were usually not recognized as such by the Germans,

During the war and afterward, the question arose if work of any kind in cooperation with the occupying German power had been justifiable. Tactically, those that were involved in the creation of the SAL intended to suggest cooperativeness, while efforts were being made to keep the lower-level government offices in the hands of the SAL and to sabotage those German plans that did not meet Latvian national interests. It was also an attempt to influence the details of Germany's post-war planning in a direction desirable for Latvia. These hopes were false. Although the SAL's role was mostly symbolic, it did help realize Nazi goals in Latvia. The SAL concurred with the mobilization of Latvia's inhabitants into police battalions and later into a "Latvian Legion," thereby supporting Nazi actions that violated the norms of international justice and giving them needed ideological justification.

At the beginning of 1945, The Nazi regime decided to allow the creation of a Latvian National Committee (LNC), with restricted Latvian governmental rights, in order to create the belief that the German government was sympathetic to attempts for Latvian national autonomy. This committee was in its way a "national billboard" for the occupational regime, since it (the committee) did not have real power and it did not enjoy support of many Latvians.

Despite the lack of popularity of the Nazi regime, resistance to it began spontaneously, with active work by communist connected to the Soviet Union, and, later, by the formation in 1943 of the Central Council of Latvia which oriented itself toward cooperation with the USA and England. The absence of a mass resistance movement in Latvia was due to three factors. First, there was no government-in-exile of Latvia in the West that could organize a non-Communist resistance. The western Allies denied the representatives of the Baltic States the right to create such a government and, moreover, did not encourage the creation of a non-communist resistance in these states. Second, such a movement could not have any Communist connections because the Soviet terror of 1940-1941 diminished popular support for a movement so connected. Thirdly, the work of the repressive apparatus of the German occupational regime was very effective.

The primary objective of the Nazi political economy was to maximize the exploitation of Latvia's economic resources for the war and in Greater Germany's interests. The political economy was institutionalized in Latvia by three different elements of the German government: Hermann Goering's Four Year Plan (*Vierjahresplan*); Alfred Rosenberg 's *Ostland* State Ministry; and the *Wehrmacht*. Each of these organizations had its own goals.[35] There were also differences of opinion on whether the primary objective was to squeeze everything possible from Latvia for the war effort, or if it was preparation for post-war colonization. Therefore economic policies were frequently contradictory. At the beginning of the war, everything possible was taken out of Latvia. Raw materials and food were sent *en masse* to Germany. Nevertheless, as the war dragged on, the Nazis came to the conclusion that the potential of Latvia's industry was better exploited on the spot because the front was not far, and this facilitated quick supply. Furthermore, Latvia's cities were much less targeted by aviation attacks than Germany's industrial centers, and Latvia also had enough qualified workers that could be used in military industry. Factories produced and repaired military equipment and material. This was also one of the reasons why Latvia's inhabitants were not sent to labor service in Germany in large numbers.

Farmers were not allowed to freely dispose of the foodstuffs they produced. As outlined in the April 10, 1943, instruction of the *Ostland Reichskommissar*, these foodstuffs were viewed as if they had been confiscated. The farmer could only act according to instructions from German institutions. Nevertheless, the expropriation of foodstuffs was not particularly successful because of widespread corruption and sabotage by local institutions. The *Ostland Reichskommissar's* supplemental instructions of January 25, 1943 declared that work in agriculture was in second place in the occupied eastern provinces, behind work in the armaments industries, and this was because of the shortage of labor particularly after the beginning of the mobilization of local people into the German army.

The nationalization accomplished by the Soviet regime in Latvia in 1940-41 greatly facilitated the realization of Nazi economic goals. All nationalized property, including land, which after nationalization was considered the property of the Soviet Union, automatically transferred to the authority of the German state as spoils of war (see Document No. 11). At the beginning of the

German occupation, only small industry and handicraft enterprises were returned to their previous owners (this was done with restrictions), but the Soviet agrarian reform was rescinded. Nevertheless, after the German defeat at Stalingrad, widespread denationalization began. On February 18, 1943, A. Rosenberg issued instructions about the renewal of private property in Estonia, Latvia and Lithuania (see Document No. 13). The denationalization of municipal buildings and plots of land was more successful, as well as that of small commercial and industrial enterprises. Farmers re-acquired about a quarter of their land. Only a few of the large industrial enterprises were returned to their former owners, however. Politically unreliable persons did not have their property rights restored. All Jewish-owned property was confiscated, of course, and became part of property available for general use (see Document No. 19).

Currency policy was one of the instruments of economic exploitation. In the occupied territories, there was a monetary unit called the *Reichmark,* which bore the same name as the money in circulation in Germany but differed from it. The circulation of German paper money in the occupied lands, however, was forbidden. Soviet rubles continued to be in circulation simultaneously with the *Reichmarks* of the eastern occupied territories. The exchange rate between rubles and *Reichmarks* set at 10 rubles = 1 *Reichmark.* At the same time, at the beginning of the occupation, it was declared that wages and prices had to remain at pre-war levels. All products were assigned permanent prices. The occupation's artificial inflation of the exchange rate of the *Reichmark* gave German soldiers and bureaucrats the ability to buy goods cheaply and to send them in great quantities to Germany. Slowly the Soviet ruble was pushed out of circulation because banks accepted rubles but did not return them to the public.

A unique method of payment was the so-called "point note" (*Punktwertschein*) – special coupons that were given to farmers for the agricultural products delivered to occupation institutions. Industrial goods could be purchased with these coupons.

As the volume of goods began to dry up, the inhabitants in Latvia and particularly German soldiers and bureaucrats held increasingly larger numbers of coupons with which they could not buy anything. Inflation increased, which led to the development of widespread "black market" and barter trade.

Another component of economic exploitation was the mobilization of human resources for labor service (see Document No. 38).

Simultaneously, the Nazis sought to involve the residents of Latvia in the realization of their military plans, thereby violating international norms. In July of 1941, the SD began to create volunteer police units in Latvia to help with guard duties. On October 6, 1941, the SS *Reichsführer*, Heinrich Himmler, issued an order for the reorganization and expansion of these units. Facing a shortage of volunteers, men were conscripted for six months, but later the term of service was extended. By the end of October 1941, the first police battalions were sent to the front. By 1944, about 40 Latvian police battalions with about 12,000 men (according to other statistics 15,000) and 7 battalions of other nationalities of former Latvian citizens (Russians, Ukrainians, and Belarussians) were formed. The majority of the police battalions fought at the front, but some battalions, following SD orders, were involved in operations in the rear of the German army (in battles against partisans in Latvia, Ukraine, Belarus, Russia, Lithuania, and Poland), as well as in the repressions of civilian inhabitants.

In 1943, the Latvian SS Volunteer Legion began to form (see Document No. 34). It was given the name "volunteer" only to circumvent the Hague conventions forbidding the conscription of inhabitants of occupied lands. Actually, the Legion used mobilization. In 1943, those born from 1918 to 1924 were conscripted; later those born from 1906 to 1926 were also mobilized (see Document No. 35). In the spring of 1943, the 15th Division was formed (14,500 soldiers), and in the fall of 1944 the 19th division (12,300 soldiers). German generals were appointed as commanders of each division, but the Latvian General Rūdolfs Bangerskis was appointed the Legion's General Inspector with unclear authority and without the right to issue orders. The divisions fought their most intensive battles near

Leningrad (now St. Petersburg) and Novgorod, as well as during their retreat into the territory of Latvia before the advancing Soviet army.

The Latvian Legion did not exercise police functions; it fought at the front. It was connected to the *Waffen*-SS only because the German SS and *Polizeiführer Lettland* formed the Legion. The Latvian Legion, in contrast with the German *Waffen*-SS units and especially the "SS Elite Guards," never had to fulfill any political obligations. The difference lay not only in the how he units were created, but also in the military rank and in the uniforms they used (see Documents No. 44 and 45).

After German capitulation in May of 1945, the 19th Division became prisoners-of-war of the Soviet forces. Legion members were sent to so-called "filtration camps," and many of them were later sent to labor camps in Russia. The 15th Division, by contrast, at the end of the war found itself in Germany where it surrendered to the Western allies. They were placed in prisoner-of-war camps, but after it was decided that the Latvian Legion could not be equated with SS units, the former Legion members were given the opportunity to emigrate to and settle in Western countries.

Even though the USSR also recognized that the majority of Legion members were mobilized by force, and therefore could not be viewed as "collaborators," they were still categorized as "politically unreliable persons" and were therefore subject to various official and unofficial restrictions of their rights in the post-1945 Latvian SSR.

The Nazi occupation took a great toll on Latvia's economy. Much greater than the material damage, however, was the loss of human life in battle, in repressions of various kinds, and as a result of the genocidal treatment of Jews. In addition, in 1944 and 1945, about 250,000 persons moved to the West through forced evacuations and voluntarily flight from a second Soviet occupation and from the repressions and horrors associated with the year 1940-41. It is believed that about 50-60,000 of these people perished during the war, or when the advancing Red (Soviet) Army came overtook them in Eastern Europe and rounded them up in Soviet camps. About 140,000 refugees arrived in the Western countries, mostly in refugee (Displaced Person) camps in Germany. After the closing of these camps at the end of the 1940s and the beginning of the 1950s, they emigrated to the USA, Great Britain, Canada, Australia, Argentina, and to other countries.

During World War II, the number of inhabitants of Latvia diminished by about one quarter. If in 1939 there were about 2 million inhabitants in the country, then by September 1, 1945, there were only 1,484,000. Even if refugees, prisoners-of-war, and those placed in filtration camps (of which some returned to Latvia), are added to this number, the loss of inhabitants was still massive. In addition to the genocide of Jews and Gypsies, the German occupation's repressive measures against other inhabitants of Latvia must also be taken into account. According to some calculations, this resulted in the loss of some 35,000 lives. Furthermore, those that died in the German Army (80,000-90,000) and in the Soviet Army (there were about 130,000 of Latvia's residents fighting on the Soviet side, and their losses were very great: the estimate is that of the 43,000 Latvian-division soldiers in the Red Army, only 6-7,000 returned to Latvia), and the civilian inhabitants who died as a result of war must be included in the total. World War II caused a massive loss of the number of Latvians in the world. If in 1935 there were 1,467,000 Latvians in Latvia then according to the 1959 Soviet census there were 1,298,000. Even including the 250,000 Latvians that fled as refugees to the West (some of whom were forced to return), the number of Latvian in the world decreased from about 1,682,000 1935, to 1,560,000 in 1959. [Sources for population figures: P. Zvidriņš and I. Vanovska, *Latvieši: Statistiski demogrāfisks portretējums* (Rīga, 1992, pp. 48, 138); B. Mežgailis, *Latvijas iedzīvotāju skaits, sastāvs un kustības izmaiņas 20. gadsimtā* (Rīga, 1996); Ē. Dunsdorfs, *Latvijas iedzīvotāji simts gados. Archīvs Vol. 23* (Melbourne, 1983, pp. 25, 106)].

DOCUMENTS NO. 1-2

THE PLANS OF THE NAZI REGIME IN THE BALTIC AND BELARUS

Document No. 1

Instructions to the Ostland *Reichskommissar* about the goals of his work in the Baltic States and Belarus

[Berlin] May 8, 1941

All of the provinces between Narva and Tilsit are permanently and closely tied to the German nation. Seven hundred years of history moved the majorities of the nations that live there toward Europe, and, despite all of the Russian threats, this region became a part of Greater Germany's living space.

The goal of the work of the Estonian, Latvian, Lithuanian, and Belarus *Reichskommissar* must be to attempt to form a German protectorate and to afterward germanize the useful elements, racially speaking, thus consolidating the German nation; and to deport the useless and transform this region into a part of Greater Germany's empire. The Baltic Sea must become an internal German Sea for the defense of Greater Germany.

Baltenland,[36] to a certain degree, is a region with a surplus of livestock products and the *Reichskommissar* must return this surplus to the German nation, and, if possible, increase it. In planning deportations [to Russia], it must be taken into account that 50% of the Estonian nation is strongly germanized, with a mix of Danish, German and Swedish blood, and thus they have to be considered a related nation. In Latvia, the part worth assimilating is much smaller than in Estonia. Here we must expect much stronger resistance and must anticipate a much larger deportation. In Lithuania, we must expect an analogous development, because here the *Reich Germans* must be part the germanization process (to the borders of East Prussia).

These three provinces are adjacent to Belarus. In any case, Belarus is a difficult assignment – it has to receive some of those that are deported from Estonia, Latvia, Lithuania, and the Polish sections. It would be useful to re-locate the Poles, not in the General Governorship of Poland, but in Eastern Belarus (the province of Smolensk), and to thereby create a middleman class with respect to the Russians. The rest of the assignment of the Generalkommissar of Belarus would be to give this region, which in economic terms does not yet have a surplus, a jolt in order to increase its productivity and to use the labor force more purposefully.

Therefore the assignment of the *Reichskommissar* stationed in Rīga will be to take positive action. The land that was conquered by German knights 700 years ago, and then was built up by the Hanseatic League, and, that thanks to the continual introduction of German blood and an element of Swedishness, became primarily a germanized land; it must be transformed into a Greater German borderland. The cultural preconditions exist throughout; and the imperial rights for future settlement there may be granted to those that distinguish themselves in this war, the descendents of those that fall in war, and, further, to those that struggle for the Baltic and never lose their manliness, even in hours of despair, and continued to fight and save the Baltic from the Bolsheviks. In other cases, the solution to settlement problems is not a Baltic, but a Greater German affair, and the plan must be realized with such understanding.

This *Reichskommissar,* together with the other *Reichskommissars,* must create a water route between the Black and Baltic Seas; in other words, begin the construction of the Daugava-Dnieper Canal. In this way the arc of Greater Germany can be closed, and this will guarantee future circulation of goods and will make the area independent of any overseas blockade. In this way the *Reichskommissar* in *Baltenlande* must solve great economic problems, concerning himself first with the national political assignments.

Source: *Niurnbergskii protsess, pp. 212-213. Original in German.*

Document No. 2

From the minutes of a conference at the German State Chancellery, led by Adolf Hitler and dealing with plans for the occupied Eastern provinces

Berlin, July 16, 1941

Following the Führer's instructions, today (16.07.41) at 15:00 there was a conference with him and State Leader Rosenberg, State Minister Lammer, Field Marshall Keitel, State Marshall [Goering] and myself [M. Bormann].

In the introduction, the Führer stressed that he first wanted to establish some basic principles. <u>It is important that we do not tell the whole world of our goals at this time.</u> It is also not necessary. The most important thing is that we know for ourselves what we want. In no case can we complicate our path with unnecessary explanations. Explanations are not needed because where our power extends, we can do everything, and in what is beyond the borders of our power, there we can do nothing.

The motivation for our actions in the eyes of the world must appear to come from tactical consideration. Here we must act exactly as in the events in Norway, Denmark, Holland and Belgium. In these cases we also said nothing about our plans and we will continue to be just as clever and not do so now.

We will stress again that we were forced to occupy some province, bring order to it, and secure it. Order is necessary because, in the interests of the populations of the occupied lands, we have had to resolve issues of peace, food, transportation, etc. It cannot be known that together with all of this final solutions are being implemented! All necessary actions – <u>shootings, deportation of people, etc.</u> – we can and will do.

Nevertheless, we do not want to make some people into our enemies prematurely and unnecessarily. We will act (externally) as if we are fulfilling some mandate. Nevertheless, we must be clear to ourselves that we will not be liberating these provinces.

In relation to this, the following must happen:

1. Nothing should be pointing to the final solution (prematurely), but it should be prepared for secretly.

2. We stress that we are the bringers of freedom.

Separately:

The Crimea must be freed of all foreigners, and Germans must be settled there for life.

In the same manner, the old Austrian Galicia must become a state province of Germany.

The foundations of our actions must be such that we can handily divide this huge cake so that first we can make it obedient, second rule over it, and third exploit it.

The Russians have now given an order for partisan warfare in the rear of our forces. This partisan war has its advantages: it gives us the ability to exterminate everyone that is against us.

Basic Questions:

The question of the creation of [antagonistic] military power west of the Urals can never again be allowed to arise even if we must fight for one hundred years.

All of our descendants must know that state security is possible only if there is no [antagonistic] military power west of the Urals. Germany takes on the job of defending this region from potential horrors. The iron law is and remains: we can never allow anyone to be armed except Germans.

This is particularly important: even if at first it would be easier to draw on military help from some foreign nation, it is still wrong. One day they will definitely and inevitably turn against us. Only a German can bear arms, not Slavs, not Czechs, not Cossacks, not Ukrainians! [...]

We must create a Garden of Eden in the newly acquired Eastern provinces. These provinces are very important to our lives. Compared to them, colonies have only a subordinate role.

If we detach some provinces (and include them in Germany), we must always show that we are acting as the defenders of justice and of the population. This is why we must choose the appropriate formulations; at first we will not talk about new German provinces, but about tasks dictated by the needs of war.

Separately:

In the Baltic, the province up to the Daugava must be handed over to (civilian) rule (German) after agreement with Field Marshall Keitel. [...]

The Führer stressed that all of the Baltic (Lithuania, Latvia, and Estonia) must become a province of Germany. [...]

After a break, the Führer stressed that we must be clear that right now Europe is only a geographic concept. That, realistically, Asia stretches to our current borders. This gigantic area, of course, must be pacified as quickly as possible. This can best be accomplished by shooting anyone who even looks askance [at a German].

In conclusion it was decided that the Baltic area must be called "Ostland."

Source: *Niurnbergskii protsess, pp. 581-584. Original in German.*

DOCUMENTS NO. 3-5
ATTITUDE TOWARDS ATTEMPTS TO RENEW LATVIAN SOVEREIGNTY

Document No. 3

From the order of Colonel Petersen, Commandant of Rīga, concerning the prohibition against the renewal of the institutions of independent Latvia

Rīga, July 9, 1941

Recently, individuals have assumed offices, and have even renewed organizations that existed before the Bolshevik times, without permission. This behavior is not allowed and is punishable. [...]

Petersen
Colonel and Commandant

Source: *Tēvija, July 11, 1941. Original in Latvian.*

Directive of the Rīga Commandant, Colonel Petersen, concerning the banning of uniforms of Latvia's Army and Home Guards

Rīga, July 11, 1941

On the basis of instructions from the Commander in Chief, the wearing of military uniform of any service and rank of the former Army of Latvia and Home Guards organization is forbidden. The ban also applies to Latvia's police auxiliary forces and to self-defense forces.

The instruction goes into force without delay.

Commander in the Field of Battle
Petersen
Colonel and Commandant

Source: *Tēvija, July 11, 1941. Original in Latvian.*

From the instruction of the Rīga Commandant about surrendering weapons, ammunition, and other war materiel, and the banning of wearing armbands with Latvian national colors

Rīga, July 25, 1941

Instruction

Following the instruction of the Commander, all shooting weapons, ammunition, hand grenades and all other military equipment must be surrendered in the municipality of Rīga on July 25, 1941.

Surrendering weapons and all other military equipment is the obligation of the entire population, including the current Latvian self-defense units and members of the Latvian auxiliary police, insofar as the latter, who have special permits and green armbands, have not been given the right to carry weapons.

Permits that were issued before July 19, 1941, and the red-white-red armbands, no longer provide the right to carry weapons. From July 25, 1941, wearing the red-white-red armband is forbidden. [...]

Commandant in the Field of Battle

Source: *Tēvija, July 26, 1941. Original in Latvian.*

DOCUMENTS NO. 6-7
LATVIA AS A PART OF OSTLAND

Document No. 6

From Hitler's instructions about the introduction of rule in the occupied Eastern provinces

July 17, 1941

In order to reestablish and maintain public order and public life in the newly occupied eastern territories, order that:

1. As soon as military activities in the newly occupied eastern territories have ended, the governance of these territories will pass from military authorities to civilian authorities. The territories in which civilian authority is to be restored, and the timing according to which this will take place, I will announce with a special decree.

2. Civilian authority in the newly occupied eastern territories will be subordinated to the "Reich Minister for the occupied eastern territories," unless these territories come under the jurisdiction of territories bordering the Reich or the General-Government.

3. Military law and authority will be applied in the newly occupied eastern territories by the *Wehrmacht* authorities using the standards of my edict of July 25, 1941. The activities of those officials who have been ordered to carry out the four-year plan in the newly occupied territories with my order of June 29, 1941, and those of the *Reichsführer-SS* and the Chief of the German Police specially regulated by my July 17, 1941, order will not be affected by subsequent regulations.

4. I appoint *Reichsleiter* Alfred Rosenberg as the *Reichsminister* for the occupied eastern territories. He will have his office in Berlin.

5. Those of the occupied eastern territories that re newly occupied and are subordinated to the *Reichsminister* will be divided into *Reichskommissariats*, which in turn will be divided into general districts and these in turn into local districts. Several local districts can be brought together into a main district. The *Reichsminister* will issue relevant orders regarding these matters.

6. At the head of each *Reichkommissariat* there will be a *Reichskommissar*, at the head of of each general district a *Generalkommissar*, and at the head of each local district a *Gebietskommissar*. In the case of the formation of a main district, this will be headed by a *Hauptkommissar*.

   The *Reichskommissars* and the *Generalkomissars* will be appointed by me; the leaders of the main offices of the *Reichskommissariat* as well as the *Hauptkommissars* and the *Generalkommissars* will be appointed by the *Reichminister* of the occupied eastern territories.

7. The establishment of law in the newly occupied eastern territories will be accomplished to the *Reichsminister* for the occupied eastern territories. He can delegate the right to establish law to the *Reichskommissars [...]*

11. The execution and completion of this order through appropriate regulations is assigned to the *Reichsminister* for the occupied eastern territories and is to be co-ordinated in consultations between the *Reichsminister*, the *Reichschancellor* and head of the Reich chancellery, and the head of the *Oberkommandos* of the *Wehrmacht*.

Führer-Headquarters, July 17, 1941
Der Führer
Adolf Hitler
The head of the *Oberkommandos* of the
Wehrmacht Keitel
The *Reichsminister* and head of the Reich
chancellery Dr. Lammers

Source: *Prozess, pp. 235-237. Original in German.*

Document No. 7

Instructions of the Ostland *Reichskommissar* H. Lohse on the takeover of property by civilian authority

1. With the establishment of civilian authority complete power is passed to the "*Reichskomissar* for Ostland." The implementation of military law and orders has been transferred by the *Führer* to the "authorized military representative in the *Ostland*," whose authority is not affected by the present directive.
2. Directives to the civilian population of the territory under the *Reichskommissar* for *Ostland* will be issued through the officials of the German civilian authorities. The ability of the officials of the authorized military representative in the *Ostland* to request activities for the security of the Reich is not affected by this order.
3. The officials of the German civilian authority are:
   The *Reichskomissar* of the *Ostland*
   the *Generalkommissars*,
   the *Hauptskommissars*, and
   the *Gebietskommissars*.
4. The German civilian authority takes over in the territory under the jurisdiction of the *Reichskommissar* for the *Ostland* all the movable and immovable properties of the Union of Soviet Socialist Republics, its member states, public entities, societies, and unions, including all claims, shares, rights, and interests existing on June 20, 1941, according to existing definitions.
   After June 20, 1941, all arrangements, changes, and alterations in the above-mentioned properties are unlawful if they have not been initiated by German officials. Regulations of German officials cannot be countermanded. The rearrangement of ownership and occupation is forbidden.
   The German Army has the right of possession of the property of the Soviet-Russian Army.

5. The official language of the *Reichskommissariat Ostland* is German. The local language is permitted in the general districts.
6. This order takes affect on the day when it is issued.

Kaunas, August 18, 1941

The Reichskommissar for the Ostland
Lohse

Source: *BA, R 6/13; Meyer. Original in German.*

DOCUMENTS NO. 8-10
LATVIA MUST BECOME A GERMAN LAND

Document No. 8

From the instructions of the Chief of Press in the Occupied Eastern Provinces concerning expressions to be used in referring to concepts prevailing there

Berlin, March 5, 1942

[…] 8) Baltic States. You must refrain from the description "Baltic States" as well as "former Baltic States" or "former peripheral states." Exceptions may only be made in judicial [language] or strictly historical compilations. You must choose the description "Baltic lands," "provinces of Baltic nations" etc. […]

Source: *LVA, P-70.f., 3. apr., 39. l., p. 5. Original in German.*

Instructions of H. Vitrock, *Kommissar* of the Rīga Municipal Province, about the renaming of streets, squares and parks in the city of Rīga

Rīga, April 16, 1942

Partially altering the renaming of Riga streets done in August of 1941, I declare the following as the official list of renamed streets, squares, and parks in Rīga city:

Former street name	New street name
Augusts Deglavs Street	Rumpenhofsche Strasse
	Rumpmuiža Street
Andrejs Pumpurs Street	Ullerspergerstrasse
	Ullersperger Sreet
Aizsargi Street	Yorkstrasse
	York Street
Alberts Street	Hollanderstrasse
	Hollander Street
Antonija Street	Ernst-von-Bergmann-Strasse
	Ernst-von-Bergmann Street
Aristide Briān Street	Wilhelm-Ostwald-Strasse
	Wilhelm-Ostwald Street
Aspazija Boulevard	Von-der-Goltz-Ring
	Von der Goltz Avenue
Auseklis Street	Wilhelm-Purvitis-Strasse
	Vilhelma Purvītis Street
Baznīca Street	Laudonstrasse
	Laudon Street
Bergmanis Street	Schweinfurthstrasse
	Schweinfurth Street
Brīvības Boulevard	Adolf-Hitler-Weg
	Adolf Hitler Way
Brīvības Street	Adolf-Hitler-Strasse
	Adolf Hitler Street
Brīvības Avenue	Livländische Landstrasse
	Vidzeme Avenue
Citadele Street	Hans-von-Manteuffel-Strasse
	Hans von Manteuffel Street
	[...]

Source: *Rīkojumu Vēstnesis, May 1, 1942. Original in Latvian.*

Comment: *According to the published instruction, altogether 54 of Rīga's streets, squares, and parks were renamed. The renaming of streets began in August of 1941. This event created considerable dissatisfaction among the inhabitants of Riga because their national pride was offended by assigning to streets the names of people who had fought against Latvia's independence in the 1918-1920 period. The change in names was further inconvenient because from 1940 to 1941, during the Soviet occupation, streets had also been renamed. This renaming process was one of the actions meant to underline "the ancient Germanic character of the Baltic lands."*

Directive of A. Rosenberg, Reich Minister of the occupied Eastern provinces, concerning the structure and functions of Latvia's Self-Administration (*Selbstverwaltung*)

Berlin, March 7, 1942

The *Reichsminister*
  for the Occupied Eastern Territories

II 1 c 401/402
  I/0

Berlin W 35, March 7, 1942
Kurfürstenstr. 134
Tel.: 21 99 51
Tel. address: Ostministerium

To the *Reichskommisar* for the *Ostland* in Riga:

Reference: Organizational Directive No. 2: Regulations for the Conduct of Governance in the *Generalbezirk Lettland.*

I. Structure of Governance

1. The *Generalkommisar* exercises supreme German authority and political leadership in the *Generalbezirk* under the leadership of the *Reichskommissar.* He conducts supervision of the entire territorial government and is authorized to take any measures necessary to keep good order in the self-government as well as to make supervision easier and more effective.
   He can take over individual matters to handle them by the German civilian government. This pertains particularly to matters relating to the conduct of the economy. These can be removed from the sphere of the territorial self-government especially insofar as the need to further the four-year plan of the wartime economy is concerned.

2. Territorial self-governance will be conducted within these general rules by its own officials within its own institutions and authorized structures. Their guidance will be in the hands of the Chief General-Director and other general-directors, whose number and authority will be determined by the *Generalkommissar.* They will be appointed by the *Generalkommissar* with the agreement of the *Reichskommissar,* and they will need to have the confidence of the *Reichskommissar* in the conduct of their offices. The proposals of the Chief General-Director are not binding on the *Generalkommissar.* The Chief General-Director transmits to the other general-directors and directors directives issued by the leaders of the institutions of German governance, and provides general guidelines for conducting their work.
   The Chief General-Director represents the self-government to the *Generalkommissar* in basic policy matters. He will determine, with the agreement of the *Generalkommissar,* the division of duties among the general-directors and their replacement in the case of difficulties.

3. The Senior Administrator conducts all governance in a rural district; he is moreover the leader of the district's self-government, if one exists. Outside his governing authority, there will exist no other independent professional staff of the self-government in the rural districts. An exception to this rule will be the courts, and, insofar as they are needed, technical staffs

whose authority reaches beyond the boundaries of the rural district. Correspondingly, the same applies to towns that are not part of the rural districts.

Matters dealt with by local self-government authority can be transferred to the district authority, if one has been set up.

The Senior Administrator of the district is as a rule its chief office-holder and will be appointed and recalled by the *Generalkommissar* after consultations with the *Gebietskommissar* and the Chief General-Director. He is subordinated to the general supervision of the Chief General-Director and the divisional supervision of the other authorized General Directors.

The organization of authority in cities, parishes, and parish-clusters, insofar as the latter exist, will be undertaken by the Chief General-Director with the agreement of the *Generalkommissar*. The appointment and recall of leaders of the cities that are independent of rural district authorities belongs to the competence of the *Gebietskommissar* and the Chief General-Director, as delegated by the *Generalkommissar*. The special regulation created for the city of Riga will remain in force.

4. The *Gebietskommissar* exercises his authority under the leadership of the *Generalkommissar*. He advises and oversees the Senior Administrators in the *Kreisen* and the officials of the territorial self administration, and represents German authority exclusively in his general purview. The *Gebietskommissar* is authorized to receive information from the officials of the territorial self-administration (including those at the *Gemeinde* level), and to halt and reverse the measures taken by the territorial self-administration. In emergencies he can order the officials of his territory to enact measures that seem to him to be necessary, even when overriding the authority of the territorial self-administration (including the administration at the *Gemeinde* level), or in special cases enact such measures himself.

5. The administration of justice in the *Generalbezirk Lettland* will be carried out by German courts or the local courts. Judges will not be subject to precedents in making their decisions.

The *Generalkommissar* can call for a review by German courts of decisions made by the local courts.

II.   The Issuance of Legal and Administrative Regulations

1. If a domain of regulations is not reserved for higher Reich officials, the *Reichskommissar* or the *Generalkommissar*, and if that domain is not reserved for German officials, the Chief General-Director, and, indeed, the officials under him, can issue regulations within that domain. These require the agreement of the *Generalkommissar*. After agreement is secured, these regulations will be prepared by the Chief General-Director for announcement in a special publication meant for such announcements. Unless otherwise indicated, such regulations will become effective eight days after their announcement, as will be declared by an order of the *Generalkommissar*.

2. The General-Directors can allocate assignments within the scope of their authority to appointed officials of the territorial self-government. The *Generalkommissar* can make the announcement of such assignments dependent on his agreement and restrict the execution of the measures issued by the territorial self-government.

III.   The Position of the Offices of the Territorial Self-Government and the Officials Who Occupy Them

1. The *Generalbezirk Lettland* is the bearer of rights and obligations. In the application of the particulars of law, it is represented by the authority of the *Generalkommissar,* the Chief General-Director, and the General Directors of the territorial self-government.

2. The General Director of Finances organizes the economy of *Generalbezirk Lettland.* This organization will be confirmed by means of the directives of the *Generalkommissar.*

    The General Director of Finances is empowered to issue directives dealing with public taxation as well as to increase such taxation, to the extent that the *Generalbezirk* has its own resources on which taxes can be levied.

3. The officials of the territorial self-government, with the exception of the General Directors, the leaders of certain central offices of the territorial self-government as well as the senior officials of the *Kreise* – are appointed and recalled by the immediately involved General-Directors through the Chief General-Director. The appointment of officials in cities, parishes, and parish clusters, insofar as the latter exist, will be regulated by the Chief General-Director with the agreement of the *Generalkommissar.* The appointment and removal of the leaders of independent cities follows this Directives paragraph I.3, as implemented by the *Generalkommissar.*

    The *Generalkommissar* can make all appointments in general or in particular dependent on his agreement, or he can make the appointments them himself.

    Administrative decisions of the officials of the territorial self-government (including the government in the local districts) are subject to supervisory regulation by the Chief General-Director with the agreement of the *Generalkommissar.* Existing directives will serve as such supervisory regulation if no other regulations have been issued.

4. If the interests of the German Reich require it, the *Generalkommissar* can, with a special order, empower a particular office of the territorial self-government (including the parish self-government) with a special assignment. This special empowerment of the officials of the self-government will remove them from control of the self-government to the limits imposed by the *Generalkommissar.*

5. The language of business of the territorial self-government in dealings with German officials is German. Within the territorial self government the languages of business are German and Latvian. More specific directions in this matter will be issued soon.

6. The official channels of the territorial self-government will be regulated by the *Generalkommissar.* Here it will be especially important to determine in what administrative matters German officials have to be informed about the activities of the self-government.

7. The officials and organs of the territorial self-government will employ special symbols and seals of their office, the use of and approval for which belongs to the *Generalkommissar.*

signed

Rosenberg

Source: *BA R 6/246 (Reichsministerium für die besitzten Ostgebiete). Original in German.*

DOCUMENTS NO. 11-13
NATIONAL SOCIALIST POLITICAL ECONOMY IN LATVIA

Document No. 11

Instruction about confiscating state farms and placing them under the army's control

Kaunas, beginning of July 1941

State farms (*sovkhozes*) established by the Soviet government, and farms confiscated by the previous government of Latvia, have been transferred completely to the control of the German army, as [transferable] property of the former Soviet government.

Any change in these farms away from what they were on June 22, 194, and any meddling in their economic activities, is forbidden. Particularly banned is the return of farms or parts of them [to former owners] or the arbitrary seizure of them by former owners or their heirs. Any returns or seizures that have already happened are voided and are rescinded immediately.

Anyone who removes inventory or takes supplies for himself [from these farms] can expect the harshest punishment.

The Farm Board in Rīga, the "LA" Group, appoints the leaders of state farms (*sovkhozes*). They are responsible for the immediate resumption of work and for running the farms according to the Board's directions.

Source: *Tēvija, July 19, 1941. Original in Latvian.*

Comment: *State farms (sovkhozes) were formed during the Soviet occupation as state agricultural production enterprises. In June of 1941, there were 31 state farms with 2,340 heads of livestock (including 1,365 cattle) and 14,458 hectares of land.*

Report of the *Generalkommissar* of Riga concerning new rations for the civilian population in the province of Latvia

April 11, 1942

Using as the basis the newly declared grocery rations of April 6, 1942 in Greater Germany, beginning on April 13, 1942, I declare the following weekly rations for the civilian population of the Latvian province:

	Grams of meat	Grams of fat	Grams of bread	Grams of Sugar		Groceries to Grams	Coffee grams
Children to 3 years	125	100	775	200	Children p.1	125	-
						500	-
Children from 3 to 6	125	160	1000	200	Children p.1	62,5	
						150	80
Youths from 6 to 18	300	230	2200	150		150	80
Average amount over 18	250	180	1700	150		150	80
Overtime and night workers	375	190	2200	150		150	80
Heavy Labor	500	260	2900	150		150	80
Heaviest labor	725	490	3700	150		150	80
Jews without work	125	90	850	75		75	40
Jews with work	125	90	1700	75		75	40
Jews working heavy labor or in war necessities	250	180	1700	150		150	80

The rations for eggs, marmalade, fish, cheese, and cottage cheese will be distributed by reference to supplies, with prior notification.

Until the introduction of new grocery ration cards, grocery rations will be distributed to all age classes equally according to the average ration. The Grocery Securing Department will distribute the special rations to workers working at night, doing overtime work, heavy work and heaviest work, in concordance with the Trade Union.

General Commissar in Rīga
Im Auftrage: Luethje

Source: *Tēvija, April 13, 1942. Original in Latvian.*

Comment*: The ration card system was introduced on September 1, 1941. The ration cards defined the amount of goods that the Latvian civilian population could buy: for example 350 grams of meat a week (175 grams for Jews), 200 grams of butter (100 grams for Jews), 400 grams of sugar (200 grams for Jews), etc. From April 13, 1942, the "average ration" per week was 250 grams of meat, 180 grams of shortening, 150 grams of sugar. Workers in heavy labor were given twice the regular ration of meat and shortening, whereas Jews received half-rations. During the last phases of the war, the butter ration was more frequently replaced with lard, and there were all sorts of additives in the bread and other grocery products. Pre-determined rations for goods were initially not applied to Germans, who could buy goods "as normally needed." Later, however, the ration card system with larger rations was used for everyone. The rationed amounts were larger than the average ration in Germany. Rīga's largest store – the Army's Economic Store – became a purchasing venue for German soldiers and administrators because they did not need any permits to shop there.*

According to a survey carried out by employees of the Latvian Republic Office of the USSR State Bank in August of 1944, in the eastern sections of Latvia occupied by the Soviet army, a worker in 1944 who earned between 60 and 80 Reichmarks per month, spent 12-16 Reichmarks buying the ration card products. At the same time, 1 kilogram of rye bread that officially was priced at 0.14 Reichmarks, cost 5 Reichmarks on the black market; 1 kilogram of butter was officially priced at 2.20 Reichmarks, but unofficially 50-120 Reichmarks; while 1 liter of gasoline was officially priced at 2.60-4.60 Reichmarks, but unofficially cost 60-120 Reich Marks (LVA, 270.f., 1.apr., 203. l., p. 3).

Document No. 13

Directive of A. Rosenberg, Reich Minister of the occupied Eastern Province, about the renewal of private property in Estonia, Latvia and Lithuania

Berlin, February 18, 1943

With this, the preconditions are set for the liquidation of the actions of the Soviet Union in the general province of Estonia, Latvia and Lithuania in which farms were confiscated.

Private property is renewed in the conviction that the owners will fulfill all the tasks that come with the property ownership, particularly [in relation to the needs of] the German military economy.

Based on the Fuehrer's decree 8 of July 17, 1941, concerning governance in the newly occupied eastern provinces, and using also the 2nd point of the instruction of May 28, 1942, concerning specific economic property in the occupied Eastern provinces (*Verordnungsblatt des Reichsministers für die besetzten Ostgebiete*, p. 21), together with the authorized agent, I order for the four-year plan:

1.

1.   In the general province of Estonia, Latvia and Lithuania, private property is again allowed.
2.   Land deed offices are to start their work, again opening land and mortgage books.

2.

1.   Persons who had their property confiscated by the Soviet government's coercive actions are [hereby] returned their property, land with buildings or without, and enterprises, upon request.

2.   The return of property takes place through the Board. The return is in force from the moment of the reception of the property document.

3.

Those that have shown themselves to be politically and economically loyal are given preference in requests.

4.

The return of property is forbidden to the extent that it is against the interests of society, particularly against the interests of military economy. For these same reasons, the return of property can be linked to tax payments.

5.

If the earlier owner has died, then the property is returned to the heirs.

6.

All rights over a parcel of land are renewed with the return of the property to the person who had these rights or to his or her heirs.

7.

A special instruction will be issued about the value of nationalized property that belonged to juridical persons in accordance with private or social rights, to German repatriates, and to other German citizens or descendents of repatriates.

8.

The *Ostland* Reich Commissar will issue the preliminary juridical documents and rules that are needed for the realization of this directive.

9.

The directive is in force from the day of its publication.

Occupied Eastern Provinces
Reich Minister Rosenberg

Source: *Verordnungsblatt, Feb. 22, 1943. Original in German.*

Documents No. 14-15
Control of media: Censorship and bans

Document No. 14

Directive of the *Wehrmacht* Propaganda Section in Rīga (*Propagandastaffel Riga*) about permission to distribute periodicals and magazines

Rīga, July 30, 1941

1) All periodicals, journals, and other such publications in Latvia need the permission of the Propaganda Section in Rīga (Elizabetes Street 51). Permission must also be requested for periodicals and journals that are already being published.

2) Non-observance of this directive will be punished according to military law.

Propaganda Section in Rīga

Source: *Tēvija, August 1, 1941. Original in Latvian.*

Document No. 15

From the directive of the *Ostland* Reich Commissar, H. Lohse, concerning the prohibition of listening to foreign radio stations

Rīga, January 13, 1942

The enemy in a modern war fights not only with military weapons, but also with other resources that are meant to influence the spirit of a nation. One of these resources is the radio. Each word that the enemy broadcasts is meant to cause losses for the German state and those nations under its defense. That is why I expect each and every inhabitant of the Eastern province who is conscious of his responsibilities will cease listening to f foreign radio stations. However, for those that lack this sense of responsibility I have issued this following directive:

1. 1) Listening to foreign radio stations is forbidden. Violations will be punished with a correctional facility. In severe cases, punishment will be prison.
   2) The equipment used to receive [radio broadcasts] will be confiscated. Confiscation can also happen when the equipment belongs to a third party.
2. Whoever with prior knowledge disseminates foreign radio news meant to threaten the ability of the German nation to resist, to threaten social peace, safety, and order in the Eastern province will be punished with a correctional facility. In particularly serious cases, the death penalty can be applied.
3. The directions in this directive do not apply to activities related to the fulfillment of service obligations. The State Commissar issues for the implementation of this directive the needed judicial and board instructions, which state who is allowed to listen to foreign radio stations in pursuit of their duties.

4. Trials for transgressions fall to the special courts.
5. The directive is in effect from its publication.

Reichskommisar for *Ostland*

Source: *Tēvija, January 20, 1942. Original in Latvian.*

DOCUMENTS NO. 16-17
THE JURIDICAL BASIS OF TERROR

Document No. 16

The directions of A. Rosenberg, the Reich Minister of the Eastern Occupied Provinces, about extraordinary courts in the occupied Eastern provinces

Berlin, January 12, 1942

Using the 8th paragraph of the *Führer's* decree of July 17, 1941, concerning governance of the newly occupied Eastern provinces[37], I decree the following.

1.

1. Serious criminal acts by the local population of the occupied Eastern provinces can be tried in general provinces as determined by the *Reichskommissar* or in jurisdictions adjacent to the regular courts, or in extraordinary courts established for this purpose.
2. German citizens and German nationals are not subject to the jurisdiction of the extraordinary courts.

2.

The extraordinary courts mentioned in paragraph 1 can operate when the trial as a specific order-keeping purpose, or if public safety and order requires an immediate trial of some criminal act and the regular court cannot be used in short order.

3.

1. The prosecutor can send the accusation to an extraordinary court if he recognizes that due to a serious threat to public order and safety the investigation of the case is appropriate for the extraordinary court.
2. The chair of the extraordinary court can transfer the case to the regular court. The transfer must happen when the guilt of the accused can only be proven through extensive gathering of evidence or when the extraordinary court considers it appropriate to change the death penalty to loss of freedom.
3. The prosecutor may make the accusation of the transferred case in the regular courts orally.

4.

1. The convening of the extraordinary court is done by the *Generalkommisar* or by his defined subordinates.
2. The extraordinary Court consists of one police officer or SS officer as chair, and two subordinates from his district.

5.

1. In investigating a case in an extraordinary court, the court must do everything that is necessary to examine the truth. If need be, the accused must be provided a translator.
2. The names of the accused and the judges, the evidence, the criminal act, the court's decision with a short explanation, as well as the day and place of the court, must be recorded in the minutes that must be signed by the Chair.
3. In other cases, an extraordinary court determines the order of its trials according to procedures of the responsible body.

6.

1. Extraordinary courts assign the death penalty, transfer the case to the security police or to a regular court for trial, or vindicate the accused.
2. Along with the death penalty, confiscation of possessions may be part of the sentence.

7.

1. The decisions of the extraordinary courts are not contestable through appeal.
2. The decision of the extraordinary court, insofar as the case is not transferred to a regular court, must be reexamined. The reexamination either ratifies the decision or rescinds it.
3. With ratification, the decision is in force and is executed.

8.

1. The right to ratify or rescind the decision of the extraordinary court belongs to the *Generalkommisar* or those delegated to be in his place. The latter can bring the decision of the extraordinary court before the *Reichskommissar* for a decision about ratification or rescinding.
2. The *Generalkommisar* can determine in what cases he chooses to decline to reexamine the ratification. In these cases, the decision remains in force and is executable upon publication.

9.

The chair of the extraordinary court suggests the manner of the execution of the decision and notes its execution in the minutes of the file.

10.

This directive comes into force in the *Ostland Reichskommissariat* as of January 30, 1942. The date of enforcement in other provinces will be determined later.

Eastern Reichsminister Rosenberg

Source: *Rīkojumu Vēstnesis, December 31, 1942. Original in Latvian.*

Document No. 17

Additional directions by A. Rosenberg, *Reichsminister* of the Eastern Occupied Provinces, regarding the law of punishments in the occupied Eastern provinces

Berlin, February 17, 1942

Based on the 8th paragraph of the **Fuehrer**'s decree of July 17, 1941 about the rule of the newly occupied Eastern provinces[38], I declare:

I.

Local inhabitants must act according to German laws and according to the instructions relevant to them that are issued by German institutions. If they are not German citizens or German nationals, then the following directions about specific punishments apply to them:

1.

Punishment with death, and in less important cases, punishment with time in a correctional house:

Those that use violence against the Greater German state or against the sovereign power established in the occupied Eastern provinces;

Those that use violence against German citizens or German nationals because of their German identity;

Those that use force against the German Armed Forces or against those in their accompanying organizations, as well as against German police, including their auxiliaries, those in the service of the state, those in German institutions or in their service, or members of the National Socialist German Workers Party (NSDAP);

Those that invite or encourage disobedience to directions or instructions issued by German institutions;

Those that purposefully sabotage the equipment of German institutions or their workplaces or those things that are meant for their work or general well-being;

Those that pursue endeavors hostile to Germans or try to maintain the organizational work of banned groups;

Those that with hostile or provocative activity demonstrate hostile opinions of Germans or in some other manner through their behavior hinder the Greater German state or the honor and welfare of German nationals or belittle them;

Those that engage in arson and in so doing hinder German interests or the property of German citizens or German nationals.

2.

In the same manner, those who converse about the punishable activities in paragraph 1, become involved in serious discussions about them, offer to do these things, or accept a request to do them, or who learn from reliable sources about such activities in time when such horrors could still be prevented and purposefully do not notify the threatened German institution or person at the right time, are also punished with death, or, in less important case, with the correctional house.

3.

The death penalty is also earned for criminal activities not covered in paragraphs 1 and 2, even if such activities are not in general German laws of punishment or in directives of German institutions, if the activities are of a particularly serious aspect or if for some other reason are particularly serious; in these cases the death penalty is also allowed for minors that have committed serious crimes.

4.

1. If the jurisdiction of an extraordinary court (*Standgericht*) has not been established, trials are carried out by the regular court.
2. This does not apply to specific directions given to the armed forces. [...]

Eastern *Reichsminister* Rosenberg

Source: *Rīkojumu Vēstnesis, December 31, 1942. Original in Latvian.*

Comment: *The October 6, 1941, directive of Reichkommisar H. Lohse concerning the creation of German courts and prosecutors in Ostland was implemented in a court system that was divided into two levels: the lower, the so-called" German court," was under the authority of Latvia's Generalkommissar; the higher, the so-called " German Supreme Court", was under the authority of the Reichkommissar. The latter could overrule the decisions of the former. Rosenberg's directive of January 12, 1942 (see Document No. 16), established extraordinary courts that paralleled the others. The extraordinary courts in their makeup were very similar to the so-called "troikas" of the USSR.*

Document No. 18

Directive of Otto Drechsler, Latvia's *Generalkommissar*, concerning restrictions of the rights of Jews and the isolation of Jews

Rīga, September 1, 1941

For the information of all Jews, the directive of Dr. Drechsler addressed to all Jews in the territory of the former free state of Latvia[39]

I

Jews must carry in a prominent place on their left breasts and in the middle of their backs the yellow six-pointed star at least 10 cm. in size.

II

Jews are forbidden to:
1. Change their place of residence or apartment without permission from the *Gebietskommisar*.
2. Use sidewalks, public transportation (for example, railroads, trams, buses, passenger steam ships, carriages).
3. Use public parks and institutions meant for rest (for example, curative and swimming institutions, parks, green belts, game and sports fields).
4. Go to movie theatres, theaters, libraries, and museums.
5. Attend any type of school.
6. Own radio apparati or powered vehicles.
7. Slaughter animals according to Jewish ritual.

III

Jewish doctors and dentists can practice medicine and give advice only to Jewish patients. Jewish pharmacists and veterinarians are not allowed to practice.

IV

Jews are also forbidden to:
1. Work as lawyers, notaries, or legal advisors.
2. Work with bank, exchange, or mortgage operations.
3. Be representatives, agents, or middlemen.
4. Carry on business in immovable properties.
5. Pursue a peripatetic occupation.

V

This directive comes into force, today at 12:00.

Source: *Tēvija, September 1, 1941. Original in Latvian.*

Comment: *In preparation for the complete extermination of Jews in Latvia as in other Nazi-occupied East European lands, the isolation of Jews from the rest of the population was the fist step. Already by July 5, 1941, in Liepāja, the order was given for Jews to sew on their clothing a piece of yellow cloth (not smaller than 10cm by 10 cm), and along with this there were created a whole list of humiliating prohibitions. Beginning with August 1, all Jews had to sew the six-pointed star on their clothes.*

Document No. 19

From the order of the *Ostland Reichskommissar*, H. Lohse, concerning the disposition of Jewish property

Rīga, October 13, 1941

1.

The movable and immovable property of all inhabitants of the Jewish nation in the provinces governed by the Ostland *Reichskommissar* is confiscated, and comes under the control of the *Kommissariat*. The confiscation is conducted according to the following directions.

2.

Property is defined as moveable and immoveable objects with all accessories, obligations, joint-property rights, and other rights and interests.

3.

1. The Ostland *Reichksommissar* or his authorized representatives confiscates the property. This can be done with an order for specific persons or generally with general directive and can also be related to specific material items.
2. The following is not seized:
    a. Household accessories needed for personal use;
    b. Money, bank, and savings accounts as well as stocks to 100 *Reichmarks*. [...]

11.

The order is in force from the day of its publication.

Ostland *Reichskommissar* Lohse

Source: *Verkundungsblatt, Oct. 24, 1941. Original in German.*

114

Order of the *Kommissar* of the Rīga municipal region concerning the creation of a ghetto in Rīga and prohibiting any contact with Jews

Rīga, October 23, 1941

1. There is a ghetto in Rīga. It is bordered by: Latgale, Vitebska, Latgale, Žīda, Lauva, Lielā Kalna, Lazdona, Katoļa, Jēkabpils, and Lāčplēsis Streets. The ghetto is cordoned off with barbed wire.
2. Non-Jews are strictly forbidden to enter the territory of the ghetto. Entry to the ghetto is allowed only with permission from the Rīga municipal region *Kommissar*.
3. Any contact with Jews outside of the borders of the ghetto is forbidden. Those who with prior intent or due to carelessness do not observe this prohibition will be punished with a prison sentence and in the worst cases with a correctional house.
4. In the case of an attempt of some kind of contact with Jews over or through the barrier, the security guards are given the order to shoot without any prior warning.
5. Requests for Jewish labor are to be submitted to the Labor Board according to its published directions.
6. Each person who uses Jews assigned from the Labor Board must transport them from the ghetto in a closed convoy to their place of work and return them in the same way.
7. The work providers must take care that the directives about contact with Jews is also observed by their employees.

Those that do not follow this order will be fined to 1,000 *Reichmarks* if a more severe punishment is not in order.

Der Gebietskommissar Riga-Stadt

Source: *Tēvija, October 24, 1941. Original in Latvian.*

Comment: *The establishment of the ghetto in Rīga began in September of 1941. The territory of the ghetto was closed off with barbed wire around October 10th. By October 25th the Rīga ghetto was finished and all Jews living in Rīga were given the order to move to the ghetto by 18:00 on October 25th. The ghetto was then sealed.*

Document No. 21

Order of the *Kommissar* of the Rīga municipal region concerning the employment of Jews and the payment of their wages after November 1, 1941

October 27, 1941

Order concerning Jewish employment

1. All of the labor documents given to Jews by the Labor Board in Rīga are not valid beginning on October 31. Beginning with November 1st, new yellow documents will only be given to individual persons (specialists). Requests and their justification for the future employment of Jews after October 31st must be submitted without delay in writing to the Labor Board's Jewish Employment Section in Rīga, on Yorck (Aizsarga) Street 29/31.
2. Anyone who employs Jews after November 1st of this year must pay their wages according to the existing norms . All wages of Jews must be paid weekly into the Rīga municipal government's finance section at, Ķēniņa Street 5. It is forbidden to pay wages to the Jews [directly].

Der Gebeitskommissar Riga-Stadt

I.V. Altemeyer

Source: *Tēvija, October 28, 1941. Original in Latvian.*

Document No. 22

From the report of the Liepāja region *Kommissar*, V. Alnor, to Latvia's *Generalkommissar* O. Drechsler

Liepāja, not later than January 1942

[...] From December 14 to 17 in Liepāja altogether 2,700 Jews were shot. In the other places in the region, for example, in Ventspils, the shooting was done to the completion of the task, that is, including primarily women and children. As has been reported to me from all sides, the shooting continued all through the day in the city, that is, in the territory of the Naval Port, and has caused a great disturbance among the [other]inhabitants. There can be no doubt that with this [action], German authority has suffered noticeably. It was pointed out to me that women, children, and babies were shot [while being] almost naked, which is hardly different from Soviet methods. Among the sailors, the belief is that the shootings took place at the urging of the *Reichskommissar* who wanted to report to the Führer on January 1st that the area was free of Jews.

At the present moment there is again shooting [going on] in large numbers, which creates anew a palpable unrest. I cannot understand why they are being killed in such a cruel way. In the December shooting 2,800 people were thrown into one pit 100 m long, 3 m wide, 3 m deep. The shooting happened without a doctor or officer being present, so that in two cases those to be killed got out of the pit at night and headed for the city [dressed only] in their shirts. In one case this was a woman who had collapsed in front of the pit and was simply thrown into the pit, where she regained consciousness during the night. Such stories circulate in great numbers and this, of course, does not serve to enhance our authority in the eyes of Latvians [...]

Source: *LVVA, P-69 f., 1.a. apr., 17. l., p. 325 (copy of original). Original in German.*

Document No. 23

From the review of the work of the SD and Security Police Second Operational Command concerning the mass extermination of Jews

From January 27 to February 6, 1942

When the German armed forces entered, there were about 70,000 Jews in Latvia. During the Bolshevik times there were many more Jews living in Latvia, but a large part of them fled with the Bolsheviks.

At the beginning, the second operational command had the goal of completing the solution of the Jewish problem by executing all of the Jews. In order to do this in the entire province, and using the aid of selected members of the Latvian auxiliary police [...], widespread cleansing actions were carried out. By the beginning of October, the operational command in the province had executed about 30,000 Jews. This included a few thousand Jews who were exterminated by self-defense forces when they were given the hint [to do so]. [...]

By the end of October, the rural provinces of Latvia were completely cleansed. In order to completely isolate those Jews from society who were still needed for labor, they were placed in ghettos set up in Rīga, Daugavpils and Liepāja.

At the same time a directive was given to mark Jews with the Jewish star. The security police in the ghettoes were assigned purely police duties, while the creation of the borders of the ghetto and its supervision, as well as payments to the confined and their supplies, were assigned to the province *Kommissars*, and the allocation of [Jewish laborers] – to the Labor Board.

At the beginning of November, 1941, there were only about 30,000 [Jews] in the Rīga ghetto, about 4,300 in Liepāja and about 7,000 in Daugavpils. Since that time, about 400 to 500 Jews have been executed. [...] In addition, within the context of larger actions, the ghettos were cleansed of those not completely fit for work and the Jews who were no longer needed. Thus, on November 9, 1941, 11,034 were executed in Daugavpils; at the beginning of December, 1941, according to the order of the SS and Police leaders, a big action happened in Rīga – 27,800; and in the middle of December 1941 in Liepāja, according to the wishes of the *Reichkommissar* – 2,350 Jews. The remaining Jews (in Rīga 2,500, in Daugavpils 950 and in Liepāja 300) were exempted from these actions because they were good specialists whose labor is still needed in the economy, particularly the war economy.

From December, 1941, Jewish transports have been arriving at short intervals from the Reich. From the Reich and the Bohemia and Moravia protectorate, altogether 19,000 Jews have been sent to Rīga. They have been placed in a section of the ghetto, as well as in the newly created barracks camp near Rīga. Of these Reich Jews only a very small number are capable of work. Women and children as well as old men incapable of work make up about 70-80%. Among the evacuated Jews, mortality is constantly increasing. The old and incapable Jews especially no longer have enough strength to resist the particularly hostile winter.

In order to avoid the horrors of an epidemic in the ghetto and both camps, individual Jews with infectious diseases (dysentery and diphtheria) are selected and executed. In order that the local Jews and the Reich Jews do not learn about this activity, the transport [of the sick] is masked as the relocation of them to a house for infirm and sick Jews. In this process, some mentally ill Jews have also been removed.

Source: *LVVA, P-1026. f., 1. apr., 3. l., pp. 262-264. Original in German.*

Comment: *According to statistics from the 1935 Latvian census, there were 93,500 Jews in Latvia (approximately 4.8% of the total number of inhabitants). Unfortunately, researchers are able to offer only differing numbers for those killed in the Holocaust in Latvia. These totals vary from 63 to 75 thousand persons. There is also a lack of precise information of how many Jews were in Latvia at the beginning of German occupation, because several thousands were arrested or deported during the time of Soviet occupation in 1940-1941, and more than 10,000 Jews fled the country to the USSR in June of 1941.*

Document No. 24

Public report of the *Kommandant* of Liepāja, Brückner, concerning the shooting of hostages

Liepāja, July 8, 1941

During the last few nights shots have been repeatedly fired at German posts. In response, 30 Bolshevik and Jewish hostages were executed.

Latvian inhabitants are asked to immediately inform the security police about all the still-hidden Bolshevik and Jewish thieves.

If attacks continue, as in the past few nights, then for every injured German soldier we will shoot 100 hostages.

Local Kommandant Brückner
Corvette Captain

Source: *Kurzemes Vārds, July 8, 1941. Original in Latvian.*

Document No. 25

Report of Latvia's Security Police Commander, Schtrauch, about the burning down of Audriņi village and the imprisonment and shooting of its inhabitants

Rīga, January 8, 1942

1. Despite several reports that persons who participate in anti-state activities will be severely punished, and that particularly severe punishments await those who give these elements refuge in their apartments or farms, hide them, or supply them with provisions, weapons, and in that manner ignore the request by German institutions to notify the police about these elements without delay, specific events have recently nevertheless demonstrated to me that these directives and requests are not being observed.

2. In Rēzekne district, in Audriņi village, the inhabitants have quartered Red Army soldiers, hidden them, given them weapons and in every possible way helped them in their anti-state activities for more than half a year. In the struggle against these elements, Latvian police have been shot.

3. Therefore in re-payment for these violations I have decided the following:
    a. To level Audriņi village to the ground,
    b. To imprison the inhabitants of Audriņi village and
    c. To publicly shoot 30 male inhabitants of Audriņi village on January 4, 1942, in the Rēzekne market square.
4. Also, in the future, I will use every resource to take action against those persons who believe that they can sabotage the existing order, as well as against those who would help such elements in any way.

Latvia's Security Police Commander Schtrauch
SS- Obersturmbannführer

Source: *Tēvija, January 8, 1942. Original in Latvian.*

DOCUMENTS NO. 26-27
ATTEMPTS TO SAVE JEWS

Document No. 26

From a story in the newspaper "Daugavpils Herald" concerning attempts to save Jewish children in Krāslava and the punishment of the participants

October 17, 1941

[…] Recently, many Jews, using the aid of some clergymen, have tried to convert to Christianity and in that way save themselves from the Star of David. In this respect, particularly scandalous conditions exist in Krāslava.

According to the report of the Krāslava police, an entire Jewish family was „christened" in a local church – the merchant Bārkans with his wife and two children. During the time when the deportation of Krāslava's Jews to camps took place, other such arrangements were uncovered. For example, Agata Tomane of Miesnieka Street 5 took in 2 Jewish children to raise. Nevertheless Tomane soon tired of Sore and Iciks and gave them to her friend Paulina Silava of Vienība Street 35. Tomane asked her friend to watch them for a few days and paid her 100 rubles. After more than a week, Tomane did not come for her „children," and therefore Silava notified the appropriate authorities. During interrogation she explained that Tomane agreed to raise the children, for which she received a large sum of money and other rewards. A Krāslava resident Anna Garancareka of St. Ludvig Square 2, took in a Jewish girl after the deportation of the Jews, the girl having been given to her by a Jew, Viškins. She gave the child to be christened. In the same way Marija Umbraško took in the child of the Jew Elija Druja to raise, and christened the child in a local church. Giršs Perelmans gave his curly offspring to Tekla Šulska to raise, along with 500 rubles for expenses. This child was also christened. Olga Jureviča of Pils Street 9 took a boy and girl from the Jew Pasternak to raise, as did Marija Vaišļa of Pagraba Street 12, who took in an unknown Jewish child.

All of these Jewish children were taken from their obliging "step-mothers" and sent to the Jewish camps. The guilty women will have to answer to the courts and a harsh penalty awaits them.

Source: *Daugavpils Vēstnesis, October 17, 1941. Original in Latvian.*

Document No. 27

From the hand-written autobiography of Z. Šepšeloviča about her experiences

October 25, 1946

I, Zelda Šepšelovič, daughter of Josif, was born in Kuldīga on Ausut 19, 1920. I finished Jewish primary school, and then the Latvian gymnasium in 1938. My parents were poor folk and I had to earn money for myself in order to buy books etc. – in 1938, I went to Rīga in order to complete my education. I began to study at the pedagogical institute of foreign languages. During the day I worked – at night I studied…

The Germans arrived (July 1, 1941). I was forced to work as a domestic. I carried the yellow star on my breast and back. I worked 14 hours a day, I was harassed, and I was forced to carry rubble in the bombed part of the city etc.

On October 14, 1941, they ordered us to go to the ghetto, where we were all imprisoned. Every morning we were taken by convoy to work and returned in the evening. When I learned that all of the women up to 25 years of age would live in a separate camp I decided to end my life by suicide. I fled from work. I took a letter about my plight to an acquaintance, Vabulis, so that he would give it to my old nanny. He read my letter in the other room and offered to take me in. That was on November 28, 1941, and on November 30 they killed 15,000 Jews. On December 7, they killed my father, mom, and 19-year-old sister. I learned that all of my family in Latvia perished, that is 60 people!

I hid at Vabulis' from November 28, 1941, to April 18, 1944. During the day I never went out onto the streets, only a few times at night when it was dark. Six or 7 times our apartment was searched (by the German Gestapo) and I always was able to crawl out my window and on to the roof. Each time when there was a ring at the door, I expected it to be for me because the Germans paid 5-10,000 marks for each Jewish [family]. All the time I kept up contact with Jews in the ghetto. They received packages of goods from me through a Jew – Ļev Kor – who worked in our courtyard. That is how I lived in Vabulis' apartment until April 18, 1944.

On that day Vabulis called me at home and said that I had to get ready to flee. In the evening he, that is Vabulis, my nanny, and I drove to the railroad station; Vabulis and I took the train to Vindava [Ventspils] and my nanny stayed in Rīga. […]

Source: *LVA, 1986.f., 1. apr., 4721. l., (handwritten). Original in Russian.*

Comment: *Jānis-Aleksandrs Vabulis (1914-1998) – lawyer, lieutenant in Latvia's army. During the time of the Nazi occupation, from August of 1941 to April of 1944 he worked in the Rīga construction office and the headquarters of the railroad commandant.*

From November 28, 1941, until February of 1942, he hid the Jewish woman, Zelda Šepšeloviča, who had fled from the ghetto, in his apartment in Stabu Street 6-24, and after that, until April 18, 1944, in Miera Street 29-1. On April 18, 1944, Vabulis forged documents and took Šepšeloviča by train to the port city Ventspils. On April 20, 1944, both of them with ten other refugees crossed the Baltic Sea to Sweden on the boat "Admirālis," captained by the fishermen Heibergs and Krautmanis.

After Nazi Germany's capitulation, Vabulis and Šepšeloviča returned to Rīga on July 18, 1945.

On February 12, 1946, Vabulis was arrested by the Soviet Latvian authorities for keeping and disseminating Swedish newspapers with allegedly anti-Soviet contents. On July 9, 1946, the Military Tribunal of the Latvian SSR Ministry of the Interior's Armed Forces sentenced Vabulis to 10 years in a labor correctional camp, with confiscation of property and suspension of rights for 5 years.

Vabulis found himself imprisoned in the Noriļsk (Russia) camp. After being freed in 1954, he lived until the end of his life in Rīga.

Šepšeloviča was arrested by Soviet Latvian authorities for the same "crime" as Vabulis on October 24, 1946.

DOCUMENTS NO. 28-29

THE TRAGEDY OF SOVIET PRISONERS OF WAR

Document No. 28

From the report of the Chief Quartermaster of the *Wehrmacht* General Commanding Officer in *Ostland* to the *Reichskommissar* of *Ostland*

Rīga, June 27, 1942

Secret

The shortage of food supplies for the needs of prisoners of war, particularly due to the poor supply of potatoes, is still very great. The supplying of prisoners of war from their homeland is no longer operative. Until now, food substitutes could be used in only limited amounts. It is necessary to review the potential amount of food supplies and food supply substitutes for prisoners of war because in the near future we must anticipate considerable growth in the number of prisoners of war. [...]

We request particularly a review of the following food supplies and food supply substitutes. [...]

4. Mill waste, mill dust. In Vilnius at Stalag 344, through the mediation of the Vilnius rural province *Kommissar*, a considerable amount was provided.
5. Waste products from the sugar and drink industry, such as cuttings, molasses, and grains. We should consider limiting livestock supplies.
6. Waste and remains from the sorting of fruit.
7. Waste from the sorting of fish.
8. Scalding water from sausage processing.
9. Bone marrow.
10. Horse meat.
    It is known that most horse meat is sent to Finland. It is requested to review if part of that horse meat could be used for prisoners of war.
11. Yeast products.
12. Cabbage, rhubarb, turnip leaves.
13. Wild plants – sorrel, nettles, dandelions.
    It is requested to consider if the gathering of wild plants could include school children, with awards being distributed. [...]

Acting [Chief Quarter Master] Meijs

Source: *LVVA, P-69.f., 1. apr., 10. l., p. 378.Original in German.*

Instructions of Acting Battlefield Commander Nehtigal concerning the ban on civilians giving food to prisoners of war

Rīga, September 2, 1941

Riga residents often sell or give bread to prisoners of war marching along the streets. Residents are reminded that the selling or giving of bread or other goods to prisoners of war, as well as general contact with them, is forbidden. The violators of this instruction will be punished.

Acting Battlefield Commander Nehtigal
Advisor to the Military Board

Source: *Tēvija, September 3, 1941. Original in German.*

Comment: *Prisoner- of- war camps were located throughout all of the territory of Latvia, the largest being near Rīga (Salaspils), Daugavpils, and Jelgava. The prisoners were used primarily in military construction, but some were also used as farm laborers. Local residents were strictly forbidden to help prisoners of war in any way. The total number of prisoners of war in the territory of Latvia is not precisely known. It also not known precisely how many perished in prisoners of war camps. After the war, Soviet investigators asserted in published materials that in the territory of Latvia about 330,000 prisoners of war perished. It is possible, however, that this figure was deliberately inflated for political purposes.*

DOCUMENTS No. 30-32

THE ROLE OF THE GERMAN OCCUPATION IN INSTITUTIONAL POLICIES PERTAINING TO CULTURE AND EVERYDAY LIFE

Document No. 30

From the instruction of the Ostland *Reichkommissar* to the Chief Railroad Directorate "Northern" about creation of special passenger carriages for Germans

Rīga, June 11, 1942

Referring to the discussion of June 8, 1942, I report: for reasons of health, it is seen as necessary to separate Germans from natives. [...]
Considering the political necessity, I request the following be created:
1. Second-class compartments for general separation; further
2. A sufficient number of compartments for further separation by service rank for more detailed grading overall.

While 2nd class carriages can be freely used by anyone, compartments reserved for ranked persons can only be used with the permission of a German institution. It will further be stated which institutions have the right to issue such permits. These compartments based on rank must be for the use of any German, if they have the appropriate proof, independently of them being or not being on assignment for some service (therefore, members of the family). Further, the ranked compartments can also be used by natives if they can show a permit from a German institution.

The division by service is not needed for trains to Jūrmala. Still, I request that on Jūrmala trains, 2nd-class wagons also be put into circulation. I refer to oral explanations for the reasons related to this.

I request that all external indicators that announce the separations of Germans and natives on railroad carriages be removed (signs such as "Only for local inhabitants" or "Local inhabitants allowed").

On assignment [of the *Reichskommissar*] Genss

Source: *LVVA, P-69. f., 1.a. apr., 1. l., pp 164-65.*

Document No. 31

Directions from the General Directorate of Education and Cultural Affairs to all heads of libraries about the removal of unwanted literature from circulation

Rīga, August 1, 1941

Authorized by the Propaganda Section of the Greater German Army, I order all libraries to remove from circulation all books and articles that are in the categories mentioned below, to draw up lists of these works, and send the lists to me no later than August 10, 1941.

The lists must be ordered alphabetically within the categories and, in addition to the author's name and the title of the book, the publisher and the date of publication must also be listed.

To fulfill this assignment, the following categories of books are considered unwanted and are to be removed from circulation:

1. Bolshevik literature in all languages that has flooded into bookstores since Latvia's occupation by the Bolsheviks;
2. Jewish literature in all languages;
3. Older German literature with Marxist tendencies;
4. Émigré literature (Albert de Lange, Querido, Behrmann-Fischer, Stockholm and other Jewish and non-Jewish literature of émigré publishers);
5. Foreign literature:
   a. English, French and American since 1933,
   b. Translations of English or French literature into German or Latvian languages;
6. Latvian literature with anti-German tendencies;

All of these categories of books refer to books with political, ideological, scientific, and literary content.

G. Brēmanis
Senior Inspector

Source: *LVVA, 4419.f., 2. apr., 1.l., p. 2. Original in Latvian.*

Directions of the Ministry of the Eastern Occupied Provinces to Ostland *Reichskommissar* H. Lohse concerning the reorganization of education in Baltic universities

Berlin, August 21, 1942

To guarantee changes of officials, teachers, lawyers, and economists in the new boards in the Estonian, Latvian, and Lithuanian General Province Self-administration, to supplement the November 19, 1941 decree, I order the following:

1. To completely re-order the lesson plan of the humanistic faculties of the universities in Tērbata, Rīga, Kaunas, and Vilnius for the practical needs of the Self-administration from the beginning of the 1942/1943 winter semester.

2. That is why special instructional courses for the preparation of Self-administration officials, judges, lawyers and prosecutors, as well as teachers, physicians, and economists, must be prepared in the above-mentioned university humanities faculties.

3. The plan of study of a special instructional course must accommodate the practical instruction of the mentioned professional groups. All branches of education that are reviewed as politically useless and that do not directly support the needs of the Self-administration are stricken from the educational plan. For example, in the special educational study plan of courses, lawyers must only take those educational subjects such as Self-administration rights, human rights, criminal rights, and procedural rights, but do not have to take state and national rights, social rights, history of rights, and philosophy of rights.

4. The special instructional course does not have to prepare for a change in scientific work.

5. Research assignments are only given to medical, physician, agricultural, and forestry faculties as well as to the educational staff of technical faculties, but not to the educational staff of the humanistic faculties.

6. After the educational work of the humanistic faculties is delimited, those academics freed from work are assigned to the Self-administration. They are to be prepared for their new position by retraining. Retraining occurs in special instructional courses.

7. Obligatory special instructional courses are drawn up in the German language in all semesters.

8. All of the needed directions are given by the Ostland *Reichskommissar*

Acting : Alfred Meyer

Source: *LVVA, P-69. f., 1.a. apr., 12. l., p. 90. Original in German..*

Comment: *During the war major changes took place in the policies regarding of education and culture. The original plans anticipated maximum restrictions on the possibilities of local inhabitants acquiring education. Universities and high schools were to be liquidated; Latvians were foreseen to need only primary and commercial education. Nevertheless, as the situation worsened at the front, policies became elastic. In November of 1941, universities were allowed to renew their work (except for the faculty of history and philosophy). High schools were also allowed to work. Still, some educational institutions were closed. Some school buildings were given over to the army for field hospitals and barracks. The educational system served the ideas of national socialist propaganda, and unwanted teachers and professors were released from their posts.*

DOCUMENTS NO. 33-37
INVOLVING LATVIA'S CITIZENS IN GERMANY'S ARMED FORCES

Document No. 33

From the report of the Liepāja Branch Commander of the Security Police and SD Command in Latvia, Kiegler, to the SS and Police garrison commander in Liepāja about the mood of the population with regard to the expected mobilization

Liepāja, February 17, 1942

[...] People speak agitatedly about the anticipated comprehensive mobilization of all Latvian men. The idea is being repeated that Germans want in this seemingly polite way to get the youngest generation into the army and then at the front to use them as cannon fodder. [...]

Kiegler
SS Untersturmführer

Source: *LVVA, P -38. f., 1.apr., 26. l., p. 29. Original in German.*

Document No. 34

Report concerning the founding of the Latvian Legion

Rīga, February 27, 1943

In recognition of the bravery of the existing volunteer Latvian units at the front, the *Führer* of Greater Germany has agreed to the formation of the Latvian SS Volunteer Legion. The newly founded Latvian Legion will include a part of the existing volunteer units as its core.

The Legion is founded as a unified battle unit added to Waffen -SS formations and the Latvian units will be commanded by Latvian officers.

All Latvian men from 17 to 45 years of age can join the Legion. Their involvement in service will continue until the end of the war. Supplies, wages, and uniforms will be the same as for German Waffen-SS formations. Supplies and benefits for relatives will be comparable to the German armed forces and be in concert with SS supply and benefits regulations.

Joining the Latvian volunteer SS Legion can be done verbally or in written form at any of the following places:

     1)   SS application office in Eastern Lands, in Rīga at Pleskava Street 16, 1st floor, telephone 33279;

     2)   All German police and gendarme posts;

     3)   All Latvian police posts.

Each Latvian who joins the Latvian Legion expresses with this act his unshakeable desire to defend his fatherland and to struggle with weapons in hand against Bolshevism and for the construction of the new Europe.

Source: *Rīkojumu Vēstnesis, February 28, 1943. Original in Latvian.*

Comment: *The Latvian Legion began to be formed in light of Hitler's order, dated, of February 10, 1943: "I order the creation of a Latvian SS volunteer legion. The size of the unit and its type will be dependent on the number of Latvian men in it. Adolf Hitler."*

Document No. 35

Instruction of the General Inspector of the Latvian Legion concerning the call-up into the Latvian Legion of men born in 1924, 1923, 1922 and 1918

Rīga, December 1, 1943

1. Based on the November 25th instruction about calling Latvian citizens into active military service, I command the calling into service in the Latvian SS Legion all men born in 1924, 1923, 1922, and 1918 who were Latvian citizens up to June 17, 1940.
   I set as the first day of the call-up, in the city of Rīga, December 6th of this year, but in the cities of Liepāja and Daugavpils and Latvia's administrative districts – December 13th of this year.

2. The rights conferred upon the Military District Commanders by the Latvian Military Service Law devolve: in Latvia's district administrative borders – to the district police chief, but in Rīga, Liepāja, and Daugavpils – to the city prefect.
   The Military Service affairs office is located in the office of the relevant district police chief, or city prefect, respectively.
   The call up is done by a Military Service Commission consisting of the following:
   In districts: chair – district police chief or his deputy – and the members – 2 doctors, one of which is from the Department of Health, but the other is a doctor chosen by the General Inspector of the Latvian Legion.
   In Rīga, Liepāja and Daugavpils: - the city prefect or his deputy and members – 2 doctors, one from the Department of Health, but the other – a doctor chosen by the General Inspector of the Latvian Legion.
   Note 1: The work of the Military Service Commission is fulfilled by the district police chief, or persons chosen by the city prefects, respectively.
   Note 2: In Rīga, several auxiliary Military Service Commissions are to be established.

3. Detailed instructions for the arrival of citizens to the medical commission's examination are issued by the district police chief, or city prefects, respectively.

4. All persons called up must bring with them: passport, military service record, provisions for 2 days, change of underwear (shirt, underpants, socks), if possible high boots, blanket, kettle or clay bowl, spoon, knife, fork, cup, soap, shaving kit, tooth brush, comb, mirror, etc., as well as wrapping material for the return of civilian clothing. Compensation will be made for boots and underwear.
   Note: Together with the called-up citizens, the representative of the parish government and labor board must also come to the commission.

5. Those citizens born in 1923 and 1924, whose passports are already stamped showing an exemption from military service in the Legion due to sickness, do not have to arrive to the call-up.

6. All institutions, enterprises and private persons must issue personal account documents

and relieve from employment responsibilities all called-up persons by the day of their call-up.

7. Citizens exempted from active military service by the decision of the Military Service Commission must, without delay, return to their existing place of work.

8. Military instructors, soldiers and citizens without military experience between 17 and 45 years of age may apply for voluntary service in the Legion at the board of the District police chief and city prefect, respectively.

9. Those found unfit and temporarily exempted will have a corresponding seal put in their passports.

10. Punishment threatens those evading the call-up, according to Latvia's military and state-of-war laws.

11. The necessary quarters for assembly and for the work of the military service commission are provided and outfitted by the local Self-government institutions following the directions of the Chair of the Military Services Commission.

12. All expenses incurred in connection with the draft are covered according to Latvia's Military Service Law, paragraph 74.

General Inspector of the Latvian Legion
General R. Bangerskis

Source: *Rīkojumu Vēstnesis, December 3, 1941. Original in Latvian.*

Document No. 36

Information in the newspaper *Tēvija* about the warning of the Rīga Prefect, R. Stieglitz, regarding avoidance of the call-up to the Legion

February 26, 1944

Final Warning

On February 24th of this year, Rīga Prefect R. Stieglitz has ordered in an instruction that all Latvian citizens born from 1906-1918, and 1919-1921 are called up to serve in the Latvian Legion.

With this and previous examinations, the physical examination of Latvian citizens born between 1906 and 1924 will end completely.

Even though in general citizens in the call-up ages, as shown by statistics, have conscientiously fulfilled their responsibility to their native land and their nation, there are signs that one or another unconscientious citizen has not followed the instruction and has not arrived at the examination at the defined time and place.

The Rīga Prefect declares that the examinations and call-up with respect to specific industrial enterprises will end this year on February 26th. Beginning Sunday, February 27th, the examinations will be done in alphabetic order in accordance with the instructions of the Prefect of February 24th of this year. In Rīga the examination and call-up will end on March 3rd of this year.

At that point, there will begin the general examination of all men in the call-up years. Examinations will be done in specified houses for entire blocks of cities, industrial enterprises, on streets, in public meeting places and elsewhere.

The supervisory institutions in these jurisdictions declare that unconscientious citizens who refrain from fulfilling their responsibility to their nation at this decisive moment and have not heeded the instructions, will not be able to live unaffected. Sooner or later they will receive the punishment they have earned.

The Rīga Prefect for one last time warns and invites all of Latvia's citizens in the mentioned years who for some reason have not appeared before the examination commission to do so without delay. With this, they are given one more opportunity to fulfill their responsibilities.

Those that do not follow this last warning and do not arrive at the examination commission and refrain from being called into the Latvian Legions will be given over to extra-ordinary Military Courts, where they face punishments according to laws of war and state of war.

Source: *Tēvija, February 26, 1944. Original in Latvian.*

Document No. 37

Top Secret Report of the People's Commissar of State Security of the USSR, V. Merkulov, to the Latvian Communist Party Central Committee about the Latvian Legion

USSR
State Security   <u>COMPLETELY SECRET</u>
People's Commissariat   Personal only
July 24, 1943
Number 1289/M
Moscow

Latvia's C(B)P Central Committee

To Comrade Kalnbērziņš

The USSR SSPK has obtained information that the Germans on Latvia's territory are forming the so-called "Latvian SS Legion."

The Germans began to form the "Legion" at the end of February 1943.

Formally, it is declared that the "Legion" is formed on the basis of volunteerism, but in fact the "Legion" was formed by mobilizing men by age groups under threat of force.

At the end of February, and the beginning of March of 1943, men born from 1919 to 1924 received notices at their places of residence with directions to report to police posts where they had to fill out registration cards and, afterward, had to go to a medical examination commission.

Those working in factories that fill orders for the German army and those working for militarized institutions (police) are exempt from being drafted into the "Legion."

The mobilized persons, according to their own wishes, are counted as either in the Latvian Legion, in German Army Auxiliary units, or are sent to Defense Construction.

The material advantages of the "Legion" in terms of security, compared to the auxiliary units of the German army and the defense work, has led to the majority of the mobilized choosing to go into the "Legion."

The formation of the first "Legion" unit took lasted until the middle of March. During this time, one regiment was formed, and Colonel Apsītis (unknown to the USSR SSPK) was appointed as its commander.

This year on March 28th, in Rīga, the "Legionnaires" took an oath. Each legionnaire gave the following oath:

"In the name of God, I promise solemnly in the struggle against Bolshevism an unlimited obedience to the supreme commander of the German military forces, Adolf Hitler; and as a brave soldier, I will always be ready to give my life for this oath." [...]

After the men born from 1919 to 1924 were mobilized, this year in April in Latvia there was the registration of another seven-year period – those born from 1912 to 1918 – who are also expected to be mobilized into the "Latvian Legion."

This year on May 16th, information was received that in Latvia there was mobilization of those born beginning in 1899, including with them fighters from units of the volunteer partisan groups. The "Legion" assembly points are organized in many of Latvia's district cities.

According to agents' information in our possession, the mood of the mobilized is unstable. We note facts about attempts to avoid mobilization and about desertions from the Legion. Many are hiding in the woods.

In Zilupe the mobilized sang Soviet songs, in Ludza there was a clash between the mobilized and the police.

Of the 500 people mobilized in the four districts of Latgale, 100 people fled even before being sent to their assembly point.

There are reports that in Rīga during the first half of April this year there was an armed "Legionnaire" clash with police (The reports are being confirmed).

According to the latest received information from agents in Latvia there have been nine Latvian regiments formed that have been sent to the Leningrad front and are concentrated in the region of Krasnogvardejsk.

The highest command ranks of the "Latvian Legion" are primarily German officers; the middle command ranks are occupied by former officers of Latvia's army.

The "Legion" has been created according to the principles of the German army. The uniforms are partially those of the former Latvia army and partially the Waffen-SS. "Legionnaires" are equipped with German, Czech, and Romanian weapons.

SSR Union State Security People's Commissar
(Merkulov)

<u>Sent to:</u>
Comrade Kalnbērziņš
Comrade Lācis

Source: *LVA PA, 101.f., 5. apr., 7. l, pp. 38-40. Original in Russian.*

Documents No. 38-41
Conscription of persons into the Reich Labor Service

Document No. 38

Information about the creation of labor camps for violators of labor discipline

March 20, 1942

The deputy chair of the Rīga Labor Board, Schmutzler, informed us: There are several confirmed occurrences in the city of Rīga and in the districts of the Rīga provincial *Kommissars* in which the residents consciously refrain from work and wander from one work place to another; even when in a workplace that is organized by the Labor Board, only 8 people show up of 100 people sent to work there. The majority of these wanderers are younger people who are able to labor. In Germany, for multiple absences from work and of wandering, the latter often having a criminal character, the punishment according to the law is the death penalty.

With the instruction of October 6th of last year, the *Reichskommissar* gave the Labor Board the right to punish those avoiding work or take up wandering with 6 weeks in a workhouse and a fine of 1,000 marks. In more serious cases, the guilty parties can be turned over for punishment to the German extraordinary courts.

In order to try to rehabilitate and to acclimate to work those that wander and are lazy and are not changed at all by threats or money fines, the Labor Board has organized in Rīga a labor camp. Here wanderers and repeat offenders of labor discipline are placed from 2 to 6 weeks. During this time the wanderers do not receive wages. If they show considerable effort in their work and promise to work [in the future], they can be freed from the labor camp before the termination of their sentence. This gives the guilty the ability to decide on their own – conscientious and honorable work for a wage, or compulsory work without a wage.

The goal of the Labor Board is not to punish the population, but the current conditions of war make such conditions necessary. In many cases, the masses do not understand or do not want to understand that their trade or work is needed for military-industrial support. When such people are transferred to a different place of work they feel mistreated and in the end feel resentful and they begin to wander. This phenomenon is temporary, and anyone who is not working in their trade or profession will be able to return to their beloved place of work at the end of the war or even sooner. But until that time, they must take on all of their assignments that are necessary for us to accomplish our *Führer's* declared goal – a New Europe.

The Labor camp in Rīga has currently been organized only for men.

Source: *Tēvija, March 20, 1942. Original in Latvian.*

Instructions by the *Reichsminister* of the Eastern Occupied Provinces, A. Rosenberg, concerning the registration of local population for fulfilling the assignments of total war

Berlin, March 29, 1943

In total war, such as Greater Germany and its allies are fighting in order to save Europe from Bolshevism , the occupied Eastern provinces must participate in order to accomplish the final victory. In order to reach this collective goal, I order, based on the 8th paragraph of the *Führer's* decree of July 17, 1941, concerning governance in the newly occupied Eastern Provinces, the following:

1.

All men from a full fifteen years of age to a full 65 years of age, and local women from a full 15 years of age until a full 45 years of age, who [are native to and] live in the occupied Eastern provinces and do not belong to the groups mentioned in paragraph 2, in line with the instructions of the *Reichskommissar,* must register at the jurisdictional regional *Kommissar* (Labor Board) of their place of residence.

2.

The following are exempt from registering:
1.   Foreigners;
2.   Men and women who are employed in service to the German military or in some official place of service;
3.   Men and women who are working primarily in the health professions;
4.   Clergy.

Reichskommissars are authorized to allow other exceptions to registration, particularly expectant mothers and women with children under 14 years of age, as well as school children who attend a general education school (high school or also some school of continuing education).

3.

The responsibility of those registering is to show to the regional *Kommissar* (Labor Board), on request, all necessary documents, as well as to give all relevant information. The region *Kommissar* (Labor Board) can also make personal visits [to inspect a case].

4.

Those who must register but violate the instructions in this decree will be punished in the relevant range of punishments by the regional *Kommissar*, and in serious cases on the request of the regional *Kommissar* (Labor Board) apply prison and monetary punishment, or one of the above.

5.

The instructions are in force from the day of their publication.

Eastern *Reichsminister* Rosenberg

Source: *Rīkojumu Vēstnesis, July 8, 1943. Original in Latvian.*

Comment: *By reference to this decree, an entire age-group of persons was mobilized for the Legion and for labor service in Latvia in 1943. Priority were given to the Legion, but about 4,800 people who were unfit for military service were placed in the labor service.*

Registration for the labor force in Latvia started in November of 1941 and involved the possibility of deportation to Germany, which paralleled the recruiting of volunteers. By the end of 1941, the authorities were able to recruit about 2,000 people from all of the Baltic. In the spring of 1942, the first mass deportation of labor to Germany took place -- the so-called "new farmers" action. At that time the farmers who had received land in 1940-1941 from the Soviet authorities were deported as politically unreliable (2,500 people). At the same time, volunteer recruitment continued, although its compulsory nature remained disguised. In May and June of 1942, the next mass action of rounding up persons happened in Latgale. In this, the leadership of the Latvian Self-Administration became involved, suggesting the deportation of "foreign national elements" – the local Russians and Poles and also of persons who were suspected of supporting partisans. As a result, 8,000 persons were sent to Germany, among them only 900 real volunteers. In August of 1943, a new action occurred in Latgale in which more than 3,000 persons were taken, of whom 1,061 were children younger than 14 years. Altogether as a result of these three actions about 12,800 people were sent to Germany by force. The total number of Latvia's residents sent to Germany, including those who were voluntarily recruited to work by the end of 1943, numbered about 15,900. With these actions the forced recruiting of labor for work in Germany ended.

At the beginning of October 1944, before the German armed forces retreated from Rīga, there took place organized hunts for civilian residents in the city in order to help the labor force in Germany – about 6,000 people were taken and these were not even given permission to contact their relatives before departure.

Document No. 40

Instructions of the Chief *Generaldirektor*, O. Dankers, concerning the involvement of workers in business enterprises in constructing fortifications
Rīga, August 17, 1944

1.

1. All workers in enterprises are now involved in the construction of fortifications if they are able to do this work, except those in enterprises dealing with the food supply, who will receive specific instructions.
2. Men older than 60 years of age, and women older than 55 years of age, are exempt from work on the construction of fortifications. This instruction does not apply to these people.

2.

1. The request for enterprises to participate in the construction of fortifications will be given directly over the telephone or over the radio to institutions capable of supplying such labor force or to organizations that are subordinate to the relevant enterprises.
2. The request will be read on the radio during the reading of the news, that is at 6:15; 12:45; 16:45; 21:00.

3.

1. All who work in an enterprise, men and women, must submit to participation in the request.
2. Those working must arrive at the meeting place noted in the request at the specified time and in a formation under the leadership of the enterprise leader or his authorized person.

4.

Participation is expected for a few weeks.

5.

1. The people participating must bring bedding and other goods necessary for sleeping overnight in a dormitory, dishes for food, warm clothing and work tools if possible, such as: shovels, axes, and saws.
2. Food must be brought for two days; afterwards, foodstuffs will be provided by the Army […]

8.

All those people, men and women, that do not belong to some enterprise and have not yet registered for work on the construction of fortifications must immediately go to the Rīga Labor Board on Yorck (Aizsarga) Street) 29/31, in the courtyard house at the agricultural division, for assignment to work in the construction of fortifications. […]

10.

Violators of this instruction face punishment according to the August 4, 1944, Report of the *Reichskommissar* concerning the hanging of saboteurs.

11.

This instruction is in force from August 17, 1944.

First *Generaldirektor* O. Dankers

Source: *Rīkojumu Vēstnesis, August 18, 1944. Original in Latvian.*

Information about the shooting deaths of saboteurs in the newspaper *Tēvija*

August 21, 1944

(ON) On August 21st of this year, the following were shot to death: the Lithuanian Balis Lacas, born March 18, 1900, the Russian Jānis Sutavs, born September 13, 1897, the Russian Aleksejs Tkajuks, born September 19, 1912, the Latvian Vladislavs Maracinskis, born July 5, 1906, and the Russian Nikolajs Oničenko, born June 12, 1925.

The above were detained by security guards because they had left their places of employment without permission, hidden from fortification work, and by wandering around had refrained from work.

Source: *Tēvija, August 21, 1944. Original in Latvian.*

DOCUMENTS NO. 42-43
RESISTANCE MOVEMENT

Document No. 42

The (draft) intelligence report of Latvia's Central Council to the General Inspector of the Latvian Legions, R. Bangerskis

Until February 29, 1944

Very respected Mr. General!

The enemy from the East is again threateningly approaching Latvia. That is the same enemy whose armed forces on June 17, 1940, occupied the Republic of Latvia militarily; the same power that soon after occupation issued, supposedly in the name of our nation, an electoral law for Latvia's *Saeima*, but afterward did not even follow the form of this supposedly democratic election; crudely violated it; only allowed one, communists and their followers, list; and still falsified the results of the elections. The results of course could not and did not produce representatives of the nation, but rather appointees of the Russian occupying power.

These appointees decided to plead to the Soviet Union that it accept the independent Republic of Latvia into its fold. After that, they declared to the entire world that the Republic of Latvia joined voluntarily. The same thing, in the same way and at the same time, happened in the independent Republics of Estonia and Lithuania.

The forced annexation of Latvia to the Soviet Union was done crudely, violating the Constitution of the Republic of Latvia and the mutual treaties between Latvia and the Soviet Union, the Pact of the League of Nations, and a whole list of international treaties. The forced annexation of Latvia to the Soviet Union is not recognized in the philosophy of international justice.

It unarguably follows from the above that according to the norms of international justice the Republic of Latvia rightfully continues to exist. That is why the official position of the Soviet Union's government and press, as well as the view of some other foreign newspapers, namely, that Latvia is a component part of the Soviet Union and should again be included into the Soviet Union, have no juridical basis. It is also undeniable that the position of the current German occupational power is unfounded, namely, that Latvia had been a component part of the Soviet Union. The practical demonstration of this position is shown in all of the political and economic behavior of the German occupational power. This approach can not be reconciled with the completed mobilization of Latvia's inhabitants into the German armed forces by the German occupational power. This kind of behavior deeply insults our nation and creates in it a deep and justified dissatisfaction.

The legal consciousness and self-respect of the Latvian nation supports the mobilization of Latvia's Army announced in the name of the legal organs of the state of Latvia state and for the defense of the state Latvia. Only such a mobilization would fully use our military power, buttressing and increasing our fighting ability.

According to our understanding of the development of the war, the moment has truly arrived when the life of our nation is threatened, the very essence of our nation - the decisive moment has come: to be or not to be.

According to all the laws of nature and man, no one can deny us the right to defend ourselves if our nation and its very essence is threatened.

Based on this understanding, we proclaim the national will of Latvia and its readiness to defend with all possible force and abilities the borders of Latvia against the attacking enemy.

Having said this, we, the undersigned, declare in the name of Latvian nation the following expectations:

1. Immediately to renew the sovereignty of he Republic of Latvia;
2. To create, according to the Constitution of 1922 of the Republic of Latvia which is still in force, a coalition-based government that would gather around it all of the Latvian nation;
3. The most important assignments of this government must be: the renewal of the state apparatus and the Army of Latvia, the defense of the territory of the state of Latvia against the threatened Soviet invasion and – as far as it is possible in war conditions – the establishment of diplomatic relations with foreign countries, first with those that recognize our declared national will and support the military challenge we face – the defense of Latvia's state.

In our view, we will pursue the establishment of close a union with Estonia and Lithuania and the transformation of this union into a Confederation of Baltic States, if the mentioned states were to agree.

Declaring this as our nation's unambiguous viewpoint concerning the legal nature of our sovereignty and our desire to renew state sovereignty, as well as undertaking to use all our powers and all our abilities to defend the state of Latvia against the attacker – we beseech you, highly respected Mr. General, to please inform the persons in power of our nation's unambiguous viewpoint and unshakeable desire, [namely, the persons who can objectively understand the meaning and necessity of the renewal of the Republic of Latvia, and who could support the Republic of Latvia's struggle for national independence and the for the security of our territory.

Signing this declaration, we have the honor of expressing to you, much esteemed Mr. General, our deep declaration of respect.

Source: *Andersons, pp. 114-146. Original in Latvian.*

Comment: *At the end of 1941, national resistance groups began to spontaneously form in Latvia; when discovered, these groups were usually liquidated.*
Latvia's Central Council (LCC) became the united national resistance center. It was created on August 13, 1943, by representatives of the four largest political parties of Latvia's last Saeima.

The LCC's first chair was Konstantīns Čakste. The LCC saw itself as the only democratic, national resistance movement that under the conditions of occupation had the right to represent all of the nation of Latvia with respect to the Constitution and laws of independent Latvia.

The LCC maintained close contacts with similar organizations in Lithuania and Estonia, informed the Western states the Nazi war crimes in Latvia, and attempted military maneuvers in the territory of Latvia.

The published memorandum (Document No. 42) had an important role in the work of the LCC. It was signed by 190 noted social and political figures. On February 29, 1944, the memorandum was taken to Sweden. It was intended to be submitted to the governments of other states, but it did not get that far.

In order to protect the signatories from reprisals, the LCC submitted the memorandum to General Inspector of the Latvian Legion, General R. Bangerskis, on March 22. He believed, however, that it would be useless and even dangerous to submit it to the German government and kept it to himself.

Arrests by the SD in April 1944 were a great blow to the work of the LCC. K. Čakste was arrested, together with a group of other LCC participants. They were put into concentration camps. K. Čakste died while imprisoned in Germany at the beginning of 1945.

The most far-reaching work accomplished by the LCC was the organizing of refugee boats to Sweden from the summer of 1944 until the end of the war. These took several thousand persons fleeing from both occupying powers across the Baltic Sea.

The 1,800 men organized around General Jānis Kurelis in the summer of 1944 can be seen as the LCC's military force. They were to be the core of a new national liberation army, because the Latvian Legion was incapable of being transformed into such a force.

In November and December of 1944, German armed forces began operations against the "Kurelieši" and, as a result, they were disbanded or liquidated. Seven "Kurelieši" staff officers were tried by the Germans and shot to death; many of the soldiers were deported to concentration camps in Germany.

Document No. 43

From the sentence imposed on LCC member, Eduards Andersons, by the Military Tribunal of the Armed Forces of the Interior Ministry of the Latvian SSR

Secret
Copy number 6

Sentence 1339
In the name of the Union of Soviet Socialist Republics

On the 28th day of August, 1946, in a closed session of the Military Tribunal of the Armed Forces of the Latvian SSR Ministry of the Interior, at the Rīga Municipal Military tribunal location. Consisting of: Chair – Captain of Justice Siņickis; members: senior lieutenant Borunovs, and junior lieutenant Zoremba, secretary – Junior Lieutenant of Justice Fiļipova, with the participation of the staff translator Hasana.

Examining indictment No. 2590 against Andersons, Eduards, son of Ernests, born in 1919, Ance parish in Buku farmstead in the Ventspils district of the Latvian SSR, Latvian, citizen of the USSR, service worker, until his arrest lived illegally, with middle-range education, non-party, unmarried, never tried in court, did not serve in the Red Army – [...]

Determined:

In the time period when the territory of the Latvian SSR was occupied by German armed forces, in 1943, the former party leaders of bourgeois Latvia established an illegal, nationalist organization, "Latvia's Central Council" – LCC, whose chief headquarters was located abroad.

This organization had as its goal the renewal of the bourgeois order in Latvia with the help of other imperialist states.

In order to realize its goals, "LCC" sent its members abroad as agents and spies to do organizational work, that is, to recruit from anti-Soviet elements new members and to involve them in the organization.

In addition, the "Latvia's Central Council" led the organizing of bandit formations in Latvia's territory and gave them directions for operational work; therefore, it was their guiding center.

The accused ANDERSONS, being hostile to the Soviet order, found himself beyond the borders in a foreign country and joined the LCC in 1943; until the moment of his arrest, he was involved in important operational assignments for the Center.

In 1944 and 1945, ANDERSONS was repeatedly sent into Latvia, transported secret instructions to the "LCC" leadership, radio receivers, radio transmitters; established contacts with "LCC" members in Rīga and other cities in the Latvian SSR; worked to recruit "LCC" members; gathered news of a secretive nature and carried them to the "LCC" aboard.

In October of 1945, a conference of "LCC" members in Rīga led by the accused ANDERSONS decided:

1. To organize the publication of an illegal newspaper in the name of the "LCC."
2. To establish contacts with bandit formations in Latvia's territory and radio contact with the "LCC" center.
3. To gather news of a secretive character and with others to deal with questions related to the leading of bandit formations.

After this conference, ANDERSONS, being in Riga and Kurzeme illegally, wrote a string of articles with openly anti-Soviet content for publication in the newspapers, and gathered news of a secretive nature that he was preparing to send to the "LCC" abroad. […]

Based on the presented evidence, the Military Tribunal found ANDERSONS guilty according to the 319th and 320th paragraphs of the RSFSR Criminal Process Code, -

Sentence

ANDERSONS, Eduards son of Ernests, according to the part 1a of the 58th paragraph of the RSFSR Criminal Code, to be punished with the supreme punishment, execution by shooting and confiscation all of his personal belongings and property. […]

The sentence can be appealed to the USSR Supreme Court Military Collegium within 72 hours from the moment when the sentenced is given a written copy of the sentence by the Military Tribunal that prepared it.

The original is appropriately signed

Latvian SSR Ministry of Interior Armed Forces Military Tribunal Seal

Copy is correct: Chair of the Investigation: signature of Captain of Justice Siņickij

Source: *LVA, 1986.f. 1. apr., 28636. l., vol. 2, pp. 80-81 (copy of original). Original in Russian.*

Comment: *After the capitulation of Nazi Germany, the LCC continued to work underground in the territory of Latvia. The LCC headquarters, after the war, was in Sweden. The Riga LCC group, under the leadership of Voldemārs Mežaks, worked in the city of Rīga and in the harbor city of Ventspils. The LCC did not pursue armed actions against Soviet institutions, but used a holding strategy by waiting for the so-called "x-hour" when the international situation would change and the Western powers would help renew Latvia's independence.*

Many of the participants in the LCC were arrested in the first months of the second Soviet occupation. In the fall of 1945, an LCC group was arrested after illegally arriving from Sweden in order to activate the organization and to resume the radio contacts that had ended after the war. The completely liquidation of all such groups in Latvia followed immediately. Individual LCC members avoided repression, but as an organization the LCC ceased to exist. .

Two participants in the LCC received the death penalty. The E. Andersons describe in the above document was one of them.

DOCUMENTS No. 44-45
THE USA DISPLACED PERSONS COMMISSION AND THE LATVIAN LEGION

Document No. 44

Letter of the Latvian *chargé d'affaires* in Washington, J. Feldmanis, to a member of the USA's Displaced Persons (refugees) Commission, N. Rosenfield, concerning the differences between the *Waffen* SS and Latvian Legion

August 2, 1950

Dear Mr. Rosenfield,

Supplementing our conversation of July 24, 1950, concerning Latvian refugees — the former soldiers of the Latvian Legion -- I have the honor to present to you some considerations and documents in my possession.

You will find enclosed my memorandum to the Secretary of State on July 21, 1949, which contains general information concerning this question.

In my *aide-memoire* of January 13, 1950, I explained the difference between the German SS and the Latvian Legion. I must stress that the soldiers of the Latvian Legion never had to perform other than military duties. Consequently, no member of the Latvian Legion participated in the dishonorable actions against the Jewish populations which were organized and executed only by the German *Waffen* SS. The latter were members of the Nationalist-Socialist Party and each had his party number. The Latvian soldiers of the Latvian Legion had no such number, of course, and were not members of the Nazi Party. The soldiers of the Latvian Legion were forbidden by an order of SS *Hauptamt* to wear the insignia "SS," but were obliged to wear a shield bearing Latvian colors; only one case is known where a Latvian officer was decorated by the Germans and received recognition as an *SS-man*. This caused astonishment among the Germans, and later it appeared that it had been a mistake. The Latvian soldiers, as a general practice, received previously worn uniforms of the members of the German SS. Before the Latvian soldiers could use this uniform, they were ordered to remove all SS insignia. At this time, the SS formation was a very much privileged one, and the Germans never thought of extending these privileges to the Latvian soldiers, who were not considered as equals of the Germans, according to their race theory.

Further, you will find a copy from a document of the Nuremberg trial, which indicates that all men fit for service were sent into the Legion. Those who were not 100% fit were sent to the Commander of the *Wehrmacht* as auxiliaries, and those who were fit for work only were placed at the disposal of *Gauleiter* Saukel, Chief of Forced Labor in Germany.

I have included here information giving the following number of mobilized men in Latvia:

Mobilized in the Latvian Legion until 1-7-44	43,564
Wehrmacht Auxiliary Force	22,744
Anti-Aircraft Pioneers	1,600
Mobilized during the period 1.7.44 to 18.8.44	13,333
Police Auxiliary Force	22,262

Remark:

The following are approximate numbers.

At the first mobilization in Feb./March 1943, there were mobilized:

a.	In the Legion	15,000
b.	*Wehrmacht* Auxiliary Force	25,000
c.	Forced Labor Service	10,000

It results that in the Latvian Legion, there were approximately 57,000 men. During our conversation, you showed me a copy of a document from the Nuremberg trial, according to which some 300 *Waffen- SS* men participated in an anti-Jewish action in Latvia. I am quite sure that they were not Latvians. And, even if we will admit that among these 300 war criminals there were also a number of Latvians, the 57,000 honest Latvians should not be held responsible for the actions in which they have never participated.

If you should wish to have any further information in this matter, I am glad to offer my full assistance.

Very truly yours,

J. Feldmanis, *chargé d'affaires* of Latvia

Source: *Latvian Legion, pp. 92-93 . Original in English.*

Document No. 45

Reply of H.N. Rosenfield to J. Feldmanis

September 12, 1950

Dear Dr. Feldmanis:

Please pardon the delayed acknowledgment of your letter of August 2, 1950. By now, of course, you know the decision of the Commission. It has approved the following motion:

"That the Baltic Waffen SS. Units (Baltic Legions) are to be considered as separate and distinct in terms of purpose, ideology, activities, and qualifications for membership from the German SS, and therefore the Commission holds them not to be a movement hostile to the Government of the United States under Section 13 of the Displaced Persons Act, as amended."

Sincerely yours,

Harry N. Rosenfield
Commissioner

Source: *Latvian Legion, pp. 93-93. Original in English.*

PART IV: SOVIET TOTALITARIANISM IN LATVIA 1945-1991

As units of the Red Army approached the territory of Latvia, the Latvian Communist Party's Central Committee, which had continued to operate after fleeing to the USSR at the end of June 1941, had already received orders in Moscow to undertake the necessary preparations for restoring the Soviet system so as to avoid an *interregnum* period of confused authority. Beginning in the first half of 1944, so-called "operational groups" began to form in Moscow who were to assume power on the ground. These groups included members of the Party and the local soviets, with the leaders of the Latvian Communist Party Central Committee and the Council of People's Commissars at their head. The operational groups attached to the 1st, 2nd, and 3rd Baltic Front Armies followed the Red Army and immediately after a region's "liberation" started the process of the region's reacquisition. Thus, for example, in the city of Abrene, representatives of Party institutions and the soviet arrived two hours after the city was freed of German control.[40] One of the most important tasks of these operational groups was to prevent local initiatives in re-creating local administrative bodies. Power was immediately assumed by the Red Army and the LC(B)P district, municipal, or parish committees and their executive committees.

In August of 1944, the Presidium of the Supreme Soviet of the USSR ratified a decree called "About the creation of Pskov Province within the USSR." A part of Latvia's territory was to be absorbed by the USSR, namely, six parishes of Abrene District (in northeastern Latvia) and the city of Abrene itself. Latvia thus lost 1,202 square kilometers of its territory. This decision by Moscow was formulated allegedly to meet the demands of the local inhabitants, even though until August of 1944, neither the Supreme Soviet of the USSR nor the Supreme Soviet of the Latvian SSR had received any such demands, nor could they have received them because units of the Red Army had only just come into these regions (see Document No. 9).

The Red Army behaved on the territory of Latvia not as if it were in liberated territory of a USSR union republic, but as if in an occupied state (see Documents No. 2, 3, 4). Local authorities were forced to comply with all demands, notwithstanding the fact that the inhabitants of Latvia and the land itself had suffered massive losses (see Document No. 5). The Red Army's behavior towards the local population in this respect was even more brutal than the behavior of the German *Wehrmacht*.

The territorial administrative divisions of Latvia were harmonized with those existing in the USSR. By a decree of the Presidium of the Supreme Soviet of the Latvian SSR, on December 31, 1949, "districts" and "parishes" were dissolved. Until the Soviet occupation, the territory of the Republic of Latvia, in line with the Constitution of 1922, consisted of the regions of Vidzeme, Latgale, Kurzeme, and Zemgale, and was further divided into 19 districts and 517 parishes. Now, in their place, 58 rural regions were created that included 1,358 hamlets. In later years many of the rural regions were consolidated. In the middle of the 1980s there were 26 rural regions, 7 municipalities under Republic jurisdiction (the capital city Rīga, as well as the cities of Ventspils, Daugavpils, Jelgava, Liepāja, Rēzekne, and Jūrmala), and 49 municipalities under the jurisdiction of regions. The structure of the Latvian Communist Party (until 1952 the Latvian Communist [Bolshevik] Party) and its local Soviets was reformulated to correspond with these new divisions (in each region there was a Party Committee and a Soviet Executive Committee).

One of the carefully obscured facts in the Soviet Union was the scope of the exploitation in post-war years of the prisoners of war from Nazi Germany. Tens of thousands of prisoners of war, placed in special camps, worked in Latvia (see Documents No. 11-13). They were allowed to return to their homeland only at the end of the 1940s, although many had died earlier. To this day there are building and other structures in Latvia which were built or reconstructed by prisoners of war.

The totalitarian system was grounded in the concept of "the socialist transformation of all spheres of societal life." Correspondingly, the "plan of socialist construction" in the Latvian SSR necessarily included the collectivization of agriculture, industrialization, and a cultural revolution.

One of the first steps towards collectivization was a "new" Soviet agrarian reform. On September 7, 1944, the Presidium of the Supreme Soviet of the Latvian SSR ratified the decree "About changes and supplements to the July 29, 1940, law on land." The goal of this new reform – which was very radical in contrast with the 1940 reform – was to create tiny, economically unviable farms in the countryside that could later be brought easily into the collectivization process (the average size of a farm was 12-13 hectares). In 1940, the maximum size of a farm had been defined as 30 hectares. In the years after the war, farms were taxed in money and in kind, with these levies increasing annually. Farmers also had to do labor services such as road construction and the cutting of lumber. Harsh punishment was imposed on those who could not pay the ever-increasing taxes (see Document No. 15). Nevertheless, despite all of these difficulties, until 1947 these small farms not only fulfilled the quotas of the state plan, but also supplied urban population with food. There was no starvation in Latvia in the post-war years as there was in other regions of the Soviet Union. These individual farms should have been saved for their economic usefulness, but, in the new regime, political interests were paramount. "The class approach" was very clearly reflected in tax policies that were in reality meant to further the dissolution of private farms (see Documents No. 16 and 17).

Even though the first *kolkhozes* were created in Latvia in 1946, farmers did not want to join them. More often than not, they sold all of their possessions and left for the cities. In 1947, the Central Committee of the CPSU and the Council of Ministers of the USSR ratified a special decree about the introduction of collectivization into the Latvian SSR, Lithuanian SSR, and Estonian SSR. This meant a change in the direction of the Latvian Communist Party's agricultural policies – *kolkhozes* were to be formed by force. Still, until the mass deportations of March 25, 1949, only about 10% of private farms had joined the *kolkhozes*. The 1949 deportation, executed according to a worked-out plan, was meant to not only drive the farmers into the *kolkhozes*, but to create an atmosphere of fear in general society. By July of 1949, almost 80% of private farms had entered *kolkhozes*, and by 1950 – 90%. Comprehensive collectivization had been accomplished. This action had catastrophic consequences. As late as 1960, agricultural production had not returned to the levels of pre-war Latvia.

In the 1950s, there took place a substantial migration of rural people to the cities. This process continued in subsequent decades. Due to state subsidies, successful collective farms also had emerged by 1970. Their numbers were small, however, and the greater part of their income did not come from agricultural production but from supplemental activities (lumber, preserves, winemaking).

The March 25, 1949, mass deportations constituted the most wide-ranging act of Stalinist terror in Latvia (see Documents No. 18-25). Archival material now available, however, demonstrates that repressive activities against the inhabitants of Latvia began right after the war with the second occupation (see Document No. 26). After Stalin's death in 1953, the scale of repression diminished. During the second half of the 1950s, those deported to the GULAG camps who were still alive began to return. Their confiscated possessions, houses, and apartments were not returned to them, however. Furthermore, these persons continued to be viewed as politically unreliable, and had to live under close surveillance by the security services (see Document No. 29).

During the first post-war years, there were in Latvia many *non-violent* protest groups, including the "Central Council" (see Documents No. 29 and 32), that believed in the "x-hour theory" (i.e. liberation by the Western allies). They consisted primarily of grade-school and university students, clergy and other members of the intelligentsia (see Document No. 33).

Members of *armed* resistance groups were most often former officers, policemen, bureaucrats, and prosperous farmers. Armed resistance against Soviet power began with Nazi Germany's "small war" policy that included the leaving of armed groups of soldiers of Latvian nationality in the Soviet army's rear in 1944. Such groups formed in Vidzeme and Latgale from deserters of both the Latvian

Legion and the Red Army that did not want to be subordinated to either occupational power. After Nazi Germany's capitulation, in the so-called "Kurzeme kettle," legionnaires who did not surrender joined the ranks of the armed national resistance. After the mass deportations of March 25, 1949, many rural inhabitants also joined the resistance. The largest of these armed resistance groups were eliminated by units of the NKVD armed forces in the first post-war years, but numerically smaller groups existed until the middle of the 1950s, by which time the "national partisans" had suffered complete military and political defeat. In the first post-war years, about 10,000 persons participated in the resistance, and about 3,000 were killed. About an equal number were killed among supporters of Soviet power. It must be noted that the majority of those that fell on the national partisan side were members of armed units, while on the side of the defenders of Soviet power those killed included Communist Party members, members of the Komsomol, NKVD informants, and other unarmed Soviet activists.

In the border regions of the country, the resistance movement established links with the Lithuanian and Estonian resistance, but overall these contacts remained weak. Also, the Latvian resistance movement was not unified; it consisted of regional partisan groups that were unable to unite.

The resistance movement did not receive aid from foreign countries. Its support came only from local inhabitants. It is difficult, however, to judge how wide that support was.

Later in the 1950s, a few dissident groups were formed. These persons believed that nothing could be accomplished against Soviet power using armed struggle, and that armed struggle only hurt the interests of local populations. Different forms of nonviolent protest continued throughout the entire time of Soviet rule (see Documents No. 35 -38).

Industrialization as such is a normal developmental step for any modern state. In the Latvian SSR, however, there took place a forced "socialist industrialization." This meant, first of all, that the emphasis was on the development of heavy industry; the production of consumer goods, which to a large degree defines a population's standard of living, remained retarded. Furthermore, industry in the Soviet Union was developed extensively and non-rationally. Enterprises were created in Latvia that did not have sufficient raw materials locally or indeed a local labor force. Industries constantly needed additional labor, and in the 1950s and 1960s such labor was brought in from other regions of the USSR in an organized manner. This induced migration (see Documents No. 39-41) influenced the structure of Latvia's population in a particularly negative direction.

In the period from 1940 until 1959 (1959 being the year of the first Soviet post-war census), the number of Latvians in Latvia decreased from 1.5 million to 1.3 million. In 1989 (according to census figures), about 1.4 million Latvians lived in Latvia. Even to the present day, the number of Latvians in Latvia in the year 1935 has not been matched. Losses from the war and those incurred during the post-war years (in the deportations of March 25, 1949, it was primarily Latvians who were deported) have not been compensated for among Latvians by natural growth or in-migration. According to census data, from 1945 to the end of the 1980s when in-migration of non-Latvians was curtailed, more than 700,000 persons of other nationalities came to live in Latvia permanently. The in-migrants from other regions of the USSR (primarily from the closest districts of the Russian Federation as well as from Belarus and Ukraine) settled primarily in cities. This is why the relative weight of national minorities is currently particularly high in urban areas. In 1989, for example, the population of Rīga contained only 36.5% Latvians (the Russian plurality was 47.3%), but in Daugavpils the relative weight of Latvians was not more than 15%.[41]

The rapid growth of Latvia's population through induced migration affected negatively not only the nationality structure, but also the standards of living. Still, the standard of living in Latvia was higher than in other regions of the Soviet Union. This is why the Baltic region was very attractive not only to civilians from other regions, but also to military personnel who were not counted in censuses (see Documents No. 42-43). The population dynamics also generated a belittling attitude toward the

Latvian language that became more pronounced with every year (see Document No.44-50). The Latvian language was pushed out of many domains of life.

These unsettling tendencies in the policies of the new regime were already evident in the 1950s. Using the partial de-Stalinization introduced by N. Khrushchev after the XXth Congress of the CPSU in 1956, a like-minded group -- they would later be termed "national communists" -- formed in the leadership ranks of the Latvian Communist Party. The 1950s "national communists" in Latvia stood for the equalization in the development of different economic sectors, for curtailing migration, and for the necessity of managers and persons working in the public sector acquiring the Latvian language (see Document No. 51), as well as for a reversal of the condescension shown by many toward the Latvian national cultural heritage. At the July 1959 Plenum of the Latvian Communist Party Central Committee, the conservative (Stalinist) wing of the party gained the upper hand, however (see Documents No. 51 and 54).

As a result of this plenum, the de-Stalinization process ended earlier in Latvia than it did in the Soviet Union as a whole. The leadership of the Latvian SSR began to implement its anti-nationalist policy by forcefully moving against such Latvian national traditions as the Midsummer's Eve (St. John's Day) festivities (see Document No. 53).

Strict censorship was brought to Latvia immediately after its re-annexation in 1945. A special institution was created for this purpose, namely, the Chief Literary Board of the Latvian SSR. Of course, the harshest censorship existed during Stalin's rule, but after his death there continued careful political censoring of all mass media and of books (see Documents No. 55-60).

The Soviet system was also characterized by its negative attitude toward churches. Soviet institutions were fearful of persons gathering together in an uncontrollable manner, particularly in churches which were the last legal organizations outside of the totalitarian system. For this reason governmental policy was directed toward gradually destroying not just churches, but also the clergy and religious life as a whole. This was to be accomplished with ideological, economic, and administrative tools.

Already in 1940-1941, the Soviet Union had shown its attitude towards religion and church affairs – an attitude that belied proclamations of tolerance. Even though the Soviet Constitution promised freedom of worship, in practice believers had to suffer various kinds of limitations, attacks, and repression. Both theological faculties (Protestant and Roman-Catholic) at the University of Latvia, the Theology Institute, and religious schools and societies were closed, publishers specializing in literature of a religious nature were shut down, church property was confiscated, religious instruction in schools was ended, and persecution was begun against the clergy.

After World War II, the church found itself under the permanent control of the Party and the government; specifically, it had to answer to and was placed under the surveillance of the authorized agent in the Latvian SSR of the Bureau of Religious Cults Affairs of the USSR's Council of Ministers (Documents No. 62-75). The church could not initiate anything without conferring with him; furthermore, the authorized agent could not ratify a decision without conferring with Moscow.[42] Usually, a person who had experience in the organs of state security was chosen as the authorized agent.

In 1944, V. Šeškens, the authorized agent for Religious Cult Affairs, began to survey local conditions so as to identify the tools needed to implement Soviet policy. Broad reviews of the mood among the upper ranks of the clergy were sent to Moscow (see Documents No. 63 and 74). The reports gathered by agents in 1940-1941 about the attitude of different pastors toward Soviet power have survived in the archives.

Latvia's Soviet government also sought to isolate the church from social life. The church had to surrender its registers of births, deaths, and marriage to the Archive of Registration of Civil Acts; moreover, it was banned from charitable activities, and clergymen were forbidden to visit hospitals and pension homes and to materially support the widows of their deceased colleagues. The church could only work with "cult" matters. But on the occasions when the regime needed help from the church, the authority of the church was exploited opportunistically. Immediately after the war, for example, the leaders of several confessions had to distribute circulars inviting partisans to come out of the woods, asking parishioners to participate in elections for representatives of Soviet power, inviting those that had gone into exile westward to return to Latvia, and inviting persons to join the *kolkhoz*. Later, religious organizations and their leaders had to participate in the peace movement, "unmask anti-Soviet propaganda," "explain" the religious conditions in the USSR, and gather resources for a "peace fund."

The church was forbidden to publish and distribute literature with religious content, or to receive it from foreign countries. At the same time, in many different ways, atheist propaganda was encouraged by the authorities, and anti-religious literature of different levels was distributed. There were special broadcasts of an anti-religious nature on television and radio. The church, however, did not have the opportunity to defend itself because it was excluded from using mass media.

All state institutions had to work at raising the atheistic spirit in the "working masses." In 1945 all church congregations had to register with the authorities, but this process was extended until 1949. Registration had long-lasting consequences. A congregation had to consist of at least 20 persons (*dvadtsatka*) who had to register with the authorized agent of religious cult affairs. Afterward, the Party's local executive committee concluded a contract with the congregation about the leasing of the church and its inventory, because, in line with the January 28, 1918, decree of the Council of People's Commissars, the church and its inventory was the property of the local executive committee. The local authorities could demand changes in the membership of the congregation's executive committee if some members seemed disloyal to Soviet power. The congregation committee represented the congregation to the state institutions. This process had the goal of isolating pastors from church authority and of facilitating supervision. The Authorized Agent had the right to close a congregation on the basis of a request from the Party's local executive committees, and to rescind its lease contract. The right to dismiss a pastor or to transfer him to a different congregation was widely used.

On July 29, 1949, the Council of Ministers of the Latvian SSR ratified a special law which banned the clergy from teaching children or youth and from preparing them for confirmation, thereby seeking to block young persons from religion. The training of new clergy was limited and controlled, and at times banned. In 1959, a law was ratified that closed cloisters and monasteries (see Document No. 68).

Just as in the struggle against the *kulaks* (successful farmers), a useful tool for reducing the size of a congregation was tax policy. Congregations that were unable to pay high taxes, no matter how baseless these were, had to close themselves down. Often, church meeting places were taken away from congregations (see Document No. 75).

The implementation of these policies was paralleled by the arrest of the clergy. As shown in archival documents, they were most frequently charged with the following: "contacts with international religious organizations in the 1920s and 1930s"; "working as pastors in the home guard organization;" "during the time of Nazi occupation, using the church for anti-Soviet, pro-fascist propaganda." But the most comprehensive charge was "anti-Soviet agitation," which could be used in any and all cases. If the charge was supported only by reports from agents or if the pastor had "considerable authority among unconscientious citizens " then the affair was examined at an Extraordinary Session (see Document No. 62).

If in many respects the time of Nikita Khrushchev tenure in office (1953-1964) can be compared to a "thaw," such a characterization cannot be used with respect to the regime's treatment of the church. Granted, in that period many pastors returned from the places to which they had been deported after arrest, but that was due to the "amnesty" law from which pastors were not exempted.

A particularly energetic attack on all religious confessions began in 1959. In the 1960s, the CPSU assigned itself the task of "the complete liquidation of the remains of religion." The form of this attack can not be compared to the attacks of the 1940s and 1950s – this time prison sentences were used relatively rarely, and the authorities limited themselves to administrative punishments and the rescinding of registration rights. The atmosphere of constant fear of arrest changed to fear of the removal of registration rights.

A new form of activity to minimize the influence of the church manifested itself with the campaign "to bring in new life traditions." For example, baptisms were replaced with name- giving ceremonies, religious ceremonies at graveside with secular rituals; and, when a church event was scheduled, the authorities organized some parallel event attractive to young persons.

Beginning in the 1970s, there was a noticeable transition from a crude disavowal of the church (and of God) to an analysis of the postulates of religion. A relative peace settled on the relationships between the church and state because the church had learned the rules of the game and followed them, and the state changed its militant atheistic policy to one of peaceful coexistence and constant surveillance. The Soviet Union also had to take into account the ideas of the international community, particularly after the signing of the final act of the 1976 Helsinki Conference. Still, as a result of the earlier policies, the numbers of parishioners and congregations had diminished considerably.

The two-faced attitude of the Soviet government toward the church was comparable to its attitude toward Latvian émigrés. On one hand, authorities encouraged the official theory that Latvians in Latvia and Latvians outside of the country were two nations that had nothing in common. On the other hand, the KGB of the Latvian SSR followed the social and cultural activities of the Latvian émigrés closely (see Documents No. 76-80), and tried to get the most notable of them to return (see Document No. 67).

Given the existence of the "iron curtain," direct contact by Latvia's population with foreigners was substantially curtailed. For example, foreigners could not be received in the home without special permission, and after official meetings where foreigners visited enterprises or institutions, those present had to write reports. This was particular true in the case of official delegations visiting Latvia (see Document No. 80). At the end of the 1970s and in the 1980s the tourist flood to Eastern European states (to the so-called "socialist bloc" states) increased considerably, but trips to "capitalist" states were still restricted and were strictly controlled (see Document No. 81).

Of course, such restrictions were politically motivated, but they were also grounded in the fact that the Soviet system had a continuing material and spiritual deficit, and the system tried to avoid through administrative procedures any undesirable comparisons. Access to benefits of any kind in the Soviet Union was determined by social position, profession, and by the 'weight' of a person and how influential he or she was.

Remarkable accomplishments in social policy was one of the arguments with which Soviet propaganda argued the superiority of socialism; Latvia, it was said, enjoyed the benefits of this social policy by being part of the Soviet Union. Without a doubt, there were certain accomplishments of this kind. All inhabitants were guaranteed a certain social minimum: a roof over their heads, work, minimum wages, a pension, guaranteed health care, and education. At the same time the level of these benefits was often low and their quality very poor. Resources above this minimum, however, were distributed according to how important a specific trade or profession was to the interests of the state or according to the amount of influence the recipient had. There existed exclusions of entire social classes and groups. For example, the general pension guarantee was not available to *kolkhozniki* until 1964. During Stalinist times, the agricultural sector was seen to be a source from which the state could constantly drain money and materials -- through taxes, food requisitions, and obligatory loans to the state (see Document No. 84). In the middle of the 1950s, state policy began to change. Agriculture became more and more subsidized, and *kolkhoz* farmers in Latvia in the 1970s and 1980s became one of the most protected classes of inhabitants.

State resources were insufficient, however, to fully implement these social policies. With one hand the state gave, but with the other it took away. This was very clear during Stalin's time when all persons had to volunteer (but actually were forced) to provide loans to the state (see Documents No. 84 and 85).

Furthermore, in the Stalin period, the budgets of social insurance and guarantees were carefully monitored and controlled. For example, so as to avoid exceeding budgeted amounts, the granting of pensions was manipulated. Many reasons could be used for withholding or diminishing a pension, especially formalistic explanations that regulations had been violated. Political criteria, such as, for example, that a person had at one time owned a house that was nationalized, or that his or her children had immigrated to foreign countries, were also brought into play. Many persons in Latvia suffered not only from the use of such political criteria, but also because in the transition from the pension system of independent Latvia to the Soviet system; in the latter case, pensions for the invalided and aged could be taken away if the earlier criteria did not match Soviet pension rules. Even though the leadership of the Latvian SSR tried to get reviewed the regulation conflicts affecting workers' pensions, most often these efforts came to naught. After the death of Stalin, social policy became more liberal, but various restrictions – social and political -- continued to exist in softened forms.

Though the ideology of the state stressed that industrial workers were the very foundation of the Soviet regime, and that their social guarantees were the cornerstone of the entire system of social benefits, in reality it was the *nomenklatura* of the Communist party and of administrative institutions, and workers in the organs of state security, that formed the privileged class. During the period of rationing , for example, they enjoyed the same rationing norms as workers in leading industries. Within this class, there were also great differences growing from where in the hierarchy each person stood. In the rationing period (until the end of 1947) such privileges became institutionalized and were retained after the rescinding of the ration card system (see Document No. 83). Formally, the pay of the highest ranking members of the *nomenklatura* was not particularly high; it was comparable to the pay of a skilled industrial worker. But there were privileges of different types of bonus, support payments, and prizes that in the aggregated frequently exceeded the official pay totals many times over. There was also the privilege of access to certain scarce goods and to goods of higher quality than were available to the average person. Even though privileges were not made public, they were still difficult to hide. The existence of privilege was contrary to the declared egalitarian ideology of the Communist Party and provoked protests among the persons who actually believed the ideology. It was characteristic of the system that such protests were labeled as "anti-party."

Side by side with the official system of the distributing material and social benefits, there also existed an unofficial system consisting of persons who worked directly in the distribution system and those who had access to it due because of their professions – workers in various trades, service enterprises, and others. Goods and benefits that were not officially available could be acquired through these persons by means of payment or by barter of other benefits. In this way a "grey" market was created paralleling the official one: the Latvian term used for it in the Soviet period was *blats*. Basically, this was a comprehensive system of corruption that involved nearly all persons and in which a person's "value" was defined by what exchangeable benefits the person had access to. These could be material and non-material. There was a shortage of books, records, and tickets to the theater just as there were shortages of shoes or furniture. The same applied for trips to foreign lands, the opportunity of convalescing at a health spa, and so forth.

The goal of the cultural revolution – which was the third component in the plan of socialist construction – was the vaguest, judging by the documents of the Communist Party. In principle, the defining goal was "bringing Marxist-Leninist ideology to life," or in other words, all of the inhabitants of the USSR had to think in the way prescribed by the Communist Party. Literature, art, humanities, and the education system was to serve this goal. The relationship between the state, on the one hand, and representatives of culture and the humanities, on the other, after World War II was a very disjointed one. During the Stalin period (to 1953), cultural creativity was regulated and controlled strictly (see Documents No. 91-100). Many cultural figures suffered repressions, lost their employment, and were deliberately degraded. In the first post-war years, "discussions" of the work of individual authors and artist work were carried out in mass meetings and publicly condemned. After such public censuring, publication or exhibitions of their work was forbidden. Such a fate, for example, befell the accomplished Latvian poet Aleksandrs Čaks.

Gradually the relations between the leading ranks of the party, artists, and writers changed. It was more advantageous for the Party to use other tools of control, mainly financial. Representatives of the so-called "creative professions" were relatively well paid, and they received awards and prizes. But in return, they had to "serve" the Soviet system. At the same time, Latvia's Communist Party carefully followed cultural developments (see Documents No. 98-99), and included its own activists in the evaluative process (see Document No. 100).

Much attention was paid to "raising youth in the spirit of Soviet patriotism" (see Documents No. 100 and 101). Until the middle of the 1980s, the institutions of state security played an active part in making sure young persons were properly indoctrinated.

It would be redundant to say that all power everywhere in the Soviet Union was concentrated in the hands of the leading functionaries of the Communist Party, in spite of the fact that, according to the Constitution, the highest organ of power in the Latvian SSR, for example, was the Supreme Soviet. The Central Committee of the Latvian Communist Party not only controlled the contents of all laws and decrees, and the processes of their ratification, but also determined the contents of such enactments at all levels of soviets (hamlet, region, municipal and Supreme Soviet) (see Document No. 106). This is why, when observing from afar, it might appear that all ranks of society were represented in the Supreme Soviet. Until the middle of the 1980s, all decisions at the highest organs of state power were ratified unanimously by a show of hands. There was simply no reason for the system to count votes.

The economic conditions of the Soviet Union deteriorated continuously from the beginning of the 1970s. During that decade, this deterioration could be offset partially by the unrelenting exploitation of natural resources, but by the early 1980s this disguise slowly lost its importance and the shrinkage of production in absolute figures became clear. The supply of goods and social welfare benefits became increasingly pathetic. The "partocracy" had an increasingly difficult time explaining this phenomenon as "post-war difficulties" because more than 30 years had passed since the end of World War II. Within the ranks of the leading structures of the CPSU and KGB, the most informed and erudite persons were very worried that the "Communist Superpower" was lagging behind the USA in the arms race. With this development, the USSR began to modify its primary argument in international dialogue: the force of arms. The leading classes of the USSR began to accept the idea that "acceleration and restructuring" must be started because otherwise an epic social explosion was predictable. This likelihood grew stronger with the USSR's unsuccessful intervention in Afghanistan. The zinc coffins returning from Afghanistan dispelled the myth cultivated by the partocracy that the CPSU leadership was able to more or less guarantee that the inhabitants of the USSR would continue a peaceful life.

In 1985 Michael Gorbachev, the newly appointed General Secretary of the Central Committee of the CPSU, and his supporters expected that the implementation of reform would bring harsh counter-measures from the ranks of the party's "orthodox" members, who were worried about the weakening of their own positions and would therefore reject any plans for liberalization. Gorbachev and his supporters, in order to strengthen their own power, needed to put pressure on the so-called "stagnators" with the help of public opinion. This was the reason why the "openness" (*glasnost'*) slogan was devised. Gorbachev and his supporters needed temporary allies to push the most conservative party members out of their positions. This explains why Communist party institutions became relatively tolerant of the creation and work of the so-called "independent groups" and "informal societal organizations."

The first opposition organization that stood outside the regime in Latvia and used the themes of "democratization" and "openness" was the human rights defense group "Helsinki – 86," which, as documents show, from beginning of its existence was for the ending of the Soviet occupation and for the idea of Latvia's freedom (see Documents No. 108-112). The "Helsinki – 86" Group's organizing of the laying of flowers at the Freedom Monument in Rīga to honor the martyrs of the June 14, 1941, deportations became the first act of the so-called "Awakening" (also referred to as the "Latvian nation's third awakening"). Essentially, the "Awakening" was the Latvians' "national revolution" through peaceful means, involving also representatives of Latvia's national minorities.

The first mass-based organization in Latvia aiming toward the reacquisition of independence was the Latvian National Movement for Independence (see Documents No. 112 and 113). Then, in the summer of 1988, attempts were made to create an organization that could unite the largest number of persons in the struggle for the democratization of society, the guaranteeing of Latvia's sovereignty, and the achieving of spiritual rebirth. The Popular Front (*Tautas Fronte*) of Latvia became this organization. The Popular Front was a mass-based social and political organization created through the nation's patriotic and political activity: a union, in other words, of democratic forces. It struggled for the guarantee of the existence and development of the Latvian nation, and the creation of respectable living conditions for all inhabitants of the country. It the beginning, Communist Party functionaries hoped that it would be a satellite organization of the Party, helping to facilitate *perestroika,* but the Front soon took up positions that were incompatible with the CPSU's strategic plans (see Document No. 104). Uniting about 300,000 supporters, Latvia's Popular Front successfully organized massive patriotic demonstrations (see Documents No. 114-115). The Front also worked successfully against the Latvian SSR International Front of the Working Masses (referred to as *Interfront*), which was created in January 1989 and gathered in its ranks high party officials, militarists, and neo-Stalinists. The goals of the Interfront were to "protect Soviet power," or, in other words, to preserve the existing imperial, ideological, administrative, and bureaucratic system. On March 18, 1990, elections to the Latvian republic's Supreme Soviet (Supreme Council) took place (see Document No. 121), and these were won convincingly by candidates nominated by the Popular Front. On May 4th of the same year, the Supreme Council ratified the Declaration of the Renewal of the independence of the Republic of Latvia (see Document 122). The majority of the inhabitants of Latvia supported this decision in a referendum on March 3, 1991.

Simultaneously with these events, the inhabitants of Latvia who considered themselves citizens and lineal descendants of the Republic of Latvia that was founded on November 18, 1918, tried to renew that republic by creating and electing a Congress of Citizens of the Republic of Latvia, in April of 1990. On May 1, 1990, at its first meeting, the Citizens' Congress' created a standing executive organ – The Committee of Latvia. Due to the influence of the position taken by the Congress of Citizens, the declaration of the renewed Republic of Latvia passed by the Supreme Council came to be linked juridically to the pre-war Republic of Latvia.

In early 1991, after Soviet soldiers attacked the television station in Vilnius, Lithuania, on January 13, and when there was a perceived threat of similar armed intervention in Latvia, the Popular Front appealed to the population to defend the buildings of the Supreme Council, the Council of Ministers, the radio and television center, and the international telephone communications center. Beginning on January 14th, persons from Riga, other cities, and rural areas began to block the streets leading to these important state structures with agricultural equipment; they also constructed barricades to defend the buildings. These barriers had little value from a military viewpoint, but the "barricade days" – lasting almost a month – showed very clearly to the world at large the Latvians' desire to protect its newly reborn state. During the time of the barricades, the basis of national non-violent resistance was reveal clearly: national self-determination, unaggressive nationalism, social integration in an independent state. These principles were appreciated across the world. The support manifested by official institutions of Western states, by the government of the Russian Federation, and by various international organizations for Latvia's independence and for the renewal of its democratic traditions was the decisive factor in preventing the USSR from destroying the renewed Republic of Latvia by force of arms. The nation defended its renewed independence on the barricades in January of 1991, and exhibited solidarity with Lithuania, which was the real focus of the USSR's military attack.

The August 19-21, 1991, failed coup in the USSR created a situation in which it was possible to break all formal political ties between Latvia and the Soviet Union. On September 6, 1991, the State Council of the USSR recognized Latvia's independence (the Russian Federation had already recognized the independence of the Republic of Latvia on August 24, 1991). With this, Latvia's chains were broken, opening the path to international recognition of the renewed state and to the liquidation of the consequences of occupation. [43]

The struggle of the Baltic States for democracy and independence became the catalyst for democratic efforts and flight from the center in all of the Soviet empire. It also influenced social processes in the USSR's satellite states.

A conference in Rīga on June 13, 1991, evaluated the practice of communist totalitarianism in Latvia and its consequences: genocide against the Latvian nation, against all of Latvia's inhabitants; the destruction of the independent Latvian state; and totalitarianism's destructive influence on culture, science, education and economics. The resolution passed by this conference at the end of the meeting (see Document No. 126) became the basis for the August 23, 1991, decision of the Supreme Council of the Republic of Latvia – immediately after the failed coup in Moscow -- to proscribe the work of Latvia's Communist Party in Latvia's territory.

Despite the August 23, 1991, decision of the Supreme Council of the Republic of Latvia, which recognized the Latvian Communist Party as anti-constitutional and ended its operation in the state, the legacy of the communist regime will still remain a part of Latvian nation for a long time. Escape from it will take much longer than one day, and that escape will be helped through the step-by-step uncovering of the historical truth.

DOCUMENTS NO. 1- 8
RESTORATION OF SOVIET POWER

Document No. 1

From the minutes of the Bureau of the Central Committee of the Latvian Communist Party concerning the contents of the anthem of the Latvian SSR

Moscow, February 10, 1944

HEARD: About the anthem of the Latvian SSR.

SPOKE: comrades Pelše, Kirchenšteins, Deglavs, Lācis, Valeskalns, Rokpelnis, Vanags

DECIDED: Enacting the February 2, 1944, decision of the CPSU Central Committee "About the anthems of the united republics," the Central Committee of the Latvian Communist (b) Party decides:
1. In the text of the Latvian SSR state anthem to insert those ideas from the anthem of the Soviet Union that are reflected in the Latvian nation's struggle and its cultural heritage, to wit:
    a. The Latvian nation's centuries-old hatred and struggle against invaders;
    b. The Russian nation's friendship and aid to the Latvian nation;
    c. How the Latvian nation gained and can maintain real national and state autonomy and independence only with the help of soviet power and as a component of the USSR.
2. The organizational work of creating the text and music of the Latvian SSR anthem is assigned to the following commission;
    a. Commission Chair: A. Pelše – Secretary of the Central Committee of the Latvian Communist (b) Party
    b. Commission Secretary: Prieže (Secretary of the Presidium of the Supreme Soviet of the Latvian SSR)
    c. Commission members: Valeskalns (Commissar of Education of the Latvian SSR)
        Rokpelnis (Secretary of the Writers Union)
        Avotiņš (Deputy of the Propaganda and Agitation Section of the Central Committee)
3. To submit the text project of the hymn to the Bureau of the Central Committee [of the Latvian Communist (b) Party] for review by April 15, and music by May 30.
4. The Soviet of People's Commissars (Sovnarkom) determines the monetary amounts for compensating the authors of the anthem's text and music. [...]

Latvian Communist (b) Party Central Committee Secretary   J. Kalnbērziņš

Source: *LVA PA, 101.f, 3. apr. 8. l., pp.13-14. Original in Russian.*

Document No. 2

Excerpts from a secret report by V. Lācis, Chair of Council of Peoples' Commissars of the Latvian SSR, to USSR Marshal L. Govorov, military commander of the Leningrad Front, about the conduct of Red Army soldiers in various districts of Kurzeme

May 1945

1. ...In many of the liberated parishes in the district of Ventspils robberies are taking place. Some of them are committed by soldiers, and the majority by Germans and Vlasov's troops hiding in the forests. In this same district, soldiers have raped 7 women.

2. In Aizpute, Ventspils, and in other liberated districts, incidents of soldiers illegally taking livestock and property from inhabitants still have not ended. In Dunalka and Cirava Parish in Aizpute District two instances were recorded of soldiers raping girls, one of whom was 14 years old.[44] In these parishes there were 15 recorded robberies and 7 cases of livestock driven away. In Cirava parish the soldier stealing a horse lost is his Glory Order, third rank, Number 291669, in the stall.

3. In Liepāja district, horses taken as booty were stampeded across winter crops and the fields sown for summer. That has also happened in other liberated districts.

4. In the port of Ventspils there is a large and valuable reserve of products, but the military unit did not allow the local soviet organs to do inventory and used instead their guards.

5. The military unit stationed in the municipality of Piltene in Ventspils district, number 67636 (unit commander Ivanov), robbed a store and the warehouse of the local cooperative society.
   When with the unit's elder official, comrade Jankovičs, the store was examined [it was found to be] in a state of complete chaos, as if after a massacre.

All of these groups of soldiers and persons manifesting anti-Soviet behavior influence negatively the morale of the inhabitants, [who are] already intimidated by German propaganda.

Chair of the Council of the People's Commissars of the Latvian SSR.
V. Lācis

Source: *LVA, 270. f., 1.s. apr., 120. l. p. 76, 77. Original in Russian.*

Document No. 3

Report of K. Novikov, Secretary of the Rīga City Committee of Latvia's Communist (Bolshevik) Party, to N. Bulganin, USSR People's Deputy Commissar of Defense, about 'marauderism'

May 14, 1945

1. From the moment that the Red Army took Rīga in the Latvian SSR, the counter-intelligence command "SMERSH" seized several good apartments that contained first-class furniture - they stationed guards in the apartments and they are still there despite the passage of seven months. All of the furniture was packed up immediately, some taken to an unknown location, but most is now in Blaumanis Street 8, apartment 4.

2. In March of 1945, a lieutenant who identified himself as a member of "SMERSH"[45] counter-intelligence broke into number 16/18,[46] the apartment of comrade Temnov, Director of the Kirov

District Party Committee on Military Affairs, and took what furniture he liked while threatening his [Temnov's] wife with a weapon – this is not an individual case; I can name many others.

3. The same kind of incident happened in N Aviation section. They took 6 apartments, placed in them 3 guards who have now lived there 7 months, and took all of the furniture from 2 apartments: crystal dishes, mirrors, gold, clocks, and other valuable goods. They do not let anyone in. There was one aviation section, which has since transferred to the Lithuanian SSR, that can be called a band of robbers – it consisted of officers who stole a lot of gold and silver, and appropriated pigs and cows which they sent to Leningrad[47] by airplane.

4. On April 2, 1945, the 7th Police Department of the City of Rīga was told of the disappearance from his apartment of the son of MAULFERTS, Teodors, son of Miķelis, senior specialist at the fruit-drink and mineral water factory – later it turned out that he was killed during an attempted robbery by a group of soldiers from the 183rd and 185th Military Civil Engineers Battalion.

This crime, like many others, was committed with the direct support of the battalion's commanding major, Nikulov, and his senior lieutenant, Milenin, who previously knew that Buslov and Petrovskis, while part of the armed forces that engaged in military action in the territory of the Estonian and Latvian SSRs, were taking cattle and other valuables from the inhabitants of the newly liberated areas for more than two months. Not only did they not turn the [offenders] over to the Field Tribunal, but participated in dividing the stolen goods; taking 3 suits, 2 coats and several wrist and pocket watches. Major Nikulov took a cow and proposed these criminals for government medals.

I have asked Lieutenant-Colonel Patusenko, the commanding officer of soviet and party organs in Rīga, about the affair and about bringing to account those in the armed forces who committed these misdeeds, but even now all of these absurdities continue.

All of these absurdities, robberies, and violent acts were the reason that the Latvian C(b)P Rīga City Committee turned to you to report the illegal activities of counter-intelligence "SMERSH" Major Bozor, Major Nikulov and many others in the aviation section.

Secretary of the Latvian C(b)P Rīga City Committee   Novikov

Source: *LVA, 102. f., 2. apr., 4. l., pp. 32-33. Original in Russian.***Document No. 4**

Information about the conditions in the municipalities and rural districts of Kurzeme after the entry of the Soviet army, compiled on the basis of local Party and local soviet reports

May 21, 1945

News has come from authorized agents about mass looting and instances of rape [in the district of Aizpute].

[…] Also, in Dunalka parish the following was discovered: an eleven-year old girl was raped and her family robbed. Those responsible: a 19-year-old woman from among the Russians the Germans had driven away, and two soldiers from local Soviet army units.

In a span of 7 days in Cirava and Dunalka parishes there were 2 rapes and 15 robberies registered [and attributed] to the Russian side; in 7 cases livestock was confiscated, foodstuffs were taken as were clothes and valuable goods in addition.

[…] In the Valtaika parish dairy, the stationed soldiers emptied 3 kegs of lubricating oil while looking for butter.

[…] In all of the parishes [of Ventspils district], robbery of inhabitants and even occurrences of rape of women were registered (In Pope 2, in Ēdole 5 incidents).

[The People's Commissar of Finance, comrade Tabaks, reports that] the Tukums War Commander, the District Party Committee Secretary, and the District Municipal Committee Chair forced the local Consumer Society to sell goods for German Marks. As a result, for two days, transactions were carried out with German Marks.

Source: *LVA, 270.f., 1.apr, 120.l., p. 11. Original in Russian.*

Document No. 5

Excerpts from the report of V. Shelepov, Deputy Commissar of the People's Finance Commissariat of the Latvian SSR, to the Central Committee of the Latvian Communist (Bolshevik) Party about the imposition of taxes on farmstead, homesteads, on tradesmen, and on merchants

September 7, 1945

The payment of state and local taxes in the Latvian SSR is defined by the CPSU CK decree of 03.10.45[48], number 1329, whose operational term is extended through 1945.

With this decree and with the USSR FTK instructions and specific exceptions from the existing rules for the whole of the USSR, the following rules apply:

Lowered profit norms and rates for farmsteads relative to other republics.

Permission of private trade in the Latvian SSR.

Permission for tradesmen to work using their materials and paid labor.

Merchants and tradesmen who have worked an incomplete year will be assessed taxes according to their actual earnings for the time worked, rather than according to annual rates.

Calculation of the war tax for tradesmen 1.5 times the decreed amount for workers and domestics, instead of raising of this tax to the profit tax level.

Processing the data about the imposition of agricultural taxes for 1944 demonstrates that most of the weight of the agricultural tax rests on the well-to do farmers, as shown:

Groups	Farms		Farm Tax	
	Number of Farms	% of Total	Sum	% of Total
Farms with no more than 10 hectares land	102,145	61.6	67010.2[49]	11.9
Farms with 10 to 20 ha land	49,559	29.9	54029.9	37.7
Farms with more than 20 ha land	13,999	8.5	72206.2	50.4
Total	165,703	100.0	143246.3	100.0

In 1945 (because of the land reform), this pattern will doubtlessly change; there will be more farms in the first and second groups, and the last group will shrink considerably. Therefore the revenues from the agricultural tax will also decrease in 1945.

The highest average farm tax in 1945 comes from the liberated districts and that is explained by large farms in these districts being taxed on all of their arable land, including that part that will be taken away from them as a result of the land reform. [...]

Deputy Finance Commissar Shelepov

Source: *LVA, 327.f., 7.apr., 39. l. pp. 29, 32-33, 36. Original in Russian.*

Document No. 6

From the reports of the Rīga Municipal Executive Committee about USSR army units occupying [the housing included] in the Rīga Municipal Accommodation Fund

September 11, 1945

{...] The complete accommodation fund includes – 8,044 houses
    with living space of – 3,107,588 sq m
Armed Forces units have taken – 532 houses
    With living space of – 387, 661 sq m
Not included are specific apartments taken, with a living space of 285, 532 sq m
Altogether in the city, the armed forces' units have taken living space of 673,193 sq m
    Or of the total municipal fund – 21.7%
    This includes:
        Headquarters and inspection points – 56 houses
          With living space of - 68,154 sq m
        War academies – 20 houses
          With space – 28,826 sq m
        Hospitals – 6 houses
          With living space – 13,740 sq m
        Stationed soldiers, officers and sub-unit headquarters – 375 houses
          With living space – 237,747 sq m
    Not included, but taken for accommodation in Rīga-Jūrmala – 90 cottages
        With living space – 28,340 sq m [...]

Source: *LVA PA, 101. f., 8. apr., 11.l., p. 40.*

Excerpts from the report of the Director of the Architectural Board of Latvian SSR Council of Ministers, E. Kiše, to the Chair of the Council of Ministers, V. Lācis, about war damages in Rēzekne

March 24, 1946[50]

During September 1944, the Architectural Board of the Latvian SSR People's Council of Commissars, under orders from the USSR's People's Council of Commissars, began preliminary work in evaluating the destruction in the city of Rēzekne as a result of the German fascist occupation. The Board gathered material concerning the city's apartment and communal homes and other questions.

The results of the evaluation determined that the ancient parts of urban Rēzekne that date to the beginning of the 13th century have been transformed into a pile of rubble[51]. Approximately 70% of all buildings (there were 1471 buildings) and other structures in the city were damaged. Furthermore, all of the largest buildings in the city are ruined.

515 buildings, 35% of the total amount, were 100% destroyed, including the buildings in Rēzekne Railroad station I and II, the former Municipal Council building, 4 schools and many other buildings.

153 buildings are 75% destroyed, including the People's Hall, the Teachers' Institute, the Land Bank, two high schools, the hotel and others.

118 buildings are 50% destroyed, and 240 buildings are 25% destroyed.

445 buildings are not damaged, [these being] primarily small residences.

The industrial properties, mills, a distillery, a creamery, a tannery, and a brewery are heavily damaged and not operational.

The city's electrical, telegraph and telephone networks are destroyed, the wells are filled, and the bridges over the Rēzekne River have been blown up. The cobblestones were removed from many of the streets for the use of the German fascist army's needs. The majority of the inhabitants were driven off to a German labor camp.

Kiše
Director of the Architectural Board of the Latvian SSR Council of Ministers

Source: *LVA, 270.f., 2. apr., 250. l., p. 34. Original in Russian.*

Document No. 8

Excerpts from a report of the Personnel Manager of Latvia's Railroad Workers, Sidelnikov, on the needs of the rail services with respect to worker's certification in 1946, and about repressive acts against uncertified workers.

1946

...Aggregate quantitative and qualitative description of professional workers.

In May of 1946, the political certification of all the railroad personnel that remained in occupied territory was completely finished: in the most important positions 25,336 persons were determined to be subject to the review for certification. The Railroad Certification Commission, using the reviewed material, denied certification to 1,195 persons, or approximately 5%.

The motives:

a. Traitor to the motherland	6 persons
b. Deserters from the Red Army	149 persons
c. Police – guards	58 persons
d. Homeguards	36 persons
e. Served in the German army	367 persons
f. Others politically unreliable	379 persons
	1,195 persons

The Verdict of the Railroad Certification Commission for the decertified:

a. Repressed	156 persons
b. Sent to railroads behind the front	37 persons
c. Placed in jobs not associated with train movement	23 persons.
d. Returned to their former posts	41 persons
e. Are working in their assigned jobs after speaking with the appropriate authorities, but the decision about returning them to their former positions has still not been made	106 persons
f. Released from work for various reasons	339 persons
including called up for the Red Army	85 persons
deserted from the railroad	31 persons

...

Director of Latvia's Railroad Workers Personnel
Administrative Service Major Engineer

Sidelnikov

Source: *LVA, 93.f., 6. apr., 5. l., p. 5. Original in Russian.*

Documents No. 9-10

Latvia loses a part of its pre-war territory

Document No. 9

Decision of the Presidium of the Supreme Soviet of the Latvian SSR entitled "About the attachment of Višgoroda, Kačanova and Tolkova parishes the Russian Soviet Federal Socialist Republic"

August 22, 1944

Taking into account the requests of the inhabitants of Višgoroda, Kačanova and Tolkova parishes, in which majority [of the population] is Russian, and noting their desires, the Presidium of the Supreme Council of the Latvian SSR decides:

To ask the Presidium of the Supreme Soviet of the USSR to attach Višgoroda, Kačanova, and Tolkova parishes, [now part of the] Latvian SSR, to the Russian Soviet Federal Socialist Republic.

Chair of the Presidium of the Supreme Soviet of the Latvian SSR
Prof. Dr. A. Kirchenšteins
Deputy Secretary of the Presidium Soviet
K. Prieže

Source: *LVA, 290. f., 2.apr., 88. l., p. 1 Original in Latvian. .*

Comment: The parishes mentioned in the document are being referred to with their old Russian names that do not match their names according to the administrative territorial division of the Republic of Latvia of 1940. Ultimately, it was Kacēna, Gaura, Augšpils, Linava, Upmale, and Purvmala parishes that were attached to the Pskov provinces of the RSFSR.

Document No. 10

From a report of the communist D. Kaupužs to G. Malenkov, the Secretary of the Central Committee of the CPSU, about events in the six parishes of Abrene District of the Latvian SSR after they were attached to the province of Pskov in the RSFSR

May 29, 1946

[…] In September of 1944, with the decision of the Presidium of the Supreme Soviet of the USSR[52] , six parishes with their ethnic Russian indigenous populations were attached to the Pskov province [after being detached] from the Latvian SSR, and on this bases there were created the regions of Pitalova and Kačanova […]

I, as a communist who illegally worked in these regions during the time of bourgeois Latvian order, and during the time of the German occupation participated there in the partisan movement, wish to inform you -- the Central Committee of the CPSU – in person about the intolerable conditions in these regions after they were attached to the Pskov province. […]

After their attachment to Pskov province, leading region-level soviet and party cadres were sent in from Pskov province's old regions (Dedovichi, Shashkino), but all of the leading local functionaries went to work in the Latvian SSR either on their own or after being released to do so. Currently, almost all of the region's leading functionaries and even village soviet chairmen and leaders of economic organizations are persons from other regions. This has created a situation in which the region's and village's soviet leaders do not know the region's peculiarities and its inhabitants. Furthermore, the local cadres were replaced primarily with cadres from those regions from which were sent the Region Committee Secretaries and Region Executive Committee Chairs.

The expulsion of and refusal to use the local cadres is related almost entirely to the mistrust [by the incomers] of all local persons, which devalues and compromises the merits of the former local anti-bourgeois activists and the anti-fascist fighters. It is almost a rule that the newly-arrived functionaries shun all contact with the former undergrounders, anti-fascists, and partisans, even belittling their merits openly. "What kind of partisans were there with you" etc. The local inhabitants get labeled with the term "Latvians," and even at times are simply cursed as "fascists." [...]

Moreover, in the Pitalova region there are incidents of persecution of notable families and individuals who have earned general respect locally [...]

After this region was attached to Pskov province, an atmosphere filled with agitation was created. There has begun a great flight of our people, who are not tied to families or farms, particularly the former partisans and anti-fascist youth, to Rīga and other regions of the Latvian SSR [...]

After soviet power was renewed, the Višgorodskij *sovkhoz* was created not far from Pitalova, on first-class land [formerly] cultivated by a manorial lord and by kulaks. The *sovkhoz* had about 100 cattle and about 40 horses; even in the beginning of 1945 there were about 40 horses and about 2000 "Leghorn" breed hens that had been brought in from the Ostrova poultry farm *sovkhoz*. As our people explained it, last winter the majority of the horses and cattle, as well as most of the sheep and hens, died. [...]

By the Lavino homes there is a protected park where festivals and other events previously took place. Last winter they began to chop down this protected park, felling most of the valuable trees. The barrier of fir trees that protected the fruit orchard from northern winds was also chopped down. Near the Svetlovo houses, a stand of oak trees, where martyrs of the White terror of 1919 are interred, was also chopped down. [...]

The leaders of [this] region have started to [acquire] unwarranted and valuable personal farms. For example, the Regional Committee's First Secretary, comrade Porucenko, took two cows, pigs and three bee hives for himself from [the farms] that were abandoned. He takes feed for his personal farm animals, including pigs, from "his" subsidiary plot of land, which consists of 30 hectares, with 15 cows and other animals. [...]

This behavior has engendered great dissatisfaction and disappointment among the Soviet masses in the region. The former supporters of the Germans and the enemies of soviet power exploit this [mood] to spread lies about soviet power.

And in this unhealthy and turbulent political atmosphere, the Pitalova Region Leaders have begun [agricultural] collectivization without any kind of transitional period involving co-operatives. By April, 43 kolkhozes had been organized. [...]

Personally, I see it as unacceptable that these regions (a similar condition is to be found in the Kačanova region) that have such a famous past and such intelligent persons have to continue to suffer such behavior.

D. Kaupužs

Source: *LVA PA, 101. f., 9. apr., 98. l., pp. 121-122, 124-26 (copy of original).*

DOCUMENTS NO. 11-13
THE USE OF GERMAN PRISONERS OF WAR AS LABOR

Document No. 11

Secret Resolution of the Bureau of the Central Committee of Latvia's Communist (Bolshevik) Party from the Special Files about the use of Nazi German Prisoners of War for Labor

August 7, 1945

The Bureau of the Central Committee of Latvia's Communist (Bolshevik) Party considers it wrong that many enterprise managers, who use prisoners of war, allow them to interact with the general population in the factories and on the streets, thereby violating the orders about how prisoners should be guarded and isolated. It is also wrong that the prisoners-of-war are dispersed throughout small and unimportant enterprises, while the most important undertakings that will renew the national economy are not guaranteed enough labor[53].

The Bureau of the Central Committee of Latvia's Communist Party decides:

1. To make clear to the People's Commissars, to the Senior Directors of the Boards of the Latvian SSR Council of People's Commissars, and to the Directors of the Municipal and District Executive Committees that prisoners-of-war they must be kept in complete isolation from the general population.

2. To prohibit the use of prisoners of war in the preparation of food in the food industry, namely, the enterprises of the People's Commissariat of Food Industry, the People's Commissariat of Fish Industry, and the People's Commissariat of Meat Industry.

3. To make it the responsibility of People's Commissars, Senior Directors of the Boards of the Latvian SSR Council of People's Commissars, and the Directors of the Municipal and District Committees to:

    a. Use prisoners of war primarily for the preparation of fuel, the acquisition of construction material, and in construction and restoration work;

    b. When using prisoners of war in enterprises, to organize them in independent shifts or brigades under the technical direction and supervision of a factory expert;

    c. When using prisoners of war in construction, to deploy them to objects or brigades that are isolated from the general population;

    d. When using prisoners of war in preparing lumber or peat, to send them to designated felling areas in forests or swamps.

4. To make it the responsibility of comrade Eglītis, the Latvian SSR People's Commissar of the Interior, to reduce the transportation of prisoners of war on the main streets of the city in daylight hours, and to allow economic organizations to transport prisoners-of-war during this time only in exceptional, urgent cases.

5. To conform to the general plan for the use of prisoners of war in the republic's economic enterprises according to the attachment.

    To allow the People's Commissar of the Interior of Latvia's SSR to send prisoners of war to other workplaces, providing that the regulations governing the contact of prisoners of war with the general population is observed.

6. To make it the responsibility of comrade Eglītis, People's Commissar of the Interior of Latvia's SSR, to provide guards for prisoners of war working in the preparation of firewood and peat, in preparation work for construction, and in the largest building projects.

7. To ask the State Defense Committee to give 4800 German prisoners of war to the supervision

of the People's Commissar of Lumber of Latvia's SSR for the preparation of lumber in felling areas, and to organize 9 camps for this intention.

8. To control the use of prisoners of war within the workforce of the Republic, to organize an inspectorate composed of three persons, and to assign to it the task of producing an overview of the republic's economic needs for prisoner-of-war labor; to supervise the use by economic organizations of prisoners of war, comrade I. Trinkler, Assistant Director of the Council of People's Commissars of Latvia's SSR, is assigned to the Director of the Labor Division Office.

Secretary of the Central Committee of Latvia's Communist (Bolshevik) Party

J. Kalnbērziņš

Attachment to the July 7, 1945[54] Decision
Of the Central Committee of the Latvian Communist (Bolshevik) Party
Minutes number 123 and 126

The placement of German Prisoners of War as laborers in enterprises and buildings in Latvia's SSR

	Name of Object and People's Commissariat	Total	Preparation of (Heating	Construction (and renovation)	Producing material for construction	Work in production
	I. LSSR People's Commissariat of Timber Industry					
1.	Vecsalaca Timber Farm	400	400	-	-	-
2.	Gaujiena Timber Farm	1000	1000	-	-	-
3.	Strenči Timber Farm	400	400	-	-	-
4.	Viļaka Timber Farm	1000	1000	-	-	-
5.	"---"[55]	400	400	-	-	-
6.	Dundaga Timber Farm	400	400	-	-	-
7.	Priekule Timber Farm	400	400	-	-	-
8.	Kuldīga Timber Farm	400	400	-	-	-
9.	Lutrina Timber Farm	400	400	-	-	-
10.	Sawmill Spars	100	-	-	100	-
11.	Sawmill Udarnik	100	-	-	100	-
12.	Sawmill Mīlgrāvis	150	-	-	150	-
13.	Sawmill Jaunciems	150	-	-	150	-
14.	Sawmill Red One	50	-	-	50	-
15.	Sawmill Proletariat	130	-	-	130	-

16.	Veneer Factory Latvia's Birch	200	-	-	200	-
17.	Veneer Factory Furnieris	100	-	-	100	-
18.	Veneer Factory Lignums	150	-	-	150	-
19	Veneer Factory Rīga	100	-	-	100	-
20.	Veneer Factory Gerniņš	100	-	-	100	-
21.	Veneer Factory Volcano	250	-	-	250	-
22.	Matchstick Factory	25	-	-	-	25
23.	Furniture Factory number 2	100	-	-	-	100
24.	Furniture Factory Number 3	60	-	-	-	60
25.	Furniture Factory Number 4	100	-	-	-	100
26.	Furniture Factory Number 5	50	-	-	-	50
27.	Furniture Factory "Labor active"	80	-	-	-	80
28.	Furniture Factory Būvgaldnieks	100	-	-	-	100
29.	Furniture Factory Rīga's Communard	150	-	-	-	150
	Total	7045	4800	-	1580	665
	II. Republican Office "Primary Timber Supply"					
1.	Loading Timber on Railroad platforms	600	600	-	-	-
2.	Valmiera Forest Works	200	200	-	-	-
3.	Viļaka Forest Works	150	150	-	-	-
4.	Jelgava Forest Works	100	100	-	-	-
5.	Rēzekne Forest Works	150	150	-	-	-
6.	Rīga Forest Works	300	300	-	-	-
7.	Valmiera Forest Works	500	500	-	-	-

8.	Daugavpils Forest Works	100	100	-	-	-
9.	Daudzeva Base	200	200	-	-	-
	Total	2300	2300	-	-	-
	III. LSSR People's Commissariat of Heating Industry					
1.	Sloka Peat Factory	1400	1400	-	-	-
2.	Olaine Peat Factory	1200	1200	-	-	-
3.	Kūka Peat Factory	500	500	-	-	-
4.	Salaspils Peat Factory	1000	1000	-	-	-
5.	Garoza Peat Factory	400	400	-	-	-
6.	Bauska Peat Factory	500	500	-	-	-
7.	Misa Peat Factory	450	450	-	-	-
8.	Skrunda Peat Factory	400	400	-	-	-
9.	Priedaine Peat Factory	250	250	-	-	-
	Total	6100	6100	-	-	-
	IV. LSSR People's Commissariat of Construction and Construction Material					
1.	Superphosphate Factory in Rīga	1000	-	1000	-	-
2.	Refrigerated Plant in Rīga	500	-	500	-	-
3.	Airport buildings in Rīga	300	-	300	-	-
4.	Cement Factory in Rīga	900	-	400	500	-
5.	Pottery Factory in Salaspils	500	-	250	250	-
6.	Flax Spinning Factory in Jelgava	200	-	200	-	-
7.	Flax Spinning Factory in Daugavpils	600	-	600	-	-
8.	Pēdagogical School in Jelgava	200	-	200	-	-
9.	Teachers Institute in Rēzekne	80	-	80	-	-

10.	High School in Lielvārde	300	-	300	-	-
11.	High School in Ērgļi	300	-	300	-	-
12.	High School in Indra	300	-	300	-	-
13.	High School in Laudona	300	-	300	-	-
14.	Hospital in Ludza	150	-	150	-	-
15.	Hospital in Rēzekne	200	-	200	-	-
16.	Dairy Factory in Rēzekne	50	-	50	-	-
17.	Jugla Paper Factory	100	-	100	-	-
18.	Līgatne Paper Factory	250	-	250	-	-
19.	Sloka Paper Factory	300	-	300	-	-
20.	Brocēni Cement Factory in Saldus	1000	400	600	-	-
21.	Saurieši Lime Quarry	250	-	250	-	-
22.	Saulkalns Lime Factory	100	-	-	100	-
23.	Kārļakalns Lime Factory	200	-	-	200	-
24.	Kalnciems Lime Factory	200	-	-	200	-
25.	Sesile Lime Quarry	200	-	-	200	-
26.	Auce Lime Factory	400	-	-	400	-
27.	Rock Quarry in Pļaviņa	200	-	-	200	-
28.	Silicate Factory in Rīga	100	-	-	100	-
29.	Ceramics Factory in Bolderāja	100	-	-	100	-
30.	Brick Factory in Jelgava	120	-	-	120	-
31.	Spartaks Brick Factory	250	-	-	250	-
32.	Progress Brick Factory	120	-	-	120	-
33.	Kaišs Brick Factory in Lielupe	2500	300	800	1400	-
34.	Kalkūns Brick Factory in Daugavpils	110	30	-	80	-

35.	Brick Factory in Krustpils	150	-	-	150	-
36.	Brick Factory in Tūja	200	-	-	200	-
37.	Brick and Lime Factory in Cēsis	600	-	-	600	-
38.	Slate Factory in Rīga	200	-	-	200	-
39.	Gypsum Factory in Rīga	150	-	-	150	-
40.	Segums Roofing Paper Factory	160	-	-	160	-
41.	Factory Number 1 in Rīga	100	-	100	-	-
42.	Factory Number 3 in Rīga	100	-	100	-	-
43.	Machine Rental Base in Rīga	50	-	-	-	50
44.	Firewood preparation in Valmiera	500	500	-	-	-
	Total	14590	1230	7630	5680	50
	V. LSSR People's Commissariat of Communal Residences					
1.	Pumping Station Construction in Ropaži	200	-	200	-	-
2.	ATK Building	80	-	80	-	-
3.	Wood Finishing Factory	100	-	100	-	-
	Total	380	-	380	-	-
	VI. Building deconstruction, new construction, major renovations and preparation of heating supplies					
1.	Executive Committee of Jelgava	2000	-	2000	-	-
2.	Executive Committee of Daugavpils	3000	-	3000	-	-
3.	Executive Committee of Daugavpils	800	-	800	-	-

4.	Executive Committee of Rēzekne	700	-	700	-	-
5.	Executive Committee of Valmiera	1500	-	1500	-	-
6.	Executive Committee of Liepāja	500	-	500	-	-
	Total	8500	-	8500	-	-
	VII. Executive Committee of Rīga					
1.	Municipal Trust Building Deconstruction and Major House Repairs	4500	-	4500	-	-
2.	Supply of heating supplies to the Pumping Station	200	-	-	-	200
3.	Supply of Peat to the Municipal Heating Office in Priedaine (650) and unloading firewood at the freight station in Rīga (300)	950	950	-	-	-
4.	Sauna and Laundry Trust for Major Sauna Renovations	120	-	120	-	-
5.	Supply of heating material to the Gas Factory	40	-	-	-	40
6.	Construction of a new tram line	600	-	600	-	-
7.	Specific renovations of local industries	400	-	-	-	400
8.	Preparation of heating material for the Forest Office	100	100	-	-	-
9.	Reconstruction of the access road to the Board of Roads and Bridges	150	-	150	-	-

10.	Municipal Apartment Boards' major renovations of uninhabited houses and schools (during days off)	500	-	500	-	-
	Total	7560	1050	5870	-	640
	VIII USSR PRTK Sugar Trust					
1.	Jelgava Factory Construction	600	-	600	-	-
2.	Krustpils Factory Construction	500	-	500	-	-
3.	Liepāja Factory Construction	250	-	250	-	-
4.	Rēzekne Factory Construction	250	-	250	-	-
	Total	1600	-	1600	-	-
	IX LSSR Council of People's Commissars Primary Transport Board					
1.	Bridge Construction in Jelgava (100), in Rēzekne (200), in Tukums (100), in Valmiera (100)	500	-	500	-	-
	X. People's Commissar of Meat and Dairy Industries					
1.	Preparation of firewood in the forest	150	150	-	-	-
2.	Bone rendering and glue factory	25	-	-	-	25
	Total	175	150	-	-	25
	XI. LSSR People's Commissar of Fishing Industry					
1.	Construction of Cannery in Tūja	100	-	100	-	-
2.	Construction of Fish Nursery in Tome near the Ķegums (ground work)	100	-	100	-	-

3.	Mangaļa Cannery	200	-	200	-	-
	Total	400	-	400	-	-
	XII. LSSR People's Commissar of Light Industry					
1.	Peat Acquisition in Plakanciems	200	200			
2.	Peat swamps near Rīga	20	20	-	-	-
3.	Rīga Cloth	400	-	400	-	-
4.	Rīga Manufactures	700	-	200	-	500
5.	Red Textile Worker	300	-	-	-	300
6.	Jugla Manufactures	500	-	-	-	500
7.	Jugla Tannery	50	-	-	-	50
8.	Rīga Thread	90	-	-	-	90
9.	Parisian Commune	150	-	-	-	150
10.	8th of March	160	-	-	-	160
11.	Worsted Factory	150	-	150	-	-
12.	Bolshevichka	150	-	20	-	130
13.	Flax Spinning Factory in Jelgava	150	-	150	-	-
14.	Red Square	200	-	-	-	200
15.	Hero	50	-	-	-	50
16.	Zasulauks Flax Spinning Factory	150	-	-	-	150
	Total	3420	220	920	-	2280
	XIII LSSR People's Commissariat of Food Industry					
1.	Preparation of Firewood	210	210	-	-	-
2.	Construction of the 1st of May Bakery	500	-	500	-	-
3.	Brewery Container Construction and Repair	100	-	-	-	100
4.	Mechanical Repair Factory	50	-	-	-	50
5.	Tobacco Factory Reconstruction	52	-	52	-	-
	Total	912	210	552	-	150

	XIV LSSR People's Commissariat of Local Industries					
1.	Red Star	200	-	-	-	200
2.	Radio equipment	150	-	-	-	150
3.	Labor Drive	50	-	-	-	50
4.	Metal Technical	100	-	-	-	100
5.	Omega	100	-	-	-	100
6.	Ardor	60	-	-	-	60
7.	Young Communard	100	-	-	-	100
8.	Liepāja Energy Factory	200	-	100	-	100
9.	Jelgava Electric Station	100	-	-	-	100
10.	Sloka Electric Station	100	-	-	-	100
11.	Daugavpils Electric Station	100	-	-	-	100
12.	First Rīga Hydro-electric Station	100	-	-	-	100
13.	Rīga Ceramics Factory	1500	550	250	-	700
14.	Rīga Porcelain Factory	200	100	-	-	100
15.	Communard	150	-	-	-	150
16.	Iļģuciems Glass Factory	200	100	-	-	100
17.	Rīga Glass Factory	300	100	-	-	200
18.	Red October	30	-	-	-	30
19.	Rīga Abrasives Factory	50	-	30	-	20
20.	Red Metal Worker	200	-	50	-	150
21.	Steel	80	-	-	-	80
22.	Metal Reinforcement Factory	50	-	-	-	50
23.	Rīga Turbine Factory	200	100	-	-	100
24.	Vezuvs	50	-	-	-	50
25.	Worktable Repair Factory	100	-	-	-	100
26.	Rīga Spring Factory	50	-	-	-	100
27.	Economizer	50	-	-	-	50
28.	Imanta	100	50	-	-	50

29.	Rīga Bolt and Nut Factory	150	-	-	-	150
30.	Weight Factory	100	-	-	-	100
31.	Superphospate Factory	400	-	200	-	200
32.	Chemical Factory	150	-	-	-	150
33.	Cleanliness	30	-	-	-	30
34.	Construction Office	600	-	600	-	-
35.	Red Metal Worker Factory in Liepāja	1400	-	300	-	1100
	Total	7500	1000	1530	-	4970
	Grand Total	60982	17060	27882	7260	8780

Source: *LVA PA, 101. f., 7. apr., 31a. l., pp. 26-29. Original in Russian.*

Document No. 12

Excerpt from a report by Mihelevic, Director of the Board, USSR People's Commissar of the Interior, prisoner-of-war camp No. 317, about the use of prisoners of war for labor

August 13, 1945

Prisoners-of-war camp No. 317 was organized in line with the order of the People's Commissar of the Interior, Comrade Beria, covering the No. 277 Board of 2nd division camps

Currently camp No. 317 is in charge of over 14,970 persons, of whom the 11,469 in the labor complement are taken to work at the following economic institutions:
Camp No. 317 labor fund has 7,171 persons, 5,006 persons are taken to work;
Camp's 1st Section labor fund has 2,165 persons, 1,788 persons are taken to work;
Camp's 2nd Section labor fund has 502 persons, 414 persons are taken to work;
Camp's 3rd Section labor fund has 2,201 persons, 1,815 persons are taken to work;
Camp's 4th Section labor fund has 1,692 persons, 1,394 persons are taken to work;
Camp's 5th Section labor fond has 1239 persons, 1021 persons are taken to work.
1,200 persons are not taken to work because of a lack of convoys.

The largest economic organizations -- Rīga Sea Construction, the Municipal Construction Trust, and the 1st Construction and Assembly Board --- ...do not fulfill their contracts and use the labor of prisoners of war only partially. The Municipal Construction Trust (Director Komarov) uses prisoners-of-war partially; the contract is for 3,500 persons, but only 1,183 persons are taken to work and their labor productivity is very low – 63%.

The contract with the 1st Construction and Assembly Board (Meat processing) is for 300 persons, but they only use 100 and their labor productivity is 50%.

The Rīga Sea Construction (organization) is building a port- and ship-repair facility (Director Kochinskis); their contract is for 5,000 persons, but they only use 3,087 persons and their labor productivity is 86%.

Officials from the Production and Plan Section of the Board of Camp No. 317 have visited the mentioned workplaces and have concluded that the low productivity of prisoner-of-war labor is due to the following: the organizations do not give the brigades duties in a timely manner and do not explain the plan to the brigades; they do not supply them with all of the needed tools; they do not begin work in a timely manner (experiencing delays), they assign the workforce incorrectly; and they are poor technical organizers. The Municipal Construction Trust is one such organization; there have been times when within an eight-hour period, the prisoners-of-war actually work only thirty minutes. The Port does not supply the prisoners-of-war with tools in a timely manner, the Meat Processing Plant does not know how to assign tasks, the Sea Fleet Repair Factory of the People's Commissariat of the Interior has reduced wages, the norms of the factory *Bolshevička* do not surpass 83%, the STK Construction Board has the lowest wages for prisoners-of-war, 4 rubles and 25 kopeks, when the state norm is 10 rubles and 50 kopecks (the 4th norm).

In addition to all of these problems, the low productivity of prisoner-of-war labor is also due to the fact that the receiving institutions do not provide incentives for work by prisoners-of-war work by using additional provisions, supplying prisoners of war with dry goods, and with tobacco products in kiosks – all of which is suggested in the order of the People's Commissariat of the Interior of the USSR

These institutions do not distribute clothing and soap, which noticeably decreases labor productivity (a clear example is the glass factory, where there is a shortage of special clothing and shoes).

On occasion, transport convoys release the prisoners of war before the end of work and thus further fail to fulfill the plan. The Board of the Camp sees it as necessary to turn to the Central Committee of Latvia's Communist (Bolshevik) Party with a request that it give instructions to these institutions that they observe their contracts with the Camp strictly and use every opportunity to raise the labor productivity of the prisoners-of-war.

The Director of the Board of the Prisoner-of-War Camp Number 317 of the People's Commissariat of the Interior of the USSR
    Guard Captain

                      Mihelevic

The Director of Production and the Plans
Lieutenant-Colonel

                      Marcenko

Source: *LVA PA, 101.f., 8. apr., 34.l., pp. 15-16. Original in Russian.*

Document No. 13

Secret Report of A. Eglītis, People's Commissar of the Interior of the Latvian SSR, to J. Kalnbērziņš, Secretary of the Central Committee of Latvia's Communist (Bolshevik) Party, about inferior working and living conditions in prisoners-of-war camp No. 277.

December 24, 1945

The completed review of the use of prisoners of war on construction at the Rīga Hydroelectric Station, and of their situation in the camp, concludes that the agreed-upon contract is being violated by the Military Construction (organization) and that the violations include the following:

-Prisoners-of-war who do heavy and dangerous work are not guaranteed additional food and do not receive the required special clothing. The dormitories are not heated because the Military Construction (organization) does not provide any heating supplies. -The prisoners of war continue to sleep on bare bunks without sheets or blankets.

In addition to extended work days, free days also are not given to all of the working prisoners of war, which precludes the opportunity for the necessary sanitary work, and as a result the camp is louse-infested.

-The Military Construction (organization) exhibits both poor organization of labor and poor technical supervision. Production percentages are very low. During the first ten days of December production was only 52%. Furthermore, their incurred debt for the labor of the prisoners of war to December 20th is now 557,000 rubles.

-This kind of attitude towards the use of prisoners of war and their upkeep leads to widespread illnesses and the weakening of the organism. Overall, during work at the Hydroelectric station, 1,500 persons have become unable to work, including 341 during the days of November and December, the number including many specialists. On occasion, illness leads to death and as a result the mortality numbers of camp No. 277 have risen to 56 persons, 15 during the days of December. [These fifteen died] during the time period when the People's Commissariat of the Interior of the USSR decreed the need for special attention to the physical well-being of prisoners of war and asked for careful examination of every incident of death. Camp No. 277 was given special attention by the People's Commissariat of the Interior of the USSR because of the high death rate.

If these conditions continue in the future, we will be forced to answer the questions of the People's Commissariat of the Interior of the USSR about [why they should continue assigning] prisoners of war in the future to these organizations, and why these prisoners should not be reassigned to organizations that can guarantee the conditions needed for their upkeep.

Please get involved and give a categorical, unconditional order to the Military Construction (organization) that they take it upon themselves to use the prisoners of war and provide for them according to the contract.

At the same time, give an order to the camp and camp section about the documented shortcomings and tell them that it is necessary to bring about increased discipline and labor productivity among the prisoners of war at the Hydroelectric Station construction site.

People's Commissar of the Interior of the Latvian SSR
Major General

Eglītis

Source: *LVA PA, 101.f., 8. apr., 34. l., pp. 33-34 Original in Russian..*

Documents No. 14-17

The path to collectivization

Document No. 14

[Confidential] report of the Latvian SSR Prosecutor, A. Misutin, about the number of criminal proceedings initiated in connection with the supplying of food to the state

October 20, 1946

Number p. k.	District	Number of Criminal Counts by paragraph	
		Criminal Code paragraph 61[56]	Criminal Code paragraphs 58-14[57]
1.	Alūksne	11	3
2.	Aizpute	9	-
3.	Bauska	9	-
4.	Valka	12	1
5.	Valmiera	12	-
6.	Ventspils	4	-
7.	Viļaka	11	1
8.	Daugavpils	11	-
9	Jēkabpils	9	1
10.	Jelgava	6	-
11.	Ilūkste	16	-
12.	Kuldīga	14	-
13.	Liepāja	9	-
14.	Ludza	7	-
15.	Madona	14	2
16.	Rēzekne	10	2
17.	Rīga	9	4
18.	Talsi	10	-
19.	Tukums	1	-
20	Cēsis	14	4
		198	17
		Total 215 persons	

In addition, according to the information of the Ministry of Justice (Oct. 20, 1946) concerning the non-fulfillment of grain supply quotas in the Republic, action has been initiated against 216 persons.

Procurator of the Latvian SSR,
    second ranking justice counselor　　　　　　　　　　　　　　Misutin

Source: *LVA PA, 101.f., 9. apr., 73.l., p. 182. Original in Russian.*

Decision Number 761 of the Council of Ministers of the Latvian SSR entitled "About characteristics of *budžu* [bourgeois] farms and the manner of imposing taxes on them." August 27, 1947

Pursuant to decision No. 2874 of August 17, 1947, of the Union Council of Ministers of the USSR and decision No. 760 of August 27, 1947, of the Council of Ministers of the Latvian SSR "About imposing taxes on farms of farmers in the Latvian SSR" the Council of Ministers of the Latvian SSR decides:

1. *Budžu* [bourgeois] farms are understood to be those that after the territory of the Latvian SSR was liberated from German occupation had one or more of the following attributes:

   a. permanently employed or employ hired labor on the farm or in the factory;

   b. systematically employed or employ seasonal or day laborers on the farm or in the factory;

   c. systematically used the labor of other citizens: at very high rates leased out the use of a horse, products, seed or agricultural machinery;

   d. systematically received income in money or seed from allowing inventory of agricultural machines (tractors, locomotives, complicated or semi-complicated threshing machines) to be used on other farms;

   e. systematically received or receive income from mills, butter churns, pearl barley mills or other enterprises that work with mechanized, water, or steam power as well as the renting of the mentioned [technology];

   f. received or receive income from sale, resale or usury.

2. To count as a *budžu* [bourgeois] farm those farms that during the [German] occupation of Latvian SSR territory took back land or possessions that had been nationalized in the 1940-1941 land reform and had the land confiscated again in the land reform after the liberation of the territory of the Latvian SSR from German occupation, as well as the farms of active supporters of the German, fascist occupiers.

3. The following farms are not to be counted as *budžu* [bourgeois] farms:

   a. those that employ paid labor during the time of sowing or harvesting only because of the sickness of one of the able-bodied members of the family, as well as farms where the only able-bodied member is fulfilling an elected position or finds himself in the ranks of the Soviet army, and if the family has no other able-bodied member; b. those that employ one paid supplemental worker in farms that work at handicrafts and therefore do not need more than one supplemental worker; c. those that in the summertime employ a paid shepherd only to herd livestock; d. those that own a horse thresher, if they do not have any of the other signs of a *budžu* [bourgeois] farm mentioned in paragraphs number 1 and 2.

4. In residential areas attached to cities, the agricultural incomes of *budžu* [bourgeois] farms and incomes on farms of an industrial character are assessed according to the April 30, 1943, USSR Supreme Soviet Presidium decree "About personal incomes taxes of " 19ᵗʰ paragraph, keeping in mind the actual manner in which income is received.

5. Lists of *budžu* [bourgeois] farms in the countryside are compiled by parish executive committees and are ratified by district executive committees.

   Budžu [Bourgeois] farm lists in the cities are compiled [by the following]: in Rīga – the region executive committee and ratified by the municipal executive committee; in Liepāja, Daugavpils, Jelgava and Ventspils – compiled and ratified by the municipal executive committee; but in the remaining municipalities - compiled by municipal executive committees and ratified by district executive committees.

6. To assign the responsibility to district and municipal executive committees of determining that the lists of *budžu* [Bourgeois] farms are correct and that taxes are collected on time from them.

7. Decree that complaints that [a farm] has been listed incorrectly as a *budžu* [bourgeois] farm are to be made to the district executive committees... [further] complaints about incorrect assignment to the *budžu* [bourgeois] farm list are to be turned in through the district executive committee to the Council of Ministers of the Latvian SSR.

8. Furthermore:

   a. If on the *budžu* [bourgeois] farm there are family members with decorations, Soviet Army officers, invalids from the Great Fatherland War – pensioners, former partisans – or, if the *budžu* [bourgeois] farm belongs to the widow or orphans of a soldier killed in the Great Fatherland War, the question of assessing agricultural taxes on these farms is to be resolved by the Council of Ministers of the Latvian SSR on a case by case basis.

   In order to prepare a proposal for the assessment of agricultural taxes on *budžu* [bourgeois] farms in light of this decision, a committee is established with the following membership: Deputy Chair of the Council of Ministers of the Latvian SSR, comrade Ronis; Minister of Finance of the Latvian SSR, comrade Tabaks, and the Deputy Minister of Agriculture of the Latvian SSR, comrade Grumslis;

   b. to ratify the circular of the Ministry of Finance of the Latvian SSR "About the order of assessing *budžu* [bourgeois] farms in the territory of the Latvian SSR."

Chair of the Council of Ministers of the Latvian SSR   V. Lācis

Affair Supervisor for the Council of Ministers of the Latvian SSR   I. Bastins

Source: *LVA 270.f., 2.apr., 396.l., p. 126-128. Original in Russian.*

Document No. 16

Excerpts from a secret report of the Prosecutor of the Latvian SSR, A. Misutin, about severe violations in the implementation of the decision of the Council of Ministers of the Latvian SSR entitled "About characteristics of *budžu* [bourgeois] farms and the manner of imposing taxes on them."

August 7, 1948

A review of the material about the decision of the Council of Ministers of the Latvian SSR (No. 761 of August 27, 1947[58]) and its implementation, as well as of individual complaints received by the office of the prosecutor from citizens [reveals that] individual parish executive committees are unprepared for and have an irresponsible attitude towards the defining of *budžu* [bourgeois] farms and, as a result, the created lists [of farms] are of an unusually poor quality (often without rationales); the flawed implementation of the decision is leading to impermissible violations of laws.

The most characteristic violations are the exclusion of farms from the *budžu* [bourgeois] farm list that have all the characteristics of kulak farms; and the inclusion [in the lists] of middle-sized farms, and farms of Soviet army soldiers and participants of the partisan movement.

Contrary to decision No. 633, June 2, 1948, of the Council of Ministers of the Latvian SSR, with which all district executive committees were assigned the task of completely clearing up of the problem of kulak farms by July 10, 1948, and the review and ratification of [this task] by no later than July 15, 1948, the office of the prosecutor in the Madona district, in a review of July 17, 1948, established that of 26 parish executive committees only 7 had submitted materials.

The materials received are in the possession of a low-level [office] worker who does not review the material and does not ask for supplemental information nor takes into account [the fact that] some of the material prepared the kulak families list very superficially, as a result, making it impossible to review the legality of the inclusion of kulaks.

This circumstance [forces us] to admit that the Madona Executive Committee allowed the determination of the kulak farms to drift and has not fulfilled the 1948 decision No. 633 of the Council of Ministers of the Latvian SSR.

Moreover, from discussion with Čarna, the Second Secretary of the District Committee, it was established that illegal distortions of class politics were allowed to enter the decisions about the characteristics of kulak farms. Many farms that systematically exploited paid labor and whose members were active supporters of the German occupiers have not been included in the kulak lists because their long-term hired help did not get counted as paid employees, but as members of the farmstead.

That kind of definition increases kulak influence on their hired help and allows the preservation of kulak farms.

The following facts testify to the use of incomplete definition of [who is a kulak]:

The following live in Prauliena parish:

> Laimone, Olga – the wife of a *šucmanis* (home guardsman). Her husband was sentenced to imprisonment for 25 years for the murder of partisans and prisoners of war. The Silenieks Village Council included her in the list of kulak farms, but the Parish Executive Committee did not ratify Laimone's [inclusion].

> The village council included Polfenders, P. in the list of kulak families. He arrived at the parish executive committee meeting with his farmhand and told them that farmhands count as a member of the farmstead, and because of this explanation his farm was not included on

the kulak farm list.

Ozola, Berta – in the "Volkalna" house, husband was a *šucmanis* (home guardsman), husband was tried. The farm uses paid labor. It is not included in the kulak farm list.

Ozoliņa, Marianna, daughter of Andrejs, in the "Stuka" house, dentist born in 1915 has 23.5 hectares of land, from 1943 to 1947 exploited labor (the peasant Cirats).

Elksnīte, Anna, daughter of Jānis – in "Lijieši," born in 1888, husband, Elksnītis, Pēteris, born in 1879, 28.8 hectares land, 6 cows, it is not known where their son is. Systematically uses labor on the farm. One of those is a renter that lives in a separately constructed farmhands' house. [...]

Analogous facts are also in Ludza, Gulbene and other districts.

District prosecutors protested the decisions of individual district executive committees that removed from the kulak farm lists those who, judging by their characteristics, should have been included.

At the same time, there was the baseless inclusion of farms in the kulak farms lists that should not have been included.

In this manner, in Rēzekne district (Ozolaine parish), the district executive committee included as a kulak citizen Barkancev for practicing usury and speculation. In reality, Barkancev owns 5.3 hectares land, 2 cows, one horse, and has no agricultural machines. He does not use hired labor. He is the father of 6 small children. His wife receives support as [the mother of many children]. Barkancev himself is sick with gastrointestinal disease and is being treated in Leningrad. On trips to Leningrad he takes along produce he has grown (potatoes, meat etc.) of which he sells a portion to pay for his treatment, [and uses the rest to cover the] cost of living and other expenses. On this basis, the sick father of many children is identified as a usurer and speculator and is counted a kulak.

In the same district (Silajānis parish), the Tolstopjatov farm is included as a kulak farm because, after the death of a daughter and after Tolstopjatov's wife got sick, they hired a day-laborer for 15 days while the wife was ill. The farm has fifteen hectares.

In the Ogre district, the family farms of the Red Army soldiers Zvidriņš and Vērsēns (in Meņģeles parish) are included in the kulak farms lists without any basis.

The district prosecutor protested these illegal decisions.

In order to insure socialist legality, to implement the decision, and to eliminate the illegalities that have led in certain places to distortions of class politics,

We ask:

1. To accept the explanations of the Chair of the Madona District Executive Committee of the execution of the 1948 decision No. 633, and to assign him the task of executing this decision correctly immediately.

2. To prohibit district executive committees from making decisions that allow [the inclusion] in the lists of kulaks farms in which family members have decorations, are [military] officers or invalids from the Great Fatherland War, or are former partisans; all such material has to be sent to the Council of Ministers for ratification.

2nd ranking State Justice Advisor of the Prosecutor of the Latvian SSR   Misutin

Source: *LVA PA, 101. f., 11. apr., 70. l., pp. 64-67. Original in Russian.*

Report of the Jaunjelgava Region Council Executive Committee, Latvian SSR, to the Deputy Chair of the Council of Ministers of the Latvian SSR, J. Ozoliņš, with a request that instructions be given for returning kolkhoz farmers to the kolkhoz

September 24, 1954

The Executive Committee of Jaunjelgava region, with its August 9, 1954, report No. 1094, asks you for help in having the Latvian SSR State Insurance Board remove immediately citizen Brions Vasiļuns, son of Andrejs, from his job at the State Insurance Inspection of Jaunjelgava region, and return him as a kolkhoz farmer to the "Mičurinietis" kolkhoz. Also, his work-record book must also be returned to the kolkhoz "Mičurinietis" because he left the [kolkhoz] of his own accord.[59]

But the Latvian SSR State Insurance Board, with its document No. 1776 of August 20, 1954, which referenced the document of August 18, 1954, No. 4/9031, of the Board of Affairs group chief, comrade Kubrakovs, of the Latvian SSR Council of Ministers, maintained that there are no grounds for removing citizen B. A. Vasiļuns from work because there is not enough proof that he is a kolkhoz farmer in the documents [submitted] by the Jaunjelgava Region Executive Committee.

The Executive Committee of the Jaunjelgava region sees the action of the Latvian SSR State Insurance Board as incorrect, because, according to the existing documents on file, that while citizen *V.P. Vasiļuns* requested on March 18, 1949, before the merging of the kolkhoz "Talava" board with the kolkhoz "Talava," in front of the general assembly of members (minutes No. 10) membership, citizen *B. A. Vasiļuns* was accepted and counted as a kolkhoz farmer in the current kolkhoz "Mičurinietis."

Based on this information, the Executive Committee of the Jaunjelgava Region asks again for your help getting the Latvian SSR State Insurance Board to fulfill the September 9, 1953 decision No. 919 of the Council of Ministers of the Latvian SSR and to release comrade B.A. Vasiļuns from work at the State Insurance Inspection of the Jaunjelgava Region without delay, and to return him to the kolkhoz "Mičurinietis" and to also send his work-record book to the board of the kolkhoz "Mičurinietis".

Attachment: 1) Citizen Vera Vasiļuna daughter of Pēteris, born July 3, 1907, lives in Birzgale parish "Vaskos," request signature.

2) The minutes of the general assembly of the agricultural artel "Tālava," number 10, written March 18, 1949.

Chair of the Executive Committee of the Jaunjelgava Region   Z. Veldze
Secretary of the Executive Committee of the Jaunjelgava Region M. Grāvlejs

Source: *LVA, 270.f., 2.apr., 5415.l., p. 4.Original in Latvian.*

Documents No. 18-25
The deportations of 1949

Document No. 18

Top secret decision of the Council of Ministers of the Latvian SSR, number 282-cs, about the deportation of "kulak" families from the Latvian SSR[60]

March 17, 1949

In connection with the USSR Council of Ministers decision number 390-138-cs of January 29, 1949[61], the Council of Ministers of the Latvian SSR decides:

1. To deport 10,000 kulak families to special camps outside of the Latvian SSR in the farthest places of the Soviet Union.
2. To ratify the lists of kulak families to be deported that was submitted by the Executive Committees of the District Councils of Deputies of the Working Masses.
3. To instruct the Latvian SSR State Security Commission to deport the kulak families.

Chair of the Council of Ministers of the Latvian SSR   V. Lācis
Affair Manager of the Council of Ministers of the Latvian SSR   I. Bastin

Source: *LVA, 270. f., 1.s. 406., l., p. 188. Original in Russian.*

Document No. 19

Top secret decision No. 297-ps of the Council of Ministers about the confiscation and use of the possessions of deportees

March 24, 1949

Supplementing the March 17, 1949, decision No. 282-cs of the Council of Ministers of the Latvian SSR[62] and in connection with the January 29, 1949, decision number 390-138-cs of the Union Council of Ministers of the USSR[63], the Council of Ministers of the Latvian SSR decides:

1. To confiscate the possessions and livestock of deportees, with the exception of the possessions that the deportees take with them.
   To use the possessions of deportees to erase their debts and state-related expenses; after the erasing of debt and payments, a part of the property (residential and agricultural buildings, productive facilities, agricultural and trade inventory as well as livestock) must be given without compensation to kolkhozes, where it must be added to the common stock . The rest of the property and potatoes must be turned over for sale to the finance organs. Produce seed, livestock feed, and plant cultures must be turned over to the state (to the office of grain supply).
2. The registration of confiscated property, its storage and use, is to be handled by the district and parish executive committees. To facilitate the registration of confiscated property and to secure its storage, the executive committees of the district and parish councils of the working masses will assign responsible, authorized agents and, to help them, the required number of persons from the lists from the pool of personnel. .

3. In order to facilitate the registration of the confiscated property of deportees, its use and storage, to assign the authorized agents of the Council of Ministers of the Latvian SSR to the districts relevant to the supplement.[64]

Chair of the Council of Ministers of the Latvian SSR   V. Lācis
Affair Manager of the Council of Ministers of the Latvian SSR   I. Bastin

Source: *LVA, 270.f., 1. s.apr., 406. l., p. 189. Original in Russian.*

Document No. 20

Top secret decision from the special file of the Bureau of the Central Committee of the Latvian Communist (Bolshevik) Party about the results of the deportation[66] operation

March 29, 1949

PROLETARIANS OF ALL LANDS UNITE!
UNION COMMUNIST (BOLSHEVIK) PARTY
LATVIAN COMMUNIST (BOLSHEVIK) PARTY CENTRAL COMMITTEE

TOP SECRET
(From the special file)

Decree
Latvian Communist (b) Party Central Committee Bureau. Minutes numbers 14, 26. March 29, 1949

About the results of the operation to deport kulaks and their families, and the families of bandits and nationalists from the Republic (comrades Novik, Golovkov)

1. To recognize that the Latvian SSR State Security Ministry with the help of the State Security Ministry of the USSR successfully prepared and carried out the deportation of kulaks and their families, and the families of bandits and nationalists.
   The decisions of the USSR Union government and the Council of Ministers of the Latvian SSR on this matter are fulfilled.
2. To recognize the active participation of the Republic's Party organization, Komsomol and active members of the Council in completing the deportation.

Secretary of the Central Committee of the Latvian Communist (b) Party   J. Kalnbērziņš

2 copies Sent: Union Communist (b) Party Central Committee 1 copy, sent April 2, 1949
                                        Z. Versinina

THE MANNER OF USING THE SECRET DOCUMENTS OF THE LATVIAN COMMUNIST (b) PARTY CENTRAL COMMITTEE

The comrade who receives secret documents can not give them or discuss them with anyone, regardless of who they are, if there is no special permission from the Central Committee of the

Latvian Communist (B) party. It is category forbidden to photocopy them, or to take notes from them. Notation about the examination of the document, and the dating of each document, must be done personally by the comrade to whom the document is addressed, and [he or she] personally signs for them. The decisions of the Central Committee are stored in separate files and in no case can be attached to the office documents of the Komsomol or trade unions.

Source: *LVA PA, 101.f., 12. apr., 38a. l., p. 3. Original in Russian.*

Comment: *In order to illustrate how complicit the Communist Party of the Latvian SSR was in terrorizing the population of the country, and to show also the secrecy that accompanied its discussions and decision making, the present document (No. 20) contains not only the text itself but also the attachment that was sent out.*

Document No. 21

Top secret report of the Deputy Section Leader of the Central Committee of the Latvian Communist (Bolshevik) Party, A. Drozdov, and Deputy Section Leader, P. Ninov, to the Secretaries of the Central Committee J. Kalnbērziņš, F. Titov, P. Litvinov, and A. Pelše about the political mood of the population of Rīga following the mass deportations of March 24/25, 1949

March 26, 1949

In the Rīga population there is growing discussion about the events that occurred on the night of March 24-25. In factories, workshops, stores, markets – everywhere there is talk about what happened. Many react to the occurrence positively, saying: "It was about time. That is what they needed. Now there will be fewer bandits. The cleansing of the people's enemies from Latvia will speed the republic's prosperity etc."

Nevertheless, with all of this there is also the spread of wrong interpretations; persons explain the event in different ways: "The cleansing of Latvia is happening because soon there will be war, the Americans and English are increasing their readiness for an attack on the Soviet Union, they are strongly re-militarizing the western section of Germany." - "They are deporting the Latvians that don't submit to the Bolsheviks." – "In Latvia for the five years after the war no one was touched, but now they are deporting the Latvians because they need persons to settle the *taiga*." – "From Rīga 20,000 Latvians were deported, 80% of whom were women and children; at Ropaži station there are about 100 troop trains that day and night have Latvians loaded into the wagons." – "They will be deporting them for another 2-3 nights."

Provocative rumors were spread at the VEF factory. Citizen Moisejeva – the janitor of the 10th shop -- arriving at work told the shopwomen that she herself had seen how an arrested woman, together with her daughter, were placed in a car, but an infant was left behind. She [Moisejeva] had picked up the infant, but on the way to work had given it to a neighbor. The party organizer on the shop floor unmasked Moisejeva. After questioning, she admitted that she had told the story out of foolishness. The pupils from the 23rd high school returning from classes told their parents that all the Latvians were sent to Siberia, that in the 2nd school 3 girls – Komsomolers -- were taken from classes, and that this created a lot of worries and anxiety for their mothers. Some of the workers at the factory "Bolševicka," retelling at work what their children had said, displayed dissatisfaction. Among other things [they complained], teachers do not put a stop to such provocative discussions because they themselves are in a panic [in the belief that] all of the Latvian intelligentsia will be deported from

Latvia. The greatest anxiety is seen in the teachers of the 2nd high school. A provocative rumor spread among the medical personnel that doctor comrade Mazgalniņa, who was known as a social activist, was apparently arrested. As a result, many doctors panicked and came to the conclusion that the action is aimed toward the deportation of all Latvians.

Unhealthy, provocative rumors create nervousness among honest workers, both men and women. B. Dambe – a worker from the "Māra" factory, and a Deputy of the City Council -- turned to the factory committee chair with the following question: "What is happening in Rīga? All sorts of horrible rumors are flying about that they are going to take all the Latvians to Siberia; for what? [I can't] raise my hands for work, nothing seems important any more." B. Mīļa – brigadier from the same factory shop and a good worker -- also showed distress about the deportations from Rīga and told the shop: "Get ready to eat dried bread." A particularly despondent mood exists at the sewing shop of the "Māra" factory and, as a result, the evening shift on March 25 prepared 1,700 articles of clothing when they usually prepare 2,200-2,300 articles. Two persons from this shop were arrested – the wife of a *šucmanis*, and the mother of a convicted man. The party organization is sending many communists to the evening and night shifts to work hard at explaining the situation. Much tension has been created at the "Vairogs" factory where there were many former members of the Latvian Legion [POWs]. In the evening of March 25, a car reinforced by guards arrived at the factory [to pick up] the prisoners of war who were working there, and their departure from the factory coincided with the end of a work shift. This created considerable confusion; many concluded that the car took away arrested factory workers. In the construction work office, many repatriates from the English zone of Germany stood by waiting to be arrested. Communists were mobilized and sent to the "Vairogs" factory to explain to the masses what had happened, but almost none of the workers turned to them for explanations, but instead continued whispering to each other.

In the "Red Star" factory, the worker Plesiņš who served in the German army, and Asiņš – a locksmith – openly expressed their dissatisfaction with the arrests of Latvians, saying that "The Russian will pay dearly for this." Druvis, the warehouse supervisor, and Duncs, a locksmith, talked among themselves: "1941 is happening again, but we will show those Russians what it means to drive the Latvians away from their birthplaces." In the same factory three workers, former legionnaires, came to work in suits. When asked why they, they replied: "They are taking persons like us directly from work and so we are ready."

In the "Bolševicka" factory rumors of a different nature were spreading, many saying that these were not arrests but relocations, and that entire families left with all their belongings. "They are only taking those [who have been] involved in some sort of work against Soviet power."

The 1st city hospital collective has become noticeably calmer. A session of political instruction was held on the evening of March 25th, and a lecture was given on the theme "About the intelligentsia's role in the fulfillment of the five-year plan." Many persons came to the lecture, more than ever before. Even Professor Balodis and intern Luris, who in four years had not gone to a single lecture, came. Persons from the polyclinic are in a funereal mood because of the arrest of Doctor Kuzminskis.

At the state university, the following statements were heard in the conversations in the corridors: "They have taken out all of the Jews, 80% of the Latvians, and only Russians –communists – remain." 410 students of 4,982 did not attend classes on March 25th. The reasons for not attending are being investigated. At the agricultural academy there is noticeable distress among students in the upper classes. Many say that they walked the streets of Rīga almost all night from the 25th to the 26th of March, fearing arrest.

One of the drivers who works for the state university said that on March 25th on the road from Bauska to the Lithuanian border there were many groups of Latvians with packed bags who asked him to take them along, which request he refused.

In the Rīga market, the availability of products has declined sharply from the normal amounts: butter by 25%, meat –50%, cream – 25%, milk – 40%, bacon – 40-50%, potatoes –25-30%, flour

– 50%. There is an increased demand for bread and fats, and in the main department store in Riga [*Universālveikals*] there was a long bread line; on March 26th they sold bread only until lunchtime. In jewelry stores, gold and other precious metals are being bought up. When the sellers asked some of the buyers why there was such a demand for precious goods, the following answer was given: "Maybe there will be war, maybe they will deport all of the Latvians, therefore it is better to secure oneself with valuables." Product prices have increased: butter and bacon by 4-5 rubles per kilogram, wheat flour by 2-3 rubles per kilogram, potatoes by 30 *kapeikas* per kilogram. Butter prices have [also] risen at agricultural co-operatives.

Deputy Leader of the Party, Trade Union and Komsomol Section of the Central Committee of the Latvian Communist (b) Party   Drozdov

Leader of the Information Section   Ninov

Source: *LVP PA, 101. f., 12. apr., 81. l., pp. 55-57. Original in Russian.*

Document No. 22

Secret report by Malahova, Secretary of the Latvian Communist (Bolshevik) Party Committee of the Red Army Region of the City of Rīga, to the Secretary of the Central Committee of the Latvian Communist (Bolshevik) Party J. Kalnbērziņš, concerning the political mood of the region's inhabitants after the mass deportations of 1949

March 26, 1949

Altogether the mood of the inhabitants in the region is sound, the persons reacting correctly to the events that have happened. Nevertheless, in the region there has been some talk . The regional committee of the Latvian Communist (Bolshevik) Party can organize the identified rumors in the following manner:

1. The event that have happened herald a war in the near future, because in 1941 an analogous event took place. Therefore it is necessary to prepare a reserve of products.
2. The events were aimed at Latvians.
3. From what has been said it is clear that there was knowledge of the event before it happened.
4. The talk contains the view that the "primary" persons were not taken, but only the "pointmen."

In the state clinical hospital the Secretary of the Party organization, comrade Kolesnikova, said that the mood of the workers in the hospital is bad. Individual members are saying that those that should have been taken were not, but that second-rank persons were taken. Moreover, but comrade Kolesnikova reported that in the hospital already a week before the events there had been talk about "the deportation of Latvians", but that she had not attached particular importance to these conversations.

Communist comrade Danilova (state clinical hospital) related that on March 24, 1949 she was at the cinema with her husband. After the end of the film a well-dressed citizen came up to them and quietly said: "May God preserve you this night." After that he hid.

During the same night, comrade Danilova heard Latvian conversations on the tram to the effect that comrade Molotov had been removed from his position as Minister of Foreign Affairs and comrade Vishinski had been brought into that position; therefore, there will soon be war.

Communist comrade Jandāla of the same party organization reported that on March 24, 1949, her apartment neighbor came to her in the evening and said that he was in the "Kurzeme bag"[65] and that is why he will be deported that night.

The secretary of the party organization at the Factory Combine, Pavlova, said that many of the combine workers knew about the planned events already on the day of March 24th and talked about them, [saying] that if anyone considered themselves guilty of something (in political terms) they should not spend the night at home because during this night there would be arrests.

At the *kombinat*, comrade Zeltmane works as the cashier and her husband is a driver. On March 24, 1949, she told the workers that her husband received news about a government assignment. Apparently he told her more than that because after her statements, the workers in the office began to cry. Moreover, comrade Pavlova related how on March 24, 1949, at 13:00 she went to the store for bread and there was a long line. A few drivers came near and asked to be sold some loaves of bread without them having to wait in line. When they left, some unknown citizen said that this evening 400 cars are going to be used to deport the "disloyal"; after making this statement, the citizen disappeared.

The Secretary of the Region Executive Committee of the Party organization, comrade Serov (he is also the head of the trade section), and the Secretary of the Party organization of the Āgenskalns market, comrade Grīnbergs, said that a few days before March 24, 1949, the sale of bread, butter and particularly smoked meat became noticeably more active. Comrade Grīnbergs related that on March 24, 1949, a farmer came to him and asked him to help him find a room in Rīga for a few days, because the Latvians were to be deported from the countryside.

The Secretary of the Party organization, comrade Kruzmane, said that the Deputy of the Regional Executive Committee, comrade Sporāns, told her that on the day of March 24th everyone at the apartment council knew about the upcoming events.

The Chair of the 11th Street Committee, comrade Usakova, told comrade Golubovska (the Secretary of the Party organization of the municipal orphanage) that soon there would be many free apartments.

At the workers' meeting of the factory "Daugava" on March 24th, where the collective labor contract was being discussed, workers asked questions that suggested that persons knew about the planned events of the night of March 24th. I will just mention a few of these questions"
1. What will be the attitude toward those that served in the German army?
2. Will there be a war soon?
3. Why have a great number of automobiles gathered in the Victory Square?

The driver of this factory, Izofatovs, let it be known to the driver Petrenko that he had received a military assignment "to deport 3 wagonfuls of persons."

The Secretary of the Party Organization of the factory "Furnieris," comrade Siektorova, said that on the day of March 24, 1949, there was excitement among the workers of the office; some cried, but when she tried to discover the causes of such behavior she found out nothing.

A Communist, Andzjanov, from the factory "Bellacord Electra," said that in the tram on the evening of March 24th, two unknown citizens provoked persons with petty arguments and later said: "It's nothing, in America they are already preparing iron boots and handcuffs for you." When the Communist wanted to make further inquiries, these citizens disappeared quickly.

On March 25, 1949 at the State clinical hospital a lecture was read to the collective by comrade Freimans entitled "About the international situation" and this was attended by twice as many persons as the last lecture. In the factory "Aurora" a communist meeting was held, in which the events that had happened were explained. In the factory "Tekstiliana," an agitators' meeting was held about the anticipated congress on the question of peace.

On March 25, 1949 a meeting of secretaries of the party organizations was held and in it the basic principles of mass political work in enterprises, institutes and in schools etc. were put forward.

Secretary of the Committee of the Red Army Region of the Latvian Communist (b) Party
Malahova
Source: *LVA PA, 101.f., 12. apr., 81. l., pp. 10-11. Original in Russian..*

A. Mucenieks, Secretary of the Latvian Communist (Bolshevik) Party Rīga District Committee, [reports] secret information to the Secretary of the Central Committee of the Latvian Communist (Bolshevik) Party, J. Kalnbērziņš, about the process of the mass deportations in the Rīga district

March 31, 1949

2,109 activists participated in the deportation of kulaks and other harmful elements from the district of Rīga, among them:

      1. communists   629 persons,
      2. Komsomol members 286 persons,
      3. non-party   1,194 persons.

In addition, from the district center 135 persons were sent to help, including: All-Union Communist (Bolshevik) Party members and candidates – 112 persons, Komsomol members – 10 persons, and non-party – 13 persons from the leading Party and Soviet workers.[67]

The activists involved in this task fulfilled their assignments with honor and a good conscience. The activists participated in the collecting of kulaks and other hostile elements for deportation, as well as in registration and in the guarding of the possessions that were left behind, for example:

1. The Komsomol member, Zelenkov, in Skulte parish worked two days and nights without rest, registering all of the possessions on kulak farms.
2. The school director of Allaži parish, Marta Kirle, who was attached to an operational group as a translator, bravely entered houses ahead of everyone else and in the most active way took part in the operations.
3. The Komsomol member from Sigulda, Koneva, who worked with an operational group, was asked by the deportee Meņģelis family to take some of their shoes for her children. She was upset by this suggestion and replied: "Don't offer such vile things to me."

Without going into details of the work done by the district activists, there were individual cases of desertion:

1. All-Union Communist (Bolshevik) Party member Dābols, who works in Sigulda parish as the bookkeeper for the machine tractor station, left the activists' meeting and thus got out of participating in the work.
2. All-Union Communist (Bolshevik) Party member Turundajev, the director of the peat factory in Olaine, categorically refused to participate in the assembling of deportee elements.

The mood of most of the district inhabitants is good:

1. Farmers in Krimulda parish, after the operation was completed, said to the Secretary of the Parish Committee: "his event should have been done a long time ago, because the kulak element put brakes on the construction of the kolkhoz in our parish."
2. In Krimulda parish, in the Gaveņa village alone, there were more than 150 requests from peasants to include them in the kolkhoz. On March 27, in Sigulda, there was an artists exhibit and its participants were in a politically enthusiastic condition.
3. The farmers of Krimulda parish, supporting the government's deportation of kulaks and other harmful groups, expressed their confusion about why not all of the kulaks were deported. For example: why were the following kulaks left behind – the Amoliņš

family of the "Ziediņi" farmstead, the Mežgailis family of the "Putniņi" farmstead, Vermulis of "Sikuļa" farmstead and others who were enemies of the persons and were now left with 8 hectares of land.

Nevertheless some of the population was in a depressed mood on the 25th and 26th of March:
1. Citizen Daniels and the veterinarian Pūce arrived at the Sigulda Municipal Executive Committee asking if they could sleep peacefully and if there would be more deportations.
2. In Ķemeri, in those two days there was a greater demand for bread and there a few cases of extreme drunkenness in restaurants, the latter involving persons who said: "We no longer care if the deportation of Latvians has now begun."
3. In Allaži parish, resignation was noticeable among some of the teachers who packed their things and waited for deportation; their mood was communicated as well to their students.

On March 26, 1949, in a school in Allaži parish there was a meeting meant to explain the events, and afterward the mood changed. In the district during the assembling of the elements to be deported the following noteworthy incidents occurred:
1. In Mārupe parish, during his arrest, the kulak Eglītis, who was slated for deportation, pointed a revolver at a member of the operational group – the Komsomol district committee worker Čapass. When the other members of the operational group got involved, the revolver was knocked out of his hand.
2. In Skulte parish in the "Jaundidiņa" farmstead, as material possessions were being registered, a group of 5 armed persons approached the farmhouse and began firing at it. The parish communist organizer Brugals, who was in the house, retuned fire, and the attackers hid themselves.
3. On March 26th at 13:00 in Allaži parish signs were posted with the phrase: "Eternal honor to the deported martyrs." The persons that posted the pamphlets were found immediately, detained, and turned over to the organs of the State Security Commission.
4. In Ropaži parish, in the class of the high school teacher Strazdiņa a farewell was organized for a student who was deported with his family, and this created empathy among the pupils.
5. In Ropaži parish, the school director, Elksnis contacted the parish executive committee by telephone, asked the chair to the phone, and told her: "Thank you, you traitor to the nation."

A panicky mood was not noticeable among the deportees, but some of them behaved provocatively:
1. The kulak Jānis Bite, a former German army officer (Skulte parish) said: "Don't worry, the times are changing, and we will meet with Cernobrov (the Parish Party Committee Secretary) again and then settle accounts."
2. The kulak Sloka from Sigulda parish yelled loudly so all could hear: "Don't worry, we will not have to wait long, the English will soon take Latvia."
3. In Sigulda, while the deportee Marta Meņģele, whose husband was sentenced to 25 years, was being detained, her sister Kolpakova, who was not being deported (she is a worker at the local consumer society), told the members of the operational group: "What kind of Latvians are you, what kind of ideas do you have, when you sell out your homeland and your nation."

From the train of the deported, letters addressed to the secretary of the Latvian Communist (b) Party Sigulda Parish Executive Committee, comrade Filips, and to Judaža Village Council Chair, comrade Kalniņš, were delivered and they had the following contents:

"We are not afraid of death, our hearts are strong. Greetings to our fertile farm fields. It is not difficult to die for your homeland. Greetings to the Great Sun of Moscow and goodbye to our pastures and groves."

"...We ... go away to the wealthiest provinces of the homeland. We go with a smile on our faces, but you – our Latvians – you did not want to stay with us."

Some activists warned some of the deportees:

1. The telephone operator of Skulte parish, Miķelsone, warned the kulak Liepiņa that she was to be deported. Miķelsone was immediately released from her position and turned over to the State Security Commission organs.
2. The authorized agent of ten farmstead in Inčukalns parish – Elza Linde -- warned the kulaks in her ten farmstead about the expected deportations. Linde was detained.
3. Many of the Riga district kulaks already knew about the deportations because for an entire week earlier the operational group was in the parish and visited only the farms of kulaks meant to be deported, forgetting about a conspiratorial response. As a result many kulaks and their families hid themselves.

The work of assembling deportees in the district happened in the allotted time.

All of the possessions [of the deportees] that remained behind were registered in a timely manner and the safeguarding of it by activists was organized.

During the operation there was some looting of property:

1. In Krimulda parish the Union Communist (b) Party member Skorov while deporting the kulak Krieviņš took a watch, money, and a radio.
2. In Mangaļi parish the Union Communist (b) Party candidate Strazdiņš took from a kulak farm 2 jars of honey and a pair of shoes.
3. The Secretary of the Komsomol Committee of Mārupe parish – Union Communist (B) Party candidate member Dombrovskis took 1,000 rubles while deporting the kulak Upmanis.

All of these events were discovered immediately and the stolen property and money was confiscated.

Currently the directive of the Council of Ministers and Central Committee of the Latvian Communist (b) Party about the use of the property that was left behind after deportation is being implemented.

Secretary of the Rīga District Committee of the Latvian Communist (B)
Party   Mucenieks

Source: *LVA PA, 101. f., 12. apr., 81.l., pp. 51-52. Original in Russian.*

Document No. 24

Top secret report of the Chief of the 1ˢᵗ Special Section of the Ministry of the Interior of the Latvian SSR and the Section's 2ⁿᵈ Section Chief about those deported from Latvia and about requests received that various persons be freed from special camps

December 20, 1954

1. In 1941, socially dangerous elements and their families deported – 5,521.
2. In 1949, convicted nationalist families deported – 4,254.
3. In 1949, kulak families deported – 9,250.
4. In 1945, ethnic Germans deported – 384 families.
5. From 1949 to 1952, 250 persons deported for other reasons
6. Total from 1941 until 1952, 59,794 persons deported.

Altogether up to January 1, 1954, there were 150 families (a total of 269 persons) freed from the special camps.

The review of submissions to the Latvian SSR Ministry of the Interior special section from January 21, 1954 to December 20ᵗʰ:

1. 9,152 submissions received from persons in special camps and their relatives. Of those, 8,487 were reviewed; 665 are still under review.
1. The number of requests judged not to be relevant to decisions of the Latvian SSR Ministry of the Interior [about special camps] – 7,310 submissions.
2. The number of requests judged to be relevant to the decisions decision of the Latvian SSR Ministry of the Interior – 1,177 submissions (about 1,162 persons).
    Of those: the Latvian SSR Council of Ministers satisfactorily handled 694 submissions (requests) for 1,162 persons.
    The special section of the Ministry of the Interior of the USSR satisfactorily handled 209 submissions (requests) for 338 persons.
3. There are 62 submissions (requests) for 105 persons at the Council of Ministers of the Latvian SSR that are still awaiting final decision.
    The 4ᵗʰ special section of the Ministry of the Interior of the USSR still has 209 submissions (requests) for 338 persons.

On average, from the special camp inmates and from their relatives, we receive about 40 submissions daily.

All of the received submissions are registered in a journal and a review card is created for each. After that, the submissions are given to the [persons] handling the catalogue and archive so that that person's camp file can be found for review. After the review file is received from the archive, it, together with the submission, are given to the 1ˢᵗ Special Section's 2ⁿᵈ Section workers for review. If in the review of the file and submission there is some confusion, the file and the submission are sent to the local police section for a review by local soviet organs and for the interrogation of witnesses. Moreover, there is also review of the file in the state archives of the Latvian SSR Ministry of the Interior and of other organs.

Many submissions are received from children of special camp inmates that do not mention the parents or relatives that they were deported with. With these kinds of submission, a request is forwarded for review of the submission to the organs of the Ministry of the Interior, and, after that, to the special camp itself, because without the head of the family being named in the submission it is not possible to find the file in the archives. In these cases, and in the cases of files that ask for additional review, the normal amount of time for the process lasts up to two months.

The review files and the submissions that do not require additional review are looked through in 10-25 days from the date that they are received.

On December 20, 1954 there were still 665 submissions from special camps that have not been reviewed.

Of those: 6 were received in May, 7 in June, 25 in July, 33 in August, 27 in September, 60 in October, 138 in November, 369 in December – all in the year 1954.

Of the submissions that have not yet been reviewed, 137 are under review with the Latvian SSR Ministry of Interior militia region sections and the special camp locations; the rest of the submissions are under review of the 2nd Section's workers.

The review process addressing complaints and submissions frees from the special camps deported families or individual persons for the following reasons:
1. mistakenly deported families,
2. mistakenly deported individuals that were incorrectly attached to deported families,
3. families of participants in the Great Fatherland war of 1941-1945,
4. members of a nationalist family who were sentenced to 5 years of loss of freedom, tried and amnestied,
5. solitary, aged persons or those have lost the ability to work because of illness as well as persons that are found in invalid homes (these persons are freed and given over to the care of relatives).

For each of the freed families or individuals from the special camps a decision is then written and submitted for ratification by the Minister of the Interior, but for nationalists and for family members of deportees who are socially dangerous elements – also for sanction by the Latvian SSR Prosecutor.

Decisions involving the freeing of family members of former kulaks from special camps are sent for final decision to the Council of Ministers of the Latvian SSR, but for nationalists and family members of socially dangerous elements the documented decision, together with archival review and investigative file, are sent for the final decision to the 4th Special Section of the Ministry of the Interior of the USSR.

After the final decision, the results are conveyed to the submitter through the intermediary of the receiving territorial organ of the Ministry of the Interior and the Latvian SSR Ministry of the Interior.

The submissions from the special camps, and the archival review process needed for removal from the special camps, involve complex questions that are difficult to settle correctly; for example:

1. The kulak family was deported but the head of the family was not deported because he was away at the time and lives in the Latvian SSR and works at a socially useful and indispensable job. But his family is in a special camp or half of the family lives together in the Latvian SSR while the other half is in special camps.

2. The deported kulak aided partisans and maintained contact with them during the Fatherland War from 1941-1945.

3. The nationalist-bandit legalized himself and is living in the Latvian SSR, but the family that was deported because of him is still in a special camp.

4. In 1945, the nationalist's wife is tried but she divorces him in 1946 and marries someone else, but in 1949 she is deported to a special camp because of her first husband.

5. During the deportation in 1941 the family was deported, and, as a result the father and mother

died; but the children – son and daughter who were deported with them when they were underage -- are still in the special camps.

6. The husband died in the special camp but his wife who was deported because of the husband is still in the special camps and has remarried and has a different family.

7. In the special camps there are solitary older persons 60 years of age and older; should they be reviewed by an expert medical commission if they are capable of working, or can they be removed from the special camp review list because of their work capacity?

It is necessary to receive explanations for these complex questions.

Chief of the 1ˢᵗ Special Section of the Ministry of the Interior of the Latvian SSR, Major
      Karpačs

Chair of the 2ⁿᵈ Section of the Special Section of the Ministry of the Interior of the Latvian SSR
Lieutenant Colonel
            Borisov

Source: *LVA PA, 101.f., 18. apr., 40a. l., pp. 54-57. Original in Russian.*

Document No. 25

Excerpts from the secret minutes of a meeting of the Secretariat of the Central Committee of the Latvian Communist Party about the administrative order concerning the review of complaints from deported citizens

March 7, 1955

[…] Kalnbērziņš: […] There should be, when looking through these complaints, some kind of barrier to slow down the return [of deported citizens]. We need to know how he behaves there on the spot, what kind of person he is now, whether is he socially dangerous or not. What is making us hurry with this work? My opinion is that there must be a commission that does not just grant permission to return here, but looks at the entire question: where will this person go, what to do with him? Has he had property or not, what will the decision be about this question? When he returns, resolving this question will be too late. After [the return] they will ruin all of our kolkhozes.

Vēvers[67]: I have a small addition. Among these numbers are not just kulaks, but also bandits and supporters of bandits. The deportation of kulaks took place according to a decision of the Council of Ministers, and now the Council of Ministers can review these cases and reach a decision. But the bandits and bandit supporter cases were decided in a special session. Who can rescind a decision of a special session? In Moscow, they are solving this question and they say that these files should be given for review by the provincial, district and supreme courts of the individual Republics to be reviewed. This question is still not decided. Somehow, we should direct this question to the administrative section of the Central Committee of the USSR in order for them to decide. […]

Kalnbērziņš: I think that we should not hurry with returns. It would be better if some of the persons did not return now. Moreover, by now they have sunk roots where they are, they work there, but when they return here, they have nothing. Then they will only be more upset. Where a mistake is obvious, they have to return, but those are in the hundreds, not the tens of thousands.

Secretary of the Central Committee of the Latvian Communist Party   J. Kalnbērziņš

Source: *LVA PA, 101.f., 18. apr., 40a. l., pp. 49-50. Original in Russian.*

DOCUMENTS NO. 26-29
VARIETIES AND INEFFICIENCIES OF REPRESSION

Document No. 26

From the verdict of the tribunal conducted by the military arm of the Latvian SSR Ministry of the Interior in the case of Eduards Andersons, a member of Latvia's Central Council[68].

August 28, 1946

Verdict 1339
In the name of the Union of Soviet Socialist Republics

On August 28, 1946, the war tribunal of the military arm of the Latvian SSR Ministry of the Interior in a closed session in a location in Rīga. Consisting of: Chair – captain of justice Sinickis, members – senior lieutenant Borunov and junior lieutenant Zoremba, secretary – junior lieutenant of justice Filipova, with the participation of the general staff translator Hasana.

After reviewing case No. 2590, the charge against Eduards Andersons, son of Ernests, born 1919 in the Buka farmstead of Ance parish in the Venstpils district of the Latvian SSR, Latvian, citizen of the USSR, servant, lived illegally up until his arrest, with an intermediate education, non-party, single, not previously tried, has not served in the Red army [...]

Determined:

During the time period when the territory of the Latvian SSR was occupied by German military forces, the leaders of the former bourgeois political parties of Latvia founded an illegal, nationalist organization in 1943, "Latvia's Central Council" – "LCC" -- whose central headquarters was based in a foreign country.

This organization chose as its goal the renewal of the bourgeois order in Latvia with the help of other imperialist states.

To realize their goals, the "LCC" sent in members from foreign countries, agents and spies to start organizational work, that is, to recruit and involve new members from among the anti-soviet elements.

Moreover, "Latvia's Central Council" organized bandit groups on the territory of Latvia and provided instructions to them for their operational work; therefore, the "LCC" was the center [of this network].

The Andersons on trial, having a hostile attitude toward Soviet order and finding himself in a foreign country, joined the "LCC" in 1943 and until the time of his arrest fulfilled important operative assignments for the Center.

In 1944-1945, Andersons was sent into Latvia several times; brought secret instructions to the "LCC" leadership as well as a radio apparatus; established contacts with "LCC" members in Rīga and in other cities in the Latvian SSR; undertook the recruitment of members; gathered information, i.e. engaged in espionage, and took the information to the "LCC" outside the Latvian borders.

In October of 1945, the Andersons on trial led a meeting in Rīga of "LCC" members that decided:

1. To organize the distribution of an illegal newspaper in the name of the "LCC."
2. To establish contacts with bandit formations in the territory of Latvia and radio contact with the "LCC" center.
3. To gather information for espionage purposes and resolve other questions related to the leadership of bandit formations.

After this meeting, Andersons, finding himself illegally in Rīga and Kurzeme, wrote many articles with openly anti-Soviet content for publication in the newspaper, and gathered information for espionage purposes that he was preparing to send to the "LCC" beyond the borders. [...]

Based on all of the mentioned, the war tribunal recognizes Andersons ... as guilty according to the RSFSR Criminal Code 58-1a p. 58-11 p. and RSFSR KPK p. 319, 320.

Sentence.

Eduards Andersons, son of Ernests, in line with the RSFSR Criminal Code 58-1ap is to be punished with the maximum punishment – execution by shooting, and the confiscation of all personal possessions. [...]

The verdict can be appealed to the USSR Supreme Court War Collegium within 72 hours of the moment that the convicted receives a written verdict from the war tribunal which prepared this verdict.

Original signed.
Copy correct: chair of the investigation of the affair, captain of justice   Sinickis

Source: *LVA, 1986. f., 1. apr., 28636. l., vol. 2, pp. 80, 81. Copy of original. Original in Russian.*

Document No. 27

Memorandum from the Free Fatherland Union, Latvia's National Partisan Union, and Representatives of Workers, Farmers and the Intelligentsia to the Chair of the Presidium of the Supreme Council of the Latvian SSR, Prof. Dr. A. Kirchenšteins, the Chair of the Council of Ministers of the Latvian SSR, V. Lācis, and the Secretary of the Central Committee of the Latvian Communist (Bolshevik) Party, J. Kalnbērziņš, demanding the end of terror against the inhabitants of Latvian and the organization of a free national referendum

August 8, 1946

The decision of the Saeima asking the Supreme Soviet of the USSR to accept the Latvian SSR as a part of the USSR -- after Latvia was occupied on June 17, 1940, and proclaimed as a Soviet socialist republic -- is illegal because it does not meet the requirements of international law recognized by the Hague Convention of 1940, and because it does not meet the requirement for a national referendum as set out in the 1922 founding law of the state, which prescribes that a take-over of the state, a change in the form of the state, or the state's attachment to another state only becomes law if there is a definite majority of votes expressed in a national referendum, if the voting is free and takes place without the presence of an occupational military force. The entire world knows that did not happen. Therefore, the attachment of Latvia to the USSR was an illegal and crude violation of international law and the founding law of the state. The charter of the United Nations in 1945 also recognizes and reinforces the idea that any large or small nation's fate is determined by the will of the people through free, equal, direct, and secret elections; consequently, the above-mentioned violent act is illegal. Moreover, the entire world knows that the USSR elections that took place on the territory of the Baltic states, whether on April 11, 1941[69] or February 10, 1946, were illegal in that the free will of the people was under the terror threat and weapons of the NKVD and the Red Army and [the elections were therefore] forced and deceitful. The Crimea Conference in 1944 recognized the principles of the Atlantic Charter[70], and the charter of the United Nations[71] says that each nation has the right to express its will and desires according to democratic principles; moreover, that every political group and every citizen is guaranteed the right to freely voice political beliefs according to these declarations without any pressure from the government. Looking at the territory of Latvia from this perspective, we see that the dictatorship of the Bolshevik Party does not allow even the slightest expression of other political beliefs, turning the weapons of the NKVD and NKGB[72] against them. In view of the fact that the Bolshevik Party in Latvia does not constitute more than 4% of the population,[73] and received less than 10% support them from the Latvian nation, the persecution of those who think differently cannot be justified in terms of internationally accepted and declared principles; moreover, such behavior is directed not only against political opponents, but the power of the NKVD and the NKGB, exercised without limits and arbitrarily, seeks to subjugate completely, economically and physically, family members of political opponents – women, children, and old persons. Theft, violence, terror, often rooted in personal animosities, are the methods with which the established power threatens the continued existence of the Latvian nation and denies even the slightest possibility of democratic freedoms. Concerning all these matters, we have in our hands the documented accounts of thousands of inhabitants. Reviewing Stalin's 4th five-year plan, we see that in comparison with other territories and economies of the USSR republics, the anticipated plan for Latvia's industrial and agricultural production, and the deductions made in the interests of the USSR, are unjustifiably greater than from other, similar republics; furthermore, the plan does not serve the economic growth of the Latvian nation, but the external and internal political objectives of the USSR. This kind of planning, which ignores the state's economic capabilities, threatens to completely exhaust the resources of our state, removing the foundation of its existence and moving the nation toward famine and destruction.

In can be ascertained that in spite of the anticipated development of national strength and the privileges accorded to specific republics in Stalin's constitution, foreigners have the leading role in the institutions and industrial enterprises of the Latvian SSR, while the most able ethnic Latvian workers are pushed to one side or are placed in ill-fitting jobs. Neither does remuneration come close to matching socialist principles. (The leading functionaries of the party and government receive between 30-40,000 rubles with no limitations on what can be purchased, but the average worker's wage is only 300 rubles and a pitiful bread ration).[74]

The cost of supplies and the cost of products, as well as taxes and the prices of essential goods, are so out of proportion in relation to each other that the situation threatens to destroy the sustainability and productivity of [the basis] our national economy – agriculture.

Summing up the facts documented above, we draw the following conclusions:

1. The existing order of the Latvian state does not correspond to international law and to the democratic principles in the charter of the United Nations concerning the self-determinations of nations.

2. The work of the People's Commissariat of the Interior and the People's Commissariat of State Security and other bureaus of Soviet power, which have targeted the unprotected majority of the nation through deportations, terror, theft, and acts of violence is leading inexorably and unavoidably to the complete destruction of the nation in the near future.

3. The economic production plan of the state has been created without taking into account the economic capacity of the country, does not serve the interests of Latvia and the Latvian nation, and threatens to destroy the material foundation of Latvia and with it the Latvian nation.

4. The government of the Latvian SSR and the members of the Latvian Communist (b) Party, both of which are only carrying out the orders of the USSR and the Communist (Bolshevik) Party that do not match the vital interests of Latvia, are leading the Latvian nation to moral, physical, and economic destruction and serve only pan-Slavism and the goals of imperialist Bolshevism, neither of which have anything in common with the Latvian nation.

Understanding the historical responsibility we have to the vital interests and the future of the Latvian nation, we, the National Partisan Union of Latvia, The Free Fatherland Union, and the representatives of the workers, peasants, and intelligentsia, speaking in the name of the expectations and desires of the majority of the Latvian nation

DEMAND THE FOLLOWING

1. The local organs of power – the police, the People's Commissariat of the Interior, and the People's Commissariat of State Security -- must end the deportations, terror, thefts and other despotic actions directed against defenseless civilian inhabitants – women, children, and old persons -- as well as against the representatives of the Latvian nation who are being repressed for political reasons.
2. Recognizing that the Stalin constitution guarantees the rights of Republics and that the government of the USSR exploits the Latvian state and the strengths of the Latvian nation to implement the goals of pan-Slavism and international Bolshevik imperialism, we ask, in the name of the vital interests and future of the Latvian nation for which you are now responsible before history just as the institutions of the German occupation were from 1941 to 1944, that all unneeded and unjustifiable Russian armed occupation forces be evacuated – the units of the Red Army, and [relevant units] of the People's Commissariat of the Interior and the People's Commissariat of State Security.
3. Without the presence and influence of occupation armed forces, free national elections should be held already in 1945 (*sic!*) on the question of whether Latvia should stay in the USSR or not, which you have a right do and which is in harmony with the Stalin (USSR) constitution. To implement this demand of the national majority, as expressed in this memorandum, you will create the necessary conditions that will give Latvia the opportunity to determine its fate as an independent state, in line with legality and justice, in the name of humanity, and in harmony with the charter of the United Nations.

In the opposite case, in order to struggle against the present lawlessness and violence that is already recognized internationally and is attracting the attention of the world, we will be forced to resist with all the means in our possession to delay the destruction of the Latvian nation and the end of the Latvian state, for which we and also you are responsible before history and international rights. We insist that these demands be met by the time there is a conflict between the Western alliance and the USSR, so that the interests of our state and our nation might suffer less and so that as a real democratic state we can build our lives on the democratic cooperation between party and class, which is the only way the state will flourish and step upon the path of progress.

Signed, in the name of the will and desires of the majority of the Latvian nation,

Representatives of the Free Fatherland Union, National Partisan Union of Latvia, and the workers, peasants, and intelligentsia.

Source: *LVA, 1986. f., 1. apr., 40012.l. , vol. 4, p. 49. Original in Latvian.*

Secret review of the deportations of segments of the population, conducted by the Latvian Communist Party Central Committee Section Instructor Vasiljev, Latvian SSR Prosecutor Assistant Prosecutor of Special Affairs Kuznecova and the Chief of the 1ˢᵗ Special Section of the Ministry of the Interior of the Latvian SSR, Karpačs

January 21, 1955

In the time period from 1941 until 1949 there were altogether three mass deportations, with the sum total of more than 60,000 persons deported. We were unable to precisely determine the number deported because the data of the Ministry of the Interior of the Latvian SSR for the 1941 operation are only approximate.

The first operation occurred in June of 1941 when the organs of the Ministry of the Interior of the Latvian SSR deported former merchants, the highest ranking officials of the Latvian bourgeois government, police, etc. and their families. Altogether there were about 18-19,000 persons[75] for whom (in most cases) the Ministry of the Interior of the Latvian SSR has surveillance files, but occasionally also investigative files (more than 6,500 files).

True, usually the heads of these families were arrested without the sanction of a prosecutor, and they were shipped to camps in the interior of the Soviet Union. Most of the criminal proceedings were begun against them there, [but these] were often interrupted by the death of the arrested person or because their cases were sent to the Ministry of the Interior of the USSR for special review since these persons were tried as "socially dangerous elements" or for "counter-revolutionary work" with the loss of freedom for 5 to 10 years.[76]

Together with arrest of and transport to the camps of the head of the family, the family members of the arrested were also deported from the Latvian SSR and their possessions confiscated and nationalized, but without a legal act for the latter action.

We were unable to determine if there was a government decision for the deportation of this contingent,[77] but these families found themselves (in the best cases) in the special camps based only on a decision grounded in the "About Deportations" document of the State Security Commission of the Latvian SSR. But at times there is not even this "Document"; on rare occasions, the action was carried out only through personal notification, i.e. that the person will be deported with no reason given.

Most of these family heads died a long time ago, their wives have also died, and currently their children who remain under arrest in the camps, or their relatives, are asking in their many complaints for an explanation: whether the children will have to be imprisoned for a long time because of charges against someone else, even if those charges are known. The arrested children, or relatives, have very often already started new families, but still remain under the original classification. There are cases in which the wife of a deceased deported person has married again and has had children from the new marriage, but is still in a special camp. More often, following the decision of the Council of Ministers of the USSR, the Minister of the Interior of the USSR issued an order (No. 00597), on July 16, 1954, which released from special camps the children that were born after December 31, 1937. According to this order, a child that was 3.5 years of age when deported from the Latvian SSR can leave the special camps and become a free citizen, but a child that was 4.5 years of age when deported still remains on the special list. This also leads to many complaints.

The second mass deportation was carried out in February of 1945, following the verbal order of the former Deputy Minister of State Security of the USSR, Merkulov. In this, 675 ethnic Germans and persons without citizenship were deported. No personal files were started for these deported persons; and in the Ministry of the Interior of the Latvian SSR there are only the personnel lists of these deported, with no signature and only a note of unknown origin in pencil -- "deported according to the verbal order of Merkulov" – and that is all. On what basis these persons were deported and are currently being maintained on the special lists is not known.

The third mass deportation occurred on March 24-25, 1949 when more than 42,000 persons were deported from the Latvian SSR (kulaks, legalized bandits, convicted nationalists and other similar families).

The deportation of the kulak elements was done in line with the decision (No. 282cs) of March 17, 1949, of the Council of Ministers of the Latvian SSR[78]; in this decision, there were no specific characterizations of a kulak farm or of the persons that were anticipated to be deported. In fact, the selection of the kulak farms and of the persons to be deported was done by organs of the State Security Ministry of the Latvian SSR. Moreover, the basic criteria for determining if someone was a kulak were archived reports, created by the bourgeois Latvian government in 1939, about the inhabitants and their views on the national economy; that is, data that at the moment of deportation were ten years old, which raises considerable doubts about them. Even so, in many files not even this information was found, and, in its place, were reports compiled by district section chiefs of the State Security Ministry of the Latvian SSR, based on information from parish and district executive committees, containing the characterization of these or other farms as kulak farms in 1947-1948. [79]

What characteristics of these farms were chosen to define them as kulak farms was not mentioned. Also, it was not mentioned if these farms were later removed from the list of kulak farms. The same district sections of the State Security Ministry also determined who was a member of a kulak family; in the deportation files, there are the reports prepared by these same organs from existing parish farm descriptions. In the files are also reports of the district sections of the State Security Ministry that say that none of the members of the anticipated deportee family served or serves in the Soviet army or with the partisans.

In this way the local organs of power and Soviet activists were essentially kept from uncovering the kulak element that hampered collectivization in the Latvian SSR.

Reviewing these categories of complaint, it is clear that many families were mistakenly deported from the Latvian SSR, and that there was falsification of the record. Often in place of persons on one farm, those on another were deported; in place of kulaks, service persons; soldiers' families were deported and families were divided – children deported, but parents left behind or vice versa. In one case, because the head of the family had been arrested in the past and imprisoned for 1-2 years, his family was deported. Now he is free from imprisonment, his punishment having been shortened; he lives in the Latvian SSR; but his family is in the special camp. Helpless and old invalids who could not look after themselves were also deported.

The deportation of the families of persons convicted of counter-revolutionary activity, and the deportation of pardoned or active "bandits", was carried out without any decisions based in the law; only some 5-6 months later did the Ministry of State Security of the USSR at a particular meeting make a [retroactive] decision about the of these individuals.

As with the kulak elements, the deportation of nationalist elements and their family members was also carried out by the state security organs of the Latvian SSR. True, the Republic's prosecutor sanctioned these acts. But about this category of the deported, attention should be drawn to the following facts.

The family of an allegedly active "bandit" was deported, but later it was determined that this person never belonged to a bandit group but had only tried to get out of serving in the Soviet army and was therefore living outside the law.

A pardoned "bandit" -- the head of his family -- was deported even though he had been pardoned at the suggestion of the Ministry of the Interior of the Latvian SSR, even though there was no proof of any criminal activity on his part, and even though until the day of the deportation he worked at a socially useful job.

The family of a person already serving a five-year sentence was deported. Now this person is free, his punishment is over, and he is a free citizen, but his family is still in the camps.

Just as with the deportation of the kulak elements, so also with the nationalist elements there was breaking up of families, incorrect facts as the basis for deportation, etc.

In a review of the complaints in the files of those in special camps, the most severe violations [in procedure] were uncovered in the use of evidence for convictions, in the implementation of the deportations themselves, and in the process of complaint review by the Ministry of State Security of the Latvian SSR. Some examples of these violations are:

On March 25, 1949, Alfreds Mārtiņšons and the family of his sister Alma Kušķe (four persons) were deported from the "Sildziņa" farmstead in Valmiera district (in the review, case No. 17031). According to the report prepared by the officials of the Ministry of State Security of the Latvian SSR, in 1939 Mārtiņšons had used 3 farmhands in his farm. After Mārtiņšons' appeal in 1950, the Ministry of State Security did a review and discovered that Mārtiņšons had never used hired labor and that his farm was small – 5 hectares of plowland, 5 hectares of fields and 10 hectares of swamp and brush. Ignoring this information, the leadership of the Ministry of State Security refused to review his file further, and only after a second complaint of March 30, 1954, did the Council of Ministers of the Latvian SSR, following the suggestion of the Ministry of the Interior of the Latvian SSR, rescind the deportation of the Mārtiņšons-Kušķe family.

The Jankaitis family was illegally deported as well (case No. 16226). The file contained written information by the same official (as above) from the Latvian SSR Ministry of State Security that the "Pekeļa" farmstead, owned by Pēteris Jankaitis in the Liepāja district, Aizviķa parish, used hired labor and that no one in the Jankaitis family had served or serves in the Soviet army. The report was signed by the Liepāja district region chief of the Ministry of State Security of the Latvian SSR, Jaunpetrovičs. In the forms that were written up while the family was being readied for deportation, Pēteris Jankaitis stated that his son had served in the Soviet army and had fallen in a battle with Germans. This information was ignored and Pēteris Jankaitis, his wife Anna, and their daughter Elvīra Elfrīda were sent to the deportation transport facility. But because the elderly parents were sick and helpless, they were not placed in the transport vehicle and only their daughter Elvīra Elfrīda was deported. After Elvīra Elfrīda Jankaitis submitted a complaint from the special camp, the Ministry of the Interior of the Latvian SSR reviewed the case and determined that, first of all, Jankaitis was not a kulak and had not used hired labor on his farm and that the witness accounts in his file did not conform with reality; and, second, that the brother of the deported woman (Elvīra Elfrīda) really was killed at the front while fighting the Germans and that his mother – Anna Jankaitis – who was supposed to be deported was actually receiving a state pension because of her son's death.

With a decision of the Council of Ministers of the Latvian SSR of March 30, 1954, the placement of Elfrīda Jankaitis in the special camps was ended.

In the same parish and district there took place the illegal deportation of the six-person family of Pēteris Cimmers, from the "Burvītis" farmstead. This was also based on his supposed use of hired labor and his not having a family member who served in the Soviet army. The appeal of Vallija Cimmera from the special camps in 1950 to the Ministry of State Security of the Latvian SSR was ignored and there was a refusal to review her file. In 1954 in a review by the Ministry of the Interior of the Latvian SSR, it was discovered that the "Burvītis" farm never used hired labor and that Pēteris Cimmers' son Žanis Cimmers served in the Soviet army.

By a decision of the Council of Ministers of the Latvian SSR of October 18, 1954, the placement of this family in the special camp was ended.

We could mention many more similar cases. In case No. 15274, in Kuldīga district in place of a kulak, a farmhand's family was deported. In case No. 15139, which is about the family of the kulak Jānis Rumbenieks who supposedly owned 34 hectares of land and exploited hired labor, the 1954 Ministry of the Interior of the Latvian SSR review uncovered that Rumbenieks did not own 34 hectares but only 3, and that he clearly never used hired labor. Rumbenieks submitted an appeal in 1951, but the Ministry of State Security of the Latvian SSR refused to review his file even though it was already known at this time that his family was deported by mistake.

A characteristically formal and unfeeling approach [to these matters] ... is shown in the language of the deportation documents in case No. 11474: the Ministry of State Security of the Latvian SSR stated that the family of Pēteris Rogāls were kulaks and supposedly the owners of the "Rogals" farm in Krustpils parish in Daugavpils district. After an appeal started a review, it was determined that the "Rogals" farm really did belong to the kulak Pēteris Rogals, the former Tukums parish[80] elder who was deported with his family in 1941; but that the 1949 deportees turned out to be the poor peasants with the same name – Pēteris Rogals.

There are cases in which, after a review, the prosecutor of the Ministry of the Interior of the Latvian SSR has come to a decision that some nationalist family was deported mistakenly ... he brings the case before the Ministry of the Interior of the USSR in order to remove the family from the special list. Nonetheless, in many cases the 4th special section of the Ministry of the Interior of the USSR then refuses to review the file, saying that "the removal from the special list of this category of persons currently lack grounds" (case No. 26273 concerning Rumda and Ozols).

Only in 1954, when on the grounds for appeal the review of files began, about 2,000 persons were released from the deportation [category].

SUGGESTIONS
1. Suggest that all relevant organs release from the special list all children in special camps who were not 16 years of age when they were deported.
2. Suggest to the Ministry of the Interior of the USSR and the prosecutor [that it has the] right to propose removing persons on the special deportation lists from the Latvian SSR in 1941.
3. Suggest the creation of a commission attached to the Council of Ministers of the Latvian SSR and the Ministry of the Interior for review of the files of all persons deported from the Latvian SSR between 1945 and 1949 [together] with an obligatory review of the information from the [deportation site] that is available from the state archives and criminal files.

Section Instructor of the Central Committee of the Latvian Communist Party Vasiljev
Assistant Prosecutor on Special Affairs of the [Office of the] Latvian SSR Prosecutor   Kuznecov
Chief of the 1st Special Section of the Ministry of the Interior of the Latvian SSR Karpač

Source: *LVA PA, 101. f., 18. apr., 40a.l., pp. 58-64. Original in Russian.*

Document No. 29

Excerpts from the top secret report of the Chair of the State Security Committee of the Council of Ministers of the Latvian SSR, Major General J. Vēvers, entitled "Concerning hostile and anti-soviet expressions by persons who were previously repressed for counter-revolutionary crimes and have now returned to the Latvian SSR"

January 2, 1958

[This report] relates to the decision of the Presidium of the Supreme Soviet of the USSR of September 17, 1955, "About amnesty for Soviet citizens who collaborated with occupiers during the Great Fatherland War of 1941-1945" and to the Commission of the Presidium of the Supreme Soviet of the USSR that is reviewing the files of persons who are in correctional labor camps and have been deported. [In light of these,] and according to incomplete reports, more than 21,000 persons previously repressed for counter-revolutionary crimes have returned to the Latvian SSR in 1956-1957. An additional 7,022 families have been removed from the special camp lists of the Council of Ministers of the Latvian SSR, for a total of 18,318 persons.

As determined, among those returning there are about 500 [former] members of armed nationalist bands and more than 500 former members of illegal nationalist organizations, and a significant number of former secret agents of foreign countries, officers from the Latvian bourgeois and German fascist armies, many former bourgeois party leaders, and prominent figures of the Ulmanis regime etc.

A significant number of those returning have settled in the largest cities and towns of the republic. 1,660 persons are registered in Rīga. In truth, the number of returnees who live in Rīga is considerably greater, because there is a known number who have registration restrictions in their passports: they register as living outside of Rīga, but in fact live with their relatives or associates in the city. For example, Emma Migla, daughter of David (the leader of the Jehovah's Witness sect), was released early from a correctional labor camp in 1955 and is registered in Sigulda at Strēlnieka Street 37.

Arturs Siļķe, son of Kriss (the Lutheran pastor who was a leader of the international anti-soviet organization „Christian Student Society" and who raised his son in this spirit), returned in 1957 and lives with his associates in Riga on Aptieka street 2, apartment 2.[81] While in the camps, he was suspected of leading an underground national organization that operated there.

More than 150 of those who are registered as living in the Rīga district in fact live in Rīga. In the Ogre region 690 persons have returned from imprisonment and deportation. Of these 100-120 persons formally registered to live in the Ogre region but did not stay. It has been discovered that 25 of them live in Rīga.

Of the 1,630 persons who have returned and live in Rīga, it has been uncovered that they include: 78 former bandits, 63 former participants of the nationalist underground, 49 persons [who were] agents of the spying agencies of the USA and Germany, 47 persons [who were] official collaborators with the SD [*Sicherheitsdienst*], 396 former participants in punitive actions, 131 persons who served in the police or police battalions, and a great many different bourgeois political party members, including the leaders of the former Latvian Social Democratic Party – F. J. Menders, K. Eliass, K. Lorencs, R. D. Bīlmanis, K. J. Būmeisters, V. J. Grēviņš, H. J. Kaupiņš and others.

In the Rīga region, of the 958 returnees, 69 have been uncovered to have been former bandits.

Of 1,149 persons who have returned to Cēsis region, more than 70% have settled in the city of Cēsis.

In Ventspils and the Ventspils region, 917 persons have returned from their places of imprisonment and deportation, and of these 401 live in the Ventspils region. Among those returning to the Ventspils region are 10 former agents of spy agencies of foreign states, 5 former so-called "Latvian Central Council"[82] members, 12 former bandits.

In Liepāja and in the Liepāja region there are 835 persons registered who have returned from their places of imprisonment or deportation. Among them are 40 persons – former German spies and counter-intelligence agents, more than 20 persons of the former nationalist organization, the so-called "Hawks of the Fatherland," active members of "Kursa" etc.

In Jelgava and Jelgava region more than 1,300 persons have returned, and among them are 33 former members of armed bands.

It is a fact that some of those returning from their places of imprisonment and deportation have tried to avoid begin identified by the organs of the State Security Commission by living with their friends and relatives for a long time without registering. [...]

Among the returnees there are many persons who have retained hostile opinions of Soviet power, [and] they anticipate or are already engaged in anti-Soviet activities. They renew their former criminal connections with these goals [in mind], establishing contact with representatives of capitalist countries and with the nationalist organizations of Latvians abroad. Some of them engage in active anti-Soviet agitation, and threaten communists or the witnesses that earlier testified against them. Among the persons who have returned are some who, while imprisoned or deported, actively engaged in anti-Soviet activity by creating nationalist organizations and groups such as the well-known, so-called "Severnij sojuz borbi" ["Northern Struggles Society"], "Latvian" etc.

For example, the former battalion commander in the German army, Laumanis, and his colleagues Zemzars, Macpāns and others, who returned in 1955 after having withstood punishment in the Vorkuta camp of the USSR Ministry of the Interior, were members of the illegal anti-soviet organization "Latvians" that operated in the camp. They produced a *samizdat* anti-Soviet journal in order to keep up their nationalist spirits. Zemzars brought one of the 26 of these publications with him from the camp.

After returning to Latvia, Laumanis, Zemzars, Macpāns did not stop their struggle against soviet power but continued to work to create a nationalist underground. (They were all arrested in March of 1957.) [...]

The leaders of the former Latvian Social Democratic Party – F.J. Menders, K. Eliass, K.K. Lorencs, R.D. Bīlmanis, K.J. Būmeisters, V.J. Grēviņš, H.J. Kaupiņš -- have retained their Menshevik political beliefs and, after returning to Rīga, have renewed contact with each other and meet regularly. They cherish the idea of renewing their Social Democratic (Menshevik) activities, but only when conditions are favorable. With this goal in mind, they look for opportunities to receive information about Latvian Social Democratic (Menshevik) activities in foreign lands.

At this moment, these Social Democratic leaders of Menshevik persuasion [continue] to discuss the work of the Communist Party and the Soviet government among themselves.

Their beliefs, and more specifically Lorencs' beliefs, have undoubtedly influenced his son – Viktors Lorencs, a student at the Moscow Cinematographic Institute – [and shaped] his ideological worldview. [The younger Lorencs' work] includes an untruthful, essentially nationalist, scenario for the film "Homeland, forgive" which has been removed from production.

A seriously harmful, and in some cases hostile, influence on persons, particularly on youth, comes from the pastors, church workers, and sectarians who have returned from their places of imprisonment. 109 clergy have returned [in the period] 1955-1957 (Catholic clergy, Lutheran pastors, Orthodox priests, Baptist preachers and persons from other confessions), 28 former activists of the Summer Festival Congregation sect, 40 former underground members of the Jehovah's Witnesses [...]

In many places, amnestied state criminals, kulaks, and other hostile elements have returned from special camps and have settled in kolkhozes, openly expressing their dissatisfaction about their situations and in many different ways trying to reclaim their former property. Individual workers in Soviet organizations, and kolkhoz leaders, agree with them in viewing the deportation episode as soviet power having punished them undeservedly. [The latter] try to satisfy their baseless claims by returning houses to them, giving them livestock, and offering them other support from the kolkhoz, thereby harming the interests of the kolkhoz. Some of those who have returned to the kolkhozes do not work, but threaten those Soviet citizens who oppose restitution. [The returnees] make fun of respectable kolkhoz farmers; seek to expel them from their [the returnees'] former homes, and spread provocative rumors about war that will result in the liquidation of soviet power and the kolkhoz regime in Latvia. [...]

The organs of the State Security Commission of the Council of Ministers of the Latvian SSR is working to end the anti-Soviet activities of these persons. In 1957, 15 persons were arrested in this category [...]

For inconsequential anti-Soviet behavior, preventive activities will begin with the persons in this category. [...]

Chair of the Sate Security Committee of the Council of Ministers of the Latvian SSR
Major General   Vēvers

Source: *LVA PA, 101.f., 21. apr., 48a.l., pp. 39-63. Original in Russian.*

DOCUMENTS NO. 30-33
RESISTANCE TO SOVIET POWER

Document No. 30

Top secret decision of the Bureau of the Central Committee of the Latvian Communist (Bolshevik) Party, from the special file about activities in the struggle against national partisans

May 28, 1945

To strengthen the struggle against banditism in the Latvian SSR, the Bureau of the Central Committee of the Latvian Communist (B) Party decrees that:
1. There be organized a military section unit of the Central Committee of the Latvian Communist (B) Party, consisting of 100 former active partisans, to help the organs of the People's Commissariat of the Interior in the struggle with banditism (the list is attached).[83]
2. That comrade Laiviņš (Chair of the Rīga District Executive Committee) be ratified as unit commander, and comrade Oškalns (Secretary of the Latvian Communist (B) Party Rīga District Committee) the unit's commissar.
3. That the unit commander, comrade Laiviņš, and the unit commissar, comrade Oškalns, be assigned the task of forming, arming, and preparing a unit for total battle preparedness in five days time.
4. That leaders of Party and soviet organizations in three days time order the persons on the attached list to take up this assignment from their enterprises and institutions, while keeping their existing positions and full wages while they are gone.
5. That the People's Commissar of the Interior of the Latvian SSR, comrade Eglītis within three days time give the unit the following armaments and ammunition for the struggle against banditism:

1.	Automatics	85 units
2.	"Dektereva" light machine guns	15 units
3.	Machine gun RGD-42	300 units
4.	Machine gun F-1	300 units

5. TT cartridges	45,000 units
6. Russian pistol cartridges	20,000 units
7. Silent weapons	2 units
8. Cartridges for silent weapons	50 units
9. Rocket pistols	4 units
10. White-colored rockets	100 units
11. Green-colored rockets	25 units
12. Red-colored rockets	25 units

6. That the Chief of the Autotransport Board of the Council of People's' Commissariats of the Latvian SSR, comrade Zīle, choose and assign to the unit in three days time the following:

Transport automobile	5 units
Light automobile "Vilis"	3 units
Motorcycles	2 units

And guarantee an unlimited supply of gasoline as requested from the unit.

7. That the People's' Commissar of Trade of the Latvian SSR, comrade Paegle, beginning with the 25th of May give to the unit 100 units of grocery supplies as well as 100 clothing units (shoes, uniform jackets, pants).

8. That the People's Commissar of Finance, comrade Tabaks, find the necessary monies to cover the expenses of the unit in its struggle with bandit organizations and for upkeep during the time of operations.

9. That the People's Commissar of the Defense of Health of the Latvian SSR, comrade Ameriks, make sure that the unit have attached to it the necessary medical personnel —one doctor and two medical orderlies -- with all of the necessary medical supplies.

10. That the leader of the Finance and Economic Sector of the Central Committee of the Latvian Communist (B) Party, comrade Komisarov, give to the unit dormitory space for the time period it is needed.

Secretary of the Central Committee of the Latvian Communist (B) Party   J. Kalnbērziņš

Source: *LVA PA, 101.f., 7. apr., 31a.l., pp. 12-13. Original in Russian.*

Document No. 31

Top secret decision from the special file of the Bureau of the Central Committee of the Latvian Communist (Bolshevik) Party about additional activities in the struggle against national partisans and the strengthening of the seek-and-destroy battalions

June 16, 1945

The Bureau of the Central Committee of the Latvian Communist (B) Party views the leadership of the seek-and-destroy battalions, led by organs of the People's Commissariat of the Interior, Party district committees, and district executive committees as completely unsatisfactory.

The December 28, 1944, and April 16, 1945, decisions[84] of the Bureau of the Central Committee of the Latvian Communist (B) Party have not been completely implemented and the conditions within the seek-and-destroy battalions are currently completely unsatisfactory.

Putting aside for the moment the serious conditions in the districts engulfed in banditism (Abrene, Ludza, Rēzekne, Daugavpils, Ilūkste, Madona, Jēkabpils, Cēsis and Rīga), the Party district committees and their first secretaries, district executive committees and their chairs, the People's

Commissariat of the Interior and People's Commissariat of State Security district section chiefs seem not to understand that the seek-and-destroy battalions are the primary armed force in the struggle against banditism in these districts.

As a result of devaluing the role of the seek-and-destroy battalions, their combat training and political instructions in most cases is not taking place.

In order to vastly improve the leadership of the seek-and-destroy battalions, to raise their level of organization, and to increase their battle strength, the Central Committee of the Latvian Communist (B) Party decrees:

1. That in order to help the People's Commissariat of the Interior district sections lead the seek-and-destroy battalions, district headquarters be created, containing: the first secretaries of the district committees of the Latvian Communist (B) Party, the People's Commissariat of the Interior district section chief, district executive committee chair and the commander of the district's seek-and-destroy battalions.

   That in the parishes that have been overwhelmed by banditism there be created a parish headquarters, consisting of the parish executive committee chair, parish Party organ, and the People's Commissariat of the Interior parish chief or authorized agent, and that they be assigned to take over the leadership of the seek-and-destroy battalion and its political instruction.

2. That the People's Commissariat of the Interior of the Latvian SSR , comrade Eglītis, is assigned the following tasks:
   a. From June 20, 1945, to finalize the following seek-and-destroy battalion structure: in the battalion there must be between 500 and 1500 fighters and not fewer than 3 persons as salaried officers; in the district, one battalion is to be organized with fighters to be located in the parishes and village councils; in the battalion there should be companies for each parish group (merging 2-5 parishes); the company should have between 100 and 200 fighters, in the parishes there must be platoons of 20-50 persons and in the village councils – squads of 5 to 15 persons;
   b. There must be a strict accounting immediately of the use of munitions, and all means must be used to keep weapons and munitions from falling into the hands of bandit elements.
   Weapons must not be assigned to untested fighters in seek-and-destroy battalions;
   c. In parishes where there is banditism, sub-units of the seek-and-destroy battalions must be housed under barracks conditions;
   d. In ten days time all locales must be sent directions drawn up by the People's Commissariat of the Interior about methods to be used in conducting battles with bandit groups;
   e. By June 20, 1945, there has to be submitted a detailed [account] of the characteristics of the seek-and-destroy battalions in each parish to the headquarters of the Central Committee of the Latvian Communist (B) Party.

3. That account be taken of the report of People's Commissar of the Interior of the Latvian SSR, comrade Eglītis, detailing that the necessary number of weapons and munitions have been sent to the districts, and that in the near future the demand for supplies will be entirely satisfied.

4. That the People's Commissar of the Interior of the Latvian SSR, comrade Eglītis, and the Party district committee secretaries review again, immediately, the personnel of the seek-and-destroyer battalions; [work] to reach the necessary levels; evaluate commanders and deputy commanders with respect to their political work; and select the best persons from among the Soviet and Party activists to lead the seek-and-destroy battalions.

5. That Party district committees be assigned the task of guaranteeing the political leadership and the training of the fighters of the seek-and-destroy battalion, and that for this goal they use the parish Party organizer.

6. That the State Planning Committee of the Council of People's Commissars of the Latvian SSR (comrade Deglavs), and the Autotransport Board of the Council of People's Commissars of the Latvian SSR (comrade Zīle) assign, no later than June 20, 1945, the use of 18 heavy trucks from captured military supplies to the seek-and-destroy battalions.

7. That the State Planning Committee of the Council of People's Commissars of the Latvian SSR (comrade Deglavs) assign the People's Commissariat of the Interior 6 tons of fuel this June-July immediately.

8. That the People's Commissar of Trade of the Latvian SSR (comrade Paegle) give the seek-and-destroy battalions of the People's Commissariat of the Interior of the Latvian SSR:
   a) 100 kilograms tobacco, b) 1000 kilograms soap, c) 2000 boxes of preserves and d) rations for the personnel of the battalions in line with the demands of the People's Commissar of the Interior of the Latvian SSR.

9. That the People's Commissar of Finance of the Latvian SSR (comrade Tabaks) give to the seek-and-destroy battalions of the People's Commissariat of the Interior of the Latvian SSR [the sum of] 3.5 million rubles for living expenses for June and July 1945 from the local budget.

10. That the chairs of the municipal and district executive committees free the families of fighters in the seek-and-destroy battalion from any kind of mobilizations and work orders.

11. That the Commissar of War of the Latvian SSR, comrade Malahovskis, send to the People's Commissariat of the Interior of the Latvian SSR 20 battle-trained officers in three days time, and assign them the duty of being battalion commanders and headquarters chiefs.

12. That the battalion headquarters mentioned above formulate and submit to the People's Commissariat of the Interior immediately planning material concerning the distribution of pensions to the families of fighters killed [while in] the seek-and-destroy battalions.

13. That control of the execution of this decree be assigned to the headquarters of the Central Committee of the Latvian Communist (B) Party.

Secretary of the Central Committee of the Latvian Communist Party   Kalnbērziņš

Source: *LVA PA, 101.f., 7. apr., 31a.l., pp. 23-24. Original in Russian.*

Excerpts from the minutes of the interrogation of A. Klibiķis[85], accused by the People's Commissariat of State Security of the Latvian SSR, about the goals of the Latvia's Central Council

December 7, 1945

Interrogation begun – 10:25, finished – 15:10
The translator of the Latvian SSR People's Commissariat of State Security, comrade Kraujietis, was warned about the consequences of incorrect translation, as laid out by the Criminal Code of the RFSR paragraph 95. [...]

Question: What goals and assignments did the "Latvia's Central Council" reveal to you?[86]

Answer: As I know and understand it, our organization "Latvia's Central Council" does not recognize Soviet Latvia and sees as its goal the creation of an autonomous, independent Latvia. My assigned goal in the "LCC" is to try ... to unite and lead all bandit groups and other anti-Soviet organizations that exist illegally on Latvia's territory. The "LCC" carries out nationalist, anti-Soviet propaganda, both in Latvia and in foreign countries, aimed at the creation of an independent Latvia. Everything shown to me about the organizational goals and assignments of the "LCC" came up in several open discussions with Mežaks and Andersons.[87]

Question: Do you now personally reject your conviction that a struggle for an "independent" Latvia is necessary?

Answer: No. To this moment, I believe that the Latvian nation needs an independent, autonomous Latvia. With respect to the need of continuing the struggle for an independent Latvia I believe that I myself, being held in isolation, cannot do it, but that our organization "LCC" right now has a good chance of reaching this goal and therefore the "LCC" must continue to struggle for an independent Latvia.

The minutes were written in accordance with my words; they were translated from the Russian language by me into Latvian, to which I testify with my signature – A. Klibiķis

Senior Lieutenant of the Investigative Section of the People's Commissariat of the Interior of the Latvian SSR did the interrogation   Denisov [...]

Source: *LVA, 1986.f., 1. apr., 99. l, vol. 3, pp. 38-39 (handwritten document). Original in Latvian.*

Top secret report of the Secretary of the Latvian Komsomol, V. Krūmiņš, to the Secretary of the Central Committee of the Latvian Communist (Bolshevik) Party, F. Titov, about the struggle against resistance organizations and groupings in educational institutions.

June 1949

The creation of kolkhozes and the accompanying liquidation of the kulak class in the Latvian SSR has caused the activization of kulaks and other elements hostile to Soviet order in some institutions of learning in the Latvian SSR.

1.   The Central Committee of Latvia's LKYA knows that in the Ogre Forestry Technical School there is a nationalist group of three persons at work. On March 25th and 29th, the days of the deportation of kulaks, this group created a disturbance in the technical school dormitory and ripped up our leader's portraits. In this group there were two Komsomolers (Mazurevics and Dzērve[88]). Organs of the State Security Ministry have arrested all of the members of all of the nationalist groups.

Many technical school students, including 8 Komsomolers, knowing of the nationalist group's organized anti-Soviet work, not only did not react properly, but became participants in the group's work by not telling the directors the school nor the Komsomol district committee.

In connection with this, the Central Committee of the LKYA has sent its work brigade to investigate the facts and has paid attention to the Bureau regarding the question of ideological training at this technical school. As a result, it has been learned that neither the directors of the school nor the Komsomol organization have guided the political, ideological training of students in an appropriate manner. After evaluating the apathy and cowardice of the Komsomol organization, which reflect apolitical [attitudes] and lack of political principles, the Bureau of the Latvian LKYA fired the technical school's Komsomol committee and expelled the Secretary from the ranks of the ULKYA. All of the Komsomolers that supported the nationalist group were expelled from the ranks of the ULKYA.

To reinvigorate the student body [of the school], 20 Komsomolers will be sent to study at the technical school in the new academic year. Also, on June 6th of this year, Latvia's LKYA lecturers' group is sending to the school lecturers to deliver presentations on the [following] themes: "Classes and class struggle," "About bourgeois nationalists as the Latvian nation's fiercest enemies," "About the international situation."

2.   In July 1945, there was founded at the Alūksne high school an underground organization of youths that set as its goal anti-Soviet propaganda. Sensing that they were soon to be uncovered, the members of this organization dispersed to the different parishes of Alūksne district. Some of them, altogether 6 persons, went to Cēsis and began studying at the Cēsis Teachers' Institute. This group was able to maneuver their way into the work at the Red Cross Primary Organization. This underground organization was not able to do any active [damage], but still, organs of the VDM arrested them. The Bureau of the Central Committee of the Latvian Communist (B) Party took under advisement the question of the Cēsis Teachers Institute.

3.   The organs of the VDM report that in the Aizupe Forestry Technical School (in Tukuma district) there is an underground organization of youths led by one of the bands that is active in this region. Currently the VDM is working at the elimination of organization.

In light of these activities of anti-Soviet elements, the Central Committee of the Latvian LKYA asks your support in having the Central Committee of the Latvian Communist (B) Party call a meeting of the representatives of those ministries that operate these institutions of learning.

Secretary of the Latvian LKYA Krūmiņš

Source: *LVA PA, 101. f., 12. apr., 74. l., pp. 41, 42. Original in Russian.*

Document No. 34

Top secret summary report of the Acting Deputy Chair of the Council of Ministers of the Latvian SSR, N. Velikanov, concerning the results of combat against armed resistance bands in the period from the fall of 1944 until the end of 1956, and the top secret report about the results of legalization (amnesty) from September 18, 1955 to the end of 1956

January 8, 1957

REPORT
    Concerning the registration of illegal persons in the time period from September 18, 1955 until December 30, 1956

	Rīga and republic regions	Through the 4th section[89]	Through the 2nd section[90]	Total for the Latvian SSR CM SSC
1	Rīga	69	10	79
2	Rīga region	25	4	29
3	Abrene region	4	-	4
4	Akniste region	2	-	2
5	Alsunga region	1	-	1
6	Aloja region	1	1	2
7	Alūksne region	2	2	4
8	Ape region	-	1	1
9	Aizpute region	5	-	5
10	Auce region	2	1	3
11	Balva region	3	-	3
12	Baldone region	5	-	5
13	Bauska region	5	2	7
14	Valka region	1	1	2
15	Valmiera region	2	-	2
16	Ventspils region	6	-	6
17	Vilani region	3	-	3
18	Gaujiena region	-	-	-
19	Gulbene region	-	-	-
20	Dagda region	7	-	7

21	Daugavpils region	2	-	2
22	Dobele region	1	-	1
23	Jelgava region	9	-	9
24	Jēkabpils region	1	2	3
25	Zilupe region	4	-	4
26	Ilūkste region	-	-	-
27	Kandava region	5	-	5
28	Kārsava region	3	-	3
29	Krāslava region	6	3	9
30	Krustpils region	1	-	1
31	Kuldīgas region	7	1	8
32	Limbaži region	4	-	4
33	Liepāja region	4	-	4
34	Līvāni region	1	-	1
35	Ludza region	2	-	2
36	Madona region	1	-	1
37	Malta region	1	-	1
38	Nereta region	2	-	2
39	Ogre region	1	3	4
40	Preiļi region	3	-	3
41	Pļaviņas region	3	-	3
42	Priekule region	-	-	-
43	Rēzekne region	1	3	4
44	Rūjiena region	5	-	5
45	Saulkrasta region	6	-	6
46	Sigulda region	7	-	7
47	Saldus region	5	1	6
48	Smiltene region	-	-	-
49	Skrunda region	-	3	3
50	Talsi region	3	-	3
51	Tukums region	5	1	6
52	Cēsis region	10	1	11
53	Cesvaisne region	2	1	3
54	Eleja region	4	-	4
55	Ērgļu region	3	-	3
56	Jaunjelgava region	1	-	1
57	Dundaga region	-	1	-
	Total	256	42	298

Reasons for extra-legal status and reasons for hiding:

1. Avoided service in the Soviet army	23
2. Served in the German army's police battalions	22
3. Deserted from the Soviet army	14
4. Former self-defense forces and šucmanis	49
5. Former *starasti*	1
6. Former bandits	14
7. Former supporters of bandits	12
8. Former "Home Guard"	6
9. Served in the German army	42
10. Former police	34
11. Former kulaks	7
12. Other supporters of the Germans	6
13. Lived with a family member that was illegal	11
14. Avoided deportation	20
15. Afraid of being held responsible for not carrying out the orders of the region executive committee	7
16. Members of an anti-Soviet nationalist organization	3
17. Fled from a special camp	4
18. Served in the SD police punitive units	5
19. Agent of the German Spy agency	5
20. For keeping an illegal weapon	3
21. Other	10
Total:	298

Number of registered illegals who were hiding:

Since 1944	53
Since 1945	88
Since 1946	34
Since 1947	21
Since 1948	47
Since 1949	37
Since 1950	13
Since 1951	3
Since 1952	2
Total:	298

Of the total number that were registered:

a. arrested	3
b. legalized (amnestied)	295

When registering with the organs of state security of the Latvian SSR, the following weapons were turned in:

1. Machine guns	1
2. Automatic rifles	11
3. Rifles	10

4. Pistols	7
5. Grenades	2
6. Flare pistols	1
7. Hunting rifles	2
8. Small caliber guns	2
9. Cartridges	2,416

Operational Authorized Agent of the 4th Section of the State Security Commission of the Council of Ministers of the Latvian SSR, Senior Lieutenant   Grūbe

Agree: Chief of the 4th Section of the State Security Committee of the Council of Ministers of the Latvian SSR, Colonel   Polikarpov

Summary report
(of the results of combat with the bandit-nationalist underground in the territory of the Latvian SSR and the amnesty of former illegals in the time period from 1944 to 1956)

In the time period from the fall of 1944 to December 31, 1956, the organs of state security of the Latvian SSR:

1. Liquidated 961 armed bandit bands.
Altogether arrested or liquidated 10,720 bandits
Including:

a. Killed or committed suicide	2,407 persons
b. Arrested and tried	4,370 persons
c. Legalized (amnestied)	3,973 persons

2. Discovered illegals – 2,735 persons
Including:

a. Killed	13 persons
b. arrested and tried	1,119 persons
c. legalized (amnestied)	1,606 persons

(Including those that registered themselves)

3. Weapons and ammunition taken from bandits, illegals, and other persons:

Mortars	5 pieces
Machine guns	738 pieces
Automatic rifles	3,287 pieces
Rifles	11,863 pieces
Pistols	3,1033 pieces
Grenades	8,835 pieces
Cartridges	1,306,445
Mines	5,177 pieces
Explosives	3,939 kg

The organized and armed bandit-nationalist underground in the territory of the Latvian SSR was completely liquidated in October of 1956 (in the current year, on October 30th, the last former bandit group led by "Pana" was liquidated).

Colonel, Chief of the 4th Section of the State Security Committee of the Council of Ministers of the Latvian SSR   Polikarpov

Source: *LVA, 270.f., 1.s. apr., 1144. l., pp. 1-8. Original in Russian.*

Excerpts from the minutes of the Limbaži Region Party meeting, featuring a speech on anti-Soviet activity by Rullis, the Limbaži region authorized agent of the Committee of State Security of the Latvian SSR Council of Ministers

July 18, 1959, in Limbaži

[…] In the meeting today we are discussing a very important question related to the Party's policy on the nationality question, which is one of the Leninist foundation principles of our lives, namely, the building of communism in the entirety of our multi-nation state.

The Communist Party of the Soviet Union, with Secretary Nikita Sergeievich Khrushchev at its head, in recent years has always carefully looked after our Party's unity, making sure that Leninist founding principles are followed and no distortions of our policies be allowed. Thus, the Central Committee unmasked, in a timely manner, the traitor to the state, Beria and his followers, as well as the anti-Party group that had taken a stand against the Party general line, and is now carefully watching that our state not allow any coarse violations of Leninist policy. As we heard in the report from the Secretary of the Central Committee of the Latvian Communist Party, comrade Krūmiņš, recently in our republic there were individual persons, as, for example, comrade Berklāvs, who allowed in their work crude violations of our policy on the national question. Again, the Central Committee, in a timely manner, uncovered these shortcomings and stopped the evil consequences that would have appeared if these incorrect policies had continued. How evil these consequences might have been we all can imagine, and so we can today congratulate with pride the decision of the Central Committee Plenum that ended Berklāvs'distorting work on the nationality question and removed him from his position.

The situation in 1953, before Beria was unmasked, comes to mind today when our republic as well as our region has felt the influence of bourgeois nationalism and the slogan "Russians out of Latvia," as bourgeois nationalists have begun to lift their heads and activate their hostile work against Soviet power. The distortions in nationality policy that Berklāvs'anti-party behavior suggested activates the hostile stance of the bourgeois nationalists, targeted against our state and the policies of the Communist Party.

From this shameful episode, our republic and also we – the region Party organization – must draw certain conclusions, so that our future work does not permit any distortions in nationality policy and so that in today's meeting we can uncover the shortcomings that are still present today.

As a member of the a regional committee bureau, I have not noticed in our region any coarse violations of nationality policy suggestive of the behavior of Berklāvs, if we disregard the fact that we also promulgated a decision about the obligatory learning of Latvian and Russian languages in two years time -- a decision that was made following the decision of the Central Committee. It is undeniably that in our region, responsible figures must know and systematically acquire both languages because otherwise we would be unable to do political training among the masses as it is needed. But in no way can we allow the administrative implementation that Berklāvs used, framing the question in the following way: if you do not learn the Latvian language, which is actually not possible in two years, then you are out of a job. That [approach] of course will only bring evil to our work.

In today's meeting I want to turn the attention of communists to the need for alertness in the continuing struggle against bourgeois nationalists and their hostile actions. That there are individual bourgeois nationalists who are seeking to slow down improvement in the living conditions of our region's working masses while being hostile toward the Soviet state and Party policies is testified by many facts from our region's life. Allow me to mention just a few of them from the past year of in our region, clearly showing how bourgeois nationalists hostile to Soviet power seek with all of their might to impair the implementation of our policies. The bourgeois nationalist Treijs, Jānis, in Pociems, after returning from filtration [camp] for the "SS" Legion, refused to join the kolkhoz and did not pay state taxes. Being hostile to Soviet power, he threatened ethnic Russian citizens and communists with a soon-to-be war that the USA would win. He openly agitated [on behalf of the idea] that America and England are stronger than the Soviet Union and that [the latter] would lose the next war. When the Americans liberated Latvia [he said], he would also help to beat up Russians and communists and destroy them. When the ethnic Russian citizen Pojarkov tried to show him that his stance was incorrect and tried to defend the interests of our state, Treijs physically assaulted this worker and kept him in the hospital for a long period of time. Obviously, this kind of enemy of our state will not benefit from preventative measure, and it was necessary to arrest him and hold him responsible for his criminal [actions].

Krūze, Edmunds, in Staicele, having distinct bourgeois nationalist attitudes, could never accept the fact that Soviet power nationalized his father's two houses and sausage factory, and [therefore] displayed hostile anti-Soviet [behavior] and threatened ethnic Russians and communists. He openly said that Russians and red communists are bandits: I shot them [in the past] and will destroy them in the future. The communists will not be in power for long, but capital and science will rule and the atomic bomb will decide all. He argued that every real Latvian must know that the communists will not [be in power] in Latvia much longer, that they will be driven from Latvia, and that he will demonstrate how it should be done. It was necessary to arrest this determined enemy and bring him to account.

We must note that in our region in the recent past there has also been organized anti-Soviet activity targeting our political order. The anti-Soviet underground organization called "Spark" in Salacgrīva testifies to that. The members of this illegal organization took an oath to struggle with all means against Soviet power: it distributed anti-Soviet leaflets, flew the bourgeois Latvian flag in Ainaži, recruited new members, prepared appeals for Estonian citizens to struggle against Soviet power, gathered weapons, tried to organize anti-Soviet organizations in our district schools, and was hoping to blow up the bridge over the Salaca River by attacking and killing the night watchman who was guarding the explosives. During the time when this anti-Soviet organization was being unmasked, one of the inhabitants of Ainaži received a typed, threatening letter from Rīga that said: "The verdict: since you have participated in the betrayal of Salacgrīva Latvians and have acted against the state, we sentence you to death." It was signed with the letters "LTA."

The leader of this anti-Soviet organization, Buliņš, was arrested and said frankly during the investigation: "Yes, I led this underground group, but I will not give evidence about the other members of the group and I do not recognize Soviet state politics." These examples, and there are many others, testify that we can not even for an instant lessen our vigilance, we have to unmask the real enemies of our state, and we have to call them to justice and not allow them to interfere with our peace-loving work. At the same time, we can not forget that every time one or two citizens exhibit behavior hostile to Soviet power they may not be doing so consciously. That is why all of these persons can not be put into the same pile with the real enemies of the state but must be educated, because they commit their crimes not out of conviction and hostility toward Soviet order, but because of political ignorance. The experience with many persons shows that preventative measures do work – after a warning they take the correct path and do no engage in anti-Soviet behavior thereafter. In one of our region's largest enterprises a worker recently voiced anti-Soviet sayings, expressed hostility toward the Soviet order, and kept a weapon. Formally speaking, he could have been called to account for this. But when his behavior was analyzed more closely, it turned out that his utterances against Soviet power were done unknowingly, and that our country's policies were unfamiliar to him. In the near future, after certain other matters are investigated, this person will need to be subjected to preventative measures – a warning about his behavior, and the revealing of his anti-Soviet work at workers' meetings so his own colleagues can decide his punishment and ask for explanations, so that he changes and won't manifest anti-Soviet attitudes and behavior in the future.

This year, on May 1st , in Aloja during the night the state flag was pulled down from its secure place near an apartment building and raised again on the latrine chimney. The guilty party was arrested. It turned out to be the tractor driver in the kolkhoz "Centība." Nevertheless, he was not held to be criminally liable because he committed this crime unknowingly, not in order to struggle against Soviet power but because of his political ignorance. He was warned, and he promised in the future not to engage in such crimes and currently he is keeping his word.

Frequently among communists you can hear the thoughts voiced that the enemy is rising up against us, we can do nothing to him, and why do we not arrest him. These communists must bear in mind that we struggle against bourgeois nationalists and other hostile reactions not only with repression; it is also necessary to use against these unbalanced persons the methods of educational pressure I have already discussed, using repression only against the real enemies of our state. But often among our district's communists there is a lack of political awareness and insufficiently principled willingness to unmask our enemies; they exhibit indecision and the desire to live together peacefully with all persons, even with hostile bourgeois nationalists. In this matter, I would like to bring your attention to the following incident.

At the beginning of this month, the Supreme Court reviewed the affair of Lanks, Arvīds, from the kolkhoz "Staicele," and his anti-state behavior. Who is this Lanks? In 1942, while living in Rēzekne, he served in the district police that took an active part in repressions against Soviet patriots, participated in the capture of Soviet partisans, and after that served in the German army. For these crimes, which occurred during the German occupation, he was sentenced to 25 years but he returned from imprisonment in 1955 because of the amnesty.

Working in the kolkhoz "Staicele," Lanks systematically disseminated anti-Soviet propaganda. Already in 1957, in the presence of the secretary of the kolkhoz Party's primary organization, Lanks stated publicly : "Communists want to build communism. Nothing will come of it. We will show them how to build communism, we had and we still have only one thing for communists – a bullet. We lived and will continue to live and we will observe how these communists will take off from here. We only need to take guns in our hands."

To the communist Krūmiņš, Lanks, pointing out Strencis, Kaņeps, and Balodis, who share his ideas and also returned from imprisonment, stated clearly: "See, our ranks are growing. You Russian black beetle, the time will come soon when our ‚sparks' will set a fire, and then we will settle the score with you and take off your heads" – and added other anti-Soviet utterance. This year, on February 9th, at the review meeting in the kolkhoz when candidates were being chosen for elections, Lanks again tried to start anti-Soviet agitation. "All that is trifling what you are saying here. No one from the kolkhoz is expressing his true thoughts, because now we can only say what is written in the newspapers, but we can't trust the newspapers. We had a good leader, Bulganin, but they quickly removed him." After this, Lanks pointed to the seated presidium and said: "Soon there will come the time when all of you will be taken away."

The chair of the kolkhoz, the communist Maniks, appointed Lanks to be supervisor of the warehouse, but later removed him for inadequate work. When the court asked comrade Maniks for an explanation about Lanks'behavior, Maniks gave a good description, but could not say anything about Lanks' outbursts at the kolkhoz meeting because, he said, he had not noticed anything even though he had led the meeting and numerous times told Lanks to stop his disruptive behavior. I believe that comrade Maniks remembers very well that before he was elected as the chair of the kolkhoz, in another meeting a group of previously imprisoned persons demonstratively left the hall, and the meeting could not finish; the regional representatives then had to drive a second time to the kolkhoz meeting in order to elect comrade Maniks as chair. Maybe comrade Maniks, though a communist but remembering the first meeting, is scared of bourgeois nationalist disruptions; and should he also not have considered that Lanks could have had a hand in making the earlier meeting fail?

The communists Puriņš had not known Lanks for a long time, but in court described him as among the best persons and stated that Lanks had been rehabilitated while in prison. But facts speak the opposite about Lanks. If comrade Puriņš knew Lanks as well as he said, then he also should have known that Lanks is involved in brewing moonshine; but perhaps he has himself taken a drink with Lanks?

The other communists were confused, and in the end the court decided to vindicate Lanks and free him from imprisonment. After returning from court, Lanks said that he had broken the communists' horns and that now they would be more passive. Lanks can now be happy, laugh about the communists who gave testimony, and be grateful to those who had returned from imprisonment and to his own relatives who denied in court any anti-Soviet activity on the part of Lanks. Lanks' wife, an active member of the church choir, had asked Pastor Ozols of the Staicele church to pray to God about those communists that wanted to kill her husband.

I turn to the Secretary of the Central Committee, comrade Krūmiņš – the representative of the Supreme Council in our region – with the request that he get involved in this affair and find out if the Supreme Court, in this instance, made only a formal gesture but did not analyze the affair carefully, referring only to the new criminal code being drawn up, which allowed it to distance itself from these unfortunate matters. I believe that this kind of [inadequate] struggle against our country's real enemies will only harm us, and I believe that the actively engaged persons will support me.

Some communist official do not approach critically enough the selection of cadres, and assign to responsible positions politically unbalanced persons with remnants of bourgeois nationalism in their thinking. Due to a lack of time I cannot discuss many of these cases, but today I wanted to draw your attention to the fact that our district is one that borders on the sea, and that therefore we must be particularly vigilant against allowing betrayals of the homeland by our enemy. There have been instances recently in our republic when fishermen have betrayed the homeland and fled to foreign lands. Our fishing artels do not always make sure that only persons loyal to the Soviet state be assigned as motorists on the boats. Here I would like to draw your attention to unexplainable behavior of the secretary of the Party's primary organization in the fishing association "Free Wave," comrade Jirgensons. With his recommendation, Francis, Hermanis, who had returned from imprisonment and whose brother had also been sentenced for anti-state crimes, was assigned to the job of motorist. Returning from exile, Francis openly expressed his thoughts on nationalist issues. For example, while fixing nets, he asked other fishermen why the masses live better in Estonia than in Latvia. And he answered this question by saying that it is because there are fewer communists in Estonia. The brigade meeting discussed these utterances by Francis, and comrade Jirgensons participated. In an election meeting, Francis openly said to the communist Dārziņš: "We can probably break you"; and later he said to the non-party ethnic Russian citizen Orlov, who during the meeting had defended the candidacy of the new Chair, comrade Šlisers: "If you are drowning then I will not help save you." Comrade Jirgensons knows about these events very well, but he still recommended Francis to work as a motorist. But who will be responsible for the potentially harmful consequences? With this kind of behavior comrade Jirgensons not only does not help the new kolkhoz Chair, comrade Šlisers, but erodes his authority, which is a shameful act on the part of a secretary of the primary organization of the Party.

I must say that comrade Jirgensons lacks overall political awareness. Why else would he have participated in the funeral of former Home Guard commander Melders, led by a pastor specifically invited from Rīga, and [why would he have] even organized a wake? We should also exert influence on comrade Jirgensons concerning his brother, who often says things like "Russians out of Latvia" and "They have no business being doing here."

I want to touch on one more question. In our district 1,080 persons have returned from imprisonment or exile. Some of them do not have positive views toward Soviet power, categorically demand the return of their nationalized property, or ask for permission to live in their former homes. We do not always approach solutions to these questions appropriately, the process make coarse mistakes, reawaken bourgeois nationalism, and create indignation among the working masses.

I do not understand how the Party's district executive committee in Salacgrīva could return to the former owner, Kariņš, a house on Smilšu Street inhabited by the authorized police representative, Gaigalīts. While there was a search for a place for the policeman to live, he was forced to reside for a long time in a corner room together with the house's former owner. Finally, new home was found for the policeman, but this house is currently being repaired by its former owner Kušķis, who has also just returned from exile and is prolonging the repairs. Maybe he, the former owner, also expects to go to the district executive committee to ask them to remove the policeman from the house so it can be returned to him. I believe that the section leader of the police, comrade Fjodorov, can testify to this matter, but it is inexplicable why he is remained so indifferent to all of this. The bourgeois nationalists laugh and are quite happy about this kind of inaction. There are many instances of this kind in our region. and we are not fulfilling the Party's and the government's decisions in these matters. Comrade Prokofjev must be more diligent in the future so as not to give free rein to persons who are inspired by bourgeois nationalists, so that the Party's and the government's decisions are strictly enforced. These occurrences give the bourgeois nationalists an opportunity to create indignation among the working masses, and to terrorize peaceful inhabitants with the threat of removal from their homes. We can find many similar examples in our district.

I will relate one more. This month we had a serious discussion with the exile returnee Osis, Jānis, who is living in Piķis house in Umurga village, and who systematically terrorized the persons currently living in his former house. I will read to you the written that he gave to the house's inhabitants: To Milda Čapiņš, born 1902, Ieva Čapiņš – 1940, Jānis Vītols – 1935, Marija Vītols – 1934: "Please vacate by October 1, 1959, the house "Inurn" in Limbaži region, Umurga village, together with all of the persons related to you and with all your belongings. The house is owned by me. Signed Ošs."

Is this incident not an insult? And this is not the only example. I believe that we can not let these things pass and that, in the first instance, the district executive committee must respond vigorously. In our district, about 18% of the population are Russians and citizens of other nationalities, but lectures about the friendship of peoples and other similar themes are still rarely presented. Also, we rarely read lectures or hold discussions or artistic events for the Russian citizens who have not yet acquired the Latvian language, and we hear many complaints about this matter.

In the future it is necessary for us to improve this work. I reiterate my belief that our region's Party organization will put forth every effort to not allow distortions in nationality policy, and that every communist will be diligent in the struggle against Latvian bourgeois nationalism and Russian chauvinism, will not allow any outrages but will unmask them in a timely manner and provide the necessary counter-action. [...]

Source: *LVA PA, 101.f., 22. apr., 91. l., pp. 28-30. Original in Russian.*

Secret report of the Chair of the State Security Committee of the Latvian SSR, L. Avdjukevičs, to the Central Committee of the Latvian Communist Party, about the discovery of a youthful underground group in Rīga.

November 10, 1977

On October 31, 1977, the Latvian State Security Committee received information [from investigators] about a group of nationalist youth in Rīga, and on November 1st, its members were identified as:

1. Krūmiņš, Pēteris, son of Vladislavs[91], born 1957, Latvian, member of the LLCYS, lives in Rīga, [...][92] works as a carpenter at the Institute of Latvian State Municipal Construction Projects, leader of the nationalist group.
2. Vilcāns, Imants, son of Vladislavs, born 1956, Latvian, lives in Rīga, [...] currently serves in the Soviet army.
3. Višs, Egons, son of Vladislavs, born 1956, Latvian, member of the LLCYS, lives in Rīga district, [...], VEF factory worker.
4. Dārziņš, Ēriks son of Harijs, born 1957, Latvian, member of the LLCYS, lives in Rīga, [...] works as a painter in the Renovation and Construction Board No. 7.
5. Krasts, Ēriks, son of Gunārs, born 1958, Latvian, lives in Rīga, [...] works as a formatter in the factory "Kosmoss."
6. Nicmanis, Andris, son of Jānis, born 1957, Latvian, lives in Rīga, [...] currently serves in the Soviet army.
7. Olehnovičs, Normunds son of Heinrihs, born 1958, Latvian, lives in Rīga, [...] currently serves in the Soviet army.
8. Putrins, Dainis, son of Laimons, born 1960, Latvian, lives in Rīga, [...] currently does not work.
9. Šēnvalds, Jānis, son of Elmars, born 1958, Latvian, lives in Rīga, [...] works as a longshoreman at the Rīga mercantile port.

In addition, the group also had 4 initiates from among the school-age youth, aged 16-17.

The group saw as its goal the creation of a nationalist organization the purpose of which would be to separate Latvia from the USSR. If reaching the goal was not possible through "peaceful" means, the use of violence was not excluded. For that purpose the group had decided to collect firearms and explosives. The group hoped to use a rotator press to prepare nationalist pamphlets.

The group's leader, Krūmiņš, P.V., willingly turned over the rotator press and other materials meant to be used in this harmful work.

These facts suggest criminal charge according to criminal code of the Latvian SSR 65th and 67th paragraphs. The investigation is ongoing, with the intention of more thoroughly understanding the group's goals and methods, and uncovering those who might have been inspired by the group.

We will inform you about the investigative process.

Chair of the State Security Committee of the Council of Ministers of the Latvian SSR
Avdjukēvičs

Source: *LVA PA, 101. f., 42.apr., 74. l., pp.. 41., 42. .Original in Russian.*

Secret report of the Chair of the State Security Committee of the Latvian SSR, L. Avdjukevics, to the Central Committee of the Latvian Communist Party about politically harmful tendencies among young persons

March 24, 1978

The Communist Party of the Soviet Union has demonstrated a lasting concern for raising the new generation in the spirit and beliefs of Marxism-Leninism, proletarian internationalism, and Soviet patriotism.

The absolute majority of Soviet Latvian youth are undivided in their support of the USSR's political struggle for peace and the construction of communism in our country, actively participate in political life, show heroism in their work, and make recognizable investments in the implementation of the decisions of our Party's XXVth Congress. Tens of thousands of the republic's young men and women work self-sacrificingly in national economic and cultural sectors, and persistently strive for an education in places of learning.

An important contribution to the raising of youth was made by the decision of the Latvian Communist Party Central Committee of 1973 concerning the strengthening their political education.[93] The implementation of this decision noticeably raised the level of the political consciousness of the young. Ideological-political training has become much more effective.

As is known, the espionage agencies of the imperialist countries, their ideological centers, and foreign anti-Soviet organizations try to influence the younger generations with ideologically harmful activities that are meant to discredit the Communist Party and social order of the Soviet state.

Recognizing the constant expansion of the role of the young in all spheres of Soviet social life, our opponents see the younger generation as the primary object of its subversive activities.

By spreading bourgeois ideology by means of several revisionist theories and nationalist ideas, they hope to diminish belief in communist ideals among the young, plant the seeds of apolitical and pessimistic attitudes, start them on them the path toward demagogy and constant criticism, and inject in them a consumerist attitude toward life.

Our opponents try to exploit such factors as the insufficient political maturity of individual young persons, the absence of necessary ideological training, inadequate life experience, and unstable character; and involve them in anti-Soviet and other harmful work.

Our opponents devote special attention to those among the young who are not involved in the work process or in social life [in order] to hasten their demoralization. Drug addiction, drinking, hooliganism and other criminal phenomena serve these goals in many cases.

To accomplish these goals, our opponents seek to affect the consciousness of young persons primarily through the use of the radio. The Latvian State Security Committee has evidence suggesting that in the Republic the number of young persons who regularly listen to the anti-Soviet broadcasts of foreign radio stations is growing.

The young are negatively influenced by the anti-Soviet, nationalist, and religious literature that our opponents send into the Republic through different channels, as well as through the publications, still retained by various person, from the periods of bourgeois Latvia and fascist occupation.

In the contemporary international situation, the hostile labors of our opponents seek to use the increasing number of international exchange opportunities. The facts testify to an increase in the number of hostile agents and emissaries of destructive foreign centers who are being sent into the Republic through the channels of tourism and scientific and cultural exchange, with the task of influencing the ideologically uncertain among the young.

The objective of the ideological centers of our opponents is to expand the influence of bourgeois nationalism in the Republic. It is known that in Latvia there are a certain number of persons who, pursuant to their anti-Soviet activities in the past, try to create connections with foreign émigré organizations.

For several reasons, in the Republic during the last few years there has been a noticeable increase in certain criminal activities among the young. A nationalist and anti-Soviet perspective is often created among them on the basis of prevailing dissatisfaction and apolitical attitudes. In 1977, the number of young persons who have been held responsible for crimes had increased by 10.5% over 1976.

Because of the ideologically diversionary activities of our opponents and the influence of hostile elements on the youth of the Republic, an undesirable mind-set is being created among certain groups of the young, which expresses itself in visibly dangerous actions.

In April of 1977, it was determined that among the young persons studying at various institutions of higher learning of Rīga, a group led by the Latvian State University student Kārlis Amoliņš, born in 1956, developed plans to detach Latvia from the USSR. For this reason Amoliņš and his colleagues sought to create an underground organization for the "liberation" of Latvia. They discussed possibilities of getting hold of reproduction machines for the preparation of anti-Soviet publications, and expressed ideas about the need to overthrowing state power in Latvia by force of arms.

Also in 1977, a Rīga Polytechnic Institute student Jānis Tutāns, born in 1955, influenced by politically harmful literature he had read, began to organize possibly anti-Soviet meetings as well as an illegal nationalist group.

Along with the creation of groups, the preparation and distribution of nationalist and anti-Soviet pamphlets and anonymous leaflets will continue. In 1976 there were 6, but in 1977 there were 11 incidents of such distribution done by young persons. In 1976, of the 56 identified anonymous authors of anti-Soviet documents and their distributors, 10 were young persons, but in 1977 there were 32 such persons out of 43. It is characteristic that the distribution of hostile documents is done by youth groups. In 1976 two such groups having five members were discovered, but in 1977 there were 7 groups with 25 members.

With respect to the contents of the 157 pamphlets distributed by young persons in 1976-1977, 111 were of nationalistic character, 19 contained lies about the Communist Party of the Soviet Union and Soviet Government policies, 7 contained threats against leaders of the Communist Party of the Soviet Union and Soviet government, and 20 pamphlets were against the policies of the Communist Party of the Soviet Union.

Regular listening to anti-Soviet radio broadcasts was the reason why Vasilij Bistrov, a student from the 17th Rīga High School, born in 1963, wrote a pamphlet slandering individual leaders of the Party and government and inviting struggle against the USSR in the name of the "RFD" (republic, freedom, democracy). He gave the text of the anti-Soviet pamphlet to his relative, Zinaida Seinkina, born in 1950, who works at the Latvian SSR Food Industry Ministry Construction Bureau, for reproduction and she helped out. Further reproduction of the pamphlet was done by Bistrov's friend – 9th High School student Aleksandrs Strelcov.

As a result of regular listening to foreign radio broadcasts, Juris Jukams, a student at the Tukuma region Jaunpils High School, born in 1961, prepared and distributed pamphlets with nationalist contents.

In November of 1977, harmful pamphlets were distributed in Rīga; these were prepared using a typographic font that stolen from a printer in Kudīga. As a result, the persons who committed this crime were detained and held responsible for their criminal acts. During investigation, it was determined that nationalist beliefs in their thinking were due to the father of one of the perpetrators -- Alberts Tilgalis, born in 1922, who systematically recounted to his sons his volunteer service in the Latvian "SS" Legion during which the German occupiers had awarded him with an "Iron Cross."

In recent years, our opponents actively used the younger generation in the [Latvian] émigré population in order to subvert our young persons. In October of 1977, as a member of a group of tourists visiting Latvia, a citizen of the German Federal Republic, Andris Ķesteris, born in 1948, in a meeting with local young persons gathered information about relationships among nationalities [in Latvia] and the role of the young in the republic's cultural life. At the same time, he tried to influence those with whom he was conversing in ways beneficial to the émigrés by using all manner of hostile expressions and nationalist ideas.

In 1976 and 1977, the State Security Committee of the Council of Ministers of the Latvian SSR uncovered attempts by young persons to send politically harmful literature beyond our borders.

A former student of the Latvian State University, Imants Kviesis, saw it necessary, as his first step in the active struggle against the Soviet order, to prepare a letter full of lies about the conditions of students and youth in the Republic and to give this document to Western mass media organs for them to use toward the goal of "unmasking" the so-called " violations of human rights permitted in USSR. " To send the document [to the West], Kviesis decided to use a person from among the foreigners visiting Rīga.

Recent years have been marked by the upswing of work by different sects – evangelical Christians, Baptist separatists, 7th day Adventists, and summer congregations – to involve young persons in the sectarian activities of churches.

Regardless of the law in the Latvian SSR concerning the work of religious societies, youth choirs and orchestras have been created in several groupings, and there are special services held and excursions with organized tent cities and tourist stops for the youth.[93]

The choir leader of the 7th day Adventists in Jelgava, who is the son of the sect's pastor Modris Zaķis, has created a vocal ensemble from young persons living in 8 different republic cities (Jelgava, Tukums, Dobele, Jēkabpils, etc.). The ensemble drives around to the sect's gatherings in order to involve other young persons in the sect's work. There have been times when individual pastors during their talks have invited the young not to surrender to atheistic training (Geide-- of the Tukums Adventist Commune, Bondarenko -- Ogre Baptist group).

The existence of hostile and ideologically harmful beliefs among the young, and the analysis of the process of how they are acquired, speaks to serious shortcomings in the organized training of the young, including in the Republic's places of learning. In the latter, primary attention is often paid only to preparation in professional skills.

Being insufficiently prepared to handle questions about the internal and external politics of the Party, young persons become vulnerable to anti-Soviet propaganda and poison themselves with nationalist ideas.

With respect to hostile propaganda from foreign lands, the question of our young persons' international training becomes very relevant.

Improvement is needed in the legal training of the young. In many instances, it is the low level of education in the law that leads to anti-social activities and crimes.

In many collectives, political training is done episodically and not in an aggressive mode. As a result, in 1972 at the 1st Sigulda High School a group of students pulled off a distinctly anti-Soviet prank. Afterward, the school leadership, Sigulda municipal organizations, and the Rīga region social organizations convened many preventive training sessions. The anti-Soviet prank at the mentioned school was soon forgotten and that led again to weakening of political training. That is why it was no accident that in November and December of 1977, at the same school, a group of students came together and began to prepare nationalist pamphlets and to distribute them; they performed other anti-social work as well.

The nationalist beliefs of some young persons are to a certain degree due to the passivity of their counselors and teachers, who avoid giving answers to the young on crucial political questions and sometimes seem to be expressing support for nationalism.

In September of 1976, at the 74th Rīga High School, pupils of the teacher Jelena Bezdelīga (born in 1941; daughter of Aleksandrs), went on an autobus excursion. During the trip, students Ilgvars Krastiņš and Agris Cimmermanis, both born in 1964, composed on the bus a nationalist song, inviting the physical destruction of those in Latvia who did not belong to the indigenous nation; they adapted this text to [the melody of] a popular song and openly sang it on the bus. J. Bezdelīga did not do anything to end this nationalist incident, and did not inform the school administration about what had happened.

There are serious shortcomings in the way that the free time of young people is organized. Many social organizations still do not put forth enough effort in getting the young to spend the time they have free from work or learning on cultural matters that would be valuable to their physical and spiritual development.

This February in Dobele region, at the Apgulde 4th Professional Technical High School, after lights-out, a group of ethnic Latvian students motivated by hooligan attitudes, organized a fight with their classmates –the tractor drivers. The initiator of the disorder was Teodors Vītiņš, born in 1962. An investigation of this event uncovered that at the beginning the differences between the ethnic Latvians and Russian students was over issues of daily life, but that afterward Vītiņš portrayed these disagreements in nationalist colors and organized a group fight, as a result of which several ethnic Russian students were wounded.

This case draws attention to the roots of much of this hostility, which is the young person's incorrect understanding of the difficulties of constructing communist society.

This year in March, the Latvian State Security Committee Collegium met and reviewed the question of how to reinforce the struggle against our opponents' ideological influence among the youth.

The Republic's State Security Committee organs have done a certain amount of work in separating young persons from our opponents' destructive efforts. Many times, with the help of operational activity, we have discovered gatherings of young persons who, while subject to hostile influences, were trying to create illegal groups. As a result of preventive work, many young persons have returned to the correct path that had earlier blocked harmful activities.

All parties concerned, including municipal and region State Security Committee sub-units, have been given training in police work meant to block off Soviet youth from our opponents'spy agencies and ideological centers, foreign and anti-Soviet organizations, and hostile elements coveting the leadership of Party organs; this work has been carried out in close connection with the Party, trade unions, the Komsomol, and other social organizations.

To improve political training and to destroy nationalist and other unhealthy phenomena among certain sections of the youth, we see the following as beneficial:

strengthening the effort in learning institutions of the Republic to provide a deeper explanation of the political questions raised by specific periods of Latvia's history; unmasking more thoroughly the essence of reactionary Latvian bourgeois nationalism and the hostile intent of our opponents' ideological centers;

organizing events meant to enhance the role of Party and Komsomol organizations and teachers in the political learning process among all youth, and doing this in a timely manner so as to start preventive work early against unhealthy tendencies;

strengthening the international training of youth at their places of learning;

activating the political training of instructor cadres at the places of learning;

using propaganda much more effectively among youth to attack and to react to in a timely manner to negative expressions and tendencies appearing in the present atmosphere;

creating a program of events meant for political training outside of school; organizing better the free time of young persons, particularly of those living in dormitories; expanding the role of the family in political training.

Chair of the State Security Committee of the Council of Ministers of the Latvian SSR
L.I. Avdjukevics

Source: *LVA PA, 101. f., 43. apr., 75. l., pp. 11-19. Original in Russian.*

Excerpts from the criminal accusation No. 26 against G. Astra for anti-Soviet activities

November 11, 1983

Astra, Gunārs, son of Larions

Born October 22, 1931 in Rīga, Latvian, citizen of the USSR, non-party, with a mid-level technical education, married, wife and minor son in the family, convicted on October 26, 1961, according to the Latvian SSR Criminal Code par. 59.1, par. 65.1 and par. 209, sentenced to imprisonment for 15 years; after serving time, freed on February 23, 1976, works for the Rīga Municipal Street Board as a worker, lives in Rīga [...][94]

[G. Astra] was convicted in 1961 for a particularly dangerous crime against the state – traitor to the homeland and anti-Soviet agitator and propagandist – but before finishing his punishment he did not change his views of Soviet power; [he] continued to hold views hostile to Soviet power and [exhibited] nationalist views seeking to undermine and weaken Soviet power; he began anti-Soviet propaganda and agitation anew, as manifested in anti-Soviet ideas, beliefs, and deceitful statements meant to discredit the Soviet state and social order; [he] invited others to struggle against Soviet power, to overthrow it, distributed literature with such [subversive] contents, as well as possessed literature with the same contents for those same reasons in the territory of Latvia from 1976 to January 6, 1983.

Astra's criminal activity concretely expressed itself in the following events:

Despite the fact that on December 11, 1979, he was given an official warning about [being involved in] prohibited activity contrary to the interests of the state security of the USSR, in the spring of 1980 at his residence in Rīga [...], he received from his acquaintance Ints Cālītis, with the intention of distribution, a document in the form of a typewritten text translated from Russian to Latvian, with anti-Soviet lies as contents, entitled: "To the government of the USSR, the governments of the GFR and GDR, to the governments of the states that signed the Atlantic Charter, to the General Secretary of the UNO Mister Kurt Waldheim." [The document claimed] that the renewal of Soviet power in the Baltic Republics was allegedly the consequence of Soviet "occupation" and that "the [Soviet] state stole the rights of the [Latvian] nation and its ability to determine its own fate"; it suggested the liquidation of Soviet order in the Baltic States. Astra wrote the text of the translation in his notebook and returned it to Ints Cālītis, together with the mentioned typewritten document in Russian, in the expectation that it would be distributed. Right away, Ints Cālītis made not less than five copies of this document in Latvian-language translation in the spring of 1980 in Rīga, using his typewriter "Moskva," and distributed the copies in Rīga among his acquaintances [...] : one copy to Ģederts Melngailis, whose copy was confiscated when the apartment was searched on January 6, 1983; a second copy – to Vilma Kļaviņa and Mirdza Celmiņa, the latter of whom gave her copy to her work colleague Zeltīte Meistere, who in turn gave it to her husband Matīss Meistars to read; finally it was read by their neighbor in the apartment Normunds Vijups, after which this copy was destroyed. Two of the mentioned copies were kept by Ints Cālītis in his residence in Rīga with the hope of distributing them later, until they were confiscated in the search of January 6, 1983. Astra also took the notebook with the mentioned translation from Ints Cālītis and kept it at his residence with the intent to distribute until it was confiscated in the search of January 6-7, 1983.

In 1981, in his residence in Rīga, using his photographic equipment, including a camera "Zenit-E," number 8100098942, he rephotographed the text of a foreign publication – a book with anti-Soviet contents by Agris Balodis [entitled] *The Baltic Republics on the Eve of the Great Fatherland War* and prepared photo-negatives of this text, which in final form he meant to distribute. In the photo-negatives of the text, there are fabrications that discredit the Soviet state and social order and lie about the USSR's foreign affairs before the beginning of World War Two. The renewal of Soviet power in Latvia, Lithuania, and Estonia is described from an anti-Soviet perspective; the essence of Soviet power in Latvia in 1940 is tarnished, and it is deceitfully claimed that the inhabitants of the Baltic states in 1940, in a few months time, had been transformed from free citizens into "inhabitants under a heavy occupation yoke," and that the acceptance of the republics into the USSR was a "violent inclusion into the Soviet Union" and "naked imperialist aggression."

In December of 1981, Astra, intending to prepare photocopies of the book, turned over the photo-negatives from his residence to the co-defendant Gunārs Freimanis, who, together with a worker from his brigade, Gunārs Subačs, in that same December, prepared in Ventspils at least three photocopies of the book [...] and distributed it further among their acquaintances.

-In the Spring of 1982, Gunārs Freimanis in Rīga [...] gave one copy to Oskars Vīndedzis for reading, but after that in the fall of 1982 at Dzervju Street 9 -- to Jānis Bērziņš where this copy was confiscated after a search on March 22, 1983.

- Gunārs Subačs on April 1, 1982, in Liepāja [...] gave two copies to Uldis Rubezis, who read a part of its contents; the book was confiscated from him on April 20, 1983.

At the beginning of 1982, Astra received the photo-negatives from Freimanis and, intending to distribute the publication again, continued to keep them at his residence, but in the spring of 1982, again with the intent to distribute and to photocopy the book's text, he gave them again to Gunārs Freimanis, and the latter, with the same intent, to Vitauts Čače in Jēkabpils. As a result, Vitatus Čače, in his residence in Jēkabpils region in Kūku village at the "New Manor," prepared from the book's photo-negatives three copies and became familiar with the contents. He kept the third at his residence where it was confiscated during a search on April 28-29, 1983. Using the photocopy of the book received from Vitauts Čače in the fall of 1982, Freimanis distributed it among many persons including the following [persons]: In Rīga [...] he gave it to a well-known person Alma Strautniece to have her distribute further [...], to Pēteris Osvalds Kreicers and his wife – Biruta Ausma Eglīte -- who got to know the photocopy text through Alma Strautniece and returned it to Gunārs Freimanis. Astra received the photo-negatives from Freimanis in the fall of 1982 and with the intent to distribute kept them in his apartment until they were confiscated in a search of January 6-7, 1983.

In 1981 at his residence in Rīga, Astra gave to Gunārs Freimanis in an electrographic copy a foreign publication – a book entitled "Andrejs Eglītis," authored by Edmunds Zirnīts, which had anti-Soviet content and in which the Soviet state and social order are cynically called "the horrible tyranny," "the communist nonsensical system," "Russian colonial prison," "the world's most inhumane power," where "mud and blood are mixed, trampled, [and] befoul the nation's soul"; and which claims that in the Soviet Union there exists so-called "slave labor," that the nationalities are supposedly suffocating in the "Soviet colonial fumes and spiritual destruction" "in conditions of the time of serfdom." It also besmirches the teaching of Marxism-Leninism and the foreign and domestic politics of the Soviet state, describing from an anti-Soviet position the conditions under which Soviet power was renewed, the reality of life in Latvia in 1940-1941, and the post-war years. It deceitfully describes Soviet power as „imprisonment and enslavement," "tragedy," and the "regime of the enemy," and claims that the "coarsest, most inhumane Eastern power" rules over the land, that communism is apparently "the enemy of its own nation and people"; at the same time, there is an invitation to become active in the struggle against Soviet power in order to topple it.

After getting to know the contents of this book, Freimanis in the very same year 1981 gave it to Vitauts Čače to read. Čače wrote in his notebook citations of an anti-Soviet nature from the book, and then Vitauts Čače gave the book back to Gunārs Freimanis, and the latter to Astra.

In October of 1981 in his residence in Rīga, Astra expounded on the book written by George Orwell in English "1984". This book also has anti-Soviet contents, and Astra gave it to Roberts Cīrulis to examine. In "1984" the teachings of Marxism-Leninism are belittled and the goal of the socialist and Soviet order is portrayed as "refusing freedom and the establishment of equality," as well as holding up progress and freezing history at a defined phase of development. The book compares Russian communists to German fascists, claims that communists "repressed all progressive movements more than the inquisition of the middle ages, using torture during which the victim confessed to all for which he was charged."

At the beginning of 1982 in his residence in Rīga, Astra used his photo equipment, including the camera "Zenit-E" number 810098942, with the intent to distribute the foreign publication of the Latvian émigré Anšlavs Eglītis book "The Lucky Ones," which had an anti-soviet content. He prepared photo-negatives of the book's text. The photo-negatives of the book's text contain deceitful fabrications that discredit the Soviet state and social order, and whose anti-Soviet lies are made in the spirit that calls for the elimination of Soviet power in Latvia. It undertakes to demonstrate the so-called "inhumane" attitude [by the Soviet state] toward the nation, and described representatives of Soviet power "sneaks, traitors, professional liars, thieves and bands of murderers," claiming also that the soldiers of the Soviet army in liberating Latvia from the German fascists in 1944 tortured and destroyed unarmed masses. There are also anti-Soviet lies about the Russian nation, and claims that Soviet Latvia in the post-war years has supposedly been "occupied," It stresses that the Russian nation made "millions of obedient persons into animal-like, unfeeling slave camp guards, into millions of occupiers and satellite lands," and that Soviet power in Latvia can be compared to a "Soviet prison."

In his residence in the spring of 1982, Astra, with the intent to distribute photocopies, handed the mentioned photo-negatives of the text of the book to Gunārs Freimanis who together with the worker in his brigade, Gunārs Subačs, in that same spring in Talsi region in Dundaga prepared two copies of the book's text and got to know the contents. They distributed it further among their acquaintances:

-Gunārs Freimanis gave one copy at the end of 1982 in Rīga [...] to Gunārs Lācis to read, who turned the copy over to the investigative organs on April 21, 1983.

-Gunārs Subačs gave the second copy on April 1, 1982 to Uldis Rubezis in his apartment in Liepāja who in part familiarized himself with the contents and this copy was confiscated from Uldis Rubezis on April 20, 1983.

Astra received the photo-negatives back from Freimanis in the summer of 1982 and with the intent to distribute kept them in his apartment until they were confiscated in the search of January 6, 1983.

In the winter of 1981-1982 in his residence in Rīga, Astra gave to Gunārs Freimanis to read an electrographic copy of the book by the foreign author Uldis Ģērmanis, "The Experiences of the Latvian Nation" a book with anti-Soviet content. This book discredits the Soviet state and social order, and contains anti-Soviet lies. It describes the renewal of Soviet power in Latvia in 1940 by saying that the Latvian nation was "confused and shocked" and that throughout the land there were so-called "strange, dark fears"; the liberation of Soviet Latvia from the fascist German attackers is compared with "the arrival of communist slavery in the world."

After familiarizing himself with the contents, at the beginning of the fall in 1982, Gunars Freimanis in Rīga gave it to Vitauts Čače through the mediation of Jānis Knāķis, but kept it at his residence in "New Manor" in Kuka village in Jēkabpils region until he gave it to his neighbor, Antons Grebze, on January 1st of 1983.

In the spring of 1982, Astra in his residence in Rīga used his photo equipment, including the camera "Zenit-E" number 8100098942, and photographed, with the intent to distribute, a book by the foreign Latvian émigré author, Anšlavs Eglītis', "Five Days," which also had anti-Soviet content. Gunārs Freimanis had brought this to him and prepared photo-negatives of this book's text. The mentioned book unashamedly lies about the Soviet state and social order, [mentioning] "violence" and "forced slave camps" and that the Soviet nation supposedly finds itself "locked in prison." It claims that the Soviet Union has supposedly created a "new ruling elite, a new aristocracy," "the red bourgeoisie" that rules the state; and it is further said that the Soviet Union supposedly is ruled by "spying, lies, faithlessness and inter-personal intrigues and lies"; that the functionaries of Soviet power and communists are "drunks, uneducated, uncultured, dim-witted, unjust, and violent persons"; that life in Soviet Latvia is "under the yoke of occupation" that is an "unending nightmare." It tarnishes the reality of the renewal of Soviet power in the Latvian SSR in 1940-1941, cynically suggesting that the Latvian nation has fallen into so-called "barbarian slavery," besmirches Latvian cultural life and education system by describing it as "an unhappy sink;" Soviet Latvia's artists and writers are called "careerists" and "party slaves."

Afterwards Astra, in his residence, using his photographic equipment, together with Gunārs Freimanis, made not less than one copy of the negatives of the photocopy of the text of Eglītis' book, and gave them to Freimanis, who after getting to know the contents, distributed the copies further among his acquaintances: at the end of the summer of 1982 Freimanis took this copy to Rīga [...] and gave it to Aivars Kalējs to read, but after receiving it back from him in the fall of 1982 in Rīga [...] gave it to Jānis Bērziņš to read, where this copy was confiscated during the search of March 22, 1983.

In the same spring of 1982 in his residence, Astra, with the intent to distribute, gave the above mentioned photo-negatives of the text of the book "Five Days" to Gunārs Freimanis, but the latter, with the same intent, to Vitauts Čače in Jēkabpils. Then the latter, in his residence in "New Manor" in Kūku village in Jēkabpils region, prepared photocopies of the book's text with his photographic equipment in not less than four copies that were confiscated during the search, together with the photo-negatives on April 28-29, 1983.

Moreover, Astra had in his residence in Rīga from 1976 until their confiscation during the search on January 6-7, 1983, with intent to distribute, the following:

-Using his photographic equipment, he prepared and for the same intent kept the following photo-negatives of pages of text of the following books with anti-Soviet lies as content:

-Jānis Grīns' "Sadzīvotāji rezonē. Swedish stories" in which it is claimed that in the Baltic Republics under Soviet power the nations are allegedly oppressed and their citizens and intelligentsia have to be isolated from the Russian nation that is supposedly occupying Latvia;

-George Orwell's, "1984," in which the teachings of Marxism-Leninism about socialism are belittled by claims that their goal is to halt progress, freeze history; and that communists are similar to fascists and have repressed any and every progressive movement;

-Jānis Jūrmalnieks' "Latvia's Inclusion in the Soviet Union" in which it is claimed that the renewal of Soviet power in Latvia in 1940 was supposedly nothing more than an aggressive act of the Soviet Union, and Soviet Latvia's acceptance into the USSR is described as "Russian-led Baltic annexation" and "Latvia's violent inclusion into the Soviet Union";

-Hermanis Kreicers' "Windows" and "Reflections" that distort the teaching of Marxism-Leninism, Soviet power, and the Communist Party's foreign and domestic politics; the essence of Soviet power and the reality of life in Soviet Latvia are described as involving a nation that finds itself "in the conditions of manorial servants" of the state;

-Matīss Kaudzīte's "New Time of the Surveyors," in which the founding of Soviet power in Latvia in 1919 is described as "a night that will come in a flood of innocent people's blood"; and Soviet power needs schools in order to train persons who are "entirely happy with torture and animal-like terrors in institutions of punishment";

-Margita Gūtmane's "Veronika Strelerte. Collections of Writing for the Poet's 70th Birthday October 10, 1982." in which the renewal of Soviet power in Latvia in 1940 is called an "occupation" and Soviet Latvia's liberation from the German fascist occupiers in 1944 is said to have been the "foundation of the red terror."

-Arnold Spekke's "Episodes of Remembrance" in which discussions about Soviet Latvia claim that it is not free, but it is [said to be] a place of "Bolshevik colonial violence" where it is easiest to see their "blatant lies";

-Aleksandr Solzhenitsyn's "Gulag Archipelago" in which, through generalizing the negative characteristics of the cult of personality, Soviet power is described has having a supposedly inhumane and pitiless attitude toward soviet persons, and it is claimed that our state supposedly is not free, that rights are formal but that the Party supposedly rules all.

The following books were found with pages containing anti-Soviet lies marked for reproduction on film:

-Abauruhman Avtarhanov's "The Rise of the Partocracy," in which Soviet power is lied about in statements that in the period during the development of the Soviet state after the Great October Socialist Revolution the Soviet Union was supposedly a "single party tyranny"; and by generalizing negative tendencies of the cult of personality it is claimed that Stalin "fought with the nation" and that he was an "absolute tyrant" and ""hated the nation";

-Using his typewriter number 494460 he prepared two texts typed in Latvian, with the intent to distribute; these texts had an anti-Soviet content, and bore the title the title "Reflections About the Nation and Homeland" in which the author, Voldemārs Zariņš, makes statements in which the life of the Latvian nation in the time of Soviet Latvia is compared to a supposed "internal émigré fate" and which echo with the call to struggle against Soviet power – the "historical enemy – Russian imperialism," and its "pressure on all of the Baltic [lands]";

-Prepared, and with the same intent, and kept a text in Latvian with anti-Soviet lies as contents, together with a hand-written note beginning with the words: "Night. February 24th, 12:00…" – in which hostility is expressed to the existing Soviet order and against the "Russian oppressors", and an invitation is made to struggle against the so-called existing "yoke"; in the text the belief is expressed that Latvians will definitely win, that Latvia will supposedly lift itself from this "yoke", and that this battle will "shock all of the world";

-20 magnetic tapes recorded on his recorder, and made with the same intent, contained anti-Soviet foreign radio broadcasts with deceitful contents, but also contained discussions, poems, and texts in which mention is made of hostility to Soviet power and against the socialist order which is compared to fascism; as well as claims that the Baltic Republics today are supposedly oppressed and that they have been "occupied by Russians" and that "Russification" is taking place; also, antagonistic expressions are heard aimed at the Communist Party, which is supposedly led guided by the politics of aggression.

In addition, in Astra's residence in Rīga […] from 1976 until their confiscation during the search of January 6-7, 1983, there was the following literature with anti-Soviet, deceitful contents, which he kept with the intent to distribute:

Books:

-two copies of Adolf Hitler's "Mein Kampf" and one book with the title "Great German Independence Struggles. The Speeches of Adolf Hitler." In these, there are described the racial superiority of the Germans, lies about the teaching of Marxism, invitations to constant struggle against the Soviet Union which is referred to as the "Bolshevik regime" and the "Hebrew-Bolshevik power-center in Moscow";

-Richard Wurmbrand's "Why I am a … Revolutionary," which contains lies about the teachings of Marxism; about the revolutionary movement, its roots and leading role; hostility toward communism is voiced and deceitful fabrications are put forward about the essence of socialist order;

-Sergei Staprāns' "Through Russian Darkness to Latvia's Sun" in which communists are slandered and it is claimed that through their "destructive and seditious" work in the [Russian] army after the Great October Socialist Revolution the communists had "incited" the Latvian riflemen [*strēlnieki*], leading the latter to stand on the side of Revolution;

-Uldis Ģērmanis' "The Experiences of the Latvian Nation" in which, as already mentioned, the Soviet state, and social order are discredited;

-George Orwell's "1984" in which, as already mentioned, the teaching of Marxism-Leninism about socialism are slandered;

-Lancelot Lawton's "Soviet Russian Economic History," in two volumes, which claim that the Bolsheviks in the period after the Revolution did not occupy themselves with bread supplies and the liquidation of famine, but that daily they had "shot many peasants"; and socialism can be compared to capitalism;

-50 copies of the magazine "Signal," published in the period from 1942-1944, in which the German fascist army is described as invincible, its "victories" over sections of the Soviet army are celebrated, and the attack of the fascist armies on the Soviet Union is justified;

-typewritten texts with the following titles:

-"Once Again about the Jews and the Lithuanians," in which, in an anti-Soviet spirit, it is claimed that the occupation period supposedly began in Lithuania in 1940, and that the Lithuanian nation did not like the Jews;

-"Mart Niklus Accuses Citizen Vavrenuk and Other Powerful Persons Whose Last Names He Has Not Been Told," in which it is claimed that in the Soviet Union the right of freedom and personal inviolability does not exist, that innocent persons are held in prison and tortured for many long months;

-Jānis Zariņš' "Latvians in Russia or How Latvia was Founded," in which the creation of the first socialist state [in Latvia] and its consolidation are slandered, as are Soviet power and the work of the Communist Party during this period [1919] ;

-"To the Governments of the USSR, GFR, GDR, the Governments which signed the Atlantic Charter, and the General Secretary of the UNO, Mr. Kurt Waldheim," in which, as already mentioned, the renewal of Soviet power in Latvia in 1940 is besmirched;

-A notebook of hand-written notes containing five poems with the general title "Latvia's monologues" and titles of the individual parts "Freedom Monologue", "Daugava Monologue", "Kronvalds Atis' Monologue", "Swedish Times Monologue", "Fallen Soldiers Monologue." In these, the reality of life in Soviet Latvia is besmirched from a bourgeois nationalist position with the backdrop of historical events. [It is] claimed that the Latvian nation under the conditions of Soviet power is supposedly not free, finds itself oppressed and enslaved, and is ruled over by foreigners and attackers; they also issue an invitation to the Latvian nation to be united in the struggle for their freedom; -

[These constitute] anti-Soviet agitation and propaganda, done by a person previously convicted of particularly dangerous state crimes, as stated in the criminal code of the Latvian SSR paragraph 65, second section.

The accusatory article compiled in Rīga on November 5-10, 1983.

Relative to the request (Latvian SSR Criminal Code paragraph 211) for criminal files to be sent to the Latvian SSR prosecutor to ratify the accusatory article and the file being used in court

Senior Investigator of the Investigative Section for Particularly Important Files of the State Security Committee of the Latvian SSR, Lieutenant Colonel,   E. Bērziņš

Agree:

Deputy Chief of the Investigative Section of the State Security Committee of the Latvian SSR, Lieutenant Colonel   S. Bravackis

Chair of the State Security Committee of the Latvian SSR, Major General   B.Pugo

Source: *LVA, 1986.f., 1.apr., 45322.l., p. 99-111.Original in Latvian.*

Documents No. 39-41
Engineered migrations

Document No. 39

Excerpts from secret explanatory paper about the balance of labor resource in the Latvian SSR in the period from 1960 to 1980, [submitted by] A. Vīndedze, Deputy Chair of the Latvian SSR State Planning Commission[95] and V. Šulcs, Director of the Labor and Wage Department

December 11, 1960

...In the period of the plan, the industrial (workforce) will increase from 286,700 persons to 396,800 persons, by 33.1%; in construction from 75,700 persons to 101,600 persons – by 34%; in transport and communications (including transport that serves nonproductive sectors and inhabitants) from 87,600 persons to 153,000 persons – by 75%; in commerce and public eating establishments from 61,500 persons to 110,700 persons – by 30%; in education and cultural organizations from 61,700 persons to 106,200 persons – by 1.7 times; in the sciences and scientific services from 9,500 persons to 22,900 persons – 2.4 times; in healthcare and social welfare from 46,600 persons to 105,000 persons – 2.3 times; in communal apartment housing from 35,000 persons to 57,000 persons – 1.7 times. In agriculture, the number of employed will decrease from 395,300 persons in 1960 to 266,000 persons in 1980, by 32.7%...

Over the next twenty years, the in the labor force of the Latvian SSR [through migration], at the expense of other republics, is expected to be 100,000 persons.[96]

Reports of the previous years' growth in the Latvian SSR demonstrate that the expected increase in population is real.

Latvian SSR State Planning Commission Deputy Chair

A. Vīndedze

Latvian SSR State Planning Commission Labor and Labor Wages Department Director
V. Šulcs

Source: *LVA, 693. f., 1.s.apr., 385. l., pp. 51, 52 . Original in Russian.*

Document No. 40

Secret information submitted by G. Uhov, First Deputy Chair of the Latvian SSR State Planning Committee, to the Latvian SSR Council of Ministers concerning the suggestion to the USSR Planning Committee that all conditionally convicted and all conditionally freed individuals be used for labor only in the territory of the Latvian SSR.

January 7, 1985

In order to guarantee that in 1985 all persons with suspended sentences and in conditionally released groups be sent to labor only in the territory of the Latvian SSR, the Latvian SSR Planning Committee submitted a project letter to N. Baibakov, the Deputy Chair of the USSR State Planning Committee.

Attachment: as mentioned in the text, Accounting Document number 21s, secret, on one page.

First Deputy Chair
G. Uhov

Project
Council of Ministers of the Latvian SSR
To the USSR State Planning Committee's Deputy Chair, N. Baibakov

January 1985
Dear Nikolaj' Konstantinovich!

Due to the severe shortage of manpower,[97] the Republic's construction organizations regularly fail to fulfill their construction plans and thus delay the availability of important components of the national economy. Last year (1984) the construction assembly sector fell short of about 3,000 persons or 5% of the planned-for number and, for this reason, could not fulfill the construction and assembly plan, falling short by about 35 million rubles of which more than 18 million rubles were in the organization of the Latvian SSR Construction Ministry.

In 1985, the plan calls for continuing work and for putting into operation entities important to the national economy, such as the Rīga Wool Manufacturing Association "Rīga Textile," Liepāja Agricultural Machine Factory, Drainage Pipe Factory "Lode", several enterprises manufacturing brick and construction material, a metal foundry/mechanical factory in Jēkabpils, a radio and telephone transmitter station in Rīga, the factory junction "Blue Hill", a mechanical robot factory, as well as other large construction objects.

In order to be able to put into operation on time the entities most important to the national economy of the republic, we request your directive that all persons with suspended sentences and all conditionally freed persons in 1985, approximately 2400 persons, be sent to work only in the republic, and not outside the Latvian SSR.

The plan to which it is hoped they will be attached has been coordinated with the Ministry of the Interior, the Ministry of Construction, as well as other interested ministries and committees; and on September 17th, 1984, the USSR's Planning Committee was also notified, with Document number 944/677s.

The Chair of the Latvian SSR Council of Ministers
J. Rubenis

Source: *LVA, 693.f., 1.s. apr., 956. l., pp. 3-4. Original in Russian.*

Excerpts from an explanatory report from the First Deputy Chair of the Latvian SSR State Planning Committee, E. Āboliņš, and the Labor, Wages, and Cadre Preparation Section Chair of the Latvian SSR State Planning Committee, V. Burtnieks, about the projected labor resources in the Latvian SSR from 1986 to 1990

1985

...the growth of labor resources in the 12[98] Five Year Plan[98] will diminish considerably, as the statistics below show clearly:

	1971-1975	1976-1980	1981-1985	1986-1990
Labor resource growth in % compared to the previous 5 years	6.0	3.5	2.1	1.4
Total growth, relative to:	100.0	100.0	100.0	100.0
Able-bodied persons, natural growth	53.6	34.4	-90.7	-22.8
Able-bodied persons, in-migration	49.8	61.9	88.7	86.4
Oldest working persons and adolescents	-3.4	3.7	42.0	36.4

The dynamics of labor resources in a longer-term perspective are detailed below:

	1971-1975	1976-1980	1981-1985	1986-1990
Labor resource growth, in thousands	86.3	53.8	32.6	28.0
Due to natural growth	46.3	18.5	-10.0	-5.0
Due to in-migration	43.0	33.3	28.9	19.0
Oldest working persons and adolescents	-3.0	2.0	13.7	14.0

Latvian SSR State Planning Committee First Deputy Chair   E. Āboliņš
Labor, Labor Wages and Cadre Preparation Section Chair   V. Burtnieks

Source: *LVA, 693.f., 1.s. apr., 956. l., pp. 157, 158. Original in Russian.*

Documents No. 42-43
Retired Soviet military personnel in Latvia

Document No. 42

Excerpts from a January 1, 1961, secret report of the Commissar of War for the Latvian SSR, I. Časa, on guaranteeing the material and living conditions of demobilized soldiers

March 31, 1961

The conditions as of January 1, 1961

After January 15, 1960, the number joining the retired   2874 persons

II. Secured with living space[99]
a) Retired officers from the armed forces who have not been assured of living space   583
    These include:
       -Retired before January 15, 1960   188
       -Retired after January 15, 1960   395
Of those that retired after January 15, 1960, after being three months on the registry but still not having living space   242

b) During the review, living space was not given to the following:
       -Retired before January 15, 1960   14
       -Retired after January 15, 1960   59

III. Additional Information

1. Those put on the registry from the Baltic Military District and the SBF   2205
       Of those, from local garrisons   1746
2. Those who have arrived from other military districts (fleets),   669
       including those that do not have living space or close relatives   400
3. Of those that have arrived, the following have registered:
    a. In Rīga   2367
    b. In cities under Republic jurisdiction   439
    c. In the countryside   68
4. The total number of retired officers placed in jobs after January 15, 1960, including officers enrolled in higher education or technical training   2038

    Of those:
       a. In Rīga   1669
       b. In cities under Republic jurisdiction   320
       c. In the countryside   49
5. Total allocated living space   579 persons/14,880 sq m
       Of those:
         a. Retired before January 15, 1960   103 persons/ 2,605 sq m
         b. Retired after January 15, 1960   476 persons/ 12,275 sq m

6. During the second quarter of 1961, the plan should allocate 4,000 sq. m. (roughly 150 apartments) of living space for retired officers.

IV. Explanation

Events taking place during the review in order to improve the material and living conditions of retired officers and to guarantee them work.

1. On March 7, 1961, the Latvian Communist Party Central Committee and the Council of Ministers of the Latvian SSR in a joint meeting approved the following decision: "Concerning the guaranteeing and distribution of living space to retired officers of the armed forces of the USSR in 1961."
2. On February 4, 1961, in an expanded session of the Rīga Municipal Executive Committee Commission (participating: the Municipal Executive Committee Chair and a representative of the Latvian Communist Party Central Committee) the results of the review, and subsequent assignments for guaranteeing the material and living conditions of retired soldiers in 1961, were [discussed and] coordinated...
3. The guaranteeing of work for retired soldiers was discussed in the offices of the Latvian Communist party Rīga Municipal Regional Committees.
4. In March of 1961, three groupings of officers were interviewed about how retired soldiers are provided with work in the following Rīga factories: "Rīgaseļmaš," the railroad carriage factory, machine factory, and the Liepāja shipping industry.

b. The arrival of retired officers, their admission to the registry, and their placement in the territory of the republic.[100]

After January 15, 1960	the following were listed on the registry:	2,874
The first quarter of 1960		113
The second quarter of 1960		214
The third quarter of 1960		1196
The fourth quarter of 1960		722
The first quarter of 1961		629

Information about the arrival of retired officers arrivals in the municipalities of the Latvian SSR.

City and Region	Total arrived	From Baltic Military District and SBF	Of those, from local garrisons	From other military districts and from fleets	Of those, those without living space or close relatives
Ventspils	24	20	15	4	-
Daugavpils	116	89	55	27	21
Jelgava	66	57	14	9	5
Liepāja	170	161	143	9	3
Rēzekne	18	11	1	7	2
Jūrmala	45	36	34	9	6

Total from all Republic cities	439	374	262	65	37	
Other Republic regions	68	39	14	29	10	
Rīga	2367	1792	1470	575	353	
Total	2874	2205	1746	669	400	

The bulk of retired soldiers have chosen Rīga for their permanent living place — 2367 persons or about 83%. Of the 507 persons who arrived in other regions, 439 chose republic cities as their permanent home and only 68 the countryside, usually rural residential centers.

We have to take note that 394 reserve officers have arrived in Rīga from other cities where they had living space – they traded that for [living] space [in Riga]...

Retired officers have arrived in Rīga who have traded their living space not just in some remote city, but in the largest cities of the USSR...

In Rīga, in 1960, there were times when local councils granted retired officers living space according to above-average norms, for example:
In the Lenin *rajons*
-Major A. J. Lisenko was granted two rooms with 42 sq. meters for four persons;
-Lieutenant Colonel N. Goncarenko was granted a three-room apartment of 42 sq. m. for four persons;
In the Proletarian *rajons*
-Lieutenant R.K. Klever was granted a 17 sq. m. of room for one person;
-Lieutenant S. H. Margosjan was granted a 20 sq. m. of room for two persons;
In the Moscow *rajons*
-Colonel A.F. Bistrov was granted a separate two-room apartment with 31.7 sq. m. for three persons;
-Lieutenant Senior Engineer J.V. Demencuk was granted a separate two-room apartment with 29.9 sq. m. for two persons.

On January 21, 1961, the Rīga Municipal Commission reviewed the errors of the Regional Executive Committee in granting living space. The Commission punished this undesirable activity.

In addition, in the Lenin *rajons* [of Riga] there have been examples of individual officers receiving living space through fraud...

F) The work of the retired reserve officer Registry and the Military Commissariats in planning and guaranteeing material and living conditions.

In each Military Commissariat, a registry is planned of those retired soldiers who need work and living space.

In those Military Commissariats where the number of retired reserve soldiers is not large, the registry is in journal form.

In the larger Military Commissariats (Moscow *rajons*, Proletarian *rajons*), a special registry card index is created, and for those who desperately need living space, a personal list (parallel with the

Region's Executive Committee list) is drawn up, with officers and senior soldiers receiving priority on the list.

The work of ensuring material and living conditions is planned out on a monthly basis.

The Republic Military Commissariat's work plans reflect the following principles:

1) The Republic Military Commissar and its officers participate in the work of the municipal commission involving jobs and living space for soldiers who have retired according to the January 15, 1960, law.

2) The Third Section officers participate in the receiving of retired officers at the Rīga Municipal Executive Committee Commission.

3) The Republic Military Commissariat's officers participate in the Commission's work on the allocation of Riga living space for retired soldiers.

4) The work of ensuring social and living conditions of retired officers is inspected by the municipal and regional military Commissariats.

5) Municipal commission members and Republic Military Commissariat officers work together in the review of the regional commissions [created for this purpose]

6) The placement of retired reserve officers in jobs is controlled by the republic's enterprises and institutions.

Latvian SSR War Commissar Guard General Major   Časa

Source: *LVA PA, 101. f., 24. apr., 96. l., pp. 63-66. Original in Russian.*

Document No. 43

Excerpts from the minutes of a meeting of the Rīga Municipal Commission about the allocation of apartments and the solving of questions related to jobs, apartments. and living conditions for retired USSR armed forces military personnel

February 28, 1984

Commission Chair:	J. Jaško
Secretary:	V. Merekina
Commission Members:	Comrades V. Agajev, V. Petkevic, V. Krinbergs, A. Bergs

Submission of Engineer Major Genadij Matveyavich Reckin: a family of four persons (himself, wife, son [born 1966, a cadet in a military academy], and daughter, born 1973) requests to be registered with his wife's sister on Pavlov Street 17, apartment 8, a two-room apartment with 23.85 sq. m., with three persons registered already; they ask to be accepted in the registry of living space.

Decision: Register and add on to the registry 3 persons (him, wife, daughter).

Warned about the length of the wait for an apartment in Rīga (4 to 5 years). Agreed to wait, refused a communal apartment.

Submission of retired Lieutenant Colonel, from the Medical Services, Jāzeps Stanislavich Lielbārdis: a family of two (himself and his wife), asks for permission to register with an acquaintance on J. Kupala Street 16, apartment 32, a two-room apartment of 39.6 sq. m. with two persons already registered, and to be placed on the registry to guarantee living space for two persons. Retired Lieutenant Colonel J. Lielbārdis of the medical services was called up in 1961 by the Military Commissariat of the Lenin *rajons* of Rīga.

232

Decision: Register and place on the registry two persons. Warned about the wait (4 to 5 years) for guaranteed living space in Rīga. Agreed to wait, refused a communal apartment...

7. Submission of Reserve Major Vissarion Vasilijevich Tokarev concerning expediting the allocation of an apartment due to unsatisfactory living conditions: four persons (himself, his wife, son, and daughter) have been on the apartment registry since September 26, 1980. They are registered in a one-room apartment on Miera Street 65, apartment 17 with 15.73 sq. m. of living space in which 5 persons live.

Decision: To guarantee with living space according to the plan in the first half of 1984.

8. Submission of Reserve Major Artur Georgijevich Dudnev: to include his new-born grandson, Denis, on the guaranteed apartment registry with himself, his wife and daughter who were accepted on the registry on September 28, 1979.

Decision: To allocate a three-room apartment with 37 sq. m.; the request to add the grandson to the registry denied.

9. Request from the Proletarian *rajons* Executive Committee about allocation of living space in the second half of 1984 to Reserve Major Viktor Ivanovich Puticev, who has been on the guaranteed living space registry since September 24, 1982, and has 3 persons in his family (himself, wife and son), and has worked since January 15, 1983 as an inspector of social conditions for the Region Executive Committee.

Decision: Grant the allowance to guarantee space in the second half of 1984.

Commission Secretary   V. Merekina

Source: *Rīgas IKA, 1400. f., 13. apr., 223. l., pp. 57-58. Original in Russian.*

Documents No. 44-50
Attitudes toward the Latvian language

Document No. 44

Excerpts from minutes of a secret meeting of the Bureau of the Central Committee of the Latvian Communist Party about the teaching of the Russian and Latvian languages in republic schools[101]

April 14, 1953

2nd paragraph: concerning the implementation of the October 30, 1951, decision of the Central Committee of the Latvian Communist Party "About the conditions of Russian and Latvian teaching in Republic schools'" (comrades Samsons, Nikonov, Kalnbērziņš)

The Bureau of the Central Committee of the Latvian Communist Party believes that the Ministry of Education of the Latvian SSR and the Party committee have implemented unsatisfactorily the October 30, 1951, decision "About the condition of teaching Russian and Latvian languages in republic schools." The educational organs and individual Party committees still do not value the Russian language – the exceptional meaning of the teaching of the language of Lenin and Stalin for the overall development of the Latvian nation's culture. [...]

The primary cause of all these serious shortcomings in the teaching of Russian and Latvian languages is the shortage of qualified teachers in the literary cadres, the unsatisfactory work in preparing teachers, their low qualifications, and the absence of improvement in their ideological-theoretical training. Of 1,553 Russian-language lecturers in Republic schools only 320 have the highest education, but 425 have only a middle-pedagogical or general education. Of the 1,311 Latvian-language teachers more than 400 do not have the relevant education. [...]

The Bureau of the Central Committee of the Latvian Communist Party has decided:

1. To assign the Ministry of Education of the Latvian SSR (comrade Samsons) the task of addressing the shortcomings mentioned in this decision, to ensure that the October 30, 1951, decision of the Bureau of the Central Committee of the Latvian Communist Party .. is implemented without any objections.

2. To increase the scientific level of instruction of the Russian and Latvian languages in republic schools. To improve the personnel education section, and the control of the school leader over the instruction of languages in the school so as to guarantee for schoolchildren an even and thorough knowledge of the Russian and Latvian languages. To ensure that by July 1st all republic schools will use the directives concerning orthographic reform and guarantee that the reform will be implemented.

3. In order to raise the qualifications of teachers in the realm of the written word, to organize in the summer of 1953 courses at the Teachers Qualification Improvement Institutes for 350 teachers from all provinces[101]. To organize preparatory courses for Russian-language teachers for 75 persons in the Ministry of Education of the Latvian SSR. To involve the best school children in the courses who will be completing the 10th grade of republic schools in 1953.

    To energetically improve language teaching at pedagogical and teacher institutes. To pay particular attention to the providing of assistance in the realm of methodology so that schools can solve the problems of teaching teachers to teach languages; to activate a commission and [develop] methodological consistency to more thoroughly research, distribute, and popularize the best instructional work.

4. To assign to the Ministry of Education of the Latvian SSR and the Board of printing plants, factories, publishers, and book sellers (comrade Puny) the task of assuring the timely publication of Russian- and Latvian-language instructional books for grades 1 to 4; these books will be part of the 1953 publishing plan, as will be their distribution to schools for the start of the academic year. To finish the manuscript on the instruction book for Latvian literary history by June 1st, and for Latvian history by December 15, 1953.

5. To request that the Ministry of Culture of the Latvian SSR (comrade P. K. Ponomarenko) allow an increase to 375 persons of the number of teachers in the philology faculties of the Pedagogical Institute in the academic year 1953-1954.

6. To assign the provincial, municipal and regional committees of the Party the task of working energetically to improve the quality of instruction of Russian and Latvian languages in the republic schools. To pay particular attention to the teaching of the Great Russian national language as significant for the raising of the level of Latvian national culture. To systematically address the question of the teaching of language in the provincial, municipal, and regional committee offices of the Party. To improve the political education of teachers.

Source: *LVA PA, 101. f., 16. apr., 21. l., pp. 35-37. Original in Russian.*

Excerpts from a speech of V. Lācis, Chair of the Council of Ministers of the Latvian SSR, at the Plenum of the Central Committee of the Latvian Communist Party on June 22-23, 1953

June 22, 1953

[…] In the former Ministry of Republic Sovkhozes, the former Minister, comrade Vācietis, and his deputy on cadre questions, comrade Lodziņš, were given the information that …of 31 sovkhoz directors only 5 were Latvians, and that of 31 deputy directors only 6 were Latvians; the same kinds of situation also exists in the machine tractor stations, in which only 23 of 107 political section chiefs are Latvian. […]

A similar circumstance exists in our republic's court system. Not long ago, the Council of Ministers reviewed the work of the Ministry of Justice with its cadres. I will submit only one example to you. In the Moscow *rajons* of the city of Rīga there are five people's courts; as a result of the political shortsightedness of the Ministry of Justice and the Moscow *rajons* Party Committee in the last election, the condition was created that not one of the five people's judges understands the Latvian language and can not hold court sessions nor review materials in the Latvian language. Therefore, rather frequently, the investigative organs and the prosecutor who have done their investigations in the Latvian language can not give their material to the Moscow *rajons* people's courts and are forced to turn to the Republic's highest court with the request that the investigation of the file and other matters be assigned to another *rajons* people's court which is capable of looking through the material and is able to hold sessions in the Latvian language. This kind of situation is absurd and, without a doubt, earns reproaches and creates little satisfaction among the people.

A similar, king-of-the-mountain attitude was shown by none other than the former head of the people's education section of Rīga, comrade Rons. At the start of his appointment, this employee began by prohibiting office work in the Latvian language and then explained all office work and instructions relating to work in the Russian language. A little later, comrade Rons openly declared that it is time for Rīga to go over completely to the Russian language. […]

I also wanted to say a few words about our general problems in placing cadres. First of all, we must speak about the large numbers of responsible and leading figures of the Party councils and the economy who show excessive fear of the so-called "shadows of the past" and demonstrate too much timidity and insecurity in the placement of Latvian national cadres, thus considerably narrowing the contingent of available cadres. Something similar to the "cult of the form" has settled in with us. We have certain kinds of employees who continue to live and work according to forms of fifteen, twenty and even more years ago, completely ignoring work needs of Soviet citizens in the Soviet era. "Home guard," "boy scout," "hawk," "scout," "fraternity brother," "legionnaire," and similar words are some of the terms used to describe living persons, their essence, and their appropriateness for this or some other job, their faith in Soviet power. In this connection, we have to examine the past. What were the conditions of employment in bourgeois Latvia? The [fact is] that the worker in any state institution, particularly in the countryside, could not get work in his specialty, but if he was able to, then he could not stay in his job if he did not join one or another organizations controlled by the ruling elite. Some joined because such organizations truly were close to their hearts and suited their class interest and reactionary disposition, but how many joined unthinkingly or so that they would not be fired from their work? Many of the latter can be found nowadays among agronomists, foresters, rural teachers, and doctors. […]

Source: *LVA PA, 101.f., 16. apr., 9. l., pp. 95-99. Original in Latvian.*

Document No. 46

Excerpts from a speech of Secretary of the Rīga Municipal Committee of the Latvian Communist Party, E. Berklavs, at the Plenary of the Latvian Communist Party Central Committee of June 22-23, 1953.

June 23, 1953

The ongoing conditions are such that about half of the inhabitants of Rīga are Latvians. In the last five months, in the meetings of the Rīga Municipal Committee and in the city's eight party *rajons* committees 8,148 speeches have been given; of those only 2,410 have been in Latvian.

An even worse example is in the Lenin *rajons*, where of 508 speeches given, but only 118 were read in Latvian. About 600 Latvians work in the factory "Zasulauks Manufacturing," but all political education work is done there only in the Russian language. The situation is similar in the factories "Red Textilist," the reserve part mechanical factory "Red Morning" and elsewhere.

In May, the conditions in the city have deteriorated; of 1,010 speeches given, only 243 were done in the Latvian language. Similarly with lectures delivered, about which comrade Kalnbērziņš already spoke. In Rīga there are about 20,000 agitators [public activists] working; among them, only 8,00 work in the Latvian language.

What the true situation is and how badly we have we worked can be seen by looking at particular factories and enterprises.

Look, two examples. I am not taking these from factories with the worst situations, but from two of our largest factories, the factory VEF [*Valsts elektrotehnikas fabrika*] and the Rīga Railroad Carriage Factory.

Of all the workers in VEF, 49.8% are Latvian, but of this year's 879 speeches and lectures, only 203, or less than one fourth, were given in the Latvian language. Seventy-three political groups exists in the factory and only 30 of those work in the Latvian language. The agitators' seminars, all the instructional meetings, all of the full meetings of the working masses either in the whole factory or in individual shops, all the meetings with the director and chief engineer, all party, trade union and Komsomol meetings occur in Russian, all of the directives and news are also written only in Russian language. In this kind of work, of course, it is not surprising that of the 510-person strong Party organization in VEF, only one fifth are Latvians. In the Rīga Railroad Carriage Factory, of the 214 communists only 28, or 13%, are Latvians. During October of 1953, not a single Latvian worker or engineer-technician has been accepted into the ranks of the Rīga Railroad Carriage Factory's party organization.

Another question to which we have so far not devoted the attention it deserves is the question of the acquisition of the Russian and Latvian languages. Almost nine years have passed since the liberation of Rīga. That is enough time in which each person, if only they were willing, could have acquired another language – at least at the conversational level. That is why today there should no longer be a language problem. Unfortunately, that is not the case today and not because we have not paid any attention to it. True, the Bureau of the Central Committee of the Latvian Communist Party, as far as I can remember, has made special decisions about this question twice. But beyond that, nothing further has been done. The Central Committee is not interested in the implementation of its decisions, and the local Party organizations did not mobilize to implement them. They did not ask Russian members to acquire the Latvian language and they did not offer anyone any help nor organize any seminars.

Source: *LVA PA, 101. f., 16. apr., 9. l., pp. 296-299. Original in Latvian.*

Top secret special report by J. Ziediņš, Deputy Chair of the State Security Committee of the Latvian SSR Council of Ministers, to the Chair of the Council of Ministers, V. Lācis, about the results of an investigation into a letter from a school child in Zosna school

September 29, 1954

On April 12, 1954, comrade V. Lācis, the Chair of the Council of Ministers of the Latvian SSR, received an anonymous letter with the post mark "Priednieki" and with the following contents:

"Greetings!
Greetings to Vilis Lācis from the Komsomol of the seven-year school in Zosna

Request
Please answer the following question: why are all of the learning materials and maps in the Latvian SSR only in the Russian language? Why were the Latvian language exams for Russians eliminated; they do not need to take them, but Latvians have to pass the Russian exam?

We are not sure about this at all, particularly because the Constitution explains that all citizens have equal rights.

But the rights are not equal. Even in Latvia, the Russians are the leading nation. We would also like maps and learning material to be in the language of [our] birth.

We await an answer."

This anonymous letter of April 1954 was forwarded from the Council of Ministers of the Latvian SSR to the State Security Committee of the Council of Ministers of the Latvian SSR.

The anonymous letter was written in the Latvian language in hurried, barely corrected handwriting, but the address on the envelope was written in good handwriting.

After conducting an investigation it was determined that the author of the anonymous letter was Kovalenoka, Eleonora, daughter of Anton, born 1939 in the Malta region, non-party, Latvian, with a 7th grade education, has not worked anywhere, lives in the Latvian SSR Malta region in Zosna.

During interrogation Kovalenoka admitted to being the author of the anonymous letter and, as to the reason for writing the letter, stated:

"Before the exams in school I started to read the Constitution of the USSR and after digesting it started to think about it, what great rights it gives and what responsibilities all citizens, have regardless of nationality. But I remembered that in our school all the maps and globes are in the Russian language, except for one map in the Latvian language in the whole school... that to me did not seem like equality as it was written in the Constitution of the USSR, but some sort of inequality, that is why I decided to write the Council of Ministers of the Latvian SSR..."

Kovalenoka also stated that she herself wrote the address on the envelope, but, as it turned out, she could not explain how in fact the envelope was addressed by someone else.

During further investigation, it was found that the envelope's author was:

Suhocka, Aleksandra, daughter of Jāzeps, born 1926 in the village of Bērziņi in the Malta region, 7th grade education, member of the Communist Party of the Soviet Union, works as the chief of the "Priednieki" post office of the Malta region of the Latvian SSR.

During interrogation, Suhocka, A. J., stated that she had written the envelope to the Chair of the Council of Ministers of the Latvian SSR.

In answering this question Suhocka, A., stated:

"…Sorting envelopes for outgoing delivery I found a letter with illegible writing that was folded like a triangle, without a stamp, addressed to the Chair of the Council of Ministers of the Latvian SSR. So that the letter would have a respectable appearance I decided to unfold the letter and from the handwriting I could tell that a school child had written it so I did not read further. I put the envelope in a standard envelope pasted a stamp on it and wrote the address by hand, that is, to the Chair of the Council of Ministers of the Latvian SSR, comrade Lācis, and sent the letter to the person [for which it was intended]…"

We had a serious discussion with the author of the anonymous letter, Kovalenoka, E. A.

Deputy Chair of the State Security Committee of the Council of Ministers of the Latvian SSR
Ziediņš

Source: *LVA, 270. f., 1. s.apr., 952. l., pp. 45-47. Original in Russian.*

Document No. 48

The decision of the Rīga Municipal Committee of the Bureau of the Latvian Communist Party, concerning the conditions of the teaching of the Latvian language in the schools where Russian is the language of instruction

1956

The Bureau of the Latvian Communist Party Municipal Committee notes that the teaching of the Latvian language in municipal schools where the Russian language is the language of instruction is unsatisfactory. The knowledge of the schoolchildren is weak; even the oldest grade-school children do not know conversational [Latvian].

The municipal sector of People's Education has allowed serious mistakes in the recruitment of cadres for Latvian-language teaching. Most of the teachers are overloaded with obligatory working hours – 78.8% of them teach above the pedagogical norm; of 85 working teachers, 32 do not have the required education; and some of them know the Latvian language badly (comrade Niedrīte – in the 20th seven-year school, comrade Razgulajeva –34th middle school, comrades Ovcinska and Sudilovska – 23rd high school and others).

In many schools, Latvian language classes are only a formality. Most teachers do not implement the program's requirements (34th, 25th, 10th, 23rd high schools, 20th, 66th, and other seven-year schools), and do not use varying teaching methods or the material that they have available for use. In learning grammar, theory is kept at a distance from the learning of conversational language. In the teaching of literature, many of the teachers do not explain the idea-content of the material to be mastered (comrade Nazarova – 25th high school, comrade Dzilna – 18th high school, comrade Greiškalne – 66th seven-year school and others).

The municipal and region People's education sectors have not worked to improve the teaching of Latvian language; they have not analyzed the reasons for the children's poor knowledge. Methodological work with the teachers has been left fallow. The internal controls of the school are carried out in an unprofessional manner.

The organizational and pedagogical collectives of the Party do not attach importance to the learning of the Latvian language; they organize poorly the explanation of this question for schoolchildren and their parents. With schoolchildren, there is almost no work in the Latvian language outside of school. In the schools' libraries there are no works of Latvian authors in the original language.

The schools are poorly supplied with Latvian-language textbooks. Books for the 6th grade are completely lacking, as well as grammars for the 8th-10th grades; and there is a shortage of textbooks for 3rd-5th and 7th grades.

The Bureau of the Latvian Communist Party Municipal Committee decides:

1. To draw the attention of the People's education sectors of the municipalities and regions to the unsatisfactory condition of teaching the Latvian language in schools where Russian is the language of instruction.

2. To assign to the municipal People's education sector (comrade Dortans) the task of:
   a. radically improving the teaching of Latvian language in schools that use Russian as the language of instruction;
   b. by November 15, reviewing the Latvian-language teacher cadres and to eliminate their teaching overload.
   c. systematically providing assistance in developing language-teaching methodology to the municipal Latvian-language teachers' methodological society, and activating a commission on methodological training in the schools;
   d. improving the testing of the teaching of Latvian language in schools
   e. adding to the school library collections books by Latvian writers in the Latvian language.

3. Order school directors and Party organizational secretaries to pay more attention to the introduction to teachers, schoolchildren, and their parents of the Latvian nation's culture, history, and revolutionary traditions, as well as the accomplishments of Soviet Latvia; and to organize Latvian-language events outside of class and outside of school.

4. For the school section of the Party municipal committee, together with the municipal People's education sector, to organize for November 15 of this year a discussion of school directors, Party organizational secretaries, and Latvian-language teachers on the theme "About projects to improve the learning of the Latvian language in schools with Russian as the language of instruction."

5. To ask the Ministry of Education of the Latvian SSR (comrade Samsons) to ensure that in the shortest period of time schools with Russian as the language of instruction have Latvian language textbooks, particularly for the 3rd, 4th, 5th, 6th, and 7th grades; to speed up the distribution of Latvian-language textbooks to high schools, and to improve the schools' supplies of methodological tools.

6. To ask the Council of Ministers of the Latvian SSR to pay for Latvian-language instruction, starting from [teachers of] the 4th grade, for groups needing instruction who have arrived here from other republics and have not learned Latvian earlier.

7. To assign to the leader of the municipal Peoples' education sector, comrade Ģībietis, the task of ensuring that by January 10, 1957, all Party municipal committees be notified about the implementation of this decision.

Source: *LVA PA, 102. f., 14. apr., 8. l., pp. 35-37. Original in Russian.*

Document No. 49

Top secret report of the Minister of the Interior of the Latvian SSR, I. Zujāns, to the Secretary of the Central Committee of the Latvian Communist Party, J. Kalnbērziņš, about the creation of new police training schools [*milicijas skolas*] and the inclusion of Latvian youths in them

June 19, 1953

We have received from the Minister of the Interior of the USSR, comrade Beria, L. P., order No. 00355, dated this year June 11th, noting that coarse mistakes occur in the preparation of cadres for the Latvian SSR Ministry of the Interior with respect to Leninist-Stalinist policy on nationalities. Among these is the failure to create operational workers of Latvian nationality.

The existing police school in Rīga is made up of mostly of citizens from the central regions of the USSR, the instruction in the school takes place in the Russian language, and there are no learning materials in Latvian.

As a result there are very few Latvians working in the organs of the Ministry of the Interior of the Latvian SSR, and that handicaps the Ministry and the police in doing their assigned work.

In order to guarantee that the Latvian SSR Ministry of the Interior and police organs have operational and supervisory functionaries from the titular nation, two schools are created in Rīga:

The Rīga Ministry of the Interior Operational (Functionary) School for 250 students for one year of instruction, and retraining courses for 50 persons with six months of instruction.

The [following] schools have to enroll Latvian youth with communist and Komsomol backgrounds: in the Ministry of the Interior Operational School – 110 persons who have finished middle education (10th grade, technical school) and 40 persons who have finished secondary school; the police operational school must consist of – 200 persons with 7th grade education and 50 persons who have finished middle education (10th grade, technical school).

Persons can be counted in the schools as students if they have useful practical and political skills, and if they are healthy enough to be useful to the service of the Ministry of the Interior and the police organs.

The training in the schools will take place in the Latvian language. The activities will begin on September 1, 1953.

Comrade Beria suggests we turn to the Central Committee of the Latvian Communist Party with a request to enroll youth from Party and Komsomol organizations into the Ministry of the Interior and police schools.

Taking into account the considerable difficulties in obtaining adequate candidates for the school, as well as with organized teaching in the Latvian language, we ask the Latvian SSR Ministry of the Interior to provide all the needed help.

It would be good if the Central Committee of the Latvian Communist Party promulgated a special law asking local Party and Komsomol organs to send a selection of candidates to the school, and in order to accomplish this, to create special selection commissions.

In addition, we ask them [the Central Committee] to make the decision to send comrade Āzis to the Ministry of the Interior Operational School as the school's Instructional Section Deputy Chair, and comrade Feldmanis in the same position at the police school; they currently work in the Ministry of Justice in the section of Corrective Labor Colonies. Both of these comrades have been employees of the Ministry of the Interior.

Also, we ask for a decision to send 10 Latvians who have finished the Republic's Party school this year, and 10 communists [who are] Latvians from the Latvian State University and graduates of the Judicial Institute to the Ministry of the Interior school to work as lecturers.

At the same time we ask for support of our request to the military that the police school be allowed to accept persons old enough to be conscripted.

The proposed Ministry of the Interior Operational (Functionaries) School should be located in the building of the current police school on Allaži Street 4.

Recognizing that this building is too small to hold 150 students as well as for the needs of the normal instructional process, we ask the Council of Ministers of the Latvian SSR and the Rīga Municipal Executive Committee that the buildings currently occupied by the Rīga Municipal 5th Police Section be turned over to the Ministry of the Interior Operational (Functionaries) School and that other buildings be found for the police section in the district in serves.

Minister of the Interior of the Latvian SSR   Zujāns

Source: *LVA PA., 101.f., 16. apr., 99. l., pp. 44-46. Original in Russian.*

Document No. 50

Secret decision of the Plenum of the Central Committee of the Latvian Communist Party, entitled "About shortcomings in the political work and in the direction of economic and cultural construction in the republic."

June 23, 1953

We have listened to and evaluated comrade J. Kalnbērziņš' report about the shortcomings in political work and in the direction of economic and cultural construction in the republic; the Plenum of the Central Committee of the Latvian SSR in its decision of this year, June 12th, about the Latvian SSR has completely, correctly and in a timely and thorough manner uncovered serious shortcomings and mistakes in the work of the Party and council organs to strengthen Soviet power in the republic.

The Central Committee of the Communist Party of the Soviet Union noted that one of the causes of most unsatisfactory political conditions in the Latvian SSR is that the Republic's party and Soviet leadership crudely damages Leninist-Stalinist nationality policies.

The Central Committee of the Latvian Communist Party, the Council of Ministers of the Republic, the Party municipal and region committees coarsely overstep Soviet nationality policy principles in the training of cadres and in their selection for leading work; the central and the region Party and Soviet organs also choose very few Latvians for work. The result of this harmful practice is that among the leading cadres of the Republic the majority of officials have not mastered the Latvian language and know only poorly the local conditions. For example, Latvians are only 47.2% of all of the Latvian Communist Party Municipal and Regional Committee Secretaries, 34% of Party Municipal and Region Committee Instructors, 31% of Primary Party Organization Secretaries, 56% of the Municipal and Region Soviet Executive Committee Chairs and Deputy Chairs are Latvians. Latvians are only 42% of the apparatus of the Central Committee of the Latvian Communist Party, 43.9% of the officials of the Council of Ministers, 38.9% of the Central Committee of the LKS.

Latvian national cadres are very unsatisfactorily chosen for leading positions in factory enterprises, Machine Tractor Stations, Soviet Farms, as well as in the Republic's finance and supply, and prosecutors and for the Ministry of the Interior organs. Of the 66 largest factory enterprise directors only 8 are Latvian; of 107 Machine Tractor Stations only 48 of the directors and 24 of the political section directors know Latvian; of the 42 directors of Soviet farms only 5 are Latvian. The number of Latvian workers on the Board of the State Bank is only 20%, 40% of the leaders of region finance sections, 37% of the region and municipal prosecutors and the authorized supply functionaries. In the Republic Ministry of the Interior until the most recent times, only 15% of all the workers were Latvian. This is completely intolerable, keeping in mind that all of the mentioned institutions and organizations must have close links to the local population. The Party and Soviet organs in the Republic do not attempt to direct the Latvian intelligentsia into leading positions.

The condition that in many leading positions of the Party and Soviet organizations there are persons that do not know the Latvian language, that do not know the people's customs, culture or social conditions, is a serous obstacle to the closeness of Soviet power and the masses, keeping in mind that local conditions of this or that kind will affect the successful realization of Party and government goals. Furthermore, all of this gives material for anti-Russian propaganda to hostile elements.

The condition has occurred because there are persons in the leading positions of the Republic Party and soviets that have not taken into account one of the primary assignments of Soviet power in national republics over all of these years – to raise and form national leading cadres. In this way one of the fundamental rules of strengthening Soviet power was breached.

An imagined alertness against bourgeois, nationalist elements in national cadres led to a cultivation of general distrust that further hindered the development of cadres and their assignment to the leading jobs in the central organs.

There are also serious shortcomings in the Republic in ideological work. The greater part of lectures and speeches in the municipalities and in the countryside are read to the working masses in the Russian language. In many enterprises and kolkhozes all agitation, mass work and meetings happen in the Russian language. Latvians account for 60% of the lecturers' group of the Central Committee of the Latvian Communist Party, but in the party Rīga Municipal Committee's lecturers' group – 10%, furthermore many of the Latvians do not read lectures in their native language. In Rīga only 1/3 of the lectures and speeches are read in the Latvian language. The Party committee staff of propagandists contains 52% Latvians.

The Party organization in the Republic organizes political and mass work among the youth unsatisfactorily, poorly leads schools, and as a result some young workers, kolkhoz farmers and school children commit amoral offenses, and fall under the influence of the clergy and other hostile elements.

The Latvian Party organization does not sufficiently take into account certain threats that the influence of the clergy creates among the people of Latvia, particularly the Catholic clergy that is hostile toward Soviet power and influences the people of Latgale. In its place we must bring in appropriate anti-religious propaganda and thoroughly explain to the masses the harmful nature of the church, but up until now primary attention was on the repression of the clergy, particularly the Catholic clergy, that even further stoked the people's discontent.

It is also completely wrong that in the Republic's universities many disciplines are taught in Russian, not in Latvian. In the Latvian State University, in 75 Latvian student units 89 different lecture courses are taught in the Russian language. The Republic also does not give appropriate attention to the preparation of scientific cadres who come from the local nationalities.

All of this, as well as the use of the Russian language in the offices of the Party, soviets, and social organizations, weakens the links between state power and the national masses even more; it elicits justifiable national grievances, and hostile elements take advantage of this situation for their own provocative ends.

There are widespread violations of Soviet laws in the Republic's crude administrative methods, and these hinder the ability of the Party and local soviet organs in building stable support among the people, particularly the farmers.

The Republic's party and soviet organs have not been able to eliminate the bourgeois- national organizations and bands that frighten citizens, kill individual soviet activists, create anti-Soviet

242

propaganda, and receive support from a certain portion of the population. The struggle against the bourgeois-nationalist underground was entrusted almost completely to the organs of the Ministry of the Interior, which confined itself primarily to punishment and the use of repression that touched many classes of the population. Hostile elements, and particularly the bourgeois-nationalist underground, exploited all of this for its anti-Soviet propaganda.

The Central Committee of the Latvian Communist Party Plenum believes that the Bureau of the Central Committee of the Latvian Communist Party, the Republic Council of Ministers, and many Party's Regional Committees permit serious shortcomings and mistakes in the construction of kolkhozes; to the present, there have no been effective efforts that would organizationally and economically strengthen those kolkhozes that have low incomes; this lowers the material well-being of the kolkhoz farmers. Furthermore, distortions were allowed in the implementation of rural tax policy when specific economic conditions of regions and kolkhozes were ignored. The assignment in the plan of cultivation and husbandry was often not properly harmonized with crediting procedures, with [the availability of] fertilizers, agricultural machinery, and the supply of material and technical equipment; this led to the repeated failures in realizing assigned increases in the amount of land sown, amounts harvested, and the amount of livestock raised in kolkhozes in the Latgale region.

The Plenum of the Central Committee of the Latvian Communist Party believes that all of this testifies to the fact that the political circumstances in the republic are still unsatisfactory.

The Plenum of the Central Committee of the Latvian Communist Party decides:

1. To ensure the complete implementation of the June 12, 1953, decision, concerning the Latvian SSR, of the Presidium of the Central Committee of the Communist Party of the Soviet Union and to do so without wavering.

2. The Plenum assigns to the Bureau of the Central Committee of the Latvian Communist Party and the Council of Ministers of the Latvian SSR the task of radically improving the conditions in the Republic and not to allow exaggerations of Soviet nationality policy; to struggle energetically against violators of Soviet laws, and against arbitrary administrative decisions affecting the population. To eliminate the bourgeois- nationalist underground in the near future, and to take the necessary steps to improve the political situation in the Republic. Using necessary punishment against the real enemies of Soviet power, to prohibit distortions that could elicit justifiable grievances from wide circles of the population.

3. To envisage as the primary task of the Latvian Party organization in the near future the preparation of Latvian national cadres for leading positions in the Party, the soviets and the economy. To end the practice of placing non-Latvian cadres in the positions of Second Secretary of the Party Region Committee and the Deputy Chair of the Working Class Deputy's Council Executive Committee. To install, by law, Latvian employees into the position of director in the Soviets, machine tractor stations, and factory enterprises.

4. To reorganize the office work in all Latvian SSR Party, state, and social organizations so that it takes place in the Latvian language. The meetings of the Council of Ministers, the meetings of the Bureau of the Central Committee of the Latvian Communist Party and its Plenums, as well as the meetings of other Party Municipal and Region Committees and Working Peoples' Councils of Deputies are to be held in the Latvian language.

5. To assign the Central Committee of the Latvian Communist Party and the Council of Ministers of the Latvian SSR the task of overcoming quickly the shortcomings in the development of kolkhozes, and to ensure the organizational and economic strengthening of kolkhozes and the improvement of the material well-being of the farmers.

   To make it a responsibility of the Bureau of the Central Committee of the Latvian Communist Party and the Republic's Council of Ministers to arrange and implement steps that will radically improve the conditions of backward kolkhozes. To show already in the present year a noticeable improvement kolkhoz incomes and an enhanced compensation for kolkhoz farmers in money and seed.

To assign the republic Council of Ministers to liquidate the mistakes that the planning and supply organs have made in planning the farms and determining the supply norms for the farms by not taking into account the economic conditions of the farms.

6. To assign the Bureau of the Central Committee of the Latvian Communist Party to raise the political work to the level that must be done in the Republic to end harmful administration, to radically purge the despotism and illegalities that some officials have developed in their relationship with the population and to begin widespread explanatory work among the population that will guarantee the active participation of the population in the undertakings that are meant to build Soviet power by improving the work of Soviet organs and by strengthening kolkhozes.

7. The Plenum assigns the Bureau of the Central Committee of the Latvian Communist Party the task of taking steps to radically improve ideological institutions – cinema, theater, artistic societies, societies for political information and science popularization, as well as the [ideological] work of cultural and educational institutions.

To improve Marxist-Leninist propaganda in the Latvian language so as to better use the press and the radio. To explain widely and, unhesitatingly, to implement in real life Communist Party's Leninist-Stalinist nationality policy; to educate the working masses in internationalism and in the spirit of the friendship of the Soviet peoples; and to give more lectures and speeches in the birth language [of the persons] in enterprises, kolkhozes, shops and brigades.

In organizing special courses and seminars, to improve the preparation and development of national propagandists – lecturers, orators, and journalists.

To improve the preparation of propagandists and anti-religious propaganda; to strengthen propaganda for the natural sciences and sciences generally; to further develop anti-religious propaganda among the Latvian intelligentsia.

8. To assign to the Bureau of the Central Committee of the Latvian Communist Party the tasks of eliminating short-sighted attitudes in such important political work as organizing instruction in the Republic's universities in the Latvian language; of seriously improving the preparation of national scientific cadres and raising their qualification; of using widely the cadres of the Latvian intelligentsia and improving their development and ideological work; and of confidently directing their best representatives to [work in] leading positions in teaching institutions, as well as in scientific, cultural, and other institutions.

9. To assign to the Bureau of the Central Committee of the Latvian Communist Party the tasks of raising the level of work in the Republic's Party organization; of helping Party committees and the primary Party organizations on a daily basis to improve their internal political work.

To implement steps to strengthen Party organization in kolkhozes, to provide help to the kolkhoz in organizational and economic matters, and to strengthen the work of mass politics.

To improve the leadership of the organization of soviets, trade unions, and Komsomol, to uncover more thoroughly the shortcomings in political organizational work through criticism and self-criticism.

To fix the shortcomings that are permitted when accepting new members into the Communist Party of the Soviet Union. To reinforce political work with active non-party persons, recruiting strictly to the Party, on an individual basis, the best of the workers, kolkhoz farmers, and representatives of the intelligentsia – particularly those of Latvian nationality.

10. To assign to the Bureau of the Central Committee of the Latvian Communist Party and the Republic Party organizations the tasks of improving the leadership of Komsomol, and in the communist training of the republic's youth, devoting particular attention to training the Latvian youth and school children.

11. Taking into account the serious shortcomings and mistakes in the work of the union organizations in developing national cadres and in implementing Soviet nationality policy, to assign to the Bureau of the Central Committee of the Latvian Communist Party and the Republic Council of Trade Unions the task of rectifying these mistakes and of succeeding in approving the work of trade unions so as to enhance the communist development of the working masses.

12. To assign to the Bureau of the Central Committee of the Latvian Communist Party and the Council of Ministers of the Latvian SSR of drawing up, in a month's time, [a list of] concrete steps that will ensure the implementation of the decision of the Central Committee of the USSR of June 12th, this year, concerning the improvement in the Latvian SSR of the work of the organs of the executive, the Party, and the soviets.

Secretary of the Central Committee of the Latvian Communist Party   J. Kalnbērziņš

Source: *LVA PA, 101.f., 16.apr., 1.a.l.., pp. 16-20. Original in Latvian.*

DOCUMENTS NO. 51-54
NATIONAL COMMUNISTS: ACTIVITIES AND RESULTS

Document No. 51

The decision of the Bureau of the Rīga Municipal Committee of the Latvian Communist Party concerning the necessity for persons working in the service sector acquiring the Latvian and Russian languages

November 30, 1956
[comrades Berklāvs, Temnovs]

Being directed by the decisions of the 20th Congress[102] of the Communist Party of the Soviet Union regarding the need for careful practical labors informed by the needs of all of the nations of the USSR and their national particularities, Party regional committees, Party primary organizations, and many leaders of enterprises that serve wide circles of the population have taken positive steps in the required direction. They have begun to pay attention to how cadres are chosen, where to place them in light of their knowledge of the Latvian and Russian languages. This has improved noticeably their dealings with the population in a language understood by the latter.

Still, the Bureau of the Party Municipal Committee recognizes that the general situation and the placement of cadres in enterprises serving a wide range of the population is still unsatisfactory. In many commercial organizations, in enterprises dealing with communal services, in medical facilities, in military organs and in other structures, a significant number of employees who on a daily basis are in contact with the working masses know only one language (Latvian or Russian). This creates inconveniences and launches justifiable complaints. In spite of this, Party regional committees, Party primary organizations, and well-known leaders of enterprises and institutions have not done the work needed to bring about the acquisition of the Latvian and Russian languages among the cadres that service wide circles of the public.

The Bureau of the Latvian Communist Party Municipal Committee decides:

1. To reprimand the lack of consideration implied in service of wide circles of the population in a language not accessible to them, and the unsatisfactory acquisition of the Latvian and Russian languages by cadres who are involved on a daily basis with the working masses.

2. To assign to the Party organization secretaries, the chairs of the labor union organization committees, and the leaders of enterprises that serve a large public, particularly trade organizations, communal services, the tram and trolleybus trust, the bus park, building boards, medical institutions, military organs and others, the task of initiating among cadres the learning of the Latvian and Russian languages so that they can acquire these languages in two years' time staring from January 1, 1957.

   Persons who avoid the learning process or, after two years, have not acquired the languages will face a review of their being kept in work that is tied to service to wide circles of the population.

   To assign to the leaders of the mentioned enterprises and institutions, when accepting cadres for work, the task of keeping in mind their knowledge of Latvian and Russian alongside other practical and political qualifications.

   To assign to leaders of enterprises and institutions, and the chairs of the trade union organization committees, the task of finding the needed materials for organizing the acquisition of the Latvian and Russian languages.

3. To assign to the leader of the People's Education Section, comrade Ģībietis, and to the Leader of the School Section of the Party Municipal Committee, comrade Lomonosov, he task of providing help to the leaders of the enterprises and institutions that service wide ranks of the population in organizing Latvian and Russian language instruction and in choosing teachers.

4. To assign the Party regional committee, Party primary organizations, chairs of the trade union organization committees and the leader of enterprises and institutions the task of explaining to the workers of the enterprises and institutions that service large publics the need for acquiring the Latvian and Russian languages.

5. To assign the Party regional committees the task of providing help to the Party organization secretaries and leaders of the mentioned enterprises and institutions in organizing Latvian- and Russian-language instruction and in assuring control over the implementation of this undertaking.

6. To assign to all of the Party municipal committee sections the control of the implementation of this decision.

Source: *LVA PA, 102. f., 14. apr., 8. l., pp. 83-84*

Top secret decision of the 7th [closed] Plenary of the Central Committee of the Latvian Communist Party, entitled "Concerning serious shortcomings and mistakes in work with cadres and in the practice of nationality policy in the Republic"

July 8, 1959

The Plenary of the Central Committee of the Latvian Communist Party notes that in the post-war period the Republic's Party organization has done a significant job in the preparation of Party, Soviet, economic, and ideological cadres. In higher and middle-level teaching institutions, special instruction courses have prepared more than 20,000 engineers and technicians and about 16,000 agricultural specialists, more than 17,000 teachers and 2,400 doctors. At the same time 1,600 persons have finished the Republic's and the Party's Higher School. All of this has created for assignment to Party, Soviet, economic, trade union and Komsomol structures many trained employees who are capable of implementing the Communist Party line.

The Latvian Party's organized efforts in preparing cadres, training them and assigning them, has affected positively economic and cultural development, and the political activities and productivity of the working masses continue to expand. Latvia's industrial production compared to before the war – 1940, has increased by 8.5 times. There have also been certain successes in agriculture: the production of milk has increased by 35% in five years, meat – by 41%. The Republic's science and culture has continued to develop. Latvia's best cultural and artistic accomplishments have become widely known outside of the borders of the Republic. The number of those in the oldest grade in middle schools compared to 1940 has increased almost four times, but [post-secondary] students – two times. The number of clubs and libraries compared to the pre-war period has increased by 14 times and the number of stationary cinemas – five times. The number of published periodicals per year in 1958 compared to 1940 has increased 3.5 times.

The Plenary of the Central Committee of the Latvian Communist Party still believes that the Republic could have accomplished even more for the nation's economic and cultural development if the Bureau of the Central Committee and the Municipal and Region Committees of the Party had not allowed serious shortcomings and mistakes in the assignment of cadres, in their placement and training. Party, Soviet and economic organizations have poor knowledge of their cadres' practical work processes, do not devote enough attention to their cadres' specific characteristics in making assignments, and frequently move cadres from one important job to another without asking if the new cadre has performed well enough in the previous job. All of this creates frequent turnover of cadres and hampers productivity. In just the last three years, more than half of the Party Municipal and Region Committee First Secretaries have been changed, as well as Chairs of Region Executive Committees, and about 60% of the Chairs of kolkhozes. In the last two years one third of enterprise directors and chief engineers have been changed within the territory of the Council of the Peoples' Economy[103]. But the situation in many of the regions, kolkhozes, and enterprises has not improved as a result of this unjustifiable and hurried turnover of cadres.

The most serious violation of Leninist principles in the assignment of cadres occurs in those situations when leaders of some Party, Soviet, and economic organs propose and assign workers while not taking into account their practical and political skills and character, but their nationality. Specific Party Municipal, and Regional Committees, Ministries and Bureaus, motivated by the concern that the cadre understand both the Latvian and the Russian languages, pursued such a line in order to change the cadres that by nationality were not Latvian. Thus the multi-national make-up of the Latvian SSR's population was often ignored.

In the Latvian Republic, Lenin's advice that workers should not be forced into language training, that strict volunteerism must be observed, has been crudely violated. The Rīga Municipal Committee, after the unending requests by the then Party Municipal Committee First Secretary comrade Berklavs,[104] in November of 1956 reached the decision that in two years' time cadres must learn the Latvian and Russian languages. As a result, leaders of enterprises, organizations, and institutions had to re-examine continuation in employment of persons who did not know the Latvian language after two years. This created unfair conditions for workers of some nationalities, because the majority of Latvians living in Rīga have known Russian for a long time, while workers who arrived in Latvia from other republics needed to learn a second language anew. The real goal of the Rīga Party Municipal Committee was to force out cadres of other nationalities by reference to the criterion that they did not know the Latvian language. This all created anxiety and insecurity among substantial numbers of workers.

The Bureau of the Central Committee of the LCP did not point out the mistakes of the Rīga Municipal Committee. In December of 1956 the Bureau also made the wrong decision that in two years time the leading cadres had to learn the Latvian and Russian languages.

The Rīga Municipal Committee Bureau and the Bureau of the Central Committee of the LCP were seen by some of the Republic's local party organizations as having issued a directive to change the cadres that were not ethnically Latvian. As a result, in the past few years a considerable number of experienced workers were let go from their positions in Party, Soviet and economic organs without sufficient reason, which in many cases hampered the work [of these units].

The restriction of the rights of persons not Latvian by nationality also occurred when the programs that used Russian as the teaching language in several Republic universities were closed or reduced in size. As a result, Russian-language high school graduates from Latvia and other Republics were essentially denied the opportunity to continue their educations in Latvia's universities.

Some leading workers in the Republic sought national self-sufficiency through decisions concerning the reorganization of schools.

In the Republic, the decision was made to supply eight-year-old pupils with textbooks that made them privileged by comparison with pupils of other union republic schools. And contrary to the general law that eleven years was period of schooling, some responsible figures in the Republic constantly asked for a twelve-year period of education.

The Party's distortions of Leninist nationality policy were also manifested in the use by the Latvian SSR Council of Ministers and Rīga Municipal Executive Committee, with the knowledge of the Central Committee of the Latvian Communist Party, of a strict interpretation of the passport regime in the city of Rīga, which placed restrictions on the population, particularly in the registration of persons of other nationality.

Thus some officials the Republic use non-party principles in selecting cadres by nationality; in considering firing persons who do not know the Latvian language; in closing Russian-language programs in several university teaching institutions; in the almost complete ban on registration in Rīga of workers and their families arriving from other regions of the country, [an action] really meant to stop the arrival in the Republic of persons from other Republics and to extrude from Latvia residents not of the Latvian nationality.

The Plenary of the Central Committee of the Latvian Communist Party notes that the Bureau of the Central Committee and the Party organization have not devoted the necessary attention to the training of leading cadres, intellectuals, and all working masses in the ideas of fraternal nationalities, Soviet patriotism, and the spirit of proletarian internationalism; they have not definitively struggled against the manifestations of bourgeois nationalism.

In the Republic, specific leading figures have tried to lead the Party organization away from the correct Leninist path and toward national limitedness and seclusion. For example, the member of the Bureau of the Central Committee of the Latvian Communist Party and Deputy Chair of the Council of

Ministers of the Latvian SSR, comrade Berklavs, in discussing the seven-year plan came out openly against the Party general line concerning the development of heavy industry, asking ceaselessly for the rescinding the expansion of the railway carriage and diesel factory in the Latvian SSR and for greater capital investment in light industries and the food industry, the products of which would be used primarily in the Republic. As one of the fundamental reasons for opposing the development of heavy industry, comrade Berklavs put forward the idea that the building of new industry and the expansion of existing enterprises would require the recruitment of labor from other republics, which would mean that the number of non-Latvians in Latvia would increase. Similar beliefs were stated by the Director of the Economics Institute of the Academy of Sciences, comrade P. Dzērve. These rightist, opportunistic suggestions were nothing more than an attempt at autarchy, national limitation, and self-sufficiency, and their implementation hinders the collective interests of the state as well as the interests of the Latvian nation because they harm Latvian economic contacts with other republics and slow the development of productive power in the Latvian SSR.

The Bureau of the Central Committee of the Latvian Communist Party and some Party Municipal and Region Committees do not occupy themselves enough with the selection and training of cadres for the press, radio, creative societies, and other ideological institutions. Some editors of periodicals and journals, as well as some creative societies, are polluted by suspicious persons to whom proletarian ideology is foreign. Because of such weak leadership and control of Party organs, materials were published in periodicals and journals such "Cīņa," "Voice of Rīga," "Soviet Youth," "Star," and "Flame" with wrongheaded political formulations suggesting Latvian uniqueness. Intellectually condemnable material (the stories of Grigulis, Laganovskis, Skujiņš, and articles by Berklāvs, Kalpiņš and others) from Republic periodicals was published subsequently in foreign countries in their local bourgeois and Latvian bourgeois émigré presses.

The Bureau of the Central Committee of the Latvian Communist Party and the Party Municipal and Regional Committees, in training cadres in Marxist-Leninism and in raising the communist consciousness of the working masses, do not take into account the fact that Latvia's population during the long years of the governing Ulmanis' clique and during the fascist occupation were deeply infected by bourgeois-nationalist propaganda. They also take little into account that the current imperialists and their lackeys – the Latvian bourgeois émigrés in their many anti-Soviet radio broadcasts, and in the letters and nationalist literature they send to the Republic's inhabitants -- try to engender hostility and distrust in the population with evil lies about Soviet order, particularly with respect to relations between the Latvian and Russian nationalities. Periodicals and journals, lectures and speeches do not devote enough attention to the ideas of the friendship of nations, Soviet patriotism, and proletarian internationalism; not enough attention is devoted to showing the Russian nation's exemplary role in the struggle for the victory in the October Revolution and in liberating Latvia from the fascist yoke during the Great Fatherland War; and it inadequately stressed that the accomplishments of the working masses of the Latvian SSR in developing the Republic's economy and culture were brought about with the help of all of the nations of the Soviet Union and first and foremost with the fraternal help of the Russian nation.

The inadequate political work in the realm of ideas and with the intelligentsia is the root cause of why nationalist beliefs and expressions have spread in the creative societies. Unhealthy moods and nationalist manifestations have also been noticed among the grade-school and university youth.

In many enterprises, kolkhozes, and Soviet farms, political work is not handled satisfactorily. The principal reason is the abnormal situation during which great majority of Party's primary organizations have not been reinforced for a long time with the best workers, kolkhoz farmers, and representatives of the intelligentsia -- particularly from among Latvians. These organizations do little to ensure that the best Latvian youth join Lenin's Komsomol.

The Bureau of the Central Committee of the Latvian Communist Party and Party Municipal and Regional Committees have inadequately developed a deep sense of responsibility in their cadres toward the work assigned to them as well as toward unquestioning acceptance of Party and state discipline; they often indulge the behavior of those leaders who do not fulfill the production plan and are lackadaisical about their socialist responsibilities, show tendencies toward localism, and project a mood of self-satisfaction and lack of care.

Negligence and errors in work with cadres, absence of leadership in ideological labors, and distortions of Leninist nationality policy -- these, as practiced by the Republic's Party organization, hinder the full use of the massive industrial and agricultural reserves and opportunities available for increasing production significantly. Even though there have been some positive accomplishments in the Republic's agricultural sector in the last few years, there are still great shortcomings. The numbers of cattle and sheep to date still have not reached pre-war levels. There has come about an abnormal situation in which the percentage share of livestock production on farms producing for general consumption has grown hardly at all though it represents 39% of all meat production and 44% of all dairy production. In the Latvian SSR there are more than 200 economically weak kolkhozes. For many of them their debt to the state exceeds their annual income. The majority of the Republic's Soviet farms continue to work with [annual] losses.

All of these shortcomings and political mistakes exist first and foremost because the Bureau of the Central Committee of the Latvian Communist Party has not been sufficiently principled in deciding many important questions, has not reacted decisively to expressions of bourgeois nationalism, and has not given a crucial counter-blow against those directly responsible for these expressions. As an example, though knowing that comrade Berklāvs, in dealing with the development of the Republic's economy, had practiced a covert nationalistic policy in selection and placement of cadres for many years and in forcing the mandatory learning of the Latvian and Russian languages, the Bureau of the Central Committee of the Latvian Communist Party did evaluate his anti-party behavior from a political perspective and did not put to an end this harmful behavior.

The Bureau of the Central Committee of the Latvian Communist Party was also tolerant of the major failures and mistakes in the work of comrade Bisenieks, the Central Committee Secretary. He acted without principles in deciding many important questions, often actively supporting the mistaken work of comrade Berklāvs, and, in evaluating the accomplishments of the agricultural sector, did not take the necessary steps to eliminate the serious shortcomings in the work of kolkhozes and sovhozes. Comrade Bisenieks is an accomplice in the creating the shortages milk and meat experienced by the population of Rīga.

The Bureau of the Central Committee of the Latvian Communist Party did not point out to Candidate Members of the Central Committee, comrades Pinksis and Pizāns, that in many questions, particularly in the implementation of nationality policy, they were indecisive and often ended by taking the wrong position.

The Plenary of the Central Committee of the Latvian Communist Party decides:

1. To accept as correct the June 21ˢᵗ decision of the Bureau of the Central Committee of the Latvian Communist Party uncovering serious shortcomings and mistakes of the Bureau of the Central Committee of the Latvian Communist Party, and of specific Bureau members and candidate members, in selecting and training cadres, in violations of party principles, in the placement of cadres, and in distorting Leninist nationality policy.

2. To assign as a responsibility to the leaders of the Bureau of the Central Committee of the Latvian Communist Party, Party Municipal and Region Committees, Ministries, Bureaus, and organizations the task of addressing the shortcomings and mistakes mentioned in this decision, and in the training and placement of all cadres to unbendingly follow Leninist principles; to persistently and consequentially implement the Party's Leninist nationality policy; and to always remember that the curtailment of any nationality's rights, no matter what such curtailment might be, can seriously hamper the working masses of all nations as they gather and mobilize for the job of building communism in our land. The Party's

organizations have to energetically struggle against any attempts to mangle the Leninist principles of cadre preparation by all kinds of bourgeois nationalism and expressions of Great Russian chauvinism, and must also energetically eradicate tolerant behavior toward such attempts.

3. To assign as a responsibility to the Bureau of the Central Committee of the Latvian Communist Party and Party Municipal and Region Committees to categorically end the un-party-like behavior in which individual Party, Soviet and economic leaders select workers not according to the characteristics of their performance and politics, but according to their nationality, personal acquaintance, and favors done in the past. To guarantee the careful evaluation of cadres according to their past performance, and to make sure of assigning to leading position younger workers who have shown their organizational abilities and loyalty to the Communist Party, keeping in mind the Party's instructions concerning appropriate relationships between older and younger cadres.

   The work of all Party organization with cadres must follow the historic decision of the June plenary of the 21st Congress of the Central Committee of Communist Party of the Soviet Union, and the successful implementation of the national economic plan for 1959 in the entire republic, as in every region, enterprise, kolkhoz, and sovkhoz.

4. To rescind as incorrect the December 6, 1956, decision of the Bureau of the Central Committee of the Latvian Communist Party, entitled "Concerning Latvian and Russian language instruction for leading cadres." To explain to Party Regional and Municipal Committees as well as primary organizations of the Party that the teaching of Latvian and Russian languages must be organized, by reference to Lenin's instructions, on strictly volunteer basis, in no cases allowing administrative pressures and coercion.

5. To rescind as incorrect the third paragraph, second section, of the October 1958 decision of the 4th plenum of the Central Committee of the Latvian Communist Party.

6. To assign as a responsibility to the Bureau of the Central Committee of the Latvian Communist Party, Party Regional and Municipal Committees, as well as primary party organizations the improvement of leadership in industry, construction, and agriculture; the expansion of socialist competition among the working masses for the early fulfillment of the 1959 seven-year plan; and the most thorough use of industrial and agricultural reserves, the mechanization of and automation of production, and technological progress. To solve all questions in Party, Soviet and economic organizations, Ministries and Bureaus by first taking into consideration the collective interests of the state.

7. Taking into account the significant shortcomings and mistakes in the development of production in kolkhozes and sovkhoz, to ensure that the Central Committee of the Latvian Communist Party, the Republic Council of Ministers, Party Municipal and Region Committees, and Region Executive Committees see as an urgent assignment the strengthening of retarded and economically weak kolkhozes or sovkhozes through the appointment of experienced organizers who are capable of using all available internal reserves to mobilize a mass struggle to obtain a sharp increase in the agricultural harvest, in the numbers of livestock, and in the production of products meant for livestock, on farms that produce for social consumption. To strengthen the cadres in kolkhoz chairmanships, it is necessary in the future to install in these jobs the best workers of the Republic, municipal, and regional organizations, agricultural specialists, as well competent persons from the same kolkhozes.

8. To assign as the responsibility of the Bureau of the Central Committee of the Latvian Communist Party, Party Municipal and Regional Committees the careful study of where to place specialists in industrial and agricultural production, so as to ensure enterprises, kolkhozes, and sovkhoz with cadres. At the same time, to assign to the National Economic Council, Republic State Planning Commission, and the Ministry of Agriculture the task of

developing and implementing programs to better prepare specialists, particularly in those branches of the national economy where the shortage of specialists is clearly evident; of preparing cadres of scientific lecturers so that in the next few years we can overcome the backwardness of the Republic's cadre preparation.

9. To make it an urgent assignment of the Bureau of the Central Committee of the Latvian Communist Party and Party Municipal and Regional Committees to use all their power to strengthen the training of leading cadres; to instill in them the ideas of the friendship of nations, Soviet patriotism and proletarian internationalism; to demand strict observation of Party and state discipline, strict responsibility toward the Party in the implementation of Party and government directives, and a deep understanding of the collective needs of the state. The Party organs have to assist Party, Soviet, and economic workers raise their skill level through the study of industrial and agricultural economics.

To organize broadly so that our cadres understand and diffuse the positive experiences in economic and cultural development that has accumulated with us as well as with other fraternal union republics.

10. To assign as a responsibility of the Bureau of the Central Committee of the Latvian Communist Party, Party Municipal and Regional Committees, and the Republic's primary party organizations of raising the quality of their political efforts with workers, kolkhoz members, and particularly intelligentsia, university and high school students so as to educate them in the spirit of the friendship of nations and proletarian internationalism; to perfect the forms and methods of mass political work. To undertake political work while keeping in mind the unique characteristics of different groups of inhabitants; to make sure that in every enterprise, institution, kolkhoz, brigade, and farmfield the working masses are influenced by the politics of the Party.

The Party's organizations must ensure that all leading workers constantly meet with the masses, and explain to them the historic decisions of the 21st Congress of the USSR and the June Plenum of the Central Committee of the Communist Party of the Soviet Union. The internal and external politics of the Soviet state must show convincingly the gains in the development of the Republic's economy and culture that have come about with the fraternal help of the people of the Soviet Union. In the press and in radio broadcasts, all political work with the masses must labor inflexibly and constantly to unmask the evil inventions of hostile propaganda which, by using lies about Soviet order, attempts to gnaw at the friendship of nations in the USSR, their trust and mutual understanding, and tries to stoke nationalistic beliefs among a certain part of the Republic's population.

The Party's organizations must ensure that the intelligentsia strengthens its contact with the everyday life of the common people, and must develop in it a strong consciousness of their social responsibilities towards their homeland.

The Bureau of the Central Committee of the Latvian Communist Party must control more strictly the work of creative societies, and must energetically exterminate all expressions of bourgeois nationalism among the creative intelligentsia.

11. Since during his extensive activities comrade Berklāvs has allowed serious political mistakes of which he has been reminded several times; and since he has still not translated these suggestions into the necessary directives, and in the Plenum of the Central Committee of the Latvian Communist Party has presented himself in a un-party-like and secretive manner, to remove comrade Berklāvs from the Bureau of the Central Committee of the Latvian Communist Party and from the ranks of the members of Central Committee, and make it impossible for him to remain in the position of Deputy Chair of the Council of Ministers of the Latvian SSR. Warn comrade Berklāvs that if he does not change his anti-party beliefs, the question of his membership in the Party will be raised.

12. Remove comrade P. Pinksis from membership in the Bureau of the Central Committee of the Latvian Communist Party for inconsistencies in many important questions, particularly those that are related to the implementation of the Party's Leninist nationality policy, and for politically incorrect behavior in the Bureau of the Central Committee of the Latvian Communist Party.

13. Candidate member of the Bureau of the Central Committee of the Latvian Communist party and editor of the periodical "Cīņa," comrade P. Pizāns, is rebuked for inconsistency in many significant political questions, and for publishing several ideologically harmful materials in the periodical "Cīņa."

14. To bring to the attention the member and secretary of the Bureau of the Central Committee of the Latvian Communist Party, comrade N. Bisenieks, the serious mistakes and failures he has allowed in his work.

15. To assign to the Bureau of the Central Committee of the Latvian Communist Party the tasks of :
    a) Explaining and reviewing the question about the work of the Economics Institute of the Latvian SSR Academy of Sciences;[105]
    b) Reinforcing the cadres at the editorial boards of the periodical "Voice of Rīga" and "Soviet Youth" as well as the journal "Star."

16. To rescind the decision of the June 23, 1953 Plenum of the Central Committee of the Latvian Communist Party, entitled "Concerning shortcomings in the direction of political work and economic and cultural development in the Republic," as politically incorrect and as imposed by the enemy of the Party and state, L. Beria.[106]

***

The Plenum of the Central Committee of the Latvian Communist Party makes known its strongest belief that the serious shortcomings and mistakes in the selection of cadres, their placement and training; as well as the mangling of the implementation of the Leninist nationality policy that was allowed in the Republic, will be eliminated by the Party organization in the shortest period of time.

The Plenum certifies to the Central Committee of the Communist Party of the Soviet Union that the primary Party organizations of Latvia will lead the working masses in the struggle to implement the peoples' greatest dream – the building of communism in our land.

Secretary of the Central Committee of the Latvian Communist Party   J. Kalnbērziņš

Source: *LVA PA, 101.f., 22.apr., 10.l., pp. 16-30.Original in Latvian.*

Informational report of L. Himelreihs, the Secretary of the Rīga Municipal Committee of the Latvian Communist Party, about the situation in the city on the day of the national festival (St. John's day)

June 24, 1961

On June 24, 1961, the first-shift workers in most of the city's industrial enterprises arrived at work in an organized manner, and in many enterprises the number arriving at work was even higher than usual. At the electro-bulb and super-phosphate factories, and others, there weren't any workers who did not show up without reasons.

At a group of enterprises a small number of workers did not show up for reasons unknown: at the Auto-electrical Equipment Factory – 8 persons, Turbo-mechanical factory – 2 persons, Diesel Construction – 4 persons, the factory named for Popov – 8 persons etc.

At the same time, there were instances of individual enterprises where more workers than usual did not show up. At the Wagon Construction Factory 90 persons did not show up, the normal numbers being 10-15; at Factory Number 85 – 40 persons did not show, when the usual number is 5-6; at this same factory in shop #2 of 200 workers 18, did not arrive; at the factory "Red Star" 13 persons did not show up, compared to the usual 5-6. At the factory "Plumber" (in the Proletarian *rajons* [of the city]) 15 persons did not show up, which number constitutes about 10% of the working total -- usually 2-3 persons do not arrive.

At the factory "Latvia's Birch" the night shift did not work from June 23rd to June 24th because earlier, without the administration's knowledge, an extra night shift had been put on from June 18th to the 19th, 1961. The particulars were explained at the Party *rajons* Committee.

In the Lenin *rajons*, during the evening of June 23rd next to the house on Dzirnciema Street No. 115, a bonfire was lit, and a group of persons sitting near the fire tried to fire off a harmless firework, but as a result of the explosion citizen Vitkovskis died.

In the city minor episodes of hooliganism could be observed, as on most days.

There were some observable expressions of a nationalist character. On the corner of Sloka Street and Uzvaras Boulevard, on a poster that depicted the liberation of the African peoples, there was written "Long Live Līgo" in the Latvian language.

At the Rīga Hydroregulating Electric Station, a hand-written sheet was found in the Latvian language, with some nationalistic paragraphs about "Līgo."

On the evening of June 23rd at 9:00 PM an oak-leaf crown was placed at the Freedom Monument, the guilty were detained, and the particulars of the affair are being investigated by the Police Board.

Secretary of the Rīga Party Committee of the Latvian Communist Party
L. Himelreihs
Source: *LVA PA, 102.f., 20. apr., 17. l., pp. 17-18. Original in Russian.*

Excerpts from the top secret report of the Secretary of the Central Committee of the Latvian Communist Party, A. Pelše, to the Central Committee of the Communist Party of the Soviet Union, about the necessity of strengthening the struggle against anti-Soviet activities and sentiment.

August 1961

The working masses of the Latvian SSR, as all Soviet people, awaited with greatest the happiness the new USSR Program.[107] Workers in factories, construction, and transport successfully fulfill and overfulfill the assignments of the seven-year plan[108] and the growing socialist relationships. The working masses of the kolkhozes successfully finished the spring sowing and brought in the harvest. The necessary conditions are being created for the future growth of agricultural production, and there is acceptance of the socialistic goal that sale of agricultural products should be made to the state.

Nevertheless, ignoring for the moment the achievements and successes of the Republic's economy, we cannot avoid the observable rebirth of the harmful work of nationalists and other anti-Soviet elements. The war psychosis stoked by the monopolists of the USA, the revenge-seeking advertised by the ruling ranks of West Germany, awaken and activate the work of harmful elements in the Republic. To a substantial degree this is supported by the Latvian nationalist émigré organizations and centers, which are backed by the intelligence agencies of the USA, GFR, Sweden and other states of the capitalist camp. Émigré organizations, exploiting the "Voice of America," and the Madrid and Vatican radio stations, systematically make anti-Soviet broadcasts in the Latvian language. With the existing technical equipment in the Republic, these broadcasts are jammed only incompletely, and that is why in some regions they can be listened to easily. The influence of these broadcasts in the Republic have led to some harmful manifestations.

Harmful influences are also spread among the growing number of the local population who receive mail each year from relatives and acquaintances who are émigrés. In 1960, correspondence with foreign countries increased by a factor of eight, in comparison with 1955. Together with letters from foreign countries, there also arrive newspapers and pamphlets published by Latvian émigré organizations. The number of subscriptions to foreign commercial magazines containing propaganda about the Western style of life, and books with religious content, are also increasing. Moreover, not a few letters containing lies about Soviet reality, requests to travel to foreign lands, and mailings to émigré centers are sent abroad from the Republic each year.

In the first half of 1960 and in 1961, from 1.7 pieces of international mail (incoming and outgoing) 34.6 thousand were confiscated, or 2% of the total.

In connection with the increase of freight transport in the last three years from 1957 to 1960, the number of foreign ships and foreign crews stopping in Rīga and Ventspils has increased by a factor of three. After the Rīga port was opened to foreigners for visits, and lodging was organized for them in Riga's Jūrmala[109], the number of tourists increased noticeably, and the number of delegations and diplomats visiting the Latvian SSR also went up.

Tourists, diplomats, and foreign sailors frequently carry anti-Soviet and ideologically harmful literature, newspapers, and journals and [make these available to the local citizenry]; [these visitors] also carry on conversations with an anti-Soviet content. The greatest activity of this kind is carried out by youth from the USA, diplomats from Israel, and sailors from West Germany.

All of this has a harmful effect on the suggestible elements among the young, and they are encouraged to genuflect before western culture.

In the Republic, there are preserved remnants of the bourgeois-nationalist intelligentsia, former leaders of political parties and organizations, the ideologues of the fascist regime, and other persons from these milieus. These persons propagate nationalist beliefs in many different and harmful ways; they encourage anti-Soviet and anti-Russian attitudes and have an unhealthy influence on a portion of Latvian youth. They use as a pretext their own and their families' anniversaries and other family celebrations, organize meetings at home, reminisce about their earlier privileged position, and long for this "lost paradise," all the time deriding and belittling all that is Soviet and communist, thus distorting our reality. All of this goes on with young people in attendance and, not infrequently, with their active participation, which keeps these beliefs alive and spreads them further.

The rebirth of these harmful manifestations was furthered by the unmasking in 1959 of the work of bourgeois-nationalists and their sympathizers. These people have not only not renounced their earlier beliefs, but continue to meet and to negatively influence the politically immature and fickle segments of the intelligentsia and youth of the Republic; they hinder the prevention of mistakes in questions of nationalism that were permitted previously, and in this way harm the building of socialism and the training of the Republic's working masses in the spirit of national friendship and proletarian internationalism.

After 1955, because of the amnesty and other reasons, and after serving their punishment, there returned to the republic more than 50,000 former bourgeois political figures; members of anti-Soviet nationalist organizations and groups; members of armed bandit groups and their supporters; members of German police units and other punitive bodies; nationalists ideologues and other harmful elements.

The majority of them have started to do socially useful work, but a certain portion hide their hostility to Soviet order and promise revenge and to settle the score with leaders, and Party and Soviet activists, at an appropriate moment created by international complications . Their hostile ideas have already become observable. These persons have for the most part fitted themselves into medium-sized organizations and enterprises in construction; certain kolkhozes and sovkhozes; and in several offices of the Automobile and Road Transport Ministry bureaus across the Republic; as well as in lumber yards. They maintain contact with each other in order to have cadres ready to turn against Soviet power at the most opportune moment. In some instances, they openly urge others "to strike communists and Russians and to chase the Russians down the Leningrad highway to where they came from." Other examples are equally visible.

The work of this element does not stop with just verbal statements, but in some instances they engage in actual activity. In the Republic, the number of incidents of a nationalist or otherwise hostile nature has increased from 117 in 1955 to 217 in 1960. The tearing down of the state flag has been particularly frequent, as have been anti-Soviet graffiti and the distribution of anti-Soviet pamphlets.

At the end of 1960, this element tried to murder comrade Bižāns, the Secretary of the Party Organization of the Krustpils region kolkhoz "Victory's Morning." In January of 1961, comrade Nikonov, the Secretary of the Party Organization of the Rēzekne region kolkhoz "Spark" was wounded. In July of 1961, the instructor of the Madona Party Committee, comrade Vics, was beaten up. At the end of 1960, the son of the kulak Ziemels in the Bauska region created an anti-Soviet group with the intention of killing the chairman of the kolkhoz "Light," comrade Laugalis. During the court case, Ziemelis shamelessly said that "the time is not far away when communist blood will flow like a river."

In the recent past, the number of fires at kolkhozes, sovkhozes, and factory enterprises also has increased. In 1960 in the republic there were 842 fires that led to losses of more than 592 thousand rubles, but this year during seven months there have been 553 fires with losses of more than 337 thousand rubles.

Many persons who actively work against Soviet power have in the past few years acquired personal automobiles and motorcycles, and now they can easily stay in touch. According to incomplete reports, they have in their possession more than 800 light automobiles and motorcycles.

A large role in the creation of hostile attitudes is played by persons association with the church. In the Republic there are 655 different religious congregations and 440 preachers. A considerable number of pastors, more than 100, served time in punishment camps and prisons for their collaboration with the German invaders, for being supporters of bandits, and for other hostile activities after the end of the war. Returning to the Latvian SSR after serving their time, these persons have continued to work in the churches. The former organizer of an armed nationalist band, Grāvītis, now works in the Lielvārde congregation in the Rīga region. In the summer of 1960, as he participated in the wedding of one Priedītis (who also had returned from imprisonment), Grāvītis invited those in attendance "to remember the great path [they had] begun [to walk]" and to remember that they were all "respected sons of the nation."

Clergy, church employees, and sect leaders held more than 70 thousand church services in 1960 and with the active help of the church worked to influence believers, taking considerable effort especially with the young.

A considerable amount of worry attaches to the defense of the Republic's regions next to its [western] borders. These and adjoining regions (the so-called Kurzeme "sack") contained the 400,000-person-strong Hitlerite army until the very day of [Germany's] capitulation. It was to here that a considerable number of German supporters fled from other regions of the USSR. Persons who hid their criminal activity under the aegis of the German [occupation] are still being discovered even today. [...]

This border region was the site from which there were organized efforts to send bourgeois-nationalist and other anti-Soviet elements to Sweden. After 1956, more than 1,500 persons returned to this region from imprisonment and special camps, having been convicted of anti-Soviet activity. The border region population contains many individuals who have relatives beyond [the Republic's] borders with whom they stay in touch.

Simultaneously, in 1960 the border defense of the state has weakened noticeably. Along the shipping lanes near the shore of the Bay of Rīga, more than 80 kilometers are not guarded. The coastal defense fleet does not patrol the waters of the Bay of Rīga.

In 1960, two of the three divisions of the coastal defense fleet that operates along the shore from Cape Kolka to the border of the People's Republic of Poland have been eliminated. The 140-mile shoreline of the Baltic Sea in the Liepāja and Aizpute region is guarded by 400 soldiers in 11 guard posts, but from on the sea itself by only one seacoast defense vessel.

Also, the number of seacoast defense vessels in the Ventspils municipal region has been decreased. It is no wonder that with such seacoast defenses, West German and Danish fishing schooners in 1961 crossed the sea border 8 times in the Liepāja municipal region, and Danish warships were near our territorial waters 4 times.

The Central Committee of the Latvian Communist Party continues to do many things to organize the decisive struggle with hostile elements in the Republic. The Party organization systematically rallies the working masses to believe in the friendship of nations, to trust in the Communist Party, and to act in the spirit of Soviet government.

The question of raising awareness was discussed in the Bureau of the Central Committee of the Latvian Communist Party in 1960 and 1961. In April of 1961 the Bureau promulgated the decision "Concerning activities to raise the awareness of the Republic's working masses." This year, in June, there was a meeting of the First Secretaries of the Municipal and Region Party Committee. At this meeting, stringent demands were addressed to the State Security Committee, to the courts, and to prosecutors in order to strengthen the struggle with hostile expressions in the Republic. In June, there was a meeting of the active organs of the State Security Committee. Events are being organized to raise the quality level of the work done by the *čekisti* [employees of the Committee of State Security].

Many persons who were fomenting hostile actions in the population have been arrested and turned over to the courts. In a year and a half – 1960 and first half of 1961 – the Supreme Court of the Latvian SSR, after reviewing material provided by the organs of the State Security Committee, sentenced 13 criminals with the highest punishment – execution by shooting. Among them were four members of bandit groups who after the war had shot and beaten up Soviet activists, five participants in mass executions and torture when they were members of the 18th police battalion during the [German] occupation years, and others. The sentences have been carried out.

Counter-propaganda has been strengthened against the ringleaders of the Latvian émigrés. It is meant to unmask and compromise them, as well as [to hinder] the development of a patriotic movement amid rank-and-file émigrés. There has been created a Latvian working group called "The committee for returning to the homeland and establishing cultural contacts with fellow nationals."

The newspaper "Voice of the Homeland," which is distributed among the émigrés, has had its publishing house moved to Rīga, while a branch of it remains in Berlin. In West Germany the progressive literary journal "Friend" is being distributed. An arts almanac "My land of birth – I long for you" has been published and sent to émigrés. Twelve times a month there are radio broadcasts aimed at émigrés – 4 broadcasts each from Rīga, Moscow and Berlin.

Anti-religious and scientific-atheistic propaganda has improved noticeably. The cloisters at Vīļāni and Aglona have been closed, as has the Orthodox Cathedral and Lutheran Dom Cathedral in Rīga.

In the past few years six Catholic clergy, four members of sects, and one Lutheran pastor have left their religious calling and have participated in publicly unmasking the anti-people essence of religion. These events have been used widely in the struggle against the influence of the church.

Nevertheless, all of the implemented measures in the struggle against hostile forces are inadequate for creating stable conditions in the Republic.

The Central Committee of the Latvian Communist Party continues to raise the awareness of the Soviet people about the international situation, the Soviet government's peaceful politics, and the larger perspectives of socialist construction as laid out in the program of the Communist Party of the Soviet Union. A growing part of the struggle against hostile and anti-social forces is being played by society at large.

In view of the conditions in the republic, the Central Committee of the Latvian Communist Party considers it necessary to strengthen the organs of the State Security Committee.

In 1960 the apparatus of State Security Committee was reduced by 268 individuals, including 217 with the rank of officer. Seventeen branches of the State Security Committee in rural regions were eliminated. Operational work in these regions has been noticeably weakened, while at the same time there is growth of hostile elements.

The Central Committee of the Latvian Communist Party asks for a review of the question of whether the rural branches of the State Security Committee should be reinstated, and of the question of creating new branches of the Committee in three districts of the city of Rīga. Each of these districts has between 150 and 250 thousand inhabitants.

In Rīga, there is a concentration of important factories – VEF, semiconductor factory and others -- that do important and secret production work for the USSR Defense Ministry. Riga also has a large seaport which is visited by foreign ships and other vessels that have an important place in the economy of the Latvian SSR.

We see it as necessary that the question of the strengthening of border protection in the Republic be reviewed and decided upon positively, and that the border defense forces be supplied with all necessary technical equipment.

In order to limit the demoralizing influence of anti-Soviet radio broadcasts by émigrés in the Latvian language, we ask the Communications Ministry of the USSR to provide aid in jamming these broadcasts because the equipment currently available in the Republic cannot do the job.

To hinder in the Republic the anti-Soviet work of nationalists and other hostile elements recently released from imprisonment, we see it as necessary that the courts increase repressive measures against these persons, and that they be exiled from the territory of the Latvian SSR as unrehabilitatable enemies of the Soviet nation.

Secretary of the Central Committee of the Latvian Communist Party   A. Pelše

Source: *LVA PA, 101. f., 24. apr., 54.a.l., pp. 139-147. Original in Russian.*

Documents No. 55-61
Political and ideological censorship

Document No. 55

Excerpts from a report of the Director of the Main Literature Department of the Latvian SSR, V. Jaunzems, about his Department's work in 1948

January 13, 1949

[...] Work concerning the cleansing of harmful literature from Republic's stock of books

Glavlit pays considerable attention to the removal of politically harmful literature from the Latvian SSR's public libraries and from the bookselling network. This has required careful work, because only during the era of Soviet power did the libraries of the Latvian SSR begin seriously to add worthwhile literature to their collections.

Notwithstanding the fact that in the republic in previous years more than 12,000,000 politically harmful books were removed, there are still books in the libraries whose use requires careful daily decisions. The majority of workers in the libraries correctly understand the importance of this work and does its job seriously in the cleansing of the library collection.

In this review period, 249,402 books were removed from Latvian SSR libraries and the bookselling network.

The removal of books is done in accordance with the lists from the USSR Glavlit, from the LSSR Glavlit, and also from the lists that we exchange with the Estonian and Lithuanian Glavlits.

Because there are many books in Latvian SSR libraries that were published in Russia before 1917, and because they are not to be found on "Alphabetic list" (Moscow),[110] or in subsequent directives, their removal is done based on the "Directions to the censor of second –hand booksellers." These are books containing religious and monarchical contents and belong to such authors as Lukasevic, Čarska, as well as anthologies of Smirnovska, Martinovka, and Galahov.

The work implementing control over library collections is organized in such a manner that there are no libraries in the [Riga] center that have not been visited by a censor for the purpose of review.

For each quarter-year and each month a work plan was drawn up listing the libraries to be reviewed in that period. During a review, the censor reviewed – selectively in large libraries and completely in medium-sized ones --- the alphabetical and systematic catalogues, book inventories, and selected books from the shelves.

[Some libraries] are found to be in an unsatisfactory condition. Such was the case with the library at the State University directed for a long time by the bourgeois-nationalist Straume. After many warnings from Glavlit [Straume] was removed from his job. Similarly, in the Fundamental Library of the Latvian SSR Academy of Sciences, despite many warnings, the Library Director Eglīte even today continues to slow down the cleansing of the library's collection of politically harmful literature. [In such cases], after the review, the censor initiates the establishment of a brigade of library workers and supplies them with all of the directives and lists in force; then, led by the censor, they tackle a full review of all books on the shelves. Concrete time frames are set [for completion of the work]. That was the procedure at the State University, where in two weeks two Glavlit censors together with a brigade removed more than three thousand books from the shelves.

At the Fundamental Library of the Latvian SSR Academy of Sciences, where the censor revealed that the Russian book section was much polluted (during the review itself 41 books were removed) with books that were on the "alphabetical list," a brigade of five persons was formed and was directed by the "specfond" leader. The brigade removed 361 books. Currently such a brigade is at work at the 1st City Library.

The Cultural Education Institution, the Ministry of Education and the Central Council of Trade Unions takes part in the work of cleansing libraries of politically harmful literature. They work in their sectors of the [Riga] center, as well as in outlying districts, to remove politically harmful literature according to the lists and directives currently in force.

For example, after the Latvian SSR Glavlit issued List No. 6, all cultural-education institutions and libraries were provided with the List, together with directions about when to cleanse the libraries. At the same time, coinciding with the beginning of the school year (the list was issued in August), and using the Rīga city's Peoples'Education Region Section organizations, brigades of communist school teachers were organized to review the school libraries. After consulting with the Latvian SSR Glavlit about how to remove books and how to document the proceedings, the brigades began their work. Such brigades were active in the following *rajonss* of the city of Rīga: Kirov, Molotov, Proletarian.

The sector censors were part of the implementation of these reviews. One hundred and three schools were reviewed in this manner.

The Central Trades Union was responsible for removing politically harmful books from its library as well as all small trade union libraries. The Union was unable to complete this job.

Because the Central Trade Union Library does not have centralized information about the local trade union libraries, at times the latter seem to come into being unexpectedly. Most of the time these newly opened libraries are polluted with politically harmful literature. That was the case with [library] in the butter and dairy plants in which, from a total of 2,000 books, we removed 1,500 (bourgeois Latvian periodicals and journals, Ulmanis' books, etc.) Granted, this library was locked, and the key was under special care; but, before Glavlit workers found the key, the Latvian ACRO did not know about the existence of the library.

Because there are no precise listings of libraries in the Republic, the Latvian SSR Glavlit proposed to the library affairs section of the Cultural and Education Institutions committee that it re-register all libraries in the Latvian SSR, regardless of the institution to which they belong.

In the cover letter to the "Alphabetical list" No. 3508, there was a notice that a part of the list's printing sent to the central authorities also be sent to libraries that have more than 50,000 books. That would have made the effort of library cleansing appear far more serious. Unfortunately, neither the committee on Cultural and Education Institutions nor the Ministry nor the Academy of Sciences have received the "Alphabetical list" from the appropriate All-Union organizations. Therefore, the few copies of the list given to special collections or maintained with the apparatus of the Latvian SSR Glavlit, are also passed out to libraries for only the short term.

In the library review, censors encountered certain difficulties that made it appear as if the libraries had been completely cleansed, while [in reality] giving librarians the opportunity to hide removed books, thus sabotaging the removal of harmful literature and using the difficulties as excuses. One of these difficulties is the mismatch between book inventories and the books actually in collections. Many of the inventories of city libraries were compiled 15 to 20 years ago. These libraries have never undertaken another inventory of their collections, and this produces a discrepancy between the inventories and the actual collections because many books were pilfered or lost, particularly during the period of German fascist occupation when many libraries had to move from one location to another; and some of the books in fact were removed by the Germans. Many books are listed as in circulation to readers when in fact they were lost at the front or were taken by the Germans or by those who fled with the Germans. Even today, these books have not been dropped from book inventories, and this creates inaccuracies in the collection descriptions. Some saboteurs, including some members of the staff of the 1st City Library, make use of these discrepancies; in the said Library the review of November 25, 1948, (in the second year) found books that earlier were said to have been removed. The record of the inspection of the 1st City Library were given to the appropriate section of he Cultural and Educational Institution committee for following up. Subsequently a committee was created to examine the entire collection and completely cleanse it, and this was completed on January 1, 1949. Administrative action was taken against the Library Director Vebers.

This learning experience with the 1st City Library is currently an object lesson for other city libraries, that, upon hearing that the library director had been called to account for hiding politically harmful literature, are re-examining collections that were formerly "hidden" from Glavlit and are giving them to Glavlit [...]

Work in cleansing rural district libraries of politically harmful literature:
In 1948, 792 libraries were examined in the rural districts of the Latvian SSR and 35, 135 books were taken from them.

The quarterly reviews:

	Libraries examined	Books removed
1st Quarter	198	16,579
2nd Quarter	137	6,578
3rd Quarter	25	2,767
4th Quarter	432	9.031
	792 libraries	35,135 books

The work of cleansing libraries and book-selling networks in the rural districts is being done by the appropriate sections of cultural-education institutions under the leadership of the Glavlit district leaders of the Latvian SSR People's Ministry of Education.

Review of bookstores
[...] During the review period, Glavlit examined 42 book stores and removed 60,712 books from their warehouses.

During 1948, there were occasions when, using bookstores, some persons attempted to infect us with harmful ideology by displaying different kinds of postcards, stamps, etc that had a politically harmful character.

At the War Trade Organization Bookstore, together with prize-winning literature (the books and paintings of artist Bogdanov-Belski, the sales of which are not restricted) brought from the warehouse, there also came Easter postcards (right around the time of Easter) which were placed in the display window as "not harmful." They had represented on them a chick that had just come from the shell, together with the salutation "Greetings for the holidays." The postcards were removed.

Another event: some bookstore sold a collection of postage stamps that included stamps already proscribed by the Latvian SSR Glavlit. An examination of the postage stamp collections at the Booksellers Trust, 3,155 packages of postage stamps were destroyed.

Second-hand bookstores are reviewed daily by s specially appointed censor, because every month from 5 to 5.5 thousand books come into these stores.

The work of the special collections (*specfondi*):

Altogether in the Republic there are four special collections. They are all located in Rīga and they are in the Latvian SSR Library, the Academy of Sciences of the Latvian SSR library, the so-called Misiņš Library (a branch of the Academy of Sciences), and the State University Library.

All of the special collections are charged with the preservation of printed military and state secrets by the decrees of the Latvian SSR Council of People's Commissars and USSR Council of Ministers.

The collections are organized according to need and have private and public reading rooms [...]

In the special collections there are more than 111,000 books removed from other collections. The staffs of the special collection are actively participating in the creation of lists of books to be removed, and are working with questionable books. The special collection staffs write out their decisions about such books and subsequently they are placed on the lists of books to be removed.

Chief of the Latvian SSR Glavlit   V. Jaunzems

Source: *LVA, 917. f., 1.s. apr., 2.l., pp. 95-101, 103-105. Original in Russian.*

Document No. 56

Report of L. Veselov, Head of the Propaganda and Agitation Section of the Latvian Communist Party Central Committee, about organizing propaganda against the Western countries

1959

The Propaganda and Agitation Section has recently undertaken the strengthening and expansion of counter-propaganda work. The Bureau of the Latvian Communist Party Central Committee discussed this question twice – in May and in December – and the relevant decisions were made. The Propaganda and Agitation Section has created two commissions now working: history and economics, and literary sciences, both of which include experienced historians, economists, linguists, literature experts, and journalists who will research and collect material about the conditions and operations of the reactionary émigré press and their literary organizations.

The question about the conditions and work of the émigrés was discussed at a seminar of the Party's RK first secretaries as well as in a meeting of the editors of the republic's newspapers and journals.

At the end of 1958, the Main Literature Board of the USSR's Council of Ministers assigned to the Republic's Glavlit the task of controlling the incoming émigré literature, which requires that this literature be sifted most diligently. Furthermore, the literature now confiscated in pursuance of the pertinent laws of the Glavlit of the USSR, is concentrated in one place – at the special collection (*specfond*) of the Fundamental Library of the Academy of Sciences. From 1959 on, the Propaganda and Agitation Section began to receive the émigré publications which are received through *Meždunarodnaja kņiga* (International books)[111]; this step helped to repulse operationally incoming émigré lies and anti-Soviet activities.

Currently, a brochure series is being prepared in Latvian, Russian, German, and English in which correctly and in considerable detail foreign, socially active people, and entire nations, will be informed about true conditions in Soviet Latvia. With the help of the Latvian SSR's Ministry of

Foreign Affairs and the Republic's Society for Friendship and Cultural Contact with Foreign Lands, these will be sent to Soviet embassies in those countries where the émigrés are concentrated.

Of course, these activities do not answer all the questions pertaining to the extensive and flexible organization of counter-propaganda, or to all of the forms and methods needed in the struggle against the spread of bourgeois ideology and its remnants. Analysis shows that currently two main approaches are needed: the organization of counter-propaganda activities in foreign countries, and the struggle against organized expression of bourgeois ideology and its remnants in the Republic.

1. The organization of counter-propaganda activities in foreign countries

The VDK of the Council of Ministers of the Latvian SSR until now has organized all of the counter-propaganda activities in foreign countries. This work is done primarily along three lines:

1. Persuading prominent figures in émigré society to return to the homeland;
2. Unmasking the reactionary ruling elite of the émigré organizations;
3. Organization in foreign countries of groups loyal to Soviet Latvia .

It is necessary to note that in the past there have been notable successes in persuading notable individual émigrés to return. Such well-known émigrés as the conductor Leons Reiters and the sculptor Vesmanis have returned to Soviet Latvia. Efforts are continuing with the author Jaunsudrabiņš, the playwright Mārtiņš Zīverts, the composer Jānis Mediņš, and others.

Noted achievements were also had in unmasking reactionary figures in émigré society.

Many émigré periodicals, specifically the newspaper "Latvija" published in West Germany, are currently in a very serious financial situation.

The most complicated work has turned to be the organization of groups in foreign countries that would act loyally to Soviet Latvia. These efforts have now moved to the foreground. In the context of our Party's struggles for peaceful coexistence, the creation of such groups would encourage the faster development of understanding [between peoples] and closer relations between nations. With the help of such groups we could disseminate accurate information about the Soviet Union generally, and about Soviet Latvia specifically. This would doubtlessly influence foreign society, which today often gleans news about our Republic from the lies widely distributed by the émigrés in German and English.

On the other hand, it is perfectly clear now that the majority of the émigrés will not return to the homeland and the process of their assimilation will speed up. Nevertheless, they will still maintain their distinctiveness for a long time. This requires us to look for ways of creating centers of loyally disposed groups. The Propaganda and Agitation Section is currently searching for means to establish regular contacts with [potentially] loyal groups in the USA (the editorial staff of the newspaper "Amērikas Latvietis" has begun to reprint a substantial amounts of positive material from our newspapers) and in Canada, [being helped] in this by former members of the Canadian Communist Party. Such activity will doubtlessly isolate the reactionary émigré elite from the masses.

The newspaper "Dzimtenes Balss" is also being moved in this direction. Much of the material in the newspaper unmasking the anti-national work of the reactionary elite has had positive results. At the same time this newspaper is a good vehicle for delivering propaganda about our reality and diffusing correct information among the émigré masses.

Nevertheless, it should be noted that in the publication of this newspaper there are many shortcomings. The newspaper "Dzimtenes Balss" is published by the Berlin Committee "Concerning the Return to the Homeland[112]" and the Berlin address of the editorial staff is given [in the paper]. For a long time émigrés did not know that the newspaper was prepared and published in Rīga, but in 1958 they found out. Then they began a strong campaign to discredit the paper, arguing that the newspaper portrayed [Soviet Latvian] life so inaccurately that it could not even be circulated in the Republic. The Republic Glavlit has found that several times the newspaper was sent [into Latvia] from foreign countries.

Of course, right now we have a formal reply – namely, that the Berlin Committee publishes and distributes the newspaper. Nevertheless, it would be useful to change this organizational site of this undertaking. The newspaper could be published in the name of a committee in Latvia and that would create the opportunity of showing a Rīga address for the editorial staff.

First, [this change] would destroy the principal argument of the émigré reactionary elite; but, second, it would also encourage direct contact with the readers. Odd as it may seen, the Berlin Committee now does not even inform the editorial staff about the émigrés who have written to the Berlin editors with questions or recommendations, etc. In fact, the newspaper is completely separated from its readership, and that cannot help it in its proper mission.

Moreover, it must be noted that the Berlin Committee does not even inform the Central Committee of the Latvian Communist Party about which countries the newspaper is sent being sent to, whether readers receive it, and how they react to the material in it. The only information received from the Berlin Committee is a yearly review.

These same shortcomings characterize Latvian radio broadcasts from Berlin, but this question is already being resolved by the Propaganda and Agitation Section of the Central Committee of the USSR.

Overall contacts with Berlin regarding counter-propaganda matters are completely unsatisfactory, even though a special KGB agent was sent there, not for operational work, but with the goal of organizing counter-propaganda.

To improve the work and organization of counter-propaganda it would be useful to create a special counter-propaganda group in the KGB of the Latvian SSR Council of Ministers; the group would consist of 3-5 persons and would be under the command of the Deputy Chairs of one of the committees (a similar group was already created in Estonia). The group's leaders should be in direct contact with the Propaganda and Agitation Section of the Central Committee of the Latvian Communist Party in order to be informed about all operations and about the correct direction in which the work has to go.

After all, we cannot accept as correct that the operationally empowered person connecting the KGB with the Propaganda and Agitation Section of the Latvian Communist Party Central Committee was, as was known for a long time, a person incapable of doing the job whom the KGB was forced to remove for reasons of immorality.

It is also necessary to rethink activities aimed at discrediting of the émigré reactionary elite in the eyes of foreign societies [where they live]. It is known that many of [this elite], such as Vilis Māsēns, Janums, Ādolfs Šilde, Hāzners and these so-called ambassadors and consuls and so forth, enjoy good relations within western circles, and this allows them to conduct an active struggle against all Soviet state activities meant to guarantee peace and peaceful coexistence.

We can mention just a few of these activities as illustrations. For example:

1. On January 8, 1958, the American Latvian Association (ALA) delivered a note to the USA's State Department about the visit of staff workers from the USA Moscow embassy to the Rīga district kolkhoz "Mārupe," to which the State Department offered an official reply.

2. On April 25, 1958, the Latvian émigré Vilis Māsēns, at the 4th Strasbourg Assembly of the so-called Captive Nations of Europe, moved the inclusion of the question "About captive nations" in discussions with leading representatives. It was also decided there that this question be taken up with the United Nations.

3. On October 6, 1958, the Subcommittee of Foreign Affairs of the US Congress listened to the chair of the ALA, P. Lejiņš, reporting on the reduction of Latvian radio broadcasts on "Voice of America."

4. On October 23-24, 1958, the same Vilis Māsēns at the annual assembly of the Captive Nations of Europe was put forward for the position of contact person with the UN. He is now touring Asia's southeastern states for this organization, with the objective of getting these states to be hostile to the USSR.

5. In November of 1958, a number of reactionary émigré organizations organized a mass protest against the decision of the US Council of Churches to recognize the People's Republic of China and to admit it to the UN (the so-called Cleveland Resolution), sending about 50,000 letters to socially and politically active persons in the US.

6. In December of 1958, the Baltic Council in a special meeting undertook to send a note to the Conference of Foreign Ministers of NATO in Paris about the Berlin question.

This list could be continued. It is enough to demonstrate that [the émigrés] organize against any peace-loving step by the USSR and try to persuade Western society [of its viewpoint]. Has the time not come to raise this question anew through the USSR's diplomatic channels and with the help of the United Nations representatives of the USSR?

In order to develop contacts, gather information, improve the work to form groups friendly to our cause, to get notable émigré figures to return to the homeland, to organize public information abroad about the true conditions in Soviet Latvia, there are needed active workers who are Latvians. Moreover, there should be at least 2 foreign correspondents from *Cīņa*. These persons must be attached to Soviet embassies in countries such as the USA, Canada, Australia, and the GDR. (It must be noted that in Lithuanian SSR embassies there are 2 such workers and that the two correspondents from the central newspaper "Tiesas" are working as correspondents in foreign countries).

2. Expanding contacts between the Republic and foreign counties in order to combat the diffusion of bourgeois ideology and its remnants

In the last several years, the Republic's contacts with foreign countries, particularly after Rīga became available to foreign visitors[113], has grown many times over. Here is the evidence:

	1953	1954	1955	1956	1957	1958
Foreign citizens visiting the Republic	21	26	156	570	783	1134
Foreign ships visiting the Republic	-	303	311	617	670	869
Soviet citizens traveling to foreign countries (with visas)	2	32	65	413	964	838
Tourist travels to foreign countries	-	-	33	381	471	669
Number of postal deliveries including:						
a) letters, postcards and printed matter (thousands)	171.3	236.6	600.0	1704.9	2501.6	More than 3000
b) packages (thousands)	9.4	5.2	15.2	73.9	102.6	86.4
c) press publications (thousands)	-	-	-	301	557	687

In addition, in 1958, in order to learn about research in various technical and scientific questions, 99 persons, including 43 from the Peoples' Economic Council, 13 from the Latvian SSR Academy of Sciences, and 43 from other organizations and specializations made business trips abroad.

In the Republic, many organizations work with questions related to international contacts. In the People's Economic Council there is, for example, a Foreign Contacts Department, and these questions are of interest as well to the Science and Technology Committee, to the Friendship and Cultural Contacts Society between Latvia and Foreign Countries, to the Latvia section of Inturist, and to the Peace Defense Committee of the Latvian Republic. Currently, the Radio and Television Committees are forming special exchanges of editorial broadcasts.

At the moment, the control, leadership, and organization of these efforts is decentralized. The Propaganda and Agitation and Cultural sections that work with these questions are unable to comprehend the totality of them in all their complexity. Often, the main problem is the lack of instruction given to persons creating objects intended for the eyes of foreigners, to those reviewing the itineraries of foreigners, and to those who deal with the reception of foreigners in the Republic.

It would be useful for the Latvian Communist Party Central Committee to create a commission to deal with international contacts. This commission could consist of a Deputy Director and 1 or 2 instructors of the Propaganda and Agitation section. Equally important for the Latvian Communist Party would be the creation of a commission of international contacts on which would be represented by the heads of all of the sections, the Economics Soviet, the Science and Technology Committee, and Republic's Labor Union Councils.

Director of the Propaganda and Agitation Section of the Central Committee of the Latvian Communist Party   Veselovs

Source: *LVA PA, 101. f., 22. apr., 48a. l., pp. 64-70. Original in Russian.*

Document No. 57

Secret report by L. Lapina, Head of the Science, Schools, and Culture Section of the Central Committee of the Latvian Communist Party, and N. Muravjov, Deputy Leader, to the Bureau of the Central Committee concerning the review of the work of the Economics Institute of the Academy of Sciences of the Latvian SSR

December 15, 1959

In pursuance of the decision of the (closed) July 7th Plenum of the Central Committee of the Latvian Communist Party,[114] the Secretariat of the Central Committee of the Latvian Communist Party has approved a commission consisting of: the head of Political Economy Department of the Latvian Agricultural Academy, Professor P. Allens; lecturer of the Central Committee of the Latvian Communist Party, A. Ronis; the dean of the Political Economy Department of Latvian State University, J. Vilks; chief of the Latvian national economy plan section of the SSR State Planning Committee, V. Sitčihins; candidate member of the Marxism-Leninism Department of the Physical Culture Institute of the Central Committee of the Latvian Communist Party, docent A. Elvihs; chief specialist of the Latvian SSR State Planning Committee, Z. Osis; Central Committee of the Latvian Communist Party member and head of the Agricultural Section of the Latvian SSR State Planning Committee, V. Rubenis; Chief of the Latvian SSR Economic Council for Economic Affairs, F. Rjumins; member of the Central Committee of the Latvian Communist Party and Minister of Communal Economics of the Latvian SSR, R. Ķīsis; Chair of the Rīga Region Executive Committee E. Bitenieks; Chief of the

Rīga Electro-machine Factory Planning Section, S. Vjazmins. [The commission] examined the work of the Economics Institute of the Academy of Sciences of the Latvian SSR.

In order to help with reviewing the work of the Institute of Economics of the Academy of Sciences of the Latvian SSR, at the request of the Central Committee of the Latvian Communist Party, the Central Committee of the Communist Party of the Soviet Union sent the following group of scientists from the USSR Academy of Sciences: CPSU CC Science, university, and school section instructor and economic sciences candidate, S. Tolpekin; USSR Academy of Sciences corresponding member in economic sciences, Doctor Professor of the USSR Academy of Sciences Economics Institute sector leader, A. Paskov; philosophical sciences Doctor Professor Moscow State University Philosophy and History Department head, I. Ščipanov; historical sciences Doctor Professor and Academy of Sciences History Institute senior scientific collaborator, A. Pjaskovski; USSR Academy of Sciences Economic Institute senior scientific collaborator and economic sciences candidates A. Kurski and I. Kacalov.

The work of the Commission, and the results of the examination of the Latvian SSR Academy of Sciences Institute of Economics work-in-progress and published work, as well discussions with the leaders of the Institute and its scientific collaborators, the Latvian SSR Academy of Sciences, State Planning Committee, and the leading figures of the Republic's People's Economic Council, point to the following conclusion. [...]

The scientific qualifications and Party consciousness of the Institute's members do not fit the complicated assignments that the Economics Institute is given to solve. Among the 46 senior members and younger scientific collaborators at the Institute, only 13 have science candidate degrees and only 18 are members or candidate members of the Communist Party of the Soviet Union [...]

The leadership of the Institute turned out to be unable to understand correctly the assigned tasks of the Institute, and to organize the collective and active research on the economic problems that flow out of the historic decision of the 21st Congress of the Communist Party of the Soviet Union. The Institute is poorly grounded in the practice of building communism. Individual projects of the Institute were discovered to contain crude distortions of a political nature. These distortions were criticized correctly in the speeches of many members during the July (1959) Plenum of the Central Committee of the Latvian Communist Party, in the Plenum's decisions, as well as in the positions taken by many communists in the press and at Party meetings.

These distortions can be blamed, in the first instance, on the Economics Institute Director P. Dzērve. In his scientific work, and his work as a communist and a director, he more than once has taken a position that can be characterized as revisionist and nationalistic.

A clear expression of these problems can be found in the research program "The Future of the Economic Development of the Peoples of the Latvian SSR," which was drawn up by the leader of the program comrade Dzērve and which was supported by the Institute's Scientific Council on June 6, 1959. The problems outlined in the "research program" for the collective work of the participants centered on untruthful, economically completely unfounded, and politically harmful juxtaposition of the interests of Latvia as against the interests of the Soviet Union and on the separation of the national economy of the Latvian SSR from the economy of the USSR.

The [Institute's] "research program" lays out a foundation that distorts Marxist-Leninist principles and planning methodology, reflects local and nationalist tendencies, and is directed against the development of heavy industry in the republic. The program essentially ignores the decisions of the 21st Congress of the Communist Party of the Soviet Union concerning the path for the building of communism in the USSR and the methods proposed for this task -- socialist, peaceful, and economic competition with capitalism.

The work of the Economics Institute should not take the form of a substitution for the general development plan of the Latvian SSR State Planning Committee, but be of assistance to the State Planning Committee in finding solutions to the complicated methodological questions for the creation of a long-term future plan and for providing theoretical constructs to aid the nation's economic development. The researchers involved in the program should orient themselves toward specifying a path that would guarantee active participation by the Latvian republic in the primary economic goal of the USSR, namely, the creation of a material and technological basis for communism that should assure more rapid growth of sectors of heavy industry in the total economy of the USSR.

Theoretical work [should be done] on the questions of how to further improve and reinforce the Republic's relations with the total national economy of the USSR; how to complete the division of social labor, specialization in production, and enhance co-operation so that the arrangements of socialist production can use more fully and rationally the Republic's natural resources in view of the collective assignment of the Soviet nation and the specific assignment in national economic development of the Latvian SSR. But the [Institute's] "research program" ignores the long-time and many-sided economic relationships between the Latvian SSR and the total national economy of the USSR; it orients labor first and foremost to production aimed at supplying the consumption needs of the inhabitants in the [Latvian] Republic.

Comrade Dzērve is trying to impose onto the practices of Soviet planning strange principles of the grouping of sectors of material production, dividing it into two groups: 1) sectors that produce primarily for other economic regions of the state and for export; and 2) sectors that produce primarily for the national economy of the Latvian SSR and the needs of its population.

This grouping principle of productive sectors, unfounded from the standpoint of economics, is put by comrade Dzērve at the very basis of the research problem; but the Marxist-Leninist grouping – the division of production into (I) a sector producing the means of production and (II) a sector for the production of consumer goods – he pushes to the back of the plan. In this, the most important foundation of the methodology for deciding proportions in the national economy is ignored.

The "research program" emphasizes "strain" in the balance of labor allocation currently and in the future. The authors of the plan for the future propose developing the Republic only in the productive sectors that can draw on local materials and labor. The "program" states that "..the future development of those sectors of production that are supported by the exploitation of imported raw material, and that do not draw on the existing capacity of the labor force, is not seen as rational from an economic perspective." (p. 6).

Knowledge of the sources of raw materials and the nature of the local labor forces are, of course, important principles in the rationalization of productive power, but they are not always the deciding ones. We cannot ignore, as comrade Dzērve does, such important factors as the historically created locations of the places of industrial production, the necessity of distributing industry more or less equally across separate republics and economic regions, and the reallocation of labor from one economic region to another; also, one cannot ignore many other important factors.

It is not difficult to see that the wrong approach suggested by the "research program," if put into practice, would do considerable harm to the general development of the national economy of the USSR; would disorganize the economy of the republic of Latvia; and would destroy not only the Republic's long-established economic ties with other regions of the USSR but also the allocation of production in the internal economy of the Republic, as dictated by the objective laws of socialist reproduction.

With the "position" he takes, comrade Dzērve is trying to direct the Latvian national economy towards the crippling path of autarchy, and away from the progressive and completely justified, many-sided, and robust path of development within the framework of the entire Soviet Union. [There is emphasis] only on the one-sided development of those sectors for which the Republic has its own raw materials and labor. The "research program" ignores the fact that the Latvian Soviet Republic, just as any other Soviet republic, can accomplish its primary economic assignment, which is the creation of the material and technological base for communism, only together with the other Soviet republics; and that each Soviet republic must contribute an investment in the development of heavy industry, including the development of the defense industry. But the "research program" orients itself only toward the consumer economy as the principal assignment of the planning of the national economy in the Latvian SSR.

As several members of the State Planning Committee noted, comrade Dzērve also suggested this incorrect approach to the Republic State Planning Committee in his speech at the June 8, 1959, meeting.

The "research program" has been developed in direct violation of the measures, entitled "Numerical indicators of the development of the national economy of the USSR, 1959-1965," which were promulgated by the 21st Congress of the Communist Party of the Soviet Union and which foresee for the Latvian SSR continuing developments in such sectors of heavy industry as construction of railroad carriages, diesel construction, apparatus construction, and electro-industry, that is, in sectors in which Latvian enterprises, as is known, work mostly with imported raw materials.

In his speech at the March 27, 1959, meeting, he [P. Dzērve] noted that the work he leads "will apparently be able to in some way to make corrections to our seven-year plan" (stenogram of the meeting, p. 76).

The facts show that the "corrections" to the economic plan for the Republic means nothing less than a revision of the decision of the 21st Congress of the Communist Party of the Soviet Union. Comrade Dzērve's position at the 16th Congress of the Latvian Communist Party when he defended the consumer focus in the development of the Latvian economy over the next seven years was in the same spirit.

We have to note that the same [approach] is suggested by the observations of Deputy Director of the Institute, comrade B. Treijs, when he discussed the projected seven-year plan in the periodical "Literature and Art" on November 22, 1958, and set out the belief that continued development of diesel construction and railroad carriage construction was not rational in the Republic of Latvia, because this sector's product was used in the republic "only on a minor scale."[115]

Comrade B. Treijs and the acting leader of the agricultural section of the Economics Institute, comrade M. Kukainis, submitted on January 9, 1959, to the agricultural section of the Central Committee of the Latvian Communist Party some notes on "the question of labor resources in agriculture in the Latvian SSR." Contained in these notes were wholly incorrect estimates of labor reserves, made in crude violation of the comprehensive methods of Soviet planning; the subsidiary plots in kolkhozes were illegally included in the estimates concerning the labor needs in the kolkhoz sector. It was said, using this "estimate," that in 1965 the labor force of the kolkhoz sector of the Republic's agricultural domain will be short by 29,000. By contrast, according to the Republic State Planning Committee and the Statistical Board, the estimates drawn up with the participation of specialists from the USSR State Planning Committee, following the instructions for such estimates, concluded that as a result of the mechanization in kolkhoz production in the period of the seven-year plan more than 45,000 kolkhoz workers will be freed, and their labor will need to be placed elsewhere.

In its "labor balance estimates" the Economic Institute was trying to show the impossibility of transferring more labor from the kolkhoz to industry. In their conclusions about the future of the development of the Republic's national economy, comrades Dzērve and Treijs ignore the possibility of importing labor from other economic regions [of he USSR].

The stated facts show that comrades Dzērve and Treijs in dealing with questions about the development plan of the national economy of the Latvian SSR have taken essentially a rightist opportunist position that seeks the approach of national seclusion and closedness. Accepting their suggestions would have done harm to the general state interests as well as to the interests of the Latvian nation because they would have disturbed Latvian economic relations with other state republics and would have delayed the development of the Latvian SSR's productive power.

From the time of the July 7th (1959) Plenum of the Central Committee of the Latvian Communist Party, when comrade Dzērve received deserved criticism, five months have passed. But even now he has not seen it necessary to step forward, admit to his mistakes, and evaluate them in the spirit of the Party.

Familiarization with the published work of comrade Dzērve showed that his theoretical and political mistakes in relation of the planning of the national economy were not accidental, because many serious mistakes can be found in his earlier work. As an example, in the book "Latvian SSR," published in 1959, comrade Dzērve writes about "undue haste" in the establishment of kolkhozes in the Latvian SSR. This conclusion is not only incorrect in its essence, but is also politically harmful, because it can disorient the kolkhoz farmers in Soviet Latvia by creating in them doubts about the correctness of Communist Party's policies on questions of collectivization. The enemies of socialism, including bourgeois nationalists, can exploit this situation by spreading their lies about collectivization and the Soviet order.

In many of his public appearances, such as, for example, at the Party meeting of the Institute on July 20, 1958, when the letter of the Central Committee of the Communist Party of the Soviet Union "About the conditions in Yugoslavia," was discussed, comrade Dzērve continually stressed that the principal threat in the current situation in the Latvian SSR was not revisionism but dogmatism; furthermore, he defined "dogmatism" as [an attitude] that in the process of building communism ignores the peculiarities of Latvia and misunderstands history of the Latvian nation.

The understanding behind comrade Dzērve's question about principal threats is incorrect and politically harmful: it is nothing more than an attempt to "theoretically" justify the rightist opportunist nationalism the July 1959 Plenum of the Central Committee of the Latvian Communist Party uncovered among the practices individual leading figures of the Republic.

Taking account of unusual circumstances in Latvia's development is, of course, necessary, and a fairly important step in the successful construction of communism in the Republic. Nonetheless, comrade Dzērve frequently uses this uniqueness to suggest a trajectory that is incorrect and dangerous to the interests of the Latvian Republic, and sets the tasks and interests of the Latvian Republic against the collective interests of all of the Soviet Union and its tasks.

Appearing at the March 27, 1959, propaganda discussion devoted to the understanding the information from the 21st Congress of the Communist Party of the Soviet Union, comrade Dzērve suggested the struggle against dogmatism in the propaganda of the decisions of the 21st Congress as the main task, and as an example of this dogmatism mentioned the slogan propagated in the press of Soviet Latvia: "to catch up and surpass the USA in the amount of milk produced per person." According to the Dzērve's conclusion, this slogan does not relate to the Latvian Republic because, he says – "we in the republic have already surpassed the USA in milk production per person thrice over." By contrast, comrade Dzērve suggested another task – to match and surpass the USA in labor productivity in this sector (meeting stenogram, p. 77).

This line of though is incorrect, first of all, because it counterposes two tasks, and because it is clear that growth in labor productivity in livestock raising will also serve the goals of increased production in milk, meat, butter. But, secondly, the task of matching and surpassing the USA in the production of milk and other livestock products was assigned by the Communist Party to all of the Soviet Union, and not to particular republics or regions. The efforts of individual republics have to be aimed at making a greater investment, according to their individual abilities, to the solving of the collective tasks of the entire Soviet Union. Nonetheless, in his conclusions comrade Dzērve separates the Soviet Latvian economy from the whole national economy of the Soviet Union, and in so doing proposes a narrow and local understanding of the questions important for the entire USSR.

Comrade Dzērve has also exhibited serious political mistakes in his published book about P. Stučka. In describing the accomplishments of P. Stučka – a noted figure in the revolutionary movement and a colleague of the great Lenin – in the creation and strengthening of the Soviet state, comrade Dzērve revealed his own inability to correctly understand the nature of P. Stučka's mistakes and their importance in the year to 1919 when P. Stučka was the leader of the Soviet Latvian government.

In that period, the Latvian Bolsheviks allowed serious mistakes in the building of the Party and the state, in agrarian questions and in many other questions, as admitted later by P. Stučka. But comrade Dzērve not only justifies these mistakes with references to the uniqueness of Latvia at that time, but even uses the mistakes as a positive example of independent and creative attempts to answer questions about socialist construction, of taking revolutionary initiative, by taking into consideration Latvia's uniqueness. Praising the mistake of merging Party and Soviet institution in Latvia in 1919, comrade Dzērve characterizes the work of the RSFSR State organs as immobile, bureaucratic, centralized, and ignorant of local conditions and peculiarities.

In his book about P. Stučka, comrade Dzērve highlights for the attention of readers not the many things that brought Soviet Latvia closer to the RSFSR, not to the similarities in building the first proletarian state in the world, but to the uniqueness of Latvia.

In the article, "Pēteris Stučka – Soviet Latvia's first Chair of the Council of Peoples' Commissars," published in the newspaper "Cīņa" of January 25, 1957, comrade Dzērve reduces the image of this noted Soviet Latvian figure. Comrade Dzērve presents P. Stučka, the communist internationalist and the fighter for the friendship between nations, as a narrow-minded official, who, because of specific local concerns, did not want Soviet Latvia in 1919 to make use of the experience of the Russian Federation and was occupied primarily with battling individual representatives of the RSFSR, "who had arrived in Soviet Latvia for their own selfish reasons and in fact hindered the building of socialism…".[116]

This out-of-place statement by comrade Dzērve does not facilitate the strengthening of friendship between the Latvian and Russian peoples; it does the exact opposite by stoking in some readers nationalist feelings.

Comrade Dzērve also permits nationalist influences in those parts of his work that are devoted to the economic and cultural history of Latvia.

Comrade Dzērve's lack of political maturity also appears in his article "Two Weeks in Sweden," which was published in 1957 in the collection "Beyond the Borders." In this article, comrade Dzērve seemingly objectively beautifies bourgeois reality and reveals his inability to evaluate correctly and critically what he sees.

In the letter submitted by comrade Dzērve to the Bureau of the Central Committee of the Latvian Communist Party on December 9, 1959, he showed his inability to understand and evaluate in the Party's spirit the coarse mistakes he introduced in his work, avoiding the primary task -- which is to acknowledge that his mistakes were of a rightist-opportunist and nationalist character.

We must note that the Party organization of the Economics Institute did not discuss the decisions of the 21st Congress of the Communist Party of the Soviet Union. The Party Bureau of the Institute ignored the signals coming from individual communists – comrades Bumbērs, Bagrads, Puriņš, Besedin and others – which said that in the work of the Institute there are serious shortcomings and political mistakes.

The Party Bureau of the Economics Institute (Secretary comrade P. Guļāns) assumed a conciliatory position toward comrades Dzērve and Treijs for their political mistakes and did not provide the necessary counter-argument against them. Using this opportunity, comrades Dzērve and Treijs were able to force the rightist-opportunist direction onto the work of the Economics Institute and to pull it away from the contemporary problems identified by the 21st Congress of the Communist Party of the Soviet Union.

The circumstances described above lead us to conclude that it is necessary to strengthen the leadership of the Institute[117] and, above all, to improve the work of the Economics Institute of the Academy of Sciences of the Latvian SSR.

Leader of the Science, School and Culture section of the Central Committee of the Latvian Communist Party   L. Lapina

Deputy Leader of the Science, School and Culture section of the Central Committee of the Latvian Communist Party   N. Muravjov

Source: *LVA PA, 101.f., 22. apr., 33. l., pp. 49-57. Original in Russian.*.

Excerpt from the decision of the Bureau of the Central Committee of the Latvian Communist Party about removing V. Kalpiņš from his position as Minister of Culture of the Latvian SSR for permitting political mistakes

December 2, 1961

About comrade V. Kalpiņš

Comrade Voldemārs Kalpiņš, son of Krišs, in his work as the Minister of Culture of the Latvian SSR permitted serious political mistakes of a bourgeois nationalist character to enter his work. He published many impermissible and politically harmful articles on questions of literature and art in the Republic's periodical press. These articles were translated and republished in the bourgeois press and in Baltic émigré newspapers. In directing the cultural establishment in its practical work, comrade V. Kalpiņš allowed serious mistakes that demonstrate national narrow-mindedness and isolationism. [...]

The Party Conference of the Proletarian *rajons* voiced its distrust of V. Kalpiņš in refusing his candidacy to be a delegate to the Latvian Communist Party 17th Congress. They also did not elect him as a delegate to the 18th Latvian Communist Party Congress. [...]

1. Comrade Kalpiņš [...] must be removed from his positions as the Minister of Culture of the Latvian SSR and the Minister of Foreign Affairs of the Latvian SSR for impermissible political mistakes of a bourgeois nationalist character, and for serious shortcomings in guiding practical work. [...]

Secretary of the Central Committee of the Latvian Communist Party   A. Voss

Source: *LVA PA, 15500.f., 2. apr., 874. l., pp. 38, 39. Original in Russian.*

Comment: *Voldemārs Kalpiņš was the Minister of Culture of the Latvian SSR and the Minister of Foreign Affairs from 1958 until the beginning of 1962.*

Document No. 59

Top secret decision by the Bureau of the Central Committee of the Latvian Communist Party, from a special file concerning the improvement of counter-propaganda efforts aimed at Latvian émigrés

May 12, 1959

To further improve counter-propaganda among Latvian émigrés the bureau of the Central Committee of the Latvian Communist Party decides:
1. To assign to the State Security Committee of the Council of Ministers of the Latvian SSR the tasks of :
    a. initiating steps so that by the beginning of June of 1959, the committee "Returning to the Homeland" distributes "The Voice of the Homeland" in the name of the Latvian Initiative Group;[118]

b. speeding up the preparation of special brochures, including a brochure concerning the life and work in Soviet Latvia of returning émigrés and those who repatriated.

2. To assign to the editorial staff of the periodical "Voice of the Homeland":
   a. To more fully describe in the pages of the periodical the accomplishments of the Soviet people, with particular attention being paid to propagandizing the materials from the XXI Congress of the Communist Party of the Soviet Union, and how they are being implemented by the working Soviet masses. In articles and reviews concerning economic accomplishments, to avoid cramming them with numbers and statistics, but, instead showing the stuff of real life in tangible ways, using interesting comparisons and diagrams and avoiding second-rate informative materials;
   b. To inform readers not only about Latvia, but about the lives of all the working people of the USSR, paying particular attention to the accomplishments of our country in technology, science, city planning, people's education, social welfare, and the raising of living conditions;
   c. Keeping in mind the character of the readership, to refrain from general statements and declarations and to reinforce all conclusions and theses with carefully chosen facts, paying attention to presentation of material in many different ways.

3. To bring the attention of the Committee on Radio Broadcasts and Television (comrade Leimanis) of the Council of Ministers of the Latvian SSR to the need for the Committee to handle seriously the organizing of radio broadcasts in the Latvian language for the committee "Returning to the Homeland" and to assign to the Committee the work of fixing the shortcomings in this sphere, with the following goals:
   a. Widely propagandizing the seven-year plan, explaining to the listeners the results of the work of the Soviet people; the many republic enterprises that have shifted to the shortened work-day and shortened work-week; the material improvements of our general nation; showing the work and conditions of all of the layers of Soviet Latvia's working people, including the intelligentsia; reflecting thoroughly their creative life, work. and living conditions. To pay particular attention to describing farming, health care, social welfare, people's education; and the accomplishments of all of the Soviet peoples in sciences and technology;
   b. Preparing special broadcasts dedicated to [the commemoration of] important dates;
   c. With the goal of unmasking reactionary émigré organizations, and of describing the patriotic work of individual compatriots living abroad, using widely the work of those who have re-migrated and those who have repatriated to the Homeland;
   d. Improving the technical quality of the broadcasts and increasing their number to 8 per month;
   e. Assigning to the Chair of the Committee the task of personally controlling the preparation of the broadcasts;
   f. Entrusting the preparation of these broadcasts to the most politically competent of the workers on the editorial staff of the social and political broadcasts;
   g. Preparing and strictly following the plan for the improvement of these broadcasts.

4. To assign to the Ministry of Foreign Affairs of the Latvian SSR, together with the Society for Friendship and Cultural Contacts between Latvia and Foreign Countries (comrade Bīrons) the tasks of:
   a. Sending to the USA, Canada, Australia, England, and Sweden political novels, literature, and other written work; Rīga Cinema Studio films and film newsreels; photo exhibits, albums and other material that describe the accomplishments of Soviet Latvia in all economic, cultural and scientific fields and in the [improvement of] social welfare of the masses;

b. Selecting and sending to Soviet embassies in the above-mentioned countries small libraries (100-150 books) in the Latvian and Russian languages.

c. Sending regularly send to the committee "Returning to the Homeland" (in Berlin) diverse literature, prospectuses, and brochures about the Latvian SSR.

5. To assign to the Ministry of Culture of the Latvian SSR:

a. Together with the Ministry of Foreign Affairs of the Latvian SSR and the State Security Committee of the Council of Ministers of the Latvian SSR the task of submitting a month to the Central Committee of the Latvian Communist Party a proposal for review [a plan] for inviting progressive Latvian émigrés to the Latvian SSR for various political and cultural activities held in the Latvian SSR;

b. Together with the Executive Committee of the Municipal Working Masses Council of Deputies, the task of creating by June 1, 1959, within the booksellers organization "Books Through the Mail" a section for ordering literature and cultural goods to be sent to foreign countries;

6. To assign the editors of the republic's periodicals and journals the task of making better use of returned émigrés and the repatriated to more fully depict the general life of émigrés beyond the borders, and the living conditions [of people] in the capitalist countries.

7. In order to improve the organization of counter-propaganda amidst Latvian émigrés and work with international contacts, to view as necessary help from the Propaganda and Agitation Section in the form of an instructor from the apparatus of the Central Committee of the Latvian Communist Party, [being paid from the budget of the Central Committee].

To assign the section of party organs (comrade Voss) the task of presenting proposals on this question at a regular meeting of the bureau.

8. To create and confirm a commission on questions of counter-propaganda – comrades:

1. A. Pelše – Secretary of the Central Committee of the Latvian Communist Party – Commission Chair;

2. K. Ozoliņš, E. Berklāvs, I. Veselovs, I. Pinksis, V. Kalpiņš, P. Pizāns, V. Lukss, M. Ziediņš, I. Lēmanis, V. Ruskulis, J. Bīrons, R. Šneiders, H. Valters

8. To request of the Central Committee of the Communist Party of the Soviet Union:

a. In order to establish contacts, achieve familiarity with the work and experience of the committee "Returning to the Homeland", and to have discussions with its leading workers, to allow a ten-day trip to Berlin for the group which deals with questions of counter-propaganda among Latvian émigrés, with the following composition -- comrades: Valters, Herberts, son of Kārlis, Deputy Chief of the Central Committee of the Latvian Communist Party Propaganda and Agitation Section; Vasiljeva, Milda, daughter of Kārlis, the Editor of the Committee "Returning to the Homeland" and the "Voice of the Homeland"; Vaivads, Jānis, son of Izidors, captain and responsible senior operational agent of the State Security Committee of the Council of Ministers of the Latvian SSR;

b. To assign the Ministry of Foreign Affairs of the USSR the task of including one Latvian member in the staff of the embassy in Australia, because there are about 25,000 Latvian émigrés in Australia;

c. To allow the editors of the newspaper "Cīņa" of the Central Committee of the Latvian Communist Party to send one special correspondent to the GFR and one to Canada as correspondents for one of the periodicals of the center.

Secretary of the Central Committee of the Latvian Communist Party   Krūmiņš

Source: *LVA PA, 101. f., 22. apr., 48a. l., pp. 17-19. Original in Russian.*

Excerpts from a secret report of A. Luceviča, head of the Board for the Defense of State Secrets in the Press (Latvian SSR Council of Ministers), to the Central Committee of the Latvian Communist Party, about the work of political censors in the year 1975-1976.

June 4, 1976

We are submitting a report about charges of an ideological-political character directed against certain publications during the last seven months of 1975 and the first five months of 1976.

As before, most of these charges can be divided conditionally into several groupings.

First, there are the figures from Latvia's bourgeois period, including ones who are now anti-Soviet émigrés, whose accomplishments are exaggerated tendentiously or who are being marketed "objectively."

Thus the House of Culture of the Education Workers was denied permission to publish a flyer for an event devoted to the 90th birthday of the singer, later émigré, A. Kaktiņš.

The publishing house Zinātne [was asked] to remove from a monograph on Latvian opera references to a book published by an émigré organization, the authors of which were A. Kaktiņš and J. Mediņš.

From a different book by the same publisher, "Critique of Contemporary Philosophical Fideism" there was removed from its reference list the book "Evangelical Dogma" by the reactionary émigré Latvian theologian V. Maldons, which had already been removed from the general access [in Latvia].

A book by the Pedagogical Sciences Research Institute of the Latvian SSR Ministry of Education, entitled "Russian Language and Literature in Latvian National Schools (from the 1890s to 1917)" did not receive permission to make frequent references and positive evaluations of the work of J. Dāvis, the blackest reactionary and a bourgeois nationalist; all of his work has been removed from general collections [in Latvia].

All of the references to reactionary bourgeois Latvian figures such as K. Goppers, L. Breikšs, and the reactionary émigré V. Veldre and his pseudonym "Exile" were removed from the Liesma Publishing House's *Collected Works of A. Čaks,* volume 1. Also the references to J. Veselis' novel "Eņģelis Ufīrs" were removed and the book itself was removed from general collections.

References to books by the Latvian émigré R. Kampe, published in foreign countries, were removed from the Latvian Society of Architect's book "Latvia's Architectural Monuments," which is intended for foreign distribution.

Corrections were made to I. Bērsons' article "Portraits of An Individualist" in the journal *Karogs,* No. 1, 1976, in which the author positions the results of his research in opposition to all of the official post-war evaluations of the artistic creativity of J. Akurāters. In the article J. Akurāters is discussed only as a progressive cultural figure.

The document-based novel about Rainis by J. Kalniņš was returned to the publishing house Liesma for corrections. In the book, the author presents much new material, including heretofore unknown information about Rainis' activities among Latvian social democrats. In the book there are serious accusations of betrayal by Rainis and J. Jansons-Brauns against each other. There are also descriptions of previously unknown details of Rainis' intimate life that could sow confusion and encourage incorrect evaluations of the People's Poet.

In the book "Aesthetic Thought in Latvia to 1940"(publishing house Liesma), the Latvian revolutionary J. Jansons-Brauns' work "Lev Tolstoy" is placed on the same level as V. I. Lenin's work "Lev Tolstoy as a mirror of the Russian Revolution." Also the names of the fascist leaders Benito Mussolini and Kārlis Ulmanis have been removed from the index at the end of the book.

In the book "Clear Affair" (publishing house Liesma), permission was not granted to publish a summary of the article with the notorious title "Cannibalism in the USSR" from the Latvian reactionary bourgeois newspaper *Segodņa*. The article mentions that cannibalism was a fact in the period of famine in 1933 in the USSR, and declares that robbery and murder were daily, common events. In a different place in the book, an excerpt was removed in which the Chief of the Daugavpils Political Police described the underground work of the Latvian Communist Party, its goals, organizational structure, cadres, conspiratorial methods, and contacts with the Comintern and the leadership in Moscow.

In issue No. 4 of the journal *Karogs* in 1976, an excerpt was removed from E. Damburs' article "The Days of Our Life." The excerpt revised our contemporary, officially accepted attitude towards the Freedom Monument and the Cemetery of the Brethren in Rīga, both of which were built during the period of bourgeois Latvia [and served as] symbols of nationalism and of trust in the West. In the article, the author praised specific details of the sculptures [on the monuments] and asserted that despite these monuments having been built during the period of bourgeois Latvia, they still expressed the interests of the working people and of the democratic intelligentsia; and that we should not follow prejudicial views and permit these culturally valued objects to be forgotten. [...]

Several poems were removed from a book of poems by J. Rokpelnis (publisher Liesma), entitled "Stars, the Shadow of A Bird and All Else" and dedicated to our contemporaries. In these the author's descriptions are cast in a dark light and in minor tones. They are poems about the tired eyes of girls always looking purposelessly out the window after heavy labor. All around there is a black bottomless pit and coldness. About a teacher unable to answer his students' simplest questions without having to read "specialized literature," etc.

Permission was refused to the journal *Liesma* to publish I. Jakaiša's poem "The Season Ends" in issue No. 3. The author wrote about a disabled veteran of World War Two in a mocking tone. The veteran, being a photographer, takes photos of vacationers in Jūrmala; his life is not happy. At the end of the season there is no longer anything to photograph in the spas, and, having read the newspaper "Cīņa," the invalid, with medals clanking, pulls the heavy camera apparatus homeward.

Several pessimistic poems were removed from „Gamma," a book by O. Vācietis published by Liesma. According to the author, our contemporary is a maimed consumer of the riches of the material and natural world. He thinks only of himself and does everything for his own comfort. He is unconcerned with what he will leave behind and how his misdeeds will influence the life of the next generations. He behaves barbarically with regards to the preservation of the environment. As a result of his deeds, the beauty of nature is lost. The author weeps for the scenic cliff of the Daugava River – Staburags -- that was in the flood zone of the Hydroelectric Station at Pļaviņas and was lost beneath the waters. The person who is responsible for all this is compared to an evil, greedy, wasteful alcoholic. In one of the poems the author asks rhetorically: in what kind of land – a giant's or a dwarf's – do we really live? On the one hand, we are praised for our great historical accomplishments, but on the other we would like to be small and invisible. We have great dreams and plans that are not always realized.

Corrections were made to the article "New Motifs are Needed" by V. Lāms in the journal *Veselība* No. 12 in 1975. The article doubted the efficacy of institutional directives in combating alcoholism. The author, calling himself a private in the battle against this evil, asserted that there is no real war against alcoholism here. But because statistics are involved in the sale of alcoholic drinks and figures about revenues from them are not available to the public, he challenges the war's colonels and generals, that is, the leading officials, to stand before society and account for what has been done and for what results regulations have had. He says that it is necessary to make public statistics about bars and liquor stores that have been closed, and to state to what extent the consumption of alcoholic drinks has increased or decreased.

Some lines were removed lines from Z. Skujiņš' article-memoir about the People's Artist V. Lācis in the journal *Literatūra un Māksla*, No. 17. The lines referred to an episode in the decision of the Central Committee of the Communist Party USSR, made in Rīga, about the magazines *Zvezda* and *Leningrad*[119]; in discussions with writers, the author (V.Lācis) doubted the correctness of this decision and defended the ideas that in literature all criteria are subjective and that each era has its own views.

Corrections were made to J. Žīgurs' book "Cross and Anchor" (publisher Liesma), which concerns life in post-war Siberia. It suggested that the only diversion and entertainment for Siberia's lumberjacks was drinking. The stores are described as almost bursting from the great variety of alcoholic beverages.

Corrections were made to the documentary story "The Century's Highway" in No. 2 of *Karogs* (1976). The story claimed that at the end of the 1950s only raw youths were sent to the virgin lands in Kazakhstan. At times these young people had to live and work with criminals released early from jail, fight with them, and even suffer beatings.

A part of B. Borg's documentary story "Spring of Victory," meant to be published in No. 6 of 1976, was returned to the editorial staff of *Karogs* for rewriting. The story was about the last days of the war in Kurzeme in 1945 and had the following episodes: soldiers from the 43rd Latvian Guards Division enter a farmer's house where during the previous night officers of the fascist Latvian Legion had been drinking. The head of the household says to our soldiers that it is good that they did not run into the fascists. But the soldiers reply that nothing would have happened if they did run into them, they would have drank together and that would have been all...

From No. 10 of the journal *Karogs* in 1975, information was removed from the documentary novel "Rock Anchor" by D. Avotiņa and A. Šlisers, which is about a fishing kolkhoz. Its ships were described as fishing in the so-called "mustard gas sectors," the areas where the remains of chemical weapons from World War II were buried. This would be dangerous for the ships and the persons on them.

Permission was denied for publication of certain excerpts from S. Vinogradov's documentary story "High Plateaus" about a Soviet fishing expeditions. The excerpts discussed how Soviet fishermen used the radio transmissions of Polish and GDR ships to find out about fishing conditions and then used this information to increase the catch of our ships; also, that Soviet fishing ships systematically violated defined boundaries and instructions, some motivated by greed, others by incompetence, etc.

.

Assertions were removed from issue No. 4 (1976) of the journal "Skola un Ģimene," from the article "The Orphans of Living Parents," that claimed that the number of abandoned children in the Republic was increasing. It was asserted that not everything was in order in the personal lives even of leaders, directors, and chairmen, and that, as a result, young people denigrate labor and are indifferent to society's interests.

The Rīga restaurant "Ruse" was denied permission the use of two posters advertising the performances of a varieté ensemble because the posters were prepared in a way that did not reflect Soviet ways of living and the principles of advertising.

The final group of actions was taken in relation to directives from the appropriate organs with respect to the mention of specific persons and wrong explanation of certain events.

Thus permission was denied to the publisher Liesma for parts of their book "The Pulse of the Planet." The book described the most important events of 1974 in the political life of the USSR, but certain parts discussed as noteworthy the activities and "theories" of academician Sakharov, and the expellee from the USSR, Solzhenitsyn. For similar reasons, the Science Society's supplemental material for lecturers was returned for the reworking of the section entitled "Peaceful coexistence and ideological struggle."

From the book, "There is My Fate" by V. Bērce (publisher Liesma) there were removed the description of the author's arrest and his persecution as a relative of an "enemy of the people" during the period of the cult of the personality. [...]

From the book "Critical Calendar" (publisher Liesma) some text was removed praising the article by I. Ziedonis in *Literatūra un Māksla*. The article commemorated the 100-year anniversary of the Latvian Song Festival, but contained some incorrect opinions and had already been directly criticized by authoritative organs.

All of the political defects mentioned above were not published because after the objections of the Propaganda and Agitation Section of the Central Committee of the Latvian Communist Party, they were completely removed or were re-worked.

The Chief of the Primary Board   A. Luceviča

Source: *LVA PA, 101. f., 41. apr., 82. l., pp. 48-55. Original in Russian.*

Document No. 61

Secret report of A. Luceviča, the Chief of the Primary Board for the Protection of State Secrets in the Press of the Latvian SSR Council of Ministers, to the Central Committee of the Latvian Communist Party about the results of political censorship during the final quarter of 1978 and in 1979

February 5, 1980

In the fourth quarter of 1978 and in 1979, the Primary Board, following the directive of the Propaganda and Agitation Section of the Latvian Communist Party Central Committee, formulated 36 objections on a political-ideological basis to various materials in the press.

Characteristically, year after year many of these objections pertain to the same publishers and editorial staffs -- the publishers Zinātne and Liesma (six objections), the editorial staffs of the journal *Karogs* and the periodical *Literatūra un Māksla* (six objections), and the publications of the Latvian SSR Ministry of Higher and Middle Special Education (four objections).

With respect to content, the objections were primarily with material that put forward a [certain kind of] evaluation of the legacy of the past in the areas of literature and science. The materials described with relish the standard of living and details of daily life in foreign lands or in bourgeois Latvia without using class-based analysis and without making clear the viewpoint of the authors. Not uncommonly, various bourgeois émigré figures are cited too often, quotes from their books are used, excerpts from books, different "theories," etc. There were also times when our [Soviet Latvian] material existence and the prevailing order were indirectly besmirched.

With respect to the publisher Zinātne, for several years now the same situation has repeated itself and at times has threatened to end in conflict. The Primary Board has often reminded the publisher that in line with the decisions of the Central Committee of the CPSU publishers have to resolve problems internally and be answerable about the ideological and political content of the work they publish; they themselves must carefully research, weigh, and harmonize or remove all of the defective sections of a work before the material is given to the printer. This is especially important in the case of the publisher Zinātne, which, as is known, publishes serious and fundamental research in many scientific fields – work of the kind that will be used as the standard for many years.

Yet the publisher continues not infrequently to submit for control unfinished and unedited materials containing political defects. And when the Primary Board begins its work to get to the bottom of things, that is, to submit its report to Propaganda and Agitation Section of the Latvian

Communist Party Central Committee, the publisher's leaders start acting nervously even to the point of making unfounded accusations against the Primary Board for delaying the material.

This in part is also the case with the magazines *Karogs* and *Zvaigzne* and the periodical *Literatūra un Māksla*.

The most serious objections were made against the following material:

1. the publisher Zinātne

In the third volume of the selected works of the linguist J. Endzelīns, next to articles on linguistics, there were placed articles concerning the contentious border question between bourgeois Latvia and Lithuania; a treatise on the name of bourgeois Latvia's parliament (which is said to resolve problems and to make laws relevant to all, as contrasted with people's soviets which can only give counsel that is not mandatory); another about the term „žīds" ["Jew"] and its proper usage; polemical notes about J. Endzelīns' argument with the court historian, now reactionary émigré, A. Švābe[120], etc.

The thesis of the conference collection "Thermal Analysis" (volume 1) asserted that the complete apparatus for thermal analysis was constructed in our land twenty years ago, and that it was an outdated relative of analogous apparati of leading foreign firms. Furthermore, that since only a limited number of apparati had been constructed, they were not available for general researchers, and that their production was terminated in 1979.

In the publication "Starry Heavens" (winter 1979/1980), an article entitled "Albert Einstein in Latvia," deals with a supposed trip to Riga by the scientist and the preparations for his trip by the Rīga Jewish Polytechnic Society and the preparatory activities of its members individually. There is, in fact, no documented proof of such a trip. If it happened as the article affirms, the scientist traveled incognito.

In the publication "Bulletin of the Latvian SSR Academy of Sciences" No. 5[121], 1979, (general series), in the article "Life's Reality Triumphs Over Counterfeits," several émigré organizations are cited frequently and listed by name, as are their publications; and reference to different "theories" of émigré organizations are presented without relevant commentary and without mentioning that the authors are members of the reactionary émigré leadership.

In I. Kiršentāle's monograph "The Latvian Novel," which discusses the origins and evolution and of this genre in Latvian literature, there is discussed alongside other works more than twenty that have been withdrawn from the free access collections [in Latvia]; moreover, the analysis lacks any objective evaluation of these works, as well as the author's [Kiršentāle's] Party-sensitive position toward these works and their authors.

b. The publisher Liesma

In three works prepared for publication, there were mentioned, without comment, the names of three persons - Gerols, Blūms, Frumins – who are widely known as having compromised themselves.

In Z. Skujiņš' book "The Bending of Lightning" contains the author's remembrances of earlier writers in the republic. Included was the author's letter to the People's Poet J. Sudrabkalns, in which he asked Sudrabkalns to use his authority to rehabilitate the poet Aspāzija who in Skujiņš'view was not adequately recognized [for her work].

In remembering the author E. Vilks, Skujiņš describes his simplicity and his considerable authority among youth. As proof of the latter, he tells the story of Vilks'arriving very drunk at a meeting with the young, even falling off his chair, but that appears not to have mattered and still everyone looked up at him with great respect.

In remembering the People's Author V. Lācis, Skujiņš describes in detail how during the period of bourgeois Latvia Lācis had been invited to the Press Ball at the palatial home of the "Press King" A. Benjāmiņš, and that during the premiere showing of [the film based on his novel] "The Fisherman's Son," Lācis sat in the same box with President Ulmanis. Further on, it is described how not long before V. Lācis was awarded the State Medal he was publicly reprimanded for his anti-Party approach to the father-son problem in his novel "Toward the New Shore," etc.

In the collection of poems, entitled "Worries," by T. Treičš, it is incorrectly stated that the memorial Cemetery of the Brethren in Rīga commemorated only the Latvian riflemen who died in World War I, even though it is commonly known that the cemetery was widely used for burials by the leaders of bourgeois Latvia and for their anti-Soviet propaganda.

c. The publications of the Ministry of Higher and Special Middle Education of the Latvian SSR

In the inter-university compendium "Bourgeois Propaganda: Concepts and Methods," A. Kupcov's article "The Anti-Lenin Core of Trotsky's Views in 1917" cites Trotsky often and refers without sufficient commentary and counter-arguments to those of his books that have been removed from free access.

In a different inter-university collection called "Nationality and Literary Relations" there was a quote from a reactionary, bourgeois author who admitted on the one hand that Latvians love and value highly Russian literature, but on the other hand called Soviet authors "narrow Soviet court scribblers."

From materials from the Ministry of Higher [and special middle] Education meant for shipment to foreign countries, there was removed reference to a book called "October Revolution and Proletarian Dictatorship" (Moscow, 1919) which is among the books taken out of free circulation.

In the inter-university collection from a seminar called "The current problems of perfecting the national economy with leading cadres," an article about labor safety was returned for re-working. It was said [in this article] that to bring the reduction of sound and vibration levels to acceptable norms as stated in the USSR State Plan, in the VACP, and in the State Labor Committee's projections, the Republic's Ministry of Light Industry Enterprises would need two five-year plans, but to completely eliminate all health-harming condition, - 20 five-year plans...

d. The magazine *Karogs*

E. Kliene's memoirs "The Spark of Memory" were returned for reworking. [In the book] the author describes his experiences in bourgeois Latvia in detail, mentioning his correspondence and his meeting with the Norwegian author K. Hamsun, his travels to Czechoslovakia to meet with the President of bourgeois Czechoslovakia E. Beneš, and his enthusiasm at seeing the festivities of the nationalist youth organization "Sokol," etc.

The magazine's editorial staff had prepared for publication J. Lapsa's novel "Bitterness" which was about the lives of fishermen and contained episodes describing Soviet fisherman fishing in forbidden parts of the world's oceans and deftly avoiding international controls because otherwise they could not fulfill the plan.

For the 100-year anniversary of Kārlis Skalbe, the editorial staff prepared I. Bērsons' article in which many bourgeois Latvian female authors and female philosophers were mentioned, and included, later in the text, the life of and quotations from the confirmed anti-Soviet émigré author Z. Mauriņa.

c. The periodical *Literatūra un Māksla*

From issue No. 21, dated May 25, 1979, there was removed an article by P. Putniņš entitled "About Latvian films in 1978"; it contained an unhealthy analysis of the work of the Rīga Kinostudio. The Rīga Kinostudio and the leaders of the Republic's State Committee of Cinematographers were accused of not fighting hard enough to have Latvian films included in its repertoire; they were said to be subservient to the demands of the USSR's State Cinematographers' Committee, to the public's taste for the "big screen", and to financial considerations, thus harming the interests of Latvian cinematography. According to the author, the chance of making a film was due primarily to its representative's ability to "talk" it into Moscow's production plans, etc.

In October of 1978, the editorial staff was given for re-working V. Avotiņš' article "More About Everything – Workdays," which commemorates the 60th anniversary of VĻKJS. In the article, Komsomol is accused in a generalized way of being divorced from reality, of passivity and selfishness, and at best replicating the methods of the Party. Also discussed is an older generation which occupies itself with drinking and servility and has a negative impact on the young. Some are accused of excusing their deficiencies by saying that they were in the war and that they had to renew the war-damaged national economy and thus had to live through great hardships, etc.

According to the leadership of the Propaganda and Agitation Sections, the article was returned to the editorial staff and attention was drawn to the impermissible tone, particularly on the anniversary of Komsomol. Nevertheless, the editorial staff did not change much and published the article in one of the following issues of the periodical.

For the centenary of K. Skalbe, the editorial staff prepared J. Kursīte's article "A Look at K. Skalbe's Poetry." The article often used quotations from those of the poet's books that have been removed from the free access collection, such as "The Breath of Grass," "Quiet Melodies," and "After Time." The article's author did not provide a clear class analysis [of these works].

In the magazine "Veselība," No. 6, 1979, from the article "On Behalf of a Higher Birth Rate," those parts were removed that described assistance and privileges accorded to mothers in the GDR, CSR, UTR that are not yet available in the USSR, which fact was used to indirectly explain the low birth rate [here].

In the journal "Draugs," starting with No. 6 of 1979, a multi-part article was planned, entitled "Swamps are Not Only for Cranes." The article expressed categorical doubts about the draining of land that had become swampy. The example cited was the drainage work of Lake Lubāns and its surroundings, where, it was said, the cleaning of local creeks destroyed breeding grounds for fish and initiated the erosion of existing plant life, etc.

In the magazine "Daugava," No. 8, 1979, there was planned the publication of Lekss Manušs' article entitled "Latvian Gypsy Songs," including some of his own songs. The material [for this article] celebrated the unique social life of the Gypsies, noted the absence of songs dedicated to work, highlighted horse thievery, and noted the stratification of the Gypsy population into the rich and the poor. The song "News Have Come from the Tsar" expressed sadness about a Gypsy called so serve in the army. There was nothing in the article about the life of Latvia's Gypsies or about the life of Soviet Gypsies generally.

In September of 1979, the Society of the Friends of the Book prepared for publication a prospectus for a volume on *ex libris* designs by the artist J. Plēpis. The best of this artist's work included *ex libris* designs prepared for the four family members of the bourgeois Latvian figure K. Goppers, for artists that included the reactionary émigré N. Strunke[122], for the bourgeois Latvian press magnate A. Benjāmiņš, the bourgeois Latvian General V. Tepfers, and others.

The magazine "Zvaigzne" prepared for publication the diary of J. Žīgurs, "The Burnt Portrait," that involved recollections about the People's Poet M. Ķempe. It used completely unedited material that cast a shadow over the Poet, who, according to the diarist, was a thoughtless and sexually unbalanced woman. Also, in the diary the life and social details of bourgeois Latvia were discussed in detail.

During the review we also discovered twelve programs for the Komsomol Youth Theater's (which is named after Lenin) production of W. Shakespeare's comedy "Much Ado About Nothing." According to the General Decree about Unclassified Publications, Par. 2, theater programs are freed from prior censorship.

On the reverse side of the programs there were printed some horoscopes for the birthdays falling in that month (we attach the programs). These are superstitious constructs both in content and in literary execution. One can only express pity that the theater could not find anything better with which to influence the young audience's minds, hearts and the formation of their worldview.

In providing information on the above-mentioned items, the Primary Board believes it to be useful to turn the attention of editors and the leaders of publishing houses to the need for more careful editing of the materials to be published, as is required by the directive of the Central Committee of the Communist Party of USSR concerning the heightened responsibilities of editors about the quality of materials they publish [...]

Chief of the Primary Board A. Luceviča

[The document also contains the following resolution of the Propaganda and Agitation Section of the Latvian Communist Party's Central Committee]:

"With respect to all the facts mentioned in Latvian SSR Glavlit letter, all of which testify to the absence of heightened concern in the evaluation of the idea-content of material to be published, the necessary work has been done with the editors of the periodicals and journals, the directorships of the publishing houses, and the leading workers of the Ministry of Higher and Special Middle Education."

May 6, 1980

L. Freibergs

Source: *LVA PA, 101. f., 45. apr., 95. l., pp. 3-9. Original in Russian.*

DOCUMENTS NO. 62-75

THE CHURCH: ALL-ENCOMPASSING CONTROLS

Document No. 62

Report of V. Šeškens, the authorized agent in the Latvian SSR of the Religious Cult Affairs Council of the USSR Council of People's Commissars, about the anti-Soviet attitudes of K. Irbe, the provisional Archbishop of the Latvian Evangelical Lutheran Church, and his activities as reflected in an NKVD investigations

October 5, 1945

Since the arrival of Soviet power in Latvia in 1944, K. Irbe has taken as the basis of his work the old slogan "the worse, the better" and holds on to it, not even always disguising it.

Through all of this time, I have not had a single concrete complaint from Irbe about the conduct of local authorities with respect to places of worship, congregation facilities, or repression against servants of the cult.

When I asked him directly about the roots of this "well-being" in his dioceses, he told me that he did not know that one could complain to soviet power about oneself, and that he did not believe that one could expect results from such complaints.

A short time after this conversation he called me from the Stalin *rajons* of the city of Rīga [to tell me] that the pastor from the Estonian Lutheran congregation had come to him and told him that in the Lutheran Church on Citadele Street, the Red Army unit stationed there (in the rooms of the church), had defiled it, torn the sacred painting, befouled the rooms, broken all of the furniture, knocked out the windows, disinterred the bishops buried under the altar and scattered their bones about, apparently stealing first from the coffins, etc.

The district executive committee created a commission to examine this complaint, but I called the garrison prosecutor who appointed his representative to this commission.

An investigation of the site showed that the pastor's complaint could be confirmed; it was determined that all of damage was the work of the Germans and resulted from the carelessness of the church's watchman.

When I protested to Irbe his clergy's insinuations, he reported to me that he did not believe the commission's statement because he did not see written in it that Germans were responsible and not the Red Army.

There have not been other complaints from him.

When I asked Irbe not long ago why the required registration and the election of an executive committee was going so poorly in his congregations, he replied directly that "people are afraid of doing anything because terror governs everything, and that when that ends then things will go well [will be organized]." To my puzzled question about what kind of terror, Irbe answered „"Well, everyone knows that all around people and clergy are being arrested, so they are afraid." To my reply that this was nothing more than a provocation he responded by shrugging his shoulders – "That is how it is, what is there to hide."

During the past month I conducted a conversation with Irbe about the request to the clergy and other believers [to issue] an invitation in the same spirit as other confessions have done.

Irbe categorically refused, emphasizing that he did not believe in the promises of soviet organs concerning the inviolability of those coming our of the forests, and that he did not see it as possible to issue such an invitation unless the government issued an amnesty decree for all those arrested starting in 1940.

"Return all of our sufferers whom you deported in 1940-1941, and then we will believe you."

To my reply that this must mean that he considers bandits and similar types being in the forests as a normal situation, Irbe replied "Well, what can you do, the church does not get involved in politics, does not want to and will not."

Individual Lutheran congregations do not want to accept those clergy, assigned [to them] by Irbe, who were formerly in Kurzeme (Sigulda and Ikšķile), saying that that they should stay with the Germans. Irbe himself visited these congregations to persuade them, telling them that refusing to accept the clergy could lead to the liquidation of the Lutheran Church in Latvia.

In sum, in all of Irbe's activities there is a hostile tone against the existing conditions, and an attempt to unite under the Lutheran Church's flag a class of anti-Soviet clergymen in a struggle against soviet power.

Authorized agent of the Latvian SSR   Šešken

Source: *LVA, 1986. f., 2. apr., 10758. l., vol 2., p. 1. Original in Russian.*

Comment: *K. Irbe was arrested on February 28th, 1946. He was charged with "belonging to a counter-revolutionary organization and with traitorous behavior during the time of German occupation." In a special meeting on March 29, 1947, using the RSFSR Criminal Code paragraphs 58-1a, 58-10 section 2, and 58-11, K. Irbe was sentenced to ten years in a correctional camp and the confiscation of his property. In 1946, because of the arrests of the Senior Board members of the Church (K. Irbe, P. Rozenbergs, and A. Siļķe), the leadership of the Evangelical Lutheran Church was paralyzed.*

Secret correspondence between, V. Šeškens, the authorized agent in the Latvian SSR of the Religious Cult Affairs Council of the USSR Council of People's Commissars, and I. Polanski, the Chair of the USSR Council of Religious Cult Affairs, about the situation in specific confessions

V. Šeškens to I. Polanski

December 31, 1945

During the last quarter, in the various confessions the most attention was required by the following events:

Catholics – after word was received from the Council that continuing work could go on in the seminary, I visited Springovičs before Christmas; he was bed-ridden for two weeks because of an illness. A few days before that, Začests, his curia's secretary, who also performed the duties of a clerk and personal aide, was arrested. Springovičs was completely alone in the curia and began with complaints about difficult times. Among other things, I noted that often people forget that those who sow the wind reap the whirlwind. Springovičs immediately changed the subject and did not return to his complaints. After many questions of an economic nature he thanked me for the rationed food[123], automobile tires etc. I told him about the permission regarding the seminary. It was apparent that he was very pleased and promised that he would pray for all of those that gave this permission; he also sought to convince me in many ways that the seminary would educate true Soviet clergy. He also said that it was good that the seminary would be starting its work now when persons had already become used to Soviet conditions and had, more or less, become familiar with Soviet laws. To my question about the leadership of the seminary, Springovičs answered that he had no other candidates except Professor Strods, and he asked for my thoughts. I agreed with him that I could not identify any other candidate. That is also how we then decided it. The question about the seminary building was raised; in the past it was a separate building, in fact an entire building complex in Pārdaugava. In 1940, however, this complex was taken over Children's Bone Tuberculosis Sanatorium. I told Springovičs not to expect this building, and that they need to renovate the building on Catholic Street 14 that had been slated for this purpose when the first requests for a seminary building had come in [...]

He declined, with thanks, any help from the State Construction Organization for renovating the building on Catholic Street 14, noting that at first there would be only a few students there and that they would make do without renovations. Personally, I had already come to believe that in this academic year they would not begin any regular studies, but that the seminary was needed primarily to raise the prestige of the church leadership and to strengthen its position in Latvia. Now they are completely satisfied. On the other hand, with respect to the decreasing number of clergymen they have experienced for a while now, the opening of the seminary has great significance to the worshiping masses as a means of dispelling the gloom. I will mention an example: a delegation of faithful Catholics in Viļaka parish came to visit me. In the two churches in Viļaka there were three clergy, all of whom were repressed not long ago and thus the parish is left without any clergymen. [...]

They came to me to ask for any kind of clergy and I sent them to the metropolitan and added, by the way, that we had already opened a seminary and that there does not exist any persecution of the churches.

I gave the letter of Prelate Vaikuls, which is known to you, to the Commission examining the brutal acts of the Germans; the letter discusses how Hitler persecuted the Catholic Church in Latvia. Since the trials of war criminals are being prepared in Rīga, Vaikuls' testimony, coming from the vicar-general, about this situation, even if the testimony is in written form (I gave his letter to comrade

Pugo) could be interesting. I will summon Vaikuls to the Commission on January 3rd to gauge his disposition.

The condition among the Lutherans has not changed. With respect to stopping the so-called evangelization, I had a serious discussion with Irbe,[124] who refused to agree to this without an official written order. I said that my formal verbal statement should be enough for him, and that I did not want excessive noise about this matter. Irbe expressed further disappointment, but suddenly became quiet and calmed down. It turned out that he had heard the bells of the Orthodox Church through the window behind me. He then continued to speak with a smile: good, there will be no evangelization, but we will take the Orthodox as an example and in place of one service as before, we will have hold our services without sermons, but have them every day - that it is that, and what are you going to do to us. […]

Irbe sent two greetings to congregations, one related to the return of bandits from the forests and the other about Christmas. Both evidence a nearly anti-Soviet character and were not cleared with me, even though I had asked him to do so. I will forward the greetings after they have been translated and rewritten.

In Rīga, there is one former Anglican church which in its time served foreigners. In 1941, according to a contract with the representative of this church, the Scotsman Lofson, who continued in his position throughout the German era, remodeled the church and brought in as pastor Professor Freijs from the bombed-out St. Peter's Church. Currently Lofson is in Rīga, and Freijs with his congregation is still in the church.

Before I began to inquire about this question officially, I went to comrade Valeskalns[125] to discuss it. He recommended that I not get involved right now and not speak with Lofson, because there was a representative from England's embassy in Moscow with him and the latter was very interested in the conditions of this church. […]

Please send your suggestions about what to do regarding this question in the future, as the congregation is registered as renters. […]

I submitted news according to the new statistical forms, but my primary difficulty with these forms is that no one knows where private property begins, and where nationalized and municipal property ends, because, as I already reported to you, not in 1940-1941 nor in 1944 or later has the Republic rendered a final decision [on ownership]. Decisions about individual houses have a local character and apparently they have no legal standing...

Personally, when I speak to the clergy, I refer to the All-Union Law About Nationalization. (Simply put, all property erected on Soviet land belongs to the Soviet people).

Authorized Agent in the Latvian SSR   Šešken

J. Sadovski's answer to V. Šeškens

The Council of Religious Cult Affairs of the Council of Peoples' Commissars of the USSR submits a reply to your questions.

We take under advisement Springovičs' reaction to the opening of the seminary.

Relating to your suggestions about Vaikuls' behavior, a supplementary instruction will be given after the question is researched.

The Council believes that, as relates to Catholics, the most vulnerable thing is Springovičs' solitude, because he has no deputies or aides. Your activity must be concentrated in this direction so as to create assistants of this type. We need to consider seriously Deacon Vaikuls' candidacy.

With respect to Lutherans, the Council believes that a stricter and more direct line must be taken. It is necessary to fashion a system of activities that would lead, as their result, to the insulation of the clergy and the believers from Irbe's views. We need to work out a tax system that would constrict the role of the Lutheran clergy, and that would create among them certain disorganization. Related to this, we need to rethink in a detailed fashion the undertakings tied to Irbe's announcement that in place of "forbidden evangelization" there would be daily church service. It can be interpreted that each single church service provides the pastor with some revenue. If there are more church services then there is more revenue. Therefore some coordination of action can be worked out with the financial organs to impose severe taxes on those pastors who hold services every day.

With respect to the announcements by Irbe and other pastors that are not cleared with you, you need to reach agreement with the organs of military censorship about how to end such announcements.

You must also reach agreement with the Peoples' Commissariat of the Interior about measures to be used against persons who, without clearance from you and without appropriate permission, travel to rural districts and parishes.

The Council requests that you inform them of your proposals in these matters [...]

4. With respect to the Anglican church, it needs to be left in the condition that it is in. Currently it does not need to be registered. At the same time, please submit more detailed news about this church. [...]

We are interested in the question of the number of working and registered congregations and their activity. We understand by that congregations that perform not only religious work but are primarily "social" [in character].

You did not mention anything about our specially formulated question about the imposition of taxes. We direct your attention to this question again and its particular importance; please study it thoroughly and send all of the information requested the Council without delay.

Similarly, you mention only as an aside that in the Latvian SSR there has not been a law promulgated dealing with the nationalization of church buildings. This information is insufficient for the Council to examine this question and to send it to the Government for its attention. It is necessary to know the opinions of the local leading organs, even if only about the number of buildings that could be nationalized, what kind of reaction that would bring from the clergy and among the believers, whether there should be nationalization of cult buildings and property or just buildings, etc. [...]

Deputy Chair of the Council of Religious Cult Affairs of the Council of Peoples' Commissariats of the USSR   Sadovski

Source: *LVA, 1448. f., 2. apr., 239. l., pp. 55-60. Original in Russian.*

Excerpt from the top secret decision of the Latvian SSR State Security Ministry about the recruitment of the Evangelical Lutheran Church pastor, A. Siļķe, and the impossibility of using him as an agent

June 26, 1946

Agent "Zaķis", Arturs[126] Kr. Siļķe, born in 1908 in the Tukums district of the Latvian SSR, citizen of the USSR, from a kulak family, served in the Latvian Army from 1930-1931 as an deputy officer, finished the University of Latvia Theological Faculty in 1939, Lutheran Church pastor, from October 10, 1944, works as Dean in the city of Riga and is a temporary member of the Lutheran Church Governing Board, was an active member of the international organization "Christian Students Society", participated in their conferences in 1936 in Oslo (Norway) and in 1937 in Oxford (England) as a delegate of this organization's Latvia branch. Lives in Rīga.

Recruited on December 6, 1944, as a volunteer. During the recruiting period, he did not submit worthwhile material. After two meetings received an assignment to shed light on the work of the German henchman, the Deputy Archbishop Irbe[127]; by December 21, 1944, had not completed his assignment and categorically refused to cooperate in secret with the Commissariat of State Security.

Since he was being detained on suspicion of conspiracy, he was held secretly and actively interrogated[128]; thereafter, when it was uncovered that had been an active German supporter in matters of Church life, he testified:

"...Because of my anti-Soviet views and personal dissatisfaction with Soviet power (on June 14, 1941, my cousin, the theology professor and pastor, Rumba, was arrested and deported to the interior regions of the USSR), and being a Lutheran pastor, during the first German occupation in the territory of the Latvian SSR I participated in the Lutheran church's active anti-Soviet, pro-fascist work directed toward the full support of fascist Germany in the war against the Soviet Union.

To my congregation, I delivered sermons that were meant to damage the authority of Soviet power; I tried to awaken hostility and anger in them against the Soviet order. I conducted anti-Soviet, pro-fascist church services: on July 3, 1941, entitled "About the German Army's successful liberation of Rīga from the Bolsheviks"; on June 14, 1942, 1943, 1944, entitled "In memory of those deported and murdered by Bolsheviks in 1941"; on November 18, 1943, entitled "The anniversary of the founding of bourgeois power in Latvia."

During every church service I invited the congregation to pray for the successes of the Latvian Waffen-SS Legion and for their good health in the battle against the Red Army; I helped in gathering material support for the Waffen-SS legionnaires.

With the German arrival, religious instruction classes were renewed in Latvia's schools. On my express wishes, I began to work as a teacher of religious instruction at the 1st Gymnasium in Rīga and I taught the children in an anti-Soviet spirit.

After the fifth night of his imprisonment, agent "Zaķis" notified us that he would like to assuage his guilt before Soviet power by providing valuable information when freed, and with honest cooperation with the State Security Ministry in uncovering the enemies of Soviet power; he then signed [the promise] for a second time with his own hand.

Because of his potential usefulness as an agent, he was freed with a cover story that guaranteed success in his work.

Nevertheless, in the recent past, agent "Zaķis" did not turn over worthwhile material and did not try to do his job; he retains anti-Soviet stances and plays a double game that has been documented by other agents with reliable information; this is also reinforced by the following facts:

> [...]"...Irbe and Siļķe share some kind of secret because Irbe frequently takes Siļķe to a separate office where he tells him things while trying not to let others hear. They are very careful and do not trust others." (source: agent "Demokrat" March 5, 1945, report.)
> "This year on July 10th Siļķe received from Acting Archbishop Irbe a March 1945 leaflet with anti-Soviet content [written] by Archbishop Grīnbergs who had fled to Laus (Germany). The leaflet for Irbe was apparently brought to Riga by Pastor Vanags." (source: agent "Demokrat" July 13, 1945, report.)

During meeting times, agent "Zaķis" not only hid the fact that he had received Grīnbergs'pamphlet from Irbe, but denied that Irbe was distributing it. :

> "This year during the July 10th meeting, there was no discussion with a political content. I can not report anything particular" (source: "Zaķis" July 19, 1945, report.)

In the analysis of the material provided by agents "Astra" and "Krupnov," it was determined that not only does agent "Zaķis" not try to uncover anti-Soviet elements, but warns the persons in his immediate circle against carrying on political, particularly anti-Soviet, conversations in his presence, of the kind the Ministry of State Security might be interested in.

In addition to his two-timing anti-Soviet work, agent "Zaķis" has revealed his connections to the State Security Ministry in front of Irbe and others. [...]

On April 24, the source "Krupnov" reported that this year, on April 23, Pastor Perlbahs told him about his meeting with the Acting Archbishop Irbe, and said:

> "...Irbe told me that Siļķe goes to the Bolsheviks every week to submit news about conditions in the church."

Being hostile to the Soviet order and notwithstanding our directions for doing patriotic work through the church, Siļķe continues to conduct anti-Soviet agitation in his close circle of friends. [...]

In addition, materials from agent "Krupnov" report that Siļķe agitates against participation in the elections for the USSR Supreme Council. This year, on November 15th, in the office of St. Gertrude's church, the agent spoke with Siļķe and Pastor Pečaks about these elections.

> Pečaks said; "We will have to vote if we want to or not."
> Siļķe replied to this: "Why think like that, we should not go at all. Why in 1940 did Dean Bergs not go? Who does not want to, shouldn't go."

Moreover, according to materials from the agents "Krupnov" and "Kalniņš," persons who need fictional documents provide fictional data about their birth and on this basis receive fictional documents from Siļķe.

We have had many counseling sessions and conversations containing strict warnings with agent "Zaķis," but he continues to be hostile to the Soviet order and also continues his anti-Soviet activities.

As an agent for dealing with anti-Soviet elements and for developing Soviet patriotism ["Zaķis"] is useless. Suggest he be removed from the network of agents, arrested, and tried for criminal behavior.

Chief of the 2nd section, Latvian SSR State Security Ministry   Lieutenant Colonel Belov

3rd Department Chief, 2nd Section, Latvian SSR State Security Ministry   Captain Smetanin

Source: *LVA, 1986. f., 2. apr., 10758. l., vol 2., pp. 28-34. Original in Russian.*

Comment: *Siļķe was arrested on February 21, 1946. He was accused of "participation in counterrevolutionary organizations and support of the German occupiers." In a special meeting on March 29, 1947, Silke was sentenced according to the KPFSR Criminal Code 58-3, 58-10, part2, 58-11 paragraphs to eight years in a corrective labor camp.*

Document No. 65

Excerpt from a top secret report of the Latvian SSR Ministry of State Security about the anti-Soviet activities of the Evangelical Lutheran Church pastor P. Rozenbergs, now under arrest

July 1, 1946

Pastor -   Rozenbergs, Pauls, Pēteris' son[129]
                  Born in 1906 in the Straupe parish of Valmiera District of the Latvian SSR, Latvian, non-party, citizen of the USSR, advanced religious education, Pastor of the Koknese Lutheran congregation of the Riga District, lives in Koknese in Rīga District.

During investigations by the secret service it was determined that Rozenbergs is from a very well-to-do family, and that Soviet organs shot his father in 1919 for anti-Soviet activities.

During the Ulmanis dictatorship, P. Rozenbergs was the Pastor of the Aizsargi Organization and was a committed supporter of the plutocratic government. In January of 1941, during the elections to the Supreme Council of the USSR, he and his family did not participate.

P. Rozenbergs' brother, Arvīds Rozenbergs, was the leader of a bandit group based near Sigulda and during the German occupation time was a German fixed-post spy, arrested in 1945.

Another of Rozenbergs' brothers worked at diversionary and terrorist activities, for which he was arrested by the Latvian SSR State Security Ministry.

By conviction and actions, Rozenbergs is a person of hostile disposition toward Soviet power and is an active Latvian bourgeois nationalist.

Being a member of the governing body of the Lutheran Church and the Rīga territory Dean,[130] he led the church's struggle against the Soviet order in Latvia, encouraging active support of the German fascist invaders.

During the [fascist] occupation, he conducted annually a church service in memory of the anti-Soviet elements deported in June of 1941, in this way eliciting in his congregation nationalist sentiment and hostility toward Soviet power. Moreover, he wrote anti-Soviet articles in the newspaper of the Church's governing body "The Church News."

He greeted with hostility the return of the Red Army in the territory of Latvia and everywhere voiced defeatist opinions about the likelihood of the triumph of Soviet power in Latvia.

Together with Irbe, they disseminated the pamphlet of the former Archbishop Grīnbergs sent to them from Germany, distributing it at the meetings of the Church's governing body.

In the meeting of the Church's governing council on September 18, 1945, the discussion centered on the proposal by the government that bandits who were still the forests be asked to return home and register.

Rozenbergs expressed doubt about this question:

> "On the one side, the government's promises are very humane, but on the other, what guarantees are there that the promises will really be fulfilled. We have learned to look at the government's promises with suspicion. What guarantees are there to the Church's governing body that the promise will be fulfilled? What guarantee is there that our clergymen will not be placed in the role of betrayers of these unfortunate refugees? What will our nation say when, after a while, these same refugees are arrested and deported for an entirely different illegality or crime? (Report of agent "Demokrat'" September 19, 1945)

The Council of the governing body of the Lutheran Church consequently did not issue a call to the bandits and their families.

Notwithstanding the fact that more than a year has gone by since instructions [on registration] were promulgated, Rozenbergs and other members of the governing body of the Church are deliberately slowing down the registration of church congregations and the election of church councils; moreover, he said, in connection with a message from Irbe which had a distinct anti-Soviet flavor, that:

> "There is another phenomenon we have no right to ignore and pass by without noticing. That is the question about saving our nation's vital strength. The great misfortune of our times is that many of our nation's brethren still are not able to return home and to work productively. That continues to trouble them and those closest to them. Let us help them in this as much as is in our power. Let us try to determine the reasons that delay their return. One of these reasons is the charges and false accusations against them – it is an evil in our nation, leading to self-destruction, when brother hates brother, accuses him falsely, and betrays him. He who loves his nation and hopes the best for it needs to turn away from this sin. The truth will come to light…" [...]

Rozenbergs was called to the Church's governing body after the arrest of Irbe and Siļķe,[130] and, upon notification of their arrest, replied:

> "I suspected this would happen."

He later said in a meeting:

> "We need to go to the authorized agent of the Religious Cult Affairs [council] and find out the reason for the arrest. We must know that, so that we can defend them. I for one am ready to suffer for my conscience, I am not afraid."

Upon the initiative of Rozenbergs and under his leadership, a delegation of the Church's governing board visited the agent of the Latvian SSR TKP Religious Cult Affairs, asking for the reasons for the arrest of Irbe and Siļķe and for their release.

Latvian SSR State Security Ministry Chief of the 2nd Section	Lieutenant Colonel Belov
Latvian SSR State Security Ministry Chief of the 3rd Section	Captain Smetanin

Source: *LVA, 1986. f., 2. apr., 10758. l., vol. 2, pp. 35-37. Original in Russian.*

Comment: *Rozenbergs was arrested on February 28, 1946. He was accused of "participation in a counterrevolutionary organization and supporting the German occupiers." In a special meeting on March 29, 1947, he was sentenced by reference to KPFSR Criminal Code 58-3, 58-10, part 2, par. 58-11 to eight years in a corrective labor camp.*

Document No. 66

Report by N. Levindato, the authorized Bishop in the Baltic Republics of the All-Union Evangelical Christian-Baptist Council, to the authorized agent in the Latvian SSR of the USSR Council of Ministers Religious Cult Affairs with a request to strengthen the church buildings in the commune's possession

March 16, 1949

The Executive Committee of the Kazdanga parish in Aizpute district refused to finalize a contract with the Kazdanga Baptist Commune about giving the church it owns, located in the "Zāģers" house in Kazdanga parish, and suggested that the Commune to completely evacuate the church halls; this, in fact, would mean the complete cessation of church services for the congregation's members.

The Executive Committee motivated its decision to break the contract with the commune with the following:

1. That the members of the commune that make up "dvadcatka"[131] live in different parishes,
2. that the commune "dvadcatka" members includes members of other communes that have
3. left the other communes,
4. that the church is located close to kolkhoz buildings and because of this there is the
5. threat of contagious diseases because for the church services, congregation members will
6. arrive from many places.

We ask you to strengthen the church's control of church buildings[132] that have been used for services for several years now.[133]

Bishop   N. Levindato

Source: *LVA, 1448. f., 1. apr., 20. l., p. 22. Original in Russian.*

Document No. 67

Information by P. Liepa, authorized agent in the Latvian SSR of the Religious Cult Affairs Council of the Council of Ministers of the USSR, to the Chair of the Religious Cult Affairs Council of the Council of Ministers of the USSR, A. Puzin, about the prohibition of burials with religious ceremonies

November 22, 1962

At the mortuary of the Rīga 1ˢᵗ Forest Cemetery, it is prohibited to have a religious funeral ceremony, in connection with the Municipal Executive Committee's decision to increase the territory of the Rainis' cemetery, where there are interments without religious ceremonies with the permission of the Municipal Executive Committee.

In the Rainis Cemetery, personal pensioners and Party and Soviet activists are interred.

Authorized Agent of the Council   P. Liepa

Source: *LVA, 1449.f., 1. apr., 160.l., p. 106. Original in Russian.*

Document No. 68

Decision No. 288 of the Council of Ministers of the Latvian SSR concerning the liquidation of monasteries in the territory of the Latvian SSR

May 20, 1959
Not for publication in the press

In view of the requests from the working masses for closing of cloisters and in view of the April 13 and 17, 1959, instructions from the Council of Ministers of the USSR, the Council of Ministers of the Latvian SSR decides:

1. To liquidate:
    a. The "Marian" congregation male cloister of the Roman Catholic Church, located in the town of Viļāni;
    b. The "Poor Jesus Child" female cloister located in Aglona in the Preiļi region;
    c. The Orthodox "Holy Trinity Sergej" female cloister in Rīga and its affiliate in the Valgunde village in the Jelgava region.
2. To assign to comrade Kibiš, the Chair of the Executive Committee of the Viļāni Regional Working Masses' Council of Deputies, to comrade Cellert, the Chair of the Executive Committee of the Preiļi Regional Working Masses Council of Deputies, to comrade Deneškans, the Chair of the Executive Committee of the Jelgava Regional Working Masses Council of Deputies, to comrade Restbergs, the authorized agent of the Committee on Religious Cult Affairs of the Council of Ministers of the USSR, and to comrade Sakharov, the authorized agent of the Council on Russian Orthodox Church Affairs in the Latvian SSR of the Council of Ministers of the USSR, the tasks of:
    a. finishing the closing of the cloisters mentioned in point 1 in the course of 1960[134];
    b. ensuring that all able-bodied monks and nuns from the liquidated cloisters and

monasteries are moved into employment, and the disabled among them into rest homes if they desire it;

  c. handing over without compensation to the relevant city and regional Working People's Councils the housing, agricultural inventory, livestock, and other possessions of the liquidated cloisters.

3. To assign the Social Security Ministry of the Latvian SSR the task of placing all monks and nuns incapable of work who so wish into rest homes.

Chair of the Council of Ministers of the Latvian SSR   V. Lācis
Affairs Supervisor of the Council of Ministers of the Latvian SSR   V.Krastiņš

Source: *LVA, 1448. f., 1. apr., 11. l., pp. 97-98. Original in Russian.*

Document No. 69

Report of J. Restbergs, the authorized agent in the Latvian SSR of the Council of Religious Cult Affairs of the Council of Ministers of the USSR, explaining the complaints of nine seminarians of the Catholic Seminary of Riga about their expulsion from the institution

September 29, 1959

Report
concerning the complaints addressed to the Chair of the Council of Ministers of the Latvian SSR, Vilis Lācis
of the Catholic Seminary seminarians:

1.	Daļeckis, O.	2.	Krapāns, J.
3.	Brencis J.,	4.	Vitko, V.,
5.	Rasnacis, J.	6.	Mukāns, J.
7.	Savičs, A.	8.	Bruzgulis, P.,
9.	Viļčinskis, Česlavs		

In researching the composition of the personnel of the Rīga Catholic Seminary[135], we decided to expel the persons who were not politically trustworthy.
It turned out that there were 9 such persons:
Short descriptions of some of them:
1. Vilcinskis, Česlavs – deserted from the ranks of the Soviet army, was sentenced to ten years in a work camp.
2. Daļeckis, Oļģerts – relative of former bandits, his family was connected with bandits.
3. Savičs, Arturs – In 1946, his uncle was shot as a bandit; the family supported bandits.
4. Krapāns, Jānis – former teacher.
5. Vitko, Vikentijs – finished the Vitebsk Construction Technical Institute
6. Pujāts, Dominiks – three brothers are clergymen.
7. Brencis, Jēkabs – relatives served in the German army and in punitive battalions; he himself is hostile to the existing order.
8. Rasnacis, Jānis – studied in the fourth-year course of the Daugavpils Teachers Institute in 1950, and then entered the Seminary.
9. Mukāns, Juris – brother is a clergyman, he himself is against the [Soviet] state. He was

refused entrance to the Seminary this year.

I see it possible to reply to each [complainant] with the following answer:

"Your submission addressed to the Chair of the Council of Ministers of the Latvian SSR, has been reviewed. There is no basis for satisfying your request."

The Council's Authorized Agent   J. Restbergs

Source: *LVA, 1448. f., 1. apr., 25. l., pp. 1-2. Original in Russian.*

Document No. 70

Informational report of J. Restbergs, the authorized agent in the Latvian SSR of the Council of Religious Cult Affairs of the Council of Ministers of the USSR, concerning the request of the executive committee of the Riga Jewish congregation to the Chair of the Council of Ministers of the Latvian SSR to allow the congregation to order a special preparation of unleavened bread (matzoh) for the Jewish religious holidays

February 3, 1960

In my view, agreeing to this request, and its execution, are not necessary because, as is well known, the Jewish high holy day fast, when special unleavened bread is used for nourishment, is not related to their religious faith, but is associated with self-sacrifice in remembrance of the escape from Egyptian enslavement in the fourteenth and thirteenth centuries [BCE].

Secondly, I believe that, from a political perspective, it would be wrong to allow devout Jews to have special rights that could be used as the basis of a request. If devout Jews wish to follow their old customs, they can make unleavened bread in the home setting in the same way Christians color Eastern eggs and bake special bread on Easter.

Authorized Agent of the Religious Cult Affairs Council   J. Restbergs

Source: *LVA, 1448 f., 1. apr., 173. l., pp. 1-2. Original in Russian.*

Document No. 71

Secret report of A. Liepa, the authorized agent in the Latvian SSR of the Council of Religious Cult Affairs of the Council of Ministers of the USSR, to the Chair of the USSR Religious Cult Affair Council, A. Puzins, about activities needed in connection with the appointment of a new archbishop

July 21, 1962

After the death of Bishop Strods, who led the Roman Catholic Church in the Latvian SSR, the curia has been led by Julijans Začests. The Vatican designated J. Začests as an apostolic administrator. While conducting church affairs, Začests sidesteps the recommendations given to him by the authorized agent and basically carries on work that is directed against the Soviet laws on cults.

In view of this, the government of the Latvian SSR believes that is impossible to leave Začests as the leader of the Roman Catholic Church in the Republic and believes it would be useful to have a different bishop assigned.

I have brought into agreement all relevant institutions that Julians Vaivods, the Dean of the St. Jacob's Cathedral in Rīga, should be the candidate for the position of bishop.

It is hoped that this goal will be accomplished in the following manner. Initially two reactionary-minded consultants -- Oļševskis and Kozlovskis -- of the Rīga Metropolitan Curia will be removed (of the nine in each church district). This will be done by Začests himself as the apostolic administrator of the curia.

After that, J. Začests will be advised to resign in writing from the responsibilities of the apostolic administrator because the government does not recognize him, and to send a telegram of his resignation to the Pope in Rome.

At the same time, Začests will be told that he can choose work in any deaconate except Rīga.

After Začests resigns from the post of apostolic administrator, two consultants (the one in Rīga metropolitan area and in Liepāja) will suggest for the bishop's position 2 or 3 candidates who would be consistent with the government's recognition decision. Among the suggested candidates will definitely be Vaivods, as the most authoritative clergyman.

Both consultants will choose the candidacy of Vaivods. After his election, he will send a telegram to Rome asking that his election be sanctioned.

After a telegram is received from Rome, the bishop of Lithuania will invest J. Vaivods into with the position of bishop.

In the event that Začests does not want to resign from his position – something that obviously is not very likely -- I will call together all of the consultants and deacons and will notify them that because of such a situation has arisen I am forced to close the curia. The pastors will be against this and will force Začests to resign.

In this way we hope to replace Začests with the more trustworthy clergyman -- Julians Vaivods.

I request your agreement in principle with the procedure outlined above.[136]

Authorized Agent of the Council   P. Liepa

Source: *LVA, 1448. f., 1. apr., 268.l., pp. 59-60. Original in Russian.*

Document No. 72

Excerpt from a report by A. Sakharov, the Deputy Authorized Agent of Religious Affairs in the Latvian SSR, about a meeting with journalists from Portugal on April 24, 1978, and the course of their conversation.

April 25, 1978

Responding to the request of the Portuguese journalists Julio Sereno de Cabral and Cezar da Silva Principe, I received them in my office on April 24, 1978. Accompanying the journalists and participating in the conversation were: the Board Secretary of the Russian Orthodox Church in Rīga, the priest Leonid Abasev; an official of the office of the Patriarch of the Russian Orthodox Church in Moscow, the senior priest Mihail Turcin, and the APN translator S. Poļakov.

After mutual introductions, the journalists announced that they represented the progressive press of Portugal. [They said] that even after only a short stay in our country, they had come to realize that in Portugal there exist completely simpleminded and wrongheaded beliefs about the USSR in general, and about the church in particular. The goal of their trip to the USSR is to learn about religious life in the Soviet Union. They believe that in Portugal the religiosity of the population is not deep, and it receives less external expression than here. Visiting Orthodox houses of worship in Kiev and Rīga, they saw more believers than in their homeland. Nonetheless, almost all Portuguese "in the depth of their souls" see themselves as believers, and thus are troubled by the widespread propaganda in Portugal that in the socialist countries, particularly in the USSR, religion is discriminated against by the law and that the state suppresses the church. In the recent past, among the ranks of the religious reactionaries there has been an anti-Soviet propaganda campaign, asking for a defense of the church in the USSR.

The journalists asked many questions. Cabral was especially active; Principe asked almost no questions but during the conversation wrote down both questions and answers.

The following questions were asked (summary of the answer in parentheses):

1. How are the relations between the church and state?
   (The separation of the church from the state, and the schools from the church, were explained, an arrangement that guarantees all citizens true freedom of conscience).

2. Bishop Zondaks told us that in Latvia there had been a Jesuit monastery, but the state had forbidden new members to join and then had closed it. Why?
   (The question apparently arose because Bishop Zondaks' response was not translated precisely enough for the guests because he speaks Russian poorly. I know that among the Latvian Roman Catholic Church clergy there are Jesuit monks. But during the years of Soviet power they did not come together to live in a monastery, but remained as deans of various congregations. Since there was no monastery, it could not be closed.)

3. But can Catholic believers establish a cloister or monastery?
   (These are religious organizations, and there is a well-defined procedure for establishing religious organizations. First, in order to found a cloister or monastery there has to be an explicit desire to do so, and then an official request to the appropriate state offices. If a request is submitted – it will be examined.)

4. Can the faithful in this country receive from abroad the newspaper "Osservatore Romano"? How can they subscribe to it?
   (This newspaper, as far as I know, is of interest to a very narrow group of persons, namely, the Roman Catholic clergy. In this Republic, the Roman Catholic bishops and individual clergy receive this newspaper. Apparently, there is a certain procedure for subscribing to foreign publications, and the interested persons make use of it. That it is used is reinforced by the fact that those who are interested do receive it.) The journalists agreed that indeed they had seen the current copies of "Osservatore Romano" in the seminary.

5. But can every believer receive the newspaper?
   (I believe that the question has to be put forward more objectively: can the citizens of our state receive, that is, subscribe to a foreign newspaper, journal, or other [foreign] literature. In our state, the rights of a citizens are in no way connected to that citizen's religious beliefs. This thesis receives particularly strong stress in the Constitution of the USSR. I can say that our state observes the statutes of the Helsinki Declarations dealing with the exchange of information: in "Sojuzpečatj" kiosks one can get the most varied newspapers and journals published in foreign lands. There is also a way of subscribing to foreign publications. It is not clear to me why everyone shows such interest in the distribution of the "O.R.")

6. Does the Roman Catholic seminary receive from the state a piece of land for the seminary's agricultural work?
   (A seminary is a teaching institution. In our state, teaching institutions can receive land if it is necessary for the process of learning. The seminary does not need this. Church organizations

can receive land for use. For example, in Rīga there is an Orthodox cloister that receives from the state for its agricultural needs 8.5 hectares of rural land. If the seminary turns to us with such requests – they will be examined. [...])

7. Can the church organize processions and ceremonies outside of the buildings of the cult?
   (The law provides for unrestricted religious rituals and related ceremonies within the buildings of the cult. The state does not control either the time of ceremonies or their character – those are the internal affairs of the church. Outside of the cult's buildings, rituals and processions can be carried out if related to funerals [...])

8. Can the Roman Catholic Church print religious literature for its own needs?
   (The journalists were shown last year's publications of the Roman Catholic Church publications and literature received from the Vatican, and it was explained to them that the church has the opportunity to print the religious literature it needs at the state printing houses.)

9. Does the church have the right to make an appearance in the press, on the radio or on television?
   (The freedom of conscience of all citizens is guaranteed by the free exercise of the cult's beliefs among believers. You saw that in our country there are many different confessions, and if every church had the opportunity to use the press (newspapers) for its confessional needs, as well as radio and television, that would become missionary work, which would conflict the principle of freedom of conscience. The periodical press, and radio and television, broadcasts the most important events of the life of our state. Naturally, when important church events happen in our state, they are in the news. There is also news about church forums, trips, church leaders' stands on questions pertaining to the struggle for peace and the most important international events, about the arrival of church delegations and about cult employees' trips to foreign lands, etc. [...])

The journalists thanked us for the information and said that they were convinced that in their country lies are being told about religious life in the USSR. Now they have seen for themselves those lies are anti-Soviet propaganda and are far from the truth. [...]

Deputy Authorized Agent of the Council   A. Sakharov

Source: *LVA, 1419. f., 3. apr., 18. l., pp. 50-54. Original in Russian.*

Document No. 73

Excerpts from the decision of the Rīga Municipal Committee of the Latvian Communist Party, entitled "Concerning the strengthening of atheistic training"

October 10, 1982

The Bureau of the Rīga Municipal Committee of the Latvian Communist Party notes that the municipal Party organization is working to raise the level of atheism among the Rīga working class and the city's population.[137] In the municipal committee, regional Party committees and [local] Party committees, atheist councils have been formed and are working to coordinate the scientific work of furthering atheistic propaganda. [A total of] 926 atheistic agitators disseminate agitation propaganda and do individualized work among believers.

Year after year, the number and quality of lectures read at factories, construction sites, learning facilities, municipal offices, and learned societies[138] increases. If in 1976 there were 1,604 lectures, then in 1981 there were 2,537 lectures.

A part of the work done in raising the atheism of individuals is done by the cultural-educational institutions.

The Atheist Council of the Party's Rīga Municipal Committee, together with the Party's Regional Committee, is undertaking sociological research about the attitudes of youth toward religion and about the work of the Roman Catholic Church in Rīga.

At the same time, the Rīga Municipal Committee Bureau of the Latvian Communist Party notes that there are serious shortcomings in atheistic training in the city. These questions are analyzed only superficially, and rarely, in many primary organizations of the Party, trade unions, and in the Komsomol; they lack concrete information about how religion expresses itself [in society]; their work in propagating the introduction and acceptance of socialist customs and rituals is insufficiently serious; and the strict Leninist principles relating to religion and the church are not realized in everyday life. Sharp rebukes are not given to those Party members and Komsomolers who have become all too comfortable with religious prejudices, reactionary customs, and superstitions. There are also administrative incidents when the feeling of believers are not observed, which is a violation of their constitutional rights.

The executive committees of the Councils of People's Deputies still have not followed precisely the laws relating to cults; they do not organize appropriate events to end the illegal work of the followers of sects.

The Rīga Customs Office in the past two years has registered 226 incidents of religious literature being brought into the country, and has confiscated 920 examples of such literature.

In Rīga there are 48 religious societies, of which 9 are Catholic, 17 Lutheran, 11 Orthodox, 6 Evangelical Christian, 2 Seventh Day Adventist, 1 Old Believer, 1 Evangelical Christian Believers ("fifties"), and 1 synagogue. Over the past few years the revenue of these religious societies has grown. There is a high percentage of baptisms in the cities – 20.2%, burials with religious rituals – 18.5%, and marriages – 3.2%.

Scientific-atheistic propaganda lacks aggressiveness and concreteness. In the city there is still a shortage of atheist cadres. Even though the majority of young boys and girls acquire a middle-level education, a segment of them do not believe in atheism.

Insufficient attention to the need for an atheistic upbringing is paid by the cultural board of the Rīga Municipal Executive Committee, by the newspaper "Rīga's Voice," by the editorial staffs of the large-edition periodicals, and by the primary Party organizations of the creative societies.

In practical efforts at the personal level, it can be noted the propaganda centers of the bourgeois countries use religion in their work against our country.

The reinforcement of atheist training takes on particular importance in the contexts of an increasingly sharp political struggle in the international arena, and the exploitation of religious slogans by reactionary powers concerning the events in Poland, Afghanistan, and Iran.

In concert with the November 3, 1882, decision of the Bureau of the Central Committee of the Latvian Communist Party, entitled "Concerning the strengthening of atheistic training," the Rīga Municipal Committee Bureau of the Latvian Communist Party decides that:

1. The Party regional committees and all of their Party primary organizations should analyze comprehensively and thoroughly the present condition of work being done to promulgate atheism, and its effectiveness in each labor collective, learning institution, and place of residence.

    By March 1, 1982, a plan should be worked out, for implementation from 1982 to 1985, of concrete steps to be taken to strengthen atheistic training among the working masses and the inhabitants of the city.

The primary organizations of the Party should work on the creation of a system of atheist training. The promotion of atheism should use a system of persuasion, employing ideological and political influence in many different forms and means, and devoting particular attention to individualized efforts among [religious] believers.

To ensure that every communist works toward the requirement of the statutes of the Communist Party of the Soviet Union namely, to resolutely struggle against religious prejudice [...]

3. The relevant sections of the Party municipal committees, Party regional organizations, municipal executive committees, municipal Komsomol committees, and Party primary organizations must report in November of 1982 and 1984 on the progress of their work in enacting this decision.

Source: *LVA PA, 102. f., 43. apr., 3. l., pp. 20-22. Original in Russian.*

Document No. 74

Information about the work of religious societies in the Latvian SSR in 1979

1980

		Total	Roman Catholic Church	Evan. Lutheran Church	Orthodox Church	Old Believers	Baptists	Adventists	Jews	Pentecostals
1	Income in 1979 (rubles)	2,110.5	453.5	324.1	921.5	138.0	125.7	74.7	65.9	7.1
2	Costs in 1979 (rubles)	2,107.4	442.2	308.8	946.6	133.1	121.8	75.5	74.1	5.3
3	Remaining money Jan. 01. 1980 (rubles)	875.7	73.5	214.4	404.5	125.6	42.7	8.9	3.8	2.3
4	Number of religious society members	370,604	247,530	38,012	34,498	38,234	5,434	1,832	4,461	153
5	Number of services in a year	42,950	9,203	6,817	12,131	3,768	4,783	2,523	3,325	400
6	Number of persons that took part in religious holidays	156,528	94,722	26,836	10,725	12,451	7,500	1,724	2,300	270

#										
7	Number of baptized children (for Baptists, Adventist and Pentecostals the number of adults) including from other Soviet republics	7,395 130	4,460 121	846 5	1,360 -	543 2	107 2	62 -	- -	17 -
8	Number of marriages	1,163	926	125	63	-	18	6	22	3
9	Number of confessions	1,061,451	983,071	12,757	46,052	15,084	4,487	-	-	-
10	First communion (Roman Catholics) and confirmation (Ev. Lutherans)	2,601	2,503	98	-	-	-	-	-	-
11	Anointment (confirmation for Catholics)	2,244	2,244	-	-	-	-	-	-	-
12	Number of funerals, number of wakes	6,881 688	3,597 -	987 -	1,069 679	845 9	182 -	45 -	155 -	1 -
13	Number of religious societies	633	178	208	89	68	61	23	4	2
14	Number of clergy	381	134	72	62	47	44	19	1	2
15	Number of choirs	3,342	571	1,061	152	124	999	390	7	38

Authorized Agent of the Council   E. Kokars-Trops

Source: *LVA PA, 101. f., 45. apr., 95. l., p. 77. Original in Russian.*

Report of E. Kokars-Trops, authorized agent in Latvia of the Council of Religious Affairs of the Council of Ministers of the USSR, to the Council of Religious Affairs about the use of cult buildings

March 20, 1986

In answer to your February 25, 1986, letter No. 716, I am reporting on those cult buildings in the Latvian SSR that have been removed from the registry and are being used for agricultural and cultural purposes.

Attachment: information on one page, only for the addressee.

Authorized Agent of the Council   E. Kokars-Trops

Information about unused cult Buildings in the Latvian SSR

		Number of Cult Building that are not used for their original purpose			
			Including:		
		Used		Unused	
Confession	Total	National economic objectives	Social and cultural objectives	Total	Of those in critical condition
Russian Orthodox Church	29	11	15	3	3
Evangelical Lutheran Church	66	30	29	7	7
Roman Catholic Church	5	1	4	-	-
Old Believers Church	7	5	1	1	1
Baptist Church	11	6	5	-	-
Total	118	53	54	11	11

Source: *LVA, 1419. f., 3. apr., 265. l., pp. 30-31 . Original in Russian.*

Documents No. 76--81

Struggling with the Émigrés

Document No. 76

Secret correspondence between the USSR Mission in Sweden via the USSR Ministry of Foreign Affairs with the Latvian SSR Ministry of Foreign Affairs, concerning information gathering about Latvian émigrés in Sweden

Moscow, Stockholm, Rīga, September-October 1946

> To the Latvian SSR Deputy Minister of Foreign Affairs
> Comrade J. Avotiņš

Enclosed is a copy of a letter from the advisor to the mission in Sweden, comrade Vazarov. If possible, please send to the Ministry of Foreign Affairs of the USSR the information requested by comrade Vazarov.

Attachment: one page.

5th European section Deputy director   M. Vetrov

Attachment

> September 5, 1946

> To the Deputy Director of the 5th European Section of the Ministry of Foreign Affairs of the USSR, comrade M. Vetrov

In this year on August 14th the USSR mission in a special note asked the Ministry of Foreign Affairs of Sweden for a list of all Soviet citizens who have arrived in Sweden after June 22, 1941, together with their current addresses.

The reply of the Ministry of Foreign Affairs has not yet been received.

However, in view of the fact that up to now the [Swedish] Ministry of Foreign Affairs as well as the Commission on Foreigners Affairs, using various pretexts, have refused to provide us with such information about refugees who are primarily Balts, we can almost certainly assume that the Swedes will also refuse to satisfy our request this time. Nonetheless, it is maximally important in our effort to repatriate Soviet citizens/Balts from Sweden to have complete information about all of our citizens who arrived here as refugees during the war.

The information we have in our possession pertaining to this question is incomplete, and it is necessary to renew it continually. We believe that some of the answers to the questions we that interest us can be obtained from our organs in the Baltic republics which for their own purposes and with their own methods are creating an account of Baltic refugees who left for foreign lands during the war, particularly for Sweden.

Consequently, we ask that you request the Ministers of Foreign Affairs of Estonia, Latvia and Lithuania for information about the number of Estonians, Latvians and Lithuanians who fled to

Sweden during the war, together with their first and last names (and, if possible, their last addresses in Sweden), and their last places of work and residence in the Soviet Union. It would also be desirable to have information about the refugees' relatives living in the USSR.

As soon as you receive this information or some part of it, please do not delay in sending it to us for its use in our repatriation efforts.

Advisor to the USSR Mission in Sweden   S. Vazarov

October 1, 1946

To Deputy Chair of the
Council of Ministers of
the Latvian SSR, comrade
Plūdonis

The Soviet mission in Sweden is compiling a list of the persons who went to Sweden from the Baltic Republics during the war. Since this kind of list is very difficult to prepare there, the mission has turned to us, via the Ministry of Foreign Affairs of the USSR, with a request for information about those persons who according to information in our possession are currently in Sweden.

In this connection, we request you to issue a directive to the Latvian SSR State Security Ministry, the Ministry of the Interior and other relevant organs to submit to the Ministry of Foreign Affairs of the Latvian SSR all the information they have on this question so that we can for notifying the Soviet mission in Stockholm. This information must include the following: last name and first name, previous residence in Latvia, previous type of work, work place, when they left Latvia, and where they currently are in Sweden, as well as the addresses of any relatives that remained behind in Latvia.

Deputy Minister of Foreign Affairs of the Latvian SSR   Avotiņš

Source: *LVA, 1051.f., 1.a. apr., 12.l., pp. 9-11. Original in Russian.*

Document No. 77

Top secret decision of the Bureau of the Central Committee of the Latvian Communist Party, from the special folder entitled "Improving counter-propaganda initiatives among Latvian émigrés"

December 2, 1958

To expand and improve counter-propaganda among Latvian émigrés, the Bureau of the Central Committee of the Latvian Communist party decides:

1. To assign to the editorial staff of the periodical "Voice of the Homeland" [139](comrade Vasiljev) the task of enlarging the descriptions of the accomplishments of the Soviet peoples in the pages of the periodical, stressing in particular Soviet scientific and technical achievements; of popularizing widely scientific and cultural figures, showing the institutional work of the Academy of Sciences of the Latvian SSR; of devoting special attention to the question of the rights of Soviet citizens; of describing to the readers of the periodical the health care and

the guarantees of the education and social system in Latvia; of using clear examples of the expansion of the well-being of the Soviet peoples; and of systematically diffusion of patriotic feelings in the [writings of the] periodical so that the enemies of Soviet peoples will not be able to recruit among them traitors, spies, and saboteurs. Also, together with state security organs, the continuation of the unmasking of the reactionary émigré elite and the publication of open letters and invitations from the relatives, associates, and friends of émigrés who live in the Latvian SSR.

2. To assign to the Radio Broadcast and Television Committee of the Council of Ministers of the Latvian SSR (comrade Lēmanis) the task of improving the Committee's radio broadcast program "About Returning to the Homeland" by enhancing broadcast quality by means of focusing primary attention on propaganda depicting the accomplishments of the USSR and Latvian Republic in economic life, culture and science; on the rights and conditions of youth; and of using the Latvian revolutionary tradition as propaganda, and in the radio broadcasts, using pointed counter-propaganda material that unmasks the anti-national work of the Latvian émigrés. To pay particular attention to the quality of the form of broadcasts by assigning the preparation to its own most qualified employees. To prepare the broadcasts according to a plan and to regularly send them to the Committee "Repatriating to the Homeland", and to submit to the Propaganda and Agitation Section of the Central Committee of the Latvian Communist Party the broadcast plans and schedules.

3. To assign the editorial staffs of the Republic's periodicals and journals the tasks of initiating the thorough unmasking of the anti-national, anti-Soviet, and counter-revolutionary work of the émigré leadership, individual émigré ringleaders, and their organization; of showing the true conditions of the masses of émigrés and for this purpose using returned, repatriated émigrés to prepare articles, carefully selecting the authors and including in the project as a whole historians, literary specialists, critics, and the most experienced journalists.

4. To support the proposal of the State Security Committee of the Latvian SSR Council of Ministers to create in the Latvian SSR a special group called "Repatriating to the Homeland" and to involve in this project notable cultural and artistic figures as well as other authorities who are known in foreign lands, include them in the preparation of propaganda material, and establish contacts with the most notable and vulnerable émigrés in order to encourage them to return to the Republic of Latvia.

5. To assign to the Latvian SSR Council of Ministers' Committee on State Security (comrade Vēvers) the tasks of :
   a. Together with the editorial staff of the periodical "Voice of the Homeland" and the Latvian State Publishers, to organize the distribution of a brochure depicting the lives of returned émigrés and repatriated persons, and unmasking the destructive work of foreign nationalist organizations, thus enabling the distribution of the brochure, with assistance of the committee "Repatriating to the Homeland," in foreign countries.
   b. To create in foreign countries groups of émigrés loyal and sympathetic towards us and to organize events.

6. To assign to the Latvian SSR State Economic Council Paper and Wood-products Industrial Board (comrade Vimba) the task of ensuring that the editorial staff of "The Voice of the Homeland" and the Latvian State Publishers have "dictionary" style thin paper for printing the materials sent to foreign countries.

7. In order to better concentrate [in one place] all Latvian-language periodicals and literature published in foreign countries:
   a. To suggest to the Committee of State Security of the Latvian SSR Council of Ministers (comrade Vēvers) that it examine the question of giving to the special collection of the Fundamental Library of the Academy of Sciences of the Latvian SSR the materials that that Committee possesses that is not needed for their operations;

b. To assign to the Latvian SSR Council of Ministers' Primary Board of Preserving Military and State Secrets in the Press (comrade Šneiders) the task of sending the aforementioned literature and periodicals to the special collection of the Fundamental Library of the Academy of Sciences of the Latvian SSR (except for the material to be destroyed or the material to be sent to the Central Committee of the Latvian Communist Party), in the order it is received and after coordination with the Latvian Communist Party Central Committee's Propaganda and Agitation Section;

c. To assign to the Fundamental Library of the Academy of Sciences of the Latvian SSR (comrade Liepiņš) the task of keeping the aforementioned literature and periodicals, and to circulate it for research purposes only with the strictest adherence to the rules of storage and use of special collections'material.

8. To assign to the Ministry of Foreign Affairs of the Latvian SSR (comrade Ostro) and the Ministry of Culture of the Latvian SSR (comrade Kalpiņš) the tasks of:

a. Sending to the USSR embassies in the countries with concentrations of émigré masses: political literature, literature, Rīga Cinema Studio art and chronicle films, photo exhibits, and albums about the life of working persons in Soviet Latvia; description of Rīga, Rīga-Jūrmala, Sigulda, Cēsis and other tourist brochures and other propaganda material;

b. Studying the possibility of, and submitting a proposal to the Central Committee of the Latvian Communist Party regarding, invitations to congenially inclined notable Latvian émigré figures to come to Latvia for organized events, and coordinating with the Soviet embassy in Sweden a proposal to explore the possibility of sending delegations of leading cultural, scientific, youth, and sport figures to Sweden and other countries where there are concentrations of émigrés, and the possibility of inviting delegations of workers from Sweden.

9. Assign to the Latvian SSR Ministry of Culture (comrade Kalpiņš), Ministry of Communications (comrade Aleksandrov) and the Ministry of Trade (comrade Jansons) the task of creating a section in the book-trade enterprise "Book through the Post" which would receive orders from and send books and cultural goods to foreign countries.

10. To assign to the Latvian State Shipping (comrade Avots) the task of making sure that the films of the Rīga Cinema Studio are placed on ships that travel to foreign countries.

11. To suggest that the Latvian SSR Council of Ministers provide the resources to the Latvian Society for Cultural Contacts with Foreign Lands for the mailing of literature and other materials, with the assistance of Soviet embassies and the committee "Repatriation to the Homeland."

12. To request the Central Committee of the Communist Party of the USSR that it:

a. Allow the Latvian SSR Communications Ministry and the Latvian SSR Council of Ministers Committee of Radio Broadcasts and Television to organize a twice weekly 40-minute evening radio broadcast in the Latvian language to the Scandinavian countries where there are Latvian émigré centers.

b. Suggest to the committee "Returning to the Homeland" that it submit a more detailed and more operationalized report on strengthening and improving the work of organizing counter-propaganda among émigrés';

c. Allow the editorial staff of the periodical "Cīņa' to have one correspondent in Germany and one in Sweden at the embassies of the USSR.

Secretary of the Central Committee of the Latvian Communist Party   Kalnbērziņš

Source: *LVA PA, 101. f., 21. apr., 48a. 1., pp. 26-28. Original in Russian.*

Excerpt from the report of the advisor to USSR Embassy in Sweden, N. Voinov, to the Minister of Foreign Affairs of the Latvian SSR, V. Kalpiņš, about popularizing the art of A. Vinters in the Latvian SSR

Stockholm, February 24, 1959

Supplementing our letter No. 141/zv, January 31, 1959, we inform you that Alfrēds Vinters, the conductor of theater orchestras, has told us that unfortunately he could not put on guest performances in Rīga in March, and has asked us to table the question of his guest performances to a later date. His statement is corroborated by the fact that the primary obstacle to the guest performance is that he has been able to secure a good position at one of the clubs in Stockholm. From the conversations with Vinters it is apparent that he fears the reaction to his Latvian trip by the Latvian émigré elite, and fears also that he will lose his job.

Putting aside the inability of A. Vinters to give guest performances in Riga now, the Embassy views it as useful to not break our work with Vinters simply because the ringleaders of the Latvian émigré community are upset with Vinters' decision to establish contacts with the Homeland and will try to "compromise" Vinters in the future. To pull Vinters even further away from the influence of the émigré ranks, the embassy views the following as possible:

1. To organize this year in March and April one more radio broadcast of Vinters' recordings and to include in them Vinters' newest work.

2. To publish in the periodical "Voice of the Homeland"[139] the text and music of the song ("May song unite us") that Vinters wrote for his concerts in Latvia, assuming the song has been composed at a respectable artistic level.

3. To place in the newspaper "Literature and Art" a mid-size review of the radio broadcast of Vinters'records in Latvia, written by Viktors Sams (who worked with Vinters in Latvia).

4. To sign a contract with Vinters through the A/O "Meždunarodnaja Kņiga[140]" concerning the distribution in Sweden of records of Soviet Latvia's classical, folk and stage music.

5. To organize the sending to Vinters from different representatives of the Latvian working masses listeners'letters about the radio broadcasts of his records, together with the question of when he will be visiting the Homeland. [...]

Advisor to the Embassy of the USSR in Sweden   N. Voinov

Source: *LVA, 678. f., 1. apr., 177.l., p. 92. Original in Russian.*

Top secret report of L. Avdjukevičs, the Chair of the State Security Committee of the Latvian SSR, to the Central Committee of the Latvian Communist Party about the activities of Latvian émigré centers

May 5, 1980

Recently the State Security Committee of the Latvian SSR received information testifying to the start of certain kinds of destructive activities aimed at Soviet Latvia and led by émigré centers abroad; behind these activities stand the spy agencies of the USA and the People's Republic of China. The Latvian émigrés who collected in the capitalist countries after World War Two currently number about 120,000 persons, of whom 60% live in North America, 20% in Australia, while the rest are distributed across the Western European countries.

The older generation of émigrés are primarily from the propertied class and the bourgeois intelligentsia; many of them collaborated with the Hitlerites and were influenced by Nazi propaganda. When the Soviet Army routed the fascist forces at the end of the war, these persons fled to foreign countries and they fundamentally maintain a position of hostility toward the USSR.

The Latvian émigrés who have settled in the West are primarily middle-class, as analysis of their situation shows; a considerable number of the younger generation have received the highest education. The USA does not place any obstacles in their paths when they are hired into jobs. More than 200 émigrés are employed in different USA governmental institutions, a substantial number of Latvians work in scientific fields as lecturers at institutions of higher learning, etc. A similar situation obtains in other countries where there are émigré colonies. Many émigrés – members of youth organizations -- have not remained neutral in the diffusion of leftist ideas, and have moved toward the improvement of contacts with the Latvian SSR in opposition to the conservative émigré elite.

In recent years in western countries there has been the so-called "new immigration." These are persons of Jewish nationality who have left the USSR under the rubric of family reunification and have settled to live primarily in Israel, the GFR and the USA. In view of the characteristics of these people (high level of education, social activism), the Jews leaving the USSR, just as the Latvian émigrés, are used by our enemies' spy agencies to carry out destructive activities aimed at the USSR.

Many objective factors have combined to produce a division of labor among the many émigré centers in their destructive activities aimed against the USSR.

The émigré centers based in the USA -- such as "The World Association of Free Latvians" (PBLA), the American Latvian Association (ALA) -- attach particular importance to anti-Soviet propaganda through political actions, campaigns of lies, and the organization of ideological diversions. Using the efforts of the central organization of Baltic-origin émigrés, they pushed through the US Congress and Senate a special Baltic resolution that asks the US government, among other things, to take the stand at international forums such as the upcoming Madrid summit[141] condemning the supposed forced annexation of the Baltic republics to the USSR.

Many organized and harmful propaganda activities are expected in connection with the forty-year anniversary of the renewal of Soviet power in the Baltic – from press conferences to official announcements by employees of the US government and the People's Republic of China. Similar activities are being prepared for the summer Olympic games in Moscow, particularly in Tallinn[142]. In advance of the Madrid summit, there has been a heightened gathering of untruthful information about the political and economic conditions in the Republic. With this goal in mind, the émigré ringleaders -- Spilners, Pavlovskis, Kadelis, Meierovics -- and other proven agents of the USA spy agency, in 1979 visited many countries with Latvian émigré colonies.

To concentrate all information, a special information office has been created by the PBLA. In view of increased international tensions because of the faults of the Carter administration and the heightened activity of the CIA, the Latvian émigré centers in the US are forming coalitions with other anti-Soviet émigré organizations, and with the support of the Department of State and some congressmen are organizing seminars, preparing propaganda material to influence public opinion, and placing emphasis on working on [the opinions] of American youth. Characteristically, a much higher level of anti-Soviet work has been achieved by the united actions of émigré organizations, their coordination and consolidation.

Because of the geographic closeness of Sweden to the Republic and the active tourism and cultural exchanges [between the two countries], Latvian émigré organizations in Sweden -- the "LSDSP AK" and the "Latvian National Foundation" (LNF) -- are particularly active along numerous channels in gathering political and economic information about the Republic. These organization interview émigrés who visit the Republic, looking for untruthful information that can be used as propaganda in international forums and to instruct other émigrés before their visits to the USSR.

They follow closely the Republic's press and the public material in radio broadcasts from Riga, and organize massive amounts of information for delivery to the spy agencies of our enemy.

Émigrés come to the Latvian SSR to fulfill certain assignments: to find approaches to persons who are ideologically close to the émigré community through relatives and other contacts; to gather negative information about the conditions in the Republic and to seek information about armed forces units; and, finally, to recruit individuals among our citizens who can be given espionage assignments, these beings masked by the interests of the Latvian anti-Soviet émigré centers.

All of the information acquired in these ways, depending on its relative value, is then used by émigré propaganda organs or in propaganda broadcasts by the radio stations "Liberty" and "Voice of America"; the most valuable information is given to the USA Department of State or the American spy agencies.

Another channel for receiving political and economic information about the Republic is by means of "scientific contacts" through the mediation of the "Association for the Advancement of Baltic Studies" [143] in the USA and the "Baltic Institute" (BI) in Sweden. These research centers organize regular scientific symposia about the wide spectrum of problems relating to the countries of the Baltic Sea basin and are also used by enemy spy agencies.

In the last few years the "AABS" and the "BI" have experienced significant changes in their politics. Following the recommendations of spy agencies, the most compromised émigré ringleaders were forced to leave these organizations, to be replaced by émigrés from the academic world who are chosen by the spy agencies. After the change in leadership, the mentioned centers have sought under the guise of scientific interest to expand contacts as much as possible with the Republic's scientists, including those who work in the humanistic sciences.

Operational work in the Republic and an analysis of the enemy's efforts both testify to the fact that the spy agencies of the USA and its NATO allies have activated Latvian and Jewish anti-Soviet émigré organizations for use in destructive purposes. Thus there is a much more purposeful use of tourism, private [contacts], scientific and cultural exchanges, as well as visits to the Republic of diplomats and journalists from the USA and major capitalist countries.

Along with the attempts at spying, the enemy is still making attempts at establishing conditions for the emergence in the Republic of an organized nationalist underground.

During 1978-1979, information from émigrés known to the State Security Committee organs showed that there were 9 attempts to express direct interest in dissidents and persons who had earlier been tried for committing particularly dangerous crimes against the state.

The anti-Soviet efforts by foreigners -- Latvian and Jewish émigrés – at targeting particular individuals in the Republic remains among the most malevolent of their activities. In 1979, 2,706 émigrés of all categories visited the Republic. From 1978-1979, about 50 instances of the involvement of Soviet citizens in anti-Soviet propaganda were found on this side. Different kinds of approaches and deceptions were used [but the émigrés] to accomplish this. The leader of the "LSDSP AK" in Sweden, B. Kalniņš, in a meeting in 1977 reported, among other things, on one such method, allegedly using for the first time the sending of undeveloped film to the LSSR containing all the issues of the newspaper "Freedom" for the past two years. Furthermore, he recommended the use of this method for sending in anti—Soviet material in the future, using persons unrelated to the "Foreign Committee."

Furthering the same goals, the enemy seeks to use the international mails as well as Soviet citizens returning from officially sanctioned foreign trips. In the period from November 1, 1978, to November 1, 1979, there were confiscated more than 4,000 harmful and ideologically dangerous periodical press publications, newspaper clippings, anti-Soviet books, journals, and items of religious propaganda.

Much material has been gathered about the methods used by spy agencies, émigré organizations, and centers in order to engender in Soviet citizens the desire to collaborate, betray the homeland, and not return to the USSR. Such propositions have been directed at Soviet citizens who are in the USA and Sweden for work-related or personal reasons, as well as at individual citizens of the Republic who have met with émigrés arriving from foreign lands with whom they have close contact. In 1978, among the Soviet citizens who had gone to capitalist states for personal reasons, 30 had had suggested to them by Latvian émigrés that they not return to the homeland, but in 1979 – 40.

Determination has been made of individual instances when inhabitants of the LSSR, on their own initiative, have sought connections with spy agencies and anti-Soviet centers.

Gathered material shows that there has been a noticeable increase in the number of trips to the Republic by emissaries of Latvian, and especially Jewish, anti-Soviet organizations. Thus the emissary of the "LSDSP AK"-- "Johanna"-- visited the Latvian SSR six times, and being on assignment from the "Foreign Committee," researched individual persons among the intelligentsia; gathered information about dissidents and about the traitors to the Homeland, Skudra and Treibergs; met with the anti-Soviet figures Kalniņš and Elsbergs with whom we conducted preventive work because of their nationalistic activities.

Many Jewish emissaries usually visited persons who had been denied the right to leave the country for reasons of state, as well as active Jewish nationalists. The emissaries took notes about the condition of Jews in the Republic currently, and conducted instructional sessions for organizing and continuing harmful activity.

All of the matters described above are being made know so that they can be put to use in the implementation of USSR's Central Committee decisions "Concerning improvements in the vigilance of Soviet people" and "Concerning further improvements in ideological and political education. "[144]

In 1979 and in the months that have passed in 1980 we have opened many operational files concerning ongoing contacts with émigrés; in the cases of more than 600 persons who have expressed nationalistic and other negative sentiments, preventive work has been carried out.

There has been a meeting of the Collegium of the Latvian State Security Committee in which a detailed review was made of the enemy's harmful efforts to use anti-Soviet Latvian and Jewish émigré organizations and centers; activities were organized as a counterweight to the enemy's aspirations in the Latvian SSR.

Chair of the Latvian SSR State Security Committee   L. Avdjukevics

Source: *LVA PA, 101. f., 42. apr., 96. l., pp. 39-44. Original in Russian.*

Secret report of J. Bojārs, advisor to the Ministry of Foreign Affairs of the Latvian SSR, about the visit to Latvia of USA General Consul in Leningrad, T. Buchanan, on February 6-9, 1978

February 13, 1978

During his time in the Latvian SSR, T. Buchanan behaved himself as could be expected from an official representative of our principal enemy. He did not forget in any situation to work the citizens of the USSR around him for interesting news about the economic and political conditions in the USSR. At the same time, he was no less energetic in expressing his views about the reality of our daily lives, which mostly slid into efforts to discredit our existing order and economic system. Furthermore, Buchanan has a habit of speaking extensively and confusedly, which caused certain difficulties in interrupting his observations.

The impression was strong that the two Americans had prepared carefully for their trip to the LSSR, and had researched ahead of time substantial amount of material about some aspects of our politics and our social and economic life.

The job of the LSSR Ministry of Foreign Affairs during T. Buchanan's visit was to make sure the Americans could not gather the information they sought, and that their provocative announcements were refuted and unmasked as being propagandistic lies. For this purpose the Ministry of Foreign Affairs used materials from our new Constitution, the Party congress, UN and other international treaties; data from US and our own statistics; positive examples from the reality of our daily life [that showed] the advantages of our system; as well as materials from the American press that were useful for us and that created considerable unease in the General Consul. Also, we have to note that in the first days of the visit Buchanan went about his work without much delicacy and made mistakes in his comments that our side exploited immediately. Understanding this, Buchanan from then on changed his tactics, and tried to work in a much more nuanced manner, no longer posing "crude" questions and making pronouncements; but he continued to attempt to gather information that was of interest to him. At the same time he tried to neutralize the officials from the Ministry of Foreign Affairs accompanying him by asking that they translate conversations for his wife.

During discussions with the Chair of the Rīga Municipal Executive Committee, Buchanan noted that in the USA and in other capitalist countries there can be years of bad harvests, but that shortages of meat are never felt. For [such shortages here], he said, the blame should attach to the "Soviet economic system and our government's poor efficiency. But maybe there is no meat here because it gets sent to Russia?" After receiving an answer about the national makeup of the inhabitants of Rīga he started to doubt these numbers, claiming that he had information that placed the city's Latvian-nationality inhabitants at 30% or less, which [to him] demonstrated russification. Buchanan asked about the nationality question at almost every meeting. He asked whether there was an observable mandatory russification process going on, and what were our thoughts about whether the LSSR would still exist in 10-15 years.

Later, at an official breakfast organized in the name of the Chair of the Rīga Municipal Executive Committee, Buchanan asked the following question: "Does the letter of the 12 Latvian Communists express the though of only these particular communists or those of the entire Latvian nation?" In response, the General Consul was told that he had apparently made a mistake, because if he were talking about document falsified by émigrés then it involves 17 communists.[145] With respect to its contents, the [letter] is a smear of lies created by émigrés and obviously could in no way reflect the thoughts of the Latvian nation.

Buchanan also asked the question – how many persons in Rīga are admitted into the Communist Party of the Soviet Union per year, and why is this number shrinking. And, could not one infer from this that the desire of the Soviet people – particularly among the young – to join the Party is diminishing, and infer further that the Party's authority among young persons has declined? Buchanan was also interested in how many of those that joined the Communist Party were Latvian.

Further, he was interested in knowing if in the LSSR there is discrimination against Latvians, and what were the competence and powers of the LSSR government in comparison with those of the Union government.

In Ventspils, the visit to a fishing kolkhoz impressed the General Consul; he reluctantly admitted that such an impressive fishing cooperative did not exist in the USA and that indeed a great deal of attention is being devoted to satisfying the social needs of our fishermen.

At the official dinner organized for him in Ventspils, the General Consul started to argue that that the Soviet press is not known for its objectivity, and that Americans are surprised that in the USSR leading political figures suddenly disappear from the political stage. Moreover, unsatisfactory explanation for this is provided in the press. The American was reminded that the in the USA many well-known presidents and political figures disappear from the stage in far more tragic circumstances when they are killed. Also, the American press is not always sufficiently objective; one simply has to remember how the Warren report was reported in the press.

Further, Buchanan began to explain in detail how in the USA there is no longer any noticeable race discrimination. The Carter government has begun actively to include Negroes in the apparatus of the state, and at present in the USA in the hiring process whites are frequently discriminated against in favor of blacks. Here, from our side, the comment was heard that apparently some states have not yet abandoned the practice, as described by Talleyrand, of hiring honest persons into diplomatic posts in order to send them to foreign countries to lie.

At the end of the American diplomatic events in Ventspils, in which American specialists from the Ventspils harbor construction project participated, the General Consul told the representative of the LSSR Ministry of Foreign Affairs that he had received complaints from the American specialists about restrictions on their freedoms "from the chekists." The representative of the Ministry of Foreign Affairs asked that these complains be described in detail so that the appropriate offices could be notified. Nevertheless, Buchanan did not submit such a report, even after he was made the offer a second time by the VURN of the Ministry of the Interior of the LSSR.

Similarly, we had prepared a meeting at the Visa and Registration Division of the Ministry of the Interior of the LSSR. We had already received a list of American complaints on specific emigration cases, and we had prepared a report on each of the persons mentioned in the complaints. Buchanan asked questions in the Visa and Registration Division about what criteria the LSSR state authorities used to permit Soviet citizens to travel to foreign countries, why is it easier to go to Israel and not the USA, and, in settling questions about family reunification, what persons are regarded [in the category of] parents. Further, he reported that Americans and the Congress did not understand why the USSR placed various obstacles in the way of family reunification.

During discussions with the Deputy Chair of the State Planning Committee of the LSSR, E. Āboliņš, the General Consul again expressed interest in the number of employed inhabitants in the LSSR; in their nationality composition; in the in-migration of labor from other republics; and in methods of raising labor productivity: was it not accomplished by intensification of labor in view of labor shortages. He also asked questions about the LSSR State Planning Committee ZPI.

He was also interested in the wage system for labor, the politics and priorities of distributing labor to construction work, and the rates of gasoline use in the republic. To all of his questions, Buchanan received considered and clear answers that left him no chance of gathering information of a strategic character, and at the same time did not offer the opportunity of provocative explanations.

The carefully prepared visit to the Northwestern Energy System United Dispatcher Board included showing the American examples of the advantages of the Soviet energy systems compared to the capitalist states, including the USA, particularly in the realm of the accident-free and secure work places.

In the end, Buchanan left the impression of being a very persistent person of the kind who is not embarrassed to ask even shameless questions as long as they provide the information he wants. He reacts unbelievably poorly to criticism, particularly criticism of the USA. In everything else the General Consul is a sociable, polite person, who uses alcohol very moderately, and never forgets about his work.

The General Consul received considerable help from the Vice Consul, Oscar Klajat. He carefully wrote down all discussions and supplied Buchanan with needed statistics in critical situations.

The General Consul's wife, Nessy Shaw, was interested in the Soviet system for teaching impaired children. During the visit she did not ask any provocative questions.

Report prepared by the advisor to the Ministry of Foreign Affairs of the LSSR

J. Bojārs

Source: *LVA PA, 101.f., 43. apr., 78. l., pp. 5-8. Original in Russian.*

Document No. 81

Secret instructions from the Secretariat of the Central Committee of the Latvian Communist Party concerning the preparation of documents for foreign travel and the review of these by departments of the Central Committee.

May 6, 1980

Applications by ministries, institutions, and organizations for travel to foreign countries, except tourist groups, are submitted for review to the Foreign Travel Commission of the Central Committee of the Latvian Communist Party through the relevant departments of the Central Committee. Materials for tourist groups are submitted to the Commission by the Trade Union Organization of the Latvian Republic and the Central Committee of the Lenin Society of Communist Youth in Latvia.

I

In order to review applications for trips to foreign countries, the following fundamental documents are necessary:

        -The application letter from the relevant ministry, institution, or organization,

        -A character recommendation,

        -An objective biographical report.

The application letter: together with the signature of the director of the ministry, institution, or organization (or the first deputy), the application must contain the following specific information: last name, name, father's name (in full), year of birth, party affiliation, workplace, trade, to what country or group of countries the trip is intended, the length of the trip (whether a one-time trip or repeated trips), purpose, and the anticipated departure time. If travel includes [the applicant's] wife, then her last name, name, father's name, year of birth, and party affiliation must be included.

The application letter must include mention of the institutional document (letter, telegram, teletype, relevant plan for international contacts) on the basis of which the trip is taking place. It is obligatory to include this document's number and date.

A letter is submitted for each individual traveler, in one copy, on the organization's letterhead.

For collectives in the arts, in sports, or [other such fields], one letter only is submitted, together with an attached list of names arranged according to proper form.

In the event that a trip to a country is changed for a trip to a different country or to several countries, or if the time period is changed, a new application must be submitted.

Character recommendation: this is submitted from the place of work (or education), and it is signed by the unit's director, the Party secretary of the unit, the Chair of the Trade Union Organization (for members of the VLKJS – also the Komsomol Committee Secretary). Only one of the signatures can be that of a substitute. Furthermore, in the character recommendation it must be stated that the Party organization (Party committee or Party bureau) [as a whole] is making the recommendation to the given country or group of countries, and there must be reference to the number of the [meeting] protocol and date.

Recommendation to capitalist and newly developing countries, Yugoslavia, Republic of Cuba, Socialist Republic of Vietnam, People's Republic of Korea for any length of time, as well as to the People's Republic of Bulgaria, People's Republic of Hungary, People's Republic of Germany, People's Republic of Mongolia, People's Republic of Poland, Socialist Republic of Romania, Socialist Republic of Czechoslovakia for one year or more, are reviewed by the Party Municipal and Region Committee and are signed by the Party Municipal Committee, Secretary of the Region Committee. Furthermore in the recommendation it is noted that the submitters were recommended by the Party Municipal Committee, Region committee for the trip to the foreign country (the country, the time, and the objective are noted).

Trips to the PB, PRH, PRG, PRM, PRP, RSR and CSR for a year or less are reviewed by the Foreign Travel Commission on the basis of the primary Party organization's recommendation.

Character recommendations are normally given [only] to workers who have been in their most recent place of work not less than a year, and are valid for one year from the moment of their issuance by the primary Party organization. They must reflect the recommendee's moral, political, and everyday-behavioral traits, their social-political traits, and their relations with their family. If they have been divorced, it should be so noted, as well as whether the administrative and Party organizations are familiar with the conditions of the divorce.

The recommendation can be submitted to the Commission as the second typewritten copy (because the first copy is sent to the All-Union Ministry and [relevant] offices).

A character recommendation of the wife is going on her husband's assignment with him or as a member of his family does not have to be submitted.

The objective biographical report: must be typewritten in three copies (for persons who are going to the PRB, RH, RG, PRM, PRP, RSR and CSR for a period of time up to one year, the biographical reports are to be submitted in one copy.)

In the report, the length of the trip, the country, and the reason for the trip must be shown.

For all of the questions on the report, clear and comprehensive answers must be given. A complete work record must be provided, showing the month and year [for each entry]; the place of work must be stated without abbreviation, and the precise name of the workplace must be shown; [in case of] service in the Russian army – in what military district and in what military unit. All requested information about nearest relatives must be given, including the mother's and wives' maiden names, if they have been tried and have received temporary or permanent punishment. Also relatives living abroad must be listed.

In all of the documents (in the application letter, objective report, character recommendation), the recommendee's name, father's name, and surname must be written in the same way, that is, consistent with the names in the passport.

The biographical report must include information from the medical commission's decision [evaluating] the foreign trip by reference to the [applicant's] health ("By reference to the medical report, there is no obstacle to a trip to … [name of country here]" […]

Source: *LVA PA, 101. f., 45. apr., 96. l., pp. 32-35. Original in Russian.*

Documents No. 82-90

The paradoxes of alleged social equality

Document No. 82

Excerpts from a secret decision of the Bureau of the Rīga Municipal Committee of the Latvian Communist Party, entitled "Bringing order to the supply of bread for the population of Rīga"

October 12, 1946

The Bureau of the Rīga Municipal Committee of the Latvian C(B)P notes that the Party's Municipal and Regional Committees, the Municipal and Regional Executive Committees, the Ministry of Trade of the LSSR, the Municipal Trade Section, the Ration Card Control and Review Board, and the leaders of the Rīga municipal Party and economic organizations have not understood and comprehended the September 27, 1946, decision of the All-Union C(B)P Central Committee and the Council of Ministers of the USSR concerning the economics of bread resources and their significance to the state. As a result, the Rīga Municipal Party, soviets, and economic institutions have allowed the uncontrolled distribution of bread ration cards[146] in October, and the haphazard validation of those cards; instead leading to the execution of the ruling of September 27, 1946, of the All-Union C(b)P Central Committee and Council of Ministers of the USSR, this [lack of procedure] has led to an increase in the use of bread in the first quarter of October of this year.

In order to bring about the tightest control in the distribution of ration cards, and the unquestioned execution of the law of September 27, 1946, as promulgated by the All-Union C(B)P Central Committee and Council of Ministers of the USSR, the Bureau of the Rīga Municipal Committee of the Latvian C(B)P Central Committee rules:

1. To assign to the Municipal Executive Committee (comrade Deglavs), the Secretaries of the Region Committees of the Latvian C(B)P and the Region Executive Committee's Chairs, from October 12 to 15 of this year and with help from the Party, councils, Komsomol, and the active elements of the labor unions, the task of ensuring that distribution of bread ration cards in all of the businesses of the city of Rīga and in all institutions and supervisory boards of buildings is being done correctly …

4. To assign the Municipal Executive Committee, the Region Executive Committee, and the leaders of businesses and institutions the task of removing without delay from the normed supply system all those uncooperative and solitary tradesmen who do contract work for the state's local and cooperative factory enterprises as well as the rest of the unemployed elements and their families.

5. To assign to the Municipal Executive Committee and the Jūrmala Region Executive Committee the task of ensuring that normed supplies go only to workers and service personnel in state enterprises and institutions, students at technical schools, and 1st and 2nd class war invalids who do not have a farmstead. Other inhabitants should be removed from the normed supply system.

6. To assign to the leaders of cooperatives, local factories, and other economic organizations the task of removing from the normed bread supply system the handicraftsmen [home workers] who do not meet their assigned quotas (excepting 1st and 2nd class war invalids)…

Secretary of the Municipal Committee of the Latvian C(B)P   K. Novikov

Source: *LVA PA, 101. f., 9. apr., 92. l., pp. 117-119. Original in Russian.*

Document No. 83

Telegram No. 50 from the government of the USSR to the Chair of the Council of Ministers of the Latvian SSR, V. Lācis, about the termination of distribution of groceries and industrial products to leading Soviet and party officials at no cost

December 23, 1947

With respect to the cancellation of the ration card system[147] for supplying the population, it is necessary to cancel also the corresponding system of distribution of products and factory goods for free to the leaders of the councils and the Party. The distribution of free products and factory goods, the use of resources from the Social and Living Conditions Betterment Fund for the distribution of free goods for summer cottages, and other forms of free distribution of products and factory goods must all be ended. In Moscow, after reviewing this questions, the Council of Ministers resolved on January 1, 1948, to end the allocation of free products and factory goods for workers of central organizations and departments and for the leading figures of the councils and the Party, but in its place to create temporary money supplements to the supplementable work wage.[148] Proceeding from this, the All-Union Council of Ministers of the USSR and the Central Committee of the All-Union Communist (b) Party proposes:

1. From January 1, 1948, to end the existing system of distributing free products and factory goods [...], to stop the use of the resources of the Social and Living Conditions Betterment Fund for the distribution of free products for summer cottages, and other forms of distribution of free products and factory goods to the leading employees of the councils and the Party.

2. From January 1, 1948, to create for leading officials of the councils and Party (not including functionaries of the Ministry of the Interior and the Ministry of State Security) who currently receive free products and factory goods a supplemental bonus to their monthly salary that is two or three times their base salary per month. To submit to the Council of Ministers of the USSR and the Central Committee of the Union Communist (b) Party the decision made on this subject, attaching the list of officials and the amount of their intended money supplement.

3. To open to the free market all of the closed types of special stores, and factory goods stores and centers, that served the leading officials of the councils and the Party.

J. Stalin
A. Zhdanov

Source: *LVA PA, 101. f., 10. apr., 100.l., pp. 92-95. Original in Russian.*

Excerpts from a circular from the Latvian SSR State Labor Savings Bank and the Chair of the State Credit Board to the heads of savings banks about procedures for submitting information for preliminary work in the creation of state loans for the economic development of the people of the USSR

April 9, 1949

The Latvian SSR State Labor Savings Bank and the Board of State Credit asks you to submit information every third day on the preparatory work for the realization of the new loan.[149] In the [submitted] information, the following must be highlighted:

1. When a decision was made by a District (Municipal, Regional) Executive Committee and District (Municipal and Regional) Committee of the Latvian Communist (B) Party about preparations for the realization of loans.
2. What number of the working commissions must be in enterprises and institutions and what number of those have been reviewed and how many organized anew.
3. The number of localities that have chosen and approved village council representatives in favor of the loan, and the number of the latter.
4. How district executive committees and district committees chose the responsible representatives for visits to the localities and when will they travel to them.
5. When were instructional meetings held:
   a. With secretaries of the enterprises, and an institution's party organizers;
   b. With the parish party organizers and the secretary of the parish party committee;
   c. With representatives of the parish executive committee;
   d. With the chair of the village council;
   e. With the chair of the kolkhoz;
   f. With the leaders of the enterprises and institutions and the chief accountants;
   g. With the chairs of the commissions for [gathering] support from subordinates;
   h. With the secretaries of the Komsomol organizations;
   i. With the school directors;
   j. With the village activists;
   k. With the responsible representatives of the Party district committees and the district executive committees who will travel to the localities.
6. When agitation and instructional material about the loans was distributed to the enterprises, institutions, localities, and village councils.
7. When the aides of the tax inspectors were given goals.
8. What number of enterprises, institutions, and localities were reviewed with respect to their preparedness to realize the loan, and when the results were discussed in meetings of executive committees and Party committees.

   The information must be submitted to the Board precisely on the 15th, 18th, 21st, 24th, and 27th of April.

   We draw your attention to the fact that the deadlines for submitting the information must be observed. [...]

The Head of the Latvian SSR State Labor Savings Bank and State Credit Board Veinbergs
The Head of the Operational Section Cirkovs

Source: *LVA, 511.f., 2. apr., 37. l., pp. 1-2 (copy of original). Original in Latvian.*

Document No. 85

Excerpts from the minutes (No. 3) of the meeting of the leaders of the district financial departments of the Latvian SSR about the pace of the state loan campaign in rural regions

May 26, 1952

[…] The agenda

1. Report of the leaders of the district financial departments about the pace of farmer subscriptions to and the collection of resources for the State Loan[149] for the People's Economic Development of the USSR (issued in 1952).

Reporting: leaders of district financial departments: comrades Ruskis, P. – Dobele, Bogdanovs, F. – Ilūkste, Seliņš, A. – Rēzekne, Stjopkins, A. – Alsunga, Robežnieks, V. – Cesvaine. […]

Comrade Seliņš – Rēzekne

This year the Rēzekne district has not reached its assigned number of subscriptions and the collection of resources is going slowly. The primary reason for the slowness of the collection is that more than 50% of the representatives did not take loans into account. Some of the directors of kolkhozes have raised the question of erasing the subscription of loans in ten months time. A different reason – the kolkhozes do not pay their kolkhozniki for the all days worked. The kolkhozniki say that they will pay the money for loans after they have received wages for all days worked. Today, the executive committee is discussing the question of loans for farmers' subscriptions, and the village council chairs and kolkhoz directors are taking part in the discussion. The primary weight must be put not on the [money] received for worked days, but on the kolkhozniki's actual wages […]

Comrade Stjopkins – Alsunga

The collection of actual money for the subscriptions is happening in a completely unsatisfactory way. In May, not enough work was done in order to prepare resources for the repayment of loans. In the kolkhoz named for Rainis, the director, his deputy and their brigade have not taken the loan into account. The kolkhoz takes little of its products to the market. The kolkhozes have not paid their kolkhozniki for the worked days of 1951. The kolkhozniki report that they will pay the money after they have received from the kolkhoz money for their worked days. Of the 12 village councils, not one has completely collected the money for the subscriptions […]

Comrade Vīndedze[150]

[…] It is wrong to raise the question of erasing the subscriptions of loans relative to the [money] received for worked days. Every kolkhoznik has his family plot and can pay independently of whether or not they have received wages for worked days. They should have organized their work correctly and in a timely manner. If some directors of kolkhozes do not pay because they receive only a salary and do not have their own farm while the members of the brigades and the kolkhozniki have their home plots, they [the directors] receive products and money for worked days and we cannot orient ourselves on the [basis of the views of] of these directors. It may be that some of these kolkhoz directors will have to extend the repayment of the loans. On Wednesday, the Council of Ministers will examine the question of loans in the four districts and this will show that some of the activists have not accounted for subscription based loans. The inhabitants of the Zilupe region not long ago paid 500,000 rubles into the Savings Bank, but collected 81,000 rubles for loans. So from this region we will also have to ask for resources to cover the loans […]

Source: *LVA, 327. f., 3. apr., 36.l., pp. 30-35. Original in Russian*

317

Decision No. 52 of the Council of Ministers of the Latvian SSR and the Bureau of the Central Committee of the Latvian Communist Party, entitled "About the obligatory supply of milk to the state in the Latvian SSR"

April 2, 1946

The Council of Ministers of the Latvian SSR and the Central Committee of the Latvian Communist (B) Party decides that:

1. Beginning with 1946, the farmsteads of the Latvian SSR, depending upon to the amount of land under their control, are assigned the following norms, in liters per homestead per cow, as the obligatory amount of milk to be supplied to the state[151]:

   farmsteads with land

to	10 hectares	300 liters milk per cow	
from	10 to 15 hectares	350 "	"
"	15 to 20 ""	400 "	"
"	20 to 25 ""	450 "	"
more than	25 hectares	500 "	"

   with a fat content of 3.6%

   For cows that have calved for the first time, for the first half year after delivery, the milk norms are reduced to 50% of the norm [stated above].

2. Farms in municipal areas and worker's villages are assigned obligatory milk delivery to the state at half the norm of the farmsteads [as stated above].

3. Persons who live in fishing and tradesmen's artels and co-operatives of invalids who live in the countryside or in summertime villages; as well as workers and service personnel who are permanently (not seasonally) employed by the state or by co-operatives and cooperative enterprises, who have a cow (or a cow that has calved for the first time) as a personal possession, are included in the obligatory milk delivery system according to the norms defined for farmsteads, depending upon the amount of land they use […].

7. The following are exempted from the system of obligatory delivery of milk to the state:
   a. the farmsteads of persons invalided by war and labor who have been classified by the organs of social insurance and social welfare as invalids of the 1st of 2nd group, if the farmsteads have been exempted from farm taxes and if their families have no work-capable members employed on the farmstead;
   b. the farmsteads of disabled persons who can not participate in farmwork or other work, if the farmsteads are exempted from farm taxes, if the farmstead has no arable land, and if their families have no work-capable members employed on the farmstead […]

Chair of the Council of Ministers of the Latvian SSR   V. Lācis
Secretary of the Central Committee of the Latvian Communist Party   J. Kalnbērziņš

Source: *LVA, 270. f., 1. apr., 204. l., pp. 87-91 (copy of original). Original in Russian*

Excerpts from the minutes (No. 25) of a meeting of the Collegium of the Ministry of Justice of the Latvian SSR, concerning the work of the people's courts in enacting the July 14, 1951, decree of the Presidium of the Supreme Soviet of the USSR concerning absence from work and absence from work without leave

September 13, 1952

Agenda:

1. The results of the summary description of the work of the people's courts in the cases relating to the July 14, 1951, decree about absence from work and absence from work without leave. [...][152]

The Collegium decides:

1. To note that the people's judges of the Latvian SSR do not appreciate the political meaning of the struggle with the violators of work discipline in manufacture, and therefore the quality of the work of the people's courts in dealing with cases involving absence from work and absence from work without leave (the July 14, 1951, decree of the Presidium of the Supreme Soviet of the USSR) is unsatisfactory:

   a. the seven-day time frame for dealing with a case is violated egregiously;
   b. punishments are light because the minimal sanction from the July 14, 1951, decree, is used;
   c. the attitude of people's judges toward the directors of enterprises and institutions is conciliatory, and the latter are not asked to observe strictly the instructions of the Ministry of Justice of the USSR that a case be prepared within three days against those absent from work and those absent without leave. [...]

Source: *LVA, 938. f., 3. apr., 15. l., pp. 58-59. Original in Russian.*

Excerpt from a report by the Chair of the Board of Statistics of the Latvian SSR to the Secretary of the Central Committee of the Latvian Communist Party, J. Kalnbērziņš, and to the Chair of the Council of Ministers, V. Lācis, about the characteristics of the working family's budget

October 12, 1955

[...] The country's economy does not come close to satisfying the growing needs of the population for other grocery products. Particularly noticeable are shortages in the supply of meat and sausage products, fats, sugar, fish and other products. There have been almost no fresh fish for sale. Shortages exist in the variety of small fish, fish products, cold smoked fish and in the supply and sale of assorted fish groups. There is no sturgeon caviar or delicatessen fish for sale. In the second quarter of this year there was no sunflower seed oil, there were shortages of sugar, and the sale of early vegetables and greens was badly organized. [...]

In the surveyed [budgets] of kolkhoz families in the first half of this year, some factory goods were bought from resellers for increased prices: wool knits, silk fabric, coats, wool kerchiefs, cotton and wool thread, boots, separators, fertilizer, livestock feed, fuel, wooden spoons, cans, clay dishes, rakes, household soap, batteries for pocket flashlights, yeast, bay leaves, potato flour, salted fish and others.

These products were bought from private persons because they were not available at consumer co-operative stores. Moreover, consumer co-operative stores did not satisfy the kolkhozniki's demands for the following factory goods: sugar, cheap candies, macaroni, margarine, laundry detergent, petroleum, different dry goods (buttons, snaps, zippers, razor blades, and others), petroleum lamps, "bat" lamps, radios, parts for motorcycles and bicycles, inventory for farms (large and small cans, shovels, flails, ropes and others), construction material (slate, bricks, cement, lead castings, etc), cotton fabrics, raincoats and tarpaulins, leather shoes and others. [...]

Chief of the Board of Statistics of the Latvian SSR   A. Drjucin

Source: *LVA, 277. f., 11. apr., 970. l., pp. 1-28. Original in Russian.*

Document No. 89

Excerpts from the report of the Latvian SSR Board of Statistics, entitled "Concerning the conditions of family apartments and communal apartments of surveyed workers"

1956

[...] The data lead to the following conclusions:
1. The apartment situation of the Republic's population get worse year after year.[153] Workers'families in Rīga are particularly inadequately supplied with living space; their average living space per person is significantly smaller than the average for all of Rīga's inhabitants.
2. Without guaranteed living space, 45.8% of the surveyed workers'families have an average living space per family member of 4.4 sq.m., and 7.6% of the workers'families are forced to rent living space as sub-tenants, which significantly increases their apartment costs.
3. The apartments inhabited by workers'families are insufficiently supplied with necessities: 24% do not have running water, 32.5% do not have plumbing, 86.5% do not have gas, and 81% do not have central heating.
4. The apartments are heated entirely inadequately even where there is central heating; this not only creates problems for the renters, but also has a ruinous effect on apartment structure itself. Moreover, the cost of heating of one sq m of living space is increasing year after year.
5. The Republic's municipalities, particularly Rīga, are completely unsatisfied with their supply of fuel. Speculators take full advantage of this, driving fuel prices higher and forcing people to spend great sums out of their [household] budgets.
6. Putting to one side the population of Rīga and the inadequate living space for working families in the city, the [general] plan for the construction of apartments is inadequately carried out, the resources earmarked for the construction of apartments are not provided year after year, and, as a result, in the Republic and particularly in Riga with its growing population, population growth noticeably exceeds the growth of the amount of allocated living space.

Chief of the Board of Statistics of the Latvian SSR   A. Drjucin

Source: *LVA, 277. f., 11. apr., 970. l., pp. 81-89. Original in Russian.*

Document No. 90

Excerpts from the regulations promulgated by the Council of Ministers of the Latvian SSR and the Council of Trade Unions of the Latvian SSR concerning the manner in which citizens in need of improved apartment housing, and who are granted living space, are placed on the waiting list

December 23, 1983

[...]

11. The following are recognized as persons in need of improvement in their housing situation: [154]

11.1 citizens who have living space that is less than 6 cubic meters per family member, but in the republic-level municipalities – less than five cubic meters.

Invalided veterans of the Great Patriotic War, family members of soldiers killed or missing (partisans), and others whose situation is analogous to these are recognized as needing to improve their living conditions if their living space is less than seven cubic meters per family member, but in the republic-level municipalities – less than six cubic meters. [...]

2.2   citizens who have lived not less than the time[155] mentioned in Par. 10 as sub-tenants in state buildings or those of the Social Living Fund, or, because of contract arrangements, in rented housing belonging to apartment construction co-operatives, or who are in individual apartment fund housing and have no other living quarters;

2.3   citizens who live in communal housing, except for temporary and contract workers, as well as citizens who live there because their are [university] students;

2.4   citizens who live in an apartment building that does not meet minimal sanitation and infrastructural requirements;

2.5   citizens who have in their families members of both sexes at least nine years or older, except for married couples, and if the object of the rent contract is a room or a one-room apartment;

2.6   citizens who because of the terms of the rent contract occupy an apartment without insulation;

2.7   citizens who have a serious form of an illness listed as such by the USSR Ministry of the Protection of Health; and, if, after review by the USSR State Labor and Social Questions Committee and VACP, [it is determined] that giving this person a separate room would give the rest of the family members the right to be included in the list;

2.8   persons who during the Civil War, the Great Patriotic War, and other combat operations in defense of [the homeland], were enlisted as active members of the military; partisan fighters in the Civil War and the great Patriotic War; as well as other persons who participated in combat operations in defense of the USSR if they have lived in badly equipped apartments for not less than 20 years;

2.9   workers and service personnel who have achieved distinction in production work and social work, have worked in the same enterprise, institution, or organization in question for not less than 20 years, and have lived in badly equipped apartments for not less than twenty years.

Citizens can be recognized as eligible for improving their apartment conditions for other reasons, as permitted by the laws of the USSR and the Latvian SSR. [...]

Source: *LVA, 425. f., 7. apr., 746. l., pp. 96-120 (copy of original). Original in Russian.*

DOCUMENTS NO. 91-101

SUBORDINATION OF CULTURE TO IDEOLOGY

Document No. 91

Directive from the Board of Artistic Affairs of the Council of People's Commissars of the Latvian SSR concerning themes that must be reflected in works of art

November-December 1944

Thematic plan and list of illustrative themes

I. Scenes from everyday life and battles of the Red Army
   The heroic work of Red Army commanders and the political officers work in the battles around Moscow, as the Army moved westward and toward the territory of Latvia.
   "Before the Assault", "Assault on an Inhabited Place", "Initiation into the Party after the Battle", "The Sniper at Work", "Keeping Quiet", "The Presentation of the Guard Flag", "Reconnaissance", "Political Information", "Tank Squad", "Air Squad", "The Medics in Battle", "Actors at the Front", etc.
   From the everyday life of the reserve battalions
   "Waking in the Morning" (sprightly morning mood), "Training" (sunny day in summer, or a rainy and muddy one in the autumn, energy and drive), "Political Training" (concentrated attention), "Rest" (evening games, joy), "Amateur Performance," "The Actors have Arrived," "Heading to the Front" etc.
II. The struggle of partisans with the occupiers
   "Partisan Headquarters", "With the Partisans in the Forest", "Partisans Reconnoitering", "Couriers", "Trial of the Oppressor", "Trial of the Traitor", "Young Partisans", "Portraits of Partisans", etc.
III. Scenes of everyday life and work among Latvians during the evacuation.
   "Smagars at Work", "Komsomol Tractor Girl", "Donor", "In the Orphanage", "In the FZO School", "Volunteering at the Kolkhoz", etc.
IV. From the history of the Latvian nation
V. The period of [German] occupation
   "The New Order in the Countryside", "Traitors to the Nation", "Hanging of Peaceful Inhabitants", "The Concentration Camp at Salesgirls", "Persons – Monsters", "Hiding the Wounded Commissar", "Killing Children", "Nobleman", "Booty", "In the Fascist Labor Camp", "Catching People", "Flee" (The Red Army is Coming), etc.
VI. Latvia liberated from occupiers
   "Liberators are Coming", "At the Shores of the Daugava after Expelling the Germans", "Renewing the Railroad", "People's Meeting on October 22, 1944", "Again the Red Flag over Rīga", "Returning to the Land", "Surveyors at Work", "Renewing Industry", "The Beginning of the School Year" etc.
   "Portraits of Shock Workers"
VII. Scenes of the Native Land
   "Devastated Rīga", "Wide is the Daugava", "The Sea", "Sown Fields", "The Forests Rustle", "Golden Autumn", "Gaiziņš Hill in Winter", "Jelgava after the Occupation," etc.
VIII. Still life
   Historical themes for painters from the struggle of the working class in Latvia

322

Theme	Subject
1) The New Current	The founding of the Social Democratic propaganda organization on January 20, 1895 (teachers, students, pupils – workers); types.
2) Organizing workers in all the regions of Latvia	1896-7 the Kuldīga seminarians establish a Social Democratic organization. Types. 1898 Founding of a workers organization in Lielsesava
3. The first organized working-class rising and strike	In Rīga, by the Alexander Gates, the demonstrating workers from "Džute" and "Phoenix" struggle with detachments of the Tsarist army and police (types – police, workers, soldiers). March 5, 1895-25 killed, 35 wounded Confrontations between police and workers near the Ģertrūde Church in Rīga in 1899
4. Continued organizing of illegal activity and groups (about 200)	1900, a workers' meeting in Rīga, 10-15 persons 1900, at a workers meeting, their leader -- a student -- gives a speech to 10-15 persons
5. Mass meetings in the forest	May 1, 1903, the first forest meeting (speaker – listeners). 1903 Zasulauka Forest meeting (speaker – worker type) 1903, Biķernieki Forest meeting (speaker – worker type)
6. The origins of the Bolshevik and Menshevik division	Workers discuss the results of the 1903 London Congress where comrade Lenin took a stand and won support for his views
7. The spread of illegal literature from 1890-1900	The spread of the 1903 proclamation in Rīga – in a church
8. Publication of first issue of "Cīņa" in 1904	In 1904, the workers look at the first issue of "Cīņa"
9. The period of maturing revolution 1904-1905	April 11, 1904, May 1 worker's meeting -- armed conflict with police in Rīga. 4-5 thousand demonstrators participating. 1903, in Rīga during the time of the performance in the theater "Uleja," proclamations are distributed
10. Years of repressions and punitive expeditions	Rendering punishments on 9 persons tried on September 11, 1/24 in the morning. Punitive expeditions. May 1, 1913, workers'demonstrations in Rīga (about 5000 persons).

11. Unmasking the imperialistic war	Conference of the Communist Faction of the Red Latvian Rifles in 1918. January 1919, the founding of Soviet power in Latvia. May 1919, the shooting of workers in the streets of Rīga. Fall of 1918, underground activists organize workers meetings.
12. Reaction in 1920	"Forest Brothers" (partisans) battle in the forest at Cesvaine with White Guards. Shooting of workers in the Matīss Cemetery in 1919. The July 25, 1920, and December 1919, funerals of communists shot in Valmiera during mass demonstrations. March 18, 1921: the Latvian Communist Party celebrates the 50th anniversary of the Paris Commune. Red flags are hung and demonstrations are held. 1923 Congress of the Latvian Communist Party. 1923, March 8, establishment of international women workers day 1925, founding of the Latvian "MOPR" section. 1928, street fighting in August against the fascists. 1934, the founding of the People's Front.
13. Reactionaries attack the proletariat	An armed Home Guard post near a factory in 1936. Widespread beatings of political prisoners in the Rīga Central Prison in 1930. At the end of 1934, Home Guards with weapons repress the workers.
14. Liberation of Latvia's proletariat	June 17, 1940: the Red Army arrives in Latvia. The people greet the armored divisions of the Red Army. Police assault the welcoming masses near the rail station's police office.
15. The liberated working class	Demonstration of workers organizations in Rīga. The nationalization of factories and large enterprises.
16. Land reform	Distributing land to workers and working farmers.
17. Socialist competition	The first Stakhanovites. Pioneers. Komsomolers.
17. Defense of Soviet Latvia	The first aviation festival in Spilve. Parade in the Red Square in Riga marking the 23rd anniversary of the October revolution

1. Relations with the Russian tribes before the German arrival. The Chronicle of Henry of Livonia.
2. The arrival of the Germans on the Daugava
   a. The first meeting with German merchants – missionaries – soldiers – robbers,
   b. The Zemgalians assault on the German castle at Ikšķile in 1187,
   c. Crusade against the Livs organized by Bishop Berthold in 1198,
   d. The second crusade against the Livs. Bishop Albert 1200.
3. The conquest of Sēlpils.
4. The origins of the state of Koknese.
5. The fall of the Latgalians.
6. The fall of Tālava. The Bear-slayer.
7. The Couronian wars with the Germans
   a. The Couronian assault on Rīga in 1210,
   b. The suppression of the Couronians in 1242,
   c. The Battle of Durbe in 1260.
8. The Zemgalians' wars for freedom
   a. The march of the Zemgalians and Couronians on Rīga,
   b. The battle near Saule in 1236,
   c. The Lithuanian assault on the Livonian knights near Aizkraukle in 1279,
   d. The Battle near Garoze in 1289,
   e. The Zemgalians' retreat to Lithuania
9. The first manor owners at the end of the 13th century. The farmers are turned into serfs – 15th century
10. The Livonian Wars, 1501
11. Ivan the Terrible's[156] march on the German Order in 1558.
12. The time of Polish rule (?).[157]
13. The Polish-Swedish War (?).[158]
14. The Swedish time (?).[159]
15. The Northern War.
16. The condition of the peasantry in the Duchy of Kurland and Zemgalia.
17. Peasant unrest in 1784 in Rauna, Krimulda, Smiltene, Dikļi, and Valmiera.
18. The unrest at Kaugurmuiža in 1801.
19. The emancipation of peasants without land in Courland and Livonia in 1817 and 1823.
20. The migration movement after emancipation to the shores of the Black Sea and the Azov Sea.
21. Peasant unrest in Vidzeme in 1841.
22. The relationships of the activists of the [Latvian] national awakening movement with the progressive Russian intelligentsia
    a. the struggle against the Germanizers,
    b. Krisjānis Valdemārs,
    c. Rainis

Source: *LVA, 627.f., 2.apr., 159.l., pp. 5-7. Original in Latvian.*

The decision of the Bureau of the Central Committee of the Latvian Communist Party concerning the performance of Latvian poets during [the program] Ten Days of Latvian Literature in Moscow

1948

The [program] Ten Days of Latvian Literature in Moscow[160] demonstrated that the historical decisions of the Central Committee of the All-Union Communist (B) Party about the journals "Zvezda" and "Leningrad,"[161] and other decisions of the Central Committee, on questions of ideological work helped Latvian Soviet literature excise many mistakes and shortcomings[162], raise its ideological and artistic level, turned it decisively to contemporary themes, and created the opportunity for the first steps in implementing solutions [...]

In the future, Soviet Latvian authors face significant and responsible assignments. Following the method of socialist realism, and [proceeding] with the best intentions and a carefully worked-out understanding of the reality of our [daily] life, the writers of Soviet Latvia must educate and arm the nation with ideas. Nonetheless, a real shortcoming of Soviet Latvian writers is the insignificant number of striking, convincing examples that describe the creative, everyday life of the working class of Soviet Latvia, showing their selfless struggle to create communist society, bravely unmasking the remains of capitalism in people's consciousness. In current Soviet Latvian poetry, the demonstration of crucial social processes and class struggles in Latvia is insufficiently deep. In the work of Alexandrs Čaks the residue of decadence is felt, and formalist elements have remained in the works of Jānis Plaudis and Jānis Grots. In many works, such as, for example, Cecīlija Dinere's poem "For my son" the poet's experiences are described, but no social interest is generated. Sometimes, in literary works the psychological motives of the hero's behavior are insufficiently shown. [...]

The Bureau of the Central Committee of the Latvian Communist (b) Party decides:

1. To assign the Board of the Latvian Soviet Writers Society (comrades Upīts and Muižnieks) the task of eliminating the mistakes and shortcomings mentioned in the decision. To assume that the chief assignments of the Writer's Society's were and still remain the continued elevation of the ideological and artistic level of all genres of literary work, and the unrelenting [incorporation] of the struggle of the spirit of the Bolshevik Party in literature. Writers in their work must show the Soviet people's selfless struggle more clearly and in a more full-blooded [fashion]; they must demonstrate Soviet patriotism, the friendship of the peoples of the USSR, and the pride of the masses in the national collective; they must reflect clearly and truthfully the creative initiatives of the Soviet masses and their ideological growth, as well as the new character traits that Bolshevik party has created raised in [the masses]; they must portray Soviet Latvia more triumphantly – both cities and countryside – as the venue of huge and important historical processes; they must show the creation of the new Soviet person. Following the methods of socialist realism, [writers must] become deeply involved with life, fervently support all that is new and communist, and struggle more resolutely with bourgeois nationalism, cosmopolitanism, and with the worship of foreignness, consistently and convincingly demonstrating the advantages of the Soviet socialist system.
2. To assign to the Board of the Latvian Soviet Writers Society (comrades Upīts and Muižnieks) the task of taking radical steps to develop and improve literary criticism. To organize comradely discussions of literary works, underlining positive phenomena and successes and uncovering shortcomings and mistakes, thus helping our literature move forward.
3. To assign to the Board of the Latvian Soviet Writers Society the task of organizing systematic instruction of young writers and of putting into practice a system of literary consultations.

The Propaganda and Agitation Section of the Central Committee of the Latvian Communist (B) Party is assigned the task of reviewing and approving the work plan for the young writers.

4. To warn comrade Muižnieks that the Board of the Latvian Soviet Writers Society is not implementing the decision of the Central Committee of the Latvian Communist (B) Party regarding the development of literature for children and youth. To suggest that the Board of the Latvian Soviet Writers Society develop activities that will ensure a radical break in the pace of development of Soviet Latvian children's and youth literature. [...]

Secretary of the Central Committee of the Latvian Communist Party   J. Kalnbērziņš

Source: *LVA PA, 101. f., 12. apr., 17. l., pp 13-16. Original in Russian.*

Document No. 93

Secret report by A. Pelše, the Secretary of the Central Committee of the Latvian Communist (B) Party, to the Deputy Minister of the USSR Ministry of Higher Education, A. Topčijev, concerning the undesirability of giving a doctor of science degree and the title of professor to B. Brežgo

July 24, 1948

In reply to your letter, we see it necessary to explain the following about B. Brežgo,[163] who has been nominated by the Latvian State University to receive a doctor of science degree and the title of professor.

Over the last two years, B. Brežgo was the Head of the Department of Slavic Philology, and for a while worked as the Associate Dean of the Philology Faculty. In the beginning of 1948, he was relieved of the deanship as not being appropriate for the position, and for attempting to carry out bourgeois-nationalistic work. The department led by B. Brežgo does its work unsatisfactorily. During the period of Soviet power, no one in the department, including B. Brežgo, has published a scientific article. Members of the department permit liberalism in their appraisal of student knowledge.

Based on this, the Central Committee of the Latvian Communist (B) Party believes that it was correct of the Latvian State University SCC[164] to rescind its request that B. Brežgo's doctorate degree in historical sciences and the professor title be approved.

Propaganda Secretary of the Central Committee of the Latvian Communist (B) Party

A Pelše

Source: *LVA PA, 101. f., 11. apr., 57.l., p. 79. Original in Russian.*

Excerpt from the secret report of O. Strods, leader of the Propaganda and Agitation Section of the Central Committee of the Latvian Communist (B) Party, to the All-Union Communist (Bolshevik) Party Central Committee Instructor, Čurkin, entitled "Concerning examples of the manifestations of bourgeois nationalism in the Latvian SSR and the struggle against them."

April 1951

[...] The manifestation of bourgeois nationalism in schools

8. In the Young Workers High School in Rīga, Kuple has been the teacher of Latvian language and literature for a long time. She minimized the value of contemporary Soviet literature in teaching her pupils, and portrayed the best representatives of Soviet literature – Gorky and Mayakovski – in a coarse and vulgar way. Describing J. Rainis, Kuple in all manner of ways depicted accomplishments as being those of Aspāzija, [saying] that if Aspāzija had not inspired Rainis it would have been unlikely for him to have reached literary glory. Kuple explained the revolutionarism of Rainis'literary drama as having been happenstance. Kuple's lessons on the literature of the pre-revolutionary years, which excluded the revolutionary democrats, were clear, substantive, colorful, emotional, and memorable; [by contrast] she discussed Soviet revolutionary literary figures in an indifferent, difficult, and twisted manner. At the same time, teacher Kuple very deftly masked what she was doing. Only after long observation of her and the results of the schoolchildren's own ideological-political upbringing, was it possible to unmask teacher Kuple, who was then forbidden from working in the school.

The same can be said about the teacher Stanga, who teaches geography at the 30th Rīga Seven-Year School. The lessons describing the climate, natural world, economies, and political systems of capitalist lands are emotional, clear, and colorful. At the same time, in her lessons concerning the natural world, economics, and political order of the USSR the children receive poor statistical information that is replete with formalism. A decision has been made to release Stanga from work in the school. [...]

Chief of the Propaganda and Agitation Section of the Central Committee of the Latvian
Communist (B) Party   O. Strods

Source: *LVA PA, 101. f., 14. apr., 71. l., pp. 18,19. Original in Russian.*

Secret report of the Chief of the School Department of the Central Committee of the Latvian Communist Party, A. Andriksons, about anti-Soviet activity among school youth and about shortcomings in the learning process

April 5, 1954

In 1953, and 1954, the Ministry of the Interior of the Latvian SSR uncovered 19 incidents of school children distributing anti-Soviet pamphlets and performing diversionary activities, including 6 such incidents in Rīga.

Anti-Soviet pamphlets were distributed and diversionary activities were carried out by youth organizations as well as by individual school children.

From only the beginning of the school year 1953/1954 anti-Soviet incidents were uncovered in Aizpute, Saldus, and Sigulda regions and in Jelgava.

On November 18, 1953[165], in Saldus, 11 anti-Soviet pamphlets were discovered, inviting persons of Latvian nationality to join the ranks of the "partisans" and to fight against communism. This pamphlet's author and distributor was an 8th grade student of the Saldus High School, Jaunpetrovičs.

In December of 1953, there was discovered an anti-Soviet organization among the schoolchildren in the Jelgava 2nd Seven-year School. The members of this organization prepared about 100 anti-Soviet pamphlets, but when the organization was discovered, they destroyed the bulk of the pamphlets.

In the Dunalka Seven-year School in the Aizpute region, the anti-Soviet youth group "Latvian Eagles," later renamed "Iron Heels," from January 18th to 29th distributed 12 anti-Soviet leaflets and calls-to-action. This group included pupils of the 6th and 7th grade as well as Pioneers[166]. The great majority of their parents were punished for counter-revolutionary work.

This year in February, pamphlets with anti-Soviet content were found in the Nītaure Village Council bookstore in the Sigulda region. The pamphlet's author and distributor was the Nītaure Seven-year School student Urjāns. Other school children also participated in the distribution of the pamphlets.

During the course of the investigation it was determined that the reason for the existence anti-Soviet organizations among children in the seven-year schools in Dunalka and Nītaure, and in other schools, was negligent etching and upbringing.

The cadre of teachers at the Dunalka school is polluted. The former 6th Aizpute Home Guard Regiment's Nīkrāce Section Leader works as the Latvian language teacher; his wife, who participated in the destruction of the portraits of Party and government leaders in June of 1941, also works in the school; the teacher Poriņa is a Baptist; and the teacher Smurģe is the daughter of a kulak, and both of her brothers have been convicted for counter-revolutionary work.

The educational discipline in this school is at a very low level.

None of the four classes we visited could be described as satisfactory.

The geography lessons (teacher Smurģe) are distant from practical work, [and] the pupils do not have the slightest idea why learning geography has relevance to their lives.

The history of the USSR in the fourth grade (teacher Ducmane) was presented chaotically. The teacher Ducmane permitted many mistakes in substance and in factual information. For example, she said that the academician Pavlov was the first to start the struggle against religion, and his accomplishment was teaching about instinct and seed vernalization – "when seeds are placed in a cold room." Ducmane claimed that Lenin and Stalin supposedly showed that if a object can not be seen, we can not think about it; and as proof of this [she] gave the following question: "Have you, for example, seen the devil?"

Teacher Tilts conducted the Latvian literature class from the position of bourgeois objectivism. He told facts to the school children without giving any evaluation [of them] and allowed the children to draw their own conclusions. Fragments of the story "The Makers of the Future" were analyzed in this way.

The work of upbringing of the children was performed very shallowly in these schools, and no one understood the children's individual idiosyncrasies. Neither the school director Ducmane nor the senior leader of the Pioneers, Freimane, know the children's parents and their predispositions, and do not know the children's interests, what they read or what interests them.

The school director Ducmane, a member of the Communist Party of the Soviet Union, does not examine her teachers' work, she carries no authority in the school, and she calls the pupils fascists.

The Aizpute Region People's Education section (RTIN leader Brumele, a member of the Communist Party of the Soviet Union) follows the work of this school only cursorily. In the academic year 1953/1954, the work of the school was not reviewed even once by inspectors.

Also, the Aizpute Regional Party Committee works poorly at reviewing the school with respect to teaching and upbringing.

In the last two years, not one person from among the Secretaries of the Party Regional Committee has visited the Dunalka Seven-year School, and many other schools.

Starting in early 1953, the Bureau of the Party Regional Committee reviewed questions about the work of schools three times, but questions about the contents of schoolwork, the ideological and theoretical level of teaching were not looked at in the Party Regional Committee. Decisions made about these matters are vague and poorly formed; some decisions are no longer enforced, even though they remain on the books. Every year, the level of accomplishment in the schools is dropping, and the number of children who repeat grades increases, but still this situation does not cause worry for the Secretaries of the Aizpute Region Party Committee.

In the academic year 1950/1951, of 2,832 school children 352 had to repeat a grade, in the academic year 1951/1952, of 2,776 – 353, in the 1952/1953 academic year, of 2,612 – 375. Progression [to the next grade] in the first quarter of the 1953/1954 academic year was 85%, but in the second quarter – 84.8%.

The Aizpute Regional Party Committee did not make the correct political assessment of the anti-Soviet expressions among the children at the Dunalka Seven-year School; it confined itself merely to looking at the facts received by the Bureau and did not even send [to the school] [some of] the Committee's staff, as was directed in the decision of the Bureau. Furthermore, the Party Committee Secretary, comrade Salajev, did not demand a thorough investigation of this question. At the moment, the identities of the two anti-Soviet authors are still not known, and nothing is known also about the contacts between the Dunalka Schools anti-Soviet youth group children at the seven-year school in Dzērve (the pupil Doršs from the Dunalka Seven-year School confirmed that in the summer of 1953 he had asked the Dzērve Seven-year School pupil Gunārs Bergs to join his group).

[Next,] the Sigulda Regional Party Committee and Regional Executive Committee also does poor work on questions having to do with the people's education, with leadership in teacher training being handled only by the People's Education Section. The Sigulda Regional Party Committee Secretary, comrade Pēda, did not make the correct political assessment of the fact that anti-Soviet pamphlets were distributed in the Nītaure Seven-year School and did not notify the Central Committee of the LKP. The questions of improving teaching and training in the Nītaure Seven-year School were not reviewed by the Regional Party Committee's Bureau.

The Jelgava Municipal Party Committee, particularly comrade Korolkevičs, handled work with schools in an unsatisfactory manner, and, as a result, from 1951-1953, in the Jelgava schools there were uncovered many anti-Soviet youth groups, and a large number of anti-Soviet pamphlets were distributed.

School Section Leader of the Central Committee of the Latvian Communist Party
Andriksons

Source: *LVA PA, 101. f., 17. apr., 60a. l., pp. 54-57. Original in Russian.*

Document No. 96

Excerpts from a meeting of the Collegium of the Latvian SSR Ministry of Culture during an excursion to view a model of a monument in the 1905 Park (with the participation of the Old Bolsheviks)

March 27, 1959

[…] Comrade Treimanis: This sculpture does to contain a full expression of the time period. The woman's figure personifying the Revolution is superfluous. The author has returned to the images of the French Revolution. For us, 1905 is important. Do we find it in these figures? Without a doubt, no. The time period related to the Revolution of 1905 cannot be captured in the figure of one worker. [This figure] is some sort of thoughtful youth pressed up against the Revolution and looking for support in it. Then [there is] the woman's raised hand. It is not a call to revolution, to battle, no, that is a call [that says] – not one step farther, stay in your place! Then [there is] the bas-relief -- in it, the persons are moving toward the central figure. If these persons were going toward the other side then it would appear that this woman were urging them toward the struggle. But they are going in a different direction. The bas-relief barely reflects the types of workers involved in the 1905 Revolution. They are closer to the images of the Kauguri peasants, not workers that are going to battle. The composition of the bas-relief is not deeply thought out. Comrade Albergs has relied solely on his strengths. But in this case a Marxist worldview is needed. The woman called "Revolution" upsets everything. This memorial needs to be monumental.

Comrade Asare: They should have invited us earlier. That aside, I completely agree with comrade Treimanis' thoughts and views that the Revolution can not be seen in the woman's figure. If it is possible to correct it, the sculpture must be corrected.

Comrade Rokpelnis: There can talk only about corrections. If we want a new symbol, then without a doubt a completely new work must be created and we have to agree to a new contract.

Comrade Kļaviņš: The monument does suit the Revolution of 1905. The Revolution of 1905 was a conscious struggle.

Comrade Lintiņš: I agree with comrade Treimanis' thoughts.

Comrade Jankovskis: The symbols of socialist realism will remain. I do not see in the worker a frightened youth, but a guardian, a thoughtful youth. The search is very rewarding. I do not feel the impulse of great struggle in the bas-relief. […]

[…] Comrade Bērce: If we accept the idea of representing the Revolution as a symbol, then it can only be a woman, just as the workers can [be represented] only by a man. Here there are two views – if struggle is to be represented, and then after all we will have the monument by the Daugava River. But Grīziņš Hill was always a meeting place and then it is correct that in the bas-relief the masses are moving toward the central figure, they are gathering for a meeting, and then the woman's hand is understandable as an invitation to gather. The bas-relief underlines the theme of Grīziņš Hill.

Comrade Bajārs: It is possible to represent the themes of revolutionary struggle with symbols. As is known, Grīziņš Hill was the first step. In the bas-relief we have to look for expressions.

Comrade Krasovskis: They should have invited us when they were discussing the conceptual model.

Comrade Edžiņš: They should put a flagpole in the man's hands. That would make him dynamic. The woman needs to be transformed. […]

The Recording Secretary of the Collegium of the Latvian SSR Ministry of Culture

M. Vidrika

Source: *LVA, 678.f., 1. apr, 126. l., pp. 86-87. Original in Latvian.*

The decision of the Collegium of the Latvian SSR Ministry of Culture about the work of the I. Kalniņš'ensemble of the Liepāja Municipal Culture House

September 14, 1970

Having heard and discussed the report of comrade Grauda, the Chief of the Board of Clubs and Libraries of the Ministry of Culture of the Latvian SSR about the work of the vocal and instrumental ensemble of the Liepāja Municipal Culture House, the Collegium of the Ministry of Culture of the Latvian SSR ascertained that the Liepāja Municipal Culture Section (Leader, comrade G. Balodis) has acted in an unprincipled and condemnable manner in approving the ensemble's artistically and ideologically unacceptable program, which is replete with pessimism, dark hopelessness, and irony concerning our contemporary views [of life].

Working as an autonomous artistic unit, the members of the ensemble received remuneration, thus violating the rules of autonomous artistic collectives.

Moreover, in view of the fact that the leader of the ensemble, I. Kalniņš[167], as well as some of the members of the ensemble, in their concert in Ogre on August 30th, behaved in a scandalous, politically ambiguous, and amoral way, they have completely compromised their ensemble, and [therefore] the Collegium of the Latvian SSR Ministry of Culture decides:

1. To order that the Chief of the Liepāja Municipal Cultural Section, Gunārs Balodis, terminate, as of October 1 of this year, the Municipal Culture House's vocal, instrumental ensemble (led by I. Kalniņš) as an illegally organized and ideologically ill-prepared collective.

2. Because she consented to the organization of the vocal, instrumental ensemble and its impermissible and irresponsible work, and to the impermissible behavior of some of the members of the ensemble, to remove the current Liepāja Municipal Culture House Director, Vita Pētersone, from her responsibilities as Director of the Liepāja Culture House as being inadequate for the responsibilities of this position.

3. To rebuke to the Director of the Ogre Region Culture House, Vilma Millere, for not notifying the Ministry of Culture of the Latvian SSR in a timely manner about the serious disorders during the concert in the Culture House of the Ogre region this year on August 29th.

4. To ask the Liepāja Municipal Committee of the Latvian Communist Party to review the incorrect actions of the Municipal Cultural Section Leader, a Party member, Gunārs Balodis, which showed themselves in the illegal organization of the ensemble, as well as in the approval of the ideologically and artistically unacceptable program of the ensemble.

5. To order all Regional and Municipal Culture Section Leaders in the seminars of regional and municipal cultural workers set for October of this year, with the invited participation of all regional and municipal territory culture house directors and club leaders (independent of their sector membership), to discuss once again the two decision of the Council of Ministers of the Latvian SSR (no. 301 of June 26, 1968, and no. 219 of April 22, 1969), as well as the directives of March 14, 1969, entitled "About stage orchestras and Soviet traditions".[168]

6. To order the Head of the Board of Clubs and Libraries of the Ministry of Culture of the Latvian SSR, F. Grauda, to be in charge of carrying out these decisions.

Chair of the Collegium, Minister of the Latvian SSR of Culture   V. Kaupužs

Source: *LVA, 678. f., 1. apr., 367. l., p. 95.Original in Latvian.*

Excerpts from a lecture by A. Voss, the First Secretary of the Central Committee of the Latvian Communist Party, at the 21ˢᵗ Congress of the Latvian Communist Party[169]

February 25, 1971

Sometimes cultural-educational institutions do not look [sufficiently] critically at [our] cultural heritage. For example, in Limbaži, Bauska, Cēsis, and in some other regions, there have opened museums of literary figures whose writings are contradictory and whose life story has been closely ties to the Latvian nationalist bourgeoisie.[170] At the same time, the exhibits in these museums explain these writings in a one-sided way, not using a Party approach or class analysis. It is completely clear that in these so-called museums, under the cover of Latvia's national cultural heritage, ideas are being put forward that are foreign to us. [...]

Source: *LVA PA, 101. f., 35. apr., 1.l., p. 36. Original in Russian.*

Excerpts from a speech by A. Voss, the First Secretary of the Central Committee of the Latvian Communist Party, at the 22ⁿᵈ Congress of the Latvian Communist Party[171]

January 22, 1976

[...] Our writers and artists still sometimes do not research sufficiently the material of everyday life on which they base their works of art; they do not immerse themselves sufficiently in the essence of the phenomena and the processes that make up our contemporary reality.

As a result, some authors introduce hurried, and sometimes mistaken, assertions that deceive readers.

Many collections of literature and art, even though based on contemporary themes, do not show fully the important social, political and spiritual processes [that affect] the people.

Works still appear with a content that is weak in terms of ideas and artistic mastery, in which author's Party position is not clear, and which poeticize personal inertia and ambiguous ideas.

Individual artists try to pass off as important experiments with „deep" philosophical meaning [works] of an obviously formalist nature. Such works were shown at the exhibits organized by the Artists Society.

Word puzzles unattached to civic ideas and artistic intent also show up in the work of individual poets. There have been attempts to relate such works to the innovativeness of contemporary stylistic expression, even though in reality they demonstrate nothing more than simplifications and a crippled understanding.

The Ministry of Culture, the Artists Society, the Writers Society, and literary and artistic criticism do not always provide sufficiently timely evaluations of the long-term illness that is called innovativeness, and periodicals such as "Literature and Art" turn their pages over to this false innovation.

During the period under review, the Republic's Party organs and the Party press provided principled criticism of the work and presentations of particular literary figures, [designating them] as efforts to illuminate historical and contemporary events without the use of class analysis.

Unfortunately, the recurrence of such phenomena has not yet been ended. An example is the fragment of the book by S. Viese – *Raganiezis* – published in the magazine "Karogs" in 1975; in this, the class differences of Latvian peasant life during the German occupation are not mentioned – the farmer and servants are shown as one family.

The Party has never reconciled itself, and never will reconcile itself, with ideological ambiguity, with even the smallest steps away from the strict criteria of class in the evaluation of social and literary phenomenon. [...]

Source: *LVA PA, 101. f., 41. apr., 1.l., pp. 46,47. Original in Russian.*

Document No. 100

Excerpts from a speech by A. Plaude, Secretary of the Rīga Municipal Arts Committee, entitled "Concerning the tasks of the municipal Party organization in improving patriotic and international training in light of the requests of the 26th Congress[172] of the All-Union Communist Party"

October 10, 1982

[..] The process of internationalization, encompassing all spheres of human life, is particularly strongly expressed in the field of culture, and that has a huge impact on the creation of an international psychology among the working masses. The majority of literary and artistic figures have adopted as their defining guidelines the Central Committee Report to the 26th Congress of the Communist Party of the Soviet Union about how to live with the interests of the nation in mind and how to attest to life's truths, to our humanitarian ideals, to active participation in the construction of communism – that is also the authentic national sense, the authentic artistic sense of belonging to the Party.

In recent years, forms of action that effectively support the internationalization of social life have firmly entrenched themselves in Latvian literature and culture. Contacts between the national cultures of our land have developed in a stable manner, attesting to the fact that mutual closeness and mutual influences among them have for a long time been the generally accepted norm. Almost one-third of the repertoire of the Rīga theatre is from the output of Russian authors and other authors of the multi-national Soviet literature and drama [...]

The unified culture of the Soviet nation has developed in many directions. First, we feel the influence of Russian Soviet culture. Research on the interests of readers shows that the most-read books are by M. Gorky, M. Sholokhov, J. Bondarev, and V. Suksin -- 80% of readers show preference for the poets and writers of Russian Soviet literature and the literature of the fraternal Soviet republics. Much popularity has been gained by readers' conferences "The sense, honor, and conscience of our time[173]," "Work adorns the person," "Take Communists as an example," and those based on the books of L. Brezhnev "Little Land," "Rebirth," "Virgin Land," and "Memories.[174]" This year in the Leningrad *rajons* on Jūrmala Boulevard there opened a Library of the Literature of the Peoples of the USSR – the second library of this kind in the USSR, after Moscow. Many of the 71 nationalities and peoples who live in the USSR are represented there, and the inhabitants of Riga have the opportunity of reading their literature in their native languages. In a short time, the Library has managed to gain considerable authority among readers. There have been friendship evenings with representatives of Ukraine and Kirghizstan, meetings with authors from the fraternal republics, and musical evenings. The Library has rightfully become a center for all municipal libraries in the methodologies of international upbringing of young people [...]

Nonetheless, some individual leaders of cultural-educational institutions still do not take sufficiently into account the spiritual interests, needs, and traditions of different peoples. The repertoires of many autonomous collectives still contain too few works by authors of Union republics and socialist states, and the principle of bilingualism is not observed everywhere. Thus, in the cultural centers of the Education Ministry, of the university, and of sciences workers everything still takes place only in the Latvian language, even though among teachers, university lecturers, and scientists there are not a few representatives of other nationalities. Or, to use another example, the Hotel Latvia varieté program this year was comprised primarily of the works of English, American, and Italian authors. The time had come to change immediately the work of the leadership of the Rīga Stage and Concert Society. These examples demonstrate the insufficient political maturity of individual leaders, and reinforces the idea that the cultural boards of the municipal executive committees need to exercise the strictest controls over the repertoires of its subordinate institutions. [...]

The centers of anti-socialism and overseas Latvian reactionary émigré organizations are increasing their ideological pressures on schools, young people who are studying and working, and on the creative intelligentsia. Their radio programs are meant for these audiences. Harmful literature is sent into the republic for that purpose. Also, particular emphasis is placed on stoking nationalist feelings in an attempt to convince the Latvian people that they are being subjected to Russification.

Magazines we have received, commercial advertising, and other literature of this type all seeks to implant in the minds of our youth bourgeois ideology and the cult of material things.

You can still meet young persons who see it acceptable to wear a shirt or sports jersey or windbreaker with a star-spangled flag[175] or the emblems of the capitalist military. This lack of selectivity in clothing is not just a little harmful.

We still do not pay enough attention to the propaganda [value] of Soviet symbols, of conversations about the Red Flag, and the coats-of-arms and flags of the state and the Union Republics. There are still incidents of damage to or ripping down of the flags of the USSR or the Union republics. Thus in November of last year, at the Electric Bulb and Ship Mechanical Factory the young workers Terezov and Tiroškevič, being drunk, took down the flag and went with it through the streets singing. When asked how they evaluated their behavior, their reply was the following: "We did not do anything wrong." [...]

Not long ago the Party Municipal Committee's Propaganda and Agitation Section analyzed the contents of the recordings made by the "Rīga Photo" Sound Recording Studio. It turned out that more than 90% of the recordings requested by persons from Rīga were from West German and American [companies] and their foreign branches. Most of them are not only unlicensed, but they were not obtained through the Soviet foreign commercial organizations.

The above [examples] permit the conclusion that there aren't and should not be spheres of activity outside of strict Party control. Musical propaganda must be in the hands of one institution. [...]

Source: *LVA PA, 102. f., 43. apr., 2. l., pp. 76-78, 80. Original in Russian.*

Report of B. Pugo, Deputy Chair of the State Security Committee of the Latvian SSR, to the Central Committee of the Latvian Communist Party, about the spread of western music in youth discotheques and the necessity of controlling the contents of programs

October 24, 1980

The intelligence agencies of the imperialist states, their ideological centers, and their overseas anti-Soviet organizations recently have activated attempts to ideologically harm and influence Soviet youth. With the help of bourgeois ideology, the objective of the enemy is to damage the beliefs of young people in communist ideals, to enlarge in them the influence of baser instincts, of a primitive worldview, and of a consumer attitude toward life. To further this goal, there is widespread use of so-called cultural exports, include music meant for the masses of youth, and in the last few years – discotheques.

The radio stations of the enemy's ideological centers, in broadcasts meant for Soviet youth, encourage an active western lifestyle and through propaganda spread apoliticism and negative attitudes towards Soviet reality, hiding [such messages] in music popular among our contemporary youth. This popular and youthful genre of music has recently become increasingly widespread in our Republic.

During the past few years in Rīga, there has been the sporadic opening of many youth discothèques. Currently there are about 20 official, permanent working discothèques and more than 50 that are open episodically. The most popular discotheques operate in the Printers'Central Club, in the Moscow Regional Culture House, and in the RPI Student Club. Several thousand young boys and girls, ranging from students to school children to young workers, go to these discotheques.

Nonetheless, in the organization and performances of these discotheques there are many features that negatively influence their idea-contents. There is practically no leadership present in the discotheque. To this day, there has been established no organizational and methodological center dealing with how discotheques should be created and managed. As a result, many discotheques are run by persons who genuflect before Western mass culture, who have no musical education, and who are poorly prepared politically; not infrequently, [such persons] exhibit purely commercial motives.

As a result, a significant part of discotheque programs is empty of ideas but overloaded with tendentious information of a doubtful character. Generally, what is performed are the works of foreign ensembles whose repertoire is politically unacceptable ("Čingishan" from the GFR and "Kiss" and others.) There is an absence of effective and competent control over the discotheque program and the contents of the repertoire, and as a result almost no Soviet disco music is played. Because the financial conditions of the discotheques is so chaotic, a situation has arisen whereby the equipment and recordings are handled directly by the leaders of the discotheques, thus opening the way for individual persons to make a killing.

Thus there is the unsolved problem of providing discotheques with quality equipment and recording material. Practically all of the recordings played at the discotheques are prepared at home. This results in the creation of conditions in which ideologically unacceptable recordings can be distributed. [...]

In order to obtain foreign records, cassettes and magnetic tapes, as well as sound systems, young persons contact visiting foreigners, including Latvian émigrés, and make shady deals with them. Also, there have been uncovered many instances of direct attempts by young people to establish contacts with western radio stations, which can lead to the enemy's exploitation of these contacts for damaging action. We are taking certain steps on this question.

We believe that the continuing unchecked work of discotheques and of ensemble concerts on stage, which not rarely has a negative psychic effect on youth, can lead to serious, politically unacceptable consequences that can become widespread in scope.

Our view is that the republic's Ministry of Culture, the Council of Latvian Republic Trade Unions, the Latvian LKJS Central Committee, and the Latvian Soviet Composers Society should develop an action plan that would lead to the creation of effective and permanent control over the working of youth discotheques, the improvement the ideological contents of their programs and repertoire. The plan [when implemented] should be assured of involving experienced and prepared cadres and having appropriate material support.

Deputy Chair of the Latvian SSR State Security Commission   B. Pugo

Source: *LVA PA, 101. f., 45. apr., 95. l., pp. 85-87. Original in Russian.*

Documents No. 102-104
The cult of personality

Document No. 102

A request by the voters of Rīga to the Municipal Working Class Council to proclaim J. Stalin an Honorary Deputy[176]

March 12, 1953

In the last election of the local Council of Working Class Deputies, we had the great fortune of voting for our dear father, leader, and teacher Josef Vissarionovich Stalin, who was unanimously elected as our Deputy to the Rīga Municipal Council and Rīga District Council of Working Class Deputies.

A great misfortune has befallen all Soviet persons [and] all of the working class of the world. Death has removed our dear beloved Josef Vissarionovich Stalin from our ranks. A heavy loss; there are not words to describe it. Josef Vissarionovich's illumined character [and] his selfless service to all persons will serve as an example to us for life. His memory will be preserved in our hearts for all time.

We ask the Rīga Municipal Council of Working Class Deputies to immortalize our dear deputy's – Josef Vissarionovich Stalin's memory – by keeping him as an Honorary Deputy of the Rīga Municipal Council of Working Class Deputies. We ask the Municipal Council to erect a memorial plaque at the Electoral Commission Building where he was a candidate for Deputy. [177]

Source: *LVA PA, 102. f., 11. apr., 177. l., p. 16. Original in Russian.*

Excerpts from the minutes of a meeting of the Bureau of the Central Committee of the Latvian Communist Party about punishing persons connected to the incorrect printing of J. Stalin's name

March 31, 1953

[...] The Bureau of the Central Committee of the Latvian Communist Party notes that in printing of the magazine "Znaņije – sila"[178] number 1 of 1953 in printing plant No. 2, a serious political mistake was permitted – the Leader's last name was mangled. The Chief of the Printing Industry, Publishers and Book Sellers Board of the Latvian SSR Council of Ministers, comrade Putniņš, J., and the Director of the Printing Trust, comrade Mihailovs, P., and the 2nd Director of Typography, comrade Erensteins H., have not provided a correct political evaluation of this mistake and have not called the guilty parties to strict account.

The Bureau of the Central Committee of the Latvian Communist Party decides that:

1. For not maintaining order in Printing Office No. 2, for a non-party attitude in evaluating the gross political mistake that was allowed in the printing of the journal "Znaņije – sila" at this Office, the Chief of the Board of the Printing Industry, Publishers and Book Sellers of the Latvian SSR Council of Ministers, comrade Putniņš, Jānis son of Pēteris, member of the Communist Party of the Soviet Union since 1933, Party card number 4762855 [and] the Director of the Printing Industry Trust, comrade Mihailov, Pimen son of Maksim, member of the Communist Party of the Soviet Union since 1947, Party card number 9175917, are given severe reprimands to be noted in their record[179]; but the Director of Number 2 Printers, comrade Erenšteins, Honon son of Mark, [is given] a reprimand.

2. The Minister of the Interior of the Latvian SSR, comrade Kovaļčuk, is assigned the task of investigating how the gross political mistake was allowed in the printing of the journal "Znaņie-sila," and of reporting his findings to the Central Committee of the Latvian Communist Party.

Source: *LVA PA, 101. f., 16. apr., 20. l., p. 88. Original in Russian.*

The decision of the Supreme Court of the Latvian SSR in the case of critical remarks about J. Stalin made by R. Adamovičs.

April 6, 1953

Decision
In the name of the Latvian SSR
On April 6, 1953, the Collegium of Criminal Affairs of the Supreme Court of the Latvian SSR, with the following composition:

Presiding officer: J. Rīdziņš; court assessors: D. Poiss, A. Brečs; secretary Seikale; with the participation of procurator V. Kuznecov and the lawyer V. Jakovlev reviewed in a closed session of the Court in Rīga the criminal affair of Adamovičs, Rudolfs, son of Jānis, born in 1924 in the village of Dagda in the Dagda region of the Daugavpils district of the Latvian SSR, from the working class and by nationality a Pole, citizen of the USSR, non-party, and with a seventh grade education, married, and before his arrest working in a cement factory in Rīga as an electrician, lives in Rīga in apartment 21 of number 2 Podraga Street – charged with the crimes mentioned in KPFSR KK 58,10.1.

Having listened to the explanations of the defendant Adamovičs, Rudolfs and to the testimony of the eyewitnesses, the court in investigating looked through previous investigative material and real evidence. The Collegium of the Criminal Court of the Supreme Court was able to clarify that the defendant Adamovičs, Rudolfs on March 6, 1953, being at work in the cement factory in Rīga, in the factory dressing room in the company of factory workers, voiced obscene lies about the death of the Head of Soviet government. [180] In addition, the defendant Adamovičs had at his apartment anti-Soviet literature that was removed from his apartment during a search and this qualifies as a crime under KPFSR KK 58.-10.1.d.

Confronted with his crimes, the defendant Adamovičs in the pre-investigation period admitted that he was guilty, but in the court proceedings did not admit his guilt and denied his earlier testimony, saying that he had lied about himself.

Reviewing the investigative material, the Court Collegium views the defendant Adamovičs' attempts to deny his testimony during investigation as an attempt by Adamovičs to escape responsibility for the crimes he committed. Convincing testimonies of Ivanov, Ronis, and Baranov, who testified in the courtroom, as well as the other real proof reveals sufficiently that Adamovičs committed the crimes of KK 58-10-1-d, that is he told obscene lies about the Head of Soviet government with respect to his death, and that he was in possession of anti-Soviet literature. Assessing the existing proof of the affair on the basis of internal proof based on the examination of all of the circumstances of the affair in their entirety, the Court Collegium views the charge of KK. 58-10-1-d against Adamovičs as proven.

On the basis of all the uncovered evidence, and following the KPSFSR KPK 319 and 320 paragraphs, the Court Collegium of the Criminal Court of the Supreme Court of the Latvian SSR decides:

Adamovičs, Rudolfs, son of Jānis, born 1924, is punished, according to KPSFS KK 58-10-1-d with imprisonment for 10 years, with the loss of rights according to KK 31-p-a, b, and c for 5 years.

The term of punishment for the convicted R. Adamovičs will begin on March 7, 1953.

The material proof in the affair, the anti-Soviet literature, will be destroyed.

The decision is final and can not be appealed.

Chair J. Rīdziņš
People's Assessors: D. Poiss, Brečs

Source: *LVA, 1986. f., 2. apr., 4494. l., pp. 79, 80. Original in Russian.*

Documents No. 105-107
Elections in the Soviet style

Document No. 105

Instructions from the Central Committee of the Latvian Communist Party about the composition of the Supreme Council of the Latvian SSR

1946

Altogether 120 deputies are needed.[181]

Of those there must be:

Women	36 persons or	30%
Non-party	26 persons or	20-25%

Expected by province	120 persons	
Of those:		
Women	36 persons or	30%
Non-party	28 persons or	23.3%
Latvians	93 persons or	77.5%
Russians	22 persons or	18.3%

Among them

Comprehend Latvian language	8 persons or	6.6%
Georgians	1 person or	1.2%
Ukrainians	1	1.2%
Belarussians	3	2.5%
Secretaries of District Committees of the LCP	10	
Secretaries of the Municipal Committees…	4	
Secretaries of the Region…	3	
Chairs of District Executive Committees	7	
Municipal	4	
From the Central Committee of the LCP	6	
From the Council of Ministers	6	
Ministers and Deputy Ministers	22	
Komsomolers	3	
Soldiers	8	
From the workers	7	
From the farmers	16	
Including:		
Chairs of Village Councils	5	
Parish Executive Committee Chairs	3	
Teachers	7	
Doctors	1	
From the Supreme Council	4	
Academicians	1	
Factory Directors	2	

Hero of the Soviet Union	1
Artists	2
Authors	2
Mother Heroines	1
Editor of a Periodical	1
Student	1
Chair, the Committee of the Republic Labor Union	1

Source: *LVA PA, 101. f., 9. apr., 35a. l., p. 202. Original in Russian.*

Document No. 106

Top secret report by A. Eglītis, the Minister of the Interior of the Latvian SSR, to the Chair of the Council of Ministers, V. Lācis, about the work of the Interior Ministry in preparation for the elections to the Supreme Council and during the elections

March 4, 1947

To ensure that the elections to the Supreme Council of the Latvian SSR [ran smoothly], the organs of the Ministry of the Interior accomplished the following:

1. To give a decisive blow to the nationalist bandit underground, to the criminal element and to thieves, and to their support base in the Republic's municipalities and districts, an operational group was created consisting of employees of the Ministry of the Interior, police, soldiers of the Ministry of the Interior, and fighters from the strike forces of the Ministry.

    The operational units were ordered to uncover and liquidate all nationalist bandits, groups of criminals, and thieves in the Republic before the elections to the Supreme Council.

2. To organize and lead this activity the following were sent to rural districts: Deputy Minister of the Interior, Colonel Sieks (Rīga district); Deputy Minister of the Interior, Colonel Zaharov (Daugavpils district); Deputy Minister of the Interior, Colonel Piesis (Liepāja district); Chief of the Section of the Fight against Bandits, Colonel Ritikov (Talsu district); and 14 other leading officials from the Ministry.

    Our operational workers were stationed in each rural electoral district and at the polling stations, and altogether 1,883 operational agents engaged in the task of liquidating banditism.

    In the city of Rīga, 13 sectors were created for the 276 operational workers who had the assignment of liquidating criminals and the maintenance of order during the elections.

    Altogether, in the Republic, the struggle against bandits and the guarding of electoral districts and the polling booths involved 2,176 operational workers from the Ministry of the Interior, 2,705 soldiers from the Ministry of the Interior, 180 students from the Ministry of the Interior School, 83 students from the Police school, 1,835 soldiers of the Soviet army, 12,690 commanders and fighters from the Ministry of the Interior's Strike Battalions[182] --- altogether 19,671 persons.

    As a result of the activities of the organs of the Ministry of the Interior in the time period from December 15, 1946 to February 15, 1947, the following were uncovered and destroyed:

    a. Bandit groups tied to the anti-Soviet underground   38

    b. Bandit and robbers' groups   45

During the course of the liquidations, the following were killed: 14 band chiefs, 49 bandits; arrested: 28 band chiefs, 261 bandits, 195 bandit supporters, 10 members of anti-Soviet organizations, 3 terrorists, 14 German henchmen, 5 traitors to the homeland, 4 deserters and persons who had avoided service in the Soviet Army, 23 persons who were in possession of illegal firearms, 154 robbers and destroyers of socialist property, and 13 other illegal elements. In addition, the following were exonerated: 12 band chiefs, 91 bandits, 1 member of an anti-Soviet organization, 448 former legionaries and German henchmen, 17 deserters and persons who had avoided service in the Soviet Army, and 12 other illegals.

Consequently, [the total of those] killed, arrested and legally exonerated were: 54 band chiefs, 401 bandits, 195 bandit supporters and 704 criminal elements.

[The following were confiscated from] from the bandits: 1 mortar, 33 machine guns, 59 automatic rifles, 186 rifles, 201 pistols, 212 grenades, 14 mines, 15 rocket shells, 44,010 cartridges, 72 kg explosives, 1 transmitter, and 6 mortar sets.[183]

3. In doing their jobs to stop planned terrorist acts, diversions, bandit attacks, and the spread of anti-Soviet pamphlets in the days before the election, the organs of the Ministry of the Interior uncovered and liquidated several terrorist and bandit groups, of whom the most characteristic were:

a. January 1, 1947, in Kuldīga district there were found, wounded during armed conflict, and captured: the leader of the diversionary terrorist and spy organization "SS Jagdverband Ostland"[184] in Latvia, the "SD" Captain Boriss Jankavs, together with the captured bandit Melesko.

From the testimony of Jankavs, on the 1st of February in Kuldīga district, the "Oļģerts'" terrorist band was crushed, and, as a result, the band chief, former German Army Lieutenant, Oļģerts Kārkliņš, was killed, as well as the band chiefs Tumpmans, "Karlitis," and three other bandits. Two were arrested, and 10 bandits were legally exonerated.

Taken from them were: 8 machine guns, 5 automatic rifles, 6 rifles, 14 pistols, 36 grenades, 3,200 cartridges, and 1 typewriter on which the bandits prepared anti-Soviet pamphlets.

b. Using the testimony of Ēvalds Pakuls, a leader of an underground nationalist band in Kurzeme who was captured earlier, on December 28, 1946, the headquarters of the Voldemārs Poļakovs'band in the district of Tukums was discovered and completely liquidated. Killed – the band's chief Poļakovs, a former German Army Lieutenant, and 7 bandits including two terrorists: "Nēģeris" and "Osis."

After the arrest of the band's signaler Ērika Launīte, she testified that the terrorists "Nēģeris" and "Osis" were preparing a terrorist act against the Secretary of the Tukums District Committee of the Latvian Communist Party, and against other notable Republic Party and Soviet officials.

Taken from the bandits: 1 machine gun, 6 automatic rifles, 2 rifles, 8 pistols and 150 cartridges.

c. On February 13, 1947, in the region of the "Roznieks" house in Lubāna parish of the Madona district, the Slavinskis' terrorist band was discovered, and after armed conflict, liquidated; 11 persons were killed, including the band's chief Ādolfs Slavinskis, a former policeman with the code-name: "Laivinieks."

From 1945-1946, the Slavinskis' band made more than twenty-five shameless bandit attacks in the territory of the districts of Madona and Viļaka, including attacks on state institutions and the murder of Soviet and Party persons. Of this band's number, in 1946, the Ministry of the Interior killed 23, arrested 10, and legally exonerated 3 bandits.

At the place of the armed conflict the following was collected: 3 machineguns, 3 automatic rifles, 6 rifles, 4 pistols, 15 grenades, and 3,000 cartridges.

d. On February 13, 1947, in the territory of the parishes of Lutriņa, Kabile, and Gaiķi in the Kuldīga district, bandits from the "Seska ūsas" band distributed 50 counter-revolutionary pamphlets that asked inhabitants not to go to the elections and threatened to shoot those that went to vote.

As a result of this activity, the distributor of the pamphlets, bandit Kārlis Rutkis, was captured on that same day, and after interrogation testified that the counter-revolutionary pamphlets were being distributed by orders of the band chief Cuša, and that the band decided to destroy the polling place in Lutriņi parish on the night of February 15th.

Using the information given by Rutkis, on February 14, 1947, the Cuša band was found in Lutriņi parish near the "Jāņkalna" farmstead, and after armed conflict, it was completely liquidated. Seven bandits were killed, including the band's chief Cusis with the code name "Seska ūsas" a former member of the diversionary, terrorist organization "SS Jagdverband Ostland."

Collected at the place of the armed conflict were: 3 machine guns, 6 automatic rifles, 2 rifles, 8 pistols, 2 grenades, 15 rocket shells, 200 cartridges; in addition, 190 counter-revolutionary pamphlets that were to be distributed on election day for the Supreme Council of the Latvian SSR.

e. On February 15, 1947, in the territory of Drusti parish in the Cēsis district a bunker was discovered, and after some gunfire the bandit was killed; with him, there was found: a typewriter, different examples of counter-revolutionary propaganda urging a boycott of the elections, a machine gun, an automatic rifle, and 1,000 cartridges.

4. In the process of conduction operations together with legally exonerated bandits and former members of fascist military organizations, the District Sections of the Ministry of the Interior discovered and liquidated three groups of bandit this year in February.

In Ludza district in Mērdzene parish, during an attempt to rob a farmer's house 2 bandits were killed, together with 1 bandit robber from a previously exonerated and liquidated group of bandits.

In the district of Daugavpils, 4 bandit robbers were arrested who happened to be legally exonerated bandits from three defeated bandit divisions of 1945-1946.

In the district of Viļaka, a bandit robber group with five persons, led by the legally exonerated bandit Stanislavs Donušs, was liquidated.

5. Using gathered information, the organs of the Ministry of the Interior discovered and confiscated three warehouses of weapons, munitions, and technical equipment during January and the first half of February in the territories of the districts of Talsi, Madona, and Viļaka. Altogether taken were: 1 mortar, 3 machineguns, 4 automatic rifles, 12 rifles, 8 pistols, 22 grenades, 3 mines, 9,500 cartridges, 1 radio station, 2 typewriters.

6. Because of all of these operations there was no bandit activity during the elections, and no violations of public order in Rīga municipality and district, except for the distribution of some illiterate, hand-written pamphlets that were discovered and quickly collected in a timely manner.

Minister of the Interior of the Latvia SSR   Major General Eglītis

Source: *LVA, 270. f., 1. s.apr., 270. l., pp. 143-147. Original in Russian.*

Document No. 107

Excerpt from the confidential minutes of a meeting of the Bureau of the Rīga Municipal Committee of the Latvian Communist Party concerning the mistake in the list of Latvian SSR Supreme Council Deputies published in the newspaper "Rīga's Balss"

March 5, 1985

[…] 2nd par. About the mistake in the newspaper "Rīga's Balss," about the need to enhance the responsibility of the leadership of the editorial board, and about the newspaper's quality.
(comrades Šveide, Ždanova, Reigass, Rubiks, Razguļajeva, Vagris)

On February 28, 1985, in the Russian version of the newspaper "Rīga's Balss," a mistake was made in the list of the deputies[185] of the Supreme Council of the Latvian SSR, namely, the last name, first name, and patronymic of the Deputy from the 85th Riga District, as well as his place of work, were separated from each other and appeared in different parts of the article. The mistake was uncovered only when the newspaper was released to be sold.

The mentioned error happened because the head of the editorial staff (editor, comrade V. Šveide), the journalists, the proofreader, and the printer showed insufficient responsibility toward the publication of the issue.

This event proves that the editorial collective of the newspaper "Rīga's Balss," and the responsible members of the Publishers Organization of the Latvian Communist Party Central Committee, do not follow the order necessary for journalists and typesetters to have accountability for their work and for the quality of the produced newspaper.

The Bureau of the Party City Committee decides:

1. For being insufficiently demanding of the workers responsible for the production of the newspaper, and for inadequate control of the preparation of the newspaper for publication that led to the appearance of the coarse mistake, the Editor of the newspaper "Rīga's Balss", member of the Communist Party of the Soviet Union, comrade Šveide, V., is reprimanded.

2. For carelessness that led to the appearance of the coarse mistake in the newspaper "Rīga's Balss," the Deputy Editor, member of the Communist Party of the USSR, Ždanova, M. is given a severe reprimand.

3. For being inadequately demanding on those assigned to him, and for a lack of necessary control over the work of the typesetters that led to the coarse mistake in the newspaper "Rīga's Balss," the Chief Engineer of the Publishers of the Latvian Communist Party Central Committee, member of the Communist Party of the Soviet Union, comrade Reigass, G., is given a severe reprimand.

4. The Party Bureau at the newspaper "Rīga's Balss", and the editorial staff, are to make sure that the editors increase the personal responsibility and executive discipline in the quality of the newspaper's publication process by improving the organization of collective work, and by enacting strict controls so that the editorial workers fulfill their responsibilities. […]

Source: *LVA PA, 102. f., 49. apr., 7. l., p. 109. Original in Russian.*

Documents No. 108-111
The group "Helsinki-86" -- the initiators of the Awakening

Document No. 108

Announcement of the founding in Latvia of the human rights group "HELSINKI – 86"
Liepāja, July 1986

In view of the 49th and 50th paragraphs of the Constitution of the Latvian SSR, we have decided to found a group that will follow how our nation's economic, cultural, and individual rights are observed.

We undertake to openly to inform international organizations, without censorship or external pressure, about violations of our nation's material and spiritual values, as well as of the nation itself.

Our basic principle is to block the path of lies and terror. To give to all nations the right to choose their path of development. To follow the principles defined in the final Document of the Helsinki conference.

The group has decided to call itself after Helsinki.

"HELSINKI – 86"

1. Grantiņš, Linards, son of Alberts, born 1950 in the Boļšerečenska region of the province of Omsk, works in the creative union "Daiļrade" as a craftsman in amber and metals. In Liepāja, M. Būka Street 47-8.

2. Bitenieks, Raimonds, son of Ernests, born in 1944 in Liepāja, in Latvia, works as a driver for the Central Hospital. In Liepāja, Grīzupe Street 102-46.

3. Bariss, Mārtiņš, son of Pēteris, born in Lēdurga hamlet in Limbaži region in Latvia, works in the Liepāja Dry Goods integrated Plant.

Source: *Helsinki-86. Original in Latvian.*

An appeal by Latvia's Human Rights Defense Group "HELSINKI – 86" in connection with the anniversary of the persons deported on June 14, 1941

May 1987

On the night of June 14-15, 1941, the first mass deportations of the Latvian nation took place, from which only a few returned.

Men were separated from women and children. People found themselves transported in livestock wagons in terrible conditions. Children and the elderly were the first to part from this world and found their gravesite by the side of the railroad in a foreign land.

This genocidal act was led by the Communist Party. Even to this day the Party has not seen it as necessary to apologize, let alone compensate people for moral and material losses. Only murky phrases about some [personality] cult are heard.

We, the group "HELSINKI –86", have decided to lay flowers at the Freedom Monument in Rīga this year on June 14th at 15:00 to pay our respects to the martyrs of genocide and sovietization.

We invite other Latvians who are not indifferent to our nation's fate to pay respects to the innocent martyrs with a moment of silence and a laying of flowers at the Freedom Monument on June 14th in Rīga.

"HELSINKI –86" group:
Grantiņš, Linards
Silaraups, Rolands
Bitenieks, Raimonds
Andersons, Guntis
Bariss, Mārtiņš

Source: *Helsinki-86. Original in Latvian.*

Document No. 110

Secret decision of the Bureau of the Central Committee of the Communist Party of Latvia, entitled "About the anti-social and nationalistic events in Rīga on August 23"

August 24, 1987

(Comrades Soboļev, Oherin, Briļs, Rubenis, Auškāps, Zitmanis, Ņukša, Zukulis, Priedītis, Brokāns, Gobelko, Rubiks, Savicka, Terehov, Gruduls, Barkāns, Astahov, Šteinbriks, Johansons, Stefanovič, Zālīte).

Recently, hostile foreign radio stations and other centers opposed to the USSR in the ideological war have expanded their urging that inhabitants of the Baltic Republics organize meetings and demonstrations this year on August 23rd to mark the anniversary of the 1939 Soviet-German Non-Aggression Pact. In line with the expectation of the Western instigators, provocative activities in Riga were announced by the extremist elements who have united in the so-called group "Helsinki – 86".

Some politically immature inhabitants of Rīga followed the provocative call of hostile propaganda. A few dozen nationalistically inclined persons organized a procession and a meeting by the Freedom Monument. After laying down flowers, some of them acted provocatively -- they shouted slogans and tried to give their activities a nationalistic, anti-Soviet character. Individual hooligan elements, primarily from among the youth, insulted members of the police and allowed other violations of social order.

All this has created indignation among the majority of the citizenry. Party and ideological activists did take explanatory actions at the site of the event. The police detained persons who violated the social order. These actions allowed the localization of anti-social behavior and prevented a demonstration or a provocative procession.

The Bureau of the Central Committee of Latvia's Communist Party views the events of August 23rd of this year the Freedom Monument as expressly negative and politically hostile. The City [Party] Committee, City Executive Committee, Region Committee, Region Executive Committees, and Rīga police organs did not take sufficient steps to prevent the anticipated gathering of nationalistically influenced elements at the Freedom Monument.

Therefore the Bureau of the Central Committee of Latvia's Communist Party decrees:

1. To assign to the Party's Rīga City Committee and the Rīga Region Party Committee to carefully analyze the events of August 23rd of this year at the Freedom Monument and to mount additional activities for energetically reinforcing training and propaganda among all categories of the city's inhabitants. Discussions must be held of the nationalistic, anti-Soviet, and anti-social work of the event's participants, and the necessary explanatory and preventative work must be carried out in places of learning, in labor collectives, and at places of residence.

   The relevant sections of the Central Committee and the sources of mass information must strengthen the unmasking of the hostile work of bourgeois radio stations and the so-called "Helsinki – 86" group's nationalistic anti-Soviet essence. The Republic's press, radio and television broadcasts must uncover the extreme character of the work of the active members [of the group].

2. In a month's time, there must be developed a long-term propaganda program dealing with the most complicated and pointed questions in Latvia's history. A report must be sent to the Party committees orienting them in the events of August 23rd, and this must include recommendations for the organization of counter-propaganda events. In September of this

year, within the setting of a day of political education, there must be organized speeches on this question by the Latvian Communist Party Central Committee. Using the Republic's House of Science in Rīga, a political discussion club must be created, which must involve more widely leading scientists, cultural and artistic workers, journalists, and activists from the Party, soviets and the Komsomol, particularly in meetings with young people.

3. City and region Party committees, trade union and Komsomol organs must strengthen their work to ensure that the working masses, particularly the young, are trained in class consciousness and high political vigilance, and are immunized against the intrigues of hostile propaganda; and must regularly investigate society's thinking, so as to unmask in a timely manner nationalistically inclined persons, to improve [the quality of] individual effort; and to enhance the influence of the labor collective on these persons, creating an atmosphere of intolerance toward any expressions of nationalism, chauvinism, and anti-Sovietism. The Party organization's reports and election campaigns must be used more energetically toward this goal.

   The Party's committees and organizations must be acquainted with the decision of the Central Committee of Latvia's Communist Party concerning the progress of international and patriotic training, and devote particular attention to achieving results in the work that is done.

4. The police must be more flexible and energetic in preventing similar provocations, while at the same time preserving strict socialist legality, the legal order, and the citizens' constitutional rights.

5. This decision must be published in the press.

6. Control over the implementation of the decision is assigned to the Secretariat of the Central Committee of Latvia's Communist Party and the Secretary of the Central Committee of Latvia's Communist Party, Comrade A.V. Gorbunovs personally.

C.C. Secretary   V. Soboļev

Source: *LVA PA, 101. f., 61. apr., 73. l., pp. 112-114. Original in Russian.*

Letter of the human rights defense group, "HELSINKI – 86"'s to the governments of the signatories of the Concluding Act of the European Security and Cooperation Conference in Helsinki

August 24, 1987

We wish to draw the attention of the international community to the egregious violations of human rights last night, August 23rd, in Rīga.

On August 6th, Latvia's human rights defense group "Helsinki – 86" invited people to place flowers at the Freedom Monument to honor the martyrs of the outrageous Molotov-Ribbentrop Secret Agreement and through this to draw the world's attention to the unresolved consequences of this criminal pact. Already by the second half of August, the press had started a campaign of crude disinformation and lies against us, and we were not given the chance to refute the lies.

On August 21, almost all of the members of "Helsinki – 86" and also Jānis Rožkalns, Boriss Grezins, and Jānis Vēveris, were summoned to see the Deputy Prosecutor of the Latvian SSR, who issued warnings and threats against placing flowers at the monument in any organized manner.

On August 22nd, all of the side streets [in the area] were closed and all traffic was detoured along the Freedom Monument in order to interfere with any attempts to approach it.

We had decided to place flowers at the monument at 17:00, but at 15:00, the police and members of the KGB arrived at our apartment on Soviet Boulevard and told us we could not leave the apartment. To our objection that this was a violation of the Constitution, we received, as an answer, threats to settle accounts with us and laughter. We were in an illegal arrest situation. The only option that remained to us was to hang out of the window a sign with the words THE HELSINKI GROUP IS IMPRISONED HERE, because our telephone was also disconnected at 15:00. Immediately the apartment was broken into [again] and with the use of crude physical measures by the representatives of state power, we were taken to the police station. There we were held for several hours. During this time of arrest, bodily damage was done to many of us, including the woman present, Gunta Barisa, who was there with a child.

At the same time, about 10,000 persons gathered at the Freedom Monument and called out: FREEDOM FOR LATVIA! RELEASE THE HELSINKI GROUP! SHAME, SHAME, SHAME!

Those that wanted to place flowers at the monument had them ripped from their hands if the color combination resembled the colors of the [old] national flag, red-white-red. The police tried to keep the masses back with curses and punches, until the police cordon was penetrated by about 2,000 persons who broke through to the monument.

At about 19:00, about 1,000 members of the police and the KGB began to try to capture people, arresting several hundred. Afterward, the entire block around the monument was blocked off by a police cordon.

The Latvian [news] broadcast "TV Panorama" on August 23rd proved again that dishonesty rules the land, because in the report it was said that a few dozen persons gathered at the monument.

During recent days, we have been followed in a completely undisguised manner. This is all just because we stood for our nation's right to know the whole truth about its history and to know the full truth also about the USSR's shameful treaty with the fascists.

Honored state leaders and parliamentarians! Europe pays considerable attention to, for example, the events in the Republic of South Africa, but when similar things happen right here in Europe, in Rīga, they are not given the appropriate attention. We believe that violence and the crude violation of human rights must be unmasked in any corner of the world. The time has come to talk about violence against society's thoughts in Latvia. The nation's demand for the truth has again been suppressed with crude violence. The only argument of the state organs in this dialogue was brutal force. It is this kind of experience that allows us to more clearly understand who are the true and pure representatives of the nation.

The process that has started in the Baltic area, in Latvia first, cannot be stopped. European society and the government of the USSR will hear our nation's voice more frequently. We appeal to your conscience. Will European society remain indifferent even when before their very eyes representatives of the Soviet government continue to violently settle scores with those who express the people's will? We ask you to pay attention and direct your activities to the processes that have begun in the Baltic area. We ask you to evaluate them objectively and support them. We invite the Soviet government to officially investigate the illegal events in Rīga on August 23rd, to identify those who are responsible, and to put them on trial.

With respect –Latvia's Human Rights Defense Group "HELSINKI - 86" leader
Jānis Barkāns

Source: *Helsinki-86. Original in Latvian.*

Comment: *The Human Rights Defense Group in Latvia – "Helsinki – 86"—called soon after its creation for an end to the occupation of Latvia by the Soviet Union and for the renewal of Latvia's independence. The laying of flowers at the Freedom Monument organized by representatives of "Helsinki – 86" in Rīga on June 14, 1987 was the first open action against Soviet power that captured the imagination of a large part of Latvian society and is considered the beginning of the "Awakening". With this action there began in Riga the so-called "calendar unrest," consisting of public gatherings meant to memorialize important events in Latvia's history (the deportations of March 25, 1949; the signing of the Molotov-Ribbentrop pact on August 23, 1939; the declaration of Latvian independence on November 18, 1918, and others). Most of these took place at the Freedom Monument in Riga. The LCP CC and KGB tried to suppress these activities, both by ordering the use of naked force against protestors and also by initiating "ideological explanatory work" (but without noticeable success). The protest actions directed against the occupation power drew international attention to the fact of the occupation of the Baltic States, and made many persons become interested in the most important events of 20th century history of Latvia. This led to doubt about how these events were portrayed in official Soviet-era histories and found a place in the developing confrontation between the "Awakening" movement for the national liberation of Latvia and continuing Soviet control.*

THE NATIONAL INDEPENDENCE MOVEMENT OF LATVIA — THE FIRST MASS-BASED ORGANIZATION SEEKING THE RETURN OF LATVIAN INDEPENDENCE

Document No. 112

Declaration of the Council of the National Independence Movement of Latvia concerning the Movement's goals

July 10, 1988

We are very worried about the situation of the Latvian nation in Latvia. For the first time in its history, it is becoming a national minority in its own land.

A part of the nation was exterminated in Stalinist mass repressions. The unjustified baseless creation of heavy industry [in Latvia] brought a massive flood of other nationalities into the Republic (in the period after the World War II, about 700,000 persons).

During the period of stagnation, illegalities [of all kinds] facilitated the decline of national culture, of morals, and of the desire to work. Because of an irresponsible and incompetent government, industry was damaged and agriculture declined, and people developed an attitude of indifference toward their surroundings. Latvia's natural environment was polluted by industrial waste, and its resources near exhaustion.

The nation's education and health care is at an impermissibly low level. Our nation's life expectancy is the lowest of any nation in Europe.

We believe that these and similar conditions threaten the vital interests of the Latvian nation, even its survival. Latvians can successfully defend their interests and solve the many mounting problems only in the condition of complete national sovereignty.

We believe that the Latvian nation's demand for a sovereign state is just and holy.

The Council of the National Independence Movement of Latvia invites all those in Latvia and beyond who support the Latvian nation's effort for national self-determination, -- regardless of their nationality, religious denomination, or party affiliation – to join the movement for the renewal of Latvia as a sovereign republic.

The primary task of the movement is to achieve the establishment of the democratic state of the Republic of Latvia and of political sovereignty, the securing of economic independence, the normalization of the demographic situation, and the defense of cultural traditions.

The movement directs itself against discrimination against the Latvian nation in any form and defends the interests of the Latvian nation. The movement is not directed against any of the nationalities living in Latvia, recognizing their legitimate political, economic and cultural interests, and invites them to work together to solve common problems.

The movement works with open, democratic, peaceful methods within the recognized human rights norms of the UN and other international organizations. The movement participates in the development of socialism, pluralism, openness, and democracy and opposes against all violence, militarism, and chauvinism.

The movement is for cooperation with all similar social organizations, societies and clubs that share its goals. Specialists of all kinds and members of the creative professions must become the pathbreakers. All ideas and suggestions can be useful.

We believe an important task in the realization of the movement's goal is to implement the resolutions of the plenary meeting of the Board of the Creative Unions of the Latvian SSR. Furthermore, we view the following as necessary:

1. Stopping immediately the flood of migrants into Latvia and facilitating the return of some of them to their homelands.
2. Defining the Latvian language as the language of state.
3. Defining the nature of Latvian citizenship and renewing national symbols.
4. Thinking of Latvians living outside of Latvia as part of the nation.
5. Freeing the territory of Latvia of nuclear weapons.
6. Giving over to the jurisdiction of the Latvian government all of the existing productive enterprises and institutions that now are under the jurisdiction of Union ministries and offices.
7. Creating Latvian national military units where Latvia's youth could do obligatory military service, and using Latvian as the language of instruction in military schools. Rescinding military training in general education schools.
8. Guaranteeing in a constitution all personal freedoms and basic rights.
9. Allowing the expression of opinions in the press, radio, and television, that differ from the official view, and the organization of meetings and demonstrations having the purpose of making political demands.
10. Allowing the publication and distribution of an independent press.
11. Creating a new and democratic electoral law that would guarantee the right to propose independent lists of candidates to all elections.
12. Allowing the establishment of independent political parties.
13. Recognizing as illegal and rejecting the July 1959 decisions of Latvia's Communist Party Plenary meeting on language, cadres, economy and other questions.
14. Ending the state's control of churches. Ensuring the access of the churches to the press, radio, and television; their right to distribute literature with religious content; and their right to do charity work.

We invite all who are concerned with the problems mentioned above to send their ideas and suggestions to the Movement's council.

The Council of the National Independence Movement of Latvia:
1. Eduards Berklavs
2. Jānis Biezais
3. Juris Dobelis
4. Aivars Jakovičs
5. Roberts Kļimovičs
6. Juris Lomanovskis
7. Visvaldis Mucenieks
8. Andris Pauls-Pāvuls
9. Ilga Pūpola
10. Einārs Repše
11. Diāna Repše
12. Anta Rudzīte
13. Dans Titavs
14. Valts Titavs

The report was ratified by the general meeting of the National Independence Movement of Latvia, which was also a public and the founding meeting, in Rīga in Arkādija on July 10, 1988.

Source: *LVA, f. 1806; see also in Tauta, pp. 11-13. Original in Latvian.*

The fundamental position of the Council of the National Independence Movement of Latvia (LNNK) on the question of the status of the Republic of Latvia

September 8, 1988

We believe that, historically and juridically, it has been shown that the Sovietization of the Republic of Latvia and its inclusion into the USSR in 1940 was illegal, and we do not recognize Latvia as a *de jure* member of the Union of Soviet Socialist Republics.

We view the *de facto* inclusion of the Republic of Latvia into the USSR as an occupation of Latvia and ask for its end.

Ratified, voted unanimously on at the meeting of the Council.

Minutes taken by:	A. PAULS-PĀVULS
Meeting Chaired by:	J. DOBELIS

The fundamental position was supported unanimously by the general meeting of the National Independence Movement of Latvia on September 17, 1988, by more than 2,000 persons.

Meeting chaired by:	J. DOBELIS
Minutes taken by:	E. REPŠE

Source: *Tauta, p. 18 Original in Latvian.*

Comment: *If "Helsinki – 86" was a small group of like-minded members, then the LNNK, founded on June 10, 1988, was already an organization that had more than 10,000 members. In meetings and other large-scale events, activists of the LNNK put forward demands and a program of steps for the elimination of the occupation in Latvia; called for the immediate and complete withdrawal of USSR armed forces from Latvia; and for Latvia's complete separation from the occupying state – the USSR. The LNNK also asked for a struggle against the large-scale relocation of other nationality populations to Latvia; called for the reinstitution of private property and for the return of confiscated property to its previous owners or their heirs; for the complete legalization of the Latvian cultural heritage and for cultural renewal; and for the return of Latvian émigrés to their homeland. LNNK chapters and support groups quickly formed in almost all of the regions of Latvia. The work of this organization radicalized large parts of the national population and did not allow the goals of the Awakening to wither in the face of "opposition of the internal regime."*

Documents No. 114-116

Latvia's Popular Front – The main national organization of the "Awakening" period

Document No. 114

Resolution establishing the organization at the founding Congress of Latvia's Popular Front (LPF)

October 8, 1988

The founding congress recognizes that Latvia's Popular Front has been created as a movement of the people's political and patriotic initiative and awakening. At this moment, groups with more than 10,000 members already support the ideas of the Popular Front. Support groups have formed in all of the Republic's regions and in many of the cities. The LPF believes that the Popular Front's self-organizational process has ended. Consequently, the congress declares that Latvia's Popular Front as the country's all-inclusive social, political organization has been established.

Source: *Fronte, p. 224. Original in Latvian.*

Comment: *Latvia's Popular Front was founded as an organization representing in its ranks a wide spectrum of beliefs and uniting the politically active section of the nation. Its demands at the beginning were relatively moderate, anticipating the Latvian SSR becoming an equal sovereign republic in a renewed Soviet federation. This moderation was justifiable because it allowed to be involved in the political process the undecided inhabitants of Latvia – those who did not believe in the possibility of renewing an independent state and were fearful of directly confronting the regime. But the position of the LPF gradually became more radical and in May of 1989 it declared as its goal the renewal of the independence of Latvia (see Document No. 115). The Popular Front played a decisive role in the realization of the slogan of independence.*

The declaration of the Council of Latvia's Popular Front's "Concerning the sovereignty of the Latvian SSR"

November 19, 1988

[…] the declaration of Latvia's *Saeima* about Latvia's inclusion into the USSR said that "Latvia's People's *Saeima* is convinced that only inclusion in the USSR guarantees our state's real sovereignty…" But this was not accomplished in the real world.

As a result of the implementation of the twisted domestic politics of Stalinism and of the period of stagnation, the actual sovereignty of the Latvian SSR was eliminated because the destiny of Latvia and the nation living there was decided not by the Supreme Soviet of the USSR and its government, but by the All-Union monopolistic ministries worried only about the realization of their narrow goals and completely ignoring the Republic's interests. As a result, the whole of the economy of the Latvian SSR finds itself in a condition of deep crisis, the ecological situation is catastrophic, and the level of the welfare of the persons living in the Latvian SSR continues to fall; moreover, the demographic situation, for the first time in the thousand-year existence of the Republic's indigenous nation, presents a real threat to that nation's continued existence.

The continuation of this situation can end the process of national awakening and the activism [resulting from it], throwing the nation into apathy and hopelessness, or even creating among some the desire to leave the USSR. Furthermore, this creates confusion among the Russian- speaking part of Latvia's population who are successfully exploited by forces of corruption bent on stoking intra-national hostility.

In order to end the crisis situation, the Council of Latvia's Popular Front believes that the continued development of Latvia must happen in a condition of sovereignty, that we must return immediately to the Leninist founding principles of the USSR and their realization in practice. The relations between the Latvian SSR and the USSR must be placed on the foundation of treaties to be concluded after the ratification of a new, democratic Latvian SSR Constitution.

At the same time, the Council of Latvia's Popular Front believes that the currently proposed corrections and alterations to the Constitution of the USSR contradict the declared course of the CPSU's 19th All-Union Conference concerning the decentralization of power and are unambiguously aimed at the creation of a unitary state.

The Council of Latvia's Popular Front believes that under current conditions there is no safe guarantee that the Supreme Soviet of the USSR will ratify those suggestions of the Commission of the Presidium of the Supreme Council of the USSR in which there are guarantees of the Republic's sovereignty. Therefore the Council of Latvia's Popular Front suggests that the Supreme Council of the Latvian SSR declare that until the Republic's sovereignty is guaranteed, only those laws accepted by the Supreme Council of the Latvian SSR are in force in the territory of the Latvian SSR.

The Council of Latvia's Popular Front suggests to the Supreme Council of the Latvian SSR to ratify this declaration in session and to make the following change to the Constitution of the Latvian SSR: edit the 71st paragraph of the Constitution of the Latvian SSR to read that "The laws of the USSR come into force in the territory of the Latvian SSR with the decision of the Supreme Council of the Latvian SSR."

At the same time, we suggest that there be put before the Supreme Soviet of the USSR that alterations and corrections to the Constitution of the USSR be ratified first by the Supreme Councils of the Union Republics.

Council of the LPF

Source: *Fronte, pp. 241-242. Original in Latvian.*

Call by the Board of the Council of Latvia's Popular Front to all members of the LPF concerning the question of the involvement of the Front in the struggle for Latvia's complete political and economic independence

May 31, 1989

From its founding, Latvia's Popular Front has had as its primary goal Latvia's true sovereignty -- guarantees of its economic, political, and legal autonomy. There is the opinion that there are two paths to acquire and implement this sovereignty – within the context of the USSR or outside of the statehood of the USSR.

Until the present, Latvia's Popular Front has based its work on the Program position accepted at the founding congress, namely, the first alternative – the federal principle. But the events of the last month testify that all of the attempts of the Baltic region and Latvia to reach this goal run into increasing political, economic and ideological opposition at the center and from internal reactionary forces, even involving the use of violence as is shown by the tragic events Tbilisi on April 9th. Also, the work of Congress of People's Deputies of the USSR testifies that in it a conservative majority has formed, standing against the attempts of the union republics to gain full state sovereignty.

Therefore, the Board of the Council of Latvia's Popular Front puts forward for discussion in all of the chapters and support groups of the Front a question vitally important to our nation: namely, how should Latvia's Popular Front enter the struggle for Latvia's complete political and economic independence?

We see the future Latvia as a democratic state, in which all citizens, regardless of their national origin or social position, political or religious beliefs, are guaranteed equal rights. Latvia must be a humane state ruled by law, and must offer opportunities for economic growth and spiritual and cultural development to any ethnic group. In relations to other states, union republics must be created on the basis of a treaty that is mutually beneficial [and incorporates] equality.

The Board of the Council of Latvia's Popular Front believes that the decisive role in the acquisition of independence will be played by Latvia's nation. The Board of the Council of Latvia's Popular Front sees the pursuit of this goal as involving both the parliamentary path, in which the existing structures of power in the state will be transformed using the wishes of the nation; and, also, direct expressions of the nation's will. The goal of the LPF is to obtain Latvia's independence as a state, and to secure juridical guarantees that would permit the people themselves to decide on the forms and mechanism of political power. We must realize that in reaching this goal we will have to travel a difficult path which will demand from all of Latvia's patriots political responsibility and immovable conviction, independent of their nationality or social standing.

Our urgent task is to make sure that in its June 16th session the Supreme Council of the Latvian SSR issues a declaration of Latvia's state sovereignty and corrections to the Constitution of the Latvian SSR concerning the Republic's property rights and concerning the ratification of the laws of the USSR, so that the Supreme Council, without delay, can ratify the law concerning Latvia's economic autonomy.

Viewing favorable electoral results as the primary precondition for the path to the development of free politics and Latvia's independence, [we urge] a coalition of all the progressive forces during the election.

The board of the Council of the LPF understands the ideas behind the creation of citizen committees, seeing them as a desperate move in the defense of the rights of Latvians and other Latvia's indigenous inhabitants against the consequences of totalitarianism. But the work [of the committees] should be resorted to only in the event that Latvia's rights to state independence and national self-determination cannot be ensured by [taking] the parliamentary path.

Source: *Fronte, pp. 253-254. Original in Latvian.*

DOCUMENTS NO. 117-122
MARCH TO INDEPENDENCE

Document No. 117

A call by the Council of Latvia's Popular Front to the nation on the eve of November 18, 1989

November 13, 1989

THE IDEA OF THE INDEPENDENCE OF THE REPUBLIC OF LATVIA IN ITS OWN LAND IS EVER-LASTING.

THE IDEA OF THE SOVIET UNION AS A GREAT POWER ON LATVIA'S LAND IS REELING.

The military superiority of the USSR in 1940 dictated to Latvia a change in the nature of the state, and with force and deception brought about Latvia's inclusion into the USSR. The Latvian nation has the right to self-determination, and only the nation can determine its future. In order for the nation's will to be freely expressed, a document of Soviet power that decrees peace says: "…the incorporating or stronger nation will withdraw its armed forces completely." The entire world is concerned about the Baltic region, expressing its sympathy to the martyrs of the Molotov-Ribbentrop Pact, but justice has not been renewed.

THE USSR'S PROBLEM IS TO LEAVE THE BALTIC REGION.

LATVIA'S PROBLEM IS TO REMAIN AND TO EXIST.

Today, when our moderate demands are constantly denied by the bureaucracy of the great power, even the most mild-mannered Latvian understands that independence is the only path to survival.

To wait inactively for an undefined future moment when destiny will grant Latvia absolute freedom is unforgivable. Because the path is already clear.

THE GREAT GOAL SHOULD NOT DELAY THE DOING OF SMALL NECESSARY DEEDS.

Let us do everything so that we live in a Latvian environment; so that the wealth in the land, water and nature belongs to Latvia; so that the Republic has its own money, imposes its own duties, has direct traffic with Europe and the world; a flag in the national colors, a seal, an anthem, a national holiday on November 18th. Everyone can add to the list of things to do. In the Latvia of today it may already be possible for society, not the Party, to choose society's leaders.

TIME MOVES ON, PEOPLE ARE BORN, BUT PEOPLE ALSO DIE.

The carriers of the nation's experience, knowledge, and goodness -- the old -- leave with but one last hope: for Latvia to be free. We the living say: „Look truth in the eye, you immense USSR." Latvia will decide its own future. All hearts want freedom, regardless of what language the tongues may speak. May parties help form the national government, working as the leading force. Our intellect will show us the way, our means are legal, our invitation unambiguous: we do not want to destroy any structure, we only want to see a Latvian house on our land. To ensure an honorable life for every worker. We want a state where the nation is not more important than the people, but also where the people are not more important than the nation.

THE UNITY OF THE PEOPLE AT THE NOVEMBER 18 DEMONSTRATIONS WILL HAVE DECISIVE IMPORTANCE.

OUR DESIRE IS FOR AN INDEPENDENT LATVIA.

We appeal to the better judgment of the USSR, to the people of Russia and of the other republics, to European society and the world, to the citizens of all lands and leaders of countries. The independence of the Baltic States, the freedom of the Republic of Latvia, is the foundation of an equitable Europe. And [this freedom] will show all people that there is Justice on Earth!

OUR HEARTS BEAT FOR LATVIA.

MAY GOD HELP US!

In the name of the Council of the LPF
ALBERTS BELS

Source: *Atmoda, November 13, 1989. Original in Latvian.*

Document No. 118

An open letter of the nation of Latvia to the President of the USSR, M. Gorbachev, and to the President of the USA, G. Bush, with an invitation that they resolve the question of the renewal of the independence of the Baltic States

November 27, 1989

We, the 500,000 participants in the grand demonstration on the occasion of Latvia's independence day, turn to you with a most important question, one that is a sacred question for the Latvian nation – the independence of the state.

Fifty years ago as a result of the Hitler-Stalin Pact, Latvia, Estonia, and Lithuania – all members of the League of Nations – had their independence destroyed by aggression. They were occupied, annexed, and incorporated into the USSR. The right of self-determination of three European states was violated in a crude way.

The Baltic nations have never been content with occupation and annexation. This was demonstrated to the entire world with the "Baltic Chain" on August 23, 1989, in which more than 2 million people expressed their desire for independence.

Latvia, Estonia, and Lithuania are the only European states which after 50 years are still the victims of the work of two dictators.

We are convinced that the question of Baltic independence in terms of its history and in terms of international rights is not a domestic affair of the USSR.

The renewal of Baltic independence must take place fully in accord with the Helsinki and Vienna Documents.

At this moment of national awakenings – during a time of awakenings in Europe -- many nations selflessly and bravely have stepped onto the path of democracy and true independence.

The nations of Latvia along with those of Estonia and Lithuania also have their Baltic path. They must reacquire full European state status and must become a friendly bridge between the East and West.

We invite you during your meeting to do everything to resolve the urgent question of Latvia's independence within the framework of the unwavering desire of the three Baltic nations for self-determination. For independence.

The text of the letter was unanimously endorsed by the participants of the November 18th demonstration in Rīga.

Source: *Atmoda, November 27, 1989. Original in Latvian.*

Announcement of the Board of the Society of Russian Latvians supporting the renewal of an independent, democratic Republic of Latvia

July 19, 1989

The board of the Latvian Society of Russia discussed on July 19, 1989, the LPF Council Board's call of May 31st of this year and came to the following conclusions.

Recently, in international and All-Union conferences there have been reports by many specialists, together with many publications in the press, that in June of 1940 Latvia was occupied and annexed by the USSR, not taking into account the interests of the Latvian nation and the other national groups living in Latvia. Latvia's social structure, and political structure and status, were changed without the referendum called for by the Constitution of Latvia.

The return to the Fatherland of Latvians living in Russia was tied to the hope to again be one with our nation, to preserve the national identity that had been destroyed by Stalinist nationality politics, and to become a part of Latvia's economic and cultural milieu. Unfortunately, Stalinism in the Latvian SSR did not provide the opportunity for these desires to be fulfilled. The deportation of inhabitants and the suppression of democratic sentiment in Latvia made us relive all of the horrors we survived in the USSR during the thirties.

Further events – forced collectivization, economically unjustifiable hypertrophic development of industry, the slowing of the cultural development of Latvian and other national groups living in Latvia, purposeful recruitment of huge numbers of migrants -- have brought us in these days to ask every nation's most basic question – about our further existence. The new reality in the Latvian SSR differs little from our previous experience in the USSR, where national minority interests were and continue to be ignored, constant assimilation and a foreign culture is forced upon one – all of which is not in accord with the declared objectives of the Constitution of the USSR.

The events of the last year in the domestic politics in the USSR and the development of the USSR Congress of People's Deputies does not bring hope for the rapid and essential changes that would guarantee to the Latvian nation and the national groups living in Latvia the essential and comprehensive development corresponding to the cultural and economic level of the rest of Europe's nations.

We believe that a critical situation has been created in Latvia's economy, culture, and ecology, and that there exists a real threat that the Latvian nation will become a minority (if that has not already happened) in its historic ethnic territory. This requires choosing the only, even though radical, path for national survival and continued existence, that is, the renewal of national statehood -- an independent, democratic Republic of Latvia -- so that the nation itself can determine its social-political structure. To reach this goal, only legal and peaceful means must be used.

No one has the right to deny a nation that was under the yoke of the German Baron and Russian Manor owner for 700 years the right to make its own choice about its future path of development. Actions that place the Latvian nation under the tutelage of another, larger nation are apolitical and amoral. We cannot accept from regional or center politicians a political game that exhibits cynicism toward a small nation's natural desire to renew its statehood. There is no known historical precedent of a nation voluntarily surrendering its own freedom and statehood.

The board of the Society of Russian Latvians supports the May 31 call of Latvia's Popular Front and supports the formulation of political and economic concepts meant to renew an independent and democratic Republic of Latvia outside of the USSR.

We rely on the common sense and responsibility of Latvia's intelligentsia – we, working people, will support you.

Board of the Society of Russian Latvians
Source: *Krievijas, n.n. (publication without pagination).Original in Russian.*

Document No. 120

Appeal of the Central Board of the *Daugavas vanagi* organization for support for the renewal of an independent, democratic Republic of Latvia

March 24, 1990

The Central Board of *Daugavas vanagi* encourages all of Latvia's inhabitants regardless of their nationality or political views to unite in the joint struggle for the renewal of independence of the state of Latvia. Let's be united in this difficult struggle for the freedom of Latvia's nation and its welfare.

"Daugavas vanagi" urges the newly elected deputies to renew without delay the 1922 Constitution of the Republic of Latvia.

In Latvia, as in exile, we understand that only in an independent state can an acceptable political and economic structure be created for the nation of Latvia.

The recent promises by Moscow concerning political independence within a federation while economic decision-making is left to the Russian center, means the unending continuation of the exploitation of our people and the environment. Today our nation should already be at the same level of well-being as Finland...

We congratulate our brother nation in Lithuania which has already declared complete independence. *Laišve Lietuvos*! Deputies of the Soviet Union in Moscow doubt if the newly elected Lithuanian parliament expresses the peoples' true desire to be separated from the Soviet Union; they must now hold a national referendum about the separation.

It is completely clear, except to the Moscow deputies and Soviet imperialists, that the Baltic States did not voluntarily join the Soviet Union; therefore there can be no talk of withdrawing from it. If there are any doubts, then there should be a plebiscite about entering. How many persons of sound mind would vote for entering into Soviet hell?

The "Daugavas vanagi" and all émigrés must mobilize without delay all their strength and resources for the renewal of the independence of the Baltic States. If not now, when?

Ratified at the March 24, 1990, meeting of the Presidium of the Central Board of the "Daugavas vanagi" in DVF "Straumēni," England.

Source: *Atmoda, April 28, 1990. Original in Latvian.*

The election platform of Latvia's Popular Front in the Supreme Council election of 1990

March 18, 1990

The new era,
About to begin --
It will not come
We must bring it in!

Honored inhabitants of Latvia!

The last year will go down in Latvia's history as the year when the nation expressed its fervent desire for social liberalization and democratization. The awakening process occurring in Eastern Europe, in the Baltic area, and in many of the regions of the USSR, is unstoppable. The Berlin Wall has fallen, the Prague Spring is reborn, the Communist Party splits apart and loses power.

Where the democratic process is hindered, innocent persons suffer through the death throes of the old power.

Shoulder to shoulder, the Baltic nations go along their peaceful and democratic path to independence.

After fifty years of repression, Latvia's nation has its first chance to choose deputies who will realize the nation's wish and desire for independence and well-being. We have to be maximally active and focused, and not allow the kind of „elections" that took place in 1940 and in the time of Stalinism and stagnation.

Voters! We are at the decisive moment. In the March 18 elections, let us state clearly our desire – to live in a free, independent and democratic Latvia! Our fate should not be decided by indifference, laziness, or happenstance.

Our goal – an independent state of Latvia that will continue and develop the democratic and parliamentary traditions of the Republic of Latvia. Independent Latvia must become a state of political equality and freedom. The state of Latvia must guarantee its inhabitants social-economic, political, and personal rights and freedoms, regardless of their national, religious, or party affiliation.

In the future, Latvia must be shaped by peaceful, friendly, and mutually beneficial relationships with all states; we must have unity and, together with Estonia and Lithuania, we must form a united position.

In developing mutually beneficial economic cooperation, we must also establish good relations with the Soviet Union.

Source: *Atmoda, March 18, 1990. Original in Latvian.*

Declaration of the Supreme Council of the Latvian Soviet Socialist Republic concerning the renewal of the Republic of Latvia

May 4, 1990

The independent state of Latvia that was proclaimed on November 18, 1918, received international recognition in 1920, and became a member of the League of Nations in 1921. The Latvian nation implemented its self-determination juridically in April of 1920 when in a universal, equal, direct, and proportional election the nation entrusted its mandate to the Constituent Assembly. On February 15, 1922, the Assembly ratified the state's basic law – the Constitution of the Republic of Latvia -- which has been in force *de jure* until this very moment.

The presentation on June 16, 1940, by the then Stalinist government of the USSR to the government of the Republic of Latvia, of an ultimatum to change its government, and the subsequent military aggression by the USSR on June 17, 1940, qualified as an international crime. The result was the occupation of Latvia and the liquidation of the sovereign state power of the Republic of Latvia. The [new] government of Latvia was created following the dictates of the representatives of the government of the USSR. From the viewpoint of international law, this government was not the executive power of the sovereign state power of the Republic of Latvia because it did not represent the interests of the Republic of Latvia, but the interests of the USSR.

On July 14th and 15th, 1940, in an atmosphere of political terror (after the illegal creation of an anti-constitutional electoral law) there took place elections to the *Saeima*. Of 17 submitted lists of candidates for the elections, only one was permitted to stand – the candidate list of the "the Working People's Bloc." In the pre-election platform of "the Working People's Bloc" there was no suggestion of the declaration of Soviet power in Latvia and of the inclusion of the Republic of Latvia into the Soviet Union. Moreover, the results of the election were rigged.

Resulting from a deception of the nation, an illegally created *Saeima* did not represent the sovereign will of Latvia's nation. It did not have the constitutional right to decide the questions of changing the nature of the state and of liquidating Latvia's sovereign statehood. These questions could only be decided legally by the nation, but a free national referendum did not take place.

In view of [these matters], the inclusion of the Republic of Latvia into the Soviet Union, from the perspective of international rights, is not in force, and the Republic of Latvia still exists *de jure* as a subject of international rights, as recognized by more than 50 countries.

Taking into account the Supreme Council of the Latvian SSR's July 28, 1989 "Declaration about Latvia's state sovereignty," the February 15, 1990 "Declaration on the Question of Latvia's State Independence," and the April 21, 1990 "Appeal of Latvia General National Deputy Assembly"; recognizing the desire of Latvia's inhabitants as was expressed unambiguously by the election of a majority deputies who in their pre-election program declared their intent to renew the independence of the Republic of Latvia; and starting on the path of the renewal of a *de facto* free, democratic, and independent Republic of Latvia,

The Supreme Council of the Latvian SSR decides:
1. To recognize the priority of the basic principles of international law concerning the norms of the rights of states and to view as illegal the August 23, 1939, agreement between the USSR and Germany, and the subsequent June 17, 1940, liquidation of the sovereign state power of the Republic of Latvia by an act of military aggression on the part of the USSR.
2. To declare as not in force from the moment of its ratification the July 21, 1940, declaration of Latvia's *Saeima* "Concerning Latvia's admission into the Union of Soviet Socialist

Republics."

3. To renew the Constitution of the Republic of Latvia as approved by the Constituent Assembly on February 15, 1922, as being in effect in all of the territory of Latvia.

The official title of the country of Latvia is the REPUBLIC OF LATVIA, in short form LATVIA.

4. To delay implementation of the Constitution of the Republic of Latvia, except for those paragraphs that define the legal constitutional foundation of the state of Latvia and that according to the 77th paragraph of the Constitution are alterable only through a national referendum, until the ratification of a new draft of the Constitution. Those paragraphs are:

Paragraph 1 – Latvia is an independent, democratic Republic;

Paragraph 2 – The sovereign state power of Latvia belongs to the people of Latvia;

Paragraph 3 – The territory of the state of Latvia in international treaties is defined by the borders of Vidzeme, Latgale, Kurzeme and Zemgale;

Paragraph 6 – The *Saeima* is elected by general, equal, direct, secret and proportional elections.

The Constitution's 6th paragraph is to be applied to the renewal of those state and administrative structures of the independent Republic of Latvia that guarantee free elections.

5. To declare a transition period in the *de facto* renewal of state power of the Republic of Latvia, ending with the election of the *Saeima* of the Republic of Latvia. During the transition period, supreme state power in the Latvia resides in the Supreme Council of the Republic of Latvia.

6. During the transition period, to consider it possible to adapt the norms of the Constitution of the Latvian SSR and other legislative acts now in effect in the territory of Latvia as long as they are not contrary to the 1st, 2nd, 3rd, and 6th paragraph of the Constitution of the Republic of Latvia.

In the event of disagreements about the adaptability of legislative acts, the Constitutional Court of the Republic of Latvia decides.

7. To create a commission to work out a new draft of the Constitution of the Republic of Latvia appropriate for the current political, economic and social conditions.

8. To guarantee to the citizens of the Republic of Latvia and the citizens of other states who permanently live on the territory of Latvia, social, economic, and cultural rights as well as political freedoms corresponding to generally recognized international human rights norms. This will apply also to those citizens of the USSR who will declare their desire to live in Latvia while not acquiring citizenship.

9. To shape the relations of the Republic of Latvia with the USSR in terms of the August 11, 1920, Peace Treaty between Latvia and Russia, which is still in force and which recognizes the independence of the state of Latvia for all eternity.

A Government Commission is created for discussions with the USSR.

The Declaration is in force from the moment of its ratification.

Chair of the Supreme Council of the Latvian SSR
A.Gorbunovs
Secretary of the Supreme Council of the Latvian SSR
I.Daudišs

Source: *Diena, May 5, 1990. Original in Latvian.*

Documents No. 123-126

The Time of the Barricades

Document No. 123

Appeal of the Writers Union, Artists Union, and Composers Union of Latvia to the Supreme Council of the Republic of Latvia and other Republics regarding the murder of civilian inhabitants by Soviet military personnel in Lithuania

January 15, 1991

The murder of unarmed civilian inhabitants, as has already happened in Lithuania, is a crime against humanity.

We invite you to quickly draw up and ratify a law on war crimes for the territory of Latvia [that would]:

1. Recognize as war criminals all military personnel who have been given weapons, if they have murdered, tortured, or humiliated unarmed civilian inhabitants who have not actually threatened military personnel or the security of military objects.
2. Recognize as war criminals those who are the actual shooters, as well as those who gave the order to shoot, as well as those that have killed unarmed civilian inhabitants with other military equipment.
3. Compile and distribute all information about these war criminals.
4. We invite you to establish contact with the Supreme Councils of other republics to explain the necessity for such a law in defending democracy, to organize an exchange of information, and to turn over criminals for punishment in the place where the crimes were committed.

> In the name of Latvia's Writers Union
> Imants AUZIŅŠ
> In the name of Latvia's Artists Union
> Egils ROZENBERGS
> In the name of Latvia's Composers Union
> Juris KARLSONS

Source: *Diena, January 17, 1991. Original in Latvian.*

Document No. 124

Appeal of the Women's League of Latvia to Raisa Gorbachev, the wife of the President of the USSR, Michael Gorbachev, to help stop the bloodletting in Lithuania

January 15, 1991

In the Republic of Latvia, January 15, 1991, 6:15

To Mrs. Raisa Gorbachev,

Last night, our children slept alone because we, their fathers and mothers, were at the Supreme Council of the Republic of Latvia, the Council of Ministers, and radio and television centers. We stood guard at vital and important objects that support our legally elected Supreme Council and the work of our government.

Respected Raisa Mihailovna !

We imagine that you have in your possession precise information about the events in Lithuania. We can understand that your heart is sad: the oldest of the party murdered was Apolinārs Povilaitis born in 1937, but the youngest – Ignass Šipuļonis born in 1973, Darjus Gerbutāvičs and Virgīlijs Druskis. Loreta Asnavičuta, born in 1966, was crushed by a tank...

You yourself have a daughter and a granddaughter [and] that is why you will be able to understand how deep the pain is that the parents of the murdered feel...

Today in Rīga we have gone into the streets with bare hands to stand against tanks. We can block them only with our bodies.

If they want to drive over people, let them – on the way to the office of your husband who is President.

We appeal to you – woman, mother, grandmother – to help stop the bloodletting in Lithuania. We appeal to you not to not become an accomplice in the crime that makes children into orphans. We appeal to you to think also about saving the souls of the soldiers who are sitting in the tanks...

Latvian Women's League

Source: *Atmoda, January 22, 1991. Original in Russian.*

Document No. 125

Appeal of the Council of the Latvia's Popular Front to the Supreme Council of the Republic of Latvia to request the UN to include Latvia in the list of states to decolonize

February 5, 1991

The majority of Latvia's nation has chosen the path of renewing state independence and democratic traditions. Nevertheless, the Communist Party of the Soviet Union and the mass media under its control have launched an unprecedented campaign of disinformation and lies concerning the domestic conditions in the Republic of Latvia. With the blessings of the reactionary forces of the Soviet Union, armed bands loyal to the Communist Party are raging in Latvia, not caring about the kinds of provocation they use and hoping to create a situation that our government cannot control. The USSR is openly bringing its corps of punitive expeditions into the Baltic States.

The collapsing leadership of the Empire is blatantly threatening us with extensive economic sanctions, hoping in that manner to force the Union Treaty on us.

The Council of Latvia's Popular Front invites the Supreme Council:

- based on the Declaration of May 4th that establishes the priority of international law in the work of the Supreme Council, and corresponding to the 103rd resolution of the 36th session of the UN, to declare Latvia as having the status of a country under foreign and colonial occupation;
- to ask the UN to include Latvia in the list of states to decolonize;
- to invite UN observers to the Republic of Latvia so that the world can obtain objective and undistorted information about our domestic situation.

Source: *Atmoda, February 5, 1991. Original in Latvian.*

Resolution entitled "Charges Against the Communist Party of the Soviet Union and its Affiliate in Latvia, the Communist Party of Latvia, for Crimes Committed against Humanity, the Nation of Latvia, and its Land" issued by the scholarly conference on "The Practice of Communist Totalitarianism and Genocide in Latvia"

June 13, 1991

More than a year has passed since the promulgation of the declaration of Latvia's independence.[186] Nonetheless, Latvia still cannot renew its state autonomy because the primary opponent to state independence, the affiliate of the Communist Party of the Soviet Union – the Communist Party of Latvia – does everything possible to keep Latvia as an annexed territory of the USSR in order to keep the CPSU in power, as it has been until the present.

The illegal, anti-state, and anti-national work of the LCP continues, creating a real threat of the renewal of the totalitarian regime. That is why, for the self-defense of the nation, it is necessary to evaluate the history and behavior Communist Party of Latvia, so as to forestall the repetition of totalitarianism and genocide in Latvia. This is even more important because the LCP has not condemned the crimes of Stalinism.

    1.   The Juridical Basis of the Charges

In paragraph 4 of the November 26, 1968, Convention of the UN General Assembly dealing with the inappropriateness of time limitations on war crimes and crimes against humanity, it was stated that crimes against humanity do not have time limitations and that, regardless of when these crimes were committed, those responsible for committing the crimes must be called account. The preamble of this Convention states that crimes against humanity are the most serious crimes. The subjects of such crimes are criminally punishable in order for peace to be preserved across the world and so that trust between nations and human rights guarantees [can be maintained].

The General Assembly of the UN, on December 11, 1946, ratified the Resolution against Genocide, and, on December 9, 1948, the Convention concerning adjudication of genocidal crimes and punishments for genocide. The Convention defines as genocide any behavior that is aimed at the partial or complete destruction of any national, ethnic, religious, or otherwise defined group, including the creation of conditions that would anticipate the physical destruction of the group. Such behavior, according to Paragraph 1 of the Convention must be held to account. Responsibility for genocide was also defined by the statutes of the military tribunals of Nuremberg and Tokyo. The June 28, 1965, UN Resolution and the August 5, 1966, Resolution create the responsibility of calling the guilty to account and of punishing them for genocide.

In line with the December 9, 1948, Convention of the UN General Assembly concerning the adjudication of genocidal crimes and the punishment of persons charged with genocide, such persons are to be tried in the courts and in the territory of the state where the genocide was committed or in international courts recognized by that state.

The CPSU and its affiliate the LCP are juridical persons that can be the objects of a prohibition, but its members are physical persons that can be the subjects in the adjudication of crimes against humanity, if their guilt in these crimes is demonstrated.

The CPSU transformed itself into an instrument of power. That is why all real and potential opposition to it was liquidated, and why all the governing system of the state, the armed forces, the police, and the state security services, were politicized; an atmosphere of total fear was created so that all of the productive power of society could be used, without opposition, for the preservation of the dominance of the Party, for its strengthening, and for its spread across the whole world. That is why the so-called world socialist system of cooperation was created, and why all of the nations of the USSR were forced to maintain it. The Party spoke in the name of the people while never asking for their real thoughts. Using the people's productive capacity, the CPSU was able to create an all-socialist cooperative system, which, particularly in the USSR, was an inclusive slave camp – a GULAG system. The destruction of persons became systematized. In a January 10, 1939, in a telegram to party organizations, for example, it was said: "the Central Committee of the All-Union Communist (Bolshevik) Party explains that physical coercion in the practices of the People's Commissariat of the Interior is used with the permission of the 1937 AC(B)P CC. [...] The AC(B)P CC believes that in the future use of the method of physical coercion must be obligatory and is [...] completely correct and appropriate." In an atmosphere suffused with fear, the people lost initiative, their moral sense was degraded; together with the destruction of private property, they lost interest in working well; and an economic and moral crisis became inevitable.

Because in the Constitution of the USSR the Party defined its own role as being determinative in all the processes of the USSR, the CPSU is juridically responsible, according to the principle of causality, for all of the crimes committed under its direction.

2.   The Practice of Totalitarianism and Genocide

In June of 1940, after the occupation of Latvia, the political and economic system of the USSR, whose primary ideologue and organizer was the CPSU, was introduced into Latvia. Its affiliate, the LC(B)P, had as is primary task the carrying out of the directions of the center and of becoming the most reliable support of the occupation regime.

Already in the 1920's and 1930's the leadership of the LCP had subordinated its work to the Comintern, that is, to the directions of the AC(B)P, and in so doing had become the USSR's "fifth column" in Latvia. The goal of the work of the LCP was to liquidate the Republic of Latvia and to attach its territory to the USSR. To realize this goal, the LCP received resources from the USSR for espionage and diversionary work in Latvia. Individual Communists or groups of Communists who sought to defend their own beliefs and tried to act independently were repressed. After the liquidation of state power in Latvia, power was assumed undemocratically by the apparatus of the newly formed LCP Central Committee. All of the decisions of the LCP were really made by a handful of persons – the Bureau of the LCP. The Commander of the Baltic Military Province and the Chair of the LSSR KGB were ex officio members of the Bureau.

The work of the Supreme Soviet and Council of Ministers of the Latvian was under strict Party control; the Party controlled all domains of social life in Latvia. Primary organizations of the Party were created in all organizations involved in production, all state organizations, and all institutions.

In order to intimidate the inhabitants of the country and to strengthen the totalitarian regime, an apparatus of terror with extraordinary authority was created, with the full and direct participation of the LCP. It began to work immediately after the occupation of Latvia on June 17, 1940.

Repressions were directed not only against the opponents of the totalitarian regime in Latvia, but also against those who, according to the thinking of the functionaries of the repressive apparatus, could become such opponents – against persons who thought differently, against the entire nation. Among the repressed were people of different social classes, professions, and nationalities, as well as children. The repressions were planned in advance and implemented according to a plan.

The principal institutions implementing repression in Latvia were the Peoples Commissariat (later Ministry) of the Interior and the State Security Committee of the Latvian SSR, including all of the units subordinate to these institutions. These organizations, along with a few other privileged state institutions, were allowed to operate outside existing laws.

A particularly heavy blow to the Latvian nation were the deportations of June 14, 1941, when in one night Latvia lost more than 20,000 of its citizens, and the March 25, 1949, deportations when 43,231 persons were deported from Latvia to the USSR. The total number of persons repressed by the Stalinist regime in Latvia is at least 200,000. As a result of the system of terror, more than 150,000 citizens of Latvia were forced to flee to the west and stay there as refugees.

Using the catchwords "a united Soviet nation" and "internationalism," the leadership of the LCP implemented a policy of russification.

As a result of the policies of genocide and russification, in 1989 the number of Latvians in Latvia (1,387,800) still did not reach the 1930 level (1,395,000).

In order to hide its crimes against the Latvian nation, the LCP has closed its archives and refuses to give them to the state for preservation.

The LCP, working closely with the institutions of Soviet occupation, is responsible for the destruction of Latvia's state, for its territorial inclusion into the USSR, and for the consolidation of the totalitarian regime.

The Army of Latvia and all organizations that could have resisted the [Communist] regime were liquidated, as were those the regime envisaged as a probable opposition to the establishment of total control.

Trade unions were liquidated, and in their place new trade unions were established using the model of the USSR – obedient instruments for the LCP to control all working people.

The system of relationships between the individual and the state created during the existence of the Republic of Latvia was crushed. Through liquidation of guarantees of citizens'[individual] rights, strict control of societal work and personal life was established under the leadership of the LCP.

The LCP took under its control not only all sources of mass information, but all means for society to express its ideas, as well as the different means of exchanging ideas between Latvia and other states. The LCP created a giant, many-branched apparatus for its ideological propaganda.

Efforts were made to transform literature and art into ideological weapons, into celebrators of Communist ideology. The Latvian language was polluted and dilutes with increasing intensity. Implementing russification, the Latvian language was extruded from the conduct of everyday affairs and from other domains in which it had been used.

The LCP tried to minimize the influence of the church on the nation, particularly on youth, popularizing atheism in order to liquidate the Christian church in Latvia and to replace it with a satanic anti-religion – Marxism-Leninism.

The LCP also took the education and training system under its control. Latvian national schools were destroyed. According to plan, the education system was russified and politicized. In the post-war years, all of Latvia's minority nationality schools were closed, as well as many of Latvia's rural schools.

Strict control over information and cultural events was introduced. These were placed under the control of censors. In 1940, all of the periodical publications of the Republic of Latvia were closed; only those published by the LC(B)P were permitted.

According to plan and [by reference to] previously compiled lists, books were destroyed. Much of the documentary record of Latvia's institution was sent to Moscow; special collections were created in libraries. Collections of national treasures were audited and their contents removed, and they were reconstituted to reflect the demands of communist ideology.

Science was given the task of serving communist ideas and the goals of Soviet imperialism. The social sciences suffered considerably. Latvia's history was falsified and interpreted tendentiously.

The LCP implemented a continuous imposition of Marxist-Leninist dogma as the only correct world view, and fought against any differences of opinion, seeking even to control the thoughts of citizens.

The LCP controlled the economy, and exploited it in order to achieve its political goals.

In 1940-1941, industrial enterprises and institutions of trade, as well as banks, buildings, and land, were nationalized.

After WWII, under the direction of the LCP, Latvian farmers were forced to join kolkhozes and state farms. The individual farmstead system was eradicated, and Latvians were forced into style of life foreign [to their traditions]. Latvian agriculture was essentially destroyed.

All of the branches of the national economy were placed under [a system of] central planning. Baseless industrialization was forced, tied to the planned influx of other nationalities, primarily Russians.

Latvia's national merchant marine was destroyed.

The influence of the military industrial complex increased sharply on the national economy of Latvia. The territory of Latvia was militarized.

As a result of incompetent leadership of the national economy, forced industrialization, and militarization, Latvia's environment was polluted. There were no serious attempts at protecting the environment.

The extreme growth of the numbers of immigrants in Latvia and the catastrophic decrease of the Latvian majority in their own land exceeded the level needed for the nation's survival. The living standards of the indigenous inhabitants declined, the societal culture and traditions of Latvians eroded. The gene pool and public health of the nation were damaged.

Having lost political power, the LCP now renews the use of violent methods against the legally established state power. Such LCP behavior was evident in the events of January 1991 in Latvia, when the so-called All-Latvian Society's Salvation Committee was formed, led by the LCP. It called for a coup, declaring the legally constituted Supreme Council of the Republic of Latvia and the Council of Ministers to be overthrown with all power transferred to the hands of this Committee. These facts are published widely and are generally known.

To reach its illegal goals and to defend its selfish interests, the LCP uses armed Special Assignment Military Units (OMON). This is attested to by the use of OMON to occupy the Press House in order to paralyze the distribution system of the democratic press, as well as the open assault on the Ministry of the Interior of the Republic of Latvia and the police of Rīga. People perished in these attacks. The decisive role of the LCP was reflected especially in its commanding the units of OMON in Jūrmala against the implementation of the decision of the Executive Committee of the Council of Peoples Deputies. Currently, OMON units are being used actively in bandit-like attacks on the stations of the Customs Department of the Council of Ministers of the Republic of Latvia. With this behavior, the LCP seeks to maintain in society a high level of anxiety.

In view of the proceedings of this conference, of published documents, and of other evidence; and in view of recognized legal norms, there is a basis for charging the CPSU and its affiliate in Latvia – LCP -- with crimes against humanity, such as genocide and the violation of

of human rights. The CPSU, being the leading and directing power in the USSR from November 7, 1917, onward, and seeking to preserve and strengthen its role, has consciously created a set of conditions in order to exploit the productive capacity of society and to strengthen the authority of its partocracy. [To further these goals] in has done the following:

> The *nomenklatura* of the CPSU was inserted into all structures of state administration, in the national economy, and in leading positions in the armed forces;
>
> So-called democratic centralism was created, through which power was concentrated in the hands of the apparatus of the CC of the CPSU, the Bureau, and in individual leading party figures;
>
> Legislation was subordinated to orders from the CPSU;
>
> In this context, the CPSU implemented illegal repressions against the nation and created an atmosphere of fear;

The terror apparatus of the state was given unlimited power; the GULAG system was created in which scores could be settled without society's knowledge;

The life of the state was militarized and its borders closed;

Individual states were annexed by force, and coups took place;

Communist ideology was imposed by force and all of social life was reordered by reference to it;

An undemocratic electoral process, in which the nation had no ability to voice their real desires, was introduced by force;

As a result, the states of the so-called socialist system were driven to complete moral and economic collapse.

Taking into account all of the above, the conference recommends:

1. That the Supreme Council of the Republic of Latvia create a state-financed Documentation Center with a collegium of experts, in order to investigate the harmful consequences of communist totalitarianism and to document the evidence.

2. That the government of the Republic of Latvia and the Prosecutor of the Republic of Latvia undertake all of the needed tasks to investigate and call to account all those guilty of genocide in Latvia.

3. That the Supreme Council of the Republic of Latvia investigate the communist totalitarian crimes committed by the work of the LCP, both in the Republic of Latvia and at an international level.

4. That the Supreme Council of the Republic of Latvia assume control, so that the affiliate of the CPSU – the LCP – can not be registered [as a legal entity] in Latvia until the completion of the investigation of the activities of the LCP.

5. That the information media report on the practice of totalitarianism and genocide and its harmful consequences for Latvia, and direct society's thinking toward the exclusion of any totalitarianism and violence.

Source: *Komunistiskā, pp. 172-178. Original in Latvian.*

APPENDICES

Appendix 1: The Population of Latvia[187]

Year	Number (in thousands)	Urban Population	Rural Population	Urban %	Rural %
1914	2,493	939	1544	38	62
1935	1.905	708	1197	37	63
1939	1,885	663	1222	35	65
1945[188]	1,484	469	1484	32	68
1947[189]	1,709	645	1064	38	62
1951	1,954	917	1037	47	53
1955	2,010	1041	966	52	48
1959	2,093	1114	979	53	47
1970	2,364	1477	887	62	38
1979	2,521	1726	795	68	32
1989	2,679	1905	774	71	29
1990	2,686	1913	773	71	29

Appendix 2: Proportion of the titular nationality in the populations of Latvia, Lithuania, and Estonia

Year	Estonia	Latvia	Lithuania
1939[190]	92.0	77.0	76.0[191]
1945[191]	94.0	83.0	80.0
1950[191]	76.0	63.0	75.0
1960	74.1	61.7	79.4
1970	68.2	56.8	80.1
1980	64.5	53.5	80.1
1989	61.2	51.8	79.2

Appendix 3: Population changes resulting from migration in Lithuania, Latvia, Estonia and Belarus from 1959 to 1988[192]

	Average increase in inhabitants per year (thousands)			Increase in number of inhabitants (hundreds)		
	1959-1969	1970-1978	1979-1988	1959-1969	1970-1978	1979-1988
Lithuania	4.7	7.3	10.0	16.0	22.3	28.3
Latvia	14.3	11.6	9.3	64.0	47.3	36.0
Estonia	8.3	6.8	5.5	65.2	48.0	36.3
Belarus	-26.0	-9.7	-0.8	-30.5	-10.4	-0.8

Appendix 4: Titular Nationalities and Slavic Nationalities in the Union Republics of the USSR from 1959-1989[193]

Republics	Titular nationality %				Slavic Nationality[194] %			
	1959	1970	1979	1989	1959	1970	1979	1989
Latvia	62.0	56.8	53.7	52.0	30.9	36.1	40.0	42.3
Estonia	74.6	68.2	64.7	61.5	22.3	28.2	32.0	35.2
Lithuania	79.3	80.1	80.0	79.6	10.5	10.0	11.6	12.3
Russia	83.3	82.8	82.6	81.5	3.6	3.3	3.4	3.8
Ukraine	76.8	74.9	73.6	72.6	17.6	20.2	21.9	22.9
Belarus	81.1	81.0	79.4	77.8	9.9	12.5	14.3	16.1
Moldavia	65.4	64.6	63.9	64.4	24.8	25.8	27.4	27.2
Georgia	64.3	66.8	68.8	70.2	11.4	9.6	8.3	7.4
Armenia	88.0	88.6	89.7	93.3	3.2	2.7	2.6	1.8
Azerbaijan	67.5	73.8	78.1	82.6	13.6	10.0	8.3	6.2
Kazakhstan	30.0	32.6	35.9	39.7	52.1	51.1	48.2	44.4
Uzbekistan	62.1	65.5	68.7	71.3	14.6	13.4	11.6	9.3
Turkmenistan	60.9	65.6	68.4	71.9	18.7	16.1	14.0	10.8
Tadzhikistan	53.1	56.2	58.7	62.2	14.7	13.0	11.3	8.5
Kirghizstan	40.5	43.8	47.9	52.8	36.7	33.3	29.0	24.3

Appendix 5: Russians in the Union Republics of the USSR and Change in the Number of Inhabitants Due to Migration, 1979-1990

Republic	Number of Russians (thousands) in 1989	Number of Russians who have learned the titular nationality's language (thousands)	Changes in the number of inhabitants due to migration		
			1979-1988	1989	1990
Latvia	906	191	+9.2	+1.2	-9.2
Estonia	475	65	+5.4	+4.6	-4.0
Lithuania	344	115	+9.9	+16.8	-11.8
Ukraine	11,356	3,722	+15.5	+44.3	+79.3
Belarus	1,342	329	-0.7	+10.3	-32.0
Moldavia	562	63	-6.0	-16.3	-29.8
Georgia	341	77	-5.6	-28.8	-39.0
Armenia	51.6	17	-31.6	-44.2	+25.1
Azerbaijan	392	56	-25.5	-40.2	-136.2
Kazakhstan	6,228	53	-77.5	-93.4	-130.9
Uzbekistan	1,653	75	-50.7	-97.9	-179.6
Turkmenistan	334	8	-8.4	-4.9	-7.3
Tadzhikistan	388	13	-10.6	-20.6	-60.3
Kirghizstan	917	11	-15.7	-17.6	-40.9

Appendix 6: Persons in Latvia Arrested, Deported, Tried in Absentia, and Obligated To Not Change Their Residence: 1945-1986[195]

Year	Arrested	Deported	Tried in absentia	Obligated to not change their residence
1945	14,702	25	-	-
1946	3,967	84	-	5
1947	2,424	22	2	-
1948	3,131	3	-	-
1949	3,542	7	-	-
1950	2,987	7	-	-
1951	2,427	8	-	-
1952	969	26	-	-
1953	616	5	3	-
1954	92	-	-	-
1955	54	-	-	-
1956	43	-	-	-
1957	101	-	1	-
1958	103	-	1	-
1959	44	-	-	-
1960	46	-	-	-
1961	71	-	1	-
1962	73	-	-	-
1963	27	-	-	-
1964	21	-	-	-
1965	17	-	3	-
1966	22	-	-	-
1967	24	-	-	-
1968	9	-	-	-
1969	16	-	-	-
1970	17	-	-	-
1971	19	-	-	-
1972	33	-		-
1973	18	-	-	-
1974	8	-	-	-
1975	2	-	-	-
1976	13	-	-	-
1977	16	-	-	-
1978	12	-	-	-
1979	8	-	-	-
1980	22	-	-	-
1981	22	-	-	-
1982	10	-	-	-
1983	24	-	-	-
1984	13	-	-	-
1985	5	-	-	1
1986	6	-	-	-

Appendix 7: The Organs of Political Repression in the Latvian SSR

Immediately after the occupation of Latvia on June 17, 1940, the structures of the political police of the Republic of Latvia were used to create political repression. The Department of Security Police and its existing Political Board was gradually replaced, starting with the leadership and later all of the employees. From August 30, 1940, the People's Commissariat of the Interior filled this function.

-On March 31, 1941, People's Commissariat of State Security (VDTK) was removed from the People's Commissariat of the Interior and was given the functions of a political police force.

-On March 24, 1946, it was renamed the Ministry of State Security.

-On April 13, 1953, the Ministry of State Security was again attached to the Ministry of the Interior.

-On April 10, 1954, the Committee for State Security of the Council of Ministers of the Latvian SSR was created.

-On September 7, 1978, the State Security Committee of the Council of Ministers of the Latvian SSR received Ministry status, keeping the title of the Committee of State Security.

-On August 23, 1991, the Supreme Council of the Republic of Latvia passed the law entitled "About the end of operation for the institutions of State Security of the USSR in the Republic of Latvia."

Appendix 8: The heads of the organs of State Security in the Latvian SSR from 1940-1988

A. Noviks and S. Šustins	1940-1941
A. Noviks	1944-1952
J. Vēvers	1953-1963
L. Avdjukevičs	1963-1980
B. Pugo	1980-1984
S. Zukulis	1984-1991

FOOTNOTES

[1] *Cīņa*, January 3, 1949.

[2] Indulis Ronis, ed. *Kārlis Ulmanis trimdā un cietumā: dokumenti un materiāli* (Rīga: 1994, p. 392).

[3] On January 10, 1941, after long discussions, Germany and the USSR signed an agreement by which those Germans still remaining in Latvia and Estonia were given the right to move to Germany until a deadline of March 25, 1941. The terms of departure had become less favorable because the amount of movable property that could be taken was restricted: the amount of food, the amount of silver, and the number of animals. According to approximate figures, about 10,500 people left Latvia during this later departure period. Some Latvians, by claiming Germanness, took this opportunity to leave Latvia in order save themselves from the Soviet regime.

[4] Joachim von Ribbentrop.

[5] Hiiumaa and Saaremaa.

[6] The discussion took place on September 27th.

[7] The discussion took place on September 28th.

[8] Paldiski.

[9] See Document No. 4.

[10] Document title.

[11] See Document No.3.

[12] The Latvia Chamber of Trade and Industry is meant.

[13] See Document No. 8.

[14] See Document No. 3.

[15] See Part I, Document No. 17

[16] LVA, Social Political document section, 102.f., 1.apr.,4.l., p. 1.

[17] LVA, 270.f., 1.apr., 2.l. p. 48.

[18] June 17, see Document No. 1.

[19] See Document No. 3.

[20] The "Legion" society that included recipients of the Lāčplēsis War Order and those soldiers that fought for Latvia's independence from 1918 to 1920 is meant.

[21] See Part I, Document No. 17.

[22] See Document No. 6.

[23] See Document No.16.

[24] See Document No.10.

[25] Mistake in document; the name should be B. Shaposhnikov

[26] England and France are meant.

[27] The Latvian SSR Gosplan is meant.

[28] This means before the November 7, 1917, coup d'etat which in the former USSR was referred to as the Great October Socialist Revolution.

[29] Latvia's War School is meant.

[30] The 24th Territorial Rifles Corps is meant.

[31] One of the methods of torture. The prisoner would be forced to stand on their feet all day and night in order to get them to submit to everything.

[32] These were: 1) the Rīga municipal region, the Commissar of which eventually came to be called the *Oberbürgermeister*, 2) Rīga rural region, 3) Jelgava region, 4) Liepāja region, 5) Valmiera region, 6) Daugavpils region.

[33] Cited in A. Ezergailis, *The Holocaust in Latvia, 1941-1944* (Riga: 1996), p. 139.

[34] K. Ducmane and E. Veciņš, *Nauda Latvijā* (Rīga: Latvijas Banka, 1995), p. 187.

[35] The rivalry and conflicts among these groupings is described well in Valdis O. Lumans, *Latvia in World War II* (New York: Fordham University Press, 2005), pp. 173-109.

[36] Later in 1941 the term *Ostland* was created for the territory referred to in the document as *Baltenland*.

[37] The 8th paragraph reads that "the power of justice in the newly occupied eastern provinces belongs to the *Reichminister* of the occupied eastern provinces. The authorization can be transferred further to *Reichskommissars*."

[38] The 8th paragraph of this decree states "the power of justice in the newly occupied eastern provinces belongs to the *Reichminister* of the occupied eastern provinces. The authorization can be transferred further to state commissars."

[39] The title of the document.

[40] LVA PA, 101.f., 3.apr., 5. l., p. 101.

[41] P. Zvidriņš and I. Vanovska, *Latvieši: statistiski demogrāfisksportretējums* (Rīga, 1992), p. 49; *Mazākumtautību vēsture Latvijā: Eksperimentāls metodisks līdzeklis* (Rīga: 1998), p. 262-263.

[42] Already on May 29, 1944, there took place the creation of the apparatus of the authorized agent of the Religious Cult Affairs inf the Latvian SSR, with the task of "bring[ing] into life the laws of the USSR on religious questions."

[43] On August 31, 1994, the withdrawal of the armed forces of the Russia from Latvia was completed, and on August 31, 1998, the last Russian military installation on Latvia's territory – the Skrunda Radio-Locator station – was closed.

[44] The occurrence of rapes in Kurzeme in May of 1945 was often noted, for example, in Ventspils district: Ēdole- 5 and Pope – 2 (LVA, 270, f., 1.s. apr., 120. l., p. 43). Fishing with explosives in the the Gulf of Rīga, resulting in the damage of fish stocks, was common.

[45] SMERSH (shortened from the Russian for "Death to Spies"), the USSR People's Commissariat of Defence, and the Naval Fleet's central counter-intelligence unit was formed in April of 1943 with very wide authority. The unit's assignment was to struggle against espionage, the infiltration of foreign intelligence agents in units of the army or navy, and also to combat sabotage at the front. SMERSH was active until May of 1946.

[46] The building on Blaumanis Street.

[47] Currently St. Petersburg.

[48] Error in the document. 1944 is meant.

[49] Error in the document. It must be 17,010.2

[50] Dated as in the document. On March 5, 1946 the USSR renamed the People's Commissariat Ministries and the Council of People's Commissariats the Council of Ministers. The relevant Decree of the Presidium of the Latvian SSR Supreme Soviet was prmulgated on March 24, 1946 (*The Bulletin of the Presidium of the Supreme Soviet of the Latvian SSR* – 1946 – number 71). The document mentions the Council of Ministers of the Latvian SSR and therefore was authored after March 24, 1946.

[51] During World War II, the wartime front was located on Latvia's territory for almost a year. As a result, all of the cities suffered, but most of all Rēzekne and Jelgava, which were almost entirely destroyed. Altogether in Latvia about 50,000 residences were destroyed, all of the important bridges, 785 businesses, the Rīga port, and almost all electric power stations and substations. In 1945 Latvia produced only 1/3 of the electrical energy that had been produced in 1940. The railroads were heavily damaged. The German occupation authorities, when leaving Latvia, gave the order to evacuate and take along the equipment of all of modern businesses, as well as other materials and resources. The inhabitants of Latvia suffered from a shortage of foodstuffs and industrial goods, which was particularly harmful in the cities.

[52] The August 23, 1944 decree of the Presidium of the Supreme Soviet of the USSR "About the creation of Pskov provinceas a part of the RSFSR" is meant.

[53] Prisoners of war played an important role in the reconstruction projects, in construction, and in factory production in post-war Latvia. The number of prisoners of war in specific branches and in specific enterprises was fairly large. For example, in 1945, 3,084 persons worked at the VEF Factory (electrical goods and electronics), including 453 prisoners-of-war (approximately 15%). In 1946, prisoners of war accounted for 16-30% of the total number of workers in the largest enterprises of the Ministry of Local Industries of the Latvian SSR (LVA, 754.f., 8. apr. 7.l., p. 270; 2.f.., 423. apr., 1.l, 4262, pp. 110-11). Beginning in 1947, prisoners of war were allowed to return to Germany. That explains why, when planning for labor deployment 1948, the Board of the Central Statistical Office of the Latvian SSR drew attention to the need for additional labor in the national economy to replace the prisoners of war.

[54] Error in the document. Must be August 7, 1945.

[55] Unable to read text; entry is erased.

[56] The 61st paragraph of the Criminal Code of the Russian Soviet Federated Socialist Republic contained the following:"For refusal to do labor service, or take on work assignments made by the state, for work with significance to the state – a monetary fine [will be imposed] by the relevant state agency until the assigned task, labor service or work is met by a multiple of five; a second violation [will bring] loss of freedom or corrective labor for up to one year. For those same violations committed by members of the *kulak* element, even if for the first time, or also other perons in critical positions; groups of persons conspiring against or actively resisting government organs of labor service, assigned tasks or the fulfillment of decreed work, [the punsihment is] loss of freedom for up to two years, total or partial confiscation of all possessions, and [possibly] deportation. " See Russian Soviet Federated Socialist Republic Criminal Code with revisions of April 15, 1944. The official text with additions and the systematic material in.

[57] Paragraph 58-14 of the Criminal Code of the Russian Soviet Federated Socialist Republic contained the following: "For counter-revolutionary sabotage, that is, for willful neglect of specific responsibilities or for purposely careless fulfillment of them with the express purpose of weakening the government's power or the work of the state apparatus, [the punishment is] loss of freedom for not less than one year, total or partial confiscation of all possessions, but, particularly under conditions of crisis, the increase [of the punishment] to the maximal instrument of defending society – execution by shooting and the confiscation of possessions." *USSR Commissariat of People's Justice Juridical Publication*, (Moscow, 1944, p. 24).

[58] See Document No. 15.

[59] In the beginning of the 1930s, when the Soviet Union began collectivization, in order toattach peasants to kolkhozes it did not issue passports to them. Without a passport in the former Soviet Union it was not possible to change one's place of residence, get a job, register, or reside somewhere for a longer period of time. The only way the kolkhoz farmer could get out of this relationship was to sign a labor contract with an industrial or construction enterprise, or as a youth, not return home after serving in the army.

The government of the USSR did not attempt to take passports away from kolkhoz farmers in the Baltic states, including Latvia. But with the implementation of one-shot collectivization, the local governing offices tried strenuously to limit the freedom of movement for the kolkhoz farmers, as shown by this document (No. 17).

[60] The top secret decision of the Council of Ministers of the USSR – entitled "About kulaks and their families, bandits and nationalists that are in an illegal status, families of bandits that fell in armed conflict or were sentenced, that continue with hostile activities and also the deportation of families of repressed bandits from Lithuanian, Latvian and Estonian SSR" – defined, first and foremost, the categories of inhabitants that have to be deported from Latvia, Lithuania and Estonia ("kulaks and their family members, bandits and nationalists, their family members, and also family members of executed and tried bandits, family members of bandit supporters"); secondly, determined the total number to be deported from the Baltic republics ("at least 29,000 families"); and thirdly, set the deportations to happen in the second half of March, 1949. The decision of the Council of Ministers of the USSR also said that the deported must be settled in camp places "forever". In connection with this decision, already in February and March of 1949 the district executive committees in Latvia together with functionaries of the Latvian SSR State Security Ministry were compiling lists of deportees in the localities affected.

[61] See Document No. 16.

[62] See Footnote 1 of Document No. 10

[63] This was not made public.

[64] In order to present a complete description of how the terror, aimed at Latvia's populaation and led by the Latvian Communist Party, manifested itself, as well as of the secretiveness that surrounded the discussion and acceptance of the decision, not only the actions themselves but the form they took must be described. We must note that the secretive and conspiratorial nature of the work of the Latvian Communist Party was characteristic not only of the first post-war years, but throughout the Soviet period, up to the time of the the in 1991 when the Communist Party was declared an illegal organization in Latvia.

[65] The „Kurzeme kettle" (or fortress) is meant. This westernmost area of Kurzeme was not occupied by the Soviet army until after the German surrender of May 8, 1945.

[66] The deportations were carried out by the USSR and the Latvian SSR Ministry of the Interior and the State Security Ministry. The Minister of the Interior of the Latvian SSR, A. Eglītis, in the month after the deportations, reported to Moscow that the day before the operation all of the ministry's district and municipal offices and militia personnel were already on barracks alert. The State Security Ministry of the Latvian SSR was assigned more than 400 police members for its use. The State Security Ministry was responsible for the deportation and it drew up the plans and determined the schedules for particular parts of the assignment, and for the soldiers as well as for the special battalions (about 10,000 persons). Just before the operation, 4,500 soldiers were sent to Latvia. But the greatest majority of those that carried out the deportations were communists, Komsomol members and "non-party activists." According to the some estimates, the "soviet and party activists" were up to 40% of the persons that carried out the deportations, and they worked in groups of 8-10 persons (group commanders usually were the operational worker of the State Security Ministry).

[67] J. Vēvers was the Chair of the State Security Committee of the Council of Ministers of the Latvian SSR (see Appendices No. 7 and 8).

[68] After the surrender of Nazi Germany, the LCC continued to work underground on Latvian territory. After the war, the LCC center was located in Sweden, but its groups in Rīga and in the port city of Ventspils were led by Voldemārs Mežaks. The LCC did not organize armed actions against Soviet institutions, but adopted a waiting tactic, namely, the arrival of the so-called „x-hour" when the international situation would change and the western countries would help renew Latvia's independence.

Many of the LCC members were arrested in the first months of the second Soviet occupation. In the fall of 1945, a LCC group that had arrived from Sweden to Latvia illegally in order to start work and renew radio communications that had ended with the war's end, was also arrested. Shortly thereafter, all of the existing LCC groups in Latvia were eliminated. Individual LCC members avoided repression but as an organization the LCC ceased to exist in Latvia.

Two members of the LCC in occupied Latvia received the death penalty. The E. Andersons dealt with in this document was one of them.

[69] Mistake in the document. The election of deputies to the Supreme Council of the USSR took place January 12, 1941.

[70] Atlantic Charter – the declaration signed on August 14, 1941, by the governments of the USA and Great Britain, saying that after the defeat of Nazi Germany they would not seek any territorial change, and would recognize the sovereignty of nations. The USSR joined the Atlantic Charter in September 24, 1941.

[71] The authors probably were thinking of the statutes of the UN that came into force on October 24, 1945.

[72] Meaning the People's Commissariat of the Interior and the People's Commissariat of State Security.

[73] The authors made a mistake in their estimates. On September 1, 1945, there were 1,483,700 inhabitants of Latvia, whereas on January 1, 1946, there were 10,987 members of the Latvian Communist (b) Party. Therefore, in the beginning of 1946, the party members were fewer than 1% of the total population. The compilers did not have data for for this assessment in August of 1946, when the document was created. Also, on January 1, 1947 the country's inhabitants numbered 1,708,800, while party memberships was 15,897 persons, thus still not surpassing the 1% mark (0.93%).

[74] During the period of rationing (until the end of 1947), even the salaries of the highest ranking officials was not large, comparatively speaking. In 1956 the Chair of the Council of Ministers of the Latvian SSR and the Chair of the Supreme Council officially received 2,000 rubles a month. At this time, the majority of industrial worker wark salaries fluctuated between 500 and 1,500 rubles a month (including bonuses and supplementals). Thus the salaries of the highest ranking

officials surpassed those of the average industrial worker – the official principal class of Soviet society – by no more than a multiple of four. But in 1956, in the period from April to December, all higher officials received a supplement of 5000 rubles to their salaries. These officials also received 80% coverage of the cost to traveling to a sanatorium, that cost being 1440 rubles. Lower officials, in the Council of Ministers, the Supreme Council, and other institutions at this level (for example the Supreme Court) received lesser supplements, but also the 80% coverage for travel to a sanatorium. Office workers in lower ranks – such as consultants, typists, chauffers – received supplements up to the level of their salaries, and one-time reimbursement for the cost of medically required travel up to the level of their salaries (LVA, 270 f., 1.s apr., 1103.l., pp. 15-20). Such a system of supplements existed also in the apparatus of the Party. The First Secretary of the Central Committee of the Latvian Communist Party received a supplement of 6000 rubles, and his deputies about 3500 rubles. The country's budget for 1957 included supplements for the highest officials – persons at the top rank, their deputies, as well as directors and office managers – that were listed as supplements to travel expenses and as "money for health" (LVA, 270 f., 1.s apr., 1103.1, pp. 31-34). Thus, for example, the aggregate actual income of the chair of the Council of Ministers in 1956 was 7000 rubles a month, with an annual supplement of 1440 for travel. It should also be kept in mind that persons of the highest rank continued to receive various special awards (*prēmijas*) for various special accomplishments – ranging from a successful harvest to a succesul metal scrap drive – so that their actual incomes were larger still. Therefore, although the authors of this document had been mistaken in their estimates of large salaries for members of the *nomenklatura*, the mistaken figures were not that far off the mark.

[75] The complete number of persons deported on June 14, 1941, from Latvia is still not clear. In the beginning of the 1990s the number mentioned was about 12,500 persons, later 14,300 and still later more than 15,000. Only a careful analysis of all review files and investigative files will permit deteermination of the real number that might match the one mentioned in this document.

[76] Analysis of the investigative files of those arrested on June 14, 1941, shows that many of those deported to GULAG camps also received the sentence. For example, of the 397 persons arrested on June 14th in the 4 Latgale districts (Abrene, Daugavpils, Ludza and Rēzekne) 50 persons received the death penalty in the camps, while 85 persons died of famine and disease while awaiting a final decision.

[77] The mass deportations from Latvia, Lithuania and Estonia occurred simultaneously pursuant to the May 14, 1941, top secret decision (No. 1299-526) of the Union Communist (b) Party Central Committee and USSR Council of People's Commissars entitled "About the deportation of socially foreign elements from the Baltic republics, western Ukraine, western Belorussia and Moldavia." The goal of the action was to "cleanse" the newly incorporated territory of the USSR of "anti-soviet, criminal and socially dangerous elements." Further, in the beginning of June the People's Commissariat of the Interior of the USSR prepared a plan for "the transportaion of the special contingent of the deported, their placement and assignment with work." The material of the investigative files of those arrested on June 14, 1941, in the Latvian State Archives testify that the functionaries of the State Security Commission in the 1960s knew about the May 14, 1941 decision.

[78] See Document No. 18.

[79] See Documents No. 24 and 25.

[80] Mistake in the document. There was no such parish in the Republic of Latvia.

[81] See Document No. 64.

[82] See Part III, Document No. 39. Mistake in the document: it should be – Latvia's Central Council.

[83] Not made public.

[84] These decrees, which were aimed at the creation of seek-and-destroy battalions in the regions of Latgale, Vidzeme, and Kurzeme (platoons operated in the parishes), laid down the principles of forming such units (Party, Komsomol and non-party activists), and [set out] their goals (primarily the struggle against national partisans). Seek-and-destroy battalions existed in Latvia until 1953 and there were more than 10,000 persons in their ranks.

[85] Alberts Klibiķis (born 1913) was arrested on October 31, 1945. A tribunal of the military arm of the Ministry of the Interior of the Latvian SSR tried him on May 16, 1946 and sentenced him to 25 years in a correctional labor camp (LVA, 1986.f., 1, apr. 99, l. 7, p. 367-375).

[86] In Latvia at the end of 1941 groups of a national resistance movement began to form spontaneously, but were usually eliminated quickly. Latvia's Central Council (LCC) tried to become a unified national resistance center; it was founded on August 13, 1943, by representatives of the four largest pre-war political parties of Latvia. The movement's first chair was Konstantīns Čakste. The LCC saw itself as the only democratic, national resistance movement in the country, and believed, that, in view of the occupation, it had the right to represent all of the Latvian nation with respect to the constitution and laws of independent Latvia. The LCC kept close contact with similar organizations in Lithuania and Estonia, and informed Western countries about Nazi war crimes and military manouevres in the territory of Latvia.

A great shock was delivered to the work of the LCC by the arrests by the SD (*Sicherheitsdiens*) in April of 1944 of K. Čakste and many other LCC figures. They were placed in concentration camps. K. Čakste died in imprisonment in Germany at the beginning of 1945.

The most significant work work accomplished later by the LCC was in organizing refugee boats to Sweden starting with the summer of 1944 until the end of the war. These boats helped to transfer several thousand persons who fled from both occupying powers across the Baltic Sea.

With respect to military force possessed by the LCC, one could view the 1,800-man group created by General Jānis Kurelis in the summer of 1944 as such a contingent. It was hoped that this could become the foundation of an army of national liberation if the Latvian Legion could not be transformed into such and army. In November and December of 1944, German forces engaged the "Kurelites" and as a result they were dispersed and eliminiated. Seven of the "Kurelite" general staff officers were tried and executed by the Germans; many of the soldiers were sent to concentration camps in Germany.

[87] See Document No. 26.

[88] Kārlis Dzērve (born 1929), Oļģerts Mazurevics (born 1930), and Leons Veinbergs (born 1928) (who was not a Komsomoler, which is why he is not mentioned in the document), were arrested May 17, 1949. The Court Collegium of the Supreme Court of Criminal Affairs of the Latvian SSR, in a closed meeting of July 13, 1949, in Rīga, found K. Dzērve, O. Mazurevics, and L. Veinbergs guilty according to the criminal code of the RSFSR 58-10, p. 1st section and sentenced K. Dzērve and O. Mazurevics to 10 years imprisonment in correctional labor camps with loss of rights for three years, but L. Veinbergs to 8 years imprisonment and loss of rights for three years. On March 25th and 29th of 1949 the three destroyed portraits of the Soviet people's leader Stalin and the poet Rainis at the Ogre Technical School Dormitory. (LVA, 1986.f., 1.apr., 2928.l., pp. 162, 163, 166, 168, 169).

[89] 4th Section of the State Security Committee of the Latvian SSR – anti-espionage section.

[90] 2nd Section of the State Security Committee of the Latvian SSR – investigative section.

[91] A criminal charge against P. Krūmiņš was instigated on November 2, 1977, but interrupted on December 29th. The other eight received official warnings from the State Security Committee of the Latvian SSR. The youths that are not mentioned in the document – Gundars Niedra (born 1961), Andris Kaufmanis (born 1961), Raimonds Šiliņš (born 1962), Andris Ozoliņš (born 1962), Arijs Grants (born 1963), Juris Mašlakovs (born 1958) were subjected to "preventive measures with called for visits to the State Security Committee of the Latvian SSR," which means they were intimidated (LVA, 1986. f., 1.apr., 45280.l., pp. 300-302).

[92] Addresses were not made public.

[93] Refers to the October 1973 decisions of the Latvian Communist Party Central Committee Plenum of "expanding the training role of the working masses in communist training"; in the Plenum and in the subsequently adopted law special weight was placed on the responsibility of the Latvian Communist Party and the LLCYA for the condition of ideological training of the young in different places of learning.

[94] Addresses were not made public.

[95] From the State Planning Commission for 1978.

[96] Actually, from 1959 to 1979, the number of inhabitants in Latvia grew by 428,000 (see Appendix No. 1). About two-thirds (almost 300,000) of this population increase was due to "increases at the expense of other republics." The increase of the urban population was particularly rapid. In the period from 1951 to 1970, Latvia's urban population increased on average by 29,000 persons annually; natural growth accounted for 8,000 while in-migration accounted for 21,000 persons a year.

[97] In all of the post-war years the flood of in-migrants from other republics of the USSR into Latvia was seen essentially as an important source of manpower for the many industrial enterprises that already existed in Latvia or were recently built. Every year, the State Planning Committee, in projecting the size of the labor force needed for industrial enterprises also sought to plan for the necessary mechanical growth (in-migration). Particularly large numbers of in-migrants were projected for the enterprises under All-Union jurisdiction and also in construction enteprises, which this published document discusses.

[98] The USSR's national economy was developed in line with five-year plans. Latvia's national economy was included in this system after World War II, beginning with the 4th Five-Year Plan (1946-1950); the 12th Five-Year Plan covered the period from 1986 until 1990.

[99] If an officer in the Soviet Army served for 25 years, after demobilization he could choose to live in any city in the USSR (except the largest cities – Moscow, Kiev, Petersburg, and others -- which had more than one million inhabitants). Local War Commissariats had to ensure apartments in good condition for these officers and their families. In all newly constructed apartment buildings, a portion of the apartments was reserved for the War Commissariat. Retired officers and their families came to Rīga first because the city was considered the USSR's "West"; furthermore, Latvia was relatively well supplied with groceries, health care was good (relative to the USSR standards), there were spas, and a good variety of local products. It is important to add that, in line with decrees of the Defence Ministry of the USSR that were not available to the compilers of this collection, retired officers did not pay income tax on their pensions, and, upon retiring, they received better pensions than civilians and could earn an additional salary if they chose to work.

[100] Many demobilized Soviet army soldiers arrived and remained in Latvia immediately after World War II. By the second half of 1945, 26,000 demobilized soldiers needed job placements in Latvia; in 1946 53,000 and by October 1, 1947, 27,000. Very few of these persons had lived in Latvia previously.

[101] This document is typical of the the politics of language that became a permanent part of the Latvian scene when Latvia was a part of the USSR. Officially, the equality of both languages was always emphasized. At the same time, in real life, everything possible was done to give the advantage to Russian. As the document shows, there were more Russian language teachers than Latvian language teachers, even though at the start of the 1950s ethnic Latvians were a majority

of the country and there were more schools with Latvian language instruction. That meant that in many schools Latvian language was not taught at all, even though Russian was. Furthermore, in the decision of the Central Committee of the Latvian Communist Party, stress was placed only on the teaching of Russian language. Russian in the Soviet Union was seen as the primary instrument of the integration necessary to unite the very different nations of the country. But, if we disregard the periodic campaigns in the Baltic Republics to strengthen the position of the Russian language in general, special, and higher education, the diffusion of the Russian language in the education system was limited. The language had a much more fundamental role in the military, in daily life, and in almost all professionals where knowledge of Russian was indispensable for surivival and accomplishment.

[102] The 20th Congress of the Communist Party of the Soviet Union took place on February 14-25, 1956, in Moscow. This congress has become notable in the history of the Soviet Union because of the closed morning session of February 25th at which First Secretary of the Communist Party of the USSR, N. Khrushchev, read the speech "Concerning the Cult of Personality and Its Consequences" in which the Stalin regime was castigated. But what was said in this voluminous speech was only part of the truth, because complete openness about the crimes of the Stalin period would have meant collapse of the state. Even N. Khrushchev had made his career during the Stalinist period, supporting the Soviet totalitarian system. Nevertheless, the decisions of the 20th Congress of the Communist Party of the Soviet Union started the partial liberalization of the Soviet system, in, among other things, the field of nationality relations.

[103] On June 5, 1957, an economic administrative region was created on the territory of the Latvian SSR. In order to control the industrial enterprises that were found in this territory, a Council of the Peoples' Economy was created, answering to the Council of Ministers of the Latvian SSR. The Chair of the Peoples' Economic Council was at the same time the First Deputy Chair of the Council of Ministers. This system of industrial control gave greater authority to the USSR's Union Republic's leading institutions and lessened the power of the All-Union Ministries. It existed until the end of 1965. After it was abolished, the influence of the All-Union Ministries in the development of USSR Union Republics increased again.

[104] See Document No. 46.

[105] See Document No. 57.

[106] See Document No. 50.

[107] The USSR's new (third) program was adopted at the 22nd Congress of the Communist Party of the Soviet Union, meeting in Moscow from October 17-31 , 1961. The program envisaged as the primary task of the Communist Party of the Soviet Union the improvement of the technological-material base, the creation of communist social relations, and the upbringing of young people. These tasks of building communism were allocated a period of twenty years.

[108] The seven-year plan covers the time period from 1958 until 1965.

[109] The city of Rīga's Jurmala was created in 1920. After World War II it was incorporated into the city of Rīga, becoming the Jurmala region. In 1959 it was re-created as a separate city.

[110] The alphabetical list and book index. The books on the lists were judged to be as "politically and ideologically harmful." Some of them were destroyed and other were taken to the special collections (specfondi). Using a book that was held in a special collection was possible only with permission from the appropriate sections of the Latvian Communist Party Central Committee.

[111] An agency of the USSR.

[112] See the Footnote 1 of Document No. 59.

[113] This happened in 1957; see Document No. 54.

[114] See Document No. 46.

[115] The article "The plan for the building of communism" by B. Treijs says: " In opposition to the conservation of resources, [the plan] anticipates the expansion in the Latvian Republic of those sectors in which there will be needed the importion of huge amounts of metal (Rīga Wagon Factory and Diesel Factory). The raw material base of this sector is thousands of kilometers from the Republic, and the finished products are used for the needs of the Republic only on a minor scale. That is why the further expansion of these sectors, as already mentioned in the press, is not economically rational."

[116] The reference here is to P. Dzērve's article "Pēteris Stučka – the First Chair of Latvia's Council of Peoples' Commissars," in which he wrote: " But some of the representatives of the RSFSR that had arrived in Soviet Latvia for selfish reasons, in fact hindered the building of socialism in Latvia and with their behavior harmed Latvian and Russian national friendship, and P. Stučka called them to order. In these important differences of opinion, P. Stučka himself, as well as other leaders of Soviet Latvia and of the Latvian Communist Party, turned to V.I. Lenin and J.M. Sverdlov, receiving from them effective support in the struggle against such unwanted phenomena. Unhappy with these activities on the part of the Soviet Latvian government, these bureaucrats and seekers of self-interest accused P. Stučka and other responsible figures in Soviet Latvia of being bourgeois nationalists."

[117] The phrase "strengthen the leadership" meant that the leadership of the enterprise, institute, or organization must be changed. P. Dzērve was demoted from the directorship of the Economics Institute, and on June 13, 1960, the Latvian SSR Academy of Sciences General Assembly rescinded his title of Corresponding Member of the Academy of Sciences of the Latvian SSR -- an unprecedented step. As a result of this affair, economics research in Latvia descended into state of ineffectuality and could no longer influence the resolution of social and economic questions. It was not until December 8, 1988, long after P. Dzērve's death, that the General Assembly of the Academy of Sciences of the Latvian SSR reinstated

his title of Corresponding Member.

[118] The periodical "Voice of the Homeland" was initially called "Returning to the Homeland" (first distributed starting in the summer of 1956). Because its original purse had no changed – ceasing to be agitation for return and becoming counter-propaganda -- in May of 1958 the periodical was renamed "The Voice of the Homeland." The periodical with the first name at first was distributed by a committee called "Returning to the Homeland", which was founded in 1955 and was located in East Berlin and which had a Latvian sector. After the periodical changed its name, from December of 1963 on it was distributed by the Committee on Cultural Contacts with Co-nationals in Foreign Lands, located in Latvia. "Voice of the Homeland" appeared until December 1989. In January of 1990 it was renamed "The Newspaper of the Fatherland."

[119] The decision of the Central Committee of the USSR, entitled "About the journals *Zvezda* and *Leningrad*," was made on August 14, 1946. It directed that literature and art in the Soviet Union had to develop "in the spirit of national and socialist realism" and went on to criticize those that according to the authors of the decree did not consider these founding principles of socialist literature. Sharp criticism was directed against the work of A. Akhmatova and M. Zoščenko. In May of 1958, the Plenary session of the Central Committee of the USSR admitted that the mentioned authors were criticized too severely and without foundation. Therefore, in 1958, the Central Committee of the Communist Party of the USSR admitted that this decision was incorrect, but the Glavlit of the Latvian SSR in 1976 still saw it as entirely valid.

[120] The authors of this document were writing about the historian Arveds Švābe and the painter Niklāvs Strunke as if they were alive. In fact, Arveds Švābe died in 1959 and Niklāvs Strunke in 1966.

[121] Error in the document. The article was published in No. 8, 1979, of the magazine.

[122] See Footnote 1 of present document.

[123] Until the end of 1947 in the Soviet Union, including Latvia, there existed a system of ration cards, which were divided into different groupss of card for different products.

[124] Candidates for the leadership of different confessions were carefully evaluated. On October 5, 1945, V. Šeškens, the authorized agent in the Latvian SSR of the Council of Cult Affairs of the Council of People's Commissars of the USSR, prepared a report about the office of temporary archbishop of the Latvian Evangelical Lutheran Church, which was to be filled by K. Irbe. In it V. Šeškens characterized Irbe's work as hostile to Soviet power. After speaking with Irbe, he concluded that the latter does not accept the orders given by Soviet power; for example, he refused to urge that those hiding in the woods come out before the government published a decree about amnesty. After a year, on February 21, 1946, Irbe was arrested for organized sabotage. He was sentenced to ten years in corrective labor camps. He was freed from his arrest on November 15, 1956 (LVA, f. 1986, apr. 2, l. P-10758, volume 1, pp. 15, 227-235, 239, 342.)

[125] At the time, P. Valeskalns was the Peoples' Commissar of Foreign Affairs of the Latvian SSR.

[126] A. Siļķe was arrested Febrary 21, 1946. He was sentenced "for participating in a counter-revolutionary organization and supporting the German occupation." In a special session on March 29, 1947 A. Siļķe was sentenced according to the RSFSR Criminal Code 58-3, 58-10 2nd section, 58-11 paragraph, to 8 years in a labor camp. In 1957, he was released and returned to Latvia (LVA, 1986.f., 2.apr., P-10758.l., volume 1, pp. 74, 227-235, 237). The State Security Committee continued to follow him (see Document No. 29).

[127] See Document No. 62.

[128] In the terminology of the State Security Ministry, this meant that the arrested person was tortured. A. Siļķe's torture lasted for five days and nights.

[129] P. Rozenbergs was arrested on February 28, 1946. He was charged with "participating in a counter-revolutionary organization and for supporting the German occupation." At a special session on March 29, 1947, and on the basis of the Criminal Code of the USSR 58-3, 58-10 2 sections, 58-11 paragraph, P. Rozenbergs was sentenced to 8 years in a labor camp. He was released from imprisonment on May 25, 1957 (LVA, f. 1986, apr. 2, l. P-10758, volume 1, pp. 227-235, 242, 343).

[130] Actually, P. Rozenbergs was the Dean of the Rīga District, a smaller territory.

[131] Translated from the Russian – 20 persons. In order to register a religious commune, in Soviet laws it was necessary to show a request with the signatures of twenty persons to the Soviet authorities along with a request to allow the registration of the congregation.

[132] From the documents in the archives it cannot be determined if the Bishop's request was fulfilled. He only received a response to his letter with the vague promise to "examine this question."

[133] The preparatory work for closing cloisters was begun immediately after Soviet occupation in 1940. After World War II, the confiscation of property continued, as did the the arrests of monks and the reorganization of and relocation of the cloisters. This decision to close the cloisters was perceived as a predictable government action against the church. Certain difficulties were caused only by a letter from the wife of H. Lübke, President of the German Federal Republic, to the USSR Embassy in West Germany, in which she asked that the sisters of the Aglona cloister be allowed to move to Holland where the primary headquarters of the "Poor Jesus Child" congregation was located. The Embassy believed it necessary to organize a negative response or some other acceptable answer on the part of the the nuns. (LVA, 1448.f., 1. apr. , 265.l., p. 21)

[134] The Roman Catholic Metropolitan, A. Springovičs, was able to get the seminary to open again in 1946, but the seminary instructors and the attendees had to suffer considerably in order to fit in with the needs of the Soviet power.

From 1948-1951, many instructors were arrested. In 1951, the seminary was closed for a while. Its work was carefully monitored. Each year, the list of accepted seminarians was vetted by the authorized agent of the Council of Religious Affairs and a number of applicants were always rejected. This practice continued until the end of the 1980s.

[135] What was planned in the document was also carried out. In September of 1962, J. Začests was called to the Council of Religious Cult Affairs and "was notified that since the government to this point had not recognized him, his remaining in the leadership of the curia was not desired by the government." It was in this way that J. Vaivods became an archbishop of the Catholic Church. In summarizing the procedure, the authorized agent observed that "the new leader of the curia would be chosen canonically" (LVA, 1448.f., 1.apr., 262.l., p. 16).

[136] Following instructions from the USSR, anti-religious propaganda was actively promoted in all the years of Soviet power. It was imposed upon the inhabitants of Latvia immediately after the occupation in the summer of 1940. Already on September 23, 1940, the Central Committee of the Latvian Communist Party accepted the decision to organize a „Society of the Godless" and to publish this society's magazine. Directions for the organization of future work was supposed to be coming from Moscow (LVA, PA, 101.f., 1.apr., 7.l., p. 54). During the years after the war, the question of anti-religious propaganda was reviewed regularly the Central Committee of the Latvian Communist Party as well as in local Party committees, as is attested to by the the present document. Work collectives also had the tasks (particularly in the 1950s and 1960s) of discussing the Party's decisions in this matter and of punishing persons "with religious prejudices and remnants [of religiosity]," as they were referred to in the documents.

[137] The Society of Knowledge of the Latvian SSR was a part of the All-Union Society of Knowledge. Founded n 1947, it worked to spread political information and to popularize science among the inhabitants of Latvia. Until 1963 it was called the Latvian SSR Political Knowledge and Science Popularization Society, and it was active in Latvia until 1992.

[138] See footnote 1 of Document No. 72.

[139] See footnote No. 1 in Document No. 72.

[140] "International book" – an agency of the USSR.

[141] The Madrid Conference took place with interruptions from November 1980 to September 1983, and the member states of the European Security and Cooperation Conference participated in it. It was dedicated to the fulfillment of the 1975 Helsinki Accords on Safety and Cooperation in Europe Final Acts. The breaks were caused by the sharpening of relations between Western and Eastern states relating to Soviet intervention in Afghanistan, the Polish events, and criticism of the USSR for human rights abuses; nevertheless, the meeting was a notable step forward in the Helsinki process.

[142] The 22nd Summer Olympic Games took place in Moscow from July 19th to August 3rd, 1980. Talllinn was the venue of the sailboat races.

[143] Also know as the AABS.

[144] These decisions were promulgated in 1979. Their execution was considered in plenary sessions of the Central Committee of the Latvian Communist Party where particular stress was placed on the need for "sharpening conditions of the ideological struggle... to strengthen political vigilance and not tolerate the appearance of any unhealthy political ideas." A set of activities was created, the goal of which was "to increase the effectiveness of the Party's work, to strengthen its rootedness in real life."

[145] With respect to the preparation and sending of this letter to foreign countries E. Berklavs wrote in his memoirs, *To Know and Not To Forget*, that in 1969, the national communists prepared an "Invitation to foreign communists," which asked the communist parties of foreign countries to try to influence the leaders of the USSR. The latter were held to be crippling the principles of Lenin's nationality policy by, in reality, pushing assimilation and violating human rights. But it was not until 1972 that it became possible to carry this invitation, or "The letter of 17 communists," to other countries (see E. Berklavs, *Zināt un neaizmirst* (Rīga: 1998, Vol. 1, p. 352).

[146] From October 1, 1944, the parts of Latvia under Soviet control experienced the introduction of controls over the supply of most essential goods. The primary model for determining the proportion of supplies for different categories of persons receiving supplies was the bread norm; this was ascribed to four basic categories of persons – workers, service personnel, children, and the state-supported (that is, adult, unemployed family members). Workers received 500 grams of bread per day, service personnel 400 grams, children 300 grams, and the state-supported 200 grams.

But these norms determined only the minimum and were operative only in the factories, enterprises, and institutions of which the Republic was in charge. The workers and service personnel at the most important enterprises were supplied by reference to increased norms, as well as receiving different kinds of additional supplies. The norms for factory workers and service personnel were used to set the norms for workers of other organizations.

The *nomenklatura* of the Party and of the state administration were supplied by reference to the highest norms for factory worker, but they also received additional supplies from the Party. The fixed supplies for the average worker or service person covered only a portion of the necessary groceries for a family. Other products had to be bought at the market or in commercial outlets, but for much higher prices. Furthermore, many of the groceries received from ration cards were of low quality; meat was often replaced with powdered eggs, sugar with cookies, etc. The higher a person had climbed the career ladder, the more of the most necessary groceries of much higher quality he or she could purchase at the low ration card prices. The highest-placed members of the *nomenklatura* did not even have to spend their salaries because all of the groceries they needed could be received for free.

[147] Ration cards were terminated on December 14, 1947. But the introduction of "free" market did not mean a surplus of goods or even of elementary necessities. This or that product was always lacking, which encouraged different kinds

of corruption and also a continuation of more or less disguised differentiation of norms. There were special stores in which only certain privileged groups of people (the *nomenklatura*, invalids of the Great War for the Fatherland, personal pensioners) could shop, including cafeterias and clothing stores. Persons who worked in the largest industrial enterprises and exemplary kolkhozes and sovkhozes also had certain privileges. This system grew and developed from the middle of the 1970s onward, and when individual incomes increased the shortages of certain goods increased as well. Different privileges and exceptions were ascribed to increasingly larger number of new groups until the connection between a person's nominal income and the real standard of living became very blurred.

[148] The supplement system mentioned in the document existed until February 1, 1957. In 1956, the system supplemented the incomes of 147 persons in the government, 48 persons in the Party apparatus, and 9 officials of the Committee of State Security. The amount of support varied from 500 to 1,200 rubles a month. (LVA 270.f., 1.apr., 1103.l., pp. 3, 4, 21). At that time 1,200 rubles a month was considered a good wage.

[149] The state's internal loans that were collected by means of subscription remained in place in the USSR from 1927 to 1957. Workers and service personnel had to subscribe for an amount approximating 3-4 weeks of wages. But that was just the minimal amount, since it was not unusual for subscriptions to be from 1 1/2 to 2 months' wages. Afterwards, the amount subscribed was deducted from wages over a 10-month period. Farmers individually did not have a defined subscription quota, but district financial departments and savings institutions were given a plan for quotas, which meant that the funds had to be collected from farmers. After collectivization, the material conditions of farmers rapidly worsened, and it was very difficult to fulfill the plan. Although the subscribed sums had to be paid in 10 months, annual instruction stressed repeatedly that it was necessary to collect all of the total sum in the first month. Pensioners, housekeepers and students had to register for loans [to pay what they owed].

From 1953 to 1957, the amount subscribed for was reduced by half, and in 1958 the subscription system was ended altogether, but at the same time the the the amounts still owed were frozen in place. The final liquidation of owed amounts resumed only in 1974, when inflation and the currency reform it inspired reduced the value of the owed amounts.

[150] At the time A. Vīndedze was the Deputy Chair of the Council of Ministers of the Latvian SSR.

[151] The system of obligatory milk delivery to the state operated also after collectivization. It was eliminated in 1956.

[152] On June 26, 1940, the USSR promulgated a decree entitled "Concerning the transition to the eight-hour work day and the seven-day work week and the prohibition against for workers and service personnel to be absent from work from enterprises and institutions without leave." The decree envisaged correctional work at the workplace, as well as a 25% reduction in wages, for [an employee] being twenty minutes late for work; and for changing workplaces without the permission of the leadership of the enterprise or institution – a prison sentence of 2 to 4 months. After Latvia's annexation to the USSR, this decree did not come into force until the war started. After Latvia was occupied for the second time, the decree went into force on March 1, 1945.

On July 14, 1951, the Presidium of the Supreme Soviet of the USSR issued a decree that substituted for criminal punishment for missing work the imposition of discipline and exertion of pressure by means of people's courts, except for long-term or chronic absence from work. The rule about twenty-minute tardiness was rescinded, with the absence of an entire day replacing it. Even though this 1951 decree for the whole of the USSR meant a certain liberalization, in Latvia it brought the opposite results – in 1951, 473 persons were punished, but in 1952 1,016, of whom 252 were sentenced to up to one year. All of these decrees were rescinded on April 25, 1956, and workers were given the option of changing their workplace on their own initiative after two weeks' notification [of the employer]. This began the process of dismantling by the Soviet regime of the worst of the Stalinist methods for enforcing social and economic discipline, though, in principle, it did not reject the use of extra-economic pressures.

[153] Soon after the war, in Latvia and particularly in Rīga there began a very rapid population increase, brought about by the demobilization of Soviet military personnel and the recruitment of labor from other republics of the USSR. But renovation of the apartments damaged by the war proceeded very slowly, and the construction of new apartments was minimal. Most new construction was in the form of barracks, that is, homes intended as temporary housing (even though persons often lived in them for several decades). The poulation was crowded into existing apartments, and large apartments became communal apartments. In the communal apartments one family usually occupied one and occasionally two rooms. Workers were often placed in dormitories in which one room contained many persons, sometimes even families together with unmarried people.

Conditions began to improve when in the second half of the 1950s the transition began toward the building of standardized apartments. Many families could now move to small, poorly constructed buildings, which, nonetheless allowed them to have a private apartment. From the end of the 1950s, the construction of apartment cooperatives speeded up, which created the chance of geting an apartment faster but also involved paying for the costs of construction. This was not feasible for all; morevoer, one qualified for a cooperative aparatment only if one had been put on the waiting list for apartments. Notwithstanding the fact that a person had paid for the construction of a cooperative apartment, he or she did not get ownership rights to it; it could not be bequeathed to someone not residing in it, and it could not officially be sold. There were also other forms of apartment construction: for example, many enterprises built apartments with their own resources, but potential renters had to work a certain number of hours in the construction project.

[154] Even though apartment construction increased substantially during the 1960s and 1970s, it did not surpass the growth

in the urban population. Moreover, the main effort was placed on on the construction of apartments; attention was paid minimally to the creation of an adequate infrastructure in the micro-regions where the aapartments buildings were located. There were few stores, dry cleaners, barber shops, pharmacies, etc.

[155] Permanent inhabitants and those registered in republic-level cities not less than five years, but in the regional centers, not less than three years.

[156] Ivan the Terrible – the Russian Tsar – is meant here.

[157] Called thus in the document.

[158] Called thus in the document

[159] Called thus in the document

[160] The program Ten Days of Latvian Literature took place in Moscow from December 22 to 28, 1948.

[161] See Footnote 1 of Document No. 60.

[162] This refers to the August 26, 1946, decision of the Central Committee of the All-Union Communist (B) Party, entitled "About the repertoire of the drama theaters and its improvement," and the September 4, 1946, decision, entitled "About the film ,The Big Life.'" These decisions criticized harshly the expressions of "harmful bourgeois ideologies'" in literature and art. After this decision, also in Latvia writers and poets were sought out, and found, who were criticized "in the light of this decision"; and on November 5, 1946, in a meeting of the Bureau of the Central Committee of the Latvian Communist (B) Party a decision was made asking responsible persons to review all of the published literature of 1945-1946 "and to decide on its conformity to the decisions of the Central Committee of the All-Union Communist (B) Party." Already on August 28, 1946, in the meeting of the Communist Party Primary Party Organization of the Latvian SSR Soviet Writers Society, the "sick and harmful phenomena" in the magazine "Karogs" and in the periodical "Literatūra un māksla" were condemned. Among those criticized were not only the persons mentioned in the present document, but also M. Ķempe, V. Brutlane, A. Balodis and others, who were said to have "become stuck in unfruitful, harmful, apolitical individualism and mystical decadence" (these descriptions were taken from the text of the decision of the Central Committee of the All-Union Communist Party). These decisions, just as the decision entitled "About the journals "Zvezda" and "Leningrad,'" were withdrawn in May of 1958.

[163] Boleslavs Brežgo (1887-1957) – an historian who worked primarily with the problems of Latgalian history. As with many other scientists who remained in Latvia after World War Two, he was persecuted as a bourgeois nationalist.

[164] The Supreme Certifying Commission (SCC) awarded all scientific degrees and scientific titles in all of the branches of the sciences, technological fields, education, and culture in all of the territory of the USSR, including Latvia until 1991.

[165] On November 18, 1918, the independent Republic of Latvia was proclaimed. Already in 1940 celebration of that day was banned. Not unil 1988 (for the first time since 1939) was this day celebrated in public with a demonstration at the Freedom Monument [in Riga]. During all the post-war years of Soviet power, the police and the employees of the State Security Committee were put on state of heightened alert on this day; and additional forces patrolled the monuments and cemeteries built in the 1920s and 1930s where pre-war government and military figures of the Republic of Latvia were buried (particularly the Freedom Monument and the Cemetery of the Brethren in Rīga).

[166] Pioneers – members of the All-Union V. I. Lenin Pioneer Organization. The Pioneers enrolled school children from the ages of 9 to 14. There were small Pioneer groups in the Latvian Republic as well, but this children's organization developed a mass base eventually. By the middle of 1945, in Latvia there were 30.3 thousand pioneers, but by the middle of the 1980s – almost 150, 000. This organization was under the control of the LLKJS and its primary assignment was ideological and political training. Thus, as in all other realms, children were also denied the right of choice, because only one children's organization existed and that, starting with the 1960s, enrolled entire school grades.

Children's summer camps were called Pioneer Camps. The first Pioneer Camp in Latvia was organized in August of 1940, and was named for Pavlik Morozov, who received the USSR' highest medal for betraying his father to the USSR People's Commissariat of the Interior in the early 1930s.

[167] The composer, I. Kalniņš, in his interview with M. Čaklais in 1998, remembered the episode in the following way: "Rock music was the original form of youth protest. I don't know what kind of politics it was, I do not want to call anyone by name, but in every way this genre – rock music -- that had already won its place in the world, here in Latvia was looked with unusual strictness, and anyone who tried to play it was brutally and inhumanely removed; permission was simply not given. This genre was not allowed into Latvia." (M. Čaklais, Im Ka. Rīga: 1998, p. 74)

[168] These decisions were not made public.

[169] The 21st Congress of the Latvian Communist Party took place in Rīga from February 25-26, 1971.

[170] Referring to memorial museums for Fricis Bārda, Vilis Plūdons, and the Brothers Kaudzīte.

[171] The 22nd Congress of the Latvian Communist Party took place in Rīga from February 22-23, 1976.

[172] The 26th Congress of the Communist party of the Soviet Union took place from February 23 to March 3rd, 1981.

[173] This was a picturesque description of the USSR.

[174] Various honors were bestowed in the USSR on the General Secretary of the USSR Leonid Brezhnev who held that post from 1966 until his death in 1982 and was Chair of the Presidium of Supreme Soviet of the USSR from 1977 on. In 1978 there were published Brezhnev's memoirs (actually just short brochures) in several volumes. These books were discussed not only in readers' meetings but also in scientific conferences. In 1979, L. Brezhnev received the highest award in the Soviet Union – the Order of Lenin – for his compilations.

[175] The flag of the USA is meant.

[176] Several similar documents are preserved in the Latvian State Archives, suggesting that this was an organized campaign to show the desires of the working class

[177] The following ten signatures are appended: B. Ivanjuk, Goldicka, Bobiljev, Valkova, Sidorovs, Trikons, Rebatins, Ivanjuk, Batova, Zandarov.

[178] The journal "Znaņije – Sila" was a popular scientific journal published in Moscow. To reduce transportation costs, the issues meant for Latvia were printed in Rīga. In the process of printing, a mistake was made that went unnoticed. Usually the workers in the printing establishment paid particular attention to the correct spelling of Stalin's last name. Mistakes were not a common phenomenon. That is why this document is interesting.

[179] Members of the Communist Party of the Soviet Union were subject to a particular Party system of punishments. The severe reprimand with notation on the record was the highest punishment. The only thing that could exceed that was expulsion from the Party, which would automatically mean losing one's employment.

[180] Stalin died on March 5, 1953. Judging by the materials of the affair one can deduce that R. Adamovičs told jokes about Stalin.

[181] The elections to the Supreme Council of the Latvian SSR took place on February 16, 1947. Its composition, however, was laid down before the elections. In harmony with Document No. 105, the candidates put forward consisted of 47 workers (39.2%), 26 farmers (21.6%), and 47 service wokers (39.2%). In the same manner, the composition of the rest of the Latvian SSR Supreme Councils was set before the elections. Over the years, the number of deputies changed. After 1950, the number of deputies was raised to 200; in 1963 it was increased to 310; and in 1980 to 325 deputies. From 1978 on, the Supreme Council was elected for a five-year term, rather than the earlier four years; and the voting age was lowered to 18 years from 21. In 1966, the Union Republics, including Latvia, increased the number of deputies to the Supreme Council of Nationalities of the USSR from 25 to 32 persons. In the 1960s and 1970s, the slogan was – the greater number of deputies, the more democracy.

[182] See also Document No. 31.

[183] See also Document No. 34.

[184] Error in the document. The correct designation is "SS Jagdverband Lettland."

[185] Elections in the Soviet Union were farcical, but great attention was paid to the formal side of the process. Any technical mistake was interpreted as a political mistake. For these, members of the Communist Party were punished first. The actual "guilty parties" that were not members of the Communist Party of the Soviet Union were punished very lightly. The Senior Proofreader was demoted for a while, and the person responsible for the issue and the Secretariat of Correspondents were put on notice. 13,100 copies of the newspaper were removed from kiosks, and 27,000 copies were printed anew for the subscribers, institutions, and libraries with the text corrected.

[186] See Document No. 122.

[187] Totals for 1935, 1959, 1970, 1979, 1989 from census materials. The permanent inhabitants from the last five censuses were the following (in thousands): 1959 – 2,080; 1970 – 2,352; 1979 – 2,503; 1989 - 2,667; 2000 – 2,430.

[188] As of September 1.

[189] As of January 1.

[190] Within the pre-war borders.

[191] Estimated.

[192] Compiled from A. Gagalaite and J. Skirius, *Lithuanian History Reader, 1861-1900, Volume III*, 11 (Kaunas: 1993, p. 339).

[193] Compiled from O. Krastiņš, B. Mežgailis, and M. Smulders, *Latvijas iedzīvotāji (statistikās izziņas)* (Rīga: 1990).

[194] Russians, Ukrainians, Belarussians.

[195] Compiled from: *No NKVD līdz KGB. Politiskās prāvas Latvijā 1940-1986. Noziegumi pret padomju valsti apsūdzēto Latvijas iedzīvotāju rādītājs* (Rīga: 1999, p, 972). The table is not complete, since it does not include persons deported by administrative order, those held in filtration camps, as well as those that were repressed but whose criminal proceedings were not in held Latvia.

Printed in the United States
147805LV00001B/3/A